On the Edge
Writing the Border between Haiti
and the Dominican Republic

American Tropics: Towards a Literary Geography

American Tropics: Towards a Literary Geography

The term 'American Tropics' refers to a kind of extended Caribbean, an area which includes the southern USA, the Atlantic littoral of Central America, the Caribbean islands, and northern South America. European colonial powers fought intensively here against indigenous populations and against each other for control of land and resources. This area shares a history in which the dominant fact is the arrival of millions of white Europeans and black Africans; shares an environment which is tropical or sub-tropical; and shares a socio-economic model (the plantation) whose effects lasted well into the twentieth century. The approach taken by the series is geographical in the sense that the focus of each volume is on a *region*. Each region is a zone of encounter, bringing together sets of writing in different languages and styles, from different literary and cultural backgrounds, all of which have in common the attention paid to the same place.

The imaginative space of the American Tropics series therefore offers a differently centred literary history from those conventionally produced as US, Caribbean, or Latin American literature. The development of the discipline of cultural geography has encouraged more sophisticated analyses of notions of place and region, which this series brings to bear on its materials. The individual volumes therefore stand at an angle to national literary histories, offering a different perspective, with each volume contributing one piece of the jigsaw towards a completely new map of the literary history of the area.

Series Editors

Maria Cristina Fumagalli (Professor in the Department of Literature, Film, and Theatre Studies at the University of Essex)

Peter Hulme (Professor in the Department of Literature, Film, and Theatre Studies at the University of Essex)

Owen Robinson (Senior Lecturer in the Department of Literature, Film, and Theatre Studies at the University of Essex)

Lesley Wylie (Lecturer in the School of Modern Languages at the University of Leicester)

On the Edge

Writing the Border between Haiti and the Dominican Republic

MARIA CRISTINA FUMAGALLI

LIVERPOOL UNIVERSITY PRESS

First published 2015 by
Liverpool University Press
4 Cambridge Street
Liverpool
L69 7ZU

This paperback edition first published 2018

British Library Cataloguing-in-Publication data
A British Library CIP record is available

ISBN 978-1-78138-160-1 cased
ISBN 978-1-78694-130-5 paperback

Typeset by Carnegie Book Production, Lancaster
Printed and bound by CPI Group (UK) Ltd, Croydon CR0 4YY

To Jon and Ernesto,
for our journey.

To Peter,
for lighting
the oven so that
everyone may
bake bread in it.

Contents

Figures

Acknowledgements

Writing the border between Haiti and the Dominican Republic has been a wonderful adventure which would not have been possible without research grants from the Arts and Humanities Research Board (2006–2010) and a Leverhulme Research Fellowship (2012–2013): to these two funding bodies goes my deepest gratitude for their assistance.

I would like to thank the University of Essex Research Endowment Fund and the Department of Literature, Film, and Theatre Studies, which funded two terms of study leave to further my research for this book. I also would like to warmly acknowledge JISLAC (Joint Initiative for the Study of Latin America and the Caribbean) and the British Academy for funding the interdisciplinary seminar 'An Island Divided and an Island Shared: Post-Earthquake Hispaniola,' which took place at the University of Essex on Saturday 26 November 2011.

I am grateful to all my students, who always have the power to re-energize me when I need a boost, and to all my colleagues, in particular Nic Blower, Shohini Chauduri, Clare Finburgh, Jeff Geiger, John and Patricia Gillies, John Haynes, Karin Littau, Jonathan Lichtenstein, Susan Oliver, and Phil Terry, for supporting the project in different ways. Sanja Bahun, Joanne Harwood, and Sarah Demelo from ESCALA deserve a special mention for persuading me to co-curate the exhibition 'Karmadavis: Art, Justice, Transition,' which took place at *firstsite*, Colchester (10 November 2012–10 March 2013), and the symposium 'Art and Politics in Hispaniola' which closed the exhibition. I would also like to salute former colleagues Leon Burnett, Richard Gray, Glyn Maxwell, Rebecca Prichard, Derek Walcott, and Marina Warner: regrettably, some of them have recently left the department in appalling circumstances and they are all deeply missed.

Many other friends and colleagues have also offered their help and supported the project in different ways: it is impossible to be comprehensive but, among many others, I would like to offer my thanks to Alessandra Benedicty, Celia Britton, Gordon Brotherston, Michael Bucknor, Paula Burnett, John Cant, Matthew Carter, Susan Castillo, Roberta Cimarosti, Anne Collett, Jordi Doce, Roberto del Valle Alcalá, Elizabeth DeLoughrey,

Hilary Emmett, Ottmar Ette, Christian Flaugh, Michelle Franke, Valerie Fraser, Mary Gallagher, Susan Gillman, Kaiama Glover, Rosemarijn Hoefte, Ben Jefferson, Michael Jonik, Maria Lauret, Bénédicte Ledent, Paola Loreto, Katherine Miranda, John Masterson, Russell McDougall, Wendy Mcmahon, Sharon Monteith, Danielle Mortimer, Pat Noxolo, Evelyn O'Callaghan, Lisa Paravisini-Gebert, Alasdair Pettinger, Kimberley Robinson-Walcott, Mayrah Rodríguez, Héctor Rodríguez Pérez, Matthias Röhrig Assunçao, Luigi Sampietro, Lúcia Sá, Anne Schröder, Mimi Sheller, Karina Smith, Roberto Strongman, Sue Thomas, Neil Whitehead, Matthew Woollard, and, last but not least, the super-efficient and super-helpful Penny Woollard.

I have shared this adventure with fellow-*tropicalistas* Leanne Haynes, Jak Peake, Owen Robinson, Lesley Wylie, and Susan Forsyth: it has been a real joy working with them. I am forever indebted to our *líder máximo* Peter Hulme for his unfaltering encouragement, guidance, and friendship: this is why he is one of the people to whom this book is dedicated.

Working on this book allowed me to meet wonderful people who so generously found the time to discuss some border-related issues with me: Elizabeth Eames Roebling – who came with me to the Dajabón/ Ouanaminthe and Pedernales/Anse à Pitre and has been a dear friend ever since – Sonia Adames, Marianella Belliard, Michael Benson, Tim Brothers, Emma Domínguez de Benson, José Emperador, Lorgia García Peña, Eve Hayes de Khalaf, Sarah Hermann, David Howard, Andrew Leak, Aurora Martínez, Anne McConnell, Robert McCormick, Daniel O'Neil, Max Puig, Giselle Rodríguez Cid, Hoyt Rogers, Alicia Sangro Blasco, Sergio Reyes and his family, Miguel Silva, Marion Traub-Werner, Martha Thayer, Eddy Tejeda, Jean Marie Théodat, Sonia Vásquez, Chiqui Vicioso, Rubén Darío Villalona, and Rafael Emilio Yunén. Bridget Wooding deserves a special mention for her enthusiastic and ongoing support – she generously opened the doors of OBMICA to me in 2009 and on 28 January 2013 she organized a one-day event in Santo Domingo which gave me the opportunity to discuss my ideas with Stephen Fischer, Wilfredo Lozano, Allison Petrozziello, and many other experts on border relations: I would really like to thank all the people who came to my talk on that day for their input and for the lively conversation that we had.

I am deeply indebted to Frank Báez, with whom I have had many illuminating conversations, Polibio Díaz, Laura Amelia Guzmán and Israel Cárdenas, Hulda Guzmán, Jean Philippe Moiseau, David Pérez Karmadavis, Pancho Rodríguez, and Evelyne Trouillot for putting up with all my questions and requests and for their astute insights. The artworks of Polibio Díaz, Hulda Guzmán, Jean Philippe Moiseau, David Pérez Karmadavis, and Pancho Rodríguez are reproduced here courtesy of the artists.

Anthony Cond has been an extremely supportive and efficient editor and I am grateful to Sue Barnes and Patrick Brereton for their assistance. The reviewers of my manuscript also deserve my gratitude for their insightful comments.

The Albert Sloman library at the University of Essex has been an amazing resource here in the United Kingdom; in Santo Domingo I worked in the Biblioteca Nacional Pedro Henríquez Ureña and in Archivo General de la Nación but mostly in the Biblioteca Juan Bosch, where I was warmly welcomed by Leonel Fernández and could rely on Rachelli Fernández and Luis Manuel De Peña, who have been wonderfully helpful to me.

Antonella Patteri has been immensely helpful, every single day, for three years; Eleonora Andricciola, Massimo Binda, Rosaria Campagnani, Antonella Moretti, Cristina Pallini, Guido Palloni, Antonello Ticozzi, Marco Zanibelli, and Stefano Zerpelloni have helped in more ways than they can possibly imagine. *Grazie per esserci. Sempre.*

On the Edge is also dedicated, with more gratitude and love that I can possibly express, to the best travel companions one could dream of: my partner Jon and my son Ernesto. They illuminate every day of my life.

Some of the material in this book first appeared in different essays; I wish to acknowledge and thank *Entertext*; *Sargasso, A Journal of Caribbean Literature, Language, and Culture*; *The New West Indian Guide*; *The Journal of Haitian Studies*; *BLAR – Bulletin of Latin American Research*; *Caribbean Quarterly*; and the publisher *Mimesis* for their permission to reprint portions of the following essays:

'Border (Un)Writing: Victor Hugo's *Bug-Jargal*', *Entertext*, 7.1 *Abolition Bicentenary: The Black Atlantic Then and Now* (2007), pp. 178–95.

'Jean Baptiste Picquenard and the Rebels, Maroons, Cannibals, *Pacotilleurs* and *Debauchés* of Hispaniola's Borderland', *Sargasso, A Journal of Caribbean Literature, Language, and Culture – Placing the Archipelago: Interconnections and Extensions*, I & II (2010–11), pp. 89–104.

'Landscaping Hispaniola: Moreau De Saint-Méry's Border Politics', *New West Indian Guide*, 85. 3&4 KITLV (2011), pp. 169–90.

'Servants Turned Masters: Carlos Esteban Deive's *Viento Negro, Bosque del Caimán* and the future of Hispaniola', *Journal of Haitian Studies*, 18.2 (2012), pp. 100–118.

'Hispaniola after the Earthquake: Confronting the Fault Lines' and 'Isla Abierta or Isla Cerrada? Karmadavis's Pre- and Post-Earthquake Hispaniola', *BLAR – Bulletin of Latin American Research*, 32.4 (2013), pp. 391–3 and pp. 431–7.

'"La carne repta entre Dajabón y Juana Méndez": Manuel Rueda's "Geography of Living Flesh" and the Borderland of Hispaniola', *Caribbean Quarterly*, 60.3 (2014), pp. 1–18.

'Une belle phrase peut changer la vie'/'A beautiful sentence can change one's life': Jean-Noel Pancrazi's *Montecristi* and the borderland of Hispaniola', *in Il valore della letteratura: scritture in onore di Luigi Sampietro/The value of literature: writing in honour of Luigi Sampietro* (Milan: Mimesis, 2014), pp. 95–104.

A note on translations

P lease note that, unless otherwise indicated, all the translations from French and Spanish are mine. Throughout the book foreign language quotations have been translated into English for the ease of the reader, but when the original language was crucial to my argument I have provided the original words alongside my translation.

Introduction
On the edge: border-crossing, borderland-dwelling, and the music of what happens

*O*n *the Edge: Writing the Border between Haiti and the Dominican Republic* was conceived as part of a project called *American Tropics: Towards a Literary Geography* and is part of a series which bears the same name. The *American Tropics* series is governed by a new approach to literary history which shifts the traditional focus on the Romantic idea of the nation state to geographical regions which do not correspond to national territories. Almost unavoidably, a literary history that derives from such an approach tends to privilege what the philosopher Edward Casey has called the 'vernacularity of place, its habitability and idiosyncrasy,' and to reveal the existence of transnational sets of allegiances, connections, and trajectories which are often disavowed in the nation-building process.[1] This is even more the case if the place in question lies 'on the edge' of two nations: while Haitian and Dominican literatures are usually studied in isolation, *On the Edge* is a literary and cultural history which brings to the fore a compelling but, so far, largely neglected body of work from Haiti and the Dominican Republic, and puts it in dialogue with texts from the rest of the world which have had the border between Haiti and the Dominican Republic at their core.

The frontier between Haiti and the Dominican Republic has been defined as the 'the longest and most significant land boundary in all the Antilles.'[2] Living on this border has always meant living 'on the edge,' both physically

---

[1] Edward Casey, *The Fate of Place: A Philosophical History* (Berkeley, CA: University of California Press, 1998), p. 77.
[2] Michel-Rolph Trouillot, *Nation, State and Society in Haiti, 1804–1984* (Washington, DC: The Wilson Center, 1985), pp. 5–6.

Figure 1a. Map of Hispaniola: borderland *Provincias* (Dominican Republic) and *Départements* (Haiti). The position of the current border is indicated with a dashed line.

and psychologically, and, in order to better understand the nature of this 'edge' it is important to pay attention to its often troubled history, to border-crossing dynamics, and to the rhythms of borderland-dwelling. The border, which is as tortuous as its troubled history, has in fact produced a complex 'contact zone' characterized by <u>conflict and violence</u> but also by many collaborative linkages, often established against the directives of the central colonial, national, and occupying authorities.[3] As it is often the case for international borders, there is no consensus on its length and estimates vary from <u>275 to 391 kilometres.</u>[4] Haiti and the Dominican Republic, moreover, still have not agreed on a name for the island as a whole – a sign, perhaps, that in the collective consciousnesses of Haitians and Dominicans there has traditionally been little space for a shared insular dimension.[5] Generally, in fact, Haitians use 'Haiti' to indicate both their nation and the island while Dominicans often refer to their country as 'Quisqueya' – a term erroneously taken to be one of the indigenous names of the island – and call the island Española or Santo Domingo.[6] 'Hispaniola,' originally a Latinization of the

---

[3] For more on 'contact-zones' see Mary Louise Pratt, *Imperial Eyes: Travel Writing and Transculturation* (London: Routledge, 1992), pp. 6–7.

[4] Marie Redon, *Des îles en partage: Haïti & République dominicaine, Saint-Martin, Timor* (Port-au-Prince/Toulouse: Editions de l'Université d'État d'Haïti et Presses Universitaires du Mirail, 2008), p. 76 note 2.

[5] Jean-Marie Théodat, *Haïti/République Dominicaine: Une île pour deux 1804–1916* (Paris: Karthala, 2003), p. 9.

[6] Theodat, pp. 8–9; Juan Daniel Balcácer, '¿Cuál es el nombre de nuestra isla?',

Figure 1b. Map of Hispaniola: main border crossings.

Spanish 'Española,' is the term I will be using here: despite its neo-colonial residues – it has been widely used by Anglophone writers since the North American occupation of Haiti (1915–34) and the Dominican Republic (1916–24) – 'Hispaniola' has been regarded as a compromise which allows one to avoid seeming biased towards one or the other country while leaving behind colonial appellatives such as 'Española,' 'Santo Domingo,' or 'Saint Domingue.'[7]

Like all frontiers, the geopolitical border which divides Hispaniola in two is defined by the social practices which animate it and by the different discourses at work in the imagined communities it simultaneously separates and connects. Amabelle Désir, the protagonist of Edwidge Danticat's *The Farming of Bones*, a text I will be looking at in Chapter 6, describes the border between Haiti and the Dominican Republic as 'a veil.'[8] Veils conjure up secrecy, inaccessibility, exclusion – their function is to keep 'out' what is not wanted, what pollutes and compromises the alleged 'purity' of what they set out to protect. Yet, their insubstantiality also suggests that veils are constantly 'on the edge' of permeability and penetrability. Historically, across-the-border exchanges have often been characterized by conflict and violence: it is perhaps no coincidence that one of the rivers along which runs

DiarioLibre, 29 September 2012, http://www.diariolibre.com/juan-daniel-balcacer/2012/09/29/i353742_cual-nombre-nuestra-islaa.html [accessed 25 November 2014].

[7] See Rafael Emilio Yunén, *La isla como es: hipótesis para su comprobación* (Santiago de los Caballeros, Dominican Republic: Universidad Católica Madre y Maestra, 1985), p.31.

[8] Edwidge Danticat, *The Farming of Bones* [1998] (New York: Penguin 1999), p. 264.

the border which divides Hispaniola in two is called River Massacre, a name
which was chosen to commemorate the slaughter of a company of French
boucaniers and border-trespassers in 1728, when the island was still officially
a Spanish colony. Toponomastics, in this case, posits the borderline – what
Richard Muir calls 'vertical interfaces between state sovereignties which
intersect the surface of the earth' – as a sharp and rough edge, where the
two colonies and nations sharing Hispaniola have often 'grated' against one
another and 'bled,' to paraphrase Anzaldua's poetic evaluation of interactions
across the US–Mexican frontier.[9] In 1937 the waters of the River Massacre
became the theatre for more 'grating' and 'bleeding,' namely the massacre of
Haitians and Haitian–Dominicans living in the Dominican border provinces
perpetrated by the dictator Rafael Leonidas Trujillo's army. Yet, as the title
of a famous and controversial Dominican book (analysed in Chapter 5)
reminds us, 'the Massacre can be crossed on foot.'[10] The ease with which
the river can be traversed blunts the sharp edges of the vertical frontier and
insists instead on the horizontal dimension of the borderland which Muir's
borderline's verticality aims to disallow; as a result, the borderland can be
seen as a site where something other than conflict, 'grating,' and 'bleeding'
can arise, and as a place 'on the edge of' positive exchanges, collaboration,
solidarity, regeneration, and cross-pollination.

The Dominican provinces situated alongside the borderline – Montecristi,
Dajabón, Elias Piña, Independencia, Pedernales – are not homogenous: the
Dominican historian Frank Moya Pons has in fact identified eight border
regions which differ in terms of distance from the country's political centre,
degree of militarization, links to Haiti, permeability of their section of
the borderline, and tolerance of Haitians on their territory.[11] It is fair to

---

[9] Richard Muir, *Modern Political Geography* (New York: Macmillan, 1975), p. 119;
Gloria Anzaldúa, *Borderlands/La Frontera: The New Mestiza* (San Francisco, CA: Aunt
Lute Books, 1999), p. 25.
[10] Freddy Prestol Castillo, *El Masacre se pasa a pie* (Santo Domingo: Editora Taller,
1973).
[11] Frank Moya Pons, 'Las Ochos Fronteras de Haití y la República Dominicana', in
La Frontera: prioridad en la agenda nacional, ed. Secretaría de Estado de las Fuerzas
Armadas (Santo Domingo: Editora de las Fuerzas Armadas Dominicanas, 2004),
pp. 441–6, p. 442. See also Haroldo Dilla Alfonso, 'Pensar la frontera', *Cuadernos
de Comunicación*, 5.4 (2013), pp. 5–11, p. 5, who highlights that Jimaní is a perfect
'non-place' which links the two capitals, Dajabón constitutes a relatively prosperous
link between Santiago de los Caballeros and Cap-Haïtien, Elias Piña is a fragmented
line made of multiple points of contact between agricultural regions, and Pedernales
has connections only with Anse à Pitre, which is very poorly connected with the rest
of Haiti.

Figure 2. The River Massacre at the border crossing between Dajabón (Dominican Republic) and Ouanaminthe (Haiti) (photograph: Maria Cristina Fumagalli).

say, however, that, despite their differences, these provinces are among the poorest and least densely populated parts of the country and – regardless of the fact that article 7 of the Dominican constitution sanctions that the development of the borderland is of the utmost national interest – many feel that the frontier region has traditionally been neglected by the central government in cultural, educational, social, and economic terms.[12] It is widely recognized, however, that the markets attended by sellers and customers from both sides of the border and which take place twice a week in different locations within the Dominican borderland, have a remarkable impact on the region's economy.[13] These markets used to take place on Haitian territory, but are now managed and controlled by Dominicans

---

[12] Adames, 'Presentación', in *Antología Literaria Contemporánea de la Frontera*, ed. Francisco Paulino Adames (Santo Domingo: FUDECESFRON, 1998), pp. 3–5, p. 3.

[13] Haroldo Dilla Alfonso, 'La nueva economía fronteriza', in *La frontera dominico-haitiana*, ed. H. Dilla Alfonso (Santo Dominigo: Editora Manatí, 2010), pp. 95–130, pp. 101–2 and maps 7, 8, 10.

(despite the fact that they are called 'bi-national'), and have an important precedent in the trade which, breaking colonial monopoly, transformed the island's borderland into a crucial conduit of exchange and communication from the second half of the sixteenth century, when the first French settlements in the western part of the island began to establish themselves.

Across the frontier, the borderland on the Haitian side is constituted by the strip of land at the extreme east of the four geographic departments of the country (Département du Nord-Est; Département du Centre; Département de l'Ouest; Département du Sud-Est): its demographic density is higher than the Dominican borderland's but lower than that of the rest of the country.[14] Infrastructures and resources are very limited but Haitian borderland-dwellers can benefit from the possibility of trading goods (generally re-exports) in the bi-national markets and can sell produce from the farming and livestock sector at various (official and unofficial) sites of interchange located all along the borderline; they can also take advantage of the opportunity to find some daily paid work across the border, mainly as agricultural labourers.[15] Haitians working at the bi-national markets, however, are not exempt from discrimination or exploitation: a recent study of the frontier market of the Dominican border town of Comendador in Elias Piña has highlighted that, allegedly for public health reasons, Haitian market sellers have at times been segregated from Dominicans or relegated to muddy and insecure areas nearer to the border crossing, rather than being allowed to carry their goods into town. Haitian sellers, moreover, are routinely charged more than Dominicans, and market fee collectors can charge arbitrary and exorbitant fees: if the Haitian sellers cannot afford to pay, a part of their merchandise is taken away by the collectors

---

[14] Map 10 in H. Dilla Alfonso (ed.), *La frontera dominico-haitiana* (Santo Dominigo: Editora Manatí, 2010) and Guy Alexandre, 'Visión Haitiana sobre la Frontera de Cara al Siglo XX', in *La Frontera: prioridad en la agenda nacional*, ed. Secretaría de Estado de las Fuerzas Armadas (Santo Domingo: Editora de las Fuerzas Armadas Dominicanas, 2004), pp. 125–34, p. 131.

[15] Haroldo Dilla Alfonso, 'Palabras preliminares' and 'La nueva economía fronteriza', in *La frontera dominico-haitiana* (Santo Dominigo: Editora Manatí, 2010), pp. 9–13, p. 10; p. 102 and maps 6, 10; Gerald Murray, *Sources of Conflict along and across the Haitian–Dominican Border* (Santo Domingo: Pan American Development Foundation, 2010), http://web.clas.ufl.edu/users/murray/Research/Dominican_Republic/Dominican_ Haitian_Conflicts.pdf [accessed 25 November 2014]. The controversial Free Trade Zone created in the poor Haitian border town of Ouanaminthe, for example, can also offer some form of employment, but it has been widely denounced as exploitative and for its appropriation of fertile land: see, for example, Mark Schuller, 'Challenges to Solidarity across Multiple Borders: Haiti's Free Trade Zone', *Caribbean Quarterly*, 58.4 (2012), pp. 87–110 and Dilla Alfonso, 'Pensar la frontera', p. 5.

Figure 3. On 17 January 2011 the border crossing of Pedernales (Dominican Republic)/Anse à Pitre (Haiti) was closed owing to the cholera epidemic and the bi-national market which normally takes place in Pedernales was suspended. Frustrated Haitian sellers, many of whom had journeyed many miles, organized a makeshift market on the Haitian side (photographs: Maria Cristina Fumagalli).

and (supposedly) put in storage until the sellers find the money to retrieve it; sometimes, if sellers refuse to comply, they can be physically abused.[16] Exploitation and discrimination notwithstanding, the protracted closure of the frontier on market days in the winter of 2010/11, a measure taken by the Dominican government to (allegedly) prevent the spread of cholera, caused chaos as well as frustration and anxiety for those who, from both sides of the island, depend on these markets for their livelihood.[17]

Owing to a special migration arrangement which allows Haitians to enter Dominican territory on market days, the frontier markets which take place on the Dominican borderland also function as one of the many routes through which illegal migrants from Haiti cross into the Dominican Republic. They are supposed to travel only as far as the town where the market is being held and then return to Haiti once the market is finished but, given the large numbers of people that cross the border on these occasions, tight control of who comes and goes is simply impossible to achieve. In 2012 it was established by Dominican authorities that Haitian occasional workers who live in the Haitian borderland should obtain a 'carnet' or 'identification card' valid for a year, which would give them permission to enter legally in the Dominican Republic. Two years later, however, these *carnets* have still not been issued and the migratory flux appears to be arbitrarily regulated, a system obviously open to abuse. The same arbitrariness affects Haitian students who cross the border to attend short-term vocational courses in the Dominican Republic.[18]

The precariousness which characterizes the lives of those who reside along the border and who cross it every day in search of work has attracted the attention of sociologists, historians, geographers, human rights activists, politicians, journalists, lawyers, anthropologists, experts in international relations, health issues, migration, and economic development, members

---

[16] Bridget Wooding and Allison Petrozziello, 'New Challenges for the Realisation of Migrants' Rights Following the Haiti 2010 Earthquake: Haitian Women on the Borderlands', *Bulletin of Latin American Research*, 32.4 (2013), pp. 407–20, p. 409, 413.

[17] In January 2011, with the journalist Elizabeth Roebling, I visited Pedernales, where, since they could not cross to the Dominican Republic, Haitian sellers put together a makeshift market on their side of the border to try to salvage the situation. See Elizabeth Eames Roebling, 'Haiti–Dominican Republic: Cholera Chokes Off Border Trade', *Global Issues*, 17 January 2011, http://www.globalissues.org/news/2011/01/17/8204 [accessed 25 November 2014] and José Luis Soto, 'Caos en el mercado binacional dominico-haitiano', *Teve Espacinsular*, 14 November 2010, http://www.youtube.com/watch?v=LCB7X7bd2TA [accessed 8 February 2014].

[18] Altair Rodríguez Grullón, *Estado del arte de las migraciones que atañen a la República Dominicana* (Santo Domingo: Editora Búho, 2014), pp. 88–90, 81–82.

of the armed forces, civil engineers, and environmentalists; a sizable number of publications have recently tried to bring into sharp focus the problems and, in some cases, also the opportunities that the border and the borderland represent for Hispaniola.[19] These investigations are mainly published locally and generally in the Dominican Republic, partly because it has more resources, but partly because there the presence of the border has more ideological weight. For a long time, in fact, Dominican dominant nationalistic discourses have been encouraging a national identification which uses Haiti as its negative foil. Based on a set of dichotomies which covers almost every aspect of life in Hispaniola, these discourses depict a very simplified and artificial picture of the island which highlights differences, posits them as incompatible traits, and denies the existence of cultural permeability: Haitians speak Creole, Dominicans speak Spanish; Haitians practise Vodou, Dominicans are Catholics; Haitians are black, Dominicans of mixed race or white; Haitian culture and society are an extension of Africa, the Dominican Republic has 'pure' Spanish origins. As Pedro San Miguel has succinctly put it, according to these discourses, 'the definition of "Dominican" [is simply] "not Haitian."'[20]

Concomitantly, the borderland has traditionally been identified as the site where this particular version of Dominicanness ('not Haitian') is most under threat (on the edge of dissolution, as it were) and as the all too porous point of entrance of the 'clandestine penetration' of Haitian migrants which can 'disintegrate the moral and ethnic values of the Dominican family.'[21] The Dominican Republic is therefore presented as a besieged nation whose only defence lies in the staunch denial of any communality with the neighbouring country. As we will see, not everyone agrees with this antagonistic and

---

[19] Among others: Rubén Silié and Carlos Segura, eds, *Hacia una nueva visión de la frontera y de las relaciones fronterizas* (Santo Domingo: Editora Búho, 2002); Secretaría de Estado de las Fuerzas Armadas (ed.), *La Frontera: prioridad en la agenda nacional* (Santo Domingo: Editora de las Fuerzas Armadas Dominicanas, 2004); Théodat, *Haïti/République Dominicaine*; Wilfredo Lozano and Bridget Wooding, eds, *Los retos del desarrollo insular: desarrollo sostenible, migraciones y derechos humanos en las relaciones domínico-haitianas en el siglo XXI* (Santo Domingo: FLACSO, 2008); Redon, *Des îles en partage*; Dilla Alfonso, *La frontera dominico-haitiana*; Manuel Rodríguez, *Las Nuevas Relaciones Domínico-Haitianas* (Centro de Información Gubernamental: Santo Domingo, 2011).
[20] Pedro Luis San Miguel, *The Imagined Island: History, Identity and Utopia in Hispaniola*, trans. J. Ramírez [1997](Chapel Hill, NC: The University of North Carolina Press, 2005), p. 39.
[21] Joaquín Balaguer, *La isla al revés: Haití y el destino dominicano* [1983] (Santo Domingo: Editora Corripio, 1994), p. 156.

apocalyptic vision, but the effects of this ideological setup on everyday
life run very deep and are all too clear in the definition that a Dominican
student of geography in a secondary school once gave of his country: 'an
island surrounded by the sea and Haitians on all sides.'[22] As a result of this
ideological framework, the Haitian–Dominican border is often a 'presence'
in the lives and minds of all Dominicans while it is much less prominent
in the imaginary and daily occurrences of the majority of Haitians.

The Dominican Republic, in fact, occupies a rather 'secondary position'
and enjoys 'low visibility' in the Haitian vision of the territory.[23] According to
the cultural anthropologist Samuel Martínez, Haitians 'tend to underestimate
the importance [to their country] of the Dominican Republic,' which is 'at
most that sugar-plantation netherworld that swallows up the most desperate
of [...] emigrants [...] the poorest and least vocal' of Haitians: 'it is little
exaggeration,' he continues, 'to say that for most Haitians the Dominican
Republic might as well be on the other side of the planet.'[24] Martínez's
views are confirmed by Guy Alexandre, former Ambassador of Haiti to
the Dominican Republic, who has argued that 'if the "Haitian issue" is a
reality for the Dominicans, there is no "Dominican issue" in Haiti.'[25] Haitian
governments, he continues, have never really invested in the development

---

[22] Yunén, *La isla como es*, p. 183. Most of the poems and short stories included in
the above-mentioned *Antología Literaria Contemporánea de la Frontera* are lyrical
and personal in content or do not engage with the landscape and history of the
borderland, but some of those which do, evoke the many battles that the Dominicans
fought against the Haitians in order to establish their independence (i.e. Norma
Holguín-Veras's 'Antesala de la Patria' and 'Evocaciones', pp. 93 and 94; Rafael Emigdio
Caamaño Castillo's 'Himno a Comendador del Rey', and 'Fucilado por equivocación,'
p. 113 and pp. 119–21, p. 119). A similar pattern is observable in Carlo Reyes (ed.),
Letras del Sol: Antología de escritores de la Línea Noroeste (San Francisco de Macorís:
Angeles de Fierro/Editora Nacional, 2009), which showcases writers from Valverde,
Mao, Dajabón, Santiago Rodríguez, and Montecristi and contains a poem dedicated
to the battle of Sabana Larga (Norma Alt. Holguín-Veras Belliard's 'Sabana Larga,'
p. 77). Moreover, in *Antología Literaria Contemporánea de la Frontera*, the presence
of Haiti is acknowledged in the introductory remarks which describe the way of life
in the provinces to highlight brotherhood and communality of intent (Carlos Julio
Félix, 'Pedernales: Breve reseña historica', pp. 165–7, p. 166), but also to proudly refer to
the function of border settlements as bulwarks of Dominican Christian and Hispanic
values under threat by the close proximity of Haiti (Rafael Leonidas Pérez y Pérez,
'Cultura de la Provincia Independencia', pp. 147–9).
[23] Théodat, *Haïti/République Dominicaine*, p. 29; Samuel Martínez, 'Not a Cockfight:
Rethinking Haitian-Dominican Relations', *Latin American Perspectives*, 30.3 (2003),
pp. 80–101, p.83.
[24] Martínez, 'Not a Cockfight', p. 83.
[25] Alexandre, 'Visión Haitiana', p. 128.

of the Haitian borderland and border-related matters tend to generate little interest in the Haitian media, in intellectual circles, and among politicians: as a result, he concludes, Haitian literature has hardly ever been preoccupied with the theme of the frontier.[26]

One could do worse here than refer to *Le mât de cocagne* (1979), by the Haitian writer René Depestre, as a primary exemplification. This novel describes life in a country called the Great Zacharian Nation which is run by an evil dictator called the Honorable Zoocrates Zachary. Zachary is Papa Doc Duvalier, and the Great Zacharian Nation is Haiti, but the fact that this is an imaginary country, and therefore an 'imagined community' par excellence, can give us some useful insights into the way in which Haitian writers – arguably, the most 'vocal' of Haitians – have perceived themselves in relation to the international frontier which divides the island in two. The Great Zacharian Nation is referred to, en passant, as 'one half of the island' and the novel contains a few Spanish words (significantly, spoken by some of the poorest characters) which signpost the vicinity of the Dominican Republic. Yet, the material existence of the international internal border does not play any role in the narrative and when the protagonist – interestingly, a former minister of the nation – organizes his escape from the capital, he plans to board a ship directed to Canada.

Haitian engagement with border-related issues, however, has increased in the last twenty years or so, partly because of the importance of commercial exchange taking place across the border, a keen interest on the part of Haitian and international NGOs in the socioeconomic needs and environmental problems of the borderland, and the realization that a remarkable number of similarities and continuities characterize the two sides of the borderland.[27] Haitian migration to the Dominican Republic is also changing in nature and, in the process, is altering the image of the Dominican Republic as a 'sugar-plantation netherworld.' The majority of Haitian migrants are still unskilled labourers who work in the agricultural sector (often informally), but most of them are not in the sugar industry; many are young people from an urban background rather than small-scale peasants and artisans; more and more women are crossing the border in search of domestic employment; while a remarkable number of students of both genders study in Dominican universities and in primary and secondary schools.[28]

---

26 Alexandre, 'Visión Haitiana', p. 126.

27 Alexandre, 'Visión Haitiana', p. 128–9.

28 Natalia Riveros, *Informe sobre la cuestión de la migración internacional en la República Dominicana para el año 2011* (Santo Domingo: Observatorio Migrantes del Caribe/Editora Búho, 2012), p. 27; Natalia Riveros, *Estado del arte de las migraciones*

From an international perspective, works such as Michele Wucker's *Why the Cocks Fight: Dominicans, Haitians, and the Struggle for Hispaniola* (1999), Eugenio Matibag's *Haitian-Dominican Counterpoint: Nation, Race and State on Hispaniola* (2003), Pedro San Miguel's *The Imagined Island: History, Identity and Utopia in Hispaniola* (1997; translated into English in 2005), Lucía Suárez's *The Tears of Hispaniola: Haitian and Dominican Diaspora Memory* (2006), Marie Redon's *Des îles en partage: Haïti & République Dominicaine, Saint-Martin, Timor* (2008), and Myriam J.A. Chancy's *From Sugar to Revolution: Women's Visions of Haiti, Cuba, and the Dominican Republic* (2012) have also contributed to making a global audience more aware of the contradictory dynamics which characterize Hispaniola and, to an extent, the Dominican–Haitian border.

The most recent publications, Chancy's *From Sugar to Revolution*, Suárez's *The Tears of Hispaniola*, and Redon's *Des îles en partage*, revisit the border of Hispaniola in broader contexts. Chancy's passionately written monograph, which revisits nationalistic discourses from the perspective of Afro-Caribbean women writers and artists, tries to forge 'a new consciousness' that could redraw the entire region in more positive and less distorted and distorting ways by bringing to the fore often neglected connections between Cuba, Haiti, and the Dominican Republic.[29] Suárez's *The Tears of Hispaniola* is a ground-breaking comparative study of Haitian and Dominican diasporic writers who engage with the troubled history of Hispaniola and whose works reveal a similar shared experience of human rights violations and trauma. Redon, instead, offers us a very insightful and scholarly comparative study of border relations in three different islands (Hispaniola, St Martin, and Timor) and investigates both the ways in which the existence of a border can influence the production of the insular space it divides and the contradictory processes of identification and dis-identification that it can trigger.

The book which has reached the widest audience, however, is probably *Why the Cocks Fight*, by the North American journalist Michele Wucker. Invoking the traditional cockfight as its governing metaphor, Wucker's depiction of Hispaniola provides a detailed and vivid analysis of the conflicts which characterize and have historically characterized the relationship between Haiti and the Dominican Republic. Informative, engaged, and engaging, *Why the Cocks Fight* has been described by some as 'an exemplary

---

que atañen a la República Dominicana 2012 (Santo Domingo: Observatorio Migrantes del Caribe/Editora Búho, 2013), pp. 55–64; Rodríguez Grullón, *Estado del arte*.

[29] Myriam Chancy, *From Sugar to Revolution: Women's Visions of Haiti, Cuba and the Dominican Republic* (Waterloo, Ontario: Wilfrid Laurier University Press, 2012), p. xxx.

book,' 'a richly textured social history [and] a powerful cultural analysis,'[30] but it has also been criticized by others for its perpetuation of 'the fatal conflict model' of Dominican–Haitian relations, a 'model' that Wucker's critics reject as reductionist because it overlooks collaboration and exchange in order to highlight antagonisms.[31]

Eugenio Matibag, who objected to Wucker's approach on this basis, has proposed instead a different model for looking at the interactions between the two nations that now share Hispaniola: the 'counterpoint' or, more precisely, the 'fugue.' 'Like the art of the fugue,' he writes, 'the island's socio-political destiny can be analysed as so many convergent–divergent narrative lines caught up in a puzzlelike unity of contrast and affinities, continuities and discontinuities.'[32] Matibag's monograph, his 'fugue,' is a thorough revisitation of the island's history from 1492 to 2003 which elegantly and astutely brings to the fore positive interactions as well as conflictual exchanges and usefully posits the border as a crucial site for our understanding of Hispaniola. A prolonged and in-depth study of literary texts was clearly beyond the scope of this monograph, which is more concerned with history than literary history, but Matibag also devotes one of his chapters to the representation of Haitians in Dominican literature: his six case studies cover the period from 1935 to 1983 and, according to Matibag, in all these texts one finds 'new imaginings of an insular community.'[33] It has been pointed out, however, that this study is not matched by what Matibag would call 'a convergent–divergent narrative' dealing with Dominicans in Haitian literary works – an oversight which for some sabotages the very notion of counterpoint which governs his monograph.[34] Nevertheless, the twenty-five pages Matibag allocates to the study of Dominican letters clearly indicate the potential of a more sustained engagement with literary and, by extension, artistic production.

Before Matibag, Pedro San Miguel had also insisted on the importance of literary texts: in his introduction to *The Imagined Island* he notes that literature and historiography (the focus of his study) are not as dissimilar as one might think, and goes as far as saying that works of fiction 'might turn out to be truer than historical works […] because of the meanings that they

[30] Madison Smartt Bell and *Kirkus Reviews*, quoted on the back cover of Michele Wucker's *Why the Cocks Fight: Dominicans, Haitians, and the Struggle for Hispaniola* (New York: Hill and Wang, 1999).
[31] Martínez, 'Not a Cockfight'.
[32] Eugenio Matibag, *Haitian-Dominican Counterpoint: Nation, Race and State on Hispaniola* (New York: Palgrave Macmillan, 2003), pp. 1–2, vii.
[33] Matibag, *Haitian-Dominican Counterpoint*, p. 186.
[34] Torres Saillant, 'Blackness and Meaning in Studying Hispaniola: A Review Essay', *Small Axe*, 19.10 (2006), pp. 180–88, p. 187.

evoke.'[35] In *The Imagined Island*, however, it is the work of Haitian (Jean Price-Mars) and Dominican (Antonio Sánchez-Valverde, Pedro Francisco Bonó, José Gabriel García, Manuel Arturo Peña-Battle, Joaquín Balaguer, Juan Bosch) historians which receives the lion's share. The only literary texts under scrutiny are some of Juan Bosch's short stories focused on the plight of Dominican *campesinos* vis-à-vis the modernization of the country, and border relations hardly figure in the analyses of these works.

Nevertheless, Matibag's and San Miguel's very brief incursions into literary history can both be seen to constitute useful precedents for *On the Edge* which, however, is not a study of the representations of Haiti and Haitians in Dominican literature nor of Dominicans and the Dominican Republic in Haitian letters; instead it brings to the fore works which engage with Hispaniola's border and borderland in different ways but mostly from the perspective of (fictional or factual) lived experiences. Overall, more than thirty fictional and non-fictional literary texts (novels, biographical narratives, memoirs, plays, poems, and travel writing) are given detailed attention alongside other forms of writing, such as geo-political-historical accounts of the status quo on the island or journalism. Mindful that writing is not the only means through which communities of a national or, in this case, transnational kind 'imagine' themselves, *On the Edge* also analyses over fifteen striking visual interventions – films, sculptures, paintings, photographs, videos, and artistic performances – many of which are sustained and complemented by different forms of writing (newspaper cuttings, graffiti, captions, song lyrics, screenplay, tattoos). Dominican and Dominican–American voices which reveal the deep contradictions inherent both in their country's dominant discourses and in its border and borderland policies are put in dialogue with works by Haitian and Haitian–Americans who also grapple with the existence of the border and borderland and the pitfalls of nationalism. As a matter of fact, there might not be a 'Dominican issue' in Haiti, as Guy Alexandre has rightly pointed out, but there certainly are works which can provide us with a Haitian perspective on the matter and, despite being less numerous than those originating from the neighbouring country and its diaspora, they definitely are as illuminating and as engaged. Furthermore, since, as Peter Hulme has elegantly put it, 'attention to place never asks to see a passport,' *On the Edge* also incorporates in this conversation writers born in Europe, the rest of the Americas, Algeria, New Zealand, and Japan who have also dealt with both the politics of borderline-crossing and the poetics of borderland-dwelling.[36]

---

[35] San Miguel, *The Imagined Island*, p. 5.
[36] Peter Hulme, *Cuba's Wild West: A Literary Geography of Oriente* (Liverpool:

Attention to place presupposes attention to time: 'place,' as Casey puts it, 'is an event, a matter of *taking place*.'[37] The politics of borderline-crossing and the poetics of borderland-dwelling explored in *On the Edge* can be understood only in relation to the time in which these activities are experienced and, simultaneously, in relation to the time in which they are narrated, reconsidered, and revisited. One can identify many different important moments in the history of the border and borderland: *On the Edge*, as we will see, touches on most of them in its eleven chapters, but the first seven chapters mainly focus on the causes, unfolding, and immediate aftermath of two events: the 1791 slave revolt (Chapters 1, 2, and 4) – because the function of border and borderland at that time often tends to be downplayed – and the 1937 massacre of Haitians and Haitian–Dominicans (Chapters 5, 6, and 7) – because it is often identified as a crucial primary exemplification of 'the fatal conflict model.' Taking its cue from a scene from a historical novel analysed in Chapter 2, Chapter 3 affords a productive detour focusing on nineteenth-, twentieth- and twenty-first-century reimaginings of the encounter between the indigenous population and the Spanish colonizers in early sixteenth-century Hispaniola; these texts also highlight how the presence of the border can cast a long (nationalistic) shadow even on reconstructions of a moment in the history of the island when the colonial and then national border had not yet been traced. Chapters 7 to 11 investigate instead contemporary works (mainly from the 1990s onwards) which, grappling with recent events and topical issues such as the 2010 earthquake, unregulated migration, and environmental degradation, continue to refute, requalify, interrogate, or reinforce dominant images of Hispaniola's border and borderland circulated or contested by the texts that figure in the preceding chapters. The fact that many of the works analysed in *On the Edge* deal with events which took place years, even centuries, before their composition, offers the possibility of opening a conversation between the portrayed settings and the contexts of production which illuminates the complex and multi-layered '*texture*' of the border and borderland: that is, what some humanist geographers identify as the ongoing processes that go

---

Liverpool University Press, 2011), p. 13. I am aware of those debates which highlight the difference of perspective between diasporic and non-diasporic Caribbean writers, but, to return to Hulme's point, attention to place never asks to see a birth certificate, an address, or a certificate of residence: the nationality, upbringing, residence, or language of the writers and artists included here are clearly crucial clues for a better understanding of their representations of borderline and borderland and their self-positioning vis-à-vis the topic, but they never constitute grounds for inclusion or exclusion.

[37] Casey, *The Fate of Place*, p. 339.

into the making and remaking of a certain place and the complex set of networks that shape it.[38]

✶✶✶

The cover of this book features *Línea Fronteriza Intermitente* ('Intermittent borderline,' 2008) by the Dominican artist David Pérez Karmadavis. Karmadavis made a model of Hispaniola and used small electric light bulbs to highlight both its perimeter and internal frontier. Yet, while the perimeter is permanently lighted, the border, which divides it in two, switches on and off intermittently. This intermittence can be interpreted in many different ways. One could argue, for example, that it powerfully reminds us that the border we now take for granted has not always been there. Before 1492, the island of Ayiti, as it was called then by the Taíno, who had been living there for centuries, was divided up into different chiefdoms or *cacicazgos* the exact boundaries of which are still disputed, although it is clear that they used to cut across the current frontier.[39] As we have seen, as a result of the landing of Christopher Columbus, Ayiti ('land of high mountains'[40]) was renamed Española ('little Spain'). The change of name presupposes a change of hands which was remarkably swift – by 1498 the socio-political structure of the Taíno had disintegrated[41] – but did not take place peacefully. The fight for control of land and resources, in fact, brought about new, fluctuating, permeable borders and contact zones between the indigenous population and the settlers. Moreover, the first enslaved Africans arrived in 1502 and a year later so many had escaped to the mountains that Governor Nicolás de Ovando had to ask for the intervention of the mother country.[42] As a

---

[38] The conceptualization of 'place as texture' comes from Paul Adams, Steven Hoelscher and Karen Till, 'Place in Context: Rethinking Humanist Geographies', in *Textures of Place: Exploring Humanist Geographies*, eds P. Adams, S. Hoelscher and K. Till (Minneapolis, MN: University of Minnesota Press, 2001), pp. xiii–xxxiii, p. xiii.

[39] The Taíno were the descendants of South American people who, over nearly five thousand years, had arrived to north-eastern South America and the Caribbean from the central Amazon. See Samuel M. Wilson, *Hispaniola: Caribbean Chiefdoms in the Age of Columbus* (Tuscaloosa, AL: The University of Alabama Press, 1990) pp. 1–2, 14–15, 17–20, fig. 2 p. 15; fig. 8 p. 110.

[40] I have chosen to use the spelling Ayiti here to avoid confusion but the spelling of the original Taíno name of the island has multiple variants, some of which will appear elsewhere in the monograph when I quote from writers and scholars who adopt them.

[41] Wilson, *Hispaniola*, p.108.

[42] Torres Saillant, 'La Condición Rayana: La Promesa Ciudadana en el Lugar del "Quicio"', in *La Frontera: prioridad en la agenda nacional*, ed. Secretaría de Estado de

result, other borders and contact zones, those which separated the territories controlled by the Spanish from those managed by the *maroons* (which often also included fugitive Taíno), became a concrete reality on the island.

The Spanish crown, however, lost interest in Hispaniola relatively quickly because the island did not have the riches it craved, and the first trespassers of European descent, mainly French *boucaniers*, slowly began to establish themselves in the north of the island and to engage in illicit trafficking with the Spanish settlers. In 1605, in order to prevent smuggling, the penetration of Protestantism, and the establishment of alternative political allegiances, Governor Osorio forced the Spanish dwellers of the north and north-west of the island to leave their land and properties and relocate in other areas closer to central power and easier to control. This further impoverished the colony and opened the door to the French occupation of the evacuated land. The French colony of Saint Domingue and the political border between France and Spain were officially established in 1777 with the Treaty of Aranjuez, the first of many documents aimed at solving territorial disputes between the two colonies and, later, the two nations of Hispaniola.

Moreau de Saint-Méry's monumental *Description Topographique et Politique de la partie espagnole de l'Isle Saint-Domingue* (1796) and *Description Topographique, Physique, Civile, Politique et Historique de la partie française de l'Isle Saint-Domingue* (1797), the point of departure for *On the Edge*, give us a clear picture of the situation in the two colonies until October 1789. The *Descriptions* highlight the political, social, geographical, and economic differences between the two sides and reveal Saint-Méry's deep anxiety over vast portions of the island which were under the control of the *maroons*, whose presence and activities were facilitated by the existence of a far too porous border. *On the Edge* continues by focusing on the 1791 slave rebellion, which was to change forever the status quo so meticulously depicted by Saint-Méry. Preceding the 1792 declaration of war between France and Spain, the events of 1791 offer us the possibility to concentrate on local across-the-border interactions 'from below' and their representations, rather than on the history of state-sanctioned interventions. One of the texts under scrutiny in Chapter 2 is a contemporary historical novel but the others are fictional and non-fictional accounts written in the immediate aftermath of the revolt, in the troubled years that followed it, and just before and after the 'reparation' that, in 1825, Haiti was required to pay to France in order to be recognized as a sovereign nation by the international community.[43] These reconstructions

---

las Fuerzas Armadas (Santo Domingo: Editora de las Fuerzas Armadas Dominicanas, 2004), pp. 220–28, p. 224.

[43] The last instalment was paid in 1922.

of the events are different in scope and aim but they all have in common the
attention they pay to the role that the 'intermittence' of the border played
before, during, and immediately after the 1791 revolt.

After the 1791 slave rebellion which was to become the Haitian Revolution,
Hispaniola became a war zone and the border often shifted or disappeared
altogether as the French, Spanish, English, and rebel armies forged and
broke alliances and alternatively secured and lost portions of territory. In
1801, Toussaint Louverture finally unified the island under French rule but
in 1804, when the formerly enslaved insurgents declared their independence
from France, the Spanish side of the island had already returned to Spanish
colonial rule. The Black Republic repeatedly tried to export the values of
the revolution to the other half of Hispaniola and, in 1822, the Haitian
president Jean-Pierre Boyer finally annexed it. The Haitian unification lasted
twenty-two years but the Haitian government did not officially recognize the
independence of the formerly Spanish part until 1855. The fear of another
Haitian occupation was so strong that, in 1861, the Dominican government
of Pedro Santana asked Spain to re-annex its former colony.[44] After years of
civil, political, and military unrest, the Dominican Republic became once
more independent from Spain in 1865, this time permanently and with the
help of the Haitians. In 1871 Haitians and Dominicans collaborated again
to prevent the annexation of the Dominican Republic to the United States,
which was supported by the Dominican President Buenaventura Báez.

These important episodes of across-the-border solidarity, however, were
quickly side-lined. Capitalizing instead on the fact that the birth of the
Dominican nation took place after twenty-two years of Haitian rule followed
by numerous attempts by Haitian leaders to reconquer Dominican territory,
influential sectors of the Dominican elite made sure that the nation-
building process was constructed on the development and consolidation of
anti-Haitianism and on the creation of the myth of the 'Dominican Indio,'
which at this point began to play a crucial role in Dominican literature and
culture (see Chapter 3). In the late nineteenth century, in fact, Dominican
'*mulattos* and *blacks* lexically disappeared in order to be replaced by *indios*,'
a stratagem to deny the existence of an Afro-Caribbean heritage in the
national make-up while accounting for the fact that blacks and mulattoes
constituted the majority of the population.[45] Literature has traditionally

---

[44] Santana, however, was also worried about the fact that the United States would
take advantage of the country's weakness in order to overthrow his government: see
Frank Moya Pons, *The Dominican Republic: A National History* [1998] (Princeton, NJ:
Markus Wiener, 2010), p. 199.
[45] Ernesto Sagás, *Race and Politics in the Dominican Republic* (Gainsville, FL:

played a part in nation-building processes and their many mystifications so it is not surprising that the 'myth of the Dominican indio' has been strategically mobilized in Dominican letters to sustain ultra-nationalistic discourses aimed at creating and consolidating a Dominicanness predicated on anti-Haitianism, negrophobia, and the demonization of the borderland as a dangerously porous territory in need of 'purging.' Nevertheless, literary and artistic interventions, as we will see, do not always support dominant discourses: most of the texts included in *On the Edge*, in fact, redefine the island's culture as a continuous process that transcends race and nationalism by highlighting patterns of identification with the borderland understood as a multi-ethnic contact zone and a transnational territory. These identifications, as we will see, are often activated by an exploration of syncretic belief systems such as Haitian Vodou or Dominican Vodú, or by revisitations of historical and mythical figures from the indigenous and colonial past. In Chapter 3, as I explained, I have put in dialogue texts which return to the beginning of the sixteenth century: they all have at their core the pre-partition figure of the Taíno Queen Anacaona and the chiefdom of Jaragua, a contact zone which straddles the current border. Chapter 4 of the monograph, instead, is focused on a historical novel published in the Dominican Republic in 2002 which deals with the 1791 revolt and its consequences on the Spanish side and provocatively recasts Toussaint's glorious entrance to Santo Domingo and his decision to immediately abolish slavery as a fugitive but glorious moment in the shared history of the island. In a long poem analysed in Chapter 8 which evokes powerful spirits of both Dominican Vodú and Haitian Vodou, it is the rebel Makandal who sustains, with his protean nature, a transnational vision and becomes a key figure in what the Dominican poet Manuel Rueda has called 'the heart-breaking epic of [the] border struggle.'[46]

It is important to remember that the present border is a legacy not just of colonialism but also of neo-colonialism. At the cusp of the nineteenth and twentieth century, Hispaniola's borderland was characterized by economic exchanges and collaborative linkages between the two peoples, but in 1907

University Press of Florida, 2000), p. 35 (italics in the text). A project to substitute the term *indio* as the official racial category and as the skin colour descriptor used in Dominican identity cards with the terms *negro* (black) and *mulato* (which for a long time have exclusively denoted Haitians) was presented in 2011. Viviano de León, 'DR será de negros, blancos y mulatos', *Listin Diario*, 11 November 2011, http://www.listin.com.do/la-republica/2011/11/11/210557/RD-sera-de-negros-blancos-y-mulatos [accessed 25 November 2014].

[46] Manuel Rueda, *La criatura terrestre* (Santo Domingo: Editora del Caribe, 1963), p. 26.

things began to slowly change when the Dominican border's customs collections were turned over to the United States, which imposed hefty fines for smuggling.[47] The United States' occupation of Hispaniola which followed shortly after also accelerated the rebirth of the sugar industry, especially in the Dominican Republic, setting the pattern for the exploitation of the Haitian workforce. In 1924, when the United States withdrew from Dominican territory, North American corporations owned eleven out of the twenty-one sugar mills operating in the country and 98 per cent of its sugar exports were absorbed by the United States' market.[48] The signing of the treaty which, in 1929, redrew the border between the two nations and sanctioned the positioning of a new line of 'pyramids' to mark the borderline, was strongly encouraged by the United States, keen to stabilize a potentially volatile situation for their own benefit. The 1929 treaty was revised in 1935 and 1936, although, until the 1936 agreement, which fixed the present line, there was no mutually recognized political divide between the Dominican Republic and Haiti.

Until 1937, however, Hispaniola's borderland continued to be a contact zone where central power was weaker than across-the-border cooperation. In October of the same year, however, Trujillo ordered the massacre of Haitians and Haitian–Dominicans in the Dominican border as part of a ferocious campaign orchestrated against Haitians, blackness, and a notion of Dominicanness which would embrace the African presence. The estimated numbers of victims vary from 14,000 to 40,000 and this carnage completely destroyed a way of life which had ethnic pluralism and a porous frontier at its core.[49] Chapters 5, 6, and 7 present fictional and non-fictional reconstructions of life on the borderland before, during, and immediately after the massacre, when a territorial reorganization on the two sides was under way with the establishment of agricultural colonies aimed at 'dominicanizing' and 'whitening' the frontier on the Dominican side, and at retaining experienced peasants on the national territory on the Haitian side. I will argue that, far

[47] Lauren Derby, 'Haitians, Magic, and Money: *Raza* and Society in the Haitian-Dominican Borderlands, 1900 to 1937', *Comparative Studies in Society and History*, 36.3 (1994), pp. 488–526, pp. 490, 499, 502.
[48] James Ferguson, *Dominican Republic: Beyond the Lighthouse* (London: Latin American Bureau, 1992), p. 17.
[49] For life in the borderland before 1937 see, for example, Richard Lee Turits, 'A World Destroyed, A Nation Imposed: The 1937 Haitian Massacre in the Dominican Republic', *Hispanic American Historical Review*, 82.3 (2002), pp. 589–635 and Derby, 'Haitians, Magic, and Money'. According to Dilla Alfonso, currently, the Dominican borderland is culturally less '*mestizada*' or cross-fertilized than many other frontier regions in the world ('Pensar la frontera', p. 5).

from being limited to (a long overdue) commemoration of those who perished in 1937, some of the fictional recreations of the fluid cultural and social dynamics of the pre-massacre borderland might also be read as protracted meditations on border relations and as political interventions which aim to propose models for cohabitation on the island. Dominican anti-Africanism and anti-Haitianism persisted and further developed after Trujillo's death with Joaquín Balaguer, one of Trujillo's closest aides and later president of the Dominican Republic from 1960 to 1962, 1966 to 1978 and 1986 to 1996. Chapter 8 includes contemporary texts which constitute valiant attempts to come to terms with and, in some cases, even undo the legacy of the 1937 massacre: they promote national identities which are not predicated against transnational solidarity, celebrate the shared history and cultural heritage of all the inhabitants of Hispaniola, and insist that Haitians and Dominicans can live together in harmony and peace only if both Haiti and the Dominican Republic commit to social and political equality and democracy.

In line with the 'on and off' pattern highlighted by Karmadavis in *Línea Fronteriza Intermitente*, the 1937 massacre and the Haitian unification of the island in 1822–44 can therefore be evoked as examples of violent enforcement and violent erasure of the border. Yet, there are also other explanations for the frontier's intermittence which do not involve warfare. Dominican and Haitian dominant classes have frequently colluded and still collude in their exploitation of Haitian migrants and, in order to facilitate the movement of this cheap workforce, the border between the two nations was/is made to become strategically intermittent by ad hoc laws or even by patently illegal but tolerated behaviour, a point that is underlined in most chapters of *On the Edge*.

Since the early 1980s the predicament of Haitian *braceros* working in the *bateyes* of the Dominican sugar industry has been the focus of international human rights campaigns, especially after the London Anti-Slavery Society denounced the Dominican Republic as a country which enslaved Haitian workers in 1979 and Jean-Bertrand Aristide criticized the neighbouring country for its inhumane treatment of the Haitian workforce at the United Nations in 1991. Works included in Chapter 9, however, show that the life and working conditions in the *bateyes* are not the only vehicle to understanding border relations, and that not all Haitians in dire straits resort to migration to the neighbouring country. Shedding light on the conditions of other migrants who cross Hispaniola's internal border both legally and illegally – and which have received less attention by the media – these texts show not only that not all the Haitians who enter the Dominican Republic are *braceros* but also that not all the migrants of Hispaniola cross the border from Haiti to the Dominican Republic. Chapter 9, moreover, also draws attention to the role that the many manifestations of what Johan Galtung calls 'structural violence' (class, gender and race discrimination, pigmentocracy, corruption, primacy of profit over human dignity, environmental degradation, overcentralization of resources[50]) can play in the continuous impoverishment and deterioration of living conditions of the inhabitants on both sides of the island: the border, as one of the writers under scrutiny in this chapter puts it, 'divides the land but not the misery of the people.'[51]

Aristide's denunciation of the *braceros*' condition at the United Nations in 1991 was concomitant with the publication of Dominican ultra-nationalistic texts such as Luis Julián Pérez's *Santo Domingo frente al destino* ('Santo Domingo facing its destiny,' 1990) and Manuel Núñez's *El ocaso de la nación dominicana* ('The twilight of the Dominican nation,' 1990), which highlighted the crucial role played by the internal border of Hispaniola in what they considered the ongoing and serious threat posed by Haitian migration.[52] Pérez went as far as suggesting the erection of a wire fence to prevent across-the-border movement and exchanges while Núñez placed at the core of the nation what he – significantly – called 'the spiritual frontier,' which comprised the 'culture, language, values' from which the nation was moving 'further and further away' owing to the 'Haitianization of the countryside.'[53] Pérez's and Núñez's texts found an important precedent in Balaguer's *La isla al revés: Haití y el destino dominicano* ('The island the wrong way round: Haiti and the Dominican destiny'), published in 1983. Based on *La realidad dominicana* ('The Dominican reality'), a book written in 1947, when he was Foreign Minister to Trujillo, *La isla al revés* depicts the country's proximity with Haiti as a grave peril for the Dominicans, who can protect themselves only by promoting the *Dominicanization* or *nacionalization* of the frontier, which has to cover four different aspects: economical, moral, political, and racial.[54] While famously describing the Dominican Republic as 'the most Spanish people/nation in the Americas,' Balaguer

[50] Johan Galtung, 'Violence, Peace, and Peace Research,' *Journal of Peace Research*, 6.3 (1969), pp. 167–91.
[51] Máximo Avilés Blonda, *Pirámide 179*, in *Teatro* (Santo Domingo: Ediciones de la Sociedad de Autores y Compositores Dramáticos de la República Dominicana, 1968), p. 168.
[52] Luis Julián Pérez, *Santo Domingo frente al destino* (Santo Domingo: Editora Taller, 1990), p. 268 and Manuel Núñez, *El ocaso de la nación dominicana* (Santo Domingo: Alfa & Omega, 1990). Pérez had served in Trujillo's administration from 1945 to 1961 and then became the leader of the right-wing political party Unión Nacionalista of which Núñez is also a member.
[53] Pérez, *Santo Domingo*, p. 268; Núñez, *El ocaso* (1990), p.55.
[54] Balaguer, *La isla al revés*, p. 77.

insists on 'Haitian imperialism,' conflict, and incompatibility between the neighbouring nations, and depicts Haitians as primitives, diseased, ignorant, and morally flawed.[55] *La isla al revés* ends with a (very vague) proposal for a 'confederation' of the two countries for (allegedly) mutual advantage; however, considering the different conditions of the two sides of the island, it is evident which partner would control the switch which would regulate the exchanges and, implicitly, which partner would benefit the most from it.[56]

La isla al revés has had multiple editions and is still widely available in Dominican bookshops, while the ultra-nationalists' position is influential and, as highlighted in the conclusion, is still heard loudly and clearly in political debates. It is important to underline, however, that many Dominican writers, artists, and scholars openly disagree with ultra-nationalist and xenophobic positions and *On the Edge* offers an impressive body of work characterized by the urge to counteract both anti-Haitianism and the demonization or mystification of the borderland that it presupposes. Chapter 10 acknowledges the endurance of Dominican anti-Haitian discourses but also the vitality of more enabling views on the borderland and border relations and presents contrasting approaches to the spectre of a Haitian 'invasion.' At the same time, Chapters 10 and 11 also focus on Haitian and Dominican texts which display a strong commitment to a transnational ethos which has the borderland at its core, and works produced after the devastating earthquake that hit Haiti on 12 January 2010 which reiterate that dismantling ultra-nationalisms is the first step towards an authentic across-the-border solidarity and the transformation of Hispaniola into a place where one could develop a national identity in relation with and not in opposition to one's neighbours. Moreover, like all the other works included in *On the Edge* – and, crucially, including *On the Edge* itself – the texts in Chapter 11 do not limit themselves to analysing the existing state of affairs; they also actively arrange and rearrange the score of 'the music of what happens' on the ground, illuminating the processes and histories that constantly weave the *text*ure of the borderland and the complex web of border relations in Hispaniola while actively participating in, and contributing to, their shaping and reshaping.[57]

---

[55] Balaguer, *La isla al revés*, p. 63. In Spanish, 'pueblo' means both 'nation' and 'people.'

[56] Balaguer, *La isla al revés*, pp. 223–31.

[57] I have borrowed the expression 'the music of what happens' – which I consider to be one of the most arresting definitions of 'place' I have ever come across – from the poem 'Song' by Seamus Heaney in *Field Work* (New York: Farrar, Straus and Giroux, 1979), p. 56.

Chapter One

Landscaping Hispaniola: Médéric Louis Élie Moreau de Saint-Méry and border politics

Médéric Louis Élie Moreau de Saint-Méry, *Description Topographique et Politique de la partie espagnole de l'Isle Saint-Domingue* (1796) and *Description Topographique, Physique, Civile, Politique et Historique de la partie française de l'Isle Saint-Domingue* (1797)

The contradictory dynamics engendered by the presence of a colonial frontier in Hispaniola are carefully highlighted in the work of Médéric Louis Élie Moreau de Saint-Méry, which concerns itself with pre-revolutionary French Saint Domingue and Spanish Santo Domingo. A prominent member of the white creole elite born in Martinique in 1750, Saint-Méry is the author of a monumental work which set out to describe Hispaniola in its entirety but within the framework of its geopolitical colonial division. The *Description Topographique et Politique de la partie espagnole de l'Isle Saint-Domingue* was published in Philadelphia in 1796 and followed, a year later, by the *Description Topographique, Physique, Civile, Politique et Historique de la partie française de l'Isle Saint-Domingue*.[1] With its neat two-fold division,

---

[1] Médéric Louis Élie Moreau de Saint-Méry, *Description Topographique et Politique de la partie espagnole de l'Isle Saint-Domingue. Avec des Observations générales sur le Climat, la Population, les Productions, le Caractère & les Mœurs des Habitans de cette Colonie et un Tableau raisonné des différents parties de son Administration; Accompagnée d'une nouvelle Carte de la totalité de l'Isle*, 2 vols (Philadelphia: chez l'auteur, 1796) and *Description Topographique, Physique, Civile, Politique et Historique de la partie française de l'Isle Saint-Domingue. Avec des Observations générales sur la Population, sur le Caractère & les Mœurs de ses divers Habitans; sur son Climat, sa Culture, ses Productions, son Administrations &c, &c. Accompagnées des détails les plus propres à faire connaître l'état de cette Colonie à l'epoque du 18 Octobre 1789; Et*

Saint-Méry's work is organized in a way that invites readers to take for granted the partition of the island between Spain and France and betrays Saint-Méry's determination to contribute to the consolidation of what Muir would call a 'vertical interface.'[2]

Saint-Méry's *Description of the partie française* has received more attention from historians and scholars, particularly because it contains his well-known detailed racial taxonomies and offers precious information on pre-revolutionary Saint Domingue. What matters here, however, is that, back in the eighteenth century, Saint-Méry had fully realized that, in order to be fully understood, the island of Hispaniola has to be approached in its entirety. While being ultimately committed to the (re)inscription of the colonial frontier, both Saint-Méry's *Descriptions* intriguingly oscillate between its erasure and its reinforcement. Moreover, as determined as he might have been to contribute to the consolidation of the colonial border, which, at the time of writing, had only very recently been officially sanctioned, Saint-Méry also reveals the existence of horizontal dimensions and dynamics which transcend and traverse this vertical interface.

Smuggling and illicit trade between the two parts of the island were an

---

d'une nouvelle Carte de la totalité de l'Isle, 2 vols (Philadelphia: chez l'auteur, 1797–98). In April 2010 I consulted the manuscript of the two volumes of the *Description de la partie espagnole* in the Archives Nationales d'Outre-Mer in Aix-en- Provence (ms F³ 102–103). The pages of the manuscript are divided into two columns, one of which contains additions or amendments presumably included during revisions. With regards to content, the manuscript is not dramatically different from the version which was printed in Philadelphia so I will be referring to the printed version, pointing out significant discrepancies from the manuscript when necessary. In the Archives Nationales d'Outre-Mer I also found the manuscript of the English translation of the *Description de la partie espagnole* (2 vols – ms F³ 104–105), which was published immediately after the French edition and which had not been catalogued yet (the *Description de la partie espagnole* erroneously appeared to be in four volumes and catalogued as ms F³ 102–105). The *Description de la partie espagnole* was translated by William Cobbett but Saint-Méry played an active role in the translation, as testified by the many letters the two exchanged and which are included in the first volume of the manuscript. Here I will be referring to this translation unless otherwise specified. The translation presents no division into columns but its pages are not always consistently numbered – volume one is especially erratic. In my references I will be giving the page number or letter on the manuscript accompanied by the page number of the 1796 printed French edition. The manuscript of the English translation will be referred to as ms, vol. I or vol. II, while the *Description de la partie espagnole* will be referred to as PE, vol. I or vol. II. Quotations from and references to the *Description de la partie française* will be referred to as PF, vol. I or vol. II and in this case all translations into English are mine.

[2] Muir, *Modern Political Geography*, p. 119.

open secret; for a long time the two colonies were prevented from trading
with one another by their respective mother countries but did so all the same,
out of necessity and mutual advantage. Santo Domingo's livestock economy
(after initial attempts, the Spanish abandoned mining and sugar plantations)
depended in great part on the contraband trade with Saint Domingue and,
as we will see, gave rise to a different relationship between masters and
slaves. Like leather and beef, slaves were bought and sold across the border
both legally and illegally and the French did sometimes 'borrow' them from
the Spanish when they needed more workers.[3] Saint Domingue's slaves
also crossed the border of their own volition and with the active assistance
and complicity of the maroon communities.[4] They were constantly drawn
to the Spanish side of the island by the enticing promises of the colonists
and authorities, who generally granted them freedom because they did not
participate in the slave trade and did not have the financial resources to
buy labour and develop a plantation economy.[5] The relative proximity of
the Spanish border has in fact been identified as one of the main causes of
marronage, a major problem for French plantation owners.[6] These across-
the-border trajectories and connections gave rise to alternative networks and
created borderlands characterized by a horizontality which cut through and
exploded the official vertical frontier.

In the *Description de la partie française*, for example, Saint-Méry identifies
the troublesome Sierra de Bahoruco as a region unto itself, a borderland
which did not really belong to either of the colonial powers. He refers in
detail to the Bahoruco maroons' protracted defiance to colonial authority
and to the intensification of their incursions from the Spanish side into the
Saint Domingue border region of Cul-de-Sac, Anse à Pitre, Fond Parisien,
Croix-de-Bouquet, and Mirebalais throughout the eighteenth century.
Saint-Méry also retraces the history of the Bahoruco region and explains
how its topography and toponymy had been deeply affected by anti-colonial
rebellions from a very early stage. The Etang-Salé, he adds, was renamed
Henriquille or Petit-Henry because it was the place where the sixteenth-
century Indian rebel leader Enriquillo or cacique Henry met François de

[3] Matibag, *Haitian-Dominican Counterpoint*, pp. 50, 58.

[4] Jean Fouchard, *The Haitian Maroons: Liberty or Death*, trans. A. Faulkner Watts
[1972] (New York: Edward W. Blyden Press, 1981), pp. 276–8.

[5] Rubén Silié, 'The *Hato* and the *Conuco*: The Emergence of Creole Culture', in
Dominican Cultures: The Making of a Caribbean Society, ed. B. Vega, trans. C. Ayorinde
(Princeton, NJ: Markus Wiener Publishers, 2007), pp. 131–60, pp. 141, 143.

[6] Matibag, *Haitian-Dominican Counterpoint*, p. 54; Fouchard, *The Haitian Maroons*,
p. 274.

Barrio Nuovo, who was on a peace-seeking mission on behalf of the Emperor Charles V.[7] Moreover, as Saint-Méry continues,

> the canton of Anses à Pitre still contains evidence of the precautions that the cacique took to avoid falling into the power of his enemy. At Anse-à-Boeuf one can find a semicircular retrenchment about four and a half feet deep, attached to a mountain at each side [....]. All around there are caves full of human bones. Anse-à-Boeuf is connected with the Etang-Salé by a gorge which widens slightly at a point called Fond-Trélinguet and which runs to the Saint-Jean de la Croix-des-Bouquets district to connect the plain of Cul-de-Sac to Fond-Parisien. This connection is described by several hunters and was verified no longer than twenty-five years ago.[8]

For more than eighty-five years, Saint-Méry writes, the region in question was occupied by the maroons, who regarded it as their own domain[9] and who continued to adapt indigenous caves to their strategic needs well into the nineteenth century.

Saint-Méry's admirably detailed volumes on Hispaniola were the product of eighteen years of work,[10] during which he benefited from direct experience of life in the two colonies and access to both local archives (private and public) and documents relevant to the colonial administration to be found in Europe. An advocate for more economic and political autonomy for the colony, Saint-Méry actively participated in the French Revolution and for a short period of time he was even in charge of the Bastille after 14 July. However, he held moderate pro-slavery and pro-monarchic views which obliged him to abandon the ranks of the Reformers and flee France in 1793. He then moved to Philadelphia, where he opened a publishing house and a bookshop and where he published both his *Descriptions*. The two volumes devoted to the Spanish side were the first to be printed, as a result of the cession of Spanish Santo Domingo to France in 1795. This geopolitical fact, Saint-Méry explains, made him think that 'the publication of the description of the Spanish part of that Isle, would be interesting to the public.'[11] Saint-Méry further discusses the possible reasons behind this interest: knowing more about Santo Domingo, the first American colony, is helpful to better understanding what he calls

---

[7] PF, vol. II, p. 496.
[8] PF, vol. II, pp. 496–7.
[9] PF, vol. II, p. 497.
[10] Ms, vol. I, p. B; PE, vol. I, p. 2.
[11] Ms, vol. I, p. D; PE, vol. I, p. 4.

'the European genius.'[12] More poignantly, since the cession had dismantled the colonial administrative system he so carefully and minutely describes, his work is precious in that it gives his readers a precise sense of what had been destroyed.[13] This declaration of purpose sustains both his *Descriptions*, which he prefaces by informing his readers that he deliberately omitted to report any changes related to or derived from 1789.[14] In the very title of the volume devoted to the French side he indicates that his analysis covers the *status quo* up to 18 October 1789, significantly, only thirteen days after Louis XVI assented to the Declaration of the Rights of Man and four days before the National Assembly accepted the petition of rights of 'free citizens of color' from Saint Domingue. In other words, the text is suspended *before* the moment in which Enlightenment emancipationism had what Saint-Méry considered lethal consequences for the colonial social and racial structure. In the 'Discours Préliminaire' of the first volume on the French side, Saint-Méry famously compares Saint Domingue to the past civilizations of Greece and Rome[15] but, by and large, his nostalgia for the past is accompanied by a strong desire to shape the future, to 'make' history, not just to report it: 'But, & I cannot give up my hopes [...] France might need some information to assist her in choosing what to do in order to turn Saint Domingue once again into a profitable colony.'[16] As we will see, Saint-Méry's projected future of further development and exploitation also had a spatial, not only a temporal, dimension which was nevertheless rife with anxieties and contradictions.

The *Description de la partie espagnole* begins with an *Abrégé Historique* or *Historical Summary* which records, at length, the vicissitudes of the colonial border from 1630, the date of the arrival of the French buccaneers on the island of Tortuga, to 1777, when the Treaty of Aranjuez between France and Spain (provisionally) finalized the frontier between the two colonies.[17] From

---

[12] Ms, vol. I, p. E; PE, vol. I, p. 5.

[13] Ms, vol. I, p. EF; PE, vol. I, pp. 5–6.

[14] Of course, this is not entirely true. For example, the 2004 reproduction of the manuscript of la *Description de la partie française* includes all the passages that Saint-Méry decided to eliminate in 1797. One can, for example, find an argument in support of a more 'humane' form of slavery written in 1788 or 1789 which Saint-Méry later decided to suppress (tome I, p. 46). Most of Saint-Méry's amendments, however, are not as significant as this particular one. See *Description Topographique, Physique, Civile, Politique et Historique de la partie française de l'Isle Saint-Domingue*, 3 vols, 3rd edition (Saint-Denis: La Société Française d'histoire d'outre-mer, 2004).

[15] PF, vol. I, p. viii.

[16] PF, vol. I, pp. V–vi.

[17] In the manuscript the Historical Summary is to be found in the first volume and is numbered rather chaotically: i–xxiii; A–Z; Aa–Ss; xli–xlix; PE, vol. I, pp. i–xxij.

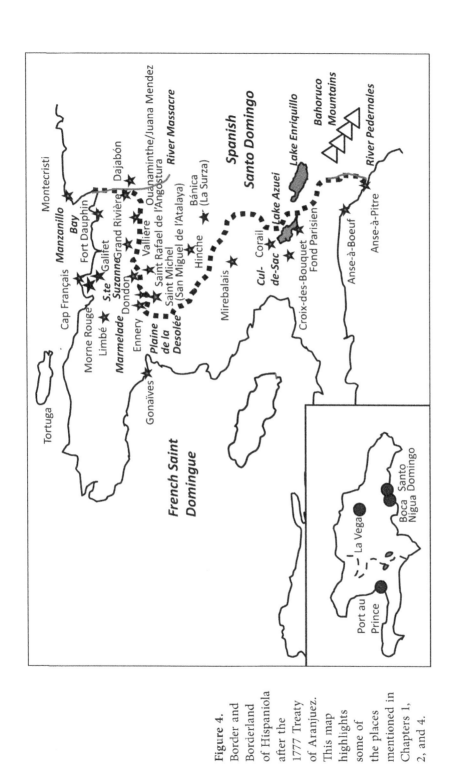

Figure 4. Border and Borderland of Hispaniola after the 1777 Treaty of Aranjuez. This map highlights some of the places mentioned in Chapters 1, 2, and 4.

the Spanish perspective, the treaty of Aranjuez legitimized the occupation of their territory by French buccaneers and other outlaws – Saint-Méry calls them 'Adventurers'[18] – but, in his unsurprisingly biased *Historical Summary*, Saint-Méry chronicles the progress of the French settlement on the island, omitting the fact that they had actually occupied the Spanish colony illegally. According to the treaty, which the conscientious and cunning Saint-Méry appends to the *Historical Summary*,[19] the border begins with the d'Ajabon or Massacre River in the north of the island and ends with the Anse à Pitre or Pedernales River in the south.[20] The treaty also determines where the line of demarcation must be signposted on the territory by 221 pairs of stone pyramids bearing the inscription 'France: Espana.'[21]

In other words, before he begins to describe the two sides of the island, Saint-Méry wants to make sure that his readers appreciate the difference between what Henri Lefebvre would call a disordered *lived in* place (the product of the territorial conflicts between the two colonies and of across-the-border activities) and the order inherent in a *conceived* place (the two colonies as defined by the vertical interface).[22] Yet, the fact that the treaty specifies that anyone caught destroying or tampering with the stone pyramids will be condemned to death, and that both colonies should do everything in their power to discourage smuggling, is symptomatic of a widespread lack of trust in the effectiveness of a legally sanctioned vertical boundary.[23] Saint-Méry includes the treaty and detailed information regarding the borderline only in the *Description de la partie espagnole* despite the fact that, arguably, they were relevant to both sides of the border. Its omission from the *Description de la partie française* was instrumental to the 'naturalization' of the French presence on Hispaniola implicit in Saint-Méry's decision to mirror the newly officialized geopolitical division of the island (*partie française* and *partie espagnole*) in the textual organization of his work.

---

[18] Ms, vol. I, p. i; PE, vol. I, p. i.

[19] In the manuscript the treaty is chaotically numbered and is to be found at K–xlviii; PE, vol. I, pp. xxiij–xlviii.

[20] Owing its name to 'ancient murderous acts reciprocally committed by the Buccaneers and the Spaniards in their disputes over the territory' (PF, vol. I, p. 108) the Massacre River still marks the internal border of the island. In both *Descriptions*, the Massacre River is also called Dajabon, d'Ajabon, Dahabon, or Daxabon (the spelling is unstable) after the small border town alongside which it runs.

[21] PE, vol. I, p. xxviij; ms, vol. I, p. U.

[22] Henri Lefebvre, *The Production of Space*, trans. D. Nicholson-Smith [1974] (Malden, MA: Blackwell, 1991), pp. 38–41.

[23] PE, vol. I, p. xlv and xlvij.

Saint-Méry's *Description de la partie espagnole* provides a picture of the political and religious structure of the Spanish side (i.e. mayors, archbishops), incorporates ethnographic material (i.e. 'Character and manners of the Spanish Creoles'), and tidily organizes his survey by administrative areas (i.e. 'Bahoruco and its vicinity') and geographical features (i.e. 'Mountains,' 'Plains,' and 'Rivers'). Similarly, his *Description de la partie française* contains topographic, ethnographic, and administrative information on the three different parts of the French colony (Partie du Nord, Partie de l'Ouest, and Partie du Sud) and it is also minutely organized parish by parish. Unsurprisingly, however, the 'neutral' word *Description* is not the most appropriate to define Saint-Méry's encyclopedic work.

Saint-Méry's survey of the territory of the French colony incessantly celebrates the fact that it is punctuated by sugar plantations and other manufactures. For example, in the small border district of Maribarou (which belongs partly to the parish of Fort Dauphin and partly to the parish of Ouanaminthe in the Partie du Nord) Saint-Méry proudly counts twenty-seven sugar plantations – that is, five more than the ones active in the whole of Santo Domingo. In his meticulous depiction of the Spanish side of the border, from Dajabón in the north to the *étangs* or lakes (currently Lake Enriquillo and Lake Azuei) in the south,[24] Saint-Méry predominantly highlights the different conditions of the two colonies. In his description of the Baye de Mancenille (Manzanillo Bay) on the northern coast of Hispaniola, for example, he observes that

> the most striking circumstance and that perhaps which is the most proper to mark the character of the two nations is to see on the west side of the River Massacre, settlements where everything bespoke an active industry, and a degree of wealth that extends even to objects of luxury, while on the other side, all appears barren.[25]

Also, further away from the border, the beauty of Santo Domingo is hardly ever contemplated for its own sake; more often than not Saint-Méry's landscaping turns into a criticism of the Spanish colonists' way of life:

> The delighted eye sweeps around over the Cape Raphael, the Pointe-de-l'Epée, all the settlement of the immense plains de Seybo and Higuey, Santo Domingo and its environs, and finds no end of its variegated pleasures till it arrives at the east of the group of Cibao.

---

[24] Ms, vol. I, pp. 243–83; PE, vol. I, pp. 252–82.
[25] Ms vol. I, pp. 10–11; PE, vol. I, pp. 206–7.

In this extensive view there are a thousand spots which, for a time, charm the sight and withhold it from the general picture by a display of more picturesque and striking beauties. All is regular confusion and majestic simplicity.

[...]

What sorrow must the beholder of all these riches feel when he considers, that nature has lavished them in vain. That they have served only to awaken the drowsy Spaniard a moment from his torpidity in order to sink the unhappy Indians to the grave in laboring to satisfy his guilty avarice, his thirst for gold, to him superior to all but in indolence.[26]

This waste of resources is widespread. On the French side one can find 793 *sucreries*, 3150 *indigoteries*, 789 *cotonneries* and 3117 *cafeteries*,[27] but Spanish Santo Domingo, despite being much larger than its French counterpart, counts only twenty-two sugar manufactures of any consequence; coffee, cotton, and cocoa are grown just to meet the need of the locals and indigo, which used to be cultivated, grows only spontaneously.[28] Many of the pastures of Santo Domingo are infested by 'lineonal,' 'mirtle,' 'wild basilick,' and other plants not suitable for the subsistence of livestock[29] and the mines of the Spanish side are rich but not exploited.[30] Overall, Saint-Méry concludes, the Spanish colony is able to survive only because of its licit and illicit trade with the French side.[31]

Spanish indolence, however, is not just a waste of resources but also a dangerous habit: as we have seen, Saint-Méry is deeply concerned about the fertile border area of the Bahoruco which, sadly neglected by the Spanish, has in fact become the 'place of refuge of the fugitive Spanish and French

---

[26] Ms, vol. I, pp. 242–3; PE, vol. I, pp. 154–5. There is a mistake in the translation because the French original refers to the west and not to the east of the group of Cibao. In the manuscript of the French version, the second part of this quotation, where Spanish indolence, torpidity, guilty avarice, and thirst for gold are emphasized, appears in the column for revisions and additions (125 Verso).

[27] PF, vol. I, p.100.

[28] Ms, vol. I, p. 60; PE, vol. I, pp. 63–4.

[29] Ms, vol. I, p. 275 and PE vol. I, p. 275.

[30] See, for example, ms, vol. I, p. 150; PE, vol. I, pp. 109; ms, vol. I, pp. 240–41; PE, vol. I, pp. 153–4.

[31] See, for example, ms, vol. I, p. 220 and pp. 272–4; PE, vol. I, p. 142 and pp. 272–4 and ms, vol. II, p. 99; PE, vol. II, p. 99.

negroes.'[32] Once again, the author remarks how one could instead advantageously mine gold there[33] and cultivate different crops, including indigo, cotton, tobacco, coffee, and, obviously, sugar.[34] More precisely, he claims, one could establish more than 250 sugar manufactures in the area.[35] All in all, Saint-Méry infers that the French (but he prudently uses passive sentences or the pronoun '*on*' all along) would make a better use of the Spanish colony's resources. For instance, he claims that Azua's 'territory might certainly have four hundred sugar plantations and furnish employment for 80000 negroes' and hypothesizes that 'it would be an easy matter to establish in the plain, between Santo Domingo and Pointe-de-l'Épée, many hundreds of sugar plantations.'[36]

The island is therefore reimagined transformed and homogenized into an extended version of Saint Domingue, with one sugar plantation after the other. In order to do so, Saint-Méry's gaze substitutes the concrete and unruly reality of 'place' with an abstract homogenous 'space' in which those dissimilarities which ironically presuppose the existence of a vertical border between the two sides of the island and which, as we will see, he explores in detail in his *oeuvre*, are conveniently neutralized. The symbolic nature of the borderland is especially altered by Saint-Méry's projections: under the reader's eyes the Bahoruco, a place qualified by underground and clandestine indigenous and black resistance, is transmuted into an ordered network of plantations, a dominated site of management and containment where everything is 'on the surface' and under surveillance. Moreover, Saint-Méry's reimaginings simultaneously explode the verticality of the international/colonial border and the horizontal dimension that characterizes the borderland of the maroons' Bahoruco and substitute them with a different form of horizontality engendered by assimilation and by the total obliteration of differences and dissent. Saint-Méry's landscaping, therefore, betrays an underlying urge to conjure up a safe perspective from which to approach border politics and to frame both borderland and the people living on it which transcends scientific, objective 'description.' This urge becomes particularly

---

[32] Ms, vol. I, p. 88; PE, vol. I, p. 80.
[33] Ms, vol. I, p. 88; PE, vol. I, p. 80.
[34] Ms, vol, p. 95; PE, vol. I, p. 83.
[35] Ms, vol. I, pp. 94–95; PE, vol. I, p. 83.
[36] Ms, vol. I, p. 124; PE, vol. I, p. 97 and ms, vol. I, p. 264; PE, vol. I, p 167. In the 'Table Générale Des Matières' ('Table of contents'), under 'Sucreries,' Saint-Méry also lists: 'Those which already are in the plain of Santo Domingo and the ones one could add to them' and 'Those one could put in the plain of La Vega'), PE, vol. II, p. 305. The 'Table Générale Des Matières' is not in the manuscript of the English translation so the above translations are mine.

poignant if one considers that, while he was revising his work in 1793,[37] the
Spanish colony was offering sanctuary to fugitive rebels from Saint Domingue
and lending them arms to support their struggle. Furthermore, in 1795, the
Peace of Basle had sanctioned the cession of Santo Domingo to the French
République and, in 1796, the date of publication of the *Description de la partie*
espagnole, Toussaint's collaboration with the Republican government (that is,
Saint-Méry's own enemies) was becoming stricter.

In his landscaping of the island Saint-Méry constantly emphasizes the
importance of human intervention to turn sterility into fertility. A plantation
estate, Saint-Méry explains in the volumes devoted to Saint Domingue, is a
'grand and fine machine'[38] which also requires the work of engineers in order
to function properly. Sugar and indigo production heavily depended on the
presence of mills and other machines and on adequate irrigation. Time and
time again, Saint-Méry proudly points out how the nature of vast areas of
the French colony destined to sterility because of annual droughts had been
dramatically altered with *ad hoc* hydraulic works. A case in point is the area
on the French side of the River Massacre, which could have been as dry and
sterile as the Spanish one if the colonists and the colonial administration
had not intervened. Since 1730 the inhabitants of the region had tried to find
ways in which the water of the River Massacre could be used to irrigate the
soil and move plantation mills. Their efforts were perfected in 1786, when it
was decided that the five *habitations* in the area would benefit from a new
water pipe from the river and their rights to the water and order of access
to it were established by law.[39] Saint-Méry's triumphal tone seems to imply
that the industriousness of the French practically 'entitles' them to ownership
of the Spanish part. This was not a new argument: for example, in 1730 it
had been put forward rather forcefully by the Jesuit Pierre François-Xavier
de Charlevoix in *Histoire de l'Isle espagnole ou de Saint-Domingue*, one of
Saint-Méry's own sources.[40] The typical colonialist recasting of someone
else's land as an 'empty space' which should be inhabited and put to good
use is applied here to a territory occupied by another colonial power rather
than to one belonging to an indigenous population. The border between

[37] Ms, vol. I, p. A; PE, vol. I, p. 1.

[38] Ms, vol. II, p. 229; PE, vol. II, p. 229.

[39] PF, vol. I, p. 127–8. In addition, when he describes Cul-de-Sac, an area close
to the border in the Partie de L'Ouest, Saint-Méry highly praises French hydraulic
engineering and its benefits: see PF, vol. II, p. 282.

[40] Pierre-François-Xavier de Charlevoix, *Histoire de l'Isle espagnole ou de*
Saint-Domingue (Amsterdam: F. L'Honoré, 1733). Saint-Méry refers to Charlevoix's
work repeatedly in the *Description de la partie française* (see vol. I, pp. 118, 218, 265,
538).

the two colonies is reimagined in a way which anticipates, albeit in a different context and historical juncture, Jackson Turner's conceptualization of the westward-receding North American frontier which is inhabited but, paradoxically, unsettled and, therefore, implicitly free land.[41]

Enthusiasm for technological advancement notwithstanding, Saint-Méry is always careful to depict Saint Domingue's sugar plantations as almost 'second nature' to the land:

> But what a delicious view is offered to the voyageur when, at the extremity of these savannahs, he discovers the rich plain of the Maribarous district!
>
> His eye glides over sugar cane fields [...] he loves the effect that is produced on these waves of green, and then some trees of a deeper green put here and there as if to vary the scene. The buildings of a great number of manufactures add some interest to the scene and the woods on the shores of the Massacre River, crown and mark the horizon.[42]

Once again Saint-Méry does not simply describe what he sees. He purposefully produces 'delicious' views which are offered to the reader as evidence of the 'progress that civilization had brought to the colony' of Saint Domingue.[43] Significantly, in the above 'vista,' the River Massacre is equated to the horizon which is 'marked' by the trees: the messy Spanish side on the other side of the border has literally and conveniently fallen off the edge of the horizon. The 'scene' that the reader is invited to share with the voyageur is both framed (the vegetation 'crowns' the horizon) and staged: Saint-Méry openly talks about 'view' ('*vue*' in the original), candidly admits that he knows one thing or two about landscaping ('as if to vary the scene'), and depicts the sugar cane plantations and the interesting buildings next to them as empty of human figures. As Raymond Williams has famously noted, 'a working country is hardly ever a landscape'; the lack of human figures in Saint-Méry's 'description' leads us to conclude that he must have been embarrassingly aware that a country where slaves were worked to death was even less so.[44]

By 1789 – that is, at the time of Saint-Méry's 'snapshot' of the colony – two-thirds of the roughly half a million slaves were African-born because

---

[41] Frederick Jackson Turner, *The Frontier in American History* (New York: Holt & Co, 1920).

[42] PF, vol. I, p. 126.

[43] PF, vol. I, p. xii.

[44] Raymond Williams, *The Country and the City* (New York: Oxford University Press, 1973), p. 120.

the slave population of Saint Domingue never really reproduced itself. The average working life of a plantation slave born in the colony was little more than fifteen years and no longer than that of creolized Africans who had survived the initial years. Slave mortality was due to overwork, undernourishment, and cruelty.[45] In Saint Domingue the field slave quarters were small, with internal partitions and no windows, and, crucially, at some distance from the master's *grande case* or *great house*.[46] Slaves were organized into *ateliers* (work groups) according to their strength and health and operated under the direct orders of a *commandeur*, frequently a creole slave who would be given better clothing than the others to mark his higher status.[47] Saint-Méry was very well aware of the different roles slaves had to play in sugar plantations: among the 200 slaves he thought were necessary to run a sugar plantation of 100 *carreaux* of land he also lists thirty artisans and domestics.[48] These domestic slaves, or *nègres a talent*, were also distinguishable from other slaves because of finer clothing, better food, and better treatment. Overall, Saint-Méry writes, in the French colony, slaves were subjected to an 'exact discipline.'[49]

The *Description de la partie espagnole* informs us that, on the Spanish side, things were a far cry from the hierarchically organized plantations of Saint Domingue. In Santo Domingo, Saint-Méry contends, 'slaves are treated with a mildness unknown of other nations'[50] and, to their masters, they are 'rather companion than slaves.'[51] This 'mildness' had pragmatic reasons rather than moral ones: Spanish slave-owners were keen to extend the lives of their slaves for as long as possible because they had no access to the slave trade and suffered from a shortage of capital.[52] However, if it is true that in the capital city slaves might have enjoyed a greater freedom than their companions who worked in plantations, in Santo Domingo's sugar mills the whip was widely used and slavery operated exactly as in other colonies.[53] In his account, Saint-Méry focuses on the fact that the Spanish creoles were

---

[45] Carolyn E. Fick, *The Making of Haiti: The Saint Domingue Revolution from Below* (Knoxville, TN: The University of Tennessee Press, 1990), pp. 25–7.

[46] Fick, *Making of Haiti*, pp. 30–31.

[47] Fick, *Making of Haiti*, pp. 27, 30.

[48] Ms vol. II, pp. 225–9; PE, vol. II, 225–9.

[49] Ms, vol. I, p. 53; PE, vol. I, p. 60.

[50] Ms, vol. I, p. 51; PE, vol. I, p. 59.

[51] Ms, vol. I, p. 53; PE, vol. I, p. 60.

[52] Silié, 'The *Hato* and the *Conuco*', p.141.

[53] Carlos Esteban Deive, 'The African Inheritance in Dominican Culture', in *Dominican Cultures: The Making of a Caribbean Society*, ed. B. Vega (Princeton, NJ: Markus Wiener Publishers, 2007), pp. 87–130, pp. 96–7, 99, 108.

more prone to raising cattle than to cultivating the land[54] and emphasizes the resulting lack of social distinction between humans and, ultimately, even between humans and animals. Animals, he explains, are raised in *hattes* usually run by members of the same family, occasionally with the help of black slaves. According to him, this lifestyle would not be suitable for the French, 'a lively, enterprising people, soon disgusted with whatever has the air of monotony.'[55] The *hattiers* live in what are disparagingly described as

> miserable huts, the sides of which are of piles or planks badly joined and the roof of straw. There is commonly a room from about 12 to 18 feet square, in which is a table, 2 to 3 stools and a hamac. The bed chamber is another room, not so large as the former containing several truckle-beds [...] If it rains, the gutters formed by the openings, make the water fall on the inside, and the floor which is not paved and which differs from the neighboring meadows only in that the continual trodding has worn off the grass, is in a moment ankle-deep in mud.[56]

The porosity of the hut, the inside of which is almost indistinguishable from the outside, mirrors Saint-Méry's suggestion that it was not easy to separate the social status of the workers who lived there and, implicitly, the conditions of humans from the conditions of livestock. Conversely, in the eyes of some planters of French Saint Domingue, their slaves *only* were not entirely distinguishable from cattle. The 1685 Black Code established that slaves were entitled to two changes of clothes per year but it was not unusual to see them move around in tatters or completely naked. When questioned by a visitor about the nakedness of his slaves, a Saint Domingue colonist is reported to have matter-of-factly replied: 'why not also ask us to put clothes on our cows, mules and dogs?'[57]

In his *Description de la partie espagnole*, Saint-Méry informs us that the population of the Spanish colony was composed of three classes: 'the Whites, the Freed-People and the Slaves. The Freed-People are few in number if compared to the Whites but their number is considerable if compared with that of the slaves.'[58] The process of 'affranchissement' or 'freeing' of slaves,

---

[54] In his description of the Spanish side of the border area Saint-Méry counts numerous *hattes* but no *sucreries* (ms, vol. I, pp. 243–87; PE, vol. I, pp. 243–87).

[55] Ms, vol. II, p. 209; PE, vol. II, p. 209.

[56] Ms, vol. I, pp. 70–71; PE, vol. I, pp. 70–71.

[57] Charles Malefant, *Des colonies et particulièrement de celle de Saint-Domingue* (Paris, 1814), p. 232, quoted in Fouchard, *The Haitian Maroons*, p. 41.

[58] Ms, vol. I, pp. 47–8; PE, vol. I, p. 57.

he continues, is extremely easy in Santo Domingo, as discriminatory laws exist but are 'absolutely disregarded.' Moreover, not only does the political constitution of the colony admit 'no distinction between the civil rights of a White inhabitant and those of a free-person'[59] but 'that prejudice with respect to color, so powerful with other nations among whom it fixes a bar between the Whites and the Freed People and their descendants, is almost unknown in the Spanish part of Santo Domingo.'[60] For his *Description* of the Spanish part as a prejudice-free colony Saint-Méry relied on the work of Antonio Sánchez Valverde Ocaña, a lawyer, theologian, and author of *Idea del valor de la isla Española, y utilitades, que de ella puede sacar su monarquia* ('On the value of the island of Hispaniola and the ways in which the monarchy can profit from it'), which was published in Madrid in 1785 and contains an accurate geographical and topographical description of Santo Domingo as well as commentaries on its history and its socio-political and racial fabric.[61]

Sánchez Valverde was a member of the elite with a very clear political and racial agenda: namely, the promotion of slavery in Santo Domingo to fully exploit the colony's potential for economic growth. He insisted, in fact, that the presence of slaves was the main reason behind the success of the French colony of Saint Domingue and, resorting to the discourse of morality to support his position, he vehemently condemned the ease with which slaves were emancipated in the Spanish colony. More often than not, he explained, manumissions were sinful acts because they were the consequence of too close a 'familiarity' between masters and female slaves.[62] Sánchez Valverde pragmatically praised the French system, which required that the masters who wanted to free one of their slaves had to pay 150 pesos to the king, because he considered it an effective way of discouraging widespread manumissions and, indirectly, of upholding social and racial discrimination.[63] However, despite this 'tax,' in Saint Domingue in 1789

[59] Ms, vol. I, p. 51; PE, vol. I, pp. 58–9.
[60] Ms, vol. I, p. 49–50; PE, vol. I, pp. 58–9. In the English translation, the adjective 'salutary' was added to 'prejudice' but later deleted.
[61] In particular, Saint-Méry praises Sánchez Valverde's work and declares that he has followed its structure in his *Description* (PE, vol. I, pp. 37–8); he then refers to his views on the irrigation of the Artibonite plain (PE, vol. I, p. 265) and to his discussion of the potential benefits of the development of agriculture and the exploitation of the mines in the Spanish part of the island (PE, vol. II, pp. 155–6).
[62] Antonio Sánchez Valverde Ocaña, *Idea del valor de la isla Española, y utilitades, que de ella puede sacar su monarquía* (Madrid: Don Pedro Marin, 1785) republished in Antonio Sánchez Valverde Ocaña, *Ensayos*, ed. A. Blanco Díaz (Santo Domingo: Ediciones de la Fundación Corripio, 1988), pp. 8–304, p. 254.
[63] Sánchez Valverde Ocaña, *Idea del Valor*, p. 225.

the number of *affranchis* had reached a near-equal balance with the white population. They owned one-third of the plantation property, one-quarter of the slaves and one-quarter of the real estate property, but they were kept in a constant state of resentment and degradation by vehemently enforced discriminatory laws aimed at maintaining white supremacy. The *affranchis* were legally defined as a distinct and subordinate social 'caste,' as it was understood that they forever retained the 'imprint' of slavery no matter how far removed they were from their black origin.[64] As Saint-Méry writes, the allegedly indelible imprint of slavery was crucial to arguments aimed at reinforcing white privilege:

> To support the opinion which does not admit the possibility of a total disappearance of the trace of intermixing and therefore wants that a prolonged ad infinitum will always separate white descendants from the rest it is understood that the hue which becomes weaker in two or three generations surfaces again and reveals the African mixture; and [it is also understood] that colour is not the best marker but the whole of the traits such as a flat nose, thick lips are very indicative of the origin.[65]

This 'opinion,' Saint-Méry insists, was the product of the 'eye of prejudice,'[66] but, ironically, and despite his affected distancing from prejudice, Saint-Méry himself does not seem exempt from it. It is worth remembering here that the title page of the volumes devoted to the French colony indicates that Saint-Méry chose to 'freeze' the colony *before* the (to him, disgraceful) moment in which the National Assembly accepted the petition of rights of 'free citizens of color' from Saint Domingue. Moreover, in his *Description de la partie française*, Saint-Méry famously includes his well-known and extremely elaborated racial classification scheme in which he claims that the presence of black parts in different quantities is responsible for various distinctive traits in an individual. Among them he identifies or, rather, 'constructs' distinct hues of whiteness (i.e. 'The Quarteron has white skin but shaded to a very pale yellow'), or physical weakness and incapacity to reproduce (i.e. 'The Métif is even weaker than the White [...] and more overpowered by the climate. He hardly reproduces himself').[67]

If read together, the two *Descriptions* give the border an important role

---

[64] Fick, *Making of Haiti*, pp. 19–21.
[65] PF, vol. I, p. 86.
[66] PF, vol. I, p. 87.
[67] PF, vol. I, pp. 76, 78.

to play in the racial politics of Hispaniola because, Saint-Méry maintains, colour and blood did not seem to be given the same significance in the social hierarchy of the French and Spanish colonies. Furthermore, Saint-Méry claims that 'it is true, and even strictly so, that the major part of the Spanish colonists are a mixed-race: this an African feature, and sometimes more than one, often betrays.'[68] Saint-Méry, however, quickly adds that many white creoles of Santo Domingo – and he mentions Sánchez Valverde as his primary example – would reject with indignation this suggestion.[69] In *Idea del valor de la isla Espanola* Sánchez Valverde sounds totally outraged by the allegations made by those metropolitan historians – he refers to the French Weuves in particular – who suggested that the mixed blood of the colonists was the reason behind their laziness and, ultimately, behind Santo Domingo's poverty.[70] According to Weuves, the indolent Spanish colonists could hardly be called 'Spanish' because they were almost invariably mixed with Caribs and blacks. Moreover, he also claimed that Spain itself did not contain a single drop of pure blood because of the presence of blacks in its colonies and, earlier on, of the Moors on its territory.[71] Sánchez Valverde replied to these assertions by saying that Spanish blood was as pure as the blood one could find in any other European nation (an interestingly ambiguous answer) and, more specifically, by insisting that the Spanish colonists of Hispaniola had better preserved their purity than their aristocratic French counterparts, who frequently married rich *mulatas*.[72] Sánchez Valverde also resorts to the term 'Indo-Hispanic' to explain the racially mixed population of the Spanish side as a combination of white and indigenous blood, thus paving the way for the Dominican discourse of indigenism that, after the nineteenth century, became expedient to deny the African presence on the territory.[73]

For these early historiographers of the island, therefore, the vertical frontier seems to have functioned also as an imagined demarcation between 'proper' and 'improper' racial relations, as they lamented that, on the other side, purity of blood was not upheld as it should have been. It was an 'imagined' demarcation because, despite its topographical and political

---

[68] Ms, vol. I, p. 49; PE, vol. I, p. 59. In the French manuscript this remark is to be found in the column for revisions and additions (54 Verso).

[69] PE, vol. I, p. 59.

[70] *Weuves, le Jeune, Réflexions historiques et politiques sur le commerce de la France avec ses colonies de l'Amerique* (Paris: L. Cellot, 1780) referred to in Sánchez Valverde Ocaña, *Idea del Valor*, p. 245.

[71] Sánchez Valverde Ocaña, *Idea del Valor*, p. 245.

[72] Sánchez Valverde Ocaña, *Idea del Valor*, pp. 245–6.

[73] Sánchez Valverde Ocaña, *Idea del Valor*, p. 345.

instability, this border was clearly inscribed on their mental map of the island. Most importantly, it was 'imagined' because miscegenation was an incontrovertible and, simultaneously, paradoxically and painstakingly denied fact on both sides of the border: Saint-Méry himself, for example, might have had a *quarteronnée* (three-quarters white) daughter called Ameinade with his housekeeper, a free woman of colour who had worked for him for several years.[74]

Saint-Méry's urge to construct the rigid racial taxonomy that he is (in)famous for is therefore better understood in the context of the 'imagined' partitioned island as a whole. His racial divisions and subdivisions pertaining to the population of Saint Domingue are concomitant to his positing of the colonial frontier as a flimsy boundary beyond which, he claims, social and racial relations were not properly policed. It has been suggested that some of the terms Saint-Méry uses to designate mixed-race individuals – such as *Marabou* and *Griffon* or *Griffe* – are borrowed from beasts and mythical monsters.[75] These onomastic practices collapse distinction between the animal world and the human beings in question and resonate with Saint-Méry's comments on the almost animalesque life and customs of the *hattiers* of the Spanish part. Things, however, were more complicated than this and Saint-Méry found himself in a tricky position vis-à-vis the exploration of the reasons underpinning Santo Domingo's pitiable state

[74] See John Garrigus, 'Redrawing the Colour Line: Gender and the Social Construction of Race in Pre-Revolutionary Haiti', *Journal of Caribbean History*, 30.1–2 (1996), pp. 28–57, p. 47. Incidentally, the presence of an international frontier does not seem to affect Haiti's current racial hierarchy nor what Jean Price-Mars famously called 'collective Bovarism' – that is, the propensity of some members of the Haitian elite to 'conceive of themselves as other than they are' by exclusively embracing French culture while denying the country's African roots: see Jean Price-Mars, *Ainsi parla l'Oncle suivi de Revisiter l'Oncle* (Montréal, Québec: Mémoire d'encrier, 2009), p. 8. In the Dominican Republic, however, the border still plays a crucial role in dominant racist discourses circulated by white supremacist ideologues who identify 'blackness' exclusively with Haiti and associate it with primitivism and savagism: it is perhaps not a coincidence that the frontier between Haiti and the Dominican Republic has recently been defined, albeit in a different context, as 'the epidermis of [Dominican] nationality': see José Miguel Soto Jiménez, 'La Frontera en la Agenda de Seguridad, Defensa y Desarrollo Nacional del Estado Dominicano en el Siglo XXI' in *La Frontera: prioridad en la agenda nacional*, ed. Secretaría de Estado de las Fuerzas Armadas, (Santo Domingo: Editora de las Fuerzas Armadas Dominicanas, 2004), pp. 3–16, p. 4.
[75] Joan Dayan, *Haiti, History and the Gods* (Berkeley, CA: University of California Press, 1998), pp. 232–3. According to Dayan, '*Marabou* is the name of a bird' and '*Griffon* has numerous meanings: a coarse-haired dog, a fabulous animal with the head and wings of an eagle and hindquarters of a lion.'

of affairs. On the one hand, he seems to inscribe himself in the French 'tradition' of blaming the bad temperament and laziness of the Spaniards for Santo Domingo's problems and has no qualms about subscribing to French mixophobic discourses when he asserts that the Spanish colonists were, for the most part, a mixed race. On the other hand, he had carefully read Sánchez Valverde's attack on French historians for what the Spanish creole called 'insolence'[76] and was aware that he could not afford to ignore the broader implications of his own xenophobic and racist remarks. Saint-Méry was a French creole very proud of his tropical origin: in the *Description de la partie française*, whenever possible, he catalogues and celebrates notable people born in the colony.[77] He also goes as far as saying that, at birth, the white creoles are endowed with a number of 'gifts' that people born elsewhere do not receive and which are partly the result of Saint Domingue's climate. Unfortunately, he adds, they lose their advantage over others because they are spoilt as children by over-indulgent parents (especially creole mothers, who tend to be excessively sensitive and delicate), by the presence of slaves who are at their beck and call, and by a regrettable lack of proper education.[78] Sadly, he contends, these important factors are never taken into consideration when those born in the Americas are branded as inept or indolent[79] and, in a short aside in the *Description de la Partie espagnole*, he feels the need to clarify that he blames Spain rather than the creole colonists who, he reveals, are abandoned to their own devices by their central government.[80] In so doing, he simultaneously circumvents raciologic and anti-American/ anti-creole discourses and also aligns himself with his fellow creole Sánchez Valverde in his firm rebuttal of the assertion that the people born in the New World were degenerate because of the unhealthy influence of the place they inhabited.[81] The border between the two colonies is at this point provisionally erased by Saint-Méry in favour of the establishment of a white creole transcolonial and transnational horizontal brotherhood which rejects tropical degeneration.[82]

---

[76] Sánchez Valverde Ocaña, *Idea del Valor*, pp. 244–5.

[77] For example, for the parish of Fort Dauphin he mentions Monsieur Croiseuil, translator of Ovid (PF, vol. I, p. 139) and for the parish of Limonade he mentions Monsieur de Chabanon de l'Académie Française and of the Académie de Belles-Lettres and his brother, Monsieur Chabanon de Maugris, translator of Horace and author of *mémoires* published by the Académie de Sciences (PF, vol. I, p. 217).

[78] PF, vol. I, pp. 12–14 and 18.

[79] PF, vol. I, p. 15.

[80] PE, vol. I, pp. 300–301.

[81] PE, vol. I, p. 301.

[82] Saint-Méry also depicts black creoles as superior to African blacks both physically

The differences in racial and social structuring between the two sides of the island presented by Saint-Méry are clearly at odds with his imaginary and appropriative landscaping of the Spanish colony: it just does not seem likely that the (allegedly) egalitarian society of Santo Domingo[83] could be as unproblematically assimilated to Saint Domingue's segregationist way of life as his territorial projections seem to suggest and, indeed, advocate. Saint-Méry's fantasy of expansionism, in fact, had a very complicated relationship with reality. At the end of the second volume on Santo Domingo he informs us that the question of a possible French acquisition of the Spanish side had actually been considered by the French since 1698.[84] Saint-Méry then proceeds to develop what seems a convincing argument which highlights six different reasons why France could benefit from the annexation of the Spanish part of Hispaniola.[85] Among other things, Saint-Méry points out that the elimination of the internal border of Hispaniola presupposed the elimination or at least the reduction of *marronage*,[86] a definite bonus for Saint Domingue's planters. This argument is, however, followed by the articulation of a more detailed and even more persuasive line of reasoning that shows instead that annexation would be a disastrous option for France and by Saint-Méry voicing his unequivocal and vehement hostility to the notion of unification. His objections are all of a practical nature: most of all, Saint-Méry insists on the impossibility of building, manning and rendering profitable the same *sucreries* that his gaze so easily conjured up in the plains of Santo Domingo. What might appear bewildering at first has instead a perfectly rational explanation.

---

and morally, but this is mainly due to their close proximity to the whites, from whom they learn how to behave (PF, vol. I, pp. 39–40).

[83] The fugitive slaves from Saint Domingue were usually taken to a settlement on the eastern side of the Ozama River which was called San Lorenzo de los Minas. They were then forced to work in the *hatos* described above or in the capital's construction sites for public buildings, or to join the border militia. They were free but racial and social prejudices condemned them to live as second-class citizens. It goes without saying, however, that as difficult as this predicament might have been, it was certainly preferable to slavery: see Frank Moya Pons, *La otra historia dominicana* (Santo Domingo: Librería La Trinitaria, 2009), pp. 86–97.

[84] Ms, vol. II, p. 189; PE, vol. II, p. 189.

[85] The six reasons that Saint-Méry enumerates and discusses are: '1) a more defensible position 2) a greater security for navigation in war time; 3) a greater certainty of subsistence; 4) an augmentation of population; 5) a more extensive cultivation 6) an augmentation of commerce (ms, vol. II, pp. 190–240; PE, vol. II, pp. 190–240).

[86] Ms, vol. II, pp. 198–9; PE, vol. II, pp. 198–9. Interestingly, a few pages later, when he argues *against* the unification of the island, Saint-Méry decides to ignore this particular point.

Saint-Méry's opposition to an *actual* appropriation of Santo Domingo is incongruous with his imaginary landscaping of the colony only if one does not consider his utopian fantasy of an extended network of sugar plantations as another perfected imperial perspective which magically removes all that is discordant with it. Undoubtedly, the difficulties that the Saint Domingue elite would have encountered in dealing with the population of Santo Domingo as described by Saint-Méry himself – that is, with a majority of *sang-mêlés* colonizers, with *affranchis* enjoying the same civil status as whites and with slaves who could easily purchase their freedom and were treated with 'mildness' – must not have escaped his meticulous reasoning on the feasibility of unification. Nevertheless, none of these considerations seem to underpin his decision to pronounce French expansion into Santo Domingo a mere *'chimère.'*[87]

Chimeras and reality, Saint-Méry insists, are poles apart but reality was most uncomfortably catching up with him. I have already pointed out that Saint-Méry was provided with the opportunity to publish his *Description* of the Spanish side by the 1795 Treaty of Basle, which officially sanctioned the cession of Spanish Santo Domingo to France and marked the end of an era in the history of Hispaniola. In his 'Advertisement' to the volume, Saint-Méry proudly declares that the new geopolitical scenario of the island has not altered his views on the acquisition of Spanish Santo Domingo and categorically denies to have curbed his 'thoughts to occasional events.'[88] Uncannily, his disquisition on the matter begins with the declaration that, since Spain will never give up her colony, a discussion about the advantages and disadvantages of the unification of the island under French administration was just a mere abstraction or, indeed, as he puts it, a *chimère*. Of course, the very fact that, in 1795, Spain had in fact relinquished Spanish Santo Domingo to the French disallowed and disallows Saint-Méry's readers to interpret his views on the matter as simple conjecture. Yet again, the *Description* is not what it claims to be: rather than a mere portrayal of the past, Saint-Méry's work is inspired by the author's ambition to intervene in and hopefully influence current border affairs. The erasure of the frontier brought about by the Peace of Basle between Spain and Republican France did not favour the interests of the white creole elite to which Saint-Méry belonged,[89] so it is not surprising that the subscribers who made the publication of the *Description de la partie espagnole* possible, and whose names are listed at the beginning

[87] Ms, vol. II, p. 234; PE, vol. II, p. 234.
[88] Ms, vol. I, p. F; PE, vol. I, p. 6.
[89] Matibag, *Haitian-Dominican Counterpoint*, pp. 71–2.

of the first volume, were mainly Saint Domingue's colonists living in the United States.[90]

Saint-Méry's and his supporters' belief in the political potential of his work was not mere wishful thinking. They might have genuinely felt that there was still some space for manoeuvre because, at the time of publication, the French acquisition of the Spanish part was sanctioned *de jure* but was not taking place *de facto*. The Treaty of Basle did not specify an exact date of the transfer of power, as it was agreed that such a date depended on Spain providing the means for evacuation to the population of the Spanish colony, a long and laborious process complicated, among other things, by the question of the slaves living and working in what was formerly Santo Domingo. The French Republicans insisted that they be allowed to stay on the island as freemen and women, while the Spanish considered them as their property and maintained that, as such, they had to follow them in their exile from the island.[91] Besides, a lack of French military personnel to substitute the Spanish garrison also delayed the transition as the French realized that a strong Spanish military presence in Santo Domingo was key to the security of the entire island.[92] English successes in the southern part of Saint Domingue further contributed to leaving things as they were and the actual unification of the island under French administration was finally achieved only in 1801 by Toussaint.

Saint-Méry, however, does not just oppose unification resolutely; he insists that, rather than acquiring Santo Domingo, France should try to reacquire Louisiana, which had been given to Spain in 1762.[93] The desire of France to recover its former North American possession had been the subject

---

[90] One finds twenty-nine Saint Domingue colonists living in Philadephia, Albany, New York, Wilmington (Delaware), Baltimore, and Elizabeth Town (Jersey). Saint-Méry also mentions four shopkeepers from Cap-Français living in the United States.

[91] Emilio Rodríguez Demorizi, 'Laveaux to García, November 1795' in *Cesión de Santo Domingo a Francia: Correspondencia de Godoy, García, Roume, Hedouville, Louverture, Rigaud y otros, 1795–1802* (Ciudad Trujillo: Impresora Dominicana, 1958), pp. 17–20.

[92] Wendell Schaffer, 'The Delayed Cession of Spanish Santo Domingo to France, 1795–1801', *The Hispanic American Review*, 29 (1949), pp. 46–68, p. 53.

[93] Saint-Méry's wife, he informs his reader, was actually from Louisiana and her father and uncle were among the French 'proscrits' who rebelled against Louisiana's cessation to Spain. In the English manuscripts the word 'proscrits' is substituted by the more emphatic 'sufferers.' Moreover, Saint-Méry refers to such 'proscrits' or 'sufferers' as patriots whose sacrifice will forever demonstrate that Frenchmen are not 'to be sold like cattle' or, in French, 'trafiqu[és] [...] comme des tropeaux' (ms, vol. II, p. 236; PE, II, p. 236). The fact that there was a connection in his mind between Louisiana and the unstable border between Santo Domingo and Saint Domingue is evidenced by Saint-Méry's choice of terminology: as we have seen, cattle and slaves were bought, sold,

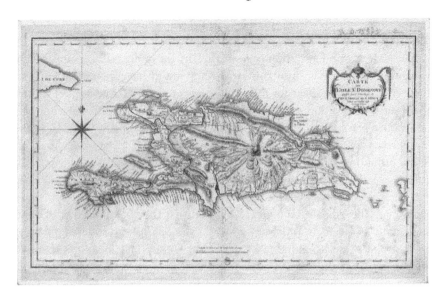

Figure 5. Carte de l'isle St Domingue dressée pour l'ouvrage de M.L.E. Moreau de St Mery. dessinée par L. Sonis, gravée par Vallance (Bibliothèque nationale de France).

of numerous political discussions since the day of its loss but it is worth mentioning that this suggestion was topical indeed when the *Description* was published. In December 1795, Spain did propose a treaty according to which Santo Domingo would be returned to Spain in exchange for Louisiana, but the French Directory firmly rejected it in June 1796.[94] If, in colonial terms and within the remit of the rhetoric of the Enlightenment, Saint-Méry's imaginary expansion into the Spanish side of Hispaniola could be regarded as a daring move forward in time along the line of 'progress' (that is, further development and exploitation), his insistence on the desirability of *re*acquiring Louisiana suggests that he was instead folding back onto the past. This is in agreement with the trajectory of his politics: from being an active participant of the French Revolution, he ended up becoming a staunch supporter of Napoleonic reaction.

Saint-Méry's commitment to the reconstitution of the *Ancien Régime*'s *status quo* that both his *Descriptions* minutely depict also compelled him to include a visual reinscription of the recently erased border of Hispaniola.

---

and, more often than not, smuggled across the border between Saint Domingue and Santo Domingo, and the French verb 'trafiquer' does gesture towards illicit activities.
[94] Schaffer, 'The Delayed Cession of Spanish Santo Domingo to France', p. 52.

His *oeuvre* is illustrated by a map of the island which, on the title page of the two *Descriptions*, is referred to as 'new' and which is positioned at the beginning of both books so that it precedes rather than follows Saint-Méry's words. A hand-written draft for a leaflet aimed at publicizing the first volume of the *Description de la Partie Espagnole* describes the book as 'A New Useful and Amusing Work' and the map it contains as 'new, elegant and correct.' Evidently, 'new' and 'correct' are highly misleading adjectives to use when describing a map that, in 1796 and 1797, was so blatantly out-of-date and Saint-Méry was of course very well aware of this. However, such deliberately misleading appellatives, combined with the fact that, prior to reading the *Descriptions*, the reader is given access to a visual source where the two sides of the island are neatly separated by a very heavily marked border, have the function of naturalizing what was no longer officially there and constitute a powerful addition to Saint-Méry's reactionary project to turn the past into the future.

Chapter Two

The 1791 revolt
and the borderland from below

Récit Historique sur les Évenemens qui se sont succédés dans les camps de la Grande-Rivière, du Dondon, de Ste.-Suzanne et autres, depuis le 26 Octobre 1791 jusqu'au 24 Decembre de la même année. Par M. Gros, Procureur-Syndic de Valière, fait prisonnier par Jeannot, chef des Brigands, augmenté du Récit historique du Citoyen Thibal, Médecin et Habitant de la Paroisse Sainte-Suzanne, détenu prisonnier, par les Brigands, depuis 16 mois et de la Déclaration du Citoyen Fauconnet, faite à la Municipalité le 16 Juin 1792 (1793), Victor Hugo, *Bug-Jargal* (1819 and 1826) and 'The Saint Domingue Revolt' (1845), Jean-Baptiste Picquenard, *Adonis, ou le bon nègre* (1798) and *Zoflora, ou la bonne negrèsse* (1801), Madison Smartt Bell, *All Souls' Rising* (1995)

As we have seen in the previous chapter, Moreau de Saint Méry's snapshot of the two sides of Hispaniola covers the *status quo* up to 18 October 1789. Four days later the National Assembly accepted for consideration the petition of rights of 'free citizens of color' from Saint Domingue: they demanded an end to racist discrimination against them, the right to vote in Saint Domingue's local assemblies, and to have representatives in the National Assembly. Saint Méry, who was a representative for Martinique in the National Assembly, was against the petitioners' requests, as he considered segregation the only way forward for the colonies. Saint Domingue's welfare, he insisted, could be guaranteed only if the National Assembly kept itself out of the colony's business and left the power firmly in the hands of the white plantocracy; it was too dangerous, he warned, to give the blacks the impression that there was a power above their white masters to which they could appeal to change their condition.[1] The Colonial Committee set up

---

[1] Médéric Louis Élie Moreau de Saint-Méry, *Considérations presentées aux vrais amis*

by the initially sympathetic Assembly was responsive to the arguments put forward by the likes of Saint Méry and a decree inspired by these views was proposed and approved on 8 March: it sanctioned that the colony would be governed by special laws unconstrained by the Declarations of the Rights of Man but did not establish whether free-coloured people should be granted the title of 'citizens' and therefore be admitted to the vote. Obviously, there was going to be trouble ahead.

In July, frustrated by the lack of progress his cause was making in Paris, the free man of colour and lawyer Vincent Ogé, one of the petitioners, resolved to go back to Saint Domingue and to organize an armed rebellion of free people of colour against the white planters. His army of 300 enthusiastic *sang-mêlés* took over Grand-Rivière but was quickly overpowered by the militia and forced to withdraw to Spanish territory via San Rafael. The Ogé case brought the border (and, as we will see, borderland) to the forefront of the island's politics: initially, in fact, his demand for political asylum was accepted and he was given a passport and a safe-conduct, but the same officer who issued these documents also instructed the authority in charge in the next village (Hinche) to arrest Ogé and to take him to Santo Domingo, where he was put in prison. Governor Blanchelande presented a petition to obtain Ogé's extradition to Joaquín García, the governor of the Spanish side. The Spanish finally handed Ogé over to the French authorities, but the case triggered a feverish exchange of views and documents between the various authorities in Santo Domingo and between the colony and Madrid.[2] Despite the fact that Ogé had not attempted to abolish slavery and had refused to mobilize the blacks to fight alongside his men, Saint Domingue's colonial authority punished him ferociously: he was tried in February 1791 and his body was tied to a wheel and broken on a scaffold.[3]

The cruel execution of Ogé sharpened the conflict between whites and free-coloureds in Saint Domingue and had repercussions in Paris, where the republicans were becoming more and more powerful among the revolutionaries. A compromise was struck between the radicals and the representatives of the planters: political rights would be given to those free people of colour who had been born to two free parents. It was a small step but a significant one as it created a dangerous precedent for those mulattoes

---

du repos et du Bonheur de France, à l'occasion des nouveaux mouvements de quelque soi-disant amis-des-noirs (Paris, 1791), p. 36–8, 44, 48.

[2] Carlos Federico Pérez, *Historia diplomática de Santo Domingo 1492–1861* (Santo Domingo: Escuela de Servicios Internacionales Universidad Nacional Pedro Henríquez Ureña, 1973), pp. 67–78.

[3] Fick, *Making of Haiti*, p. 83.

born of one free parent and those still in slavery; it also threatened to bring closer the abolition of slavery. Outraged, the Saint Domingue whites refused to comply with this and they were so vociferous that in July the legislative powers of the colony were reinstated. Saint Domingue, however, was on its way to exploding: the insurrection that was going to destroy the Pearl of the Antilles was only a month away.

On the night of 14 August a group of slave representatives (mainly *commandeurs*) from the major plantation of the north met on the Lenormand de Mézy plantation in Morne-Rouge. The purpose of their meeting was to fix a date for a mass uprising that the slaves had been planning for a while. It appears that during the meeting a man (mulatto or quarteroon) read a statement announcing that the king and the National Assembly in Paris had passed a law which gave slaves three free days a week and prohibited the use of the whip. This statement also informed the participants that royal troops were on their way to force the local planters to comply with it because they had refused to obey. This was not true but the chiefs of the insurgents invoked the royal authority for a number of reasons: not only was the king the only authority above their masters' but, by referring to him, they could also take advantage of the internal divisions among their enemies. Most importantly, from a border perspective, a royalist rhetoric was the best way to secure the collaboration of the Spanish, who lived on the other side of the internal frontier of Hispaniola and whose support was crucial to the success of the revolt. This trick worked so well that several delegates insisted on taking action before the arrival of the royal troops. A plan for an armed rebellion was therefore prepared: the date was fixed for 22 August and the leaders of the insurrection were Boukman Dutty, Jeannot Bullet, Jean-François, and Georges Biassou.[4]

***

This chapter will focus on three autobiographical captivity narratives by white eyewitnesses who were taken prisoners by the rebels just after the revolt; these texts are put in dialogue with five fictional reconstructions of the rebellion and its aftermath, four of which were published in the early nineteenth century and one in the 1990s. All these non-fictional and fictional narratives contain numerous, but generally overlooked, references to the role played by the colonial frontier and the borderland in the unfolding of the events.

---

[4] Fick, *Making of Haiti*, pp. 91–2 and 'Bois Caïman and the August Revolt', Appendix B, pp. 260–66.

The three captivity narratives under scrutiny here – or, as they were called then, *récits historiques* ('historical accounts') – were published in 1793 in Cap-Français. The shortest is actually a *déclaration* by Citizen Fauconnet from Fort Dauphin, a parish of the Partie du Nord which shared one of its borders with Santo Domingo.[5] Imprisoned by the rebels on 15 November 1791, Fauconnet tried to escape into the Spanish colony twice. The first time he was intercepted by two black insurgents (p. 81). The second time he crossed into Santo Domingo by taking advantage of a *passeport* issued by the rebel Grégoire which allowed him to move freely around the *quartier* of Sans-Souci, situated between the parishes of Vallière and Grande Rivière and close to the border (pp. 81–2). It is quite clear from this account that the rebels were in control of the territory and of the various routes which led to the other side; they were also trading with the Spanish for food and ammunition. Citizen Fauconnet reports having seen a Spaniard selling three barrels of gunpowder, beef, and pork to the insurgents, which were paid for with coffee and mules stolen from raided plantations and with a coupon payable in fifteen days (p. 83). Fauconnet re-entered into Saint Domingue in May 1792, via Saint-Michel, south of the parish of Marmelade (p. 83).

Fauconnet also features in the more detailed *récit* by Citizen Thibal, a doctor who lived in the parish of Sainte-Suzanne and was captured in August 1791.[6] This is a longer account with some dramatic twists – at some point Thibal is saved from being executed while on the scaffold (p. 68) – but overall it reveals how, most of the time, he was reasonably well-treated and allowed to stay in the relatively comfortable *habitations* still belonging to white planters held captives by the rebels. Nevertheless, Thibal was constantly planning his escape into Spanish territory and his account chronicles various attempts to reach and cross the border, only the last of which was successful. During the first attempt Thibal and Fauconnet got lost in a wood and were captured by black insurgents who removed their clothes, cut their hair, tied

---

[5] *Déclaration du Citoyen Fauconnet, fait à la Municipalite le 16 Juin 1792*, in *Récit Historique sur les Évenemens qui se sont succédés dans les camps de la Grande-Rivière, du Dondon, de Ste.-Suzanne et autres, depuis le 26 Octobre 1791 jusqu'au 24 Decembre de la même année. Par M. Gros, Procureur-Syndic de Valière, fait prisonnier par Jeannot, chef des Brigands, augmenté du Récit historique du Citoyen Thibal, Médecin et Habitant de la Paroisse Sainte-Suzanne, détenu prisonnier, par les Brigands, depuis 16 mois et de la Déclaration du Citoyen Fauconnet, faite à la Municipalité le 16 Juin 1792* (Cap-François: Chez Parent, 1793), pp. 81–3. From now on page references to Fauconnet's account will be given in parentheses in the text.

[6] *Récit historique du Citoyen Thibal, Médecin et Habitant de la Paroisse Sainte-Suzanne, détenu prisonnier, par les Brigands, depuis 16 mois*, in *Récit Historique*, pp. 63–80. From now on page references to Thibal's account will be given in parentheses in the text.

them up, and humiliated them in different ways (p. 70). They were then taken to a nearby *habitation*, where they concocted another plan to run away. Fauconnet, we are told, took advantage of the arrangements made and successfully crossed the border without assisting Thibal as planned (p. 72). Disappointed by Fauconnet's betrayal, Thibal did not give up his dream to cross the frontier and demanded to be transferred to Ouanaminthe, then controlled by Jean-François, who received him 'with kindness' (p. 73). There Thibal looked for a guide who would take him to the neighbouring Spanish town of Laxavon (Dajabón), but was twice betrayed by the very people he was persuading to assist him (p. 73). In Ouanaminthe he witnessed the trafficking of ammunitions, weapons, and food that was taking place between the rebels and Spanish traders (pp. 74–6). Jean-François also informed him that he was in fact obeying king's orders, which he had received on 21 August at Le Cap, where he was taken during the night from Petite Anse. Thibal adds that the rebels did not appear afraid of Governor Blanchelande and spoke of Monsieur de Cambefort, colonel of the regiment of Le Cap, 'as if he were their best friend' (p. 75). On 7 January Thibal managed to escape with the help of two citizens of colour who were hiding and waiting for an opportunity to run away: they travelled during the night, crossing a thick forest, and finally made it to the frontier, where the Spanish helped and protected them from the group of rebels who were sent to recapture them (pp. 78–9). Thibal later returned to Saint Domingue, crossing the border by Ennery (pp. 79–80).

Thibal and Fauconnet were not the first who saw the border with Santo Domingo as a threshold to freedom and had to negotiate the often hostile geography of the northern region (high mountains, thick woods, rivers) in order to cross to the Spanish side. As we have seen, fugitive slaves from Saint Domingue had taken 'the Spanish route' to freedom for many years. The proximity of the Spanish colony was indeed one of the main causes of *marronage* in the French side and since 1721 the Partie du Nord had its own *maréchaussée*, a special para-military group mostly composed of mulattoes, in charge, among other things, of capturing fugitive slaves.[7] We do not have access to many maroons' and fugitive slaves' accounts but we could put Thibal's and Fauconnet's snapshots of the borderland to good use if we treated them as the few 'positive' counterparts of a massive heap of potential master negatives long soaked in runaways' minds but never developed, or simply developed in other forms (i.e. oral accounts, songs, dances). The continuities and discontinuities between Thibal's and Fauconnet's accounts

---

[7] See Saint-Méry, PF, vol. I, p. 449; Matibag, *Haitian-Dominican Counterpoint*, p. 54; Fouchard, *The Haitian Maroons*, pp. 273–4.

and what must have been the equally adventurous across-the-border journeys of fugitive slaves are arresting. Like the two citizens in question, slaves were animated by a burning urge to flee from a state of captivity where they could be subjected to all sorts of atrocities; despite their protestations, these particular prisoners were actually treated much better than the average Saint Domingue slave. Evidence suggests, however, that slaves also wanted to escape when they were treated 'well,' as was the case for the two white hostages. At times, the relatively privileged domestic slaves took advantage of the passes given to them by their masters and ran away when they were sent out on a job: as we have seen, Fauconnet and Thibal do exactly the same with the *passeports* given to them by the rebels' chiefs. Many fugitive slaves travelled during the night, as Thibal does once and as the maroon leader Jean-François claims to have done for his trip to Le Cap in Thibal's account. Like Thibal, slaves planning to escape could be betrayed by those with whom they plotted to do so and would have been punished for trying to run away. Both sets of fugitives had to make sure that they would reach the border faster than their pursuers – the *maréchaussée* for the slaves, the rebel bands for Thibal and Fauconnet. At their first attempt to leave the trodden path, Thibal and Fauconnet get disoriented and lose their way: fugitive slaves, too, ran the risk of getting lost, especially if they had only just arrived in Saint Domingue; at times, however, they could rely on the help of maroon groups who would assist them.[8]

In the northern border region that is the theatre of these *récits* there were a number of maroon hiding places and secret routes heading to the Spanish side, especially in the mountains, while in Dominican border towns Haitian maroons were the majority.[9] In his description of Vallière, one of the parishes of the area, Saint Méry points out how its very toponymy – *piton des Nègres* ('Negro peak'), *piton des Flambeaux* ('Torch peak'), *piton des Ténèbres* ('Darkness peak') and *crête à Congo* ('crest of the Congos') – suggests that it used to give shelter to the maroons and concludes by urging the colonial administration to further populate the mountain areas of Saint Domingue in order to limit the number of places where the maroons could hide.[10] Alongside the maroons' assistance, most slave fugitives benefited from the help of the Spanish, who hid and protected them as they did with Thibal and Fauconnet. Happy to secure manpower at very low cost, the Spaniards did not return the majority of slaves who

---

[8] Fouchard, *The Haitian Maroons*, pp. 253, 262–3, 256–7, 276.
[9] Mats Lundhal, *The Haitian Economy: Man, Land and Markets* (New York: St Martin's Press, 1983), pp. 112–13.
[10] Saint-Méry, PF, vol. I, p. 154.

were drawn into Spanish territory by the enticing promises of contraband sharks but also of colonists and authorities.[11] According to official estimates, in 1751 some 3000 maroons had escaped from Saint Domingue and established themselves in Santo Domingo. Despite the reversal of roles that Thibal's and Fauconnet's experiences entail, their accounts still cast the border with Santo Domingo as a powerful signifier of freedom for those who were held in captivity in Saint Domingue; from the point of view of the Spanish merchants, the 1791 uprising reinforced their notion of the frontier as a place where one could circumvent the monopolistic laws of the mother country and make money.

The third *récit* I would like to consider here is by M. Gros, *Procureur-Syndic* of Vallière.[12] Longer and more complicated than the previous two, when it was published with them it was undergoing its second reprint. The place and time at its core are defined from the outset: *On the events which took place in the camps of Grande-Rivière, Dondon, Sainte-Suzanne and others from 26 October 1791 to 24 December of the same year.* The camps mentioned above were places where the black insurgents established their headquarters, or *salles de gouvernement*, and were all close to the Spanish side; the parish of Vallière, where Gros lived and worked, shared a border with the Spanish colony to the south. At the very beginning of his account, Gros makes it clear that, in order to appreciate what happened in the Partie du Nord in 1791, it is vital to keep in mind the vicinity of the colonial frontier to the theatre of the events (p. 1A).

At the start of the revolt Gros, who had the option to escape to neighbouring Santo Domingo, decided to stay and join forces with other volunteers from the area in order to keep the insurgents at bay. His self-sacrifice, he soon found out to his despair, was in vain. Governor Blanchelande obstinately (and, to Gros, suspiciously) refused to follow Gros's advice to organize the French soldiers in a formation aimed at enclosing the rebels in a circumscribed area while gathering the necessary military strength to defeat them once and for all (pp. 9–10). Pichon, captain of the second regiment of the Cap and the person chosen to lead the volunteers in their counter-offensive, also proved himself to be strategically incompetent. Unlike Gros, who supported the French Revolution, Pichon was a royalist and, Gros

---

[11] Fouchard, *The Haitian Maroons*, pp. 276–8, 260.

[12] *Récit Historique sur les Évenemens qui se sont succédés dans les camps de la Grande-Rivière, du Dondon, de Ste.-Suzanne et autres, depuis le 26 Octobre 1791 jusqu'au 24 Decembre de la même année. Par M. Gros, Procureur-Syndic de Valière, fait prisonnier par Jeannot, chef des Brigands*, in *Récit Historique*, pp. 1–62. From now on page references to Gros's account will be given in parentheses in the text.

suggests, a traitor (p. 13). Blanchelande's and Pichon's duplicitous leadership proved disastrous to Gros and his companions, who were soon captured by a group of rebels under the command of the ferocious Sans-Souci. From Sans-Souci's camp they were soon handed over to the cruel Jeannot. In Jeannot's camp, Gros and the other prisoners had to endure and witness terrible tortures and were even threatened with being roasted alive (p. 19). Luckily for them, Jean-François came to their rescue, defeated Jeannot and had him executed as a punishment for his excessive cruelty (pp. 19–20). Gros then became Jean-François' secretary, gained his confidence and Biassou's, and played an important part in the delicate and complex peace negotiations. Gros concludes his *récit* by including a facsimile of the *passeports* necessary to circulate freely in the Spanish side; he claims to have prepared more than one hundred of these documents during his captivity (p. 62).

The events narrated by Gros, as we have seen, take place in the part of the northern province of Saint Domingue which bordered on Santo Domingo. Gros repeatedly declares that he has no experience as a soldier, but he engages with the territory around him in purely strategic terms. Former *habitations* turned into military camps by the white volunteers are safe havens where he can gather strength and hope and discuss the necessity of establishing camps and outposts at important crossroads and of forming defensive cordons (pp. 1–6). The rebels' camps (often also former *habitations*) are generally depicted as places of despair, fear, atrocious deeds, betrayal, and secret manoeuvring (pp. 14, 16–18, 20–25, 27–9, 57–9).

Unsurprisingly, Gros (like Fauconnet and Thibal) does not offer any rhapsodic description of the landscape: clearly he had more impending matters to deal with than the *philosophe-voyageur* Saint Méry. Geographical features such as 'gorges' (p. 4), 'mountains' (p. 34[13]), 'impracticable rivers' (p. 7), 'woods' (p. 17), 'plains', 'peaks and narrow passes on the mountains' (pp. 7–13) are presented merely as tactical sites. As Gros closely observes the behaviour of the black masses, the black generals, and the mulattoes involved in the rebellion, it becomes increasingly clear to him that the revolt had been initiated not by the black rebels but by the counter-revolutionary aristocracy (pp. 20–21). In order to mobilize the blacks in the *ateliers*, Gros explains, the counter-revolutionaries first stirred the mulattoes, especially those who were still enraged by the way in which Ogé had been treated by the local authorities (p. 16). The slaves had then been informed that the king had sanctioned that they should have three days off per week and, for this reason, was under attack by the white planters and their representatives. All the black insurgents that Gros met believed that they were defending their

---

[13] Gros uses *morne*, the local term for mountain.

king (p. 30): 'the slave revolt,' he declared, 'is a counter-revolution' (p. 28). This was confirmed by Aubert, a 'well-intentioned mulatto' who opened his heart to him, and later by Jean-François, when Gros eavesdropped on him (pp. 23, 35). Gros found further evidence of the royalist conspiracy in the fact that the black insurgents considered Monsieur de Cambefort their 'protector' and their 'idol': his artillery, Gros points out, 'always aimed too high or too low' (p. 56).

Scholars are divided on the reliability of early sources such as this one which suggest the existence of a royalist plot, but of interest here is the crucial role played by the border in this (counter)revolution.[14] With unflinching accuracy and precision Gros reveals that on Sunday 7 November 1791 at 8 a.m. a sergeant-major of the Spanish army delivered two large barrels of gunpowder to the insurgents in Jean-François's camp (p. 28). It is significant that Gros reports having seen a soldier, while Fauconnet or Thibal spotted only Spanish merchants. Thibal, who also refers to Blanchelande and Cambefort in suspicious terms, does not spare the Spanish government his indictment and suggests that if the Spanish authorities did not openly permit smuggling with the rebels they certainly tolerated it (pp. 75–6). Gros goes much further with his accusations. He reveals that the military envoy he saw on 7 November was neither the first nor the last one who crossed the border to assist the rebels (p. 28). Following the sergeant-major's arrival, he adds, all the chiefs of the insurgents discussed with him over dinner their plans to avenge the threatened French monarchy and the clergy. Their conversation took place in Spanish, a language Gros was able to understand and the insurgents were all able to speak (p. 28).

French and Spanish are both romance languages and therefore similar to one another but it is likely that, living in Vallière, Gros was familiar with Spanish because he had been exposed, one way or another, to the licit and illicit across-the-border trafficking which constituted a major source of income for the Spanish side.[15] The black rebels' bilingualism is also easily

---

[14] For the controversy on the Bois-Caiman ceremony see, for example: David Geggus, *Haitian Revolutionary Studies* (Bloomington, IN: Indiana University Press, 2002), pp. 81–92; Fick, *Making of Haiti*, p. 93 and Appendix B; Léon-François Hoffman, 'Un Myth national: La cérémonie du Bois-Caïman', in *La République haïtienne: Etat des lieux et perspectives*, ed. G. Barthélemy and C. Girault (Paris: Karthala, 1993), pp. 434–48; Michel-Rolph Trouillot, 'Bodies and Souls: The Haitian Revolution and Madison Smartt Bell's *All Soul's Rising*' and Madison Smartt Bell, 'Engaging the Past', in *Novel History: Historian and Novelists confront America's past and each other*, ed. M. Carnes (New York: Simon & Schuster, 2001), pp. 191–2, 199–200.

[15] See, for example, Saint-Méry ms, vol. I, p. 220 and pp. 272–4; PE, vol. I, p. 142 and pp. 272–4 and ms, vol. II, p. 99; PE, vol. II, p. 99.

explained: slaves were routinely bought, sold, and even borrowed across the border and, in order to survive, they always had to acquire at least the rudiments of the language spoken by their masters. However, Gros attaches deeper significance to linguistic allocations. Apart from Spanish, Jean-François also speaks very good French and so does Aubert, a reluctant mulatto rebel whom Gros calls his 'liberator' (p. 21). The only insurgent whose words are reported in Creole ('pai z'autres, bon père après dromi,' p. 14) is Sans-Souci, whom Gros describes as an 'evil character' (p. 14). Gros never provides a translation of Sans-Souci's words – presumably he assumed that those who would read his account in Cap-Français were familiar enough with Creole to understand its meaning – but one could also argue that Sans-Souci's utter 'otherness' is signposted here by his untranslatability.

Gros's narrative identifies the aristocratic counter-revolutionary royalists, the Spanish, at least part of Saint Domingue's clergy, and the segment of the mulatto population who still shared Ogé's views as the originators of the rebellion. Overall, Jean-François is presented as a puppet in the hands of the black insurgents, of the counter-revolutionary plotters who gave him his 'royal' orders, and also of his Spanish neighbours: 'Whenever involved in important negotiations, Jean-François used to say that he could not take any decision without consulting those he was accountable to and we have always suspected that these were on the Spanish side' (p. 43). Historians, however, have demonstrated that if the insurgents had allied with the counter-revolutionary forces to begin with, they were neither controlled nor directed by them.[16] Notably, just a few lines before being informed of Jean-François's subservience to the Spanish, we are told that he had decided to raise the price of the sugar that he was selling to his buyers from across the border (p. 43). Rather than being a mere pawn in someone else's game, Jean-François is portrayed as a capable (read ruthless) businessman who knew how to take advantage of the presence of the border in many ways; incidentally, like Biassou and Toussaint, he would defect to the Spanish side in 1793. In a quoted speech delivered in a 'language uncommon amongst the blacks' for the 'common sense' and 'humanity' it contained, Jean-François confessed to Gros that he was almost a hostage to the mass of black rebels who had different ambitions from his own:

It is not I who have decided to become the general of the slaves. I was given this title by those who had the power to do so: in taking up arms, I never pretended to fight for general emancipation, which I am well aware, is just a chimera, partly because of France's need for its colonies

---

16 Fick, *Making of Haiti*, pp. 109, 112.

> and partly because it is dangerous to fight to give uncivilized hordes
> a right which would become infinitely dangerous for them and that
> would certainly lead to the complete annihilation of the colony. (p. 38)

Gros wants us to take what he reports as Jane-François's words at face value. Even if the transcription is accurate, it would be prudent to consider the fact that the insurgents' leader knew he was talking to a member of the group he had been fighting against: when the above-mentioned speech was (allegedly) delivered, Jean-François was hoping for peace and feared he would be held accountable for the devastations caused by the revolt. During the peace negotiations Jean-François and the other leaders committed themselves to persuading the insurgents to go back to work in exchange for liberty for the revolt's chiefs and several hundreds of the officers, an unconditional amnesty for all the rebels, and an amelioration of the condition for the slaves. The mass of slaves, however, became increasingly suspicious of the frequent exchanges their leaders were having with the whites and threatened to kill all the white prisoners, including Gros. Only Toussaint's intercession saved them and they were finally brought safely to *habitation* Saint Michel on 24 December 1791. Negotiations between the rebels and the whites broke off and soon afterwards Jean-François and the other rebel leaders unanimously decided to continue the war.

These three accounts were among the sources of the authors of the fictional texts I will be looking at next, namely Victor Hugo's *Bug-Jargal* (1819 and 1826) and 'The Saint Domingue Revolt' (1845), Jean-Baptiste Picquenard's *Adonis, ou le bon nègre* (1798) and *Zoflora, ou la bonne nègresse* (1801), and Madison Smartt Bell's *All Souls' Rising* (1995), which also highlight the central role played by the border and the borderland in the unfolding of the events.

✳✳✳

Victor Hugo's *Bug-Jargal* was written as a short story in 1819 and substantially revised in 1826; it deals with the Saint Domingue slave uprising but also transposes back onto 1791 events which took place later in the Revolution. A towering figure in nineteenth-century French literature, Victor Hugo was born in Besançon in 1802 and, after a State funeral, buried in the Panthéon of Paris in 1885; he is the author of novels (*Les Misérables*, 1802; *Notre-Dame de Paris*, 1831), poems (the three series of *La Légende des siècles*, 1859, 1877, and 1883), plays (*Cromwell*, 1827; *Hernani*, 1830; *Ruy Blas*, 1838) and other literary interventions (Preface to *Cromwell*, 1827; Preface to *Hernani*, 1830; *William Shakespeare*, 1864) which have been translated in many languages and have become landmarks in the history of literature and in the establishment of French Romanticism. Hugo was also a politically engaged writer who believed that literature could play an active role in political debates; he took an active part in the struggle against absolutism and, after supporting Louis Napoleon's candidacy to the presidency of the Republic, switched allegiances and led a failed insurrection against the prince-president. As a result, Hugo had to leave France and move to Jersey and, later, Guernsey, where he spent nineteen years in exile: he returned to his country only when Napoleon III was deposed and the Third Republic was proclaimed in 1870. Hugo is generally referred to as a champion of human rights and a defender of the oppressed but, as we will see, his depictions of blacks and, in particular, of the revolutionary masses of Saint Domingue/ Haiti, are highly problematic. I would also argue that in the texts under scrutiny here, namely his two versions of *Bug-Jargal* (written, respectively, in 1819 and 1826) and 'The Saint Domingue Revolt' (1845), Hugo echoes Saint-Méry in his desire to make the border between the French and the Spanish sides of Hispaniola as impermeable as possible.

'The Saint Domingue Revolt' is in fact a frightening cautionary tale and a good example of the anxiety that the erasure of the border and the concomitant threat of a subsequent successful overseas exportation of the Haitian revolution engendered in the colonial world; *Bug-Jargal* is a productive exploration of both the tension between the vertical borderline and the horizontality of kinship that characterizes the borderland and the global forces that play a part in constituting both borderline and borderland. Hugo, in fact, was well aware of the global dimension of the Haitian revolution: in the preface to the 1832 edition (a re-edition of 1826 version) he defines 'the revolt of the Saint Domingue blacks in 1791 [as] a struggle of giants, three worlds having a stake in the matter – Europe and Africa as the combatants, and America as the field of battle.'[17] Saint Domingue and the New World in general, however, are reduced to nothing but background despite the fact that by 1826 not only Haiti but also the United States and Simon Bolívar's Gran Colombía had proved that the Americas should no longer be considered as mere backdrop and inert landscape where global politics 'took place.'

In the Preface for the 1826 edition of *Bug-Jargal* Hugo asserts that by that time his 'subject matter ha[d] acquired a new degree of interest' (p. 57). Many critics have pointed out that Hugo was probably referring to the fact

---

[17] Victor Hugo, *Bug-Jargal*, trans. and ed. C. Bongie (Peterborough, Ontario: Broadview, 2004), p. 58. This edition includes both the 1926 and the 1919 versions of *Bug-Jargal* (pp. 53–212 and pp. 213–47). I will be referring to this English translation with page numbers in parentheses in the text.

that in 1825 Haiti had just agreed to pay France an indemnity for property lost by the colonists during the Revolution in order to have its independence officially recognized. If the indemnity that Haiti had to pay to France was the event that made it topical once again in 1826, Hugo does not sound too enthusiastic about his country's decision to officially recognize Haiti. In a note to the text he explains: 'Our readers will doubtless not be unaware that [Hispaniola] was the first name given to Saint Domingue, by Christopher Columbus, at the time of the discovery in December 1492' (p. 75). This short account of the history of the island is inflected by Hugo's political views: by calling Hispaniola 'Saint Domingue,' Hugo does not acknowledge *de facto* the existence of Haiti. He was not alone, of course: in 1819, for example, Baron de Vastey, the secretary to King Henry Christophe, wrote that 'while we uniformly adopt these new names [Haiti, Haitians], the French pertinaciously adhere to the term Saint Domingue, both in their acts and writing.'[18] It is noteworthy, however, that Vastey's declaration precedes the Franco-Haitian agreement of 1825, while Hugo's footnote to the second version of Bug-Jargal follows it.

Unsurprisingly, Hugo's landscaping of Saint Domingue (a place he never visited) follows well-established conventions which are aimed at domesticizing and edenizing the land while diverting the reader's gaze from what was really happening on the territory prior to the rebellion: the colony of Saint Domingue is a place 'where the summer is eternal and nature reveals itself in all its glory' (p. 69), where tropical lianas look like 'meadows still wet with dew' (p. 105), and which smells like 'the first roses of Eden' (p. 180). Yet, there is no paradise without hell: the predicament of slaves is mentioned *en passant* but what is foregrounded is the colonist's perspective, for whom the hellish aspect of this landscape is embodied in what eludes his/her control and gaze: its grottoes, caves, vaults, and man-made prisons and, crucially, the dangerous porosity of their borders and walls (pp. 85, 167, 177, 181). Hugo's obsession with porous borders is not entirely surprising: in 1819, when the first version of Bug-Jargal was written, the Spanish part of the island, previously captured by the rebels, had been re-Hispanized and the frontier reinstated. Moreover, Haiti was effectively divided in two: the north under the black King Henry Christophe and the south a Republic led by the mulatto Alexandre Pétion. When Hugo revised the novel in 1826 things were very different indeed, because the Haitian state had then taken over Santo Domingo: this means that when Hugo returned to his short story he was writing about a border that no longer existed and, most importantly,

---

[18] Pompée Valentin de Vastey, *An Essay on the Causes of the Revolution and Civil Wars in Hayti* [1819] (Exeter 1823), p. 44.

about a border whose erasure magnified the threat that a unified Haiti represented to the rest of the colonial world – if not as a belligerent force, at least as a dangerous example. Hugo's attempt to reinscribe the border that had been erased by Saint Domingue's insurgents is an attempt to reorganize international politics. In both versions of *Bug-Jargal* the events in Saint Domingue are framed by European ones, namely the wars that Republican and Napoleonic France were engaged in against the rest of Europe (in 1792–93 and 1806–08 respectively), but Hugo's anxiety about the existence of a linguistic and cultural plurality on the island percolates through his writing, informs the two versions of *Bug-Jargal*, and provides a very plausible explanation for the substantial variations contained in the second version.

The first version revolves around the friendship between the noble black slave Pierrot and the white narrator Delmar. Delmar is the nephew of a rich slaveholder of Saint Domingue and Pierrot is also Bug-Jargal, one of the leaders of the revolt and the son of the King of Kakongo. The second version complicates things with the introduction of Marie, the narrator's fiancée (later wife) and the white woman Bug-Jargal is in love with, and of Habibrah, a house servant, fool, and dwarf of Spanish origin who is also a *griffe de couleur*. According to Saint-Méry's racial taxonomy, to which Hugo makes explicit reference in the text, a *griffe* is a type of mixed-race individual who is the result of five different combinations.[19] Saint-Méry, however, describes *griffes* as endowed with 'an altogether pleasant figure,' while Hugo turns him into a grotesque monster, further stigmatizing mixed-race identities. In the second version, the name of the white narrator changes from Delmar to D'Auverney, a name derived from Auverné, the place of birth of Hugo's mother's father, Jean-François Trébuchet. Hugo's grandfather actively participated in the Middle Passage and it is possible, although unsubstantiated, that Hugo might have had some biographical connections with Saint Domingue.[20] In a letter dated 18 December 1829 Hugo claims that his family belonged to the list of Saint Domingue's colonists who had been financially ruined by the revolution and, interestingly, holds the Haitian president Jean-Pierre Boyer responsible for withholding his family's indemnity. However, if Hugo was indeed entitled to any compensation (and historians are still debating if this is the case) Boyer himself had nothing to do with the repartition of the money (or lack of thereof) since French

---

[19] Saint-Méry, PF, vol. I, p. 80.

[20] See Graham Robb, *Victor Hugo* (London: Picador, 1997), p. 4 and, for a more detailed discussion of the issue, Jacques Cauna, 'Les sources historiques de *Bug-Jargal*: Hugo et la Revolution Haitienne', *Conjonction: Revue Franco-Haitienne*, 166 (1985), pp. 21–36, pp. 23–6.

officials, not the Haitian president, were in charge of distributing it.[21] Hugo's animosity towards Boyer can be better understood if one considers that in 1829, when the letter was written, Boyer was synonymous with an officially recognized and unified Haiti.

The novel and the short story begin in French territory, a plantation near Fort Galifet, roughly thirty kilometres from what was then the border between Saint Domingue and Santo Domingo.[22] In both versions, however, a Spanish song sung by Pierrot and entitled *Yo que soy contrabandista* ('A smuggler am I') reminds the reader that the border is not too far away and that it can be (and was) easily crossed. Significantly, Hugo leaves the title of the song in Spanish in the text and includes his translation in French in a note (pp. 87 and 157). *Yo que soy contrabandista* is the title of a famous early nineteenth-century *aria* by the Spanish singer Manuel García, who made his international debut in Paris in 1807 – that is, sixteen years after the events recounted in *Bug-Jargal*. Anachronism notwithstanding, I would argue that the fact that Hugo chose this particular song – a reconfirmed choice because it appears in both versions of *Bug-Jargal* – carries substantial weight if we consider it in the context of the internal borderland of Hispaniola. We have seen that slaves and livestock were legally and, more often than not, illegally bought and sold across the border: indeed, in the second version of *Bug-Jargal*, Hugo informs us that the livestock eaten in the French part of the island were actually raised in the Spanish side (p. 139).

In both versions Pierrot, the slave who sings the song of the *contrabandista*,

---

[21] Cauna, 'Les sources historiques', p. 25.

[22] In *Description de la partie francaise* Saint-Méry refers to the fact that 'happy as one of Galifet's slaves' was a proverbial expression in Saint Domingue which testified to the fact that the Marquis de Galifet, who owned three plantations not far from Le Cap, 'is able turn slavery into a condition that even free men might envy' (vol. I, p. 277). In reality the Marquis de Galifet was the first President of the Club Massiac, which was committed to maintaining slavery: see Laurent Dubois, *Avengers of the New World: The Story of the Haitian Revolution* (Cambridge, MA: Harvard University Press, 2004), p. 75. In *Bug-Jargal* the owner of Fort Galifet plantation is a very cruel master and Hugo seems to follow another source, namely *Histoire de la révolution de Saint Domingue*, 2 vols (1793?; Paris: Mame frères, 1814), by Antoine Dalmas, who reports that the slaves on La Gossette, the smallest plantation in the Gallifet's estate, had begun the 1791 revolt a day earlier with the attempted assassination of their manager (*Histoire de la revolution de Saint Dominque*, 2 vols [1793?] (Paris: Mame frères, 1814), vol. I, pp. 116–21). David Geggus found evidence of a 'strike' which had taken place in 1789: for two months the slaves withdrew into the woods in order to have the *commandeur* removed –see 'Les esclaves de la plaine du Nord à la veille de la Révolution Française, part III', *Revue de la Société haïtienne d'histoire*, 144 (1984), pp. 15–44, p. 32.

recounts that before arriving in Saint Domingue he was brought to Santo Domingo by a Spanish captain and then sold 'to different masters as one sells a head of cattle' (p. 171).[23] The symbolic function of the border as a signpost of freedom for the slaves on the French side is clearly illustrated in *Bug-Jargal*: when the rebel army feels threatened, its leaders decide to 'head for the Spanish frontier' (p. 178). Interestingly, while the title of the song is repeated twice in each version, the lyrics are withheld in both: this seems to suggest that what mattered to Hugo was mainly the reference to contraband contained in the title and what it signified in relation to border politics, while the figure of the *contrabandista* clearly represents the existence of a border that dangerously lacked impermeability.[24]

In the second version of *Bug-Jargal* Pierrot sings another Spanish song right at the beginning of the novel. Accompanied by a guitar, his voice suddenly disturbs the peace of the plantation of Fort Galifet and, in particular, of the pavilion where the lovely Marie normally retreats with her beloved Leopold. A Spanish song emphasizes once again the vicinity of the colonial frontier, a frontier that, at the time of writing, it is worth remembering, did not exist anymore. When Leopold sets off to ambush the unknown singing intruder, he finds himself fighting against someone who easily escapes him and who can speak both Spanish and French: his words are *Te tengo, te tengo* – '(I am holding you' Spanish translated in a note by Hugo himself) and the French for 'no! no! she would weep too much!'(p. 72). Undeterred by Leopold's attack, Pierrot comes back the following night and sings another Spanish serenade to the lovely Marie, who he calls *Maria* in the Spanish fashion (p. 75). The politics of translation are illuminating here: this time Hugo includes in the text *all* the lyrics of the song but, crucially, translated into French. In a note he explains: 'it was deemed unnecessary to reproduce here in their entirety the words of the Spanish song' (p. 75). In other words, a translation (crucially deprived of the original language version) becomes a useful tool to reinstate his preferred hierarchy between the languages that the presence of the border made readily available (French and Spanish) and to absorb and neutralize the disorder that the lyrics of the song seem instead to uphold. Here is the concluding stanza of the song:

---

[23] The slave merchant is identified as Spanish in both versions.

[24] Nature also reveals the danger inherent in the border: the river of the plantation near the border has 'a monstrous crocodile' in it (p. 78) – notably, according to Saint-Méry, the Massacre River, which forms a natural border between the two sides of the island, was infested with crocodiles (PE, vol. I, pp. 205–6). The closer one gets to the border the more 'fateful' the 'savannah' becomes (p. 176) and the revengeful Habibrah is finally swallowed by the place, crucially in a subterranean chamber through which an impetuous torrent ominously runs (p. 181 and pp. 188–91).

"You are white, and I am black, but the day needs to join with the night to bring forth the dawn and the sunset which are more beautiful than it!'" (p. 76). These are words directed to the 'white daughter of Hispaniola,' Marie/ Maria, by the black Pierrot/Bug-Jargal, but the *griffe de couleur* Habibrah defiantly claims the song as a description of himself:

> Now, if this song speaks the truth, the griffe Habibrah, your humble slave, born of a negress and a white man, is more beautiful than you, *señorito de amor*. I am the issue of the joining of day and night. I am the dawn or the sunset referred to in the Spanish song, and you are only the day. So I am more beautiful than you, *si usted quiere*,* more beautiful than a white man.

> *If you will. (pp. 77–8; Hugo's translation)

It goes without saying that the undertext is the threat of miscegenation and Habibrah has been rightly identified as the tragic mulatto and scapegoat of this mixophobic text.[25] Yet, I would like to focus here not on what Habibrah says but on how he speaks. Overall, the *griffe* Habibrah speaks Spanish as well as French, plus Latin, English, and Creole, but he mixes all these languages in a confusing fashion. In the above quotation, for example, some Spanish words pronounced by Habibrah are translated by Hugo in the text, while others are not: this is a repeated pattern throughout the novel and adds to the threatening confusion that Habibrah is supposed to represent. Habibrah's code-switching and his 'opacity,'[26] however, reveal Hugo's anxiety in relation to a border that did not hold and, as a result, was eventually erased by the Haitians. The simultaneous presence of different languages in the territory testifies to the permeability of the internal border of the island and signposts the existence of locally derived multilinguistic and multicultural formations which refuse homogenization. The multilingualism of the text comes hand in hand with Hugo's attempt to absorb the threat to the established order that such Babel entails. After all, Hugo's use of notes and translations chimes with his other strategies of containment, such as his decision to end both versions of *Bug-Jargal* by foregrounding the weakness of the rebel army which is seen retreating after the death of

---

[25] See, for example, Chris Bongie, *Islands and Exiles: The Creole Identities of Post/Colonial Literature* (Stanford, CA: Stanford University Press, 1998), pp. 231–61.

[26] Édouard Glissant's views on 'opacity' and 'transparency' are relevant here – see *Poetics of Relation*, trans. B. Wing (Ann Arbor, MI: The University of Michigan Press, 1997), in particular, pp. 111–20.

one of its leaders. We know instead that the revolt continued and, crucially, expanded into a war partly because of the support that the Spanish side was lending to the insurgents.[27] Moreover, as one of Hugo's critics pointed out in 1850, 'Why is it that [the author] nowhere acknowledges Spain's role in inciting the negro insurrection and assisting it? No doubt the Spanish titles that the leaders of the revolt assume were extremely ridiculous, but their relations with Spain are nonetheless an established fact, one which can no longer be omitted from the historical record.'[28]

Hugo's omission is consistent with the fact that, in the second version in particular, in order to counterbalance the function of the border as a signifier of freedom, he repeatedly mentions the Ogé case. In Hugo's first version, Bug-Jargal tells Delmar that his father was tortured and killed with Ogé (despite the fact that, historically, Ogé avoided the mobilization of the slaves[29]) but never mentions his extradition. In the second version, the rebel Biassou makes an explicit reference to it when he declares that he would not mind raiding the Spanish side of the island for cattle because he would be 'delighted to punish those damnable Spanish planters; they are the ones who handed over Ogé' (p. 139).[30] Biassou's words, ironically, undermine Hugo's attempt to portray the border as a colonial frontier whose gates are opened and closed exclusively by colonial powers, once again attract our attention to the illicit activities that took place across it, and reveal that colonial powers were incapable of stopping or at least controlling them.

In his preface to the 1826 version, Hugo declares that 'several distinguished people who either as colonists or as functionaries found themselves mixed up in Saint Domingue's troubles contributed to his revision by passing along to him unpublished materials and documents' (p. 57). Some of these documents and testimonials must have been concerned with one of the legendary slave leaders referred to in the revised version, namely Romaine Rivière or Romaine

---

[27] Apropos of strategies of containment, it had been noted that Saint Beuve's review of *Bug-Jargal*, a comparative study of the two versions, omits any reference to the slave revolt of 22 August 1791 and to the Haitian Revolution – Charles Augustin Sainte-Beuve, 'Les Romans de Victor Hugo', *Journal des débats*, 24 July 1832, quoted in Hugo, *Bug-Jargal*, pp. 287–90. It is worth mentioning that Sainte-Beuve wrote his review in 1832 – that is, when the island was unified under the Haitian flag.
[28] C.A. Chauvet, 'Des Roman de M. Victor Hugo,' *Revue encyclopédique* 50 (April–June 1831), quoted in Hugo, *Bug-Jargal*, pp. 285–7, p. 287.
[29] Some of his men, however, seem to have been more inclined to turn to the slaves for assistance – Dubois, *Avengers of the New World*, p. 88.
[30] In *La isla al revés* (p. 75) Balaguer refers to Biassou's words in Hugo's novel as evidence of Haitian aggression and violation of Dominican territory even if, strictly speaking, Haiti had not yet been founded in 1791.

the Prophetess.[31] Maintaining that he was the Virgin Mary's 'grandson,' Romaine the Prophetess is well-known for his subversive appropriation of the Virgin Mary symbol which, from the arrival of Columbus on the Santa Maria, was deployed to legitimate Hispanic colonization, significantly also described as 'Marian colonization.'[32] After 1697, when Saint Domingue became officially French, the Virgin Mary continued to enjoy a privileged iconic status as moral authority.[33] According to some sources, Rivière was a *griffe* of Spanish origin[34] who set up quarters in an abandoned church near Trou-Coffy and preached mass before an inverted cross with a saber in his hand.[35] In the novel he is disparagingly described by Bug-Jargal as 'a mulatto charlatan [who] profanes the sacred mass [...] incites his comrades to murder and pillage, all in the name of *Maria!*' (p. 162; italics in the text). His blasphemous attitude is not the only trait that he has in common with Hugo's Habibrah, who is depicted while preaching mass on a sugar box instead of an altar, using his dagger as a cross (p. 119).

In *Bug-Jargal*, the *griffe* Habibrah's practices as an *obi* and Romaine the Prophetess's 'religious' activities are revealed as fake and as a strategic move to keep the superstitious insurgents under a spell.[36] According to some sources, Rivière might have adopted a shamanistic pretence to reinforce his influence on his army of former slaves.[37] Others have insisted that, despite the fact that Rivière's religious practice was very different from those of other leaders of the rebellion, he should still be considered as a Vodou

---

[31] It is unclear why this male rebel chose to call himself Romain*e la* prophét*esse*: we know that he was married to a mulattress and was a father of two children (Fick, *Making of Haiti*, p. 128).

[32] Nicholas Perry and Loreto Echeverria, *Under the Heal of Mary* (New York: Routledge, 1988), p. 31.

[33] See Terry Rey, 'The Virgin Mary and the Revolution in Sainte Domingue: The Charisma of Romaine-la- Prophetèsse', *Journal of Historical Sociology*, 11 (1998), pp. 341–69, p. 345 and 'The Politics of Patron Sainthood in Haiti: 500 Years of Iconic Struggle', *The Catholic Historical Review*, 88.3 (2002), pp. 519–45, pp. 519–26.

[34] Thomas Madiou refers to Romaine as a '*grif espagnol,*' which should be taken to mean that he was originally from the Spanish side of the island and a native speaker of Spanish. See Rey, 'The Virgin Mary', p. 365.

[35] Fick, *Making of Haiti*, p. 127.

[36] Romaine is called a 'charlatan [who] persuades his followers that he is in contact with the Virgin Mary, whose supposed oracles he listens to by placing his head in the tabernacle', and, later, a 'trickster.' Moreover, Bug-Jargal tells Biassou that a 'common bond' between the rebels should have been created 'through other means than a ferocious fanaticism and ridiculous superstitions' (pp. 162–3).

[37] See Fick, *Making of Haiti*, pp. 127–8 and Matibag, *Haitian-Dominican Counterpoint*, p. 54.

practitioner: his activities testify to the diversity one finds among Vodouisant cults of the time and his appropriation of Mariology could identify him as Kongolese – that is, from a part of Africa which had been exposed to and freely adapted Catholic symbolism for 300 years.[38] In the second version, Bug-Jargal is also Kongolese (the son of the King of Kakongo[39]) and his interracial love for Marie/Maria can be seen as a disturbing version of Rivière's devotion to the Virgin.[40] Importantly, however, Bug-Jargal renounces in order to (sexually) appropriate Marie/Maria, efficiently polices his subversive (blasphemous) desire for her, and, after saving her, generously gives her back to D'Auverney.[41]

Romaine operated in the area surrounding Jacmel and Léogâne, which is a great distance from the border, but the fact that he was an *affranchi* who had actually crossed over from the Spanish part makes him a 'vector of revolution' and the very embodiment of the danger that a porous border represented at the time:[42] indeed, some of the insurgents in *Bug-Jargal* are reported as coming from the Spanish side (p. 127). It is easy to argue here that Hugo tries to reduce the threat implicit in such border-crossing by turning the free rebel Romaine into the house slave/fool and dwarfish Habibrah.

Hugo's sources also mention the maroon leader Pierrot, interestingly Bug-Jargal's slave name, who became an ally of the Republican Sonthonax and Polverel's in 1793 and defeated Galbaud's royalist army at Le Cap. Far from being Hugo's compassionate, generous, and restrained leader who seems more concerned with saving his white masters than with the actual success of the rebellion, the real Pierrot and his 'hordes of barbarians' are described by Lacroix as having 'a great thirst for blood and pillaging.'[43] Once again, therefore, Hugo dramatically departs from his sources: as a reviewer noted in 1826, 'Everything is belittled or misconstrued' in the novel.[44]

---

[38] Rey, 'The Virgin Mary', pp. 354, 350, 343.

[39] He was from Gamboa (Senegal) in the first version.

[40] When Bug-Jargal mentions the Virgin Mary as the alleged inspiration for the unlawful activities of Romaine la Prophetess he calls her *Maria* (in italics in the text) – that is, with the same name he uses when he refers to D'Auverney's beloved.

[41] At the end, Marie/Maria will be lost to both: she will perish 'in the first conflagration of Le Cap' (p. 197).

[42] See Peter Linebaugh and Marcus Rediker, *The Many-Headed Hydra: Sailors, Slaves, Commoners, and the Hidden History of the Revolutionary Atlantic* (Boston, MA: Beacon Press, 2000), p. 241.

[43] Pamphile de Lacroix, *Mémoires pour servir à l'histoire de la Révolution de Saint Domingue*, vol. 1 (Paris: Pillet ainé, 1819), p. 245.

[44] Henri Latouche, *Le Mercure du dix-neuvième siècle*, 12 (1826), quoted in Hugo,

Another example of misconstruction (but not belittlement) is the anachronism concerning the insignificant help extended by British Jamaica to the whites of Saint Domingue. When, at the outbreak of the 1791 rebellion, one of the participants to the informal council at the residence of the Governor Blanchelande suggests that the Governor of Jamaica should be notified, a deputy of the provincial assembly retorts: 'Yes [...] so that he can once again bestow upon us the inconsequential assistance of five hundred rifles' (p. 97). These 500 rifles were in fact sent to the white colonist in response to a request for help following the revolt of 22 August 1791, not preceding it. Hugo's urge to blame British Jamaica for the lack of assistance that the colony of Saint Domingue received from it might underlie this anachronism, which chimes with the fact that the perfidious villain of the second version, the Spanish *griffe* Habibrah, was actually given to the narrator's uncle 'as a toy monkey of sorts by Lord Effingham, Governor of Jamaica' (p. 67). It is noteworthy that, before joining Biassou's army as a *obi*, Habibrah treacherously kills his master, stabbing him with his dagger while he was still in bed. Moreover, another leader of the revolt and a crucial vector of revolution, the maroon Boukman Dutty, was also from Jamaica[45] and not the only Jamaican who participated in the Saint Domingue revolt: in *Bug-Jargal*, English is in fact one of the languages spoken by the composite rebel army.[46] It is noteworthy, however, that when Boukman is mentioned by Hugo much more is made of his capture and death and their detrimental effect on the rebels' army than of his victories as a leader.

Despite their differences, the Spanish *griffe* Habibrah and the *contrabandista* Pierrot/Bug-Jargal are both actively involved in the Saint Domingue revolt and their fluency in Spanish coupled with their revolutionary activities remind Hugo's readers of the existence of licit and illicit trafficking across the border. In both versions of *Bug-Jargal* the action progressively moves

---

Bug-Jargal, pp. 282–5, p. 283. The best example of a much debated 'misconstruction' has perhaps to do with a reference to the Massiac Club: in contrast to the assertion of one of d'Auverney's companions (p. 66), far from being an association of negrophiles, the Massiac Club was a pro-slavery club.

[45] Boukman was sold in contraband by an English slaver (Fouchard, *The Haitian Maroons*, p. 339); he is supposed to have given 'the signal for the revolt' (Fick, *Making of Haiti*, p. 92) and to have delivered a call to arms to the slaves who participated in the Vodou ceremony that was held at Bois Caiman, which is, however, not mentioned by Hugo and his known sources.

[46] 'A collective roar from the rebels stifled the colonist's response "*Muerte! Muerte! Death! Mort! Touyé! Touyé!*"' (p. 141, italics in the text; 'Death' is in English in the French original).

towards the border and, the closer one gets to it, the more disorderly things become. In the second version the number of Spanish words also increases exponentially. Many critics have declared themselves baffled by the presence of so much Spanish in the text, especially considering that Hugo had only an approximate knowledge of the language, as testified by his frequent 'mistakes.'[47] However, such 'mistakes' could well be deliberate and an attempt to both represent and vilify the language spoken by the rebels: the narrator himself explains that 'many negroes' who had originally belonged to colonists in Santo Domingo or were born there 'mixed the Spanish language with their own jargon' (p. 80).[48]

In chapter thirty-eight of the second version D'Auverney is offered the possibility of saving his life if (like Gros) he becomes Biassou's 'diplomatic orthographer' (p. 153): Biassou and Jean-François have just finished writing a letter addressed to the assembly in which they outline their conditions for surrender. They fear, however, that their letter might be full of grammatical mistakes so they ask D'Auverney to get rid of any error that, as Biassou puts it 'could provoke the arrogant *burlerias* of our former masters' (p. 153). Biassou's use of the Spanish word *burlerias* (in italics and untranslated in the text) is a reminder of his connection with the other side of the border: in the second version we are told that Biassou was sold by his first master in Saint Domingue to 'a dealer from Santo Domingo for thirteen piastres-gourdes' (p. 134). The principled D'Auverney predictably refuses to help Biassou but what is interesting here is the fact that Hugo presents us with multilingual rebels who are seemingly willing to have their own heterogeneity erased in favour of what they call '*style blanc*' or 'the white style' (p. 179; italics in French original). The rebels' multilingualism and multiculturalism, however, had deep cultural, historical, and political roots which could not be as easily 'translated' and ignored as Hugo hoped.

In a note to the text Hugo explains that Jean-François's and Biassou's 'ridiculously characteristic letter was indeed sent to the assembly' (p. 153) but what he offers us in the pages of *Bug-Jargal* is instead a pastiche of

---

[47] Cauna, Les sources historiques', p. 31; Léon-François Hoffman, 'Victor Hugo, les noirs et l'esclavage', *Francofonia: studi e ricerche sulle letterature di lingua francese*, 31 (1966), pp. 47–90, pp. 71–2.

[48] Hugo means Creole when he writes 'jargon.' The Spanish spoken by Pierrot, Biassou, Habibrah, and the other rebels appears in the text alongside the French language as it was spoken in Saint Domingue – words such as *chica* (113) or *ajoupa* (115) are a good example, as are *griffe* or *sacatra* (67) – but also alongside African words such as *obi* (69), *balafo* (113), *griot* (112), and *wanga* (112), Creole expressions such as *Zoté cordé! Zoté cordé!* (113), *bon Giu* (119), and *Guetté blan si la la* (121), and, as we have seen, English (*Death*).

three different dispatches that he found in one of his sources – namely, Lacroix's *Mémoires*.[49] One in particular records the response that in June 1793 Macaya, Pierrot's lieutenant, gave to the Republican Commissioner Étienne Polverel when the latter was trying to convince the rebel to return to support the Republic after he had sworn allegiance to the king of Spain. Macaya's words to Polverel are copied almost verbatim and then attributed by Hugo to Biassou and Jean-François:

> We are the subject of three kings: the king of Congo, born-master of all the blacks; the King of France, who represents our fathers; and the King of Spain who represents our mothers. These three kings are the descendants of those who, guided by a star, went to worship the Man-God. (pp. 151–3)[50]

These words do not necessarily prove that the rebels were backward-looking and royalist, that in their camps reigned what Pierre Laforgue calls 'a confusion of symbols,' and that all they aspired to was a 'carnivalesque royalty.'[51] In the 1780s Kongolese slaves made up 60 per cent of the slaves in the North Province, where the rebellion began: like the fictional Bug-Jargal, who also has an immediate African background, the real Macaya, his name suggests, was actually from Congo.[52] As John Thornton has pointed out, Kongolese society was resolutely monarchic but absolutism was not the only way: its opposing political model was one that required the king to rule by consent and to make decision after consultation.[53] In the eighteenth century Kongo became so heavily involved in the slave trade precisely because of numerous civil wars partly fought to determine what powers the king of Kongo was allowed to have. The Kongolese presence was so remarkable that

---

[49] See Bongie's note on p. 153.

[50] Compare with Macaya's oral statement 'I am the subject of three kings: the king of Congo, master of all the Blacks; the king of France, who represents my father; and the king of Spain who represents my mother. These three kings are the descendants of those who, guided by a star, went to worship the Man-God,' reproduced in Lacroix, *Mémoires*, p. 253, quoted in Hugo, *Bug-Jargal*, pp. 301–23, p. 315.

[51] See, for example, Thomas Madiou, *Histoire d'Haiti* [1814–1884] (Port-au-Prince, 1947), p. 104 and Pierre Laforgue, '*Bug-Jargal*, ou de la difficulté d'écrire in *style blanc*', *Romantisme*, 69 (1990), pp. 29–42, pp. 30, 32.

[52] John Thornton, '"I Am the Subject of the King of Congo": African Political Ideology and the Haitian Revolution', *Journal of World History*, 4.2 (1993), pp. 181–214, p. 185. Congolese also constituted the most numerous ethnic grouping among the maroons (Fick, *Making of Haiti*, p. 59).

[53] Thornton, '"I Am the Subject of the King of Congo"', p. 186.

even if many of the leaders of the revolution had never been to Africa they still had to take into consideration the ideology of their followers. Important cases in point are, for example, Romaine the Prophetess, who was probably either Kongolese or heavily influenced by Kongolese religious culture, but also Boukman, who, despite the fact that he was not from Kongo, was still known among the rebels as Kakongo or by a Kakongo nickname, Zamba (from *nzamba*, elephant).[54]

The different views of the Kongolese on monarchical powers and leadership were imported in the New World and, concomitantly with European political ideas, informed ideological perspectives on the revolution which were also complicated by the rebels' ability to take advantage of the fact that the island was divided in two. The interests of two monarchical (and, lately, a republican) governments which, for the fulfilment of their own agenda, were ready to appeal to the rebels and make different concessions to them in order to enlist their services, have certainly been extremely important.[55] Far from being a weak and disorderly 'agglomeration of means without an end' (p. 150), as Hugo disparagingly suggests, the heterogeneous and multilingual rebel force was actually able to make the most of the French's internecine conflicts, of the Kongolese political, cultural, military, and religious traditions, and, most importantly, of the presence of a disputed colonial border. The rebels' appropriation of European uniforms seriously undermined the colonizers' authority and substituted it with a different one. Moreover, the disorderly uniforms worn by the rebels and vilified by Hugo because of their mixed, often contradicting nature offer further evidence of the rebels' capacity to take advantage of a strikingly confusing situation and to adopt the 'style' that, on a particular occasion, would give them the best result.[56] In other words, the 'white style' that the maroons Biassou and Jean François are keen to be identified with seems to imply a purely strategical change rather than a substantial one.

---

[54] Rey, 'The Virgin Mary and the Revolution', p. 350. On Boukman's name see Fick, *Making of Haiti*, pp. 92, 297 note 5 and Thornton, '"I Am the Subject of the King of Congo"', pp. 185 and 186.

[55] One could add another monarchy to the list, as in 1798 Britain offered to recognize Toussaint as King of Haiti.

[56] 'First came gangs of negroes, absolutely naked [...] then it was a battalion of mulattoes, fitted out in the Spanish or English fashion [...] Fluttering above all these heads were flags of every colour, displaying every slogan imaginable: white ones, red ones, tricoloured ones, flags with the fleur-de-lis or topped with the bonnet of liberty, and bearing such inscriptions as "Death to priests and to aristocrats!" ... "Long live religion!" ... "Liberty!" ... "Equality!" ... "Long live the king!" ... "Down with France!" ... "Viva España!" ... "No more tyrants!"' (p. 150).

In the second version of *Bug-Jargal* multilingualism and code-switching are not limited to Habibrah's and other rebels' interventions. Leopold/the narrator seems incapable of keeping himself to standard French when he approximates the border and describes life in the rebels' camp:

> The time had come for [the] *almuerzo*.* A large turtle shell was brought before the *mariscal de campo de su magestad catolica*: steaming inside it was a sort of *olla podrida*, abundantly seasoned with slabs of lard, turtle flesh substituting for the *carnero*# and sweet potatoes for the *garganzas* §. An enourmous Caribbean cabbage flowed on the surface of this *puchero*. On each side of the shell [...] were two cups made out of coconut husks and filled with raisins, *sandias***, yams, and figs; this was the *postre*##.

*lunch // # lamb // § chickpeas // ** watermelon // ## dessert
(p. 147, Hugo's translation)

Notably, Hugo deals with his narrator's bilingualism exactly as he did with Habibrah's: some of the words are translated in French in the text, but others are left untranslated. Overall, the presence of different languages on the page, which can overwhelm the reader despite notes and partial translation, articulates the intersection of a metropolitan/colonial culture with a local and global culture from below. Strategies of containment notwithstanding, Hugo's metropolitan representation of the 1791 rebellion ultimately reveals the revolutionary potential of the border by depicting it as a dangerously interactive contact zone through which emancipatory and revolutionary ideas and people could and did flow.[57] Apart from the 1791 revolt with which the plot is directly concerned, it is fair to say that *Bug-Jargal* presents us (albeit unwillingly) with another powerful rebellion: the insurrection of a discredited transcultural and multilingual borderland which brings to the fore a different linguistic and cultural landscape and a literary geography that goes well beyond national languages and colonial mappings.

Hugo went back to the topic of the Haitian Revolution twenty years after the second version of *Bug-Jargal* was published in 1826 with 'The Saint Domingue Revolt,' a short account of a dream that he apparently dictated to his wife in 1845. 'The Saint Domingue Revolt' has been described as a blatantly racist text or, more generously, as a 'therapeutic attempt at giving

---

[57] Hugo's ineffective strategies of containment reflect Leopold's uncle's order to guard the 'border' of the plantation 'more strictly than ever' because he erroneously assumed that Marie's 'new suitor could have come only from outside his domains' (p. 74).

novelistic form to a shapeless nightmare.'[58] One definition does not exclude the other, but I would argue that the short story is also a document that confirms Hugo's interest and anxiety vis-à-vis border relations on the island. The reader is presented with a sequence of grotesque and violent scenes of pillage and destruction occurring (presumably) in the city of Le Cap, but Hugo's focus on an urban scenario does not prevent him from meditating on the danger that porous borders constitute. On the contrary, he positions himself as the narrator very close to the city gate, 'a flimsy lattice barrier'[59] which is utterly inadequate to contain the political, sexual, and criminal excesses which are taking place inside: as a matter of fact, 'a massive file of vehicles [was] exiting through the city gates' forming, 'far off in the distance [...] battalions of soldiers in rags and tatters' (p. 253). Hugo invites us to project this 'minute portion' on a much larger scale: 'multiply these details to infinity,' he writes, 'and you will have the overall picture' (p. 250). In other words, the nightmarish 'overall picture' he wants us to imagine features a centre that does not hold precisely because of the flimsiness of its 'borders.' To hammer the message home more decisively, readers of 'The Saint Domingue Revolt' are given the impression that, contrarily to what actually happened, the rebellion began in the city only to be exported outside, to the conventionally (but both ahistorical and unhistorical) 'calm, delightful' countryside (p. 253).

That the 'The Saint Domingue Revolt' is a cautionary tale at heart can be also corroborated by the fact that, to add poignancy to the description of what, at the beginning of the story, he calls 'a dream,' Hugo insists on depicting himself as an 'ocular' witness of the rebellion: 'I will simply tell you what was right there in from of my eyes' (p. 250). Of course, when Le Cap was pillaged by Pierrot's and Macaya's troops in 1793, he was safe and sound in Paris. If it is true that in 1845, when Hugo dictated 'The Saint Domingue Revolt,' the border between the Spanish and the Haitian side of the island had just been reinstated (in 1844), we also know that the Haitians relentlessly tried to reconquer the re-Hispanized Eastern side for more than ten years. As we have seen, Hugo was obviously disturbed by the possibility of Haiti (re)exporting the revolution inside and outside the perimeter of Hispaniola, whether directly (with an army) or indirectly (as a model for all slaves). In this respect, 'The Saint Domingue Revolt' did not work as a therapeutic attempt to keep his fears under control due to the turbulent

---

[58] See Hoffman, 'Victor Hugo, les noirs et l'esclavage', pp. 47–90 and Chris Bongie's notes to 'The Saint Domingue Revolt' (1845), in Hugo, *Bug-Jargal*, p. 249.

[59] Hugo, 'The Saint Domingue Revolt' in *Bug-Jargal*, p. 250. Further references to this translation text will be given in parentheses in the text.

political reality of the island: Faustin Soulouque, a former slave who was president and then Emperor of Haiti between 1847 and 1859, was particularly keen to reappropriate Santo Domingo and masterminded many expeditions aimed at a reunification of the island under Haitian rule. Interestingly, in the 1850s Hugo ridiculed and criticized Soulouque both vehemently and repeatedly in his poetry: Hoffman reads Hugo's verbal assaults on the Emperor Faustin I as indirect attacks on an Emperor closer to home, that is Napoleon III, but I would argue that Soulouque's expansionistic efforts should not be neglected.[60] Hugo's animosity towards Soulouque reminds one of his hostility towards Boyer, former ruler of the entire island of Hispaniola, and Toussaint, the man who had brought the whole island under the control of the rebels in 1801. Despite the fact that Toussaint is never mentioned in the text, in a number of notes that the author appended to the second version of *Bug-Jargal* the black leader is repeatedly (and conveniently) conflated with Biassou (pp. 120, 147, 149).

✳✳✳

Unlike Hugo, the Republican Jean-Baptiste Picquenard, author of two of Hugo's most probable literary sources, had actually spent time in Saint Domingue, probably between 1791 and 1793. Picquenard is as determined as Hugo to investigate the role that the border played in the Revolution in his two 'colonial anecdotes' *Adonis* and *Zoflora*, the first novels which deal with the Haitian Revolution.[61] In *Adonis, ou le bon nègre* ('Adonis, or the good negro'), set in 1791 at the time of the slave revolt, the action begins in Vallière, a place that signposted 'the border between the French and the English sides' (p. 7).[62] Picquenard's second novel, *Zoflora, ou la bonne negrèsse* ('Zoflora or the good negro girl'), deals more explicitly with the division of what it calls the 'old island of Ohaïti' (p. 85).[63] Written two

---

[60] Hoffman, 'Victor Hugo, les noirs et l'esclavage', pp. 57–8.

[61] Jean-Baptiste Picquenard, *Adonis, ou le bon nègre* (Paris: Didot jeune, 1798) and *Zoflora, ou la bonne negrèsse*, 2 vols (Paris: Didot jeune, 1800). For more information on Picquenard's life and sojourn in Saint Domingue see Chris Bongie's Introduction to Jean-Baptiste Picquenard, *Adonis suivi de Zoflora et de documents inédits*, ed. C. Bongie (Paris: L'Harmattan, 2006) vii–xl. It is certain that Hugo read *Adonis* and it is very likely but not certain that Hugo read *Zoflora* –see 'Literary Sources' in Hugo, *Bug-Jargal*, pp. 326–38.

[62] Picquenard, *Adonis suivi de Zoflora et de documents inédits*, p. 332. References to these texts will be given in parentheses in the text followed by my translations into English.

[63] The name 'Ohaiti' does not signpost Picquenard's sympathy for the Republic of

years after *Adonis*, it begins with a description of the island in which he acknowledges the presence of two nations and emphasizes 'the difference in their customs' (p. 85). As we will see, *Zoflora* is so border-conscious that it ends with a surprisingly bold alteration of the historical chronology for a novel that 'depends on history' (p. 86): according to Picquenard's plot, the war between Spain and France declared in 1793 significantly precedes rather than follows the 1791 rebellion.

Picquenard's political views strongly influence his fiction and the ways in which he represents border and borderland. Initially he was an ally of the Republicans Polverel and Sonthonax and a committed supporter of equality. In January 1793 he found himself under threat from the white creole population of Saint Domingue, who identified him with the National Assembly's decree of 4 April 1792 which gave full rights of citizenship to mulattoes and free blacks and gave the power to enforce it to a new three-man Commission (namely, Sonthonax, Polverel, and Ailhaud). Picquenard's friendship with Sonthonax, however, did not last long: in August 1793 Sonthonax had him arrested for what the commissioner called his (unspecified) 'blatant lack of sense of civic duty' (p. xxi). When he wrote the two novels in question, Picquenard had been in jail and was deported to Brest, where he also worked as a journalist, this time keen to denounce the excesses related to the period of *la Terreur* rather than to fully support the Jacobins.

Adonis and *Zoflora*, written in 1798 and 1800 respectively, are the products of the historico-political climate that marked France from the fall of Robespierre to the rise of Napoleon: for example, *Adonis* begins with Picquenard's striking attempt to position himself outside the political debate: 'I will not try here to decide whether the sudden abolition of slavery in the French colonies really was a good thing for mankind' (p. 5). However, if he was very keen to disentangle himself from what he calls the 'inextricable maze' of the events in Saint Domingue (p. 178), he was also eager to demonstrate that this maze was made even more inextricable by the presence of a permeable colonial frontier on the island. In 1793, when Picquenard was still in Saint Domingue, Biassou, Jean François, and Toussaint had joined the Spanish army and were fighting (and winning) against the French Republicans. One should note, moreover, that if both novels are set around 1791, they were written and published at a time when

---

Haiti, which did not yet exist at the time of writing, but, being the name the indigenous population had given to their island, acknowledges their presence on the territory before the arrival of the colonizers. Hugo does the same in a note to chapter 29 of the second version of *Bug-Jargal*.

the border between Saint Domingue and Santo Domingo had been erased *de jure* (if not *de facto*) by the Treaty of Basle. After 1795, as we have seen, Hispaniola's border politics turned into a form of suspended animation and, until May 1798, the presence of the British on the island complicated the matter further.

In Picquenard's account, the colonial frontier is never a site connected with the political activities of the insurgents, who are never credited with an emancipatory agenda of any kind; he is in fact more interested in highlighting the role that the French royalists, Spain, and Britain played in the fall of Saint Domingue than in understanding, or even acknowledging, the revolution 'from below' that Hugo's account unwittingly brings to the fore. As a result, Picquenard's border crossers are never vectors of revolutionary ideas. They are treacherous and *debauchés* French creoles, black petty criminals and bandits, the French and Spanish colonial armies, and the emissaries of the perfidious royalist Blanchelande who helps to organize the black rebellion precisely by crossing what is presented to us as a dangerously porous colonial frontier (p. 17). In *Adonis*, Picquenard takes for granted the hypothesis that the 1791 revolt originated in a badly conceived royalist plot and his depiction of the black insurgents is consistent with this: no political agenda characterizes them and they are unfailingly presented as savage, revengeful but disorganized puppets in the hands of the perfidious royalist Blanchelande who, in turn, is but a puppet of the British.[64] As noted above, historians have instead shown how, even at this early stage of the rebellion, the blacks had learnt to trade with the Spanish for additional weapons and ammunition and, most importantly, how, if they had allied with the counter-revolutionaries, they were neither controlled nor directed by them.[65] Moreover, if it is fair to say that at the beginning of the revolt rebel leaders such as Biassou, Boukman, or Jean-François did not really have a clear long-term revolutionary plan, one should not forget that from 1793 to 1800 (the date of publication of *Zoflora*) Toussaint had put in place an impressive and successful military and political strategy which was aimed at (and later achieved), among other things, the unification of Hispaniola. Picquenard's chosen timeframe for the novels' settings allows him to completely ignore Toussaint's activities while focusing instead on

[64] The Anglophobia of the text is evident everywhere, especially in the first edition of the text – see Bongie for the alterations implemented in the 1817 edition. Towards the end of the story, Adonis and D'Herouville are also kidnapped by English pirates characterized by 'barbarism [...] profound immorality [...] greed' and who are 'encouraged' and 'protected' by their government (p. 77).

[65] Fick, *Making of Haiti*, pp. 109, 112.

Boukman and Biassou. As we have seen, Hugo followed Picquenard in this but he put in place a different tactic to occlude and/or diminish Toussaint's achievement: he conflated him with Biassou.

Picquenard's depoliticization and criminalization of the rebels goes hand in hand, unavoidably, with a depoliticization and criminalization of the borderland. Picquenard's *Adonis* begins in a *habitation* very close to the frontier between the French and the Spanish side: it belongs to the virtuous Parisian white planter D'Herouville and it is the place where the *bon nègre* Adonis works as a *commandeur*.[66] There are obvious similarities between Hugo's noble slave Pierrot and Adonis who, on non-working days, plays the *banza*, 'an instrument much cherished by the blacks and a rough imitation of the guitar' (note 3, p. 8). However, unlike Pierrot, who sings and plays the guitar to give voice to his sadness, Adonis is a very happy slave because D'Herouville treats his slaves much better that do most Saint Domingue planters – he even plans to free them once he can afford to do so.[67] This is interesting because, being in the mountains, the parish of Vallière also used to be a famous refuge for maroons, who obviously signpost a very different type of freedom from the bestowed one that D'Herouville represents. As we have seen, Saint Méry concluded his 'description' of Vallière by urging the colonial administration to further populate the mountain areas of Saint Domingue in order to limit the number of places where the maroons could hide.[68]

In *Adonis*, the maroons appear in Vallière as a result of the 1791 revolt; they ruin D'Herouville's generous plans and turn him into a prisoner of the cruel rebel Biassou, who establishes his 'palace' not far away from the *habitation* and the border (p. 12). The arrival of Biassou dramatically changes the nature of the borderland which, nonetheless, remains fundamental

---

[66] Notably, Vallière had been praised by the creole Saint-Méry as a place where both white and coloured people could live a moral and healthy life (PF vol. I, p. 154). The mountains of Vallière mainly produced coffee, not sugar (Saint-Méry PF, vol. I, p. 151), and D'Herouville actually owns a coffee plantation. However, slaves' mortality rate and living and working conditions in coffee plantation were as bad as in sugar plantations (see Fick, *Making of Haiti*, p. 29).

[67] Manumissions were taxed in Saint Domingue and were an important part of the financial resources of the colony: in 1788, for example, the liberty tax generated 463,025 livres, more than the income and slave head tax revenue of the colony: see Stewart King, 'The Maréchaussée of Saint-Domingue Balancing the Ancient Régime and Modernity', *Journal of Colonialism and Colonial History*, 5.2 (2004), http://muse.jhu.edu/journals/journal_of_colonialism_and_colonial_history/toc/cch5.2.html [accessed 25 November 2014].

[68] Saint-Méry, PF, vol. I, p. 154.

to the action. Under D'Herouville's control it was an abstractly utopian place of relative independence from a much contested colonial centre and, for his slaves, it represents the hope of a – crucially deferred – freedom; in the hands of the rebels, instead, the border region becomes a vehicle for anti-revolutionary, royalist oppression, a dystopian site of cannibalism (pp. 14–15) and all sorts of dissolution and atrocity (pp. 37–40).[69] In his notes to the text, Bongie has pointed out that Picquenard's innovative mixture of fictional and historical characters contributed to the birth of the historical novel (p. 6). If he is right, it is useful to emphasize not only that the origin of this genre is inextricably linked to the Haitian Revolution but also to the need to vilify, demonize, criminalize, and neutralize black insurgents and to neuter the revolutionary potential of the borderland.

From the Plaine du Nord, which remains firmly in the hands of Biassou, the action moves across the Plaine de la Desolée to the west of the island. Further from the 1777 border than Vallière, the Plaine de la Desolée had nevertheless been a disputed borderland of the island. It is in fact located in the parish of Gonaïves, where buccaneers from Tortuga – that is, those we could call, simultaneously, the first border-keepers and -trespassers of Hispaniola – had found refuge in the seventeenth century. In 1633, according

---

[69] When the cruel and bloodthirsty Père Philémon, an ally of Biassou, decides to get rid of the virtuous white protagonist of the novel (who, in the meantime, has been forced to become Biassou's secretary in exchange for his life and the life of his wife and children), he plans to send him on a (false) mission to the Spanish side of the island, where he is supposed to represent Biassou at a royalist meeting but where his killers are instead waiting for him. However, Père Philémon's plans are thrown up in the air when a courier, crucially arriving from the Spanish colony, reveals that Blanchelande wishes to inform the blacks of the arrival of a powerful army which could defeat them (p. 45). It is not surprising that a Jacobin such as Picquenard should include in his novel a corrupted and malevolent priest, but it is worth remembering that, in *Adonis*, Père Philémon is a border crosser who, after seeking refuge in the Spanish side of the island, returned to join the black rebels in order to take revenge against all supporters of the French Revolution (p. 40). In a note to the text, Picquenard affirms that he was in Cap-Français when Père Philémon was sentenced to death and reports that the priest looked like 'crime personified' (p. 48). In 1793 two priests (also border crossers), Padre José Vásquez and Padre Vives, persuaded the Haitian leadership to join Spanish forces against the French. When Jean François's army entered Fort Dauphin on 6 July 1794, after celebrating mass for the former slaves, Padre José Vásquez incited the blacks to kill the white colonist of the city: 950 French colonists – children, women, and men – were killed in the massacre – see Selden Rodman, *Quisqueya: A History of the Dominican Republic* (Seattle, WA: University of Washington Press, 1964), p. 36. In Picquenard's novel Père Philémon is equally guilty of inciting the blacks to kill the whites.

to Saint Méry, their number was so remarkable that the Spanish decided to attack them to send them back to the islet. The Spanish lost their battle and, in 1666, the famous marauder François l'Olonnois used the bay of Gonaïves to divide up the bounty derived from his raid of Maracaibo. In 1730 the territory of Gonaïves counted twenty-seven indigo plantations, and, in 1737, it was once again invaded by the Spanish, who were worried about the establishment of more and more French colonists in the area.[70] In the novel, these historical layers are left unmentioned but the Plaine de la Desolée shares with the border region some of its qualifications, namely a strong symbolic association with conquered, not bestowed, freedom from colonial authority. Picquenard himself highlights this connection when he informs us that the revolt had actually transformed what used to be the refuge of the maroons into an uninhabited region because they had all joined Biassou's army of rebels (p. 59). *Marronage* was indeed a problem in this area and, according to Saint Méry, Gonaïves had its own *maréchaussée* as early as 1775.[71] Consistently with his depiction of the insurgents as bloodthirsty but gullible murderers, Picquenard turns the maroons into petty outlaws: in a note to the text, a maroon is defined as 'one who escaped his/her masters because he/she was lazy or because he/she wanted to avoid being punished and went to hide in the woods to hunt and to steal' (p. 59).

The Plaine de la Desolée is a desolate land where nothing grows and with no natural water springs and, Picquenard writes, had been the grave of many travellers who got lost in it. When Adonis and D'Herouville cross it, they also run the risk of dying of thirst until they discover that a noble and altruistic 'Frenchman' had actually built a fountain in the middle of the wasteland to assist those who were crossing it (p. 63). This human intervention on the territory tames the surrounding area and reminds us that places are always produced, qualified, and animated by their content and inhabitants.[72] It is in this radically transformed and transforming landscape that Picquenard allows his political commitment to surface in full: in fact, after relinquishing the utopian northern border to what to him were unmanageable and uncontrollable forces, Picquenard appropriates the free land of the maroons in order to reorganize it into his own political platform. Despite his initial declaration that he would not get involved in politics, Picquenard resorts to the rhetorical form of a fictional dialogue

---

[70] Saint-Méry, PF, vol. 2, pp. 89–91.

[71] Saint-Méry, PF, vol. 2, p. 110.

[72] Edward Casey, 'How to Get from Space to Place in a Fairly Short Stretch of Time: Phenomenological Prolegomena', in *Senses of Place*, ed. S. Field and K.H. Basso (Santa Fe, NM: School of American Research Press, 1996), pp. 13–52.

between D'Herouville and Adonis in order to reveal his views on equality, on morality, and on the *science de la vérité* ('science of truth', p. 72). The politics of language and translation are also very evident in this dialogue, where the standard French spoken by D'Herouville is openly contrasted with Adonis's (or rather Picquenard's) version of Creole.

Picquenard's linguistic practices testify to and reinforce his dismissive attitude towards both rebels and borderland. Adonis (but also, as we will see, Zoflora) express themselves in what Picquenard himself describes as a 'purified' version of 'Creole,' an intervention justified by the fact that he wanted to make available to those readers who could not speak Creole what he considered the 'spirit' of the language (p. 10). When he was a member of Saint Domingue Commission Civile, Picquenard understood the importance of Creole as a means of communication and there is evidence that some of the proclamations issued when he was working with Polverel and Sonthonax were translated into Creole for the benefit of the population of African descent.[73] It has been suggested, therefore, that the rudimentary, childlike language spoken by Adonis and Zoflora should not be too quickly dismissed as patronizing and infantilizing because it has its roots in the revolutionary language spoken and written by Picquenard when he was at the service of the Commission Civile, operating in what was a 'bilingual environment.'[74] I am not entirely convinced by this argument, and not simply because Picquenard himself admits that he edited the language spoken by Adonis; what interests me, however, is the fact that Biassou does not speak Creole in the novel – incidentally, contrarily to what happens in Hugo's account, one does not hear a word of African, Spanish, or English among his troops.[75] Picquenard's erasure of the multilingualism of the rebels is unhistorical but chimes very well with his denial of the horizontal dimension of the borderland that Hugo so obsessively demonizes in *Bug-Jargal* and which played such a decisive part in the revolution.

Picquenard's second novel *Zoflora* marginally but, perhaps, significantly, departs from *Adonis* in terms of multilingualism (or lack of it): the text includes one Spanish word ('*cortejo*' translated in a note as 'suitor' p. 193) and the words *Cazoucan* (p. 116) and *Fé-touté* (p. 221), translated in the notes as 'African word meaning *respect to the good*' and 'Creator of the universe.

---

[73] Bongie's introduction to Picquenard, *Adonis suivi de Zoflora et de documents inédits*, p. xix.

[74] Bongie's introduction to Picquenard, *Adonis suivi de Zoflora et de documents inédits*, p. xix.

[75] We are only told that the slaves come from Africa and the names of their tribes are listed (pp. 14, 46).

(African term)', respectively. The word *Fé-touté* is pronounced by a black rebel who tries to prevent (unsuccessfully) the execution of a white villain: despite this invocation of a black divinity, the black rebels proceed to kill the white man, tearing his body apart with their teeth. *Cazoucan* is what an old and virtuous black instructs the white protagonist to say in order to cross the land of the maroons unharmed. The password *Cazoucan* is accompanied by the leg of a *fétiche* and together they function as bodyguards for the white traveller who, without them, would not be able to move freely around the colony. Picquenard is obviously keen to demonstrate – perhaps echoing Saint Méry, who was the first to provide a detailed (and prejudiced) description of Vodou rituals in Saint Domingue – how superstitious the blacks could be.[76] Yet, the need for a password and a *fétiche* to freely circulate and the fact that they do guarantee the white man's safety highlight the power of the maroons, their management of the territory, the strength of their culture, and their self-control and discipline: traits that Picquenard ends up emphasizing despite himself.

The white protagonist of *Zoflora* also witnesses the cruelty of the maroons who live in the Plaine de la Desolée. They are led by Boukman,[77] who, unlike Biassou in *Adonis*, does speak (Picquenard's) Creole. Yet, far from being presented as the language of a revolutionary, Creole is associated with a cannibal who hates the whites and eats their 'half-grilled breasts,' but would also eat the flesh of black men if necessary (p. 120). The dichotomy between civilized and uncivilized is made even more dramatic here by the fact that *Zoflora* begins in Paris, very far from 'primitive' areas. The young protagonist, whose name is Justin (*nomen est omen*), is sent to Saint Domingue by his father because his rich colonist uncle is unwell and needs help managing his plantations. Upon his arrival Justin depicts 'the old island of Ohaïti' as 'the island of happiness [...] the old Eden' (p. 97).[78] Justin's definition of Saint Domingue as Eden is predictable enough: Hugo's D'Auverney, for example, uses the same imagery in *Bug-Jargal*; Picquenard's repeated evocation of Bernardin de Saint-Pierre's landscaping abilities and idyllic depictions of racial relations also sheds light on the conventional and bookish nature of his own descriptions (pp. 3, 4, 196).[79] Nevertheless, one

---

[76] Saint-Méry, PF vol. I, pp. 46–51.
[77] In his notes to the text Bongie points out that the identification of Boukman as a maroon chief might originate precisely in Picquenard's novel (p. 135).
[78] In a note to the text Picquenard explains his terminology in the following way: 'Ohaïti, name given to Saint Domingue by the first inhabitants of the island' (p. 97).
[79] In a footnote to the text Picquenard explains that Bernardin de Saint Pierre actually had read *Adonis* at his request and subsequently encouraged him to publish it (p. 4).

could suggest that Picquenard does try to engage with the territory in its own terms. In the *avant-propos* to the novel Picquenard complains about the fact that, before him, the majority of those who had written about the island were more interested in depicting it as a 'new Eldorado' (p. 85) and a source of material gain rather than as a land with beauties and imperfections. He also utilizes a remarkable number of what he calls 'local terms' to describe the land (*morne* p. 7), its flora and fauna (*mapou* p. 55; *raquette* p. 60; *pitre* p. 121; *caïman* p. 121; *bois-chandelle* p. 131; *colibri* p. 141; *couleuvres* p. 148; *dorade* p. 197), its crops and produce (*tafia* p. 15; *patate, igname, manioc* p. 36), and the way in which the hierarchical organization of space landscapes the territory (*atelier, grande case* p. 8; *cafier* p. 11; *ajoupas* p. 14).[80]

The economic exploitation of the island ostensibly denounced by Picquenard, however, is not the only form of abuse. In *Adonis*, Picquenard's exploitative transformation of the Plaine de la Desolée from free land of the maroons into a setting for his own political agenda is a case in point. As a strategy, it chimes perfectly well with the fact that, in both his novels, Picquenard reduces both island and borderland to being just the backdrop of Europe's utopias and dystopias and of its political and economic interests. Not only does Picquenard share Hugo's desire to consider America as no more than the revolt's background but (somewhat ironically for a believer in racial equality) he does not even treat Africa and the rebels as serious and dignified contenders: as we have seen, the insurgents are always depicted as nothing more than mindless, vicious savages. Picquenard was writing before Haiti's Declaration of Independence, which took place in 1804, but one should not forget that, by 1800, Toussaint had officially become commander in chief of all French armies in Saint Domingue after fighting – and winning – for the Spanish for more than a year, had expelled all Spanish forces from the French part of the island, stipulated the complete British withdrawal from Saint Domingue, rejected Britain's offer to recognize him as King of Haiti, and repressed the mulatto revolt in the Artibonite area. It is clear, therefore, that Picquenard was prepared to praise (and patronize) the virtuous, naïve, and ultimately submissive *Adonis* and *Zoflora* (Rousseauesque *bons savages* in captivity), but his dream of racial equality never included the rebels.

In *Zoflora*, after his arrival in the colony, Justin discovers that his uncle died without arranging for him to inherit his fortune, which was in the hands of the colonial administration. His newly found friend

---

De Saint-Pierre's encouragement, Picquenard writes, also made him bold enough to publish *Zoflora* (p. 85).

[80] All these terms appear in the novel in italics and are translated in note by the author.

Simon explains to Justin how people live and behave on the island: in his description, the white creoles appear as unsurprisingly corrupted and cruel but, Simon insists, up in the mountains, in the least accessible *habitations* closer to the border with the Spanish part, one can find slave-holders who treat their slaves as if they were their children despite the ostracism of the white community (p. 107). Once again the borderland is presented, at first, as a place where the control of the establishment is loose and where 'eccentric' (but, in this case, 'enlightened') ways of life can flourish. Since Justin wants to remain in Saint Domingue and start his own business there, Simon encourages him to travel around the colony as a *pacotilleur* to familiarize himself with the place and the people (p. 111). *Pacotilleurs* dealt and sold merchandise around the colony and possibly also across the border (not unlike *contrabandistas*) and it is worth mentioning that *pacotilleurs* were not uncommon among slaves and free blacks who offered their services in the slave quarters. Most importantly, a source relates that in the year preceding the 1758 revolt Makandal recruited his most trusted fellow insurgents precisely among the *pacotilleurs*.[81] Once again, therefore, Picquenard appropriates and simultaneously neuters a politically charged figure: the naïve and generous Justin is in fact not a vector of black revolt but an ultimately anti-revolutionary figure.[82] Justin's wanderings take him all around the French part of the island and later to Santo Domingo as well; he travels mainly along the border with the Spanish side from the north to the west, from Le Cap to Port-au-Prince, falls in love (reciprocated) with the lovely Amicie, is captured by the cannibal Boukman and later by Biassou, and fights against the Spanish invaders.

The presence of Boukman enables Picquenard to refer to what he considers to be Jamaica's and, by extension, England's responsibilities not only for the island's tension and violence but also for the excesses of its inhabitants. Such 'excesses,' moreover, appear to take 'place' in the borderland and not far from the area which had been occupied by the Spanish under Touissant's command, and by the British. During his peregrinations around the colony Justin comes across the plantations of Amicie's father, the perfidious Valbona, a rich and merciless slave-holder. Valbona's behaviour is totally reprehensible and the result of the bad influence of the rich and powerful but morally corrupted Lord Durcley, former Governor of Jamaica. It is not entirely clear where Valbona's many plantations are because Picquenard

---

[81] Fick, *Making of Haiti*, p. 60.
[82] We have seen what a faithful *commandeur* Adonis is. Yet, the leaders of the 1791 rebellion were *commandeurs* as well as the vast majority of the 200 slave delegates to the Morne-Rouge assembly –see Fick, *Making of Haiti*, p. 241.

declares that, 'wishing to offend nobody,' he deliberately tried to 'disorient' his readers and moved the setting by, at times, more than twenty 'leagues' (p. 123). However, Cul-de-Sac (p. 122, a rift valley that was once a marine strait and that extends for thirty-two kilometres from Port Au-Prince Bay to the Haiti/Dominican Republic border) and later Corail (p. 131, very close to the border then and now, as the Spanish resonance in the name also suggests) are repeatedly named.[83]

Beneath his property in Corail Valbona had discovered, by chance, one of the underground galleries where, the narrator informs us, the indigenous population of Hispaniola used to bury their dead.[84] One of the many entries of this vast system of galleries had access to his *grande case* through a secret path only he had the keys for. As Picquenard emphatically puts it, 'it was the place where he dragged the victims of his lust and ferocity' (p. 210). Picquenard's reference to a pre-'discovery' hallowed ground deconsecrated by colonial powers shows unexpected sensitivity to the layers of history or to what Casey calls the changing qualifications of a place which distinguish it from timeless, homogenous space.[85] Picquenard's landscaping also dramatizes the tensions and contradictions inherent in Saint Domingue and almost lays bare the device: if the *grande case* stands for the respectable façade of colonial slavery, the horrifying caves more than adequately reveal its corrupted and gory core. Simultaneously, these underground and clandestine galleries represent a powerful revolutionary kernel that the *grande case* has tried to repress but has not been able to fully neutralize. Most importantly, despite Picquenard's disorienting strategies, Valbona's caves cannot be very far from those that Saint Méry describes as the network of hiding places for Enriquillo and his rebels and, later, the maroons; indeed, they might even be the very same ones.[86] It is difficult

---

[83] In *Zoflora*, Corail also becomes the theatre of 'the first battle between the French and the Spanish,' p. 212.

[84] According to Taíno mythology, the cave is the primeval uterus – see Henry Petitjean Roget, 'Notes on Caribbean Art and Mythology' in *The Indigenous People of the Caribbean*, ed. S.M. Wilson (Gainesville, FL: University of Florida Press, 1997), pp. 100–108, p. 104. Caves were also used for ritual purposes and provided access to the underworld: see Antonio M. Stevens-Arroyo, *Cave of the Jagua: The Mythological World of the Taíno* (Albuquerque, NM: University of New Mexico Press, 1988), pp. 138 and 185.

[85] Casey, 'How to Get from Space to Place'. The reference to early colonial times also indicates the existence of an ancient and superseded border, the one that had divided the indigenous inhabitants of the island from the Spanish *conquistadores* and to which I return in Chapter 3.

[86] According to Saint-Méry, the Étang Sumâtre (or Lac Azuei) was at the western

to prove that this is not a mere coincidence, as Picquenard's deliberate vagueness does not help one way or the other, but it is significant that the refuge of the maroons in a border area characterized by a two-century-long tradition of resistance is here depoliticized and transformed into a place of 'horror' in which all morality and humanity is forfeited.

After *la bonne négresse* Zoflora denounces his illicit activities, the perfidious Valbona crosses the border and moves to Santo Domingo with his daughter. When the war is declared between France and Spain, he enlists in the Spanish army and offers his Corail *habitation* to them to use as their headquarters. In *Zoflora*, the 1791 revolt is preceded, not followed, by the war between France and Spain: thanks to an impassioned speech by Justin, *grands* and *petits blancs* of Saint Domingue (momentarily) leave behind their differences and unite to defend the border and to fight their common enemy – in this case, the Spanish. Significantly, contrarily to what really happened, both armies are rigorously monoracial and the fierce Boukman appears on the scene simply because he sees the war between the two colonies as his opportunity to rob the defeated party, whichever it would be. When the French army wins the day at Corail, Valbona's dungeon is blown up by the French General, who is appalled by the horrors it conceals; Boukman, instead, kidnaps Valbona and his daughter and will later kill him but not her. Ironically, the French success at Corail is crucial to the revolt: claimed as *their* victory by all the different parties which had contributed to the defeat of the Spanish, it triggers division and conflicts among the French. Desertions became so numerous that the army could no longer defend the frontier and, at that point – it is quite unclear why – a slave revolt quickly spread among the *ateliers*, fomented, Picquenard quickly adds, by the dishonest royalist Blanchelande and supported by the Spanish who provided the rebels with weapons (p. 214). In other words, as far as the 1791 revolt is concerned, Picquenard insists that the weaknesses and inner divisions of the French, the assistance of the Spanish, and the presence of an all-too-permeable colonial frontier were much more important factors than the slaves' desire for freedom, a point that, as we have seen, Hugo also reiterates in his own writing.

Hugo and Picquenard's dismissive and disparaging attitude towards the rebels confirms, as Michel-Rolph Trouillot would put it, that the 1791 revolt and the Haitian Revolution were utterly 'unthinkable' for their contemporaries and those who wrote about these events in their immediate

---

extremity of the Plaine de Cul-de-Sac and the border between the French and Spanish side of the island cut the Étang Sumâtre in the middle. Lake Enriquillo is approximately ten kilometres south-east of it (PE, vol. I, p. 283).

aftermath.[87] Arguably, equally 'unthinkable' was the fact that far from being simply a vertical frontier controlled and traversed exclusively by the colonial powers, the borderland of Hispaniola could also be a place where 'the self-liberation ethos of the enslaved blacks'[88] could thrive and find new ways to articulate itself: in other words, in order to _un_think the revolution, both Picquenard and Hugo compellingly denied the existence of, or eagerly misrepresented, the horizontal borderland and its inhabitants.

✸✸✸

Madison Smartt Bell's historical novel _All Souls' Rising_ (1995) offers instead a thorough rethinking of Hispaniola's borderland. Written by a self-defining 'white southerner,'[89] _All Souls' Rising_ is the first of a trilogy of novels which deals with the Haitian Revolution and which took Smartt Bell almost ten years to complete. _All Souls' Rising_ was a finalist for the National Book Award in 1995 and the PEN/Faulkner Award in 1996, when it won the Anisfield-Wolf Award. It was followed by _Master of the Crossroads: A Novel of Haiti_ (2000), _The Stone that the Builder Refused_ (2004), and, in 2007, a biography of Toussaint Louverture. Smartt Bell's sustained engagement with Hispaniola's border and borderland derives from the fact that among his sources were some of the fictional and non-fictional 'captivity narratives' discussed in this chapter which, as we have seen, have in common the attention they pay to the crucial role played, at the time, by the colonial frontier and the borderland.[90] Central to the plot of _All Souls' Rising_ is the royal plot and the smuggling of weapons destined for the black insurgents organized by the Saint Domingue Royalists. To finalize the purchase of weapons, the seller/smuggler Xavier Tocquet and the buyer/creole plantocrat Michel Arnaud – chosen by fellow royalists to acquire and distribute the rifles to the rebels – meet by the River Massacre in the northern borderland.[91] We

[87] Michel-Rolph Trouillot, _Silencing the Past: Power and the Production of History_ (Boston, MA: Beacon Press, 1995).

[88] I owe this definition to Hilary McD Beckles, 'Caribbean Anti-Slavery: The Self Liberation Ethos of Enslaved Blacks', _Journal of Caribbean History_, 22.1-2 (1988), pp. 1–19 rprt in _Caribbean Slavery in the Atlantic World_, ed. V. Shepherd and H. McD Beckles (Kingston: Ian Randle, 2000), pp. 869–78.

[89] Madison Smartt Bell, 'Engaging the Past', p. 198.

[90] See Jeremy D. Popkin, 'Facing Racial Revolution: Captivity Narratives and Identity in the Saint-Domingue Insurrection', _Eighteenth-Century Studies_, 36.4 (2003), pp. 511–33.

[91] Madison Smartt Bell, _All Souls' Rising_ [1995] (New York: Penguin, 1996). From now on page references will appear in parentheses in the text.

are told that Arnaud is profoundly disturbed by Tocquet's familiarity with his two black fellow smugglers as the three of them eat together sitting around a fire. Arnaud, in fact, used to know Tocquet as a member of the *maréchaussée*: more agile than most whites, he used to climb mountains barefooted with mulatto and black slave-catchers in order to capture runaway slaves and prevent them from crossing the border into freedom. A short pointed Spaniard's beard and his shocking behaviour, however, prompt Arnaud to ask: 'You've become altogether a Spaniard, Xavier?' (p. 191). Tocquet's answer, 'What does it matter *here*? [...] This place was here before our nations' (p. 192; my emphasis), explodes the vertical border and requalifies the borderland as a special place where rules are subverted, colonial/national discourses undermined, and their contradictions exposed.

Refusing to partake of Tocquet's dinner because the two blacks are too close for comfort, Arnaud posits himself as the bulwark of Saint Domingue royalist, segregationist, and racist values at a time where such values were simultaneously undercut by revolutionary ideas from France and the 'lax' attitude of slave-holders from the Spanish colony. Yet, one should not forget that, in order to 'stabilize' the French part of the island, Arnaud and his fellow royalists rely on material help from the Spanish side. Tocquet, instead, embodies the island's borderland history in more than one way: dressed as a *boucanier*, he eats 'shreds of meat and roasted plantains still in their skin, spread on a glossy banana leaf' next to 'the vestige of a clearing with banana suckers sprouting from what might have been [...] the dwelling place of the maroon bands' (pp. 190, 191, 188). The word *boucanier* derives from the Carib *boucan*, the gridiron used to smoke and broil the meat of wild cattle, or *cimarrones*, as the Spanish used to call them. The fact that Tocquet points out that the place where he is standing was 'there' before the colonial/national border was established acquires more piquancy if one considers that he utters these words dressed like a *boucanier* and eating *à la* Carib.

Despite his disapproval for Tocquet's behaviour, during their 1791 encounter by the River Massacre Arnaud's manners are also affected by the 'place' in which he finds himself: we are told that he would have never addressed Tocquet by his first name 'on the plain or in the coast towns' (p. 191). Arnaud's attempts to maintain a binary opposition between the (allegedly) uncouth and uncivilized borderland and the civilized *habitations* or the palaces of the urban elite rings hollow in a novel which repeatedly demonstrates the artificial nature of such binarism, even if one takes into account the legal and moral (implicit or explicit) codes of the time: *habitations* and plantations, in fact, are described as places where slaves are raped and tortured in flagrant breach of the *Code Noir*. If, during the revolt, atrocities against former white planters are indeed perpetrated (and graphically described) in both Jeannot's and Biassou's camps, which are situated near Grand Rivière, close to the northern border, the novel also makes it crystal clear that the insurgents might have learnt a thing or two about how to rape, torture, maim, and kill from their former, allegedly civilized, owners.[92] Smartt Bell's borderland, therefore, does not stand out as a site characterized by particular or exceptional ferocity: it is merely a part of a colony where widespread cruelty had always been commonplace, before and after the 1791 revolt, and a site which merely discloses what the centre tries to hide behind closed doors and under the veneer of appearances. The rooms of (more or less) sophisticated urban dwellings are in fact the theatre of interracial and interclass *liaisons dangereuses* involving, for example, a wealthy white creole female (Isabelle Cigny) and a free man of colour (Choufleur), or a white French doctor (Antoine Hébert) and a free mulatto 'prostitute' (Nanon).

In *All Souls' Rising* the encounter between Tocquet and Arnaud also reveals the unease that breaches in the racial divide engendered at the time: from a 'personal' perspective, what Arnaud sees in Tocquet's familiarity with his fellow smugglers is perhaps a disturbing version of his abhorred and aborted mixed-race family: early in the novel we are told that he had many illegitimate children and his wife Claudine tortures and murders a black slave who was carrying his child (pp. 82–95). As Saint Méry's complex subracial categorizations confirm, white masters like the fictional Arnaud customarily abused their female slaves in Saint Domingue and Doris Garraway has interestingly investigated the ways in which the libidinal became highly politicized in the colony.[93] Arguably, as we have seen, border politics also played a role in this process, as the presence of a neighbouring colony where interracial intercourse and its reproductive consequences were not as stigmatized was bound to make the French colonial administration even more anxious to produce discourses and enforce laws aimed at neutralizing or at least (somehow) managing miscegenation. It is noteworthy, in fact, that Macaya's words to Polverel reported by Lacroix and redeployed, as we have seen, in Hugo's *Bug-Jargal* reveal that the rebels identified themselves

---

[92] Without his master Bullet, the narrator argues, 'Jeannot could have never been all that he was [as] he learned many of his torture tricks from [him]' (p. 318). The only thing that prevented Biassou's prisoners from escaping from his camp, where they were allowed to roam freely, was his threat of cutting off their legs: 'they believed this because they had done this thing to [their former slaves] many times before' (p. 287).

[93] Doris Garraway, *The Libertine Colony: Creolization in the Early French Caribbean* (Durham, NC: Duke University Press, 2005), p. 197.

as the offspring of an imaginary mixed family which had progenitors in Africa and, crucially, on both sides of the island.[94]

As noted above, discriminatory laws, especially those which targeted and humiliated the *affranchis*, were among the causes of Ogé's 1790 rebellion. Hugo exploits Ogé's story in order to emphasize the across-the-border complicity between the two colonial powers; Smartt Bell, instead, unveils a side of the same story that was completely ignored by Hugo and recasts the borderland as a rebels' hotbed. One of his characters informs us that, after being sentenced *in absentia*, 'many, if not most of Ogé's party had remained at large after the leaders were taken' (p. 149); as a matter of fact, despite the fact that in 1790 Ogé had refused slave support for fear that it would jeopardize his cause, in 1791 his supporters were among the mulattoes who joined the rebels voluntarily.[95] In Smartt Bell's novel, the white and unchaste Père Bonne-chance declares to have spotted Ogé's co-conspirators close to the River Massacre. The river runs just behind his church and the *ajoupa* where he lives with what Saint-Méry would call a *quarteronnée* woman (Fontelle) and their many *sang-mêlés* children. The presence of Ogé's mulatto supporters and Père Bonne-chance's illegitimate but (contrarily to Arnaud's) beloved family once again qualifies the borderland as a place characterized by the inescapable heterogeneity of the colony.

Smartt Bell's sensitivity to the plurality of voices that characterize the borderland brings to the fore forms of knowledge that are related to it and had been silenced or subalternized. The smuggler Tocquet speaks Spanish, French, and Creole fluently and represents 'local' (that is, 'of the borderland') knowledge. Significantly, this is the kind of knowledge that Saint-Méry, for all his attention to *paroisses* and minute details, rates as inferior to that possessed by those who had studied one or more aspects of the colonies.[96] The knowledge of the island that Saint-Méry displays in his *Descriptions* is unashamedly at the service of power, based on the vilification or dismissal of alternative forms of knowing (such as Vodou), and does not put the living, experiencing body at the centre: (in)famously, as we have seen, Saint-Méry always removes black slaves from his idyllic landscaping of plantations. Smartt Bell's trilogy, instead, begins exactly with what Saint-Méry occludes,

---

[94] See Lacroix, *Mémoires*, p. 253, quoted in Hugo, *Bug-Jargal*, pp. 301–23, p. 315.

[95] Fick, *Making of Haiti*, note 17 p. 298 and note 111 p. 304.

[96] 'Where are those who know the colonies? I do not mean those who have seen them or even those who have inhabited them but those who have studied them in any way and who are in a position to talk about them in an informed way' (PF, vol. I, p. x). Smartt Bell instead emphasizes throughout Toussaint's knowledge of the local herbs and medical plants, echoing Casey's argument that 'local knowledge is at one with lived experience' – 'How to Get from Space to Place', p. 18.

the objectification of black bodies: the opening pages of *All Souls' Rising* focus on the tortured body of a female slave. Poignantly, the only first-person narrator in the novel, the maroon Riau, gives a voice to the revolution from below and highlights the fundamental role that Vodou practices played among the rebels. Smartt Bell, in fact, does not only foreground the royal plot but he also insists on the crucial role played by the Vodou ceremony of Bois Caiman.[97]

Unlike Saint-Méry, Hugo, and Picquenard, who vilify the religious beliefs of the Afro-Caribbean population, Smartt Bell treats with the utmost respect Riau's experiences of listening to his *ti-bon-ange* or being mounted by Ogûn (pp. 28, 33, 170, 174, 274), and the novel is dedicated to the Haitian spirits: 'For les Morts et les Mystères, and for all souls bound in living bodies.' Arguably Riau, who, at the end of the novel, runs away to join the Bahoruco maroons, stands for a different form of knowledge which resonates with what Walter Mignolo has defined as 'border gnosis.' Gnosis, he explains, using Valentin Mudimbe's work as a springboard, includes what epistemology and Western philosophy tend to discard as esoteric or unscientific knowing.[98] *Border* gnosis, more specifically, is 'knowledge from a subaltern perspective conceived from the exterior borders of the modern/colonial world system.'[99] Mignolo's 'border' has, at various places and times, intersected and physically overlapped with the geopolitical frontier of Hispaniola, which often corresponded to the boundary which separated the 'colony' from the free space of the maroons and rebels.

Riau, like Arnaud, is puzzled by Tocquet, the strangest white man he has ever seen: in the raciological society of Saint Domingue Tocquet's behaviour makes Riau wonder if he is not in front of 'some strange pale kind of *homme de couleur*' who, being always accompanied by two black men, lives in the mountains with them 'like maroons' (p. 470). Later on in the novel Tocquet denies having black blood in his veins but is happy to admit that his great-grandfather was among the pirates who secured Saint Domingue as a French colony while his great-grandmother was probably a Carib (p. 460). Tocquet makes this claim two years later, in 1793: his interlocutor is no longer Arnaud but Captain Maillart, a 'turncoat' French soldier who has left Saint Domingue to enlist in the Spanish army. When the conversation between Tocquet and Maillart takes place, the two men are relaxing in hot springs situated along a disused Carib mountain path which connects the Spanish

---

[97] 'Bois Cayman' is also the title of the first 129 pages of the novel.
[98] Walter Mignolo, *Local Histories/Global Designs: Coloniality, Subaltern Knowledges, and Border Thinking* (Princeton, NJ: Princeton University Press, 2000), pp. 11, 10.
[99] Mignolo, *Local Histories/Global Designs*, p. 11.

and the French sides of the island. 'I belong here,' Tocquet proudly says (p. 460): his mixed ancestry reveals the intrinsic complexity of place and, in particular, the complicated nature of his geohistorical *locus* of enunciation.

Tocquet and Maillart are in the north-eastern portion of the borderland, between Saint Raphael and Dondon. In the parish of Dondon, Saint-Méry writes, one could find numerous examples of indigenous artefacts. In a long passage in which he describes the *Voûte à Minguet*, an Indian temple that was famous at the time, he combines a ferociously racist content with a distressingly patronizing tone and ridicules the ethnocentricity of the *caciques*, who believed that they were superior to the rest of mankind.[100] For Saint-Méry, the fallacy of their belief is proved by the fact that they were annihilated by 'a handful of Spaniards'[101] – a rather ironic comment if one considers that he had witnessed how Saint Domingue, a 'colonial Hercules,' had been rapidly reduced to a 'skeleton' by an army of mostly uneducated slaves.[102] Tocquet, instead, celebrates the indigenous population of Hispaniola: 'The *caciques* might have held out forever here […] The Spanish would not have reached them with an army, in these mountains […] they died of grief […] They would not be slaves. They threw themselves from the cliffs in droves […] it's not the first time this island has been washed in blood' (460). In other words, by implicitly creating a connection between the indigenous and the black rebels, and unlike Hugo and Picquenard, who tried to neuter the insurrectionary nature of the borderland, Smartt Bell requalifies it as a site of continuous resistance to colonizing and centralizing projects. This is a move which, as we will see in Chapter 3 (and onwards), also characterizes the work of many other writers who, before and after Smartt Bell, have focused on the borderland at different historical junctures in order to reveal a more enabling past on which to build a better future for Hispaniola.

---

[100] Saint-Méry, PF, vol. I, pp. 263–4.
[101] Saint-Méry, PF, vol. I, p. 264.
[102] Saint-Méry, PF, vol. I, p. v.

Chapter Three

This place was here before our nations: Anacaona's Jaragua

Salomé Ureña de Henríquez, *Anacaona* (1880); Jean Métellus, *Anacaona* (1986); Edwidge Danticat, *Anacaona: Golden Flower: Haiti, 1490* (2005)

In Smartt Bell's *All Souls' Rising*, discussed at the end of Chapter 2, the readiness with which the contrabandist Tocquet admits to a Carib heritage, matched with his concomitant denial of the possibility of having African blood, can also be read as a 'prefiguration' of the way in which the discourse of *indigenism* or the myth of the 'Dominican Indio' was later embraced by the Dominican elites in the process of fashioning a national identity after independence from Spain was declared in 1865.[1] Famously, the text that most poignantly encapsulates this effort is *Enriquillo: novela historica* (1882), by Manuel de Jesús Galván. *Enriquillo* tells the story of the Taíno chief Guarocuya, (re)baptized Enrique and educated in a Franciscan convent at the request of the Spanish *encomendero* Valenzuela, who took him as his protégé.[2] When Valenzuela died, his son, who did not favour Enriquillo, tried to violate Enriquillo's beloved Mencia. Disgusted by such outrageous behaviour and by the numerous wrongs suffered by his people at the hands of other cruel Spanish colonists, Enriquillo decided to take to the mountains, where he soon became the leader of the Bahoruco rebels.[3]

---

[1] Sagás, *Race and Politics*, p. 35.

[2] Manuel de Jesús Galván, *Enriquillo: novela historica* (1882). I will be quoting from Robert Graves's English translation of the novel, which is entitled *The Cross and the Sword* (Bloomington, IN: Indiana University Press, 1954), and page references will be in parentheses in the text.

[3] In *Los guerrilleros negros: esclavos fugitivos y cimarrones en Santo Domingo* (Santo Domingo: Fundación Cultural Dominicana, 1989), Carlos Esteban Deive does not mention Enriquillo's love story with Mencia as a possible cause for his rebellion but focuses exclusively on the Spaniards' wrongdoings (p. 29).

Figure 6. 'Monumento del Cacique': a statue that celebrates the rebel Enriquillo and positioned at the southeast corner of Lake Enriquillo (Cruce de Neyba), at the feet of the Bahoruco mountains. The juxtaposition of Enriquillo and the Dominican flag signposts his role in the national narrative of the country (photograph: Maria Cristina Fumagalli).

After fourteen years of resistance Enriquillo and his people were finally given their liberty by Charles V, to whom they remained, however, loyal vassals. *Enriquillo* has been famously defined by Doris Sommer as 'a kind of national epic of the Dominican Republic' and as a 'romance' whose purpose was 'to influence history rather than describe it' by denying 'the historical ties between [a] mulatto-black country and the revolutionary black tradition of Haiti.'[4] Even leaving these crucial ties aside, the simple fact that Enriquillo himself is appropriated as a 'Dominican' icon is in itself a move which privileges national narrative over island history: as Smartt Bell's Tocquet would put it, Enriquillo's 'place' was there well before the two nations which now share Hispaniola.

These observations are equally applicable to a less-studied text that

---

[4] Doris Sommer, *One Master for Another: Populism as Patriarchal Rhetoric in Dominican Novels* (Lanham, MD: University Press of America, 1983), pp. 51, 78, 54.

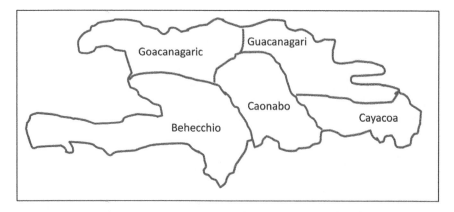

Figure 7a. Maps of the chiefdoms or *cacicazgos* of Hispaniola: interpretation of Charlevoix (1730) based on the names of the caciques. Adapted from M. Wilson, *Hispaniola: Caribbean Chiefdoms in the Age of Columbus* (1990).

appeared two years earlier, namely Salomé Ureña de Henríquez's long poem *Anacaona* (1880).[5] The Taíno Queen Anacaona, who is the protagonist of Ureña's poem, is an important figure in early modern Hispaniola: this chapter will investigate three fictional reconstructions of her life from the nineteenth, twenty and twenty-first centuries by writers born in the Dominican Republic and Haiti. These texts, I will argue, dramatize precisely the ongoing tension between national narratives and island history while revisiting Anacaona's complex renegotiations of the 'border,' which, in her time, was supposed to ring-fence the indigenous population from the Spanish colonists. Poignantly, the *locus* of Anacaona's renegotiations is an area which partly overlaps with the current borderland.

Anacaona was born in the *cacicazgo* or chiefdom of Jaragua; she was the sister of the *cacique* (chief) Behechio, who ruled over Jaragua and the wife (and later widow) of Caonabo, the chief of Maguana. The boundaries of the chiefdoms of Hispaniola are still being debated, partly because they shifted and a considerable part of the island was not recognized as belonging to any of them.[6] Scholars, however, tend to agree on the fact that the central area of Jaragua covered the Cul-de-Sac plain, near modern Port-au-Prince and extended to the current Haitian–Dominican border, and believe that the overall province comprised the area around the Bahoruco mountains, Lake

---

[5] Salomé Ureña de Henríquez, *Anacaona* (Santo Domingo: Publicaciones América, 1974). From now on page numbers will appear in parentheses in the text.

[6] Wilson, *Hispaniola*, p. 14.

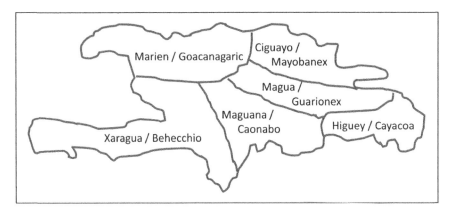

Figure 7b. Maps of the chiefdoms or *cacicazgos* of Hispaniola, interpreted by Rouse (1948), with names of *caciques* and *cacicazgos*. Adapted from M. Wilson, *Hispaniola: Caribbean Chiefdoms in the Age of Columbus* (1990).

Enriquillo and the peninsula of Pedernales, now located in the Dominican Republic.[7] Maguana, in contrast, was in the centre of the island, near the current city of San Juan de la Maguana and close to the current border.[8] After Behechio's death (between 1496 and 1502), Anacaona became *cacica* of Jaragua. In 1503, during the destruction of what Galván has called the 'wonderful, rich and contented [...] Jaragua' (p. 3), Anacaona was captured by the Spaniards and hanged in Santo Domingo.[9]

Early historians have offered different explanations for the massacre of Anacaona's people and her execution. According to Gonzalo Fernández de Oviedo, the Governor Nicolás de Ovando travelled to Jaragua because he needed to crush a secret rebellion against the Spanish which had been planned by the *caciques* of the south-west of the island. Ovando invited the *caciques* into a hut with the pretence of discussion, and then locked them in and burned more than forty of them alive. As a mark of respect for her high status, Anacaona was taken for trial to Santo Domingo and then hanged

[7] Wilson, *Hispaniola*, pp. 15, 16, 110, 115, 116; Bernardo Vega, *Los cacicazgos de la Hispaniola* (Santo Domingo: Museo del Hombre Dominicano, 1980), pp. 34–5. Jaragua is also spelled Xaragua or Xaraguá in some of the texts I will be quoting from; for the sake of consistency here I have always used Jaragua.

[8] Wilson, *Hispaniola*, p.110.

[9] See William F. Keegan, *Taíno Indian Myth and Practice: The Arrival of the Stranger King* (Gainesville, FL: University Press of Florida, 2007), pp. 32–3 and Wilson, *Hispaniola*, pp. 116–18, who also explains that their rules of inheritance are very complex but that the Taíno were predominately a matrilineal society.

there.[10] Antonio de Herrera y Tordesillas tells his readers that Ovando realized that he was going to be attacked while he was Anacaona's host in Jaragua and that he had to act quickly to defend himself.[11] The account of Bartolomé de las Casas, in contrast, does not mention the existence of a conspiracy on the part of the *caciques* but foregrounds the cruelty and duplicity of the Spaniards.[12]

In 1503 Jaragua had become a very problematic place for the Spanish crown. At the turn of the fifteenth and the sixteenth centuries the mother country and its representatives on the island were finding some of the disaffected Spanish colonists of Hispaniola more and more difficult to control. Francisco Roldán Ximeno was one of the most vociferous rebels and the leader of a remarkable revolt against the Columbus family; his surname was used to christen the *roldánistas*, the first political movement in the New World.[13] Roldán had arrived in Hispaniola as Christopher Colombus' squire and was appointed *alcade mayor* by the Admiral, despite his humble origins. An *alcade mayor* had a very important administrative role and Roldán took his position very seriously, leaving his mark on the history of colonial Spain.[14] Initially, he represented the interests of the poor Spaniards and also became a champion for social justice for the Indios, for whom he acted as a self-proclaimed defender and liberator.[15] In 1497 Roldán and his rebellious companions moved to Jaragua, where they established 'a permanent centre of protest' against Columbus's authority.[16] Later, however, Roldán left Jaragua, turned his back on the Indians, and became responsible for the *encomiendas* – a system of forced labour without salary to which the Taíno agreed in order to avoid the gold tribute they had been asked to pay by the Columbus family.[17]

---

[10] Gonazalo Fernández de Oviedo, *Historia general y natural de las Indias*, ed. J. Pérez de Tudela Bueso [1535] (Madrid: Ediciones Atlas, 1959), vol. I, pp. 82–3.

[11] Antonio de Herrera y Tordesillas, *Historia general de los hechos de los castellanos en las islas y tierra firme del mar Océano* [1726] (Madrid: Academia de la Historia, 1935), vol. III, p. 22 (Dec. I, chap. 4).

[12] Bartolomé de las Casas, *A Short Account of the Destruction of the Indies* [1522] (London: Penguin, 1992), p. 22. I would like to thank Peter Hulme for sharing with me his views on this episode of colonial history.

[13] Pedro Mir, *Tres leyendas de colores: ensayo de interpretación de las tres primeras revoluciones del Nuevo Mundo* (Santo Domingo: Editora Taller, 1984), p. 37.

[14] For more information on the role of an Alcade Mayor see Mir, *Tres leyendas*, pp. 39–44.

[15] Mir, *Tres leyendas*, p. 48.

[16] Mir, *Tres leyendas*, p. 59.

[17] The *encomiendas* or *repartimientos* allotted each settler large parcels of Indian

When Anacaona's people were massacred by Ovando in 1503 Roldán had already left Jaragua, but the place remained *sui generis* and continued to attract disenchanted settlers and renegades: it has been estimated that there were more than one hundred Spaniards living in the region – a collection of former followers of Roldán and people who had jumped ship to stay there.[18] Despite the conspicuous presence of the Spanish, Jaragua still had powerful indigenous leaders, such as Behechio and Anacaona. When Bartolomé Colombus visited Jaragua in 1496, Behechio and Anacaona had managed to persuade him that the region had no gold but could instead produce plenty of cassava bread and cotton, and the relative absence of forced labour made it an attractive place for the natives.[19] Most importantly, Jaragua was turning rapidly into a creole community where the Spaniards had to learn from the Taíno how to sleep in hamacas, how to eat native food such as cassava bread, yucca, sweet potato, and plantain, and how to cook iguanas and other animals of the island.[20]

After a short while the coexistence of Spanish men and Taíno women began to bear its fruits as the settlers formed familial but often polygamous relationships with the women of Jaragua. Interestingly, one of the requests made by the Spanish–Jaraguan rebels when they were invited to enter into negotiations with central power in 1498 was precisely to take their native wives back to Spain, 'some of whom were pregnant and some of whom had only recently given birth.'[21] It goes without saying that these gender relationships were not predicated on equality – as a matter of fact, the same request by the rebels specifies, rather ambivalently, that these women would be taken back to Spain 'instead of slaves.'[22] Yet, the emphasis that

---

land with all the Indians that were on it. During a period of time, generally six or eight months, the natives were supposed to work for the Spanish; for the rest of the year they were allowed to work for themselves. See, for example, Mir, *Tres leyendas*, p. 81 and Rodman, *Quisqueya*, p. 14.

[18] Troy Floyd, *The Columbus Dynasty in the Caribbean, 1492–1526* (Albuquerque, NM: University of New Mexico Press, 1973), p. 60.

[19] Wilson, *Hispaniola*, pp. 125–6. In *Tres leyendas* (p. 109), Mir underlines that there were no *encomiendas* in Jaraguá, which was *encomendada* after Anacaona's death in 1503.

[20] For more information on the Spanish settlers having to learn the indigenous way of life see Moya Pons (*La otra historia dominicana*), who calls this 'the birth the Creole': pp. 119–21.

[21] One of the stipulations of the roldánistas reads as follows: 'And, since many of the people have indigenous "natural" wives, some pregnant and some who have recently given birth to their children, they will be allowed to bring their women with them': quoted in Mir, *Tres leyendas*, p. 74.

[22] Mir, *Tres leyendas*, p. 74.

the *roldánistas* put on the presence of offspring (some already born and
some on their way) might suggest that, for their fathers, they were more
important than mere chattel. It is probably fair to say, therefore, that, as
Jaragua's ruler, Anacaona seems to have presided over a creole community in
which the boundaries between the indigenous population of the island and
the Spanish settlers were becoming increasingly blurred. Moreover, some
of the women with whom the Spaniards were having relationships were
daughters of *caciques* and, according to the Taíno's complex matrilinear
system, which was not unknown to the Spanish authorities, their husbands
could have inherited their land from them.[23] It is evident that the Spanish
crown and its representatives on Hispaniola could neither tolerate nor
afford this potentially destabilizing development.

In 1502, desperate to find a strong ruler to subjugate the rebellious
colonists and to represent its interests, the Spanish monarchy sent Nicolás
de Ovando to Hispaniola to 'reorganize' the island. He was well aware of
the necessity to establish large areas of food production to supply the gold
miners and these areas included Jaragua, which, in his view, had been
underexploited.[24] As we have seen, Ovando was responsible for slaughtering
the inhabitants of Jaragua and for the execution of Anacaona. The massacre
orchestrated by Ovando, however, did not target the Indians exclusively but
also included the Spaniards who were still living in Jaragua, apparently as
many as fifty.[25] After the massacre Jaragua was renamed Santa Maria de
la Vera Paz ('Santa Maria of the true peace') because, as Oviedo explains,
after that tragic moment Anacaona's people never rebelled again.[26] Most
importantly, Jaragua was also *encomendada* – that is, turned into a network
of places where the domestic economy was destroyed and interethnic
relationships were carefully policed.[27]

Some contemporary scholars have suggested that the massacre was
aimed at the subjugation of a Spanish–Jaraguan alliance of *caciques* and
renegades who had been evading demands from Santo Domingo for food
and labourers to work in the mines.[28] Others argue that the fact that it

---

[23] See Wilson, *Hispaniola*, pp. 116–18 and de Oviedo, *Historia*, vol. I, p. 373.

[24] Wilson, *Hispaniola*, p. 133.

[25] Floyd, *The Columbus Dynasty*, p. 62.

[26] Oviedo, *Historia*, vol. I, p. 83.

[27] Mir, *Tres leyendas*, p. 109.

[28] Juan Peréz de Tudela, 'Política de poblamiento y política de contratación de las
Indias (1502–1505)', *Revista des Indias*, 15.61–62 (1955), pp. 371–420, pp. 378–9; Ursula
Lamb, *Frey Nicolás de Ovando, Governador de Indias (1501–1509)* (Madrid: Consejo
Superior de Investigaciónes Científicas, 1956), p. 126; Floyd, *The Columbus Dynasty*,
pp. 60–64.

housed the mixed community established by Roldán was probably the reason behind Ovando's decision to destroy Jaragua; the conspiracy of the *caciques* whose existence is argued for (albeit in conflicting terms) by both Oviedo and Herrera is dismissed as nothing but a pretext.[29] As we have seen, Las Casas did not confirm that Ovando's real task was to eliminate the creole community of Jaragua, but his account highlights another important point:

> When one or two Spaniards tried to save some of the children, either because they genuinely pitied them or perhaps because they wanted them for themselves, and swung them up behind them on to their horses, one of their compatriots rode up behind and ran them through with his lance. Yet another member of the governor's party galloped about cutting the legs off all the children as they lay sprawling on the ground.[30]

The violence perpetrated against these children is not unusual; what is highly unusual, instead, is the desperate attempt of some of the Spanish colonists, possibly their fathers, to save them, a fact that highlights the interethnic nature of Jaragua.

✳✳✳

Ureña is not the only writer from Hispaniola who found Anacaona's story inspiring: many different writers have capitalized on different aspects of her experience but her poem is a good place to start because it is strictly linked to Dominican nation-building. Ureña, who was born in Santo Domingo in 1850, was a prominent figure in nineteenth-century Dominican letters and a champion of the education of women. In her poem, geographical features (plains, mountains, woods, waters, seas pp. 14–15) are often rhapsodized and the island is always referred to as 'Quisqueya' (pp. 13, 14, 21, 53, 62, 67, 82, 84), a term which was believed to have been the indigenous name for the entire island. This, however, does not imply that Ureña was promoting a pan-insular perspective: at the time of writing, the term Quisqueya was in fact being used as a poetic alternative to 'República Dominicana.' This trend was sanctioned in 1883, three years after the publication of Ureña's poem, when Emilio Prud'homme wrote the lyrics for the Dominican national anthem in which 'Quisqueya' is the Dominican Republic (and not

[29] Peréz, *Historia diplomática de Santo Domingo*, p. 21.
[30] Las Casas, *Short Account*, p. 22.

the entire island) and 'Quisqueyanos' is understood as a term that refers exclusively to Dominicans.[31]

Ureña's poem, therefore, contributed to the nation-building project by engaging in a tacit but powerful projection of the national border – which was being forcefully upheld at the time of writing – onto a historical and geographical landscape to which it was entirely alien. *Anacaona*'s insertion into the national effort depended on its ability to turn into an important precedent the past sufferings of the Indians who, like the Dominicans, fought against Spain: the 'infamous Ojeda' (p. 38), killer of Anacaona's husband Caonabo, the 'cruel' Governor Ovando (p. 84), and Roldán, in fact, are all depicted as villains. Ureña's task, however, was further complicated by the fact that the Spanish legacy could not be totally bypassed but had to be salvaged if the new Dominican Republic wanted to fashion itself as different from neighbouring Haiti. The evil Roldán, in fact, is set against the 'handsome and attractive' Hernando de Guevara and the massacre of Anacaona and her people are presented to readers as an aberration masterminded by evil characters rather than one of the many manifestations of the violence inherent in colonialism (p. 73). Overall, despite her heartfelt sympathy for Anacaona and her people, Ureña, a mulatto member of the Dominican elite, ultimately identifies with and embraces Hispanic heritage rather than identifying with Jaragua's creole community, and in her poem the Jaragua massacre features the Taíno as its only victims.

The 'race' of Quisqueya is celebrated by Ureña as a monoethnic 'indigenous family' (p. 14). This includes the 'beautiful' Anacaona, 'singer of the people of Quisqueya' (pp. 69, 91), and Behechio, 'the good old man' (p. 82), both from Jaragua; Guacanarix, from Marién, who is depicted as 'the weak one' because he welcomed the Spaniards when they first arrived on the island (p. 82); Guarionex, 'undefeated chief' of Magua (p. 83); the 'arrogant' Maniocatex (p. 47) and Caonabo, 'the strong chief' of the 'fierce' tribe of Maguana (p. 82). According to early historians, Caonabo was not a Taíno but a foreigner: for Las Casas he came from the Lucayan islands, while Ovando describes him as a Carib.[32] If this is true, Anacaona's ability to create interethnic bonds was manifest in her family as she married a 'foreigner' and gave birth to a daughter (Higuenamota) with a mixed (Taíno–Carib) ethnic background.

---

[31] For more on this see Max Henríquez Ureña (incidentally, the son of Salomé Ureña de Henríquez), *Panorama histórico de la literatura dominicana* (Santo Domingo: Librería Dominicana, 1966), p. 282.

[32] In *Taíno Indian Myth and Practice*, Keegan highlights the ethnological incongruences of Oviedo's and Las Casas' conclusions and proposes instead that references to Caonabo as a king who came from across the waters were in fact allegorical (pp. 34–44).

Ureña, however, omits this aspect of the story but foregrounds instead the interracial love between the 'good' Hernando Guevara and Higuenamota in order to gesture towards a possible and peaceful coexistence of Taíno and Spaniards.

Notably, in Ureña's poem acculturation is not in reverse: Guevara wants to marry Higuenamota with a Christian rite and Anacaona regards favourably such a union, which entails the cultural and religious 'whitening' of Higuenamota, who, during the ceremony, will joyfully embrace Hernando's God and renounce the 'false' indigenous system of belief (p. 77). Their marriage is antagonized by the perfidious Roldán, who wants Higuenamota for himself and whose intervention turns the possibility of the intermarriage between Guevara and Higuenamota into an unattainable dream.[33] The two young lovers, the potential father and mother of the nation, disappear from the poem very quickly, a fact that reveals that the nation-building project was not exempt from deeply felt, but not always openly acknowledged, anxieties which, in this case, might have been magnified by Ureña's own position as a member of the mulatto elite. A couple of years after the publication of *Anacaona*, Galván tried to neutralise these anxieties by making sure that Guevara's civilizing mission was completed: in *Enriquillo*, Anacaona's daughter marries Guevara and becomes known as Doña Ana. The two have a daughter, Mencia, who, after overcoming numerous obstacles, becomes the wife of Enriquillo. Interestingly, in Galván's reconstruction, Jaragua is inhabited only by Taíno, 'a benign, intelligent and handsome people' butchered by the 'bloodthirsty' Ovando (p. 3); there is no mention of the creole community depicted by Las Casas who, however, appears as a character in the novel.

Anacaona, a play by the Haitian poet, novelist, playwright, and neurologist Jean Métellus, ends instead with Yaquimex, a Taíno survivor of Ovando's massacre, seeking refuge in the Bahoruco mountains. Métellus's *Anacaona* was published in 1986, the same year which saw the end of the Duvalier era, and performed in the Theatre National de Chaillot in Paris in 1988.[34] Like many Haitian writers and intellectuals, Métellus was forced to leave Haiti by Duvalier and moved to the French capital in 1959. A self-defined 'advocate of the memory of his people,' Métellus has declared that he wanted to 'avenge Anacaona [and] resuscitate her memory,'[35] and his rediscovery and celebration of the indigenous past of the island and of the creolizing processes

[33] See Mir, *Tres leyendas*, pp. 97–102.
[34] Jean Métellus, *Anacaona* [1986] (Paris: Éditions Hatier, 2002).
[35] Mohamed B. Taleb-Khyar, 'Jean Métellus', *Callaloo*, 15.2, *Haitian Literature and Culture, Part 1* (1992), pp. 338–41, pp. 338–9.

which have shaped it from its very beginning can also be seen as an indirect attack on the Afrocentrism promoted by Duvalier to legitimize his regime.

Unlike Ureña, Métellus follows Oviedo and identifies Caonabo as a Carib: he is characterized by 'ferocity' and an 'appetite for power' (p. 23) and Métellus underlines that not everyone in Jaragua approves of him or of his marriage to Anacaona (p. 22). Significantly, the words of one of the characters who regards the wedding favourably and who calls for inter-island solidarity could also be addressed to those who promote divisive discourses and policies inside Hispaniola: 'A Carib is not a foreigner / He is a brother from another island' (p. 22). Métellus also circumvents nationalistic discourse by mostly referring to the island as 'Ayti-Quisqueya-Bohio' – that is, with the three indigenous names it has traditionally been associated with (pp. 14, 34, 39, 42, 50, 63). This choice of a compound name is significant because Métellus, a neurologist specialized in speech impediments, is particularly aware of the importance of words which, as his Anacaona points out, presumably giving voice to the author's views on the potential of literature, 'have the strength to metamorphose the objects they touch' (p. 36) and are 'formidable weapons' (p. 52).

In the play Anacaona's 'words' are a decisive factor in the establishment of a multiethnic community in Jaragua; some of the Spaniards who had been sent there to learn her language for the profit of the Spanish crown are persuaded to settle down in her chiefdom by the poetess-queen's poetic eloquence. In Métellus's play Anacaona's entourage is acknowledged as the creole community that Ovando set out to destroy. A horrified representative of the Spanish authority highlights how Anacaona's 'court is attended by a curious mixture of gentlemen and brigands' and adds that 'a group of officers went to stay for a while in Xaragua, dreaming of mixing their blood with that of the Indian women' (p. 75). Among these men is Fernand de Guevara who, we are told, wants to marry Higuemota, embrace her culture, and 'spend his life in Xaragua / with savages and under Anacaona's rule' (p. 75). The response of the Spanish authorities is swift and ruthless: they imprison Guevara following an armed encounter, while his companions, equally enamoured of the women of Jaragua, are slaughtered (pp. 75, 77).

Métellus's characters are complex, and at times behave in contradictory ways, but overall one could argue that Anacaona favours exchange and dialogue and hopes that a peaceful resolution to the conflict between the indigenous population and Spanish could be achieved (p. 89). Unlike Ureña's protagonist, Métellus' Anacaona firmly resists assimilation: 'Why do you want us to be like you?' she asks one of the Spanish missionaries (p. 97). Sadly, when she finally decides to trust the invaders she is betrayed and her people are massacred. As noted above, the play ends with a defiant note portraying the Indian Yaquimex on his way to the mountains, where,

he continues, 'our brothers from Africa preceded us' (p. 138). Yaquimex
is referring to the enslaved blacks who had arrived on the island in 1502
on the same fleet as Governor Ovando and who soon ran away from
forced labour and formed alliances with the Indios.[36] Galván and Ureña,
who occluded the existence of a multiethnic community in Jaragua, never
mentioned the presence of blacks on the island, while Métellus's characters
are all aware of both slaves and black rebels; his Ovando, in fact, appears
extremely concerned about a possible alliance between them and the Taíno
(pp. 131–2). Métellus's revisitation of early modern Hispaniola, therefore,
foregrounds both interethnic (Taíno and Carib) and interracial (Indian and
black, Spanish and Taíno) alliances which also counteract Oviedo's claim
that 'the punishment [...] for Anacaona and her followers was so frightful for
the indios that, from that moment onwards [...] they never rebelled again.'[37]

Using Pedro Mir as a springboard, Torres Saillant has criticized Métellus
for suggesting a connection between the 1791 revolt and the rebellion of the
cacique Enriquillo, and for 'evok[ing] the history one would have wished
rather than the one that actually happened': Enriquillo, Torres Saillant
reminds us, in the end betrayed the anti-colonial struggle.[38] This is a fair
point which, however, is valid only if we focus only on Enriquillo rather
than on the mass movement that, for a while, he was leading. Enriquillo's
betrayal, in fact, did not mark the end of the Bahoruco maroons and the
help that his men gave to the Spanish for the capture of the blacks did
not prevent or deter marronage: in the *Description de la partie française*,
in fact, Saint-Méry still identifies the borderland region of the Bahoruco
as a free-standing place where neither of the colonial powers could exert
any power or authority. By and large, therefore, Métellus's *Anacaona* (like
Smartt Bell's *All Souls' Rising*) celebrates both the Bahoruco's autonomy and
its heterogeneity – that is, the very characteristics which deeply disturbed
the colonial order and, later, when the region of the Bahoruco became part
of Hispaniola's borderland, the national order.

In 2005 the Haitian–American writer Edwidge Danticat decided to
write her own version of Anacaona's story. Born in Port-au-Prince in 1969,
Danticat moved to New York in 1981 to be reunited with her parents who
had migrated to the United States when Edwidge was a little girl, leaving
both her and her brother in the care of their uncle and aunt. After moving
to the United States, she learnt English, graduated in French Literature

---

[36] Deive, *Los guerrilleros negros*, p. 19.

[37] Oviedo, *Historia*, vol. I, p. 83.

[38] Silvio Torres Saillant, *An Intellectual History of the Caribbean* (New York: Palgrave Macmillan, 2006), pp. 210–11.

from Barnard College, and then enrolled in the Brown University Fine Arts programme. Her thesis, a series of short stories inspired by her experience as a Haitian migrant in New York, was accepted for publication by Soho Press before it was actually completed. It was published in 1994 under the title of *Breath, Eyes, Memory* and was an instant success. She is now one of the best-known Haitian–American writers and has been the recipient of numerous literary awards, such as the American Book Award (1999) and the National Book Critics Circle Award (2007); her oeuvre includes novels, short stories, travel writing, memoir, and children literature.

Danticat's *Anacaona: Golden Flower: Haiti, 1490* is a reconstruction of Anacaona's life for the 'Royal Diaries,' a series devoted to young adults: each book of the series is a diary (allegedly) written by an important woman during her adolescence. Among the featured women are Cleopatra, Elizabeth I, Marie Antoinette, and Nzingha, the Warrior Queen of Matamba. Danticat has explained that her interest in this historical figure and her self-description as one of the 'most faithful subject[s] of Anacaona' are due to the fact that her mother is from Léogâne, the Haitian town which is generally thought to have been the centre of Jaragua.[39]

The novel begins with Anacaona explaining the subtitle herself: 'I am Anacaona. In my language, the Taíno language, *ana* means "flower" and *caona* means "golden". Thus I am called the "golden flower"' (p. 5). *Ana* and *caona* are not the only words in Taíno language included in the novel: there are several instances of native words in italics, followed by a translation or brief explanation in English.[40] For reasons that have, at least partly, to do with the Royal Diaries template, Danticat mainly deals with Anacaona's adolescence in Jaragua, her life as Caonabo's wife, the birth of her daughter Huguemota in Maguana, and her participation in a raid against the Spanish port city of La Navidad (now Môle-Saint-Nicolas) in Marién. Jaragua, as we have seen, straddled Haiti and the Dominican Republic; the *cacicazgo* of Marién was situated mostly in Haiti, while Maguana was located mainly in the Dominican Republic, with a small portion in Haiti. Therefore, the very trajectories and local affiliations of the first part of Anacaona's life, as described in Danticat's fictional account, criss-cross rather than uphold the then non-existing border between Haiti and the Dominican Republic.

The 'Historical Note' appended at the end of the novel explains that the island's name has changed over the centuries: before 1492, we are informed,

---

[39] Edwidge Danticat, *Anacaona: Golden Flower: Haiti, 1490* (New York: Scholastic, 2005), p. 181. Further page references will be given in parentheses in the text.

[40] At the end of the novel, we find a glossary of Taíno words followed by an English translation (pp. 175–7).

'the island which would later be called Espanola (little Spain) and Hispaniola, by the Spanish, was interchangeably called Quisqueya, Bohio, and Ayiti by the Taíno. We set this story in Haiti because Jaragua, the region Anacaona ruled, is believed to have been part of what is now modern Haiti' (p. 166). As we have seen, Haitians tend to use Haiti to refer both to the island as a whole and to their nation, a slippage which can have unwelcome repercussions. Strictly speaking, in fact, if one follows the 'Historical Note,' the sub-subtitle of the novel, '*Haiti 1490*', is rather puzzling: all you had in 1490 was Ayiti, not Haiti. Moreover, among the documentary evidence which accompanies the novel, one can also find a map of contemporary Hispaniola. The border between Haiti and the Dominican Republic is clearly marked and the names of the two countries are clearly visible. The caption, however, cuts the Dominican Republic out by referring to the map as a 'contemporary map of Haiti' and insists that Jaragua was located 'in the southwestern part of modern-day Haiti' (p. 174). If 'Haiti' is meant to signify the island, this is true; however, if 'Haiti' here stands for the current nation of Haiti, the information provided is not entirely accurate: the central area of Jaragua was probably in current Haiti but, according to Las Casas, at the end of the fifteenth century, Anacaona's Jaragua 'was really the heart and core of the whole island' and, as we have seen, it probably also included the Pedernales Peninsula and what is now called the Jaragua National Park, both of which are part of the Dominican Republic.[41]

What seems to be an implicit privileging of a 'Haitian narrative' in *Anacaona* is further confirmed by Danticat's assertions in 'We Are Ugly, but We Are Here,' a short non-fiction piece in which she celebrates with great pride the inner strength and resilience of Haitian women. Danticat refers to herself, her female relatives, and all Haitian women as 'the daughters of Queen Anacaona,' and writes:

Anacaona's land is now the poorest country in the Western hemisphere, a place of continuous political unrest. Thus, for some, it is easy to forget that this land was the first Black republic, home to the first people of African descent to uproot slavery and create an independent nation in 1804.[42]

---

[41] Las Casas, *Short Account*, p. 21. For the boundaries of Jaragua see Figures 7a and 7b Wilson, *Hispaniola*, fig. 10 p. 115. Metellus's *Anacaona* is also prefaced by a map of the chiefdom of Hispaniola that he calls a map of 'L'île d' "Ayti" ou d'Haïti' but where Jaragua clearly straddles the current border (p. 7).

[42] Edwidge Danticat, 'We Are Ugly but We Are Here', *The Caribbean Writer* 10 (1996), http://www2.webster.edu/~corbetre/haiti/literature/danticat-ugly.htm [accessed 26 November 2013].

It is evident here that Danticat places Anacaona firmly within the national boundaries of Haiti ('the poorest country in the Western hemisphere,' 'a place of continuous political unrest,' 'the first Black republic') and not of the island of Ayiti as a whole.[43] It is worth remembering that 'We Are Ugly, but We Are Here' is not a jingoistic, ultra-nationalist piece and that Danticat is well aware of the existence of the Haitian–Dominican border and of the history of the interactions of the two nations in question: as we will see, in 1998 she published *The Farming of Bones*, a moving and insightful novel on the 1937 massacre of Haitians and Haitian–Dominicans ordered by Trujillo. Yet, these facts make even more poignant Danticat's uncharacteristically unsubtle appropriation of Anacaona as a Haitian icon, a move which superimposes the current border of the island on a geo-political reality in which it was entirely non-existent. I am not suggesting here that, as the ultra-nationalist Dominican Núñez would have it, Haitian writers and intellectuals do not have the right to claim this part of the history of the island as their own.[44] I am arguing, instead, that the recognition of Anacaona (or Enriquillo, for that matter) as a figure important for the island as a whole rather than (exclusively) for one or the other of the two nations which share its territory is crucial to the transcendence of pernicious nationalistic discourses predicated on exclusion as well as, incidentally, being central to a better understanding of the history of this particular place which later became a portion of Hispaniola's borderland.

Places, Casey argues, have the power to 'gather' and 'hold' memories and experiences which give them their 'peculiar perduringness' and to which one can return for 'empowerment, much like Antheus touching the earth for renewed strength.'[45] In Danticat's novel Caonabo maintains some links with the Kalinas (or Caribs) through his servant, an old Kalina woman living among the Taíno who teaches Caonabo 'many of the Kalinas' ways (p. 121), but the rebel Francisco Roldán, on the other hand, is not mentioned and neither is the interethnic community of Jaragua. This seems like a missed opportunity because when Danticat asks, in 'We Are Ugly but We Are Here,' 'what is the legacy of the daughters of Anacaona?'[46] it seems that one could legitimately claim as her historical legacy a tentative form of ethnologic pluralism which is at the core of the transnational creole culture currently binding the island of Hispaniola together and which has Taíno, European, and, after the arrivals of the African slaves, African origins.

---

[43] Incidentally, Anacaona was killed in Santo Domingo.

[44] Manuel Núñez, *El ocaso de la nación dominicana* (Santo Domingo: Letra Gráfica, 2001), pp. 331–80.

[45] Casey, 'How to Get from Space to Place', pp. 25–6.

[46] Danticat, 'We Are Ugly but We Are Here'.

Chapter Four

Servants turned masters:
Santo Domingo and the black revolt

Carlos Esteban Deive, *Viento Negro, bosque del caimán* (2002)

The texts analysed in the previous chapters highlight the existence of areas overlapping with the current borderland of Hispaniola which, like the chiefdom of Jaragua and the indigenous strongholds in the Bahoruco mountains, were characterized by a rebellious ethos before and after the two European colonies established themselves on the island. The same can be said, as we have seen, for the 'borderland from below', which played a decisive role in the 1791 slave uprising and the Haitian Revolution that followed it and erased forever the French colony of Saint Domingue from the world map. Unavoidably, these events also had social, political, racial, and religious repercussions on the Spanish side of Hispaniola. Esteban Deive's *Viento Negro, bosque del caimán* ('Black Wind, Bois Caiman', 2002) reconstructs the effects of this earth-shattering historical moment on Spanish Santo Domingo – a usually neglected perspective – while recasting the borderland as a site for rich cross-cultural exchange. Born in Spain in 1935, Deive moved to Santo Domingo in 1955 and, ten years later, was given Dominican nationality. Deive lives in Santo Domingo and is currently a member of the *Academia Dominicana de la Lengua*; he is the author of many books on Dominican history and cultural anthropology as well as of novels and plays for which he has received numerous awards – among others, Premio Nacional de Literatura in 1962 and 2001; Premio Nacional de Ensayo in 1976 and 1981; Premio Siboney de Literatura in 1978; and Premio Alonso de Suazo de Historia in 1980.

Deive's *Viento Negro* criss-crosses Hispaniola at a crucial time in its past and from the point of view of a problematic and tense present, and insists that a better future for the island depends on a transcolonial and transnational understanding of its history and on the elimination, once and for all, of xenophobic nationalism. A revisitation of dominant discourses related to the magical world of the island and to the representation of Vodou plays an important part in Deive's recasting of the past and in his creative narrative which, in a way like Vodou itself, aims to go beyond differences and previous enmities to highlight and gain strength from connections, mutual influences, and shared (but disavowed) empowering experiences.[1]

Vodou is one of the many manifestations of the process of creolization which shaped the life and culture of the slaves: its *lwas* (spirits) are a fusion of African and creole gods, syncretized manifestation of Catholic saints and the spirits of deified ancestors and, as we have seen, it played an important role in the history of resistance and emancipation of the island.[2] However, despite Vodou's contribution to the liberation struggle, in 1804 it was the colonists' religion and not Vodou that was made the official religion of the state, partly to secure international acceptance of Haitian independence. Yet, if Vodou was forbidden by law, the services of Vodouisants continued to be solicited in matters of health and politics.[3] The Catholic Church, which did not wish to work with the new Haitian state, left Haiti in 1805 and did not return until 1860, enabling Vodou to further establish itself in the absence of competing official religions. When Catholicism returned to Haiti, the repression of Vodou was high on its agenda and persecutions also intensified during the American Occupation of Haiti (1915–34). So-called 'anti-superstition campaigns,' promoted by the Catholic Church, were organized in 1896, 1913, and 1941: temples were destroyed and Vodou practitioners slaughtered by the hundreds.[4] During the Duvalier era, in order to control local institutions, the national religious space, and, ultimately, the Haitian masses, the dictator adopted the strategy of openly supporting Vodou. Many Vodou priests, coopted by the regime, became powerful *Tontons Macoutes* and influential

---

[1] 'The millions of slaves brought to the New World […] were […] varied in language, religion, customs and political institutions […] While it is true that the massive influx of slaves to Saint-Domingue […] were shipped predominantly from the coasts of the Kongo and Benin, they were brought there from multiple locations in the interior as prisoners of war waged against and among each other […] It was the shared trauma of defeat, slavery, banishment, and the horrors of the Atlantic crossing and plantation labour that Vodou, in a burst of cultural creation, transformed into a community of trust': Susan Buck-Morrs, *Hegel, Haiti and Universal History* (Pittsburgh, PA: Pittsburgh University Press, 2009), pp. 125–6.

[2] Margarite Fernández Olmos and Lizabeth Paravisini-Gebert, *Creole Religions of the Caribbean: An Introduction from Vodou and Santería to Obeah and Espiritismo* (New York: New York University Press, 2003), pp. 102–3.

[3] Michel Laguerre, *Voodoo and Politics in Haiti* (London: Macmillan, 1989), pp. 18–21.

[4] Fernández Olmos and Paravisini-Gebert, *Creole Religions*, p. 104.

community leaders and Vodou temples were used to propagandize and gain support for the government.[5] Catholicism, however, remained the official religion of Haiti until 1987, when a new Constitution recognized freedom of belief, but the post-Duvalier era (1986–93) was also characterized by fierce persecutions of Vodouists, especially because of the links that they had established with the Duvaliers. Vodou and Catholicism coexist in Haiti and are both practised by the majority of Haitians who, for the most part, do not see any conflict between the two.[6]

Vodou has always been an important factor in the demonization of Haitian culture as brutal, primitive, savage, and, ultimately, 'other' and, in the Dominican Republic, Vodou has long been associated exclusively with Haiti. Contrarily to what Hispanophile discourses purport, however, Dominican Vodú exists and has existed for a long time but some prefer to refer to it as 'folk religion.'[7] As an Afro-Caribbean syncretic belief, Dominican Vodú testifies to Glissant's open insularity and to Paul Gilroy's Black Atlantic, but it also points to the occluded cross-cultural exchanges that characterize the island itself. The origins of Dominican Vodú, in fact, are difficult to establish: it is possible that it originally developed independently from Haitian Vodou as a result of slavery. Deive and other anthropologists have observed that in Dominican Vodú there is a category of *luases* (a morphologic variation of the Haitian *lwa*) which, apparently, is not to be found in Haitian Vodou: they are the *luases* of the Division India or of the Water, which comprises real or imaginary *caciques* among whom, for example, we find Anacaona herself but also, as counterparts of the Haitian *lwa Monsieur Polisson*, the Dominican *luases Polizón* and, crucially, *Polizón Frontié* (Border Policeman) and *Cabo Polizón Frontié* (Captain of the Border Police).[8]

It is important to remember, however, that the border between the two colonies has always been porous: those slaves who were bought, sold, and borrowed across the border and escaped from French Saint Domingue to Spanish Santo Domingo obviously carried to their destination their system

---

[5] Laguerre, *Voodoo and Politics*, pp. 101–20.

[6] Fernández Olmos and Paravisini-Gebert, *Creole Religions*, pp. 105.

[7] Dagoberto Tejeda Ortíz, *Cultura popular e identidad nacional* (Santo Domingo: Consejo Presidencial de Cultura-Instituto Dominicano de Folklore, 1998); Carlos Esteban Deive, *Vodú y magia en Santo Domingo* (Santo Domingo: Fundación Cultural Dominicana, 1988), pp. 9–19; pp. 160–61; Martha Ellen Davis, 'Vodú of the Dominican Republic: Devotion to "La Veintiuna División"', *Afro-Hispanic Review*, 26.1 (2007), pp. 75–90.

[8] Deive, *Vodú y magia*, p. 163; 175–6; Davis 'Vodú of the Dominican Republic', pp. 75–6.

of belief, which then changed according to the circumstances in which they found themselves.[9] In the Dominican Republic the Catholic Church has not resorted to extreme repressive measures such as those adopted in Haiti during the anti-superstition campaigns, but Vodú is still considered illegal and its practitioners can be prosecuted. The current law which outlaws Vodou is a legacy of Trujillo's regime (it was passed in 1943) and is characterized, predictably, by anti-Haitian sentiments. Vodou is described as 'absolutely alien' to the Dominican way of life and those who are caught practising it can be fined, put in jail, or even 'deported,' suggesting that they are, ultimately, Haitians and not Dominicans.[10] Moreover, the complex socio-religious system of Gagá, a Vodou-derived cult practised in the Dominican Republic which has developed mainly along the Dominican borderland and in the areas with a high presence of Haitians working in sugar mills,[11] constitutes an important example of Haitian–Dominican syncretism and a local version of the 'culture of the poor' which has established itself in situations of marginality throughout the Caribbean.[12] Incidentally, in the last ten years, scholars have confirmed that Dominican Vodú is on the rise and that also members of the diaspora tend to resort to it often in order to solve migration-related and other problems.[13]

Haitian Vodou appears prominently in the chapter of *Viento Negro* which describes the role played by Boukman, Jean François, Biassou, and Toussaint Louverture during the famous windy night of 22 August 1791 in Bois Caiman. Toussaint is present at the assembly as a double agent. We are told that he is entrusted by French royalist conspirators with a falsified document which promised the slaves two days of rest per week and the abolition of the use of the whip.[14] He had been instructed to foment a rebellion the royalists thought they could easily put an end to once they had defeated the whites of Saint Domingue, who followed revolutionary ideas and threatened the *status quo*. Toussaint, however, had his own emancipatory

---

[9] Deive, *Vodú y magia*, p. 161.
[10] Dagoberto Tejeda Ortíz, *El Vudú en Dominincana y en Haití* (Republica Dominicana: Ediciones Indefolk, 2013), pp. 91–102.
[11] June Rosenberg, *El Gagá: Religión y Sociedad de un Culto Dominicano: Un Estudio Comparativo* (Santo Domingo: Universidad de Santo Domingo, 1979), p. 37.
[12] See Deive, 'The African Heritage', pp. 110, 127 and Rosenberg, *El Gagá*, p. 199.
[13] Davis, '*Vodú* of the Dominican Republic', pp. 86–7; Cristina Sánchez-Carretero '*Santos y Misterios* as Channels of Communication in the Diaspora: Afro-Dominican Religious Practices Abroad', *Journal of American Folklore*, 118.469 (2005), pp. 308–26.
[14] Carlos Esteban Deive, *Viento Negro, bosque del caimán* (Santo Domingo: Editora Centenario, 2002), p. 65. Subsequent references to this novel will be given in parentheses in the text.

agenda.[15] In *Viento Negro* the assembly of the conspirators is followed by
a Vodou ceremony: like the accounts on which it is based, the ceremony
described by Deive takes place in the midst of a terrible storm, is officiated
by Boukman and a female priestess, and includes the killing of a sacrificial
pig and an inspirational oration by Boukman – not reported but referred
to as 'short but vibrant' (p. 68).[16] Despite his somewhat irreverent approach
– at some point, the forcefully evoked Ogun Ferraille arrives, seemingly in
person, on his (literal, not ritualistic) horse and accepts three bottles of rum
and some money as a tribute (p. 68) – Deive's inclusion of Bois Caiman in his
novel suggests that he considers it to be at least a crucial and inspirational
symbol of the insurrection if not an actual, verifiable event.

Being a *novela*, *Viento Negro* features fictional characters alongside
historical figures and, while relying heavily on established chronology and
facts, it also alters them in significant ways. As a historian, anthropologist,
and novelist, Deive knows well the role that narrative plays when one tries
to map the relationship between past, present, and future and must be
particularly conscious of the 'content of the form' – that is, of the effects
that genre and formal features can have on the understanding, shaping,
and transmission of history.[17] The relationship between genre and the
Haitian revolution has been recently investigated by David Scott, who has
observed that, owing to the anticolonial organization of the relation between
past, present, and future, the transition from colonialism to postcolo-
nialism tends to be presented predominantly as a romance – that is, as a
story of overcoming and vindication, of salvation and redemption.[18] Using
C.L.R. James's *Black Jacobins* as a springboard, Scott argues that tragedy
might be a more useful narrative frame to assess the Haitian revolution,
as it is 'not driven by the confident hubris of teleologies that extract the
future seamlessly from the past, and [is] more attuned at the same time to
the intricacies, ambiguities, and paradoxes of the relations between actions

---

[15] For more on Toussaint as a double agent see Fick, *Making of Haiti*, p. 92.
[16] For an account of the ceremony see Fick, *Making of Haiti*, pp. 260–66. The woman
is erroneously identified by Deive as Romaine la Prophétesse, who was instead a man
who used to dress up as a woman – see Chapter 2 and Fick, *Making of Haiti*, pp. 127–8
– and conflated with the *mambo* Cécile Fatiman, who is supposed to have participated
to the historical ceremony: see Dubois, *Avengers of the New World*, pp. 99–100 and
Fick, *Making of Haiti*, p. 93.
[17] I am echoing Hayden White, *The Content of the Form: Narrative Discourse and
Historical Representation* (Baltimore, MD: The Johns Hopkins University Press, 2009).
[18] David Scott, *Conscripts of Modernity: The Tragedy of Colonial Enlightenment*
(Durham, NC: Duke University Press, 2004), pp. 7–8.

and their consequences, and intentions and the chance contingencies that sometimes undo them.'[19]

Deive's *Viento Negro* constitutes a departure from both romance and tragedy. It might instead be categorized as a *sui generis* comedy or even as an *opera buffa*, if one considers that the narrative is constantly underscored, often in a contrapuntal manner, by the arias of the soprano Angiolina Falconelli, who criss-crosses the island of Hispaniola singing for the French, the Spanish, and the Black Jacobins. At the outset of the 1791 rebellion, for example, it is Falconelli's performance of Pergolesi's *La Serva Padrona* (*The Maid Turned Mistress*) which provides the ironic soundtrack to historical events in Le Cap (p. 71). Comedies, it is well known, can be intrinsically conservative and ultimately support the reconstitution and conservation of the order they seem to disrupt. Admittedly, therefore, the comedic genre of *opera buffa* might not be an obvious choice for a historical novel which, as we will see, aims to make important points about Hispaniola's past and present while fostering a much-needed transformation of the ways in which Haiti and the Dominican Republic perceive one another and themselves. Furthermore, references to *The Maid Turned Mistress* might initially suggest that readers will be exposed to a (Dominican) mockery of the Haitian revolution and its leaders, but I would argue, instead, that Deive adapts the comedic template of the *opera buffa* to serve his purpose of reimagining the future of Hispaniola, disallowing what Reinhardt Koselleck has called 'futures pasts.'[20]

Unlike tragedies but like romances, comedies and *opere buffe* tend to 'end well.' Unlike romances, however, comedies and *opere buffe* do not dramatize the victory of good over evil and do not stage the 'ultimate transcendence of man over the world in which he was imprisoned by the Fall.'[21] Initially written to work as *intermezzi* given in the long waits between the acts of the *opera seria* and considered to be inferior to it, *opere buffe* treat serious matters with humour. Like Scott's tragedies, they are full of intricacies and ambiguities and thrive on paradoxes and reversals of fortune, but their protagonists lack the stature of tragic heroes and heroines and are instead everymen and women who operate in everyday situations. As for 'the confident hubris of teleologies,' *opere buffe* tend to follow rather closely the pattern that White has identified for all comedic texts, where, he writes, 'hope is held out for the temporary triumph of man over his world by the prospect

---

[19] Scott, *Conscripts of Modernity*, p. 210.

[20] Reinhardt Koselleck, *Futures Past: On the Semantics of Historical Time* (New York: Columbia University Press, 1985).

[21] Hayden White, *Metahistory: The Historical Imagination in Nineteenth-Century Europe* (Baltimore, MD: The Johns Hopkins University Press, 1973), pp. 8–9.

of occasional reconciliations of the forces at play in the social and natural worlds.'[22] 'Temporary' is the key word here. Aptly, in *Viento Negro*, authority, finality, and irreversibility are forcefully undermined but, I will argue, the novel's 'happy ending,' despite its momentariness, functions as a stepping stone towards an effective rejection of a deterministically bleak view of the future. The novel, in fact, does not support the reconstitution of a previous order and does not solicit nor obtain the reader's sympathy for the dominant social interests which upheld that order: ultimately, the emphasis falls on the emancipatory aspects of the (momentary) resolution and revolution and not on their ephemeral status and inherent contradictions.[23]

Viento Negro begins with a comedy sketch which introduces us to the profound religious, cultural, and social changes that the French Revolution brought about in the Spanish colony. On 27 November 1790, we are told, Guy Millon, a self-defining French scientist–philosopher just arrived from Le Cap, held a spectacular demonstration in the central square of the capital city of Santo Domingo. He shared his discoveries on 'medicinal electricity' with his audience and allowed them to buy 'at a very good price' a number of essential products such as 'water of light,' 'vitriolic ether,' and 'poultice for hysterical paralysis' (p. 19). At the end of the show, Millon was planning to fly over the capital city in a balloon. Millon's announcement created great excitement and expectations: in particular, we are told that Joaquín García y Moreno, governor of the Spanish colony, planned to attend the show because he hoped to apply the Frenchman's findings to military weaponry, become a successful inventor, and leave Santo Domingo once and for all (p. 22). Deive is careful to point out, however, that not everyone in Santo Domingo shared García y Moreno's enthusiasm for Millon's work. Fray

---

[22] White, *Metahistory*, p. 9.
[23] The 'happy endings' of Picquenard's two novels are not very different from Hugo's unhappy ones but they all support (like Saint-Méry's texts) the pre-revolutionary *status quo*. In both versions of *Bug-Jargal* Pierrot/Bug-Jargal is unjustly executed, Maria is lost (she dies when Le Cap is pillaged), and, in the second version, D'Auverney is also killed in battle on European territory. Most importantly, the island of Hispaniola and its all too permeable border is left behind as an Eden turned into chaotic hell and as the site of a personal and political nightmare too horrible to be dealt with. The protagonists of *Adonis* and *Zoflora* can only find peace and happiness by leaving the Caribbean island and its colonial frontier which has contributed so much to shatter Picquenard's (alleged) dream of racial and social equality and move to other places, namely Virginia, Philadelphia (incidentally, where Saint-Méry published his *Descriptions*), and then France itself. D'Herouville, his family, Adonis, and his wife find refuge in Norfolk, Virginia, while Justin, his family, and the faithful Zoflora go to Philadelphia and later to France.

Fernando Portillo y Torres, archbishop of Santo Domingo, was extremely anxious about the arrival in the Spanish colony not only of Millon but of all kinds of 'fetishists, necromancers, miracle-workers [and] swindlers' (p. 23). After the French Revolution, in fact, Spanish Santo Domingo as a whole and its border region in particular had been radically transformed by the continuous influx of refugees from Saint Domingue. In *Viento Negro* the northern border town of Dajabón, where most of them were housed, becomes a huge market where all manner of things – including a mud replica of a famous vampire – were bought, sold, and exchanged (p. 42). In Montecristi, situated by the border on the northern coast, a local priest proclaims the Declaration of the Rights of the Man and Citizen to be the only revealed truth and establishes the Culto Teodóxico Universal, a civic–religious brotherhood which soon becomes extremely popular and spreads to other border areas (Hincha, Bánica, Neyba y San Miguel de la Atalaya). Among its followers the Culto counts Sor Transfiguración des Citoyens, formerly Sor Eufrosina de la Perpetua Consolación (p. 113), and the above-mentioned Guy Millon who, tired of Portillo y Torres's persecutions in the capital, decides to move to the border area where he can thrive unmolested. The reference to the Culto Teodóxico Universal is one of Deive's many deliberate anachronisms: it was actually an esoteric and freemasonic cult funded in 1824 by Antoine Fabre d'Olivet and is conflated here with the activity of a real-life priest called Quiñones (as is Deive's character), who tried to combine Christianity with French Republicanism.[24] Deive's implicit reference to freemasonry is reinforced by the – also anachronistic – appearance, in the *novela*, of Martinez De Pasqually, the controversial historical founder of the order Elus Cohens (a mystical Masonry) who died in 1774, perhaps in Saint Domingue. In *Viento Negro*, Deive's narrator insists that his real name was Eleuterio Martínez Pascual, that he had travelled to France to become better acquainted with esoterism and then moved to the island of Hispaniola, where, with Jacques Cazotte (another real-life esoterist who was to become one of his followers and who was beheaded in France 1792), he had settled in Spanish Santo Domingo (pp. 56–7).

Freemasonry was well established in the New World: apparently, in French Saint Domingue there was at least one lodge in every major town and, owing to its generally equalitarian ethos, freemasonry might have played a crucial role in the uprising of the French colony.[25] Most white Masons

[24]   Carlos Esteban Deive, *Heterodoxia e inquisición en Santo Domingo* (Santo Domingo: Editora Taller, 1983), pp. 318–19.
[25]   André Combes, 'La Franc-Maçonnerie aux Antilles et en Guyane Française de 1789 à 1848,' in *La Période Révolutionnaire aux Antilles: Images et Résonances*, Actes du

fled or were killed in the aftermath of 1791, but it has been suggested that some of those who survived and stayed on the island continued their practice – in *Viento Negro*, De Pasqually joins the army of the rebels after their abolition of slavery (p. 107) – and, among others, they inducted (clandestinely) Toussaint Louverture.[26] The reference to De Pasqually and his esoterism also brings to the fore the fact that the much vilified Vodou assemblies were not the only 'hieratic sites' on the island: Vodou, in fact, had been described by a commentator of the time as 'a sort of religious and dancing masonry.'[27] Intriguingly, in the cosmologic diagrams for Haitian Vodou scholars have identified, interspersed along *vévé* ground signs, the secret signs of freemasonry (such as, for example, the compass-upon-the-square)[28] and, as Susan Buck-Morrs insists, 'we cannot be blind to the possibility of reciprocal influences, that the secret signs of Freemasonry were themselves affected by the ritual practices of the revolutionary slaves of Saint-Domingue.'[29]

Deive's freemason De Pasqually lives in the region of La Vega, 'a desolate landscape where only mad people, maroons and the souls of the dead walked about' (p. 54). The majority of the maroons referred to here were probably fugitives from Saint Domingue and, in the early 1790s, Deive's narrator informs us, the area around La Vega was plagued by the presence of one of these maroons from Saint Domingue, who was perpetrating 'atrocious crimes': the well-known *Voras Carnefice* or *Negro Incógnito* or *Comegente* ('Voracious Torturer' or 'Unknown Negro' or 'Cannibal' p. 53). Historically, the criminal activities of the *Negro Incógnito* were first recorded by the Spanish authorities in March 1790, when they received the news of various murders and the disappearance of two children. His killings

---

Colloque International Pluridisciplinaire, 26–30 November 1986, ed. Roger Toumson (Faculté des Lettres et des Sciences Humaines, Université des Antilles et de la Guyane: GRELCA, n.d.), p. 162, quoted in Sybille Fischer, *Modernity Disavowed, Haiti and the Cultures of Slavery in the Age of Revolution* (Durham, NC: Duke University Press, 2004), pp. 51–2.

[26] Combes, p. 162 quoted in Fischer, *Modernity Disavowed*, pp. 51–2. Fischer, however, suggests that we should take some of Combes's data with a degree of scepticism, considering that his institutional affiliation is the *Institut d'études maçonniques* in Paris (p. 311).

[27] Dayan, *Haiti, History and the Gods*, p. 251; *Lettre annuelle de l'Ordre de Notre Dame*, qtd in Fick, *Making of Haiti*, p. 265.

[28] See Buck-Morrs, *Hegel, Haiti and Universal History*, p. 70 fig. 1 and pp. 123–4 fig. 2 and Alfred Métraux, *Voodoo in Haiti* (New York: Oxford University Press, 1959), p. 140.

[29] Buck-Morrs, *Hegel, Haiti and Universal History*, p. 65.

were accompanied by arsonist attacks, rapes (of bodies and corpses alike), mutilation of genitalia, and cannibalism. A reward of 200 pesos was promised to those who could assist in the criminal's capture and almost one thousand soldiers and civilians were mobilized to bring him to justice. In the course of this operation twenty-four maroons, thieves, and vagrants were apprehended by the authorities but, since the *Negro Incógnito* proved impossible to locate, he was declared to be a legendary figure conjured up by the people's fantasy. In 1792, in Cercado Alto, near La Vega, a man who was identified as the *Negro Incógnito* was captured by some hunters with the help of their dogs. Despite this, the colonial authorities continued to deny that the *Negro Incógnito* ever existed and concluded that all the crimes that had been attributed to him had either been committed by French fugitive slaves who lived in the area or were otherwise 'inspired' by their presence, which provided a very bad example for the blacks of Santo Domingo.[30]

In *Viento Negro* 'ocular witnesses' explain the elusiveness of the *Negro Incógnito* with the fact that he had learnt his witchcraft from a Carabalí slave in a plantation in the Limbé district of Saint Domingue (p. 53). Limbé is a place with a symbolic significance because some historians believe that the 1791 revolt in Saint Domingue began 'unofficially' with the activities of some slaves from Limbé who either misunderstood the final instructions imparted by the leaders or were too impatient to wait for the established date to begin the uprising.[31] In other words, here Deive attracts our attention to those discourses which, creating spurious links between disparate events, aimed to criminalize the 1791 revolt, the Haitian Revolution, and, later Haiti and the Haitians as a whole. Crucially, the narrator reports that, according to the same 'ocular witnesses,' the pitch-black ferocious killer could rely on the unconditional protection of a '*galipote*' (p. 53).

On the Spanish side of the island, the theatre of the *Negro Incógnito*'s rampage, the word '*galipote*' is a Haitianism which (still) describes a magical shape-shifter who makes a pact with the devil and turns into animal, plant, or rock or, more rarely, into a human being, and who can therefore become impossible to capture and almost invulnerable.[32] *Galipotes* are also

---

[30]   Carlos Esteban Deive, *La mala vida: delincuencia y picaresca en la colonia española de Santo Domingo* (Santo Domingo: Fundación Cultural Dominicana, 1997), pp. 233–5.

[31]   Fick, *Making of Haiti*, p. 95.

[32]   Sergio Reyes, *Cuentos y leyendas de la frontera* (Santo Domingo: Editora Universitaria-UASD, 1996), pp. 254, 41–2. Like Reyes, Pedro Henríquez Ureña describes the word as a 'Haitianismo' and places the '*galipote*' firmly in the Domincan villages on the border with Haiti: see *Diccionario dominicano* (Santo Domingo: Editorial del Nordeste, 1983). Deive also defines the term as a Haitianism in his *Diccionario de dominicanismos* (Santo Domingo: Ediciones Librería Trinitaria/Editora Manatí, 2002).

foregrounded when the novel returns to the border town of Dajabón in 1793, when Spain and France were at war and the island was in complete turmoil. During a visit to Padre Vázquez, the priest of Dajabón, Commander don Andrés de Heredia, comes across 'a creature on a leash with a semblance of a human' (p. 143). This creature is in fact a *galipote* and, as Vázquez explains to a puzzled de Heredia, *galipotes* are 'the bodyguards of Barón Samedi, *loa* of the cemeteries' (p. 143): coming from beyond the grave, they are fluorescent, and wander around villages and fields looking for people to tear apart with their tentacles.[33] Ocular witnesses, he adds, have seen them rape young girls, sodomizing women, and steeping in pickle old females they could not do much more with (p. 143) – that is, engaging in crimes not dissimilar from those perpetrated by the *Negro Incógnito*, with whom they also share Haitian provenance. In *Viento Negro* Deive's narrator explains that de Heredia considers Padre Vázquez to be a good but superstitious man, inclined to believe in the sortileges of the 'black behiques' (p. 144) – a '*behique*' is a Taíno shaman or witch doctor. However, De Heredia himself (and, indeed, the narrator) must be under a sort of a spell too, because in the novel the *galipote* is actually described as a real presence (p. 43).

The ambivalent matter-of-factness with which the *galipote* is introduced also alerts us to the fact that, rather than being a vestige of the past, *galipotes* still play a role in contemporary Dominican society.[34] For example, in 1974, two centuries after the 1791 rebellion, the newspaper *El Caribe* reported accounts of black-skinned people who had signed a pact with the Devil, insisted that those who could turn themselves into animals or inanimate objects were Haitian in origin, and repeatedly qualified Haitians as *galipotes*.[35] However, if anti-Haitian ideology is still a powerful reality, real life – what

---

The *galipote*'s zoomorphism reminds one of the powerful rebel maroon and *houngan* Makandal who, incidentally, worked in the Limbé plantation fifty years or so before the 1791 revolt and who, according to a well-known legend, escaped his execution by flying away from the burning stake as a fly or a mosquito (see Chapter 8).

[33] In *Viento Negro* Deive uses *loa* instead of *lua*, the preferred term in *Vodú y magia en Santo Domingo*.

[34] Emilio Jorge Rodríguez, *Haiti and Trans-Caribbean Literary Identity / Haiti y la transcaribeñidad literaria* (Philipsburg, San Martin: House of Nehesi Editores, 2011), p. 202, makes an interesting comparison between the 'Haitian' *galipote* and the 'indigenous' *ciguapa* and argues that 'in the course of time [...] the overlapping and mutual influence of Haiti and the Dominican Republic, has modified folkloric figures first attributed to aboriginal or Afro-Haitian culture [...] submitting them to a process of creolization with the resulting encroachment of geographic, cultural and mental borders.'

[35] Rodríguez, *Literary Identity*, pp. 194.

Scott calls 'the intricacies, ambiguities, and paradoxes of the relations between actions and their consequences, and intentions and the chance contingencies that sometimes undo them' – does not always chime with it.[36] In his 1996 account of his childhood in Loma de Cabrera, near Dajabón, the Dominican writer and journalist Sergio Reyes offers a perspective on *galipotes* which seem inflected more by class than ethnicity or race. In the Dominican borderland the shape-shifting *galipote* seemed frightening because he watched over the property and life of the rich landowners and wealthy personalities of the area, rather than because of his phenotype, colour, or Haitian provenance.[37] Haitian influences, moreover, have always been part of the cultural and spiritual syncretism which characterizes the Spanish side of the island (especially the rural and popular segments of society), despite the fact that certain sectors of the Dominican elite have always tried to minimize or even demonize them.[38] The dynamics of acceptance and rejection of such influences are complex but their very existence testifies to the fact that, by focusing exclusively on dominant discourses, one can hardly get the full picture. In *Viento Negro*, for example, in order to prevent the *galipote* from spreading the evil eye and in order to protect himself from the traps prepared by his followers, Padre Vázquez sets fire to some tobacco leaves, spreads a handful of flour on the floor in a circular shape, and then blesses it three times. This ritualistic spreading of powders echoes Vodou practices, while tobacco firmly signposts Taíno agriculture. In *Vodú y magia en Santo Domingo* Deive argues that the Taíno influence is stronger in Dominican Vodú than in Haitian Vodou; in *Viento Negro*, De Heredia's reference to '*behiques negros*' (emphasis mine p. 144), capitalizing on the multiple meanings of the word 'negro' in Spanish, seems to gesture towards this transcultural aspect, which here firmly characterizes the northern borderland of Hispaniola.[39]

In line with his decision to recount historical events following the genre of comedy, Deive's narrator undercuts all his characters, from the French and Spanish colonial authorities to the leaders of the revolution. For example, Joaquín García y Moreno, governor of the Spanish colony, Fray Fernando Portillo y Torres, archbishop of Santo Domingo, and Léger-Félicité Sonthonax, the civil commissioner in charge of the French troops during part of the Haitian Revolution, are ferociously ridiculed and their weaknesses and pettiness unmercifully revealed. Boukman is impressive and revered by his

---

[36] Scott, *Conscripts of Modernity*, p. 210.

[37] Reyes, *Cuentos y leyendas*, p. 41. See also Chapter 7.

[38] See Deive, 'The African Inheritance', p. 87 and Sergio Reyes, *Sincretismo: Formas de Expresión en la Frontera* (Santo Domingo: Editora Universitaria-UASD, 1999), p. 5.

[39] 'Negro' is used to describe black people and the colour black.

companions (including Toussaint) but during the assembly at Bois Caiman he drinks *clerén* because, he explains, '"*Gren mwe frét*" […] "My testicles are cold"' (p. 65).[40] When they arrive in Ouanaminthe on 24 December 1792 the impossibly vain 'Generalísimo' Jean-François and the 'Vicerrey' Biassou rush to the tailor to get a new set of extravagant and flamboyant clothes, issue an edict which abolishes, among other things, 'black magic,' 'black shadows,' 'black dirt under fingernails,' and 'the black behind the ears,'[41] because they are 'derogatory, fallacious, racist and contrary to the rights of man' (pp. 97–8), and also declare as public holidays dates which are 'Gregorian, revolutionary […] patriotic, […] Muslim, Jewish and Buddhist, because here we discriminate nobody' (p. 99).

Toussaint is also caricatured: we are told that, in order to allocate to the leaders of the rebel army the most comfortable houses of the occupied villages, he requisitioned properties proffering sincere apologies (p. 100). Overall, however, Touissant is taken very seriously by Deive: from the beginning he is described as an astute, opportunistic, inscrutable, persuasive strategist, and as a statesman-in the-making (p. 227). He is also depicted as 'enigmatic as a sphinx' – that is, exactly like Francisco Sopo (p. 132), the leader of a slave insurrection described in *Viento Negro* and which took place in Boca Nigua, on the Spanish side of the island, a few years after the 1791 revolt in Saint Domingue. The fact that, in his turn, Sopo is once identified with the *Negro Incógnito* (p. 196) highlights the continuities and discontinuities that exist between spontaneous reaction and organized rebellion, survival strategies and emancipatory agendas, not only within each colony but also across the island's border.

Sopo appears for the first time in the second chapter of the novel. Here we follow the Boca Nigua slave-holder and plantocrat Ignacio de Oyarzábal crossing the border before 1791 in an attempt to accelerate the arrival, in the Spanish colony, of a new era that 'would forever bury as a most remote memory this repetitive time of sacristies and confessionals' (p. 28). This is a rather problematic statement to process because the modernization that de Oyarzábal is welcoming so warmly must coincide with the opening of Santo Domingo to the slave trade in 1786; yet de Oyarzábal is very ambivalent towards slavery, the practice of which, he believes, creates 'the most miserable and despicable world one could possibly imagine' (p. 27). His disquiet notwithstanding, de Oyarzábal crosses into Saint Domingue to visit the Bréda plantation of Haut-du-Cap in order to study the technical

---

[40] *Clerén* is a Haitian alcoholic drink.
[41] An expression which means that one person who can 'pass' for white has instead black ancestors.

innovations which Count Noé, the owner of the Saint Domingue *habitation*, had enumerated to his father in a Parisian café where (ironically) the revolutionary theses of the *sans-culottes* were being discussed at the same time. De Oyarzábal is hosted in a luxury *grande case* with a Pompeian façade and tapestries from Damascus and, during a tour of the *ingenio* with Francisco Sopo, his favourite slave who had accompanied him from Boca Nigua, he meets a certain Touissant, who was working there as an overseer. Touissant and Sopo do not speak to one another but Deive's narrator points out that they share the same resentment towards slavery and 'a dangerous disposition, a craving painfully dragged along for years' (p. 32).

Historically, the Boca Nigua revolt took place in October 1796, when the plantation had about 200 slaves: it was the largest and best run in Santo Domingo, it was fairly new (probably set up after 1786), and was managed by a certain Juan Bautista Oyarzábal (who shares his name with the father of Deive's Ignacio de Oyarzábal), the nephew of the absentee owner, the Marqués de Yranda.[42] The four different sources which relate the historical revolt identify its origin in an act of revenge on the part of a black slave driver called Francisco Sopó, who had recently lost two godsons at the hands of the plantation's white staff – the distiller had falsely accused one of his godsons of stealing rum (the youth had committed suicide as a result), while the other had died in the plantation hospital. However, when the date for the uprising had been set, Sopó changed his mind, approached the white distiller and informed him of the rebels' plan; later, he also revealed it to Oyarzábal himself. During the rebellion Sopó allied with the whites and protected their escape from the plantation. When the news of the revolt in Boca Nigua reached Santo Domingo, fifty troops were dispatched to re-establish the order, the uprising was quickly crushed, and all but two of the rebelling slaves were recaptured and sent to the capital's hospital or jail. Sopó and the chiefs of the rebellion were sentenced to death and hanged, beheaded, and quartered: their arms and legs were cut off and nailed up in public places in the city, while their heads were sent back to the plantation for display.[43]

Contemporary historians disagree on whether Sopó's revolt was an authentic cry for freedom and equality.[44] It is undeniable, however, that the

[42] David Geggus, 'Slave Resistance in the Spanish Caribbean in the Mid-1970s', in *A Turbulent Time: The French Revolution and the Greater Caribbean*, ed. D.B. Gaspar and D.P. Geggus (Bloomington, IN: Indiana University Press, 2003), pp. 131–55, p. 141.
[43] Geggus, 'Slave Resistance', pp. 139–40.
[44] For a positive assessment see, for example, Blas Jiménez, *Africano por elección, negro por nacimiento* (Santo Domingo: Editora Manatí, 2008), pp. 75–81 and Deive,

Saint Domingue revolt was influential in the Boca Nigua uprising because it provided a precedent the rebels wanted to learn from.[45] The connection between the 1791 uprising in the French part and the rebellion in Santo Domingo is further strengthened by Deive when he informs us that, just before the revolt, one of the Boca Nigua conspirators had gone to Marmelade 'to find out the details of what happened in Bois Caiman from Touissant Louverture in order to act in the same way' (p. 196).[46] However, despite Toussaint's alleged prompting, Sopo's uprising, unlike the 1791 rebellion but like Sopó's revolt, is crushed by governmental forces and he is sentenced to death. Deive's foregrounding of the rebellion of Boca Nigua is an effective move which demystifies anti-Haitian historiography: the very existence of the conspiracy calls into question the long-rehearsed claim that the slaves from the Spanish part preferred to 'remain [...] slave[s] under the Spaniards than to be free along with the Haitians who, led by Toussaint and Dessalines, attempted to make the island "one and undivided"'.[47] In order to make this point as forcefully as possible, Deive also introduces some crucial alterations to historical facts.

Sopo (unlike the historical Sopó) never betrays his comrades and is seen leading the blacks in their attack against de Oyarzábal's house. Deive's decision to change Sopó's betrayal into Sopo's determination is also to be regarded as part of his ongoing effort to undermine the representation of Spanish Santo Domingo as a safe haven and a place of freedom for blacks and to reject what he calls an 'idyllic image of slavery,' according to which master and slave relations were generally predicated upon humanitarian sentiments – slavery in Santo Domingo, he insists, 'operated exactly as in other countries.'[48] In order to offer as diversified a picture as possible of the

---

Los guerrilleros negros, p. 22, where he asserts that the historical rebellion 'aimed to proclaim freedom for all the blacks of the colony and to establish a popular and revolutionary government'; David Geggus instead insists on the fact that Sopó's revolt was not characterized by a libertarian rhetoric: 'Slave Resistance', pp. 147–8.

[45] Despite his reservations, Geggus is happy to concede as much: see 'Slave Resistance', p. 147.

[46] In reality, Sopó did approach, for advice, three former soldiers of Jean-François's auxiliary army who were working nearby and asked them to take him and some of his fellow conspirators to Saint Domingue, but the former soldiers refused to get involved in the plot: see Geggus, 'Slave Resistance', p. 142.

[47] Deive, 'The African Inheritance', pp. 105–06.

[48] Deive, 'The African Inheritance', pp. 107, 99, 108. Deive also insists on the importance of endoculturation, a mechanism by which an individual is encouraged not only to adopt the culture that is imposed on him or her but to consider it superior to his own (p. 91). What he calls 'the dual and often contradictory psychological processes that made slaves oscillate between servility and rebellion' (p. 107), which can be seen

predicament of black people in the colony, the novel begins with the voice of black women selling their produce in the streets of the capital (p. 7). In the city both free blacks and slaves enjoyed greater freedom than their companions in the sugar mills[49] but, in the following chapters of *Viento Negro*, Deive foregrounds the predicament of the latter by focusing on the Boca Nigua plantation before the revolt. We are invited to witness the agony of the slave Filemon Congo, who was a 'victim of the exhaustion caused by days of hard work' (p. 129), and the deep effect it has on Sopo. Sopo, whom de Oyarzábal describes as the most faithful and trustworthy of his slaves, according to Agripiliano Brizuela, a former Jesuit who administers the Boca Nigua plantation when Oyarzábal travels to the capital, is instead 'as enigmatic' as a sphinx' (p. 132). Before the revolt, Brizuela warns the excessively trustworthy Oyarzábal with these truly prophetic words: 'do not forget the black wind which, not long ago, blew in Bois Caiman. You cannot trust any of them, not even their mothers' (p. 132).

Brizuela's words are central to the novel because they contain Deive's title and, most importantly, because they point to the existence of a libertarian impulse which geopolitical borders could not stop: at the outset of their revolt the insurgents of Boca Nigua hoped that their rebellion was going to bring slavery to a permanent end and believed that it sanctioned the beginning of a new life (p. 195). In *Viento Negro*, moreover, toponymy allows Deive to trace a continuity between eighteenth-century anti-slavery rebellion and sixteenth-century marronage: the city gate where Sopo is executed is called the 'puerta de Lemba' ('Lemba's gate') because it was the place where Sebastián Lemba Calembo, a powerful maroon leader who burned and ransacked his way from Higüey to the Bahoruco, was (allegedly) executed in 1548 and his severed head hanged as an example to others who would dare rebel against their white masters. A statue of Lemba is now to be found in front of the *Museo del Hombre Dominicano* alongside two others that embody Enriquillo and Bartolomé de las Casas. The three figures are meant to represent the three components of Dominican identity (African, Indio/a and Spanish) but the inclusion of Lemba did create some opposition because not everyone considered it appropriate to celebrate the African heritage.[50]

Deive here seems to propose not only Lemba but also Sopó as valiant ancestors who fought for the right values and who deserve the utmost respect

---

at work in the behaviour of the historical Sopó, might be explained, at least partly, by the influence of endoculturation.

[49] See Deive, 'The African Inheritance', pp. 95–7.

[50] David Howard, *Coloring the Nation: Race and Ethnicity in the Dominican Republic* (Oxford: Signal Books, 2001), p. 8.

Figure 8. Statues of Lemba, Bartolomé de las Casas and Enriquillo in front of the Museo del Hombre Dominicano, Santo Domingo. The three figures are meant to represent the three components of Dominican identity: African, Spanish and Indio/a (photograph: Maria Cristina Fumagalli).

of contemporary Dominicans. Crucially, while Sopo is being beheaded, the *viento negro* is still blowing (p. 200) and García y Moreno is (anachronistically) informed that Touissant has reached San Rafael de la Angostura and San Miguel de la Atalaya and that Spain has ceded the colony of Santo Domingo to France with the Treaty of Basle (p. 201). Deive's altered historical chronology – in his account the Boca Nigua revolt precedes rather than follows the Treaty of Basle – draws his readers' attention to the profound political repercussions that the 1791 revolt and the *viento negro* had for the island as a whole.

Altered chronologies and anachronisms contribute to highlighting how this historical novel, like most historical novels, is preoccupied with the present and with present – not only past – forms of social injustice.[51] For example, we are told that one of the characters, the vizconde de Fontanges, is stuck in the Spanish part of the island because, at the onset of the rebellion, he found himself in the spa of La Surza, close to the border town of Bánica (p. 84). In 1791 Bánica's thermal waters had been famous for over forty years

---

[51] For more examples of anachronisms see Rita de Maeseneer, *Encuentro con la narrativa dominicana contemporánea* (Madrid: Iberoamericana, 2006), note 27 p. 39.

and Saint-Méry explains that the French used to go there in considerable numbers: in 1776, for example, the spa could accommodate more than sixty people at one time, some of whom went there purely for pleasure rather than for health reasons.[52] However, Saint-Méry adds that in 1776 French travellers began to avoid Bánica's thermal waters because, while on their way there, all too often they were being 'disturbed' by the Spanish authorities, who were trying to contain across-the-border contraband.[53] Aware that Bánica's spa could constitute an important source of income, however, the Spanish did all they could to allure as many 'health tourists' as possible from the then richer side of the island. An article from the *Gazette du Cap* dated 18 September 1776 and quoted in full by Saint-Méry informs the citizens of Saint Domingue that all abuses perpetrated against French voyageurs will be suspended. Moreover, it explains that four new residences will be built and the wood around the spa will be felled to create a much more picturesque view and a pleasant path through the *savane* where one will be able to find some 'pretty gardens' and herbs for hair treatment. Most importantly, all the French will be able to cross the border with their servants and property and will have the right to hunt and fish in the area.[54]

The plan to transform this portion of the Spanish borderland into a French enclave where the French could behave as if they were in Saint Domingue seems to pioneer the creation of those all-inclusive destinations which are currently spoiling the coast of the Dominican Republic and the rest of the Caribbean. Permeable and impermeable borders are fundamental to these tourists' heavens: impermeable boundaries keep out undesirable realities and people, while permeable ones erase, or at least minimize, the difference between 'home and away' by allowing the familiar to comfortably intermesh with a domesticated unfamiliar. In 1776 similar forms of occlusion and disavowal informed the proposed landscaping of the borderland around Bánica as the plan to grant special rights to a selected group of foreigners was an attempt to deny the tensions brought about by the existence of a colonial frontier separating an affluent French colony from its poorer Spanish counterpart – tensions that Deive clearly highlights by focusing on the privileged experience of de Fontanges. Nowadays, La Surza has been claimed back by the population of the borderland and, far from being an exclusive all-inclusive, has become an important holy site where an Indian spirit called *Rey del Agua*, or King of the Water, is worshipped.[55]

---

[52] PE, vol. I, p. 279.

[53] PE, vol. I, p. 279.

[54] PE, vol. I, pp. 279–80.

[55] Jan Lundius and Mats Lundhal, *Peasants and Religion: A Socioeconomis Study*

Deive ends his novel when Toussaint's glory is at its highest point: that is, with his triumphal entrance in Santo Domingo on 26 January 1801, when, against Bonaparte's will, he finally brought Santo Domingo *de facto* under French domination as stipulated by the Treaty of Basle. As soon as the keys of the city are in his hands Deive's Toussaint decrees, to their utter delight, that all the slaves of Santo Domingo are free men and women (p.243). This is historically accurate: approximately fifteen thousand slaves were freed on that day. We also know that Toussaint soon abolished all colour distinctions, so that the mulattos could gain entry to those higher levels in the power structure which had previously been reserved for the whites. Touissant encouraged the white men of Santo Domingo to marry their concubines and also promised security of land tenure to the *hateros* (the owners of pastures and woodland).[56] The plantocrat Ignacio de Oyarzábal, one of the people who witness Toussaint's arrival in the capital, is astonished when he realizes that the supreme and only authority on the island is in fact the former overseer he met during his visit to the Bréda plantation. In other words, as *prophesized* in 1791 by Angiolina Falconelli's performance of Pergolesi's *opera buffa*, servants, here, have literally turned masters and, crucially, the novel seems to suggest to his readers that this is a positive outcome.

The novel's last words are García y Moreno's, who points out that 'never before had Santo Domingo been so festive' (p. 244). This is most appropriate for an *opera buffa*: as White has pointed out, the temporary reconciliations and happy endings which characterize comedies 'are symbolized in the festive occasions that the Comic writer uses to terminate his dramatic accounts of change and transformation.'[57] Historically speaking, however, this festive mood was soon to end. In his position of supreme command, Toussaint called for the formation of electoral assemblies to choose deputies to a central assembly that would write a constitution for the entire island. According to the July 1801 constitution Toussaint abolished slavery, became governor-for-life with the power to name his own successor, and established that, despite the fact that Hispaniola remained part of France's colonial Empire, no French representative was allowed to play any role in the colony's administrative structure. However, Toussaint also disallowed the political and economic participation in the new social order of the formerly enslaved masses. Controversially, he was determined to maintain the plantation system of large holdings and sanctioned, in his constitution, that all citizens

---

of Dios Olivorio and the Palma Sola Movement in the Dominican Republic (London: Routledge, 2000), p. 368.

[56] Matibag, *Haitian-Dominican Counterpoint*, pp. 73–4.

[57] White, *Metahistory*, p. 9.

owed their services to the land that fed them.[58] In other words, those who were no longer slaves were still required to work in the plantations and to surrender their individual freedom to the new state in order to support, paradoxically, what was, fundamentally, a project of emancipation.[59] Predictably, Toussaint's agrarian reforms were met with hostility; in addition, his abolition of Vodou did not prove to be a popular decision among the former slaves.[60]

In Spanish Santo Domingo, despite the equalitarian measures which gained him the distrust of most of the Spanish Dominican oligarchy, Toussaint did not enjoy for long the unconditional support of all freed blacks and *hateros*. In fact, he tried to convert the Dominican economy of *hatos* into a plantation-based one and, in order to counteract the parcelization of the territory, he proscribed the unauthorized sale of land, thus making it very difficult for the emancipated slaves to acquire their own small properties; he also devalued the *peso* and, as we have seen, instituted an unpopular compulsory labour system.[61] In 1802, after the arrival of the French army whose aim was to expel the black insurgents from the western part of the island, the Dominican elites reinstated slavery and the latifundist economy of the *hateros*. Touissant was captured, taken to France, and imprisoned in the castle of Joux, where he finally died while different armies continued to fight, reducing Spanish Santo Domingo to a devastated war zone.[62] Deive knows that what happened after Toussaint's triumphal entrance to Santo Domingo is well known to his readers, and especially to his Dominican readers: decades of anti-Haitian propaganda have urged them to think of the Black Jacobins' domination, but also of Boyer's occupation, of the existence of Haiti across the border, and of the presence of 'needed but unwanted' Haitian migrants on the territory of the Dominican Republic as an unfolding tragedy.[63] All this, however, is omitted from the narrative: the emphasis is decisively on the emancipatory potential of Toussaint's arrival and not on the controversial nature of his subsequent reforms or on his tragic demise. Deive's novel leaves its readers with a sense of elation and possibility, as if the entire island were on the brink of a new era predicated upon racial equality and social justice rather than racism, discrimination, and privilege.

---

[58] Dubois, *Avengers of the New World*, p. 245; Fick, *Making of Haiti*, pp. 206–7.

[59] Dubois, *Avengers of the New World*, p. 245.

[60] Dubois, *Avengers of the New World*, p. 244.

[61] Matibag, *Haitian-Dominican Counterpoint*, p. 75.

[62] Fischer, *Modernity Disavowed*, p. 149.

[63] I am borrowing the title from Bridget Wooding and Richard Moseley-Williams, *Needed but Unwanted: Haitian Immigrants and their Descendants in the Dominican Republic* (London: The Catholic Institute for International relations, 2004).

Deive's decision to end his novel with a 'happy ending' which coincides with the French domination of Hispaniola is therefore noteworthy and a sign that he is not afraid to venture into dangerous territory. It is true that French domination is not the same as Haitian domination – in 1801 Haiti did not exist yet and Toussaint was, at least officially, still acting on behalf of Bonaparte – but the '*une et indivisible*' question in the Dominican Republic is still a very delicate matter as testified by the furore caused by Haitian President Michel Martelly's fumbled response to a question on the unification of the island posed to him by a Dominican journalist during his 2011 election campaign.[64] In 2008 the historian Frank Moya Pons devoted two chapters of his *La otra historia dominicana* to the 'one and undivided' issue in which he insisted that, contrarily to what the anti-Haitian propaganda maintains, the Haitian constitution does not actually sanction that the island is one and indivisible and therefore does not contain an implicit threat to Dominican sovereignty. The Haitian constitutions that have used such terminology, Moya Pons explains, deployed it to declare that the Republic of Haiti (not the island) was one and indivisible. The only exception is the 1806 constitution, which did not contain the expression *une et indivisible* but defined the entire island as Haitian territory following the 1801 colonial constitution promulgated by Toussaint, which mirrored the territorial unification legitimized by the 1795 Treaty of Basle.[65]

That Deive's 'happy ending' revolves around the origins of what anti-Haitian discourse has promoted and still promotes as the Dominican's tragedy and nightmare *par excellence* – the Haitian invasion – is not only provocative but chimes with Franklin Franco's invitation to revisit relations between Haiti and the Dominican Republic by starting from their colonial roots.[66]

---

[64] See 'Haitian President Michel Martelly wants to unify Haiti and Dominican Republic', Martelly interviewed by Nuria Piera, http://www.youtube.com/watch?v=kvaU-4zZwis [accessed 27 November 2014]. Martelly decided to do this interview with Nuria Piera for Dominican television without an interpreter but did not appear too sure-footed and it is at least debatable if he really advocated the 'unification' of Hispaniola, as some have argued. For the controversy which followed see 'Have you guys read what lunatic said?', *Dominican Republic Forums* (DR1), http://www.dr1.com/forums/general-stuff/112313-have-you-guys-read-what-lunatic-said.html [accessed 27 November 2012]. In 2002, the same year in which Deive's novel was published, Silvio Torres Saillant pointed out how José Quezada, ex-consul General of the Dominica Republic in New York still 'maintained' that the Haitian constitution explicitly undermined Dominican sovereignty: see *El tigueraje intellectual* (Santo Domingo: Editora Manatí, 2002), p. 27.
[65] Moya Pons, *La otra historia dominicana*, pp. 272–6.
[66] Franklin Franco, *Sobre racismo y antihaitianismo (y otros ensayos)* (Santo Domingo: Sociedad Editorial Dominicana, 2003), p. 67.

Franco also pointed out that the Haitian and Dominican people had been made to interiorize conflicts which originated instead with the dominant classes of both nations and for the dissemination of which the ruling classes adopted all the available media.[67] These reflections, published in 2003, were included in a paper that Franco delivered in 1986 in Haina, at the *Coloquio domínico-haitiano de educadores*; almost thirty years later there is still a lot of work to be done to counteract this pernicious anti-Haitian influence and to promote rapprochement, solidarity, cooperation, and mutual understanding between the two nations. Deive's resolve to terminate the continuum of his narrative by presenting the arrival of Toussaint in Santo Domingo as a happy moment in the history of the island as a whole is not an attempt to simplify otherwise complex border dynamics or to smooth the rough edges of history; it derives instead from the realization that it is crucial to reject what Raymond Williams, in *Modern Tragedy*, had distressingly called the 'slowly settling loss of any acceptable future.'[68] In this context, therefore, Deive's *opera buffa* clearly emerges as a counterhegemonic tool which attempts to demystify the past in order to recast and confront the present and, hopefully, reimagine the future of Hispaniola.

[67] Franco, *Sobre racismo y antihaitianismo*, p. 67.
[68] Raymond Williams, *Modern Tragedy* (London: Verso, 1979), p. 209.

Chapter Five

A fragile and beautiful world: the northern borderland and the 1937 massacre

José Martí, *War Diaries* (1895), Manuel Rueda, *Bienvenida y la noche: Crónicas de Montecristi* (1994), Freddy Prestol Castillo, *El Masacre se pasa a pie* (1937; 1973) and *Paisajes y meditaciones de una frontera* (1943), Manuel Rueda, *La criatura terrestre* (1963), Polibio Díaz, *Rayano* (1993)

U p to this point *On the Edge* has concerned itself with texts – mostly *a posteriori* revisitations – which have sixteenth- and eighteenth-century Hispaniola at their core. This chapter and the two which follow, shed light instead on one of the most traumatic events in the history of the island: the 1937 massacre of Haitians and Haitian–Dominicans living in the Dominican borderland. We will be looking at works which help us understand the causes of the onslaught, the ways in which it unfolded, and its dramatic consequences for the areas it affected. This chapter takes as its focus visitors, natives, or residents' personal accounts of daily life in the Dominican border province of Montecristi prior to, during, and after the massacre; their narratives enable us to 'understand' in a more 'empathetic' way both the character and the significance of the borderland, rather than simply allowing us to 'know about facts and features' in an 'objective' way.[1]

The Cuban hero José Martí – incidentally, one of the first readers of Galván's *Enriquillo*, discussed in Chapter 3[2] – was in Haiti and the Dominican Republic briefly in September 1892; between February and April 1895 he again visited Hispaniola's borderland before disembarking clandestinely in Cuba. He travelled between Dajabón and Ouanaminthe and, while in the

---

[1] Adams, Hoelscher and Till, 'Place in Context', p. xix.
[2] Sommer, pp. 66–7.

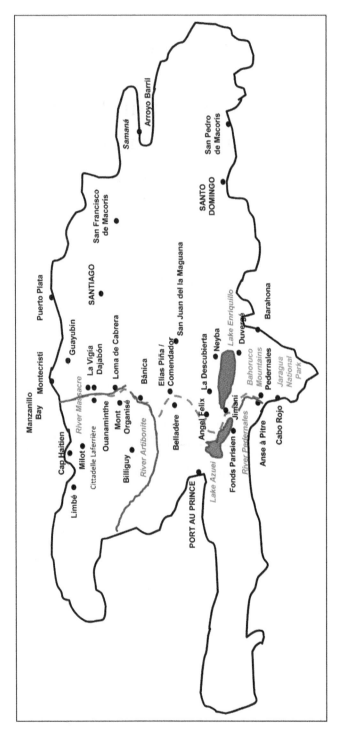

Figure 9. Map of the border and borderland of Hispaniola. The borderline was agreed on in 1936 and remains the same today. This map highlights some of the places mentioned in Chapters 5 to 11.

Dominican Republic, resided temporarily in Montecristi, also close to the border. Martí was not the only Cuban who found sanctuary in Montecristi: Antonio Maceo, for example, had preceded him in March 1880 and one of his daughters was buried in the local cemetery for a long time.[3] As a matter of fact, Montecristi played an important role in the Cuban War of Liberation not only because it gave shelter to Martí and other Cuban revolutionaries but because it was there that the official document of the Cuban Revolutionary Party – the Manifesto of Montecristi – was written by Martí and signed by him and Máximo Gómez in Gómez's house on 25 March 1895.[4] Maximo Gómez, who was a Dominican, was born in Baní, in the south of the Dominican Republic; he owned tobacco in the area around Montecristi and this was an influential factor in his decision to temporarily relocate there.

At the end of the nineteenth century, in fact, Montecristi was an attractive place for foreign businessmen, tradesmen, and workers. The arrival of Spanish, Italians, Haitians, Arabs, Germans, Cubans, North Americans, and *cocolos* (a term which generally defines coloured people from the Anglophone and Francophone Caribbean) contributed to create an 'authentic ethnic mosaic.'[5] The architectonic profile of the entire province of Montecristi, which, at the time, also included the areas around Dajabón and Santiago Rodríguez, was influenced by the presence of Anglo-Caribbean migrants as witnessed by the numerous buildings of Victorian and Anglo-Caribbean style which are still to be found there, such as the Victorian summerhouse or bandstand in the park of Dajabón, which has been identified as one of the four main landmarks of the northern borderland.[6]

Significantly, another important landmark of the area is the imposing clock tower of Montecristi, apparently built by the same engineering company that constructed the Eiffel Tower in Paris: when it was positioned in the very centre of the city Martí is supposed to have exclaimed: 'this clock will mark the exact time of Cuba's independence.'[7] This impressive clock was

---

[3] Rafael Darío Herrera, *Montecristi entre campeches y bananos* (Santo Domingo: Editora Búho, 2006), p. 46 note 49.

[4] Gómez's house in the centre of the city has now become a museum where one can still see the very table on which the two revolutionaries signed the Manifesto.

[5] Herrera, *Montecristi entre campeches y bananos*, p. 67.

[6] Herrera, *Montecristi entre campeches y bananos*, p. 69. The others are the tower clock of Montecristi, the Altar Votivo de la República Dominicana in Dajabón, and the Church of Altagracia in Loma de Cabrera: see Reyes, *Cuentos y leyendas*, drawings pp. 15, 13, 14, and 16 respectively.

[7] Herrera, *Montecristi entre campeches y bananos*, p. 78. Dates, however, do not seem to agree here as Herrera, who reports Martí's words, also reports that the clock tower was inaugurated on 29 June 1895, when Martí was already dead.

Figure 10. Victorian summerhouse or bandstand in the park of Dajabón (photograph: Maria Cristina Fumagalli).

meant to celebrate the town's cosmopolitanism and economic stability and was purchased as a result of a public fundraising operation masterminded by Don Benigno Daniel Conde Váquez, a wealthy Venezuelan who had lived in Montecristi and worked for a long time for Casa Jimenes, an important exporting company based in the city.

The proximity of a major city such as Cap-Haïtien, the political and economic independence of the Dominican borderland from central government, and the liberalization of commerce with Haiti established in 1874 clearly benefited Casa Jimenes, whose founder entertained solid relationships with Haitian tradesmen and could speak French fluently because he had lived in Haiti as a child.[8] To begin with, the activities of Casa Jimenes rested primarily on the exportation of *campeche* or campeachy-wood, a small, thorny tree (*Haematoxylon campechianum*) whose brown-red heartwood is the source of haematoxylin, a purple textile dye which is

---

[8] Herrera, *Montecristi entre campeches y bananos*, p. 91. In the Dominican Republic Spanish was proclaimed as the official language in 1812.

Figure 11.
The clocktower
of Montecristi
(photograph: Maria
Cristina Fumagalli).

still used today. The campeachy-wood industry gave the impulse for the unregulated exploitation of natural resources for private interests: as a matter of fact, by 1940, the province of Montecristi was left with only a few trees of commercial value.[9] Casa Jimenes soon began to export products other than campeachy-wood, such as coffee, cotton, vegetable wool, honey, and agave, all of which were cultivated by Haitians and Dominicans in the mountains. A significant portion of these products was obtained from Haitian peasants via more than two thousand agents operating between Montecristi and Dajabón, in the northern part of Haiti and along the border.[10] Casa Jimenes, in fact, absorbed all the goods produced by Haitian and Dominican peasants but also controlled all the commercial activities of the frontier, the majority of which were realized with the *gourde*, the Haitian currency that, at the time, circulated as far inland as Santiago.[11]

---

[9] Herrera, *Montecristi entre campeches y bananos*, pp. 44–5.
[10] Herrera, *Montecristi entre campeches y bananos*, p. 48.
[11] Derby, 'Haitians, Magic, and Money', p. 500. The Dominican peso was introduced

In his *War Diaries* Martí noted that the prosperity of the city of Montecristi had not filtered through to other parts of the Dominican borderland. Crossing the River Massacre between Dajabón and Ouanaminthe, Martí highlighted, as Moreau de Saint-Méry had done more than a century earlier, the difference between 'sad Dajabón,' with its 'tumble-down houses, a few scattered gardens, dry ground, and the tight clusters of trees around the Bel Air fort,' and what he called 'the Negro side,' where, 'suddenly,' one could find 'mango, guanabana, custard apple, palm, and banana trees everywhere.' Martí managed to take a good look around while his passport was being stamped by the Dominican consul and observed that the houses in Ouanaminthe were not 'built of palm leaves and yagua, [and] leprous and dusty,' as on the Dominican side. The sugar-mill compound was 'clean and full of fruit trees, with a good fence'; the houses were 'plastered with unpainted mud [...] with roofs of dried blackish straw and doors and windows of planed wood, with solid latches,' and carefully decorated; he also spotted 'Viennese chairs' in the 'big houses' with 'cheerful hanging balconies.' Overall, Martí found Ouanaminthe to be 'an animated border town' where he detected the presence of 'life and faith' and the Dajabón–Ouanaminthe border crossing a busy place where people came and went and Haitians and Dominicans talked to one another 'at the edge of the ford.'[12]

What particularly captured Martí's attention, however, was the presence of smugglers and contrabandists. As we have seen, smuggling had always been a feature of the area, but in the nineteenth century it intensified, particularly during the War of Restoration (1863–65), when Dominican patriots exchanged arms for agricultural products and livestock with Haitian tradesmen.[13] In 1893, two years before Martí arrived in Montecristi, President Ulises Heureux, anxious to secure his position against foreign and internal threats, and pressed by financial difficulties, had allowed a number of capitalists from the United States (including the Secretary of State and government officials), who operated under the name of San Domingo Improvement Company, to take over the interests of the Dutch Westerndorp & Company. Westerndorp had repeatedly loaned vast amounts of money to Heureux in exchange for 30 per cent of the revenues of the custom houses

---

in 1844 to replace the Haitian *gourde* but was not established as a national currency until the Trujillo administration.

[12] José Martí, 'War Diaries: Part I – From Montecristi to Cap-Haïtien', in *Selected Writings*, trans. and ed. E. Allen (New York: Penguin, 2002), pp. 350–414, pp. 361–3. Before the 1940s, overall, Haitian border towns were more opulent and refined than the Dominican ones (Derby, 'Haitians, Magic, and Money', p. 513).

[13] Herrera, *Montecristi entre campeches y bananos*, p. 50.

of the country. This takeover gave the United States unprecedented influence in Dominican affairs: by 1895–96 the Dominican Republic was completely mortgaged to the Improvement Company without any hope of recuperating its customs revenues, a fact that brings to the fore, once again, the link between global politics and the Hispaniola borderland.[14] The presence of *contrabandistas* and smugglers in Dajabón–Ouanaminthe prompted Martí to write that 'when tariffs are unjust, or border justice is vengeful, smuggling is the people's right of insurrection. The smuggler is the brave man who takes risks, the cunning man who deceives the powerful, and the rebel in whom others see and admire themselves.' Martí adds that he was not the only one who regarded illicit trading activities favourably: 'smuggling,' he explains, 'comes to be loved and defended, as the true justice.' Martí also celebrates the mutual advantage that the permeability of the border afforded to the locals by sketching this fictional encounter between two smugglers: 'A Haitian goes past on his way to Dajabón to sell his coffee; a Dominican comes up the road toward him, on his way to Haiti to sell his chewing tobacco, his famous *andullo*: "Saludo." "Saludo."'[15]

At the beginning of the twentieth century political unrest began to put Montecristi's economic affluence under threat: in 1902 it was ransacked by the troops of General Horatio Vásquez during the struggle between his supporters and the faction following Juan Isidro Jimenes, the owner of Casa Jimenes.[16] During the government of Ramón Cáceres (1906–11), many of his opponents operated in the province of Montecristi, which, as a result, was officially declared to be in a state of siege. In 1912 the so-called *Linea Noroeste* (the north-west line, the area between Santiago and Montecristi) became the theatre of a bloody civil war between those loyal to President Eladio Victoria and those who sided with General Desiderio Arias, who had been a supporter of Jimenes.[17] Arias seized the border customs and facilitated Haitian immigration along with his sidekick, a Haitian called Rosilien – a fact that reinforced the notion that the residents of the borderland from both sides of the frontier were colluding against state power.[18] Considered a bandit by the North Americans who occupied the country in 1916, Arias was imprisoned and spent the majority of the occupation under custody.

---

[14] Moya Pons, *The Dominican Republic*, pp. 271, 267, 274.

[15] Martí, 'War Diaries', pp. 363–4, italics in the text.

[16] Herrera, *Montecristi entre campeches y bananos*, p. 83.

[17] Nancie L. González, 'Desiderio Arias: Caudillo, Bandit, and Culture Hero', *The Journal of American Folklore*, 85. 335 (1972), pp. 42–50, p. 48.

[18] Matibag, *Haitian-Dominican Counterpoint*, p. 131; Derby, 'Haitians, Magic, and Money', p. 503.

In 1930 he supported Trujillo against Vásquez (whom he considered to be too pro-American) but soon turned against the future *Jefe*, who ordered his assassination in 1931: according to some, his head was cut off and brought to Trujillo; others claim that it was paraded in the streets of Santiago as a warning before his remains were buried in Montecristi, his native province; others have recorded (or 'fabricated') the 'legend' according to which a 'ghost' of Arias haunted the borderland after his death.[19] Arias clearly embodies the rebellious and unstable borderland: for some of its current inhabitants, such a turbulent past is the reason behind the neglect on the part of the central government from which the area has since suffered and something they want to distance themselves from as much as possible; for others, it is still a history to be proud of, in particular Arias's resistance to the interference of the United States in Dominican affairs, which also had a huge impact on border relations.[20]

In 1907 the porous frontier between the two countries became even more enmeshed in global politics when the Dominican–American Convention 'brought the state into the daily lives of border residents for the first time' by turning over customs collections directly to the United States (no longer a company such as the San Domingo Improvement Company) and by imposing, for the first time, 'effective accounting on Haitian–Dominican trade with high fines exacted from contraband violation.'[21] These restrictions on commerce were not popular with the locals: the rich families of Dajabón lamented the imposition of taxes on imports from Haiti such as silk, wines, and fish and the same could be said for other measures aimed at regulating and constricting across-the-border activities. For example, the border was militarized with the introduction of a *Guardia de Frontera* in 1907 and, in the late 1920s, an identification card was required to cross the border; this was to be substituted, in the 1930s, by a passport, visa, or certificate of good conduct, and even by a certificate of good health.[22]

Such legal requirements confirm Derby's suggestion that the United States' occupation of both countries (Haiti 1915–34 and Dominican Republic 1916–24) contributed to changing the way in which frontier residents perceived their relationship to the two states, even if the border remained relatively porous. The businessmen of the borderland regretted the fact

---

[19] González, 'Desiderio Arias', pp. 43–4; Marcio Veloz Maggiolo, 'La dictadura y su magia', in *Los retornos del Jefe*, Bismar Galán and Marcio Veloz Maggiolo (Santo Domingo: Editorial Santuario, 2009), pp. 9–45, pp. 20–21.

[20] Herrera, *Montecristi entre campeches y bananos*, p. 84.

[21] Derby, 'Haitians, Magic, and Money', pp. 490, 499, 502.

[22] Derby, 'Haitians, Magic, and Money', p. 502.

that the bureaucratization of the Dominican state had transformed their 'territory' – characterized by a very permeable border – into what they considered an over-bureaucratized 'province' controlled by a central power.[23] Local customs inspectors, however, illicitly benefited from the across-the-border trade they were supposed to control and most local officials realized that it was in their interests to cooperate with Haiti.[24] Montecristi was one of the municipal authorities that did not agree with restrictions on border transit: in 1920, for example, it petitioned for 'the free passage of Haitians' because this was absolutely 'indispensable for commerce.'[25] Despite these restrictions, after 1916, the date when the United States' occupation of the Dominican Republic began, Montecristi was still an important commercial hub and saw the establishment of various vice-consulates (Spain, Italy, Denmark, Norway, United States). Many international banks opened their branches there and in the early 1930s salt, which had always been important for the economy of the city, became crucial to its prosperity to the point that it was widely recognized that Montecristi 'marched forward at the pace of the salt production.'[26] Trujillo's later expropriation of the local *salinas* to create the *Salinera Nacional* – a monopoly from which he gained a net profit of US $6 million per year – gave rise to strong feelings of aversion towards the dictatorship among the citizens of Montecristi, as testified by their massive participation in the *Movimiento 14 de Junio*, an anti-Trujillo left-wing clandestine movement.[27]

✳✳✳

The poet, playwright, novelist, literary critic, and musician Manuel Rueda was born in Montecristi in 1921. At that point 21 per cent of the population of the town were considered to be of Haitian origin and in the province resided 38 or 39 per cent of all 'Haitians' living in the Dominican Republic.[28] Demographic figures, however, are quite problematic if one considers that, at the time, it was not entirely clear how to define what being 'Haitian' or 'Dominican' might have meant: many 'Haitians' had lived in the province

---

[23] Prestol Castillo, *El Masacre*, pp. 47–8.
[24] Derby, 'Haitians, Magic, and Money', pp. 500–501.
[25] Gobernación de Monte Cristy 21 (1919–21), 10 January 1920, quoted in Derby, 'Haitians, Magic, and Money', p. 501.
[26] Herrera, *Montecristi entre campeches y bananos*, pp. 57–60.
[27] Herrera, *Montecristi entre campeches y bananos*, p. 60.
[28] Herrera, *Montecristi entre campeches y bananos*, p. 72; Bernardo Vega, *Trujillo y Haití*, 3 vols (Santo Domingo: Fundación Cultural Dominicana, 1988–2009), vol. II, p. 344.

for a very long time and many had been born in the Montecristi area and were, according to the Constitution, Dominican citizens.[29] Ethnic 'Haitians' were well integrated into the life of the city and had incorporated Dominican idioms and habits: some were artisans and some doctors who practised in the area.[30] In the countryside many were cultivating land which had been neglected by Dominicans or looking after their fields and livestock for very little pay – a local commentator went as far as equating their predicament, repeatedly, with the plight of 'slaves.'[31] Between 1870 and 1930 many wealthy households employed 'Haitian' servants.[32]

In *Bienvenida y la noche: Crónicas de Montecristi* (1994), where he recounts the 1929 wedding between Rafael Trujillo, who at the time was still an army colonel, and Bienvenida Ricardo, a member of the local elite, Rueda repeatedly refers to a Haitian servant buried under shopping parcels.[33] Rueda, who was only eight years old at the time of the wedding, remembers this important event in the life of his native town because his grandmother (reluctantly) allowed her friend Eustasinia Ricardo, Bienvenida's mother, to organize the wedding party in a spacious house which was slowly being built for the Rueda family. Rueda's young age at the time of the wedding probably explains the simultaneous presence, in the title, of *crónica* ('chronicle'), a term which signposts his attempt at a faithful transposition of events, and *novela* ('novel'), a label which acknowledges both his impossibility to recall with exactitude what really happened and also an unwillingness to separate 'naked facts' from the 'colouration' that retrospective recollection, governed by hindsight and sixty-five years of experience, imparted to them.

In 1929, we are told, the wedding had to be celebrated in Rueda's house because this was Trujillo's second marriage and he could not marry

---

[29] Lauren Derby and Richard Turits, 'Temwayaj Kout Kouto, 1937 / Eyewitness to the Genocide', in *Revolutionary Freedoms: A History of Survival, Strength and Imagination in Haiti*, ed. C. Accilien, J. Adams and E. Méléance (Coconut Creek, FL: Caribbean Studies Press, 2006), pp. 137–43, p. 138; Herrera, *Montecristi entre campeches y bananos*, p. 72.

[30] Herrera, *Montecristi entre campeches y bananos*, p. 73; Prestol Castillo, *El Masacre*, p. 51.

[31] Prestol Castillo, *El Masacre*, pp. 48, 89, 120.

[32] Prestol Castillo, *El Masacre*, pp. 48, 89, 120.

[33] Manuel Rueda, *Bienvenida y la noche: Crónicas de Montecristi: A novela* (Santo Domingo: Fundación Cultural Dominicana, 1994), pp. 61, 66, 85. Subsequent page references will be given in parentheses in the text. Bienvenida Ricardo was a member of the business elite of Montecristi which had relatively recently arrived in town from Navarrete and succeeded, with some difficulties, in being accepted by the locals. Her father was a close relative of Balaguer (Herrera, *Montecristi entre campeches y bananos*, p. 96; Rueda, *Bienvenida y la noche*, p. 43).

Bienvenida in a church; he had planned to use Montecristi's *Club del Comercio* – which had played an important role in the social life of Montecristi since the beginning of the twentieth century[34] – but he was refused access (allegedly) because the correct procedure for the request had not been followed (p. 86). The committee, in fact, had denied access to Trujillo because, for Montecristi's high society, despite his prospective brilliant military career, the overly ambitious colonel was lacking in social stature and aiming too high with Bienvenida: Rueda remembers that he was deeply resented for marrying her in order to force his way into a superior class which was resisting him (p. 42).

The *Club del Comercio*, moreover, was fairly cosmopolitan and counted black people among its members, including individuals from Turks, Curaçao, and Haiti. Admission to the club, in fact, did not have overt economic, political, racial, or ethnical restrictions but depended on the prospective member's ability to conform to certain ethical standards, which went hand in hand with a relatively high level of education: professionals and educated people, in fact, were admitted almost by default.[35] During his wedding party Trujillo clearly perceived the hostility of the locals and, after the wedding, before leaving Montecristi with his wife, he delivered a threatening speech in which he swore that he was going to take revenge for all the insults that he had received during his visit (p. 154). Trujillo, however, was very grateful to Rueda's grandmother for letting him use her house: while thanking her for her kindness, he reassured her that she would be compensated for it (p. 145). It is well known that Trujillo's power as a dictator depended to a large degree on his distribution of (often overgenerous) 'gifts' which immediately transformed their recipients into indebted subjects.[36] Rueda's grandmother, with remarkable foresight, made it abundantly clear that she had no desire to consent to the subjection which would have resulted from accepting Trujillo's offer: 'I have put my house at your disposal in the spirit of friendship,' she replied, 'you do not have to return the favour' (p. 146).

In *Bienvenida y la noche* the 'borrowed house' plays a central role in the development of the narrative. Rueda describes in detail how it was quickly transformed as soon as Trujillo was permitted to use it. Things which had been there for a long time were removed and discarded (pp. 94–5), while army vans, unashamedly redeployed for private purposes, transported and put in place furniture which suddenly appeared as if from nowhere, as well

---

[34] Herrera, *Montecristi entre campeches y bananos*, p. 98.

[35] Herrera, *Montecristi entre campeches y bananos*, pp. 98–9.

[36] Lauren Derby, *The Dictator's Seduction: Politics and the Popular Imagination in the Era of Trujillo* (Durham, NC: Duke University Press, 2009), pp. 257–66.

as palm trees which decorated the outside of the house (p. 96). This display
of power was Trujillo's way of responding to the 'offences' he had received
from the local population; it was clear that, at that point, as Rueda explains,
he felt confident that his glory was both unquestionable and imminent and
acted accordingly and with typical arrogance (p. 113). In actual fact, during
his wedding party the colonel displayed many traits which later characterized
him as a dictator: he was self-conscious, self-obsessed, and immensely vain.
Rueda explains that 'he did not care about what was happening around
him but at the same time nothing escaped him. He changed men into
objects, and favourable or unfavourable situations in conjunctures he was
perfectly able to manage' (p. 147). Observing Trujillo's behaviour, Rueda's
grandmother realized 'that he was more interested in appearances rather
than in substance' (p. 147). Trujillo's choice of music for the wedding
party was also significant: he invited a *conjunto típico* (musical band) that
specialized in *merengue*, his favourite dance, which, as Rueda reminds us,
became one of the dictator's most powerful vehicles of populistic propaganda
(pp. 117–19). There are several other moments in Rueda's book when the
events in Montecristi in 1929 can be read as a prefiguration of what was
to come. Trujillo's arrival in Montecristi, for example, is perceived as the
entrance of a general to a conquered city (p. 80); unexpectedly, the military
convoy which accompanied him did not go straight to Bienvenida's house
but defiantly passed by the park with the public clock and climbed the hill
where the Fortaleza is situated. From its top, Trujillo contemplated at length
a landscape on which, in less than ten years, he was going to leave his mark
by orchestrating an utter transformation of the social fabric of the area.

In 1937, eight years after his stay in Montecristi, Trujillo, who had become
president of the Dominican Republic in 1930, ordered his army to slaughter
all 'Haitians' living in what was then the northern military department of
the country.[37] The killings began on 28 September 1937, intensified on 2
October and lasted until 8 October, but sporadic murders continued until
5 November.[38] The massacre – also known as *el corte* ('the cutting,' 'the
harvesting,' or 'the mowing-down' in Spanish) or *kout kouto* ('stabbing' in

---

[37] At the time the country was divided into two military departments: the Southern
Department and the Northern Department – the military outpost of La Cumbre,
in the north of Villa Altagracia, was the main point of separation between the two
departments (Vega, *Trujillo y Haití*, vol. II, p. 39).
[38] Vega, *Trujillo y Haití*, vol. II, p. 39.

Haitian Creole) – took place mostly in the north-west of the country. Apart from the area around Bánica, which is adjacent to the northern district, there were no killings in the southern provinces in October 1937 but, during the first half of 1938, hundreds of ethnic Haitians were killed there and thousands deported to Haiti.[39] Estimates of the number of *el corte*'s victims are still disputed and range from 10,000 to 40,000;[40] the executions were carried out mostly with machetes and knives instead of guns and rifles to make it look like a popular insurrection against Haitians who were stealing livestock.

In *El Masacre se pasa a pie* the then magistrate of Dajabón, Freddy Prestol Castillo, repeatedly mentions the fact that Haitians 'came in the night' to steal cattle; he also claims that their thieving ruined some Dominican families who had members in the army and who were particularly keen to take part in the massacre to take revenge.[41] Unlike *Bienvenida y la noche*, which was composed years after the momentous wedding was witnessed by a very young Rueda, Prestol Castillo's book, which was written in secret in 1937 but published only in 1973 for fear of repercussions, is a personal account of the massacre seen from the eyes of an adult who had arrived in Dajabón precisely during *el corte* (p. 25). Prestol Castillo, in fact, was not from the borderland: his landowning sugar family had lost its fortune and he had lived and studied in Santo Domingo until, in need of a job, he had to accept, reluctantly, a post in Dajabón, a place he considered a remote outpost. The 'Haitians' he met there are described as a 'primitive race' (p. 95) and even animalized: they can 'smell' livestock like 'leopard[s]'; their feet are 'enormous' 'paws'; their language is like 'an animal's howl' and when they speak they are as 'noisy and annoying' as 'parrots' (pp. 97–100).[42] Despite his obvious prejudices, however, Prestol Castillo was deeply shocked by the 1937 violence and calls himself an 'accomplice-witness' of the events for not speaking up against the atrocities (p. 173).

El Masacre se pasa a pie, in fact, is often contradictory and betrays the author's deep anxiety as well as his inability and unwillingness to either fully embrace or resolutely reject dominant discourses. As we have seen, in line with the regime's propaganda, Prestol Castillo refers to 'Haitians' as

---

[39] Turits, 'A World Destroyed', p. 591; Vega, *Trujillo y Haití*, vol. II, p. 40.
[40] Vega, *Trujillo y Haití*, vol. II, pp. 352–3.
[41] Prestol Castillo, *El Masacre*, pp. 95–101, 107–8, 127. From now one-page references to this text will be given in parentheses in the text.
[42] Prestol Castillo does not distinguish between long-term residents and occasional border-crossers but goes along with the regime in the identification of Haitian–Dominicans as, unequivocally, Haitians.

'thieves' but he also explains that they mostly returned in the night to steal
the produce they had grown on Dominican land for years, or came to take
the livestock they had long nurtured 'as if it were family' (pp. 93–4, 99). This
suggests that at least some of the thievery took place *after* the massacre and
also that the 'Haitians' might even have been somehow 'entitled' to do it:
'Haiti had sown the Dominican land for many years. Now it wanted to come
back for the harvest' (pp. 97, 94). Prestol Castillo goes as far as wondering
to whom the land really belonged: to the 'Haitians', who had transformed
it into orchards, or to those Dominicans who had left it uncultivated before
1937 and would continue to do so after the elimination of the Haitians?
(p. 89). We are also introduced to Don Francisco, whose land straddled the
frontier and was cultivated by 'Haitians', who also looked after his livestock:
before the massacre, when some of his cattle were stolen, Don Francisco
was not too worried because he knew that he was still making a huge profit
with the low salary he was paying those who worked for (and occasionally
stole from) him. While he normally cursed the government for introducing
taxes and other measures which hampered his profitable trade with the
neighbouring country, when his property was visited by the army engaged in
el corte he complained, hypocritically, about the Haitians and their 'stealing'
(pp. 117–22). The example of Don Francisco provides us with a different
perspective on 'Haitian thefts' which were identified, crucially, *a posteriori*,
as one of the 1937 massacre's causes.[43] Prestol Castillo also points out that,
after *el corte*, those who had found refuge in Haiti were somehow forced
to turn to criminality because of their and their children's 'hunger' and
adds that some of them even resorted to supernatural assistance to secure
protection and their family's survival: he mentions a desperate father who
went to Limbé – a significant site, as it is considered to be the place where
the 1791 revolt began[44] – to solicit the help of a powerful *bocó* (sorcerer).
His story shows how Dominicans strongly believed in and deeply feared the
power of Haitian magic and how the two peoples shared the same system of
belief, even if Haitians here seem to have had the 'monopoly of the sacred'
(pp. 95, 97, 98, 100).[45]

The way in which traditional discourses which identified Haitians with
black magic, horrific violence, and savagism could affect the Dominicans'
collective unconscious is vividly illustrated by a nightmare that Prestol
Castillo recounts having had while feverish after *el corte*. During his delirium
Prestol Castillo is 'visited' by Touissant who, asserting that the island is 'one

---

[43]   Vega, *Trujillo y Haití*, vol. II, pp. 33, 39; vol. I, p. 323.

[44]   Fick, *Making of Haiti*, p. 95.

[45]   Derby, 'Haitians, Magic, and Money', p. 517.

and indivisible,' professes that he will kill all the inhabitants of the Spanish side (pp. 179–80). In a bloodbath in which the 'fierce Haitian cannibals' destroy churches and houses and kill both whites and blacks from Santo Domingo, Dessalines, the border-crosser Padre Vásquez,[46] and the Emperor Faustin Soulouque also make an appearance (pp. 181–82). The trail of death and destruction left by the Haitian army led by Dessalines and Christophe in 1805, the abuses committed by Boyer during the unification of the island (1822–44), and the policy of aggression orchestrated by Soulouque in 1849 and 1855 have all been amply documented and capitalized upon to highlight what Martínez has called 'the fatal conflict model.' Arguably, however, this nightmare can also be seen as a projection, on its very victims, of the violence that, in 1937, the Dominican state was perpetrating against the 'Haitians': interestingly, in fact, Prestol Castillo ends his account by 'meditating' on the 'present history' 'written in blood' that was unfolding in front of his very eyes, and the history of the crimes committed by the Haitians that he had learnt 'at school' when he was a 'child' (p. 182). We do not know the conclusions that Prestol Castillo drew from his 'meditation' – he does not reveal his thoughts to us – but the mere contraposition and comparison between Dominican and Haitian brutality somehow explodes the received notion that barbarism and ferocity pertained only to one side of the border. On the other hand, however, when he envisages that 'hungry' Haitians will forever cross the border to steal from Dominicans, Prestol Castillo ends up fostering the notion of an ongoing threat of 'invasion' which has traditionally characterized anti-Haitian discourse both before and, as we will see in the following chapters, after 1937 (p. 101).

In 1937 Dominican civilians and local authorities responded in different ways to the massacre. Prestol Castillo reports how many risked their own lives by hiding and helping 'Haitians' to flee the military (pp. 39–40, 65–9, 99). Others, usually civil local authorities loyal to Trujillo, collaborated with the regime, locating and identifying 'Haitians' for the guards. Some civilians were given the task of burying and burning the corpses but it appears that, generally, they did not take an active part in the massacre, with the exception of prisoners recruited in Dominican jails (the so-called *reservistas* or 'reserves'), who were promised both land and freedom for their services. Prestol Castillo calls them 'criminal workhands' (p. 53), points out that many of them were callous murderers who had no problem with the atrocities they were asked to commit, and denounces various episodes

---

[46] Padre Vásquez is the 'border-crosser' priest accompanied by a *galipote* in Deive's *Viento Negro* (Chapter 4) and one of the targets of Picquenard's hatred in *Adonis*, where he vilifies Père Philémon (Chapter 2).

in which the Dominican military and these 'reserves' stole the properties of those they had killed or went as far as trying to steal gold teeth from corpses (pp. 72–4, 91,137–43). Prestol Castillo, however, also insists that other *reservistas* were just petty thieves who found it extremely difficult to participate in the killings and to cope with the pressure and the violence they were forced to witness and take part in, and is very sympathetic towards them, considering them victims of the 'dictatorship' that, rather problematically, is what he ultimately blames for *el corte*. Going as far as calling them 'martyrs like the Haitians,' Prestol Castillo explains how some lost their minds or were turned into 'alcoholic panthers' by the events (pp. 40, 53–7, 108–9; 113, 123–8; 131–4).

The province of Montecristi was the area which was most affected by the murderous activity of Trujillo's army. Here the massacre began in La Granja, a small village near Montecristi whose mayor was himself a political exile from Haiti. Three or four days before the massacre began in earnest he was informed that some Haitians and Haitian–Dominicans had been killed in a way that, according to him, clearly implicated the *guardia* or local police. He desperately tried to convince the Haitians and Haitian–Dominicans residing in his community to flee to Haiti but, unfortunately, many did not listen to him and, as a result, the Haitian and Haitian–Dominican population of La Granja was exterminated. After that, because of its proximity to the sea, La Granja became a *matadero* ('slaughterhouse'): corpses were thrown in the ocean to be devoured by sharks and thousands were forced off the pier at the port of Montecristi by Trujillo's military. This was one of the few instances in which the soldiers were not careful to convey the impression that the slaughter of Haitians and Haitian–Dominicans was the result of a spontaneous uprising of local civilians. The waves carried limbs and other body parts to the shore, where they were taken by dogs as far as the city of Montecristi itself.[47]

There is still a fair amount of debate surrounding what actually triggered the massacre, as the idea that it might have been a reaction to Haitians crossing the border to steal Dominican properties has been discarded as an after-the-fact justification.[48] Border relations at that point were as complex as ever: in 1936 Trujillo and the Haitian president Sténio Vincent, encouraged by the government of the United States, which considered it a useful move to maintain political stability on the island, had signed additional clauses

---

[47] Herrera, *Montecristi entre campeches y bananos*, p. 136; Eric Paul Roorda, *The Dictator Next Door: The Good Neighbour Policy and the Trujillo Regime in the Dominican Republic, 1930–1945* (Durham, NC: Duke University Press, 1998), p. 131.
[48] Vega, *Trujillo y Haití*, vol. II, p. 33, 39, vol. I, p. 323.

to the 1929 border delimitation agreement previously subscribed to by both countries. Yet, despite laws which aimed at making border crossings more difficult, migration from Haiti to the Dominican Republic was continuing relatively undisturbed and people still circulated more or less freely between the two countries, whose governments did not have much control on the borderland.[49] The Dominican historian Bernardo Vega has argued that there is evidence that, after Trujillo became president in 1930, the Haitian presence in the province dramatically fluctuated. Initially, Vega writes, it diminished, partly owing to an overall reduction of agricultural production and to the effects of the salt monopoly created by Trujillo: he quotes as evidence the official census of 1935, which counts only 3816 'Haitians,' as opposed to the 10,872 reported in the 1920 census. However, Vega continues, in the years following 1935, owing to the return to Haiti of tens of thousands of *braceros* who had been expelled from Cuba, the number of Haitian migrants in the Dominican northern borderland might have risen quite substantially, bringing the overall Haitian presence to more than 11,000. Such a dramatic increase in less than two years, Vega insists, was bound to create social and political tensions: according to Vega, in fact, one of the main factors which caused the massacre was the desire of the Dominican ruling classes to 'whiten' their nation.[50]

Lauren Derby and Richard Turits agree that the 'Haitian' presence in the area was substantial in 1937, but they dismiss the 1935 census as unrepresentative because it is restricted to documented Haitian migrants and does not provide information on the number of ethnic Haitians, mostly small farmers, who lived in the province and who, in many cases, were actually born in the Dominican Republic and were therefore, legally speaking, Dominicans. Alternative sources estimate that residents of Haitian descent in the area between Dajabón and Restauración numbered 17,000 or even 30,000 out of a total population of 35,000, while, in the province of Montecristi, they were about 50,000.[51] Derby and Turits, moreover, insist that the real aim of the massacre was not only to 'whiten' the nation but to destroy the frontier's bicultural, bilingual, and transnational Haitian–Dominican communities.[52]

---

[49] Samuel Martínez, *Peripheral Migrants: Haitians and Dominican Republic Sugar Plantations* (Knoxville, TN: The University of Tennessee Press, 1995), p. 44; Turits, 'A World Destroyed'; Derby, 'Haitians, Magic, and Money'; Derby and Turits, 'Temwayaj Kout Kouto, 1937'.

[50] Vega, *Trujillo y Haití*, vol. II, pp. 343–4, 23–6.

[51] Derby and Turits, 'Temwayaj Kout Kouto, 1937', p. 142 note 4.

[52] Turits, 'A World Destroyed'; Derby, 'Haitians, Magic, and Money'; Derby and Turits, 'Temwayaj Kout Kouto, 1937'.

In the fluid world of the northern borderland, in fact, <u>bilingualism</u> <u>(Spanish and Haitian Creole</u>) was widespread and all sorts of people crossed the border every day, often more than once a day: for example, in a primary school in Ouanaminthe which was attended by numerous pupils whose families lived in Dajabón and its surroundings, 176 out of 267 students lost their parents during the massacre.[53] As noted above, Haitian and Dominican families often had relatives and owned properties on both sides of the border; many Haitian and Haitian–Dominicans who lived in the province of Montecristi were reasonably wealthy and some had many children with local concubines: most of these children escaped to Haiti or were eliminated during the massacre, together with women and children who sold fried fish and other types of food or were employed as domestic workers by the wealthy families of the city. In some cases murders were preceded by expropriation: many Haitian and Haitian–Dominican farmers, artisans, and enterpreneurs were forced to sell their estates at very low prices to Dominican mayors and businessmen in exchange for their lives. During the night, however, they were slaughtered and robbed of the money they had received for their properties: it has been estimated that 20 to 30 per cent of the houses in the town centre of Montecristi used to belong to ethnic Haitians and that many of these residences still belong to the descendants of those who expropriated them at the time.[54]

After the massacre Montecristi also became the stage for what has been called *el gran teatro* ('the great theatre'), as it was there that, in order to be seen to be responding to international pressure, the regime staged the trials and imprisonment of some of the (alleged) civilian perpetrators of the massacre.[55] For that purpose the *alcaldes pedáneos* (submunicipal political authorities) of those sites where the killings took place were asked to select four or five youths who were 'friends of Trujillo'; these young men were then taken to the prison of Montecristi (the *Fortaleza*) and photographed firstly dressed as convicts and then next to other inmates, who were made to pose as dead 'Haitians.' During the trials, for which these 'friends of Trujillo' and some *reservistas* were given clear instructions on what to say by the judges themselves, they were given thirty- to forty-year prison sentences for 'their' crimes. They were, however, freed after only a couple of months of incarceration and rewarded with a substantial sum of money which was delivered to some of them by Trujillo himself.[56]

---

[53] Derby and Turits, 'Temwayaj Kout Kouto, 1937', pp. 138–9.
[54] Herrera, *Montecristi entre campeches y bananos*, p. 138.
[55] Herrera, *Montecristi entre campeches y bananos*, p. 139.
[56] Herrera, *Montecristi entre campeches y bananos*, pp. 139–40; Eudaldo Antonio

Overall, the legacy of the 1937 massacre was a heavy one for the province of Montecristi and had a negative impact upon the cosmopolitan and multi-ethnic nature for which its capital had become famous. It is likely that Trujillo's assassins were given special orders not to eliminate the many Anglo-Caribbean migrants, or *cocolos*, who lived in the province because the British crown protected them, but many left the area after 1937, afraid of being confused with 'Haitians' and eliminated or persecuted.[57] Moreover, until the 1980s the presence of 'Haitians,' so prevalent beforehand, became almost insignificant: as Prestol Castillo put it, *el corte* is synonymous not only with killings but also with 'Exodus' (p. 27). Haitian workers, Prestol Castillo explains, were initially substituted by people recruited in the city's underbelly and by peasants with no land who had been declared 'vagrants' and were transported to the borderland in army trucks. The difference between the Haitians and Haitian–Dominicans who cultivated the land and made it productive and these new arrivals, especially the urban 'riff raff,' he insists, was very striking, as they did not seem keen or able to work and only longed to go back to the city (pp. 163–7). A year after their arrival most of them were sent back to the capital, more destitute than when they arrived (p. 172). By and large, in Prestol Castillo's account, *el corte* seems to have achieved very little and the writer highlights only negative outcomes: if anything, the border appears to be far from sealed, at least as far as 'criminal' activities were concerned; moreover, when productive interactions were brought to an end, the local economy was damaged by the departure and/or elimination of the wealthy professionals who lived in Montecristi and by the sudden lack of a cheap workforce which comprised competent peasants and experienced cattle farmers.

Prestol Castillo also described the post-1937 borderland in *Paisajes y meditaciones de una frontera* ('Landscapes of and meditations on the frontier,' 1943), where, however, the massacre of Haitians and Haitian–Dominicans which had outraged and shocked him so much is never mentioned.[58] This is unsurprising if one considers that *El Masacre se pasa a pie* was published in 1973 (that is, twelve years after Trujillo's death) while *Paisajes y meditaciones* is a collection of short essays published in 1943 which uncritically embraces

---

Hiciano, *Cronología de un pueblo: antología de mitos* (Santo Domingo: Alfa y Omega, 1998) pp. 49–55; Prestol Castillo, *El Masacre*, pp. 134–5, 137–43, 145–9, 151–5, 157–61.

[57] Vega, *Trujillo y Haití*, vol. II, p. 36; Herrera, *Montecristi entre campeches y bananos*, p. 71.

[58] We are just told that in 1938 'the Haitians […] had gone back to their country': see Freddy Prestol Castillo, *Paisajes y meditaciones de una frontera* (Ciudad Trujillo: Editorial Cosmopolita, 1943), p. 27. Page references will be given in parentheses in the text.

the ideological framework of the Trujillato. We are repeatedly told that Trujillo (to whom the volume is dedicated) had dramatically improved the situation in an area of the Dominican Republic which was in need of being claimed back by the state. Every chapter ends with praise for the dictator and, at the end of the book, Prestol Castillo identifies Trujillo as 'the only Dominican leader who has seen the borderland problem clearly' (p. 63). Prestol Castillo argues, in fact, that owing to the pervasive smuggling – he refers to Martí's observations on the topic (pp. 13–14) – and different waves of invasion (the incursions of the buccaneers in colonial times, the political and military occupation of the nineteenth century, and the arrival of migrants and cattle thieves at the beginning of the twentieth century), the borderland was not in line with the rest of the country. Prestol Castillo suggests that, while the Haitians were the 'least evolved blacks of the Antilles' because, when they were slaves, they never assimilated the traits of their European masters (pp. 54, 44), the former slaves on the Dominican side had instead moved away from their African roots and become 'spiritually Spanish' thanks to the fact that they became part of the 'family' in which they worked. Their Spanish masters, in fact (unlike the French) were not simply ruthless slaveholders and businessmen, but pious men who shared their religious beliefs with their slaves (pp. 44–54). Unfortunately, owing to their proximity to Haiti, the inhabitants of the borderland had turned into a hybrid population of *rayanos* or *catisos* 'alien to the [Dominican] authentic reality' and characterized by a 'backward, fetishist and primitive spirit' (pp. 21, 22). Trujillo's 'extraordinary actions' and his plan for Dominicanization of the frontier, Prestol Castillo concludes, were successfully emancipating these people from their 'barbaric isolation,' reintegrating them into the nation, and enabling them to share its authentically Spanish spirit (pp. 11, 32, 56, 46).

∗∗∗

In 1963, in open contrast to Prestol Castillo's enthusiasm for Trujillo's Dominicanization of the borderland – a plan which continued to be supported, after his death, by subsequent administrations – the Montecristeño Rueda referred to the frontier which Trujillo so forcefully imposed during his regime as a *línea* ('line') 'that divides in two, in addition to the land, the spiritual freedom of the islander.'[59] In 'La canción del rayano' ('The song of the borderland dweller') Rueda remembers the happy time before the formal establishment and violent enforcement of the *línea*, as a consequence

---

[59] Rueda, *La criatura terrestre*, p. 26. Page references to this collection will be given in parentheses in the text. I will go back to this collection also in Chapter 8.

Figure 12. Polibio Díaz, *Rayano* (1993) (photograph: Polibio Díaz).

of which his 'ambidextrous' self lost 'any hope of resurrection' (pp. 32, 33). Before the *línea*, he writes, 'the world was entire' and the sea was the only barrier he encountered (pp. 32, 31). When the line on the ground was traced, he felt 'exiled from Eden,' because the same line also cut across him with a curse: 'you will forever be divided' (p. 32). This sense of self-alienation and deep self-division is still evident in *Rayano*, a photograph taken in 1993 by the Dominican artist Polibio Díaz, which constitutes a powerful visual counterpart to Rueda's lines. Polibio Díaz, whose mother was also from Montecristi, was born in Barahona, studied photography in the United States, and is a well-established and internationally recognized artist who has been awarded many prizes for his work; three of his photographs have been selected for the UNESCO permanent collection in Paris and some have been collected in four books entitled *Interiores* (2006), *Una Isla, Un Paisaje* (1998) – which includes a poem by Manuel Rueda dedicated to him – *Espantapájaros del Sur* (1994), and *Imágenes de Carnaval* (1993). *Rayano*, which purposefully does not locate his subjects in any specific part of the borderland in order to represent the *rayana* condition as a whole, portrays a world which is no longer intact: the space in the photograph is roughly split into two halves by the long thin cement threshold of a house we can see only the lower half of. The shadow of the little boy in the middle of the image, which runs parallel to the threshold, does not only underline the division of space at the core of the photograph but also indicates in an evocative and lyrical manner how this division strikes at the very heart of the young boy whose body projects, but also appears to be sliced in two, by his own shadow. None of the people next to him is fully visible to us: we have only access to fragments of their bodies as the frame cuts across them as if it were the curse/*línea* that Rueda denounces in his poem.[60]

Interestingly, Rueda's description, in *Bienvenida y la noche*, of the way in which Trujillo 'cut across' and destroyed the locally-produced wedding cake, richly decorated with swans, angels, flowers, and lace, constitutes one of most evocative metaphors for Trujillo's borderland policy. Contemptuously and menacingly brandishing his solid gold sword instead of the cake cutter, Trujillo smashed into pieces both the 'fragile and beautiful world' of the cake and the mirror tray on which it was standing (p. 150). Rueda recalls that when his grandmother saw the 'line of death' of Trujillo's sword destroying the wedding cake and cracking the mirror, she considered it as a bad omen (p. 152). Rueda's grandmother was right in her interpretation: not only was Bienvenida's marriage with Trujillo an unhappy one but the 'fragile and beautiful world' devastated by Trujillo reminds one of the pre-massacre borderland whose equilibrium and social dynamics were soon to be completely shattered.

Prior to 1937, as we have seen, the largely bilingual population of the borderland formed a bicultural and transnational community which included Dominicans, Haitian–Dominicans, and Haitians and in which ethnic Haitians were not necessarily considered inferior. The 'fragility' of that world identified by Rueda has to do with the fact that processes of nation-building and state formation were slowly beginning to impinge on the way in which Haitians and Haitian–Dominicans were being perceived and in which Dominicans perceived themselves. Derby argues that the groundwork for a new conceptualization of what was labelled as the 'Haitian problem' was being laid in the years which preceded the 1937 massacre; it revolved around the progressive identification of Haitians with dangerous magic, money which self-multiplied, filth, disorder, and the callous pursuit of self-interest.[61] These forms of differentiation, however, were gradually being processed and negotiated and did not necessarily translate into notions

---

[60] Sagás explains that interviews carried out in the 1990s suggested that most conservatives still considered the *rayanos* as merely Haitians who happened to have been born on Dominican territory rather than fully-fledged Dominican citizens (*Race and Politics*, p. 92).

[61] Derby, 'Haitians, Magic, and Money'.

of otherness or marginality and did not prevent integration and bonds of intimacy: one Haitian refugee from the massacre, for example, recalled that 'although there were two sides, the people were one, united.'[62]

---

[62] Derby, 'Haitians, Magic, and Money'; Derby and Turits, 'Temwayaj Kout Kouto, 1937', p. 140.

Chapter Six

The dream of creating one people from two lands mixed together: 1937 and borderland Utopia

Marcio Veloz Maggiolo, *El hombre del acordeón* (2003), Jacques Stephen Alexis, 'Of the Marvellous Realism of the Haitians' (1956) and *Compère Général Soleil* (1955), René Philoctète, *Le peuple des terres mêlées* (1989), Edwidge Danticat, *The Farming of Bones* (1998)

The fluid world of Rueda's *raya* where, as we have seen, according to one of the eyewitnesses of the massacre, the people from the two sides of the border felt a deep sense of unity,[1] is vividly reconstructed in *El hombre del acordeón* ('The accordion man,' 2003), one of the novels under scrutiny here. This chapter presents four fictional recreations of the events written between 1955 and 2003 by writers who had not directly experienced the 1937 events: three of the authors featured here were born in Haiti, one in the Dominican Republic; two have resided mostly on the island while two have spent a remarkable part of their lives abroad. Yet, despite their differences of origin, context, and approach, they can all be seen as committed utopian thinkers animated by an urge to investigate the complex and troubled past of the borderland in order to identify in it a promise for a better future. Crucially, they all seem to imply, more or less forcefully, that this promise can be kept.

The first of the works analysed here is the most recent: *El hombre del acordeón*, by the Dominican poet, novelist, archaeologist, anthropologist, and critic Marcio Veloz Maggiolo, who weaves a vivid and diversified tapestry with the complex human, political, and cultural fabric of the northern borderland.[2] Born in Santo Domingo in 1963, Veloz Maggiolo is a

---

[1] Derby and Turits, 'Temwayaj Kout Kouto, 1937', p. 140.

[2] Marcio Veloz Maggiolo, *El hombre del acordeón* (Madrid: Siruela, 2003). Page references will be given in parentheses in the text.

prolific author who has received multiple awards (Premio Nacional de Poesía in 1961; Premio Nacional de Novela in 1962, 1981, and 1992, and Premio Nacional de Cuento in 1981) for his literary works, many of which have been translated in various languages. Veloz Maggiolo has long been committed to dismantling the ideological apparatus of Trujllo and his followers, and *El hombre del acordeón*, set in the years just before and after the 1937 massacre, presents and investigates the often contradictory dynamics of a society deeply traumatized by a murderous dictatorial regime which violently ripped apart a well-established way of life. It also presents us with a deeply damaged but ultimately defiant borderland which, despite being abused by central power, is not entirely reduced to silence or compliance. As we will see, Afro-Caribbean culture and Vodou/Vodú in particular play an important part in Veloz Maggiolo's recreation of the *raya*.

The euphoric sound of *merengue*, widely recognized as a quintessential expression of Dominican identity, also plays a crucial role in Veloz Maggiolo's novel. The accordion man of the title is Honorio Lora, the *merenguero* who, the novel claims, had taught Trujillo how to dance and enjoy *merengue* (p. 11). According to Veloz Maggiolo's narrator, *merengue* was the most important music of the area: originating in the Dominican Republic, it crossed into Haitian territory (where it was called *meringue*) as part of an intense exchange of products and the establishment of families and friendships on both sides of the border (pp. 17–18). Not everyone agrees with this theory – for some scholars Dominican *merengue* developed from Haitian *mereng* or *meringue*[3] – but what is interesting here is the novel's identification of Trujillo's 'teacher' and favourite *merenguero* as a *rayano*, a move which, in a way, points to the inner contradictions of the regime's *nationalistic* project for which *merengue* became a powerful soundtrack. Such a project, in fact, labelled *rayanos* as potential enemies of the fatherland whose way of life was alien to it and who had to be brought back, at all costs, to the proper 'patriotic' fold. *Merengue* had been considered a *regional* form (in particular from the Cibao) until Trujillo transformed it into a state symbol which could be mobilized to encourage Dominicans to imagine themselves as members of the same community/nation and as a tool for his deification and glorification: during his dictatorship hundreds of *merengue* pieces were dedicated to him by highly regarded composers.[4]

---

[3] Jean Fouchard, *La méringue, le danse nacional de Haiti* (Pétionville, Haiti: Henri Deschamps, 1988), p. 66 quoted in Paul Austerlitz, *Merengue: Dominican Music and Dominican Identity* (Philadelphia, PA: Temple University Press, 1997), p. 2. See also Chapter 8 for more on this.

[4] Austerlitz, p. 60.

Veloz Maggiolo's novel does present us with a *merenguera* loyal to the regime, namely La Postalita, a female accordionist who sings her support for the 1937 massacre. Honorio, however, is clearly a dissident. Despite the fact that his accordion is a present from Trujillo himself, he refuses to join the pro-Trujillo choir and taps instead into *merengue*'s history of rebellion against central power: before Trujillo's appropriation, the accordion-based *merengue* typical of the Cibao area had in fact epitomized the country's resistance to North American occupation.[5] In Honorio's hands, therefore, *merengue* becomes a weapon against the regime: after 1937, the narrator explains, he no longer wrote licentious love songs but 'songs of protest and bitterness' against Trujillo's murderous activities (pp. 11, 35, 52–3).

At the very beginning of Veloz Maggiolo's novel we discover that Honorio is actually dead and that there are many discordant accounts of the circumstances of his demise and burial(s). The narrator and, to a certain extent, the reader struggle to make sense of the different tales told by various eyewitnesses and interested parties as the same story is retold, years later, in a number of contradictory versions where, more often than not, the natural and the supernatural are hard to disentangle. Moreover, the digressions and repetitions typical of oral narratives make the piecing together of all the different fragments a challenging exercise for everyone involved. It is safe to say, however, that, to begin with, the bare facts are presented as follows: Honorio Lora died in the *gallera* of his friend Juan Florio where, after winning a bet on a cockfight, he had a few drinks and could not stop laughing. After vomiting blood, he collapsed on the floor. He was then carried on his horse to Ignacia Marsán, one of Honorio's many women (but, apparently, the only one he really loved) and then buried in the Dominican village of La Salada with his accordion. It was initially suggested by Enemesio and Tantán, the *güira* (a metal musical instrument) and *tambora* (a two-headed drum of African origin) players of his musical band, that Honorio had died of intemperance because he had drunk too much 'rum or clerén' on an empty stomach – *clerén* is a type of homemade rum produced in Haiti which circulated widely in the borderland. This explanation, however, never really convinced anyone. According to Ignacia Marsán, Honorio was poisoned by supporters of Trujillo for his *merengues*, which condemned the regime for the 1937 massacre and, in particular, for the death of his good friend, the '*rayano* Tocay' (pp. 42, 51). Various people, Ignacia recalls, including the '*cuentero* ('story-teller') and inventor of biographies' Vetemit Alzaga, were actually informing the authorities of Honorio's subversive lyrics.[6]

---

[5] Austerlitz, pp. 31, 63.

[6] In Spanish the word *cuentero* means both 'story-teller' and 'liar.'

Vetemit Alzaga is also one of the narrator's informants. During his interview with the narrator, which took place many years after Honorio's death, Vetemit laments the fading away of popular poets such as the *cuenteros* and, even more so, the traditional *decimeros* or composers of *decimas* (ten octosyllabic lines rhyming *abbaaccddc*; p. 13). It is worth mentioning that in 1938 Emilio Rodríguez Demorizi, the most prolific historian of the regime, compiled an anthology entitled *Poesia popular dominicana* in which he collected some of the 'poetic treasures' of what he calls 'the people's muse,' which, he felt, were being forgotten or adulterated and which contained, he claimed, 'the true spirit of Hispanic America.'[7] The exaltation of the Hispanic origins which characterizes Demorizi's text – which also insist on portraying Haiti as an alien, ferocious enemy – goes hand in hand, as we will see, with Vetemit's mission in the *raya*. A schoolteacher born in San Pedro de Macorís, Vetemit was sent to the northern borderland by Trujillo to create an 'official history' for it, and, for its dwellers, a line of ancestry in keeping with the ideology of the regime. When he arrived in La Salada, Vetemit recalls, smuggling with Haiti was rife and its inhabitants were only 'poor peasants, mulatto *rayanos* – a mixture of white and blacks – and black Dominicans' (p. 17). Vetemit's job was to persuade them that their *rayana* identity, deemed 'unpatriotic' by the regime, was neither their real identity nor a proper identity *tout court* (p. 69). Throughout his residency in the borderland Vetemit enthusiastically contributed to the nation-building project launched by Trujillo, carefully inventing an alternative local history and, for the borderland dwellers, new Hispanic surnames and eminent and 'pure' lineages in line with the regime's fictional (or at least incomplete) notion of a Dominican Republic as the repository of Demorizi's 'true spirit of Hispanic America.'

Vetemit reveals to the narrator how he had invented illustrious biographies for the ancestors of the *rayanos*, including Honorio's fellow musician Enemesio, a petty thief who began to use the aristocratic surname 'Osorio' after Vetemit declared that he had 'discovered' that the Spanish governor Antonio de Osorio was in fact one of his ancestors. Honorio, who had written a *merengue* which mocked Vetemit's invented surnames, publicly ridiculed Enemesio for his vanity and frowned at his desire to be associated with such a controversial figure as Osorio (pp. 72–3). Governor Osorio, in fact, masterminded the devastation of the northern part of Hispaniola where, feeling abandoned by the Spanish crown, the local population had begun to break the monopoly sanctioned by the 1556 Real Cédula and trade with the

---

[7] Emilio Rodríguez Demorizi, *Poesia popular dominicana* (Santiago, República Dominicana: Universidad Católica Madre y Maestra, 1979), pp. 9–10, 100.

French, Dutch, and English. In 1605, in order to prevent smuggling (which damaged Spanish trade and the Seville's merchants), the penetration of anti-Catholic religious ideas, and the possible creation of political allegiances contrary to the interest of Spain, Osorio declared a general pardon for those involved in illicit trade with foreigners in exchange for their 'voluntary' relocation. In other words, the inhabitants of the north and north-west of the island were basically forced to collect their belongings, vacate their lands, and move to other (less profitable) parts of the colony allocated to them by the authorities. When Osorio met with resistance, he made his soldiers burn all buildings and cultivated land belonging to the rebels, dramatically impoverishing the colony as a whole.[8]

After being teased by Honorio for embracing his 'invented' surname, Enemesio (apparently) bore a grudge against his bandleader for the rest of his life. The symbolism of the conflictual relationship between Enemesio *Osorio* and the rebel Honorio is better understood once the latter's (alleged) ancestry is revealed. Honorio's progenitor was (apparently) Hernando Montoro or Montero, the 'king of the *contrabandistas*' and mulatto or '*blanco de la tierra*,' who organized an armed resistance against Osorio's *devastaciones*. The mutual hostility between Enemesio *Osorio* and Honorio Lora (previously *Montoro*) reproduces the historical fight between central authorities and the inhabitants of an area which, once the island was divided in two between France and Spain, was going to become part of the borderland (p. 36).[9] It also brings to the fore the historical moment which facilitated the settlement of the French in the parts of Hispaniola which Osorio had emptied and devastated, laying (albeit involuntarily) the basis for the creation of the current international border.

Vetemit was particularly keen to flatter the vain Enemesio because the musician provided him with information regarding 'unpatriotic' activities

---

[8] Matibag, *Haitian-Dominican Counterpoint*, pp. 34–5; Pedro Mir, *El gran incendio* (Santo Domingo: Editora Taller, 1974) especially 107 onwards; Moya Pons, *The Dominican Republic*, pp. 45–50.

[9] The narrator explains that, after the *devastaciones*, Honorio's ancestors came back to the borderland, changed their surname to Lora, and established themselves there permanently. Hernando de Montero really existed and was one of the mulattoes who put up a fight with the authorities, who had forced them to give up their lands and relocate in other parts of the country. In seventeenth-century Hispaniola the mulattoes were becoming more and more powerful and, together with the 'free blacks,' they became landowners or *blancos de la tierra* ('whites of the land'): see Tirso Mejía Ricart, 'Haití en la formacion de la nacionalidad Dominicana', *Eme Eme: Estudios Dominicanos*, XIV.79 (1985), pp. 61–75, p. 64; Mir *El gran incendio*, pp. 107, 137; Moya Pons, *La otra historia dominicana*, p. 139.

that he then passed on to the regime. Years later, an old Vetemit also confesses to the narrator that, just before the 1937 massacre, he was the one who had helped to identify the 'Haitians' among the population of the area and instructed the army on their whereabouts. Vetemit claims, however, that he did not know that so many of his 'friends from the borderland' would be killed – many of them were actually supporters of Trujillo 'whose grandmother was also Haitian' – and explains that many *rayanos* and black Dominicans were killed too (p. 14). Official discourses, he continues, presented the 'Haitians' as 'a threat' and as land usurpers but Vetemit argues that he believed that he was providing data for a statistical study when he informed on them; when he realized what the army was really up to, he decided to go into hiding because he did not want to be used as a 'guide' by the killers (p. 14). The novel, however, does not invite us to fully trust Vetemit, whose reliability and good faith are exposed as dubious; on separate occasions, in fact, he praises Trujillo for the great things he had achieved for his country, claims that they were worthy of 'thousands of executions' (p. 93), and, ventriloquizing the official ideology of the regime, insists that the Dominicanization of the borderland was necessary because 'the *gourde* was being used throughout the Dominican Republic' (p. 75).

In conversation with the narrator, Vetemit also declares that, during *el corte*, he was hiding for fear of being confused with a *rayano* and therefore killed by the military. Significantly, by highlighting Vetemit's anxiety about being identified as one of the designated victims, the novel underlines how, in the pre-1937 borderland, (ethnic) Haitians, *rayanos*, and Dominicans were not so easy to tell apart. Notably, in the lyrics of three *merengues* written by Honorio to denounce the 1937 massacre and quoted by the narrator, the word 'Haitian' is conspicuously absent: the victims are called *negros* (once) and *rayanos* (twice) and, on one occasion, these *rayanos* actually identify themselves as Dominicans when they tell their persecutors 'son *también* dominicano' (pp. 35, 42, 59). Being *'también dominicano'* presupposes an identification with the killers as fellow countrymen but also implies the possibility of being Dominican *as well as* (*también*) something else: the fact that, according to this particular *merengue*, death did not spare those *rayanos* who screamed these words to their assassins, suggests that, in 1937, what was necessary to save one's life was to embrace a fixed identity and decide to be *only* and *exclusively dominicano* in the specific, exclusionary terms in which the regime understood the word: in short, Hispanic, Catholic, and obedient to Trujillo. It is also significant that the word *negros* is used in a *merengue* where Honorio mourns the death of Ma Misién, the wife of his friend Tocay Palavé; husband and wife were killed 'by mistake' during *el corte*, probably owing to their dark skin (p. 94). Veloz Maggiolo's novel, therefore, suggests that the urge to destroy a way of life which mocked the presence of a geopolitical border (highlighted by Turits and Derby) and the desire to 'whiten' the race (privileged by Vega) were both important and, at times, inextricable factors behind the 1937 massacre.

In his reconstruction of Honorio's death and posthumous life, the narrator does not rely only on Vetemit. As we have seen, Ignacia Marsán also shares her version with him and so does Remigia Aquines, Honorio's youngest lover and, according to one of Vetemit's extravagant genealogies, a descendant of Juan de Aquines – that is, <u>John Hawkins, the English pioneer of the triangular slave trade</u> (p. 68).[10] First of all, the two women explain, Honorio was buried not just once but three times. The first syncretic burial took place in La Salada, with a Christian ceremony celebrated in the church of Friar Anthony and preceded by a procession with the music of the *palos*, three long-drums of African origin. Friar Antón, the local priest, had in fact fully embraced the syncretic culture of the area and the existence and flourishing of 'vudú' (pp. 28, 126). The service for Honorio and the procession in his honour were also attended by *rayanos*, who were hiding in Haiti after 1937 and came to pay their respects despite the fact that re-entering Dominican territory had become extremely dangerous for them (p. 62). The massacre here seems to have therefore succeeded in sealing the frontier, forcing people to embrace fixed national identities and to discard their affiliation to the complex and variegated world of the *raya*. The novel, however, also shows that there was still space for resistance, as the 'illegal' presence of those *rayanos* who were forced to identify themselves with, and move to, Haiti testifies; yet, as one of them puts it, their presence on Dominican territory was no longer a matter of everyday practice but cause for 'anxiety and fear.'[11]

After his first burial Honorio's body was exhumed by Ignacia and Remigia, who brought it to the western shore of the River Massacre, in Haitian

---

[10] Elsewhere Veloz Maggiolo has told the story of Eulogio León, whose job was (like Vetemit's) to create heroic stories about the villages and people of the borderland during Trujillo's regime. Eulogio, for example, asserted that the village of Hatillo Palma had been founded by Hawkins and that Hernando Montoro had established contraband in the area: see 'Eulogio, inventor de memoria' in *La memoria fermentada. Ensayos biblioliterarios* (Austin, TX: University of Texas Press, 2000), pp. 87–92, pp. 88–9.

[11] It is noteworthy that these *rayanos* who are no longer allowed to live on Dominican soil use the word *angutia* to mean 'anxiety': *angutia* is a Dominican variation of the Spanish word *angustia* and the fact that they drop the 's,' as is customary in the Dominican Republic, shows that, at least as far as their linguistic inflection is concerned, they fully belong to the land they are being exiled from. See Gerald Murray, 'Lenguaje y raza en la frontera dominico-haitiana: Apuntes antropológicos' in *La frontera dominico-haitiana*, pp. 241–82, p. 255.

territory. There it was received by Polysona Françoise, a *bruja* and *volandera* from Ouanaminthe, according to whom, in order to allow Honorio to take revenge against those who had killed him, it was necessary to perform a *desunén* (pp. 51, 84–5). *Brujas* and *volanderas* (a particular type of *brujas* who can fly) are powerful magical beings who can also be threatening and are usually associated with Haitian magic:[12] the narrator explains that, in 1889, the Dominican dictator Ulises Heureux protected them with a special decree which identified them as an endangered species (p. 40). Remigia, who, at the time of her interview with the narrator had permanently moved to Ouanaminthe to serve the 'loás' (p. 84),[13] describes the *desunén* as a ceremony which enables the 'three parts' which constitute the being of the deceased ('*Go bon angé*,' '*Ti bon angé*,' and '*Metet*') to join together and come back as a spirit whose power, preserved in a bottle, can be released and incarnated in a *loá* or spirit who can intervene to influence the life of the living (p. 85).[14] The *desunén* for Honorio takes place on Haitian territory and not on Dominican soil, but it is clear that practitioners of or believers in Vodou/Vodú were to be found on both sides of the river: as the 'Haitian' Remigia puts it, Barón Samedi, 'for the *rayanos* of the other side [is] San Elías' (p. 84). Honorio, we are told, was never a practitioner but, since he died for criticizing *el corte*, Polysona trusted that he had earned the right to be treated as one of the believers (p. 85). Remigia remembers that, during the *desunén*, Honorio, metamorphosed into a *lwa*, was in charge of the rites, and, smiling while he was mounting Polysona 'as a horse,' outlined the different stages in which he was going to take his revenge (p. 87).[15] Significantly, the *lwas* Guedé (guardian of the dead and 'the deification of the common people of Haiti'[16]) and Legbá (the spirit of rituals, keeper and remover of

---

[12] Derby, 'Haitians, Magic, and Money', p. 518.

[13] The Dominican counterparts of the Haitian *lwas* are generally referred to as *loa/luases* in the plural (Deive, *Vodú y magia*, p. 170), but here I am following Veloz Maggiolo's spelling *loá* (italics in the text).

[14] According to Métraux, the mystic bond between a *lwa* and a devotee or an exceptionally talented person such as Honorio Lora, whose extraordinary ability is considered to be of a supernatural nature, has to be broken after death or the *lwa* will rain vengeance on his/her relatives. The ceremony by which this separation is effected is the *déssunin* (from the French *déssonner*), or *dégradation*. After the *déssunin*, the *lwa* is free to take up residence in 'some person who, appointed by him, will immediately become [...] the spiritual heir of the deceased' (*Voodoo in Haiti*, p. 245).

[15] The relationship between a *lwa* and the person possessed by him/her is compared to that which joins a rider to his horse (Métraux, *Voodoo in Haiti*, p. 120).

[16] Zora Neale Hurston, *Tell My Horse: Voodoo and Life in Haiti and Jamaica* [1938] (New York: Harper and Row, 1990), p. 219.

barriers and boundaries) were both present at the *desunén*, proud (at least, according to Remigia) to be close to the *merenguero* 'who had besieged, with his music, those who had caused so many deaths' (p. 88). After the ceremony, testifying to the accommodating nature of Vodou, where new *loas* are constantly being created, Honorio became himself a permanent '*ser*' or *lwa/loá* of the 'pantheon *rayano*' and the effects of Honorio's hatred for his enemies began to become discernible.[17]

When Honorio's body was taken to Polysona both Remigia and Ignacia realized that his beloved accordion was missing from the box in which it had been (allegedly) buried with its owner. It later transpired that, at least according to the women, Enemesio and Tantán had stolen Honorio's accordion to sell it in a shop in Santiago and that the two musicians were also the material executors of his murder, probably acting with the complicity of the *gallero* Juan Florio. Florio later cried himself to death on Honorio's grave (p. 106), while Enemesio *Osorio* and Tantán were executed with a gun which, significantly, had belonged firstly to Desiderio Arias, one of the mythical revolutionary figures of the borderland eliminated by Trujillo, and later to Honorio Lora, who had used it to murder the killer of his friend Tocay and then left it to his son Honorio Leonidas (pp. 128, 137). On the chests of Enemesio and Tantán's corpses someone had pinned a sign saying 'They betrayed *El Jefe*'; it was not uncommon for Trujillo's enemies to be identified in this way and left unburied in order to caution Dominicans against anti-regime activities but the words 'El Jefe' here might secretly refer to Honorio (the chief or *jefe* of their musical band), an ambiguity which highlights the borderland's set of alternative allegiances.[18]

The young Honorio Leonidas (possibly Enemesio and Tantán's executor) was also the mastermind behind Honorio's spectacular final revenge which, significantly, took the shape of a musical duel '*a meringazo limpio*' ('of hard-core *merengue*' p. 25) between the regime-supporter La Postalita and the accordionist Acedonio Fernández (p. 183). What was at stake was Honorio's accordion, the one that Trujillo had given him and which was, at that point, in the hands of La Postalita. The accordionist Acedonio, the narrator reveals, was the secret son of Honorio and his one-time lover

---

[17] See Métraux, *Voodoo in Haiti*, p. 82. In Dominican *Vodú*, for example, other anti-Trujillo leaders such as Enrique Blanco and Ciprián Bencosme have become part of the pantheon (Deive, *Vodú y magia*, p. 171).

[18] It is worth remembering that on 15 November 1921 the pro-Haitian party proclaimed their independence from Spain in the border towns of Dajabón and Montecristi and demanded Haitian protection (Moya Pons, *The Dominican Republic*, p. 121).

Rutilia Fernández; on finding out the truth after Honorio's death, Acedonio did not hesitate to join forces with his step-brother Honorio Leonidas to avenge their father. Despite the fact that La Postalita was playing Honorio's accordion while Acedonio only had a 'crappy little accordion' and was not a very experienced player, he managed to win the musical contest because he felt someone else's fingers (presumably Honorio's) guiding his own (p. 143). The *merengue* he produced was so good that people ran to the *gallera* from all the villages nearby shouting 'Honorio has been resuscitated!' (p. 142). The music symbolically reunified both *raya* and *rayanos*, as it also reached the bones of those who, on the other side of the River Massacre, were waiting for the trumpet of the Last Judgment after being slaughtered (p. 142).

Despite the resistance of the new Spanish priests, who were sent to the borderland to uphold Christianity and eradicate primitive and satanic practices such as cockfights and *Haitian* Vodou, the duel took place in the *gallera* where Honorio had died, one of the spaces in which, prior to 1937, the *rayanos* from both sides used to come together to enjoy themselves. In this very *gallera* the complex syncretic cosmology of the *raya* is reconstituted and is able to exert its power. Acedonio was accompanied by the Marassa Tocay y Tocaya – that is, Tocay Palavé and Ma Misién's twin orphans. In Haitian and Dominican Vodou the Marassa represent children's sacredness; the fact these two were rendered orphans by the 1937 massacre turns them into living icons of their parents' 'martyrdom' and into haunting representatives of the *raya* before *el corte*. The potential negativity which Haitian and Dominican Vodou – but also Catholicism – associates with twins[19] is offset by their participation in a musical trio with Acedonio, who is also part of another set of 'triplets,' the one which comprises him, his brother Honorio Leonidas, and their (dead) father Honorio, three figures often mixed up by other (mostly female) characters. While Acedonio and the twins were playing, a mysterious and dark horseman with an accordion entered the *gallera*: for some, it was Tocay Palavé (p. 144), himself a good musician, who had come to witness his children's debut, thus recomposing the supernatural trio of the saints Cosmos and Damiano (who generally represent the Marassa in chromolithographs) and their father Saint Nicholas. Another important triad in the novel is the one constituted by Remigia, Polysona, and Ignacia, three women who embody an alternative *her*story which has Vodou/Vodú and magic at its core. Their popular *her*story counters Vetemit's own (official but fictional) history which privileges instead Hispanophilism, Catholicism, and patriarchy, three of the pillars of the nationalist ideology promoted by Trujillo: when Acedonio declares his willingness to revenge Honorio with

---

[19] Derby, *The Dictator's Seduction*, pp. 213–14.

his brother, he makes his allegiances clear and refuses the gift of a scapular which, according to his mother, should protect him from the *volanderas* by saying: 'the *volanderas* made me a new man' (p. 122).[20]

At the end of the *merengueros*' duel a triumphant Acedonio receives Honorio's stolen accordion from a devastated and defeated Postalita. According to one of the versions collected by the narrator, La Postalita had obtained it from a lover who had bought it in Santiago from the shop where Remigia saw Enemesio and Tantán selling it to the owner. Honorio Leonidas and Acedonio Fernández – who, after his victory against the Postalita, changed his surname into Lora – are the ones who put the accordion in Honorio's third and last grave, a grave which inaugurated the new cemetery of La Salada. Being the first to be buried there, the narrator explains, gave Honorio the opportunity to turn into no less than Barón Samedi/San Elías, head of the *lwas* who personify the world of the dead, and the best known *loá* among Dominicans (p. 145). The narrator informs us that the 'crappy' accordion used by Acedonio was rescued by Friar Anthony, who stored it in an old wardrobe from where it was retrieved only when Trujillo's soldiers came to look for Honorio Lora's 'original' accordion for the Museo Nacional – highlighting, one last time, the fictionality of the official national history promoted by the dictator and his associates (pp. 144–6).

The man who, in the novel, confesses to have been instrumental to the creation of this fiction, the *cuentero* Vetemit Alzaga, appears to be not only unrepentant but also proud of his conduct; as a matter of fact, he is confident that, in time, there will be a statue to commemorate him and his efforts (p. 91). Vetemit's 'wished-for' monument for his contribution to the construction of the Dominican nation as an imagined community which would not tolerate the way of life of the *raya*, would demonize Haitian culture, and would privilege Hispanophilism powerfully contrasts with the 'statue in motion' of 'man, horse and accordion' which Ignacia saw when they brought Honorio's corpse to her after his mysterious death at the *gallera*. The statue Ignacia describes is 'in motion' because it resists the fixity of nationalist discourses, championing instead the fluidity of the *raya*.[21]

---

[20] In another short story by Veloz Maggiolo entitled 'La dictatura y su magia,' also focused on the *raya* at the time of Trujillo, the character who challenges Trujillo's authority is also a female.

[21] There are no monuments that commemorate the victims of the 1937 massacre. In a valiant effort to remember and honour those who lost their lives, the organization *Border of Lights* has organized a number of activities during October 2012 (75th anniversary of *el corte*) and October 2013 which have seen the support and participation of writers and artists such as, among others, Julia Alvarez, Edwidge Danticat, Chiqui

This same ensemble or equestrian statue visited Ignatia in a dream where, after turning into the warrior spirit of Ogún Balendyó or San Santiago – a white saint who protects the blacks – Honorio, his mare, and his accordion rose up from the grave and, in a final display of transnational, interethnic, and 'transcolour' *rayana* solidarity, joined all those who had died in 1937 (pp. 28, 56). Once it is shared with the narrator (and the readers), Ignatia's dream assumes a crucial social and collective dimension, articulating, as it does, a sharp and critical analysis of the conditions which triggered it and a compelling formulation of different possibilities. This kind of dream – and this kind of storytelling – are among the social practices in which the German philosopher Ernst Bloch identifies little shards of utopian thinking which transcend the moment and become socio-political projections or, rather, anticipations of a new viable reality.[22] As we will see, utopian thinking which goes beyond mere wishfulness but fully engages in, and commits to, the actualization of what can be, is traceable in all the texts examined in this chapter.

It is worth pointing out, however, that given his commitment to a definition of Dominicanness which steers away from Hispanophilism, anti-Haitianism, racism, fixity, exclusivity, and impermeability, it is rather puzzling that, only one year before the publication of *El hombre del acordeón* (2003), Veloz Maggiolo had been one of the judges who awarded the 2001 re-edition of *El ocaso de la nación dominicana* by Manuel Núñez the prestigious Premio Nacional Feria del Libro León Jimenes. Núñez's text, as noted above, rejects the very notion of a fluid Dominican identity that Veloz Maggiolo so enthusiastically celebrates in his depiction of the *raya* and is instead informed by, and aims to promote, the same fictional notion of the Dominican Republic as the repository of, exclusively and homogenously, the true spirit of Hispanic America, embraced by Veloz Maggiolo's Vetemit and endorsed by, among others, Demorizi and Balaguer.[23] Notably, Carlos

---

Vicioso, Rita Dove, Michele Wucker, Rhina Espaillat, Polibio Díaz, and Sherazade Garcia: see http://www.borderoflights.org/ [accessed 27 November 2014].

[22] Peter Thompson and Slavoj Žižek, eds, *The Privatization of Hope: Ernst Bloch and the Future of Utopia* (Durham, NC: Duke University Press, 2013).

[23] For a systematic and sustained critique of *El ocaso de la nación dominicana* (2001) see, for example, Odalís Peréz, *La ideología rota: el derrumbe del pensamiento pseudonacionalista dominicano* (Santo Domingo: Editora Manatí, 2002) and Dió-genes Abreu, *Perejil: el ocaso de la 'hispanindad' dominicana, celebracion de la multiplicidad cultural desde New York* (República Dominicana: Imp. Mediabyte, 2004). In *Africano por elección, negro por nacimiento*, Blas Jiménez also attacks the notion of a monolithic and pure identity and the conflation of nationalism with anti-Haitianism proposed by Núñez and defines Dominicans as a 'mixed ethnicity,' exhorting them to be 'proud'

Esteban Deive, author of *Viento Negro, bosque del caimán* (analysed in Chapter 4) and of many works which highlight the Afro-Caribbean heritage of Dominican culture, was the president of the committee which awarded the prize to Núñez, a prize that, in a way, can be seen as the actualization of the monument Vetemit imagined would be dedicated to his efforts.

At the time, a deeply disappointed Torres Saillant described Deive and Veloz Maggiolo's decision to award the prize to Núñez as a 'public retraction' of all they had, up to that point, represented in the intellectual life of the Dominican Republic.[24] The fact that *Viento Negro* and *El hombre del acordeón* were published in the same year and one year after Núñez received his award further complicates this already contradictory scenario: the two novels, in fact, can be read only as a 'public retraction' of the 'public retraction' that their authors' endorsement of Núñez's text might have constituted. It is impossible to establish with certainty the reasoning behind Veloz Maggiolo and Deive's decision – different explanations have been offered by different observers and interested parties[25]– but it seems that they were definitely aware of the 'controversial' content of Núñez's book because, in their impassioned defence of their decision, they argued that the reasons for the award had nothing to do with the content of the monograph but were instead based on other qualities, such as contribution to scholarship and clarity of language.[26]

In 2003, the year of *El hombre del acordeón*'s publication, Núñez reiterated many of the ideas he discussed in *El ocaso de la nación dominicana* in a predictable paper entitled 'La Frontera y la Fractura del Territorio Nacional: Obstáculos en la Percepción del Problema' ('The frontier and the fracture of the national territory: obstacles to the perception of the problem') delivered at a conference organized, in Santo Domingo, by the Secretary of the Armed Forces. It is interesting to compare Núñez's view of *la frontera* with the

of their 'bastardy' (p. 20). Néstor Rodríguez has also commented on the discrepancy between Deive's work and his decision to award the prize to Nuñez, and has denounced the ongoing connection between an officially sanctioned culture and political and economic power by drawing attention to the fact that the Fiera Internacional del Libro is founded by the tobacco company Léon Jimenes: see Néstor Rodríguez, *Escrituras de desencuentro en la República dominicana* (Santo Domingo: Editora Nacional, 2007), pp. 85–6.

[24] Torres Saillant, *El tigueraje intellectual*, p. 22.

[25] See, in Pérez, *La ideología rota*, 'Addenda: La memoria de estos días, o, cómo escuchar las voces de la protesta y la esperanza' pp. 385–466.

[26] Carlos Esteban Deive, Andrés L. Mateo, Marcio Veloz Maggiolo, Tomás Castro Burdiez and José Chez Checo, 'En defensa de nuestro honor', *Listin Diario*, 4 May 2002, seccion B, p. 9, reprinted in Pérez, *La ideología rota*, pp. 391–3.

approach of a self-defined 'dissident' intellectual such as Torres Saillant, who also was among the delegates.[27] While, for Núñez, as the title of his paper suggests, *la frontera* is primarily a 'fracture in the national territory' and a 'problem,' for Torres Saillant it is a place which facilitates a better knowledge and understanding of the *quicio* or 'hinge' around which the question of citizenship revolves:[28] clearly, 'hinge' and 'fracture' are very telling terms which, alone, define the approaches of the two panellists. For Núñez the border is nothing but a far too porous barrier crossed by migrants – or rather, as he argues, 'colonizers' – who have the support of various international organizations whose only purpose is 'to demoralize the authorities[,] discredit the application of the law [and] paralyse the exercise of sovereignty of the Dominican State.'[29] He warns his audience of the existence of a 'crusade' against the Dominican Republic which is being 'denationalized' in terms of labour, language, religion, culture, territory and of registry offices (pp. 48–58). Invoking the historian Arturo Peña Battle (another staunch supporter of Trujillo), Núñez also argues that the current division of the island is the fruit of Haitian usurpation and blames on the Haitian 'copious and relentless colonization' of the Dominican territory the 'sad episode' of the massacre of 1937. Most importantly, the existence of the fluid *rayana* community which Veloz Maggiolo brings to life in his novel and which various historians before him have amply documented is purposefully ignored.[30] The differences in 'culture, history origin and language' between Haiti and the Dominican Republic are instead highlighted and the two nations proposed as impermeable, internally homogeneous, and incommensurable entities one of which, Haiti, is in ruin. Given these circumstances, the border is a threat which can destabilize the Dominican Republic because it is the site through which drugs, weapons, goods which destroy the Dominican economy, and waves of illegal migrants enter the country every day: the solution proposed by Núñez is the establishment of a vaguely outlined 'trust' which would enable the reconstruction of Haiti, a 'titanic task' which, however, he regards as the only way to safeguard and further impermeabilize Dominican territory and culture.[31]

Torres Saillant, instead, immediately identifies *la frontera* not only as

---

[27] Torres Saillant, 'La Condición Rayana', p. 222.
[28] Torres Saillant, 'La Condición Rayana'.
[29] Núñez, 'La Frontera y la Fractura del Territorio Nacional: Obstáculos en la Percepción del Problema', in *La Frontera: prioridad en la agenda nacional*, ed. Secretaría de Estado de las Fuerzas Armadas (Santo Domingo: Editora de las Fuerzas Armadas Dominicanas, 2004), pp. 47–61, pp. 47, 56.
[30] Núñez, 'La Frontera y la Fractura', p. 52.
[31] Núñez, 'La Frontera y la Fractura', pp. 53, 58–9.

a line traversed by different people and goods but as a place and, more broadly, a way of life, which deserves to be studied and better known: to him it is evident that a misconception of the frontier as an alien and threatening place goes hand in hand with a misconception of the nation as a homogenous entity.[32] A revisitation of the history of the country which brings to the fore its multicultural, transracial, and interethnic composition is at the core of Torre-Saillant's reconfiguration of the borderland as 'fertile ground' on which to rethink the internal diversity which composes the Dominican social and cultural fabric. To paraphrase his words: 'the Dominican experience [...] is fundamentally *rayana*.'[33] Distressingly, during the Q&A which followed the presentation, the questions addressed to Torres Saillant revealed that those who formulated them considered his views as evidence of his lack of loyalty to the Dominican Republic: 'Do Dominicans have the right to have a nation and a national identity?'; 'In your interior frontier are you Dominican or Haitian?'; 'Are you a staunch supporter of the unification of the island?'[34] A dispiriting result, if one considers that the conference had been envisaged as an occasion to rethink the frontier as a 'goldmine of opportunities [...] to establish a respect for differences,' but one which reveals how easy it is for Núñez's ultra-nationalist approach to find support.[35]

The proceedings of this conference were successively published in a collection of essays of over 550 pages which showcases the views of more than sixty panellists of mixed provenance and with different, often opposing, views on border-related issues which are approached from a variety of perspectives, namely historical, military, economic, environmental, political, anthropological, educational, ethical, and medical. Veloz Maggiolo did not take part in the conference but, arguably, *El hombre del acordeón* contributes to the debate from an aesthetic, ethic, and political standpoint, which is much more in line with Torres Saillant's intervention than with award-winning Núñez's, bringing to the fore, as it does, what the Cuban Alejo Carpentier and, after him, the Haitian Jacques Stephen Alexis had

[32] Torres Saillant, 'La Condición Rayana', pp. 223–4.
[33] Torres Saillant, 'La Condición Rayana', pp. 223–7 – italics mine. Torres Saillant's interventions chime with Odalís Pérez's paper where he insists on regarding the borderland as a productive intercultural space: see 'Leer la Frontera Hoy: Un Espacio para la Interculturalidad' in *La Frontera: prioridad en la agenda nacional*, ed. Secretaría de Estado de las Fuerzas Armadas (Santo Domingo: Editora de las Fuerzas Armadas Dominicanas, 2004), pp. 157–71.
[34] 'Foro de Discusión', in *La Frontera: prioridad en la agenda nacional*, pp. 229–31, p. 231.
[35] Torres Saillant, 'La Condición Rayana', pp. 222–3; 226–7.

called marvellous reality and marvellous realism.[36] Moreover, while both Carpentier and Alexis firmly linked their experience of the marvellous with Haiti, Veloz Maggiolo's novel testifies to a cultural continuity between the two sides of the island which has the *raya* at its core.

For Alexis, marvellous realism is 'the imagery on which a people wraps its experience, reflects its conception of the world and of life'; it is a state of being which thrives on 'the treasury of tales and legends.'[37] Such tales and legends come from the people and 'are there to help the nation in solving its problems,' providing it with an alternative to Eurocentric forms and modes which 'surpass' the 'analytical and reasoning realism' they champion.[38] Similarly, Veloz Maggiolo's novel is engaged in a rejection of Dominican Hispanophilism and its Eurocentric and exclusionary notion of civilization and, like Alexis, he directs his interests to aspects of popular culture which are the product of the complicated history of the island but have traditionally been occluded or appropriated by dominant discourses (Vodú; magic; popular 'tales and legends'; *merengue*). In so doing, Veloz Maggiolo brings to the fore a different kind of sensibility, forged by the refusal to differentiate between the real and the mythological; as his narrator puts it: 'sometimes it is easier to believe in certain things without analysing them rather than denying them altogether' (p. 89).[39]

Alexis also championed sensual representations of reality and the inspiring presence of the landscape;[40] in *El hombre del acordeón* the primacy of senses over reason is testified by the centrality of music, which, in the *raya*, is produced by instruments such as the accordion but also by the landscape itself: 'in the arid land of Montecristi [...] even the brambles produce music when the wind batters their thorns' (p. 12).[41] Veloz Maggiolo's

---

[36] Alejo Carpentier, 'Preface', *El reino de este mundo* (Lima: Editora Latinoamericana, 1958) and Jacques Stephen Alexis, 'Of the Marvellous Realism of the Haitians', *Presence Africaine*, 8–10 (1956), pp. 249–75 (English translation).

[37] Alexis, 'Of the Marvellous Realism of the Haitians', pp. 270–71.

[38] Alexis, 'Of the Marvellous Realism of the Haitians', pp. 271–2; 266–7.

[39] It is worth mentioning that in his intervention at the conference, which was blessed, at its opening, by the army vicar, Torres Saillant expressed his reservation regarding the validity of the effort, sanctioned in the Dominican constitution, to promote the dissemination of the 'culture and religious tradition of the Dominican people,' which is identified, exclusively, with the Catholic church, thus replicating if not the physical then the 'conceptual violence' of the past ('La Condición Rayana', p. 227).

[40] Alexis, 'Of the Marvellous Realism of the Haitians', pp. 267, 272.

[41] Arguably, echoes of Alexis's novel *Les arbres musiciens*, set on a different part of the borderland, namely a forest near Lake Azuei which 'never stops whistling and humming with the wind,' might not have been intentional but are certainly intriguing:

novel, moreover, does not reinforce the sensationalism that has traditionally characterized depictions of Haiti, and, by extension, of the *raya*, where the proximity with Haiti is identified as the cause for the moral, physical, and racial degradation of Dominicans.[42] *El hombre del acordeón* chimes instead with Alexis's commitment to the forging of a national consciousness based on an understanding of culture which goes beyond nationalism and which is instead 'an incessant happening.'[43] 'Ideas,' Alexis explains, 'cross frontiers without a passport,' and the geopolitical borders of a nation are never impermeable because 'nations are subject to other cultural influences, those of other nations which live in the same geographical zone as them, where relations are made frequent'; in order to understand what happens in Haiti on a political and cultural level it is crucial, he insists, to 'pay attention to all the cultural movements of the Dominican Republic' as well as those of other parts of the Caribbean and Latin America.[44] Alexis's anti-isolationist approach chimes with Veloz Maggiolo's determination to show the two neighbouring nations which share the island of Hispaniola as participating in the creation and recreation of the island's syncretic culture as it was being negotiated, in a specific way, in and by the borderland itself at the time of the 1937 massacre. Veloz Maggiolo's novel, in a way, becomes a collection of those 'tales and legends' which Alexis thought could 'help the nation in solving its problems' but the assistance they can provide here is channelled towards a better understanding of the past and the creation of a less sectarian future for Hispaniola as a whole.[45]

✳✳✳

Opening up a conversation between Veloz Maggiolo and Alexis is particularly useful in this context because in 1955 Alexis devoted a third of his novel *Compère Général Soleil* (*General Sun, My Brother*) to the 1937 massacre.[46] Born in 1922 in Gonaïves, Alexis was deeply attached to Haiti and, as we

---

see Alexis, *Les arbres musiciens* (Paris: Gallimard, 1957), p. 385, which will also be discussed in Chapter 10.

[42] See, among many, Prestol Castillo's *Paisajes y meditaciones de una frontera* or Balaguer's *La isla al revés*, previously discussed.

[43] Alexis, 'Of the Marvellous Realism of the Haitians', p. 255.

[44] Alexis, 'Of the Marvellous Realism of the Haitians', pp. 261–2.

[45] Alexis, 'Of the Marvellous Realism of the Haitians', p. 272.

[46] Alexis, *Compère Général Soleil* (1955); Here I will be quoting from Jacques Stephen Alexis, *General Sun, My Brother*, trans. C.F. Coates (Charlottesville, VA: The University Press of Virginia, 1999) and from now on page numbers to this translation will be given in parentheses in the text.

have seen, he identified in the ability 'to sing the beauties of the Haitian motherland, its greatness and its wretchedness,'[47] one of the crucial tenets of marvellous realism. *Compère Général Soleil* contains a sustained description of the Artibonite River as a 'monstruous liquid boa' which flows to the Haitian coast from the mountains of the Cibao, in the Dominican Republic, at the time of a catastrophic flood (p. 134). The river is also personified as a 'great fellow with muscular, powerful arms [who] walks tall' (p. 134); characterized by 'inexhaustible kindness' and 'savage […] madness,' the Artibonite 'knows' and encapsulates the history of the island, from its indigenous past (Anacaona's Jaragua is powerfully evoked) to the United States' occupation, during which it 'carried the peasant patriots and aided their ambushes' (pp. 136, 135). Anti-American resistance took place on both sides of the river and there is compelling evidence that the two movements led, in Haiti, by Charlemagne Péralte (who, incidentally, was a native of Hinche, in the borderland) and, in the Dominican Republic, by Olivorio Mateo Ledesma or Liborio (who was based in the border area of San Juan de la Maguana), were in fact interconnected.[48] Alexis draws attention to this interconnection when he calls the North Americans those 'crucifiers of men' (p. 136): after they were captured and executed by the marines, both Péralte and Liborio's dead bodies were displayed as public warnings against anti-American insurrection in a fashion that reminded one of a crucifixion. Overall, therefore, Alexis's Artibonite hints at across-the-border continuities despite the fact that, as Rueda has pointed out in 'Cantos de la frontera,' the *línea* which destroyed the permeable world of the *raya* had been brutally superimposed on a substantial section of the river.

Unlike Veloz Maggiolo's *El hombre del acordeón*, *Compère Général Soleil* does not focus on the borderland. The part which reports on the 1937 killings begins in the cane fields of Macorís, where the two protagonists, Hilarion and Claire Heureuse, had migrated so that Hilarion could find a job as a *bracero*. Unlike other sites mentioned in the novel, Alexis's Macorís, a city where life was 'completely tied to sugar' (p. 224), is not immediately identifiable as a geographical place. The name, in fact, can suggest two different cities of the Dominican Republic, namely San Francisco de Macorís, in the north, and San Pedro de Macorís, on the southern coast. Both cities are some distance from the actual border (more than 300 kilometres from it), but, while San Francisco is situated in the northern military department of the country (that is, in the area targeted by Trujillo's army) and is listed by the Haitian historian Jean Price-Mars as one of the places where ethnic Haitians were slaughtered,

---

47 Alexis, 'Of the Marvellous Realism of the Haitians', p. 272.
48 Lundius and Lundhal, *Peasants and Religion*, pp. 103–11, 489.

San Pedro is located in what is normally referred to as the 'spared' southern department.[49] Of the two cities, however, San Pedro is the one which has the strongest connection with cane fields. As early as 1893 a sugar estate near San Pedro received the first shipment of foreign *braceros* recruited by the newly created Immigration Society of Macorís, which aimed to import cheap labour from abroad, mainly the West Indies, to assist struggling estate owners. In the early twentieth century, San Pedro de Macorís was dramatically transformed by the sugar boom initiated and stimulated by North American interests; in Alexis's novel, Macorís is a city 'under the boot heel of Trujillista fascism and the Yankee imperialism of the surrounding sugar refineries, a city without horizons' (p. 225).[50] Arguably, Alexis here wanted to bring to the fore the responsibility of the United States in implementing a labour policy based on the exploitation and importation of thousands of Haitians as cheap labour to support the booming sugar industry and, more generally, for its meddling in Hispaniola and in its borderland's affairs.

There are also other considerations: if, at the time in which the novel is set, Trujillo had shown very little interest in the sugar industry, *Compère Général Soleil* was published when sugar production in the Dominican Republic was beginning to increase vertiginously; it doubled between 1950 and 1960. The profitability of this industry had not remained unnoticed by Trujillo, who, after World War II, slowly began to acquire most of the foreign mills operating in the country and to establish himself as a prominent and, eventually, the largest sugar producer of the Dominican Republic.[51] In 1952, three years before the publication of *Compère Général Soleil*, an agreement signed by Trujillo and 'Papa Doc' Duvalier enabled Trujillo to control and channel the flux of migrants and allowed Duvalier and the

---

[49] Jean Price-Mars, *La República de Haití y la República Dominicana: diversos aspectos de un problema historico, geografico y etnologico*, trans. Martín Aldao and José Luis Muñoz Azpiri, 2 vols (Santo Domingo: Taller, 2000), vol. II, p. 780. In 1938, however, the governor of the province of San Pedro affirmed that the Haitian consul had ordered his compatriots to get ready to return to Haiti but was referring only to those who did not work in cane fields (Vega, *Trujillo y Haití*, vol. II, p. 366).

[50] See Derby, *The Dictator's Seduction*, pp. 48–50 and her discussion of the Dominican novel *El hombre alucinado* (1938), by Luis Henríquez Castillo, which is set in San Pedro de Macorís in the 1920s. More recently, the film *Sugar* (dirs Anna Boden and Ryan Fleck, 2008) portrays the experience of a young baseball player born in San Pedro de Macorís whose nickname is 'Sugar' and who is signed (and exploited) by a North American team to play baseball in the United States. Significantly, in one of the initial scenes we see a group of children playing baseball close to old sugar cane trains.

[51] Moya Pons, *The Dominican Republic*, p. 364; Martínez, *Peripheral Migrants*, p. 46.

Haitian authorities to cash US $15 for each of the 30,000 workers that they supplied to the Dominican Republic plus a cut of 50 per cent of each worker's wage for a total of US $7 million per year.[52] This agreement benefited the political elites of both countries at the expense of the dispossessed and, as such, was not too dissimilar from the 1939 out-of-court settlement between Trujillo and Sténio Vincent which established the indemnity that Haiti was to receive from the Dominican government for the victims of *el corte* at US $750,000. The amount was later reduced to US $525,000 but, distressingly, only very few of the victims received any form of compensation.[53]Arguably, therefore, alongside North American influence, Trujillo's dictatorial regime and his involvement in the sugar industry, Haitian politics, and border relations thriving on corruption were also among Alexis's targets and, possibly, motivated his decision to link so decisively the massacre with the predicament of those who were working (or rather, were exploited) in the Dominican cane fields.

There seems to be historical evidence, in fact, that in 1937 Trujillo's soldiers did not target *braceros*: with very few exceptions (namely the Quinigua plantation, Barahona, and Puerto Plata) Haitian *braceros* mostly lived outside the borderland and the area where the October massacre was carried out, where ethnic Haitians cultivated mainly coffee and subsistence crops.[54] The Haitian cane-cutters, who, according to some sources, represented more than 40 per cent of the Haitians who resided in the country, were spared by the killers because, at the time, most of the sugar cane plantations and *bateyes* belonged to North Americans and the regime did not consider it prudent to antagonize foreign investors and the United States. Moreover, the *braceros* of the *bateyes* were fairly isolated from the rest of the population and therefore did not really represent a huge threat to what Trujillo and his supporters promoted as the 'authentic' Dominican way of life.[55] Overall, therefore, as Martínez has eloquently put it, 'regardless of the dictator's intentions, no more chilling way could be imagined of conveying to Haitian immigrants that the sugar *bateyes* would thereafter be the only secure place on Dominican soil'; *braceros*, in fact, continued to come to the Dominican Republic in substantial numbers also immediately after the massacre.[56]

---

[52] Martínez, *Peripheral Migrants*, p. 46; Matibag, *Haitian-Dominican Counterpoint*, p. 155.

[53] Matibag, *Haitian-Dominican Counterpoint*, pp. 148–9.

[54] Vega, *Trujillo y Haití*, vol. I, p. 399; Turits, 'A World Destroyed', p. 597.

[55] Vega, *Trujillo y Haití*, vol. I, p. 399.

[56] Martínez, *Peripheral Migrants*, p. 44. In response to *el corte*, in fact, the Haitian government did suspend permission for recruitment of *braceros* until 1941 but agents of the sugar companies may have begun to recruit covertly in Haiti within months

In Alexis's Macorís, the exploited *braceros* are both Haitians and
Dominicans: in 1934 and 1935 (and again in 1938) the Dominican Congress
passed laws which established that all businesses had to employ at least 70 per
cent Dominicans but sugar estates often managed to negotiate the possibility
to hire a higher percentage of foreign workers than that established by the
government.[57] In Alexis's novel Dominicans and Haitians form part of a
close-knit bilingual and bicultural community where everyone speaks a
mixture of Haitian Creole and Dominican Spanish. Haitians, we are told,
'remained quite Haitians [...] but were no longer the same [because] they
had their own way of thinking, their own gestures, and their special way
of doing things' and Dominicans 'were not like other Dominicans' as 'the
two national cultures mingled [t]here' (p. 218). As for Michel De Certeau,
according to Alexis, the practice of everyday life did 'not imply a return
to individuality [for] the dominated element in society.'[58] 'Everyday life,'
in fact, had the power to create something new and precious: 'something
was being woven [in Macorís] that would eventually create one heart and
one soul for two peoples chained in the same servitude' (p. 218). The glue
which keeps together the bicultural community of Alexis's Macorís is a set of
transnational everyday social practices and internationalist beliefs shaped by
anti-capitalist resistance rather than by the geographical proximity of the two
nations, which, in Hispaniola's borderland, had forged the well-established
tradition of exchanges and allegiances contrary to the interest of central
powers later revisited by Veloz Maggiolo. Veloz Maggiolo's pre-1937 *raya*
and Alexis's Macorís, however, can both be seen as 'everyday utopias' – that
is, places where daily life is experienced and performed in ways which are
radically different and characterized by innovative practices and imaginative,
counterhegemonic thinking. These practices and this thinking are sustained
by a sense of hope and potential which anticipates something which is both
beyond and other to what can be realized at that moment but conceivably
tangible at the same time; as Alexis puts it: 'Who knew what the future
held in store?' (p. 218).[59]

It is not surprising that in *Compère Général Soleil* Alexis presents Macorís
as an inspiring place where it was possible to forge new alliances between

---

from the killings. In 1942 the Haitian president Lescot interrupted official recruitment
once again and also tried to stop clandestine emigration, but to no avail (p. 45).

[57] Martínez, *Peripheral Migrants*, p. 44.

[58] Michel de Certeau, *The Practice of Everyday Life* [1984] (Berkeley, CA: University
of California Press, 1988), pp. xi–xii.

[59] See Davina Cooper's conceptualization of 'everyday utopias' in *Everyday Utopias:
The Conceptual Life of Promising Spaces* (Durham, NC: Duke University Press, 2013).

political dissidents and the disenfranchised of the two nations of Hispaniola in order to bring social justice to the island as a whole. Alexis, in fact, died while trying to overthrow Duvalier's dictatorship in 1961 after spending time in Paris – where he continued to work to bring about political change in Haiti – the USSR, Cuba, and China; his entire *oeuvre* reveals a deep commitment to proletarian solidarity and a better future for his people. To paraphrase Oscar Wilde in *The Soul of Man under Socialism*, one could argue that, for Alexis, a geographically and historically accurate map of Hispaniola which did not include Utopia or, as we have seen, the 'everyday utopia' represented by his Macorís, was not even worth glancing at.[60] In Macorís, in fact, Hilarion, who had befriended Communist militants in Haiti, becomes acquainted with a group of Dominican activists who are organizing a *huelga* (strike; in Spanish in the text) to get better salaries for cane-cutters. There were no such activities in 1937 San Pedro de Macorís: under Trujillo, the Labour Confederation 'survived but in dormancy' until about the end of the Second World War, when unions multiplied rapidly and the first Dominican party with a Communist agenda (Partido Democratico Revolucionario Dominicano) was funded in 1943.[61] In January 1946, however, a strike of cane-cutters did break out at La Romana and soon spread to San Pedro de Macorís. The strike went on for two weeks and was the only important and successful strike in the thirty-one years of the Trujillo regime. The workers obtained what they had sought and, while it lasted, the government exercised no violence against the strikers; after the settlement, however, a number of leaders were killed by the regime, which made their deaths pass for suicides.[62] This strike and the deaths of those involved might have inspired Alexis in his description of the Macorís's *huelga* even though Pedro Torres, its fictional leader, is unashamedly and publicly executed by Dominican armed forces while inciting Haitian workers to join their Dominican *companeros* to demand better salaries (pp. 235–6).

Macorís's close transnational community of exploited *braceros* is weakened when the soldiers, knowing the strategic value of 'divide and rule,' round up all the workers, confiscate their machetes, and order the 'Dominicans'

---

[60] Oscar Wilde, 'The Soul of Man under Socialism', in *Collected Works of Oscar Wilde: The Plays, the Poems, the Stories and the Essays including De Profundis* (Ware: Wordsworth Editions,1997), pp. 895–922, p. 907.

[61] Roberto Cassá, *Movimiento obrero y lucha socialista en la República Dominicana: desde los origins hasta 1960* (Santo Domingo: Taller, 1990), p. 265.

[62] Robert Crassweller, *Trujillo: The Life and Times of a Caribbean Dictator* (New York: Macmillan, 1966), pp. 216–17; Cassá, *Movimiento obrero y lucha socialista en la República Dominicana*, pp. 427–86.

to move aside and form a separate grouping. One by one, the 'Dominicans' are invited to pronounce the word '*perejil*' (parsley) because the 'Haitians,' Alexis writes, 'had a great deal of trouble pronouncing the *r* in this word' (p. 256). The assumption was that, mispronouncing it, they would have revealed their real provenance. Once they were certain that there were no infiltrated 'Haitians' in the group, the soldiers sent the 'Dominicans' away and began to kill the 'Haitians,' shooting into the crowd and finishing off the wounded ones with bayonet thrusts (pp. 256–9).[63] *El corte*, in fact, is also known as the 'Parsley Massacre' because, since there were few physical and cultural markers to separate Haitians from Haitian–Dominicans and Dominicans in the borderland region, in an effort to identify ethnic Haitians in the mixed population of *rayanos* some historians have reported that Dominican soldiers asked their prospective victims to pronounce the word *perejil*. Since Haitian Creole uses a wide, flat *r*, Haitian Creole native speakers find it difficult to pronounce the trilled *r* in the Spanish word for *perejil*: if the word came out as the Haitian *pe'sil* or a bastardized Spanish *pewehi* the victim was condemned to die.[64]

According to some scholars, however, in the fluid world of the *raya* the purpose of the *perejil* test was not to establish provenance beyond any reasonable doubt: ethnic Haitians who had deep roots in the Dominican borderland were in fact able to pronounce *perejil* as well as natives, so this litmus test could help only to differentiate recent Haitian immigrants (like Hilarion) from those who were born in the Dominican Republic or had lived there for a long time and were perfectly assimilated. The *perejil* test, these scholars suggest, was instead used to dramatize as incompatible and

---

[63] In reality, as we have seen, only a few Haitians were shot – mainly those who were trying to escape – because the regime was keen to present the genocide as a popular insurrection; a few pages later (p. 264) Alexis refers to the practice of using knives, bayonets, or blows to eliminate Haitians but only as a strategy to conserve ammunitions.

[64] See, for example, Suzy Castor, *Migración y relaciones internacionales: el caso haitiano-dominicano* (Santo Domingo: Editora Universitaria-UASD, 1987), p. 26 or Miguel Aquino García, *Holocausto en el Caribe; perfiles de una tiranía sin precedents - La matanza de haitianos por Trujillo* (Santo Domingo: Editora Corripio, 1995), p. 120, where he specifies that the '*perejil* test' targeted in particular dark-skinned people. The fact that it was very hard to distinguish Dominicans from Haitians is also highlighted in 'Fusilado par equivocación,' where Rafael Emigdio Caamaño Castillo tells the story of a Dominican soldier who was killed by accident by the Dominican army because he was mistaken for a Haitian national: this event does not have a precise date (we are told that it took place around the time of the end of the North American occupation of the country) but seems to have preceded the 1937 massacre – in *Antología Literaria Contemporánea de la Frontera*, p. 119.

mutually exclusionary the linguistic and, by extension, cultural peculiarities of Haitians and Dominicans.[65] Alexis, too, seems aware of the inadequacy of the test and ponders on the complex question of national identification and self-identification in bilingual, transnational, and internationalist Macorís when, referring to a mortally wounded man who was yelling '¡*Pelehil, pelehil, pelehil!*' he wonders: 'Was he Haitian or Dominican?' (p. 259).[66]

Nevertheless, despite the horrific carnage which takes place around them, the inhabitants of Macorís show a great deal of bravery and solidarity towards the victims: 'the Dominican people were waging a battle with all their hearts and strength, trying to save each life from the fascist murderers and death. The Dominican democrats had emerged from the great darkness in which they had been carrying on their obscure debates. The Communists had gone out into the streets to organize evacuation under the very noses of the police, the soldiers, and the Trujillistas' (p. 265). While it is impossible not to notice the way in which the 'Dominican people' helping Haitians become 'the Communists' in the space of a few lines, it is fair to point out that Alexis also highlights that Claire Heureuse and Hilarion were hidden and protected by Dominicans who were not members of the Communist party, such as, for example, the dancer Concepción[67] (who, however, believes that 'the spirit of dance could only survive in working-class neighbourhoods,' p. 222) and even a group of soldiers disgusted by the orders imparted to them and unable and unwilling to carry them out (p. 262).

After escaping from the massacre, Hilarion and Claire Heureuse arrive on foot in the area around Bánica, a small Dominican border town where the River Artibonite is the line of demarcation between Haiti and the Dominican Republic.[68] As we have seen, the massacre took place mostly in the Northern Military Department of the country; however, Bánica, in the south but in close proximity to the northern department, was an unfortunate exception. On the shores of the Artibonite Hilarion, Claire Heureuse, and their baby

---

[65] Turits, 'A World Destroyed', p. 617.

[66] In 1983 the North American poet Rita Dove, who in 1993 became the first African American Poet Laureate of the United States, also foregrounded the '*perejil* test' in her poem 'Parsley' and, like Alexis, she connected the massacre with sugar cane plantation workers. Notably, in a note appended to the poem, Trujillo's victims are simply defined as 'blacks' and there is no mention of their nationality or ethnicity. Rita Dove, 'Parsley', *Poetry Foundation*, http://www.poetryfoundation.org/poem/172128 [accessed 27 November 2014].

[67] Alexis's mother was a Dominican dancer.

[68] The long distance between San Pedro and Bánica is very difficult to cover on foot in the short time that Alexis affords to Hilarion and Claire Heureuse.

son Désiré are attacked by dogs unleashed by the Dominican army to hunt the fugitives who were trying to cross the border into Haiti.[69] Despite the fact that Hilarion fights valiantly against the animals, Désiré, who was conceived in Haiti but born in the Dominican Republic, is mortally wounded and his death becomes a replica, in a way, of the 'death' of the bilingual, bicultural, and transnational Macorís. The two continue their flight, carrying their dead baby with them, until they arrive at the River Massacre, which marks the border between Haiti and the Dominican Republic north of the Artibonite. When the three cross the river, they are intercepted by a patrol of soldiers, who shoot and fatally wound Hilarion (p. 283). Crawling onto Haitian territory, Hilarion finally manages to touch 'the border marker on which was inscribed the Haitian coats of arms,' and hopes 'to hear the soft Haitian speech' (p. 284). The dying Hilarion, therefore, realigns himself with his country, actually embracing (both physically and metaphorically) two symbols of his nation, both of which, in different ways, signpost the division of the island. Yet, Hilarion, who incites Claire Heureuse to have a new life and 'other Désirés' (p. 289), does not fully renounce the utopian possibilities inherent in his Macorís where, Alexis writes, the blood of all the victims of the massacre spilt by Trujillo's henchmen 'will retain [for as long as the land shall last] the imprint of the pools of fraternal blood, and Dominican children of future generations will bow their heads before these infamous stains' (p. 265). Hilarion, whose eyes are riveted to the landscape of 'Ayti Toma,' also exhorts Claire Heureuse to draw inspiration from both his Haitian Communist friends and the Dominican Paco Torres's belief in equality and in the bright socialist future personified by the rising 'General Sun' of the title (p. 290).

✲✲✲

Transnational solidarity among workers is also highlighted in René Philoctète's novel *Le peuple des terres mêlées* ('The people of the mixed lands,' 1989) which, additionally, like Veloz Maggiolo's *El hombre del acordeón*, brings to the fore the bilingual and bicultural world of the *raya* at the time of the massacre.[70] *Le peuple des terres mêlées* is set in the Dominican

---

[69] The novel mentions the Bánica woods and the Bánica River, which is in fact the Artibonite (pp. 276, 280).

[70] René Philoctète, *Le peuple des terres mêlées* (Port-au-Prince: Deschamps, 1989). Here I will be quoting from René Philoctète, *Massacre River*, trans. L. Coverdale (New York: New Direction Books, 2005) and page references to this translation will be given in parentheses in the text. In 'A note to the Translation,' Linda Coverdale explains that

border town of Elías Piña, the capital of the only province in the southern military district in which ethnic Haitians were killed in October 1937. Born in Jérémie in 1932, Philoctète was a poet, playwright, short story writer, and novelist who spent most of his life in Haiti – before his death in 1995, he left only twice: in 1966, when he spent six months in Canada with other political dissidents who were escaping Duvalier's Haiti, and in 1992, when he accepted a literary award in Argentina. The years immediately preceding the publication of *Le peuple des terres mêlées* saw the fall of Jean-Claude Duvalier and a period of chaos, social unrest, and violent repression: hundreds of people who protested against the eleven governments which came and went in the space of four years were ruthlessly slaughtered. By the end of their first year in office Henri Namphy and the generals had killed 'more civilians than Jean-Claude Duvalier's government had done in fifteen years.'[71] Philoctète, however, was determined to demonstrate that Haiti had a vibrant cultural scene which dictatorships, corruption, and political violence could not silence: all his books (which he published in Haiti at his own expense) are informed by a strong belief in the possibility of a better future for his country and his people.

Le peuple des terres mêlées, which gives the borderland a central role to play in the creation of this better future, is a complex verbal *tour de force* inspired by the poetics of the Spiraliste literary movement which, in the 1970s, he co-founded in Haiti with the writers Claude Fignolé and Frankétienne as a way to deal with the chaotic situation of the country under Duvalier. Its central symbol, the spiral, insists on the relational aspect of every being and is therefore perfectly suited to inform a novel preoccupied with the porous world of the borderland of Hispaniola, an island formed by two different entities which, like the strands of the double helix of an individual's

---

she felt that a literal translation of the original French title ('The People of the Mixed Lands') would not work in English so she decided to opt instead for *Massacre River* because its 'appalling symbolism' makes it 'a more striking title' (p. 219). As Coverdale herself points out, however, the positive ending of Philoctète's novel, with its promise of a better future, jars with the connotations of the Massacre River, which highlight instead the conflictual and violent nature of border relations dating back to the time of the buccaneers. Coverdale's reference to the Massacre River is also 'out of place' for another reason: there is in fact no mention of this river in Philoctète's novel because it runs more than 100 kilometres north of the town where the novel is set and the river that marks the borderline by Elias Piña is in fact the Artibonite, not the Massacre.

[71] See Michel-Rolph Trouillot, *Haiti, State against Nation: The Origins and Legacy of Duvalierism* (New York: Monthly Review Press, 1990), p. 222 and Peter Hallward, *Damning the Flood: Haiti, Aristide, and the Politics of Containment* (London: Verso, 2007) p. 27–9.

DNA are, however, deeply interconnected.[72] Like *El hombre del acordeón*, Philoctète's spiralist novel follows the oral tradition with its unfolding of stories which resist linear narrative and thrive on accumulation, circularity, repetition, digressions, contradictions; redeploying and transforming Alexis's marvellous realism, the texture of Philoctète's prose is further enriched and complicated by endless and frenetic wordplay.

Among the main characters of *Le peuple des terres mêlées* we find the 'the lovers of the border' (p. 126) – that is, '*el mulato Dominicano*' and labour activist Pedro Alvarez Brito and his wife Adèle, '*la chiquita negrita haitiana*' (italics in the text; Spanish in original, p. 26). Adèle and Pedro met at the market of Maribaroux, according to him, or of Thomassique, according to her (pp. 102, 76). The suggestion that the two cannot agree on the exact location of their first encounter signposts the fact that the markets which were held (then) on Haitian territory were visited by both Haitians and Dominicans on a regular basis: before the massacre, Philoctète explains, the priest of Elias Piña used to purchase his eggs in Belladère, the Dominican sergeant in Bánica bought his *clairin* in Mont-Organisé, and Atilo Francisco Manuel y Pérez, a merchant of Jimaní, sold his wares in Fond Parisien (pp. 146–7). These transnational markets are posited here as powerful 'everyday utopias' which, providing the opportunity for across-the-border bonds of intimacy, were instrumental in the forging of alternative individual and collective identities. Pedro and Adèle, in fact, are by no means the only 'mixed' couple in Elias Piña but are part of a heterogeneous, transnational community where, as Pedro announces at the beginning of the novel and prior to *el corte*, 'we people from here and over there – we are, in the end, the people of a single land' (pp. 34, 36). The same idea of unity is strongly conveyed by the title which, in the original French identifies a 'single people' ('*le peuple*') on these '*terres mêlées*' ('mixed lands'). Despite the plural *terres* (lands), the adjective *mêlées* ('mixed') implies the impossibility of distinguishing between them and intimates that, through the continuity of their 'mingled' nature, these two lands can become a single but diversified one, as diversified as the mixed or *mêlée* nature of the *rayanos* who inhabit it.

In Philoctète's novel, local flora and fauna fully participate in the communality of the *raya*: when the threat of the massacre approaches, 'mountains, flowers, insects, rivers and streams, rodents, plains, birds' join in the protest of the people of the borderland, who talk 'to one another in a language that only they can understand – the language of the border, nourished by local customs, history, the human heart' (p. 150). In the face

---

[72] For a study of Spiralisme see Kaiama Glover, *Haiti Unbound: A Spiralist Challenge to the Postcolonial Canon* (Liverpool: Liverpool University Press, 2010).

of the massacre, however, words 'are floundering' (p. 151). The peasants Urbain and Prospero are perhaps the best example of the devastating blow that, in 1937, Trujillo's divisive ideology landed on the way of life of the borderland: Urbain was (probably) born in Haitian territory, grew up 'somewhere between the two lands' and lived in Cercado-Cercado, near Neyba in the Dominican Republic; Prospero was born in Dajabón but also lived in Cercado-Cercado. They 'cultivate[d] their garden together without worrying whether the corn ripen[ed] in Haitian territory or the potato flourish[ed] in the Dominican Republic [...] Their four wives [were] devoted to them' and their 'twenty-eight children [...] play[ed] in the same courtyard' but 'not one of them [knew] for sure whether Urbain or Prospero [was] his or her father.' We are told, however, that the two friends stopped talking to one another when they realized that death would 'soon come to sit down between them, and they [were] growing desperately sad' (pp, 149–50).

The same sadness and desperation are revealed in the frantic attempt by 'the Dominican people of both lands' to teach 'the Haitian people of both lands the proper pronunciation of "*perejil*"', a word, Philoctète insists, 'that both people of both lands [strove] desperately to say well so that one people may not be the other's guilty conscience, but the blazing hearth of their home' (pp. 143; 145). Fefa Rodriguez of Dajabón, for example, 'nailed it to the lips of Pierre Charmant of Vallière'; César Gómez of Jimaní 'nestled it between the breasts of Rose Antoine of Boucan-Bois,' while 'between two glasses of Bermudez rum, Julian Nuñez y Jiménez hefted, handled, and gargled it for his friend Serge Laplanche, a teacher in Cerca la Souce' (pp. 143–4). Philoctète's exuberant rhythmic prose, based on accumulation and on multiple variations on the same theme, creatively counteracts the repetitiveness with which the '*perejil* test' was performed in its attempt to dramatize, time and time again, the (alleged) incompatibility, untransferability, incommunicability, and impermeableness of Dominican and Haitian culture. In Malpasse/Malpaso the word rises 'from thousands of Haitian and Dominican throats, like a slow, thick, heavy incantation'; in Pedernales 'hundreds of Dominican men and women with jugs of honey and sweet melon juice spend their days doling out the mixture to hundreds of Haitians [...] Lips touched by this drink soften, grow more flexible, and [...] will be able to pronounce the word with ease' (pp. 144–5). The most moving and tender story that Philoctète offers us, however, is the one of 'two black children,' both born in Bahoruco, the girl of Dominican origin and the boy of Haitian descent. They are respectively five and four years old and live in Hinche, where they play on both sides of the border. When the girl realizes that the boy cannot pronounce *perejil* properly, she makes him rehearse the word over and over again until night falls. They are found the next morning, we are told, 'holding hands around a bouquet of parsley' and not even the callous border guards had the courage to cut their heads off (p. 146).

In Philoctète's novel, the massacre is announced by the arrival of a mysterious flying creature (p. 24). Alerted by this presence, Pedro and Adèle realize that 'the day of blood is coming closer' and that 'death has set shop in [their] life' (pp. 27, 29). They are convinced that their 'only protection' against abuse of 'power turn[ed] stupid' is 'love' and the humanity they share with those who want to kill them: 'don't forget our common humanity,' says Pedro. Adèle, however, warns him: 'love is crippled, *hombre!*' (p. 27). Like the Haitian Hilarion, the *rayano* Pedro is a sugar cane cutter involved in the political struggle of workers; as soon as he realizes that the worst is about to happen he travels 'for more than a hundred kilometers' (p. 29) to discuss with his Haitian and Dominican *companeros* a plan of action to resist 'the horror of the beast' (pp. 33, 31).[73] As we have seen, there is no evidence, as far as 1937 is concerned, of a powerful transnational labour movement and, on a couple of occasions, Philoctète's novel acknowledges as much (pp. 99; 117). Yet, his decision to build on Alexis's internationalist dream might be due to the fact that in the 1980s things were, slowly, starting to change. In 1981, the French investigative journalist Maurice Lemoine reported that, despite the presence of Duvalier's *Tontons Macoutes* in the Dominican *bateyes*, where they were sent to control the Haitian workers and prevent any contact with the unions, the *braceros* were beginning to mobilize with the support of some Dominican union leaders.[74]

Lemoine's *Sucre Amer: Esclaves aujourd'hui dans les Caraïbes*, a harrowing reportage on the predicament of the Haitian cane-cutters in Dominican *bateyes*, was one of the many interventions in the international campaign for human rights which, in the late seventies and early to mid-eighties, was directed against the Dominican Republic. Activists equated the conditions of the Haitian *braceros* to those of 'slaves' and objected to the system of official contract migration between Haiti and the Dominican Republic, which had begun with the 1952 accord between Duvalier and Trujillo. The 1952 accord, renewed in 1959 and modified in 1966 to reflect the nationalization of Trujillo's sugar estates, was in fact regarded as a highly

---

[73] Most of the *braceros* living and working in the Dominican Republic in 1937 were based in the *bateyes* of the area around Barahona, which is in fact located about 160 kilometres from Elias Piña (Vega, *Trujillo y Haití*, vol. I, p. 399).

[74] Maurice Lemoine, *Sucre Amer: Esclaves aujourd'hui dans les Caraïbes* (Paris: Encre, 1981). From now on I will be quoting from the English translation: Maurice Lemoine, *Bitter Sugar*, trans. A. Johnston (London: Zed Books, 1985), pp. 217, 68, 91.

corrupt bilateral system of exploitation.[75] In 1986, the last year in which the 1966 agreement was valid and only three years before Philoctète's novel was published, the Dominican sugar industry's dependence on Haitian labour became dramatically evident when Baby Doc Duvalier fled to France, the money paid to the Haitian government for recruitment 'disappeared,' and the Haitian *braceros* never arrived. The harvest was declared a national emergency; the government formed brigades of civil servants to cut cane at weekends, exhorted Dominican citizens to join in, and mobilized the military, a move which, however, did not prove very cost effective.[76] Overall, the harvest was ruined and the country deeply damaged because, as one of Pedro's *companeros* puts it, 'the Dominican economy r[a]n on Haitian sweat' (p. 117), an affirmation which was probably truer in 1986 than in 1937. Philoctète's Dominican workers are as sympathetic to the predicament of ethnic Haitians as the ones depicted by Alexis in *Compère Général Soleil*. Their reaction to news of the massacre presents us with a transnational community with strong bonds of intimacy as the emphasis is put on deep and personal connections: 'one man worries about a Haitian friend; another remembers his Haitian godfather; yet another is in despair over a Haitian cousin. A husband already weeps for his Haitian wife' (p. 50). 'It's our cause as well,' they conclude, and some of them, including their leader Guillermo Sanchez y Santana, actually pay with their lives for their solidarity (p. 120).

In Alexis's and Veloz Maggiolo's novels, as we have seen, the executors of the massacre are Trujillo's soldiers; Philoctète, too, highlights that *el corte* was 'opposed with the utmost rigour by the people' (p. 153) and seems to mainly implicate the military. Two notable exceptions, however, are the government civil representative in Elias Piña, Pérez Agustín de Cortoba, and the *alcade* Preguntas Feliz, the second-in-command in the town. The 'dirty fingernails' of Preguntas Feliz, we are informed, 'perforated ninety-seven little black girls from five to seven years old' (p. 158) and, after receiving superior orders, Don Pérez began to manically whirl his machete around. The depiction of his hectic murderous activities relies on verbal excess: the narrative bends, twists, and curves only to explode in a myriad of details which resist rationality: 'The machete amputates, mutilates, decapitates'

---

[75] Martínez, *Peripheral Migrants*, p. 48; Wooding and Moseley-Williams, *Needed but Unwanted*, p. 38. Unlike the 1952 agreement, which put the onus on private companies, the 1966 accord committed the Dominican government to pay Port-au-Prince for organizing the recruitment.

[76] Martínez, *Peripheral Migrants*, pp. 49–50; Wooding and Moseley-Williams, *Needed but Unwanted*, p. 38.

and, while Don Pérez 'sings, shouts and bellows,' limbs and body parts are scattered around him: a 'head rolls at his feet [...] An arm moans. Some teeth grimace [...] guts tumble at [his] feet' (p. 67). The chronicling of the events becomes as chaotic and as fragmented as the frenzied, gory scenes it depicts and the butchered bodies it describes. In the confusion, Adèle might be Don Pérez's next victim: she suddenly appears to 'lose' her head ('Neighbor, tell me! Where is my head?') while 'her right leg rolls in the dust beside the dog [...] her left leg goes off to frolic around Don Augustin [...] [Her] left arm has snagged itself on [...] barbed wire' (pp. 77–8). As Adèle had foreseen, love among neighbours has now become 'crippled,' and there is no point in reminding the killers that once they all belonged to the same mixed community; actually, this might even make things worse, since Don Pérez had a Haitian concubine who left him just before the massacre began: he appears to be obsessed with her and fantasizes about her body, sexualized and partitioned, while he perpetrates his atrocities. After being severed from Adèle's body, her head begins to wander around Elias Piña despite her repeated efforts to 'get hold of [it], put it back on, shove it down on her shoulders, nail it, cement it, rivet it to her neck' (p. 163): among other things, it 'begins to dance a *merengue*' (p. 164), 'enters an establishment purveying strong drink, downs a neat shot, coughs' (p. 165), confabulates with other heads of ethnic Haitians (p. 168), becomes a 'community activist head' who 'protest [...] in the name of national dignity [...] Of human rights [...] Of democracy' but 'gets a resounding slap [and] slinks away crestfallen,' dreaming of her beloved Pedro (pp. 167, 173). Adèle's head is not the only one which is spinning around out of control: 'Haitian heads are marching silently through villages as a form of peaceful, unarmed protest' (p. 159). Both vivid and clearly implausible, these descriptions might document hallucinations rather than reality: Adèle, we are told, suffers from depression (p. 36) and it is obvious that scenes of extreme violence such as the ones forced on the massacre's eyewitnesses could make anyone 'lose' one's head.

Philoctète's meandering, graphic, and hallucinatory accounts of the killings are often interrupted by radio bulletins which proclaim that 'Operation Haitian Heads' is well under way and, while broadcasting weather forecasts or advertisements for 'Bermudez, the macho rum' (pp. 79, 92), they update the population with lists of locations in which mass murder is taking place and the latest figures from the massacre. These radio reports, in fact, are entirely fictional: the regime tried to hide things for as long as possible and only faced up to the facts when pressed by the international community.[77] In addition, their insertion, clearly, does not aim to provide historically

---

[77] Vega, *Trujillo y Haití*, vol. II, pp. 42–81.

accurate information: in some of the locations mentioned there were no killings in October 1937 and, as we have seen, the actual death toll is still being disputed. The inclusion of these fake radio bulletins, however, adds to the acute chaos of the nightmarish events described and further disorients readers who are forced, in a way, to share the utter confusion and the blind horror of the participants. The reference to the power of radio also introduces us to the power of discourse and propaganda: Trujillo not only recruited a substantial number of intellectuals and historians to foment anti-Haitianism but also owned and controlled the only television station, two major daily newspapers, and many radio stations.[78] Trujillo also appears in the novel as one of the characters. From a very early age he appears to be obsessed by Henry Christophe's Citadel, a fortress and a powerful rhetorical statement which he dreams of owning and transporting onto Dominican territory. Carpentier too, was impressed by the 'imposing bulk' of the Citadel[79] when he visited Haiti, but to (Philoctète's) Trujillo the fortress is simply the 'phantasm' of Haiti, which he considered, first and foremost, an 'adversary' (p. 41). According to the novel, it was precisely in order to counteract this phantasm that Trujillo concocted the myth of Dominican whiteness which found its most horrific expression in the 1937 massacre. Trujillo's plans to appropriate the Citadel and to whiten the Dominican race are recounted in self-contained chapters which alternate with accounts of the massacre and with Adèle and Pedro's story.

When Pedro, who had left Adèle behind to go and meet his *companeros*, returns to Elias Piña, he is presented with a horrifying, inconceivable scenario. Adèle's head comes to huddle against his crumpled legs and explains to him, in very confused and confusing terms, what has just happened: 'I'm done for. I was cut on the fly, on the sly, on the prowl by Don Pérez Agustin de Cortoba who – with Don Preguntas Feliz [...] has been industriously chasing other heads, slicing-dicing with tongue and sword, spitting: "*¡Perejil! ¡Perejil!*"'(p. 193). Pedro then collapses on the ground (is he hit by a machete or simply overwhelmed?) and, while lying in the dust, he watches Elias Piña as if it 'had fallen over backwards' (p. 195). We are told that he soon gets back on his feet, but at this point it is not entirely clear who is dead, alive, or dying. While desperately looking for his house, which has mysteriously disappeared, Pedro spots Chicha Calma, 'the crazy *guagua* [...] of the border' (p. 56), which just brought him back from his labour meeting (p. 198).[80]

---

[78] Moya Pons, *The Dominican Republic*, p. 375.
[79] Carpentier, 'Preface', p. 5.
[80] In the Dominican Republic a *guagua* is a small public coach which transports people around

Together with its driver, the Dominican Papito Consuelo Pipo y González, with whom she forms an almost symbiotic union, Chicha Calma plays a central role in the novel. Philoctète, in fact, endows it with her own narrative voice, with which she addresses the reader directly while commenting on what is happening around her and intervening in the action.

Chicha Calma's voice, the voice of the borderland, can be seen as the counterpart of the official radio, which is the voice of power 'turn[ed] stupid' and murderous (p. 27). Infused, as it is, with the spirit of the people of the *raya*, whom she had been 'lugging around the two lands for more than twenty years' (p. 121), Chicha Calma is clearly the embodiment of those practices of everyday life that Alexis had already singled out as potentially revolutionary, and that defined Veloz Maggiolo's *raya* as a non-dominated space whose *mêlée*, or heterogeneous, hybrid nature Trujillo aimed to destroy in order to fully subjugate. As we have seen, Philoctète's novel provides us with many examples of the way of life obliterated by the 1937 massacre, while, in the *guagua*'s microcosm, solidarity among the travellers is brought to the fore. The driver is as determined as his *guagua* to honour their contract and 'serve the people of the border': when he realizes what is happening, 'he is raring to go' and transport the borderland people to safety because 'no one can remain indifferent to slaughter' (pp. 200; 210). Pedro, while on the *guagua*, repeatedly tries to teach a *negrita* and fellow-passenger how to pronounce the word *perejil* which, however, sticks in her throat, makes her cough, besieges her, subdues her, makes her vomit (pp. 115; 118; 139). Despite Pedro's dedication and the young woman's efforts, she dies, 'struck down' by the word itself, and her legs end up sticking out one of the windows of the overcrowded *guagua* when Chicha Calma is boarded by a 'multitude' of people of all ages, genders, and colours heading for Haitian soil (p. 199). When they get to the border, refugees are piling one on top of the other 'with their furniture, tools, saints, smells, songs, legends, their ways of walking, and talking. Their way of life' (p. 210).

The novel ends with a description of these refugees: they are of 'every color, every walk of life, every belief, every character, every kind of memory and beauty' (p. 213). Significantly, the narrator cannot tell (and does not care to know) if they are Haitians or Dominicans: all he knows is that they have 'so many things in common, share so many wounds and joys that trying to distinguish between the two peoples violates their tacit understanding to live as one' and their 'dream of creating one people from two lands mixed together' (pp. 213–14). In Philoctète's novel, therefore, the massacre does not abolish, once and for all, the deep connections which characterized the people of the borderland but brings about the promise of a new beginning, of a new 'world to build' (p. 214). Hence, the original title (*Le peuple des terres mêlées*) does not limit itself to the important task of describing, reviving, and commemorating the dead but it aims to reassert, strongly and decisively, the necessity for a future of communality for all the inhabitants of Hispaniola. Philoctète acknowledges from the outset the difficulties which are inherent in such a project – in Creole, the word *mêlé*, in fact, can also mean 'troubled.' Yet, it is evident that the dream of creating one people from two lands mixed together is posited not as an impossible-to-maintain promise or consolatory wishful thinking – what Bloch would call an 'abstract utopia' – but rather as a 'concrete utopia' which anticipates 'something that *is not yet* but *could be* (because it is possible).'[81]

Philoctète's belief in the importance of mutual respect and collaboration for all the denizens of Hispaniola informs ('translated' into a diasporic scenario) Edwidge Danticat's 'Acknowledgements' for her novel *The Farming of Bones* (1998), which also revisits the 1937 massacre.[82] In the list of the people Danticat thanks for their help and assistance in writing the book we find, among others, Dominican–American writers Julia Alvarez, Junot Díaz, and Angie Cruz, and Bernardo Vega, at the time Dominican Ambassador to the United States and author of a multi-volume book on Trujillo and Haiti. Crucially, these thanks are given in Haitian Creole (*Mèsi Anpil*), Spanish (*Mucho[sic] Gracias*) and English (*Thank You Very Much*), the two languages spoken on Hispaniola and the language shared by the members of its diaspora in the United States. As we have seen in Chapter 3, Danticat moved from Haiti to the United States, where she currently lives, when she was twelve years old. Danticat and her family draw comfort from the fact that the community into which they moved in Brooklyn never really severed its connection with Haiti; yet it was hard to grow up in New York at a time when Haitian–Americans and Haitian migrants were heavily discriminated against, accused of being HIV-carriers, imprisoned in special detention camps and routinely refused asylum. Unavoidably, Danticat's reconstruction of the tension and allegiances which characterized Hispaniola's borderland in 1937 is also inflected by her personal life as a diasporic Haitian in the United States.

---

[81] Rainer E. Zimmermann, 'Transforming Utopian into Metopian Systems: Bloch's *Principle of Hope* Revisited', in *The Privatization of Hope*, eds P. Thompson and S. Žižek (Durham, NC: Duke University Press, 2013), pp. 246–68, p. 248 (emphasis in the original).

[82] Danticat, *The Farming of Bones*. Page references to this edition will be given in parentheses in the text.

The Farming of Bones is an award-winning novel written in English, a feature which gave it immediate access to a wide audience. It is a compelling and distressing fictional first-person account which presents itself as a *testimonio*[83] and provides its readers with a poetic and moving recreation of the perspective of an individual caught up in a ferocious but (at least up to that point) little-known mass slaughter. Arguably, in fact, together with the 1999 translation into English of Alexis's *Compère Général Soleil* and, in 2005, of Philoctète's *Le peuple des terres mêlées*, Danticat's novel firmly contributed to raise awareness of the 1937 massacre in the Anglophone world.[84] The protagonist and narrator of *The Farming of Bones* is Amabelle Désir, an eyewitness who survives the horrors of the bloodbath; her linear narrative details what happened before, during, and after the killings, and is interjected by chapters (in bold font to differentiate them from the others) where we are invited to share her inner life, her dreams, her nightmares, and her longing for her fiancé Sebastien, who 'disappeared' during the massacre. Amabelle was born in Haiti but went to live as a servant with a rich Dominican family when, as a child, she was found by them on the Dominican bank of the River Massacre. This encounter took place shortly after the drowning of Amabelle's parents, with whom she was on her way back to Haiti after visiting Dajabón to buy some cooking pots. Border crossing, the novel explains, was an everyday activity, facilitated by a bridge, stepping stones, and the presence of young boys, both Haitian and Dominican, who 'for food or one or two coins [...] carr[ied] people and their merchandise across the river on their backs' (p. 51); another character, the Dominican Doctor Javier, crosses the River Massacre to work in a little hospital in Haitian territory (p. 21).

As Alexis and Philoctète had done before her, Danticat explains that not all Dominicans supported the massacre: Dr Javier is killed by the military while trying to smuggle some Haitians and Haitian-Dominicans across the border into safety, and Amabelle reveals that some 'Dominicans' gave her and her fellow fugitives on their way to Haiti 'looks that showed that they pitied [them]' (p. 190). The *mêlée* nature of the local population foregrounded by her predecessors is also alluded to when, during their escape towards the border, Amabelle and her companions come across Dolores and Doloritas, 'two Dominicanas' or, Amabelle continues, 'a mix of Haitian and Dominican

---

[83] For example, the dedication to Metrès Dlo is signed by the character and not by Danticat.

[84] Danticat acknowledges Alexis' novel in the Acknowledgement to *The Farming of Bones* (p. 312) and the translation of Philoctète's novel from which I have been quoting has a Preface by Danticat (pp. 7–9).

– in some cases it was hard to tell' (p. 171). The two sisters are in search of Ilestbien, Doloritas's beloved husband who was of Haitian descent and had been captured by the military: they cannot speak Haitian Creole and identify themselves as Dominicans but are as terrified of Trujillo's army as Amabelle. The novel also maintains that in Haitian territory, in the tent clinics where those who had escaped the massacre received some medical care, Amabelle meets a 'Dominican' man who could speak only Spanish but was mistaken for a Haitian because of his blackness: 'there were many like him,' she asserts (p. 217).

Yet, despite the fact that she recounts moments of solidarity and communality, Danticat's novel decisively brings to the fore the presence of anti-Haitianism in the borderland: compared to Veloz Maggiolo's *raya* and Philoctète's *terres mêlées* inhabited by 'one' people (but also to Alexis's Macorís), Danticat's borderland comes across, by and large, as a much less integrated place despite the fact that the Dajabón province, where the novel is set, was home to a close-knit *rayana* community – in fact, one of the most affected during the massacre. At the time of the massacre Amabelle had spent most of her life working as a maid for the rich family who found her by the river and lived in Alegría, a Dominican border settlement in the Dajabón area. The name of the location is significant: as one of the characters points out, 'Alegría [is] a name to evoke joy […] perhaps this is what its founders – those who named it – had in mind. Perhaps there had been joy for them in finding that sugar could be made from blood' (p. 271). Work in the sugar fields is also evoked by the very title: the 'farming of bones,' the novel explains, is the English translation of the Haitian Creole expression *travay tè pou zo*, which refers to what one of the characters describes as 'cane life' (p. 55). Moreover, the first page alone contains three references to sugar cane ('cane stalks'; 'sugarcane harvest'; 'cut the cane'), Amabelle's fiancé and many of her friends are *braceros*, and the last words of the book are a dedication to those 'who still toil in the canefields' (p. 312). In establishing a link between the 1937 massacre and the sugar industry, Danticat follows Alexis and Philoctète, a decision that might have influenced the modalities of interaction depicted in the novel. In Danticat's Alegría, moreover, the owner of the nearby sugar mill is the white-skinned Don Carlos: according to Vega, in the Dajabón area there were no *bateyes* belonging to Dominicans but, in *El Masacre se pasa a pie*, Prestol Castillo talks about 'cane fields' in Santiago de la Cruz (near Dajabón) which belonged to a certain Don Francisco, which, according to the writer, were cultivated by 'negroes' who appear to be 'Haitians' because they speak Creole (pp. 118–19).[85]

---

[85] 'Bernardo Vega y Edwidge Danticat discuten la matanza de 1937', *Hoy*, 5 June 2004,

In *The Farming of Bones* the population of Alegría is described as ethnically diversified at all levels and, in contrast with the previously discussed novels, which present us with a much more homogeneous picture, Danticat's characters tend to belong to very different social classes. The big villas on the hill are owned not only by affluent Dominicans (Don Carlos and Dona Eva) and well-to-do former European immigrants (the Spanish Papi, the owner of the house where Amabelle lives) but also by rich Haitians such as Dona Sabine and Don Gilbert, who appear to be, at least prior to the massacre, perfectly integrated into Alegría's elite. Their wealth derives from a rum enterprise that had been in Don Gilbert's family for five generations, first on Haitian soil and then on what became Dominican soil. Their villa is surrounded by a wall and protected by Dominican guards; we are told that, during the massacre, the guards were dismissed for fear that they would turn against their former employers and that the villa was used by its owners to help and hide poor and middle-class ethnic Haitians (pp. 71–2; 162–4). The poor Dominicans and ethnic Haitians who work as servants and maids (like Amabelle) live within the perimeters of these villas, while those who work as *braceros* in Don Carlos's mill live in the compound next to it. They share small shacks and a common cooking hut, wash in the nearby stream, and consider themselves as *vwayaje*, or wayfarers, people who do not belong anywhere: Sebastien, Amabelle's fiancé, one of the *braceros*, regards both himself and Amabelle as members of this category despite the fact that, unlike him, Amabelle had spent most of her life in Alegría (p. 56). The novel shows no solidarity between *braceros* and Dominicans: for example, the food stand of the compound belongs to a Dominican woman called Mercedes (possibly a distant relative of Don Carlos), who is hostile to Haitian immigrants: she blames them for bringing down the salaries of those poor Dominicans who find themselves obliged to work in the cane fields to make ends meet (p. 105).

Between the stream and Don Carlos's mill are the houses of the stable, or *non-vwayajè*, 'Haitians,' who are better off than the cane cutters but not as wealthy as Don Gilbert. They had 'proper' houses made of cement or wood, often with gardens and yards full of fruit trees; among them were landowners, farmers, metal-workers, stonemasons, dressmakers, shoemakers, and teachers; many had intermarried with Dominicans, had been born in Alegría, and had never been to Haiti (p. 68).[86] In the novel, the *non-vwayajè* 'Haitians' are the first group slaughtered by the military (pp. 153–8) while,

---

http://hoy.com.do/bernardo-vega-y-edwidge-danticat-discuten-la-matanza-de-1937/ [accessed 27 November 2014].

[86] Despite this, the novel identifies them as Haitians.

also in line with what happened in 1937 to those who were working in North American sugar mills, the *braceros* who work for Don Carlos are not targeted (p. 300). Sebastien is captured, and presumably killed, because he did not remain in the compound but, encouraged by Amabelle, tried to escape. Amabelle was due to run away with him but was late for their appointment and the novel describes how she could not help but feel responsible for his death and agonizes over it for the rest of her life. Prior to the massacre, the *non-vwayajè* were regarded by the *braceros* and poor Haitians as 'people who had their destiny in their hands' (p. 68). Alexis and Philoctète foreground a high level of integration and transnational solidarity in the mixed communities they depict, but Danticat's novel presents us with Alegrían ethnic Haitians who feel an intense sense of alienation and rejection which, crucially, is deep-rooted and predates the massacre: they lament the fact that they cannot send their children to proper schools and that they are denied equal rights, official papers, and birth certificates; in particular, they seem to be acutely aware that the Dominicans always regard them as 'foreigners,' no matter how long their families had lived there (p. 69). In her 'Acknowledgements', Danticat explains that *The Farming of Bones* is 'a work of fiction based on historical events' whose 'inaccuracies [and] inconsistencies' are due to the demands of 'narrative flow' and 'artistic license' (p. 311). Arguably, however, the novel is also shaped by and intervenes in debates surrounding the conditions of Haitian *braceros* working for the Dominican sugar industry and the disregard for the human rights of Haitian–Dominicans (i.e. the denial of official papers such as birth certificates and children's lack of access to education) which were strongly debated and controversial issues when Danticat wrote her novel and, as we will see in the following chapters, continue to be so.

Following Alexis and Philoctète, in her epigraph to the novel Danticat refers to the '*perejil* test' by quoting the Bible (Judges 12), where the Gileadites identify Ephraimites because they say 'sibboleth' instead of 'shibboleth' and then proceed to murder thousands of them. Most of the ethnic Haitians in Alegría, Danticat reminds us, spoke Alegrían Creole and Spanish, 'the tangled language of those who always stuttered as they spoke, caught as they were on the narrow ridge between two nearly native tongues' (p. 69). However, after spending most of her life in the Dominican Republic, Amabelle tells us that she could actually say the word *perejil* properly if given 'a chance' (p. 193). Sadly, she is denied this chance when she is severely beaten up and almost killed by a group of fired-up young Dominicans who, brandishing handfuls of parsley sprigs, attack her and other fugitives who were passing through the border town of Dajabón on their way to Haiti. Here the '*perejil* test' serves no practical purpose and is not even properly conducted: in fact, before their victims can actually respond and (linguistically) perform 'Dominicanness,' the thugs stuff the parsley into their mouths and almost choke them to death (p. 193). This is a very disturbing scene, particularly because those who unleash their violence against Amabelle and her companions are actually civilians gathered in the main square of Dajabón, eager to catch a glimpse of Trujillo, who is visiting the town. Ironically, Amabelle owes her life to the Generalissimo himself because, when her torturers hear that he is approaching, they lose interest in their victims and leave them wounded on the ground while the Orquestra Presidente Trujillo plays the Dominican national anthem (p. 194).

In a public exchange of letters with Danticat, Vega strongly criticized this reconstruction of the events because it gives the impression that Dominican civil society actually approved of and took part in the massacre. Vega insists that the only civilians who were involved in the episodes of violence and in the actual killings of ethnic Haitians were convicted criminals and *asimilados* – that is, local people who knew where the 'Haitians' lived and were temporarily militarized for the purposes of the massacre.[87] In her response Danticat asserts that she doubts that a massacre of that magnitude could have taken place without at least some degree of complicity by Dominican civil society and some of the eyewitnesses interviewed by historians confirm that some civilians were in fact among the killers, even though their direct participation was more of an exception rather than the rule.[88] Danticat also reveals that the episode in the novel where Amabelle is forced to eat parsley and is beaten up by a group of civilians is actually based on the direct experience of her great-uncle, who

---

[87] 'Bernardo Vega y Edwidge Danticat discuten la matanza de 1937'. Arguably, the characterization of those civilians who took part in the massacre as 'temporarily militarized' is not entirely satisfactory in terms of excluding 'civilians' as such but see also Vega, *Trujillo y Haití*, vol. I, pp. 349–60, where Vega includes the official depositions of twenty-six eyewitnesses which invariably implicate soldiers and policemen; in a few instances, however, civil authorities are also mentioned and in one case we are told that the soldiers were accompanied by a civilian 'guide' who, however, did not take part in the killings. See also Prestol Castillo, *El Masacre*, p. 50 and Hiciano, *Cronología de un pueblo*, pp. 45–8.

[88] In *Holocausto en el Caribe* Aquino García reports the involvement of civilians coerced by the military to take active part in the killings (pp. 121–33, especially pp. 124–6), as does Hiciano in *Cronología de un pueblo*, p. 46. Turits also reports the involvement of civilians but he highlights in addition that that many local 'guides' refused to kill 'Haitians' when asked to do so by the military and adds that 'Haitians and Dominicans overall, and most state documents, rarely mentioned any civilians killing Haitians' ('A World Destroyed', pp. 619–20), an assertion echoed by Prestol Castillo, *El Masacre*, p. 50 and Hiciano, *Cronología de un pueblo*, pp. 45–8.

had been attacked in that very same way when he was living and working in the Dominican Republic (she does not specify where) as a young man.[89] The nature of Vega and Danticat's exchange highlights how difficult it is to piece together the past of the borderland, a past which was occluded for a long time and traversed by multiple inconsistencies and contradictions, and reminds us that its reconstruction is also always inflected by the urgencies of the present.

In point of fact, Danticat's novel begins by bringing to the fore some of these 'urgencies' by focusing on the birth of Señora Valencia and Senor Pico's twins. Señora Valencia was a child when her father brought home the orphaned and lost Amabelle, at the time a little girl roughly the same age as Valencia's. As children they used to play together but their different class, status (mistress and servant), and ethnicity (Valencia is a Dominican who, apparently, descends directly from the Conquistadores; p. 18) turned their relationship into a progressively more awkward one, 'always dangling between being strangers and being friends' (p. 300). When Valencia gives birth to a boy and a girl, Amabelle acts as a midwife. The boy is 'a Spanish prince,' 'coconut-cream colored' like his mother (pp. 29, 9); the girl, half his size, was born with the umbilical cord around her neck, 'as if [her brother] tried to strangle her' (p. 19). The boy appears to be reasonably strong, while the tiny girl's health is a source of anxiety for Dr Javier; readers are indirectly warned that she might not survive (p. 20). Named after Valencia's dead mother, little Rosalinda is 'a dusky rose' who resembles Pico, with his 'honey-almond skin and charcoal eyes' (pp. 19, 35), and could be easily mistaken, as Valencia says with apprehension, 'for one of [Amabelle's] people' (pp. 35, 12). This suggestion of a possible Afro-Caribbean heritage for Rosalinda (and, implicitly, Pico) – reinforced by Dr Javier's 'impolite assertion' that Rosalinda 'has a little charcoal behind her ears'[90] – is 'undone' a few pages later by Valencia herself, who, resorting to the discourse of indigenism, describes Rosalinda as an 'Indian princess' (pp. 17–18; 29). If, as we have seen, Señora Valencia chooses her daughter's name, it is her husband Pico, employed in Trujillo's army and one of the officers in charge of *el corte*, who christens their son 'Rafael' as an homage to the Generalissimo (p. 36). It is clear that Pico favours his son, whose gender identifies him as his 'heir' and whose colour does not create any embarrassment for the family (p. 36). A few hours after their birth, however, Rafi mysteriously dies in his bed.

---

[89] 'Bernardo Vega y Edwidge Danticat discuten la matanza de 1937'.
[90] A Dominican expression which alludes to the presence of African blood in an individual's ancestry.

The significance of Rafi's death is easier to understand if read in the context of Vodou, according to which twins (or Marassa) are exceptionally powerful beings who occupy a very privileged place beside the *lwas*. Yet, the birth of twins puts a lot of responsibility on their parents: it is crucial, in fact, that twins should be treated exactly alike if jealousy is to be avoided and they must be carefully supervised to prevent one from harming the other.[91] As we have seen, Rafi and Rosalinda are not treated or regarded exactly the same: when he first meets the twins Pico does not even look at Rosalinda, whose skin places her outside the racial, ethnical, and colourist parameters which were used to define Dominicanness. Ultimately, however, what causes Rafi's death is not, simplistically, Rosalinda's 'jealousy,' but rather the way in which their parents embrace the regime's privileging of Hispanophilism, their denial and occlusion of the importance of an Afro-Caribbean heritage, and their (indirect) promotion of antagonism between the two nations of Hispaniola. These discourses, as we have seen, found their most violent expression in the 1937 massacre and, counter-intuitively perhaps, one could argue that Danticat's novel presents Rafi as the first victim of *el corte* and of the divisive and murderous ideology which sustained it and, later, continued to shape the project of Dominicanization of the borderland and promote anti-Haitianism.

It is no coincidence that, in their public exchange of letters regarding the reality of 1937, both Danticat and Vega refer to the Dominican politician of Haitian descent Peña Gómez, who had recently died. Peña Gómez, Vega reminds us, is an excellent example of the solidarity which Dominicans extended to Haitians and Haitian-Dominicans in 1937: an infant at the time of the massacre, he was saved from certain death by a Dominican couple who adopted and protected him. In the 1990s Peña Gómez's Haitian origin was used as a weapon against his candidature for the presidency of the Republic and Danticat remembers how upset her great-uncle was when he saw political enemies challenging Peña Gómez 'to say *perejil*' during one of his political speeches, forcing him to 'prove' his 'Dominicanness' according to the 1937 test. This episode brought back to Danticat's great-uncle the aggression he suffered in the Dominican Republic as a young man and from which he managed to escape thanks to the help of some Dominicans of goodwill, who saved him from harm.[92]

Vega's and Danticat's references to Peña Gómez highlight the distressing continuities between 1937 and the 1994 shameful electoral campaign against Peña Gómez conducted by Balaguer. It is worth remembering that, in

---

[91]   Métraux, *Voodoo in Haiti*, pp. 146–53.
[92]   'Bernardo Vega y Edwidge Danticat discuten la matanza de 1937'.

October 1937, Balaguer was Trujillo's Foreign Minister *ad interim* and, when *The Farming of Bones* was published, he had been in power for twenty-four years (1960–62; 1966–78; 1986–96), had published some of the most ferociously anti-Haitian and racist Dominican texts, had concluded advantageous deals with the Haitian government to exploit Haitian *braceros*, but had also orchestrated mass deportations of Haitian migrants. Similar continuities can be traced between the '*perejil* test' with which Peña Gómez was challenged and the questions addressed to Torres Saillant in the above mentioned conference of 2003, when he was challenged to prove his 'Dominicanness,' which was deemed dubious on the account of his status as '*dominicanyork*' and his defence of pluralism (p. 231). However, the triangulation of the past, the (at the time of Danticat's writing) present of Hispaniola, and the diasporic position from which Torres Saillant's intervention and Danticat's novel spring forth also engenders a glimpse of hope for the future of the island: Amabelle's surname 'Désir,' in fact, might well identify her as one of the 'new Désiré(e)s' wished for by Alexis's Hilarion. 'Desires,' which often arise from the darkest of circumstances, according to Bloch, are frequently projected onto day-dreams: the collective '[day-] dream of creating one people from two lands mixed together' in Philoctete's novel can be seen precisely as one of these projections which also shares with Ignatia Marsan's dream of a (re)unified borderland in *El hombre del acordeón*, Alexis's 'Désirés,' and Danticat's 'Désir' the potential to activate 'the expansive dreams [...] of [...] utopian designs' which play such a crucial role in Bloch's utopian thinking.[93]

At the end of the novel, betrayed by both native and adoptive country (the second part of the book recounts how the money that Trujillo paid to the Haitian government to compensate the victims of the massacre never actually reached them), Amabelle realizes that she has never belonged to either of them in an exclusive and exclusivist way, positively identifies herself as a *rayana* ('I knew as well how to say pesi [parsley in Haitian Creole] as to say perejil'; p. 265), and reclaims a composite identity for herself. After a short and disappointing visit to Alegría after Trujillo's death Amabelle stops by the River Massacre, where her parents had drowned, where she was found by Valencia's father, and where many were killed while trying to cross into Haiti back in 1937. The novel closes with the image of Amabelle lying in the river, 'paddling like a newborn in a washbasin,' and 'looking for the dawn' (p. 310). The fragile possibility of a new beginning for Amabelle and

---

[93] Francesca Vidal and Welf Schröter, 'Can We Hope to Walk Tall in a Computerized World of Work?', in *The Privatization of Hope*, eds P. Thompson and S. Žižek (Durham, NC: Duke University Press, 2013), pp. 288–99, pp. 288–89.

Hispaniola as a whole that this open ending might contain is inscribed, as it was for Veloz Maggiolo, Philoctète, and (albeit indirectly) Alexis, in the very core of the borderland. Amabelle's self-positioning in the river which signposts the border is an effort to reconfigure what Rueda had called a *'línea de muerte'* ('a [border]line of death') into a place where all cultural components are valued and considered equal, different accents do not decide on an individual's life or death, and the ability to call parsley *perejil* or *pesi* is embraced as an asset. Veloz Maggiolo, Alexis, Philoctète, and Danticat, albeit in different ways and degrees, have all revisited the past, 'training their imagination,' as Torres Saillant would put it, in order to meet the challenges of the present and pave the way to the potentialities of the future.[94] The novels in question do not offer us merely wishful compensatory fantasies or impossible-to-achieve blueprints but force their readers to train their own imagination so as to credit an occluded (and still antagonized) 'alternative' history of the island which, if acknowledged, can contribute to the development of a healthier state of affairs and a more egalitarian future. Veloz Maggiolo, Alexis, Philoctète, and Danticat truly cast the borderland as 'a goldmine of opportunities' in their articulation of what Bloch would call a 'concrete utopia,' something both 'deliberate and determined,' which 'anticipate[s] and reach[es] forward toward a *real possible* future.'[95] It is apt and important, in relation to the transnational dialogue in which the writers considered in this chapter are engaged, that Bloch's operative word 'concrete' actually derives from *concretus*, the past participle of the Latin verb *concrescere*, which means 'to grow *together*.'[96]

[94] Torres Saillant, 'La Condición Rayana', pp. 226–7.
[95] Cooper, *Everyday Utopias*, p. 3 (emphasis mine).
[96] Peter Thompson, 'Introduction', in *The Privatization of Hope*, eds P. Thompson and S. Žižek (Durham, NC: Duke University Press, 2013), pp. 1–20, p. 12.

Chapter Seven

A geography of living flesh: bearing the unbearable

Sergio Reyes, *Cuentos y leyendas de la frontera* (1996), *La Fiesta de los Reyes y otros cuentos de la frontera* (2004) and 'La Vigía: destellos del "Sol Naciente" en la frontera' (2009), Kenzaburo Oe, *Sayonara, watashi no yon yo!* (2005), Anthony Lespès, *Les semences de la colère* (1949), Jesús María Ramírez, *Mis 43 años en La Descubierta* (2000), Luis Vencedor Bello Mancebo, *Memorias de Pedernales: Vencedor Bello y Alcoa Exploration Co* (2013), Bernard Diederich, *Seeds of Fiction: Graham Greene Adventures in Haiti and Central America 1954–1983* (2012), Graham Greene, *The Comedians* (1966)

Rueda's *Bienvenida y la noche*, as we have seen, ends with Trujillo departing from the city of Montecristi in 1929 after delivering a threatening speech (p. 154). On 2 October 1937, after he had ruled the country for seven years, Trujillo addressed the inhabitants of the Montecristi province again in order to make very clear his intention to eradicate, once and for all, the Haitian presence from the Dominican borderland.[1] After accusing the Haitians of stealing from the Dominicans he promised his compatriots that he would 'solve the problem. Indeed,' he said, 'we have already begun. Around three hundred Haitians were killed in Bánica. The solution must continue.'[2] Trujillo's solution was to forcibly include the unruly and disorderly *raya* into his geography of management by turning it into the dominated 'Dominicanized' and modernized frontier. This not only caused the death of thousands of people but also impacted on the lives of the *rayanos* who continued to live on the borderland and had to pay the price of modernization, and transformed the lives of the settlers of the

---

[1] The province of Montecristi and Dajabón were split in two in 1938.
[2] Wucker, *Why the Cocks Fight*, p. 48.

agricultural colonies which were established on both sides of the border in the aftermath of the massacre.

The human and environmental costs of post-1937 modernization are brought to the fore by some of the texts included in this chapter. Others reveal the incongruities which emerge when both the Dominicanized borderland, which up to that point existed only at the level of discourse, and the model agricultural colonies as they were planned and envisaged 'on paper' – what Lefebvre would call 'conceived' or even 'representational' spaces – are approached from the perspective of those for whom they were places in which they had to live and develop practices of daily life informed by mechanisms of survival and resistance against abusive governments often supported by exploitative foreign interests.[3] The writing analysed here spans from journalism to fiction (mostly with a strong autobiographical element) and from memoirs to travel writing, by not only Dominican and Haitian but also Japanese, English, and New Zealand authors. Overall, the works under scrutiny both document and elaborate upon the many different circumstances in which those living in the borderland were made 'to bear the unbearable' (as a local commentator eloquently put it), piecing together what, borrowing Rueda's words, we might call 'a geography of living flesh.'[4]

✳✳✳

In *Cuentos y leyendas de la frontera* (Tales and legends from the frontier,' 1996) and *La Fiesta de los Reyes y otros cuentos de la frontera* ('The Epiphany/ celebration of the Reyes and other tales from the frontier,' 2004) Sergio Reyes has collected a series of life sketches, experiences, memories, legends, and stories which constitute an important record of the oral history of the area around Dajabón.[5] Reyes, who currently lives in New York, is a writer

---

[3] Lefebvre, *The Production of Space*, pp. 38–9.

[4] For the expression 'bearing the unbearable' see Sergio Hipólito Reyes Arriaga, 'La Vigía: destellos del "Sol Naciente" en la frontera' (Tercer Lugar), in *Premio Periodismo Rafael Herrera* (Santo Domingo: Colleción Premios Funglode/GFDD 2009 Periodismo), pp. 76–103, p. 97, which will be discussed later in this chapter. Rueda talks about a 'geography of living flesh' in his long poem *Las metamorfosis de Makandal* (Santo Domingo: Banco Central de la República Dominicana, 1999), p. 184. I will return to this poem in Chapter 8.

[5] Reyes, *Cuentos y leyendas*, p. 29 from now on, page references to this text will be in parentheses preceded by CL) and Sergio Reyes, *La Fiesta de los Reyes y otros cuentos de la frontera* (Santo Domingo: Editora Universitaria-UASD, 2004). La 'Fiesta de los Reyes' is the Epiphany but the title here is a pun which also refers to the family of the Reyes (which also means 'Wise Men' in Spanish), whose lives and

and an established journalist particularly interested in the way of life in the Dajabón border province; he was born in El Seybo in 1956 but in the 1960s and 1970s he spent part of his childhood and adolescence in Pueblo Nuevo, by Loma de Cabrera and Dajabón, less than two kilometres from the border with Haiti. The key figures in these books and from Reyes's childhood are his grandparents, Hipólito Reyes and Vitalina Jiménez, who had moved to the Haitian–Dominican borderland from what was then the province of Salcedo during Trujillo's programme of Dominicanization of the frontier. Like other *colonos* (settlers), Vitalina and Hipólito were given a house of wood and corrugated iron, a plot of land, farm animals, and tools, and had the possibility of receiving a loan to establish their activities (CL p. 18). Apart from being peasants and developing agriculture in the area, their job was to form a 'human wall' against the Haitian 'enemy' which was depicted as an 'aggressor' and a 'bloody cannibal' (CL pp. 18–19).

In the aftermath of the 1937 massacre, the land which was being distributed to the newly arrived farmers used to belong, for the most part, to the Haitians or Haitian–Dominicans expropriated or massacred by Trujillo. Reyes recounts that it was not unusual for the settlers to find in the ploughland skeletons and human remains of those who had been murdered, while those who had escaped and lost everything as a result of Trujillo's politics looked across the river with deep sadness at what was once their land and was now owned by others (CL p. 34). At least initially, many of the newly arrived felt that their new properties were haunted by the souls of the slaughtered Haitians and Haitian–Dominicans and some believed that the victims were coming back as *luciérnagas* (CL p. 42) and *animitas* (CL p. 89) (glow-worms; fireflies) to reclaim their own.

Given the circumstances, many settlers felt uncomfortable with the expropriation and, unable to cope with the pressure, they wanted to leave; the government, however, deemed their presence necessary for the transformation of the borderland, so the newly arrived became 'prisoners in the huge jail which was called *La Frontera*' (CL p. 19). Their 'jailers' were those soldiers who, selected according to, among other things, the colour of their skin (they had to be as white as possible) and their lack of any previous connection with the borderland and its people, had been sent by the government to police the border. The oppressive presence of the military police is recorded in the story of Alberto, Reyes's uncle, who was

---

experiences the volume celebrates. From now on, page references to this text will be in parentheses preceded by FR. The short stories 'La "*baja*"', 'Una macabra venganza,' and 'El secuestro,' included in FR, had also been anthologized in *Antología Literaria Contemporánea de la Frontera*, pp. 83–91.

caught gambling by a military patrol, resisted arrest, ran away, and was forced to hide in the capital for years. The fact that he managed to reach Santo Domingo and survive there undisturbed, Reyes proudly asserts, had to do with the fact that his grandparents were highly respected in the area and could count on the help of many 'anonymous heroes' who risked their lives in order to help Alberto (FR pp. 115–19). Another anonymous hero is eulogized in a story entitled 'Una macabra vengeanza,' which recounts the posthumous supernatural revenge of a neighbour who was murdered by the military police for his 'subversive' activities (FR pp. 179–85). Both Reyes's books also celebrate famous local figures who resisted the power of the centralized state: from the *caudillo liniero* Desiderio Arias, with whom Reyes's grandfather had fought in his youth (CL pp. 39–40; 243–4), to Henry Segarra Santos, a political left-wing activist killed by the Balaguer regime in 1969 (FR pp. 157–62). Alberto's story and the admiration with which figures such as Arias and Segarra Santos were regarded by the borderland's inhabitants highlight that the Dominicanization of the borderland had succeeded only up to a point in creating loyal subjects to Trujillo and Balaguer and subduing the traditional insurrectionary and subversive nature of the area.

For some of the settlers, as we have seen, the initial encounter with their new home was highly problematic and traumatic, but Reyes explains that they slowly began to appreciate and bond with the landscape: the land around Pueblo Nuevo was fertile and Haitians and Haitian–Dominicans had left behind many mango, cashew, and avocado trees. The new dwellers also learnt how to coexist with the fauna of the area, which comprised different species of birds and fish, many of which became an integral part of the peasants' diet (CL pp. 20–22). Farm and domestic animals, especially pigs (CL pp. 220–35), dogs (CL pp. 187–94), hens (CL pp. 175–80; 123–6; FR p. 104), cocks (FR pp. 173–7), and horses (CL pp. 195–200; 209–14), feature prominently in Reyes' books alongside local predators such as ferrets (CL pp. 187–94), guaraguaos (CL pp. 123–6), and snakes (CL pp. 175–80). Overall, Reyes's sustained attentiveness to their presence gives us access to a society in which animals and humans are highly dependent on one another: we learn about the elaborate preparation of an Easter dish for which every part of a suckling pig is put to good use (CL pp. 235–9) and, while one brave horse saves the life of his rider during a storm (CL pp. 209–14), guaraguaos, snakes, and rats repeatedly damage, in various ways, subsistence farming and the peasants' livelihood (CL pp. 91, 187–94; 123–6; 175–80; FR pp. 45–53). Other aspects of daily life are carefully illustrated: for example, forms of corporal punishment for children and their favourite playing spots (CL pp. 95–8; FR pp. 25–8; 31–3; 55–9); the beneficial properties and unwelcome effects of local plants (FR pp. 21–3; 35–9; CL pp. 133–9); local feuds (FR pp. 129–37); and the daily routine of the peasants (CL pp. 99–102; FR pp. 17–20).

Reyes's borderland is also a place where complex negotiations of the natural–supernatural boundary occur. Animals, for example, are sometimes endowed with supernatural powers or traits. We have already seen how glow-worms were initially associated with the victims of the 1937 massacre, but Reyes also mentions butterflies, known as *guéperes* (a transcription of the way in which the word *huésped* –'guest'– is pronounced in the rural borderline), whose arrival preannounces important visits; owls, we are told, were particularly feared because it was believed that they always brought bad luck (CL pp. 103–08). Natural phenomena such as storms and tempests are also read as demonstrations of the anger of superior powers; lightning strikes are described by Reyes's grandparents as black stones which fall from the sky at high speed and can cause great destruction once they reach the surface of the earth. Owing to the velocity with which they reach the ground, these thunderstones, or *piedras de rayo*, generally end up being buried seven feet underground, where they remain for seven years until they resurface of their own accord and can be used for protection against bad luck (CL p. 151; FR pp. 42–4).

We are also introduced to supernatural beings such as *la solitaria*, a woman-spectre who, during the full moon, wears a white dress and offers sexual favours to men who cross her path in the attempt to make them creatures of the underworld forever linked to her. According to the legend (which sounds like a cautionary tale to suppress women's sexuality), she was run over by a truck whose driver who had not seen her when, affected by an unspecified disease which made her sexually insatiable, she used to stand on the side of the road to seduce passers-by (CL pp. 164–74). *Galipotes* are described as shape-shifters and blood-suckers whose legend first developed in Haiti (CL pp. 41, 254). As anticipated in Chapter 4, anti-Haitian discourses have often conflated *galipotes* with dark-skinned Haitians[6] but Reyes explains that, among the peasants of the *frontera*, the threat of *galipotes*, who generally watched over the property and livese of rich landowners, had more to do with class than ethnicity or race (CL pp. 41–2). In *La Fiesta de los Reyes*, the connection between money and evil is reiterated with the legend of Don Pedro, a local Dominican wealthy landowner who had made a pact with the devil in order to become increasingly affluent: according to their agreement, the devil would carry on piling up riches for his 'associate' in exchange for the lives of some of his workers. After a while, the landowner

---

[6] Rodríguez, *Haiti and Trans-Caribbean Literary Identity*, p. 194.

began to feel uncomfortable with the presence of so many widows on his land and tried to change the terms of his agreement with the devil, who, predictably, found a way to frame Don Pedro even further (FR pp. 121–8).[7]

In Reyes's *frontera* the natural–supernatural boundary is negotiated *according to* but often, at the same time, *against* the dominant discourses which enforced (and still enforce) the geopolitical border of the island. Alexis, as we have seen in the previous chapter, was theorizing the marvellous realism of the Haitians at roughly the same time that the Dominican settlers on the other side of the border were in the process of 'wrapping up' their experiences in their own 'treasury of tales and legends' which reflected their 'new conception of the world and of life' strictly informed by the locality in which they were slowly settling down.[8] Again paraphrasing Alexis (whose focus, however, was on the Haiti vs Europe dichotomy rather than on borderland vs nation), one could argue that these tales and legends come about to assist the borderland in solving its peculiar problems, providing it with an alternative to national discourses.[9] In *Cuentos y leyendas*, for example, we are presented with a situation in which everyone believed that an infant had died because of the intervention of a *bruja* or witch (CL p. 153). *Brujas* and *brujos* are powerful but also menacing figures who, like *galipotes*, are usually associated with Haiti, while *curanderos*, popular healers, tend to be Dominicans and are considered less powerful and more benign than their Haitian counterparts.[10] In Reyes's account, however, the evil *bruja* is never openly associated with Haiti; on the other hand, the neighbouring country is identified as a potentially helpful resource. Unlike the Dominican *guajiro*, who, in a famous nineteenth-century poem,[11] refuses to take part in Vodou by insisting that '*como soy dominicano / yo si no bailo judu*,' ('since

[7] The story of Don Pedro is an elaboration on the figure of the *bacá* who often protects his owner, as later illustrated in this chapter, but who can also bring wealth to him, usually requesting a sacrifice, such as the death of a family member (Derby, *The Dictator's Seduction*, p. 214). It is interesting here that those who are being sacrificed are Don Pedro's employees, thus suggesting a certain tension in the class dynamics of the area.

[8] Alexis, 'Of the Marvellous Realism of the Haitians', pp. 271–70.

[9] Alexis, 'Of the Marvellous Realism of the Haitians', p. 272.

[10] Derby, 'Haitians, Magic, and Money', p. 518.

[11] Juan Antonio Alix, 'Dialogo cantado entre un Guajiro dominicano y un Papá bocó haitiano in un fandango en Dajabón' (1874), in *Poesia popular dominicana*, ed. Emilio Rodríguez Demorizi, pp. 267–86. In this poem, Vodú appears as a threat to Dominican identity and integrity and it begins with the Dominican asserting that he will have to put an end to Haitian *brujeria*, which he disparagingly calls *poiquería* ('rubbish').

I am Dominican / I do not dance Vodou'), when his child gets very ill the desperate father portrayed by Reyes does not hesitate to cross the border to secure the assistance of a Haitian *brujo* or *Papabocó*, who prepares a potion and instructs him on how to confront the *bruja* to neutralize her. Unfortunately, when this particular father returns to his native village his child is already dead, 'taken away by the witch' (CL pp. 155–6).

Similarly, the short story 'Bacá' introduces us to two women in a difficult predicament who are prepared to face a long and difficult journey to a village in the Dominican border province of San Juan de la Maguana in order to visit a famous *Papabocó* to better their condition. San Juan de la Maguana is a significant destination as it has traditionally been associated with one of the most powerful messianic leaders of the borderland, the faith healer Dios Olivorio Mateo Ledesma, or Papá Liborio. A contemporary of other leaders of peasant rebel movements in Hispaniola, such as Desiderio Arías in the north of the Dominican Republic, the Gavilleros in the east, and Charlemagne Pèralte in Haiti (with whom, as we have seen in Chapter 6, he had important contacts), Liborio operated in the valley of San Juan, in the central portion of the border between Haiti and the Dominican Republic, at the beginning of the century. He was assassinated in 1922 by United States marines after becoming a powerful symbol of both the borderland's defiance to central power and national resistance against occupying forces. Liborismo, however, did not die with Liborio, and his devotees continued to visit the holy sites where he used to practise: during Trujillo's regime worship continued in secret owing to periodic campaigns against popular healers which instilled fear in both practitioners and believers. In 1961, upon Trujillo's death, the borderland community of Palma Sola – an alternative 'nation in miniature' – became an important centre for a new millenarian movement whose founders, the Ventura Rodríguez twins – also known as the *Mellizos* – were said to embody the spirit of Liborio.[12] Palma Sola was a community organized according to a complex set of social and spiritual principles which were often in open contrast with national rules: for example, they rejected 'the evil of money, medicine, politics, and even CARE food aid,' and its members' children were withdrawn from the local school.[13] Notably, the Catholic bishop of San Juan de la Maguana regarded Palma Sola as a centre for Vodouistic witchcraft: while pointing towards the borderland's across-the-border syncretism, this association testifies to the reputation of

---

[12] Derby, *The Dictator's Seduction*, p. 243; Lundius and Lundhal, *Peasants and Religion*, pp. 172–8.
[13] Derby, *The Dictator's Seduction*, p. 228; Lundius and Lundhal, *Peasants and Religion*, pp. 179–220.

Haitian magic, which has traditionally been considered more potent than its Dominican counterpart.[14]

At the end of 1962 Palma Sola, suspected of being a political organization which was engineering either a return of pro-Trujillo forces via Haiti or a communist coup, was attacked by the military and destroyed: the contemporary press reported forty deaths, but, according to some sources, more than 800 people were killed, hundreds were wounded and 673 were taken into police custody.[15] The visit described by Reyes must have taken place after the assault and testifies to the fact that, despite this ruthless attack, the area around San Juan de la Maguana did not lose its association with powerful supernatural forces. When they approach the *Papabocó*'s dwelling, the two women in Reyes's story are confronted by a *bacá*, a magic creature which prowls around the property of witch-doctors and which, after a pact with the devil, defends and preserves their estate. The two women manage to neutralize the *bacá* by fervently reciting an *oración* – which in Spanish means both 'Christian prayer' and 'magic charm.' After this encounter they are received by the *Papabocó*, whose 'doors are open to those who come in peace asking for help' and who readily assisted the two in their attempt to improve their situation (CL pp. 201–8).

Reyes also remembers how, as a child, he was instructed never to cross into Haiti, which was defined by his elders as the house of the Devil whose favourite food was disobedient children who traversed the border against their parents' will. The association between Haiti and evil here seems to be motivated by fear of possible retaliations for *el corte* but also by the necessity to prevent children from drowning while fording the river on their own. It goes without saying that Reyes and his little friends crossed the river anyhow, especially because they knew that on the Haitian side they could find delicious cashews. In so doing, they discovered that, as a result of 1937, Haitian children were afraid of Dominicans: when their neighbours spotted Reyes and his companions they would run away in terror even if they were, legitimately, in their territory (CL p. 36). On one occasion, however, a little Haitian boy was bold enough to talk to the Dominican children and, much to their surprise, he declared that, despite their different nationalities, they

[14] Derby, *The Dictator's Seduction*, note 2 p. 337 and 'Haitians, Magic, and Money'.
[15] Lundius and Lundhal, *Peasants and Religion*, pp. 221–52, 560–600; Derby, *The Dictator's Seduction*, p. 228 and note 2. Pp. 336–7 lists a number of important sources and comprehensive studies of the movement. Luis Francesco Lizardo Lasocé, *Palma Sola: La tragedia de un pueblo* (Santo Domingo: Editora Manatí, 2003) reproduces the confusion which governed both the planning and the execution of the attack on Palmasola.

could become friends. Reyes remembers this episode as a revelation, as it was at that point that he realized that there were neither enemies nor 'demons' on the other side of the river and that such enmity was, he explains, a creation of those who oppressed the Dominican and Haitian people alike (CL pp. 79–85, 33).[16]

In *La Fiesta de los Reyes* we find another example of a 'Haitian' reaching out to a Dominican in the legend of the settler Ricardo and the ghost of the Haitian *Fransuá* (italics in the text), killed and robbed in 1937 by the Dominican army captain Tizón. Fransuá had lived for many years in the area, namely in Santiago de la Cruz, where, thanks to his entrepreneurial abilities, he had managed to open a general store and become reasonably wealthy; being an illegal immigrant, however, he could not put his money in a bank and had to hide it away. He was honest and generous with his customers and generally liked and respected for his fairness but there were those who were envious of his good fortune, and rumours began to circulate about a treasure and a mysterious hiding place.[17] Taking advantage of *el corte*, two local troublemakers struck a deal with Captain Tizón, who had been sent to the area to supervise the killings, and decided to torture and kill Fransuá to steal his buried treasure. Before dying, Fransuá cursed them with his last breath. As soon as they dug up two large jars in which Fransuá had hidden his money, Capitain Tizón shot his accomplices and reburied the treasure in a different spot, from where he planned to retrieve it at a later date. Suddenly relocated by the army to a different area of the country, Tizón was able to return only many years later, by which time the landscape had changed so much after the arrival of the settlers that he struggled to remember the exact spot where he had hidden the money. When he finally thought he had identified it and began digging, the ghost of Fransuá appeared to him and 'demons, spectres, birds of prey, terrifying witches, hideous goblins, all disgusting inhabitants of the caverns of Avernus' began to come out of his mouth (FR p. 153). The terrified Tizón was so scared that he lost his mind and was last seen walking towards the River Massacre and Haiti – that is, 'towards the descendants of those he had done so much evil to. Nobody heard from him ever again' (FR p. 154).

The curse pronounced in 1937 finally reached Tizón, the last of Fransuá's three killers, but the Haitian's hatred for his murderers did not extend to all

---

[16] The cover of Reyes's book highlights the existence of across-the-border correspondences by utilizing a painting by the Haitian Gèrald Valsin entitled 'La reunión' to illustrate the way in which, in the evening, Dominican families used to get together around the fire to drink, eat, and tell stories (cover and p. 46).

[17] For more on this see Derby, 'Haitians, Magic, and Money'.

Dominicans. Fransuá's ghost, in fact, appeared to the 'good-hearted' settler Ricardo to reveal to him that his money was buried in the local cemetery and to invite him to take it and use it for himself and his family. Ricardo followed the ghost's instructions, retrieved the money, lit a few candles, and recited a prayer for the Haitian who had chosen to give him such a gift (FR pp. 147–56). Clearly, this story/legend is aimed at distancing the settlers from the 1937 murderers and at sanctioning their presence in the borderland by dramatizing a form of 'blessing' given to them by the previous occupiers of that territory. Eventually, in fact, the settlers managed to process and overcome the trauma associated with the violence which preceded their arrival in the borderland: as time went by, significantly, they no longer associated glow-worms with the souls of murdered Haitians coming back but, rather, perceived them as wonders of nature which fascinated children (FR pp. 29–30).[18]

Reyes is in fact very keen to demonstrate that, despite the initial distrust, Haitians and Dominicans of the *frontera* managed to put aside mutual fear and developed different forms of collaborative linkages.[19] Smuggling – on a small, domestic scale – was rife: for example, Haitian *clerén* and *Barbancourt* were routinely smuggled in, usually at night, and widely consumed on the Dominican side (CL p. 143). *Clerén*, in fact, plays an important part in the *junta*, a form of collaborative work which, Reyes argues, was crucial to the creation of a sense of community among the first Dominican settlers. For a *junta*, a group of peasants voluntarily come together to help one another perform agricultural tasks: the farmer who asks for help offers music, plenty

---

[18] *Antología Literaria Contemporánea de la Frontera* contains a short story entitled 'La botija' ('The earthen jug'), by Ramón Emilio Helena Campos, which recounts how the Devil himself revealed to a local peasant the presence of buried treasure near his home in Dajabón. Unfortunately, when the Devil shares with someone such information he wants to be paid by a human life and, despite the fact that the poor peasant does all he can to protect his family and retrieve the much-needed treasure, his little daughter dies as soon as he digs it up. The fact that the exact location of the treasure is confirmed by the presence of glow-worms suggests that this treasure too might have been hidden by a 'Haitian' on the run because of the 1937 massacre. This 'Haitian' is conflated with the Devil rather than with a good-hearted man. The short story's tragic ending, moreover, seems to indicate that some settlers were still feeling uncomfortable in the borderland (pp. 41–7).

[19] Despite the existence of welcome rapprochements that Reyes highlights in both his books Haitian–Dominican relations were not always or necessarily predicated on equality. For example, Reyes remembers that his grandmother Vitalina at one point had a little Haitian boy who worked for her as a servant: he was not badly treated but, significantly, his name is never revealed – he is referred throughout as *haitianito*, *negrito*, or *chiquillo* (pp. 175–80) – and we are told that he is the first to be (wrongly) suspected of theft when a snake steals some eggs during the night (p. 176).

of food, and, crucially, *clerén*. He will pay back his helpers by assisting them for free when required (CL pp. 55–7).[20] *Clerén* is also essential for *baquiní*, the special funeral rites normally officiated after the death of a young child: *baquiní* has to be a festive occasion to make sure that the infant will intercede for their relatives from heaven (CL p. 159), so vast quantities of *clerén* are served while the *palos* or *atabales* (three long-drums of African origin which are also played to entertain those who participate in the *junta*) intone their music and the children who take part are treated to special sweets.[21]

Music and *clerén* also played a central role in the rapprochement of Haitians and Dominicans: from Pueblo Nuevo, in fact, Haitians were not just *visible* across the river: they were also *audible* when, during their parties, they played their drums and accordions (CL p. 43). Reyes informs us that, little by little, the men of Pueblo Nuevo began to cross the river to take part in these celebrations while their women resented them and blamed on *clerén*, Haitian *mereng*, and the 'sensual gazes and bodies' of the Haitian women the origin of many extramarital love affairs (CL p. 74). In *Cuentos y leyendas* we are not told if the love affairs which began during parties on the Haitian side actually consolidated into more permanent relations, but the anxiety displayed by Dominican women when they see their husbands crossing the border does suggest that at least some of these encounters tended to become more than a simple adventure. Reyes's books relate that it was not uncommon for Dominican men to keep multiple wives and to have children from different women, but he never specifies if these multiple wives were all Dominicans (CL pp. 215–18; FR pp. 39–40).[22]

Traditional anti-Haitian discourses are detectable, at least *prima facie*, in the account of these transnational parties: Dominican women are 'good' mothers and wives whose only 'defence' is the 'rosary,' while Haitian women are sexual predators and *femmes fatales*; Haiti, moreover, is the 'dangerous' '*tierra del Vudú*' ('land of Vodou') in opposition to a Catholic and civilized Dominican Republic (CL pp. 74–5), and the demonization of Haitian music as '*non sancta*' ('unholy') is perfectly in line with the way in which Reyes tells us it was perceived in the rest of the country and 'in the ballrooms

---

[20] In Haiti this form of collaborative work is called *convite* or *konbit* and it is most likely that it shares its African (Dahomey) origin with the *junta* (Deive, 'The African Inheritance', pp. 117–18).

[21] Deive traces the etymology of *baquiní* back to Africa, namely eastern Dahomey ('The African Inheritance', p. 113). In 'La cultura en Dajabón,' Rubén Darío Villalona explains that 'Los Palos' are an important musical genre in the province: see *Antología Literaria Contemporánea de la Frontera*, ed. Francisco Paulino Adames (Santo Domingo: FUDECESFRON, 1998), pp. 52–6, p. 53.

[22] Derby describes these practices in 'Haitians, Magic, and Money', p. 515.

of the puritan society of Dajabón' (FR p. 85). Reyes, however, is well aware of how anti-Haitian discourses have succeeded in creating enmity between the two people (FR p. 84), and he often alerts his readers to the fact that the binary oppositions on which they are predicated (i.e. Christianity/Vodú; Spain/Africa; whiteness/blackness) are not as sound as they might seem. For instance, in his *Sincretismo: Formas de Expresión en la Frontera*, rosaries are listed among different objects used by Dominicans to gain protection against negative forces and we are urged to consider their deployment in a context in which Catholic saints and paraphernalia coexist and often conceal Afro-diasporic beliefs.[23] When Reyes describes Vitalina's house in *Cuentos y leyendas* he highlights how in one corner of the kitchen one could find an 'altar' with 'candles,' decorated with flowers and with the images of numerous Catholic saints including, for example, the Virgin of Altagracia, el Santo Niño de Atocha, and Santa Clara, who have their counterparts, in Dominican Vodú, in Alaila Ezili, Legbá Carfú, and *La Señorita* respectively. Vitalina also had the effigies of La Tres Divinas Personas (the Divine Trinity) and Los Santos Médicos (the twins Cosma and Damiano), which represent, side-by-side, the generally benevolent Trinitarian logic and the often malevolent – or at least ambivalent – logic of 'two' which characterize Haitian and Dominican Vodú as well as Catholicism (CL p. 50).[24]

✳✳✳

In 1956 Dominican settlers such as Vitalina and Hipólito, who had been invited by Trujillo to people the borderland, were joined by another group of colonists who came from far away to became part of the 'human wall' that Trujillo was trying to build to keep at bay the Haitian 'menace.'[25] In In 'La Vigía: destellos del "Sol Naciente" en la frontera' ('La Vigía: Sparkles of the "Rising Sun" in the Borderland'), a series of articles written in 2009 and dedicated to Tania Mukai and his cousins Shigeru, Yuki, and Hideki Kamanaka, Reyes celebrates the 53rd anniversary of the arrival in the *colonia agricola* of La Vigía, near Dajabón, of those members of his family who are of Japanese origin. Invited by Trujillo, who had long been keen to promote

---

[23] Reyes, *Sincretismo*, pp. 9–10.
[24] In *Sincretismo*, Reyes describes such altars and practices as 'subterfuge[s]' (pp. 9–10). See also Deive, *Vodú y magia*, pp. 171, 177; *Las 21 Divisiones – Dominican Vodou*, http://las21divisiones.com/misterios-of-las-21-divisiones-dominican-vodou [accessed 25 November 2014]; Derby, *The Dictator's Seduction*, pp. 212–13.
[25] Reyes Arriaga, 'La Vigía', pp. 76–103, pp. 79, 84. From now on, page references will be in parentheses in the text preceded by PP.

the establishment of colonies of white immigrants in the borderland, Japanese arrived in the Dominican Republic in 1956. In an effort to regain international approval after the 1937 massacre of Haitians and, simulta- neously, to 'whiten' the nation, Trujillo had also invited Spanish refugees from the Civil War and Jews who were escaping from Nazi persecution in Europe (PP p. 83). The Spanish refugees he had welcomed, however, did not prove very useful in the rural context in which he had placed them (they mainly came from a urban background) and soon departed from the Dominican Republic for other destinations in Latin America; the same happened with the Jewish colony he established in Sosua – most of the colonists were ultimately repatriated or left for other locations and those who stayed quickly relocated in the capital (PP pp. 84, 87).[26]

In 1954, when Trujillo approached the Japanese government with an offer to establish communities of Japanese farmers and fishermen in the Dominican Republic, Japan was struggling to accommodate the nearly seven million people who had been repatriated from its former colonies. Negotiations regarding the assignment of houses and land and the payment of financial subsidies commenced straight away and the Japanese government began to advertise the Dominican Republic as a 'Caribbean Paradise' in which Japanese citizens would have a real chance to thrive (PP pp. 85, 87–8).[27] Trujillo, this time, made sure that the immigrants were experienced farmers and fishermen and had financial resources of their own; moreover, he authorized the entrance only of families composed of at least three males between the age of fifteen and fifty (PP p. 88).[28] According to the agreement stipulated by the two nations, the Japanese government was in charge of the recruitment and selection of the colonists, of the cost of transportation, and of the supervision of the facilities provided; the Dominican Republic was supposed to allocate to each family a furnished home, roughly two square kilometres of land ready for sowing, and a daily subsidy for the first six months (PP p. 88).

The twenty-eight families that were destined to La Vigía arrived in Santo Domingo in July 1956. When they reached their final destination in the borderland, they were asked to focus on the cultivation of rice and peanuts, but they soon realised that the situation in which they had to operate did not match the promises with which they had been enticed: poor soil, inadequate irrigation, and lack of proper transport facilities from La

---

[26] Oscar H. Horst and Katsuhiro Asagiri, 'The Odyssey of Japanese Colonists in the Dominican Republic', *Geographical Review*, 90.3 (2000), pp. 335–58, p. 341.

[27] Horst and Asagiri, 'Japanese Colonists', pp. 341–2.

[28] Horst and Asagiri, 'Japanese Colonists', p. 342.

Vigía to the markets of the capital made their lives extremely difficult (PP pp. 91, 93).[29] Often they also found themselves involved in conflicts between Haitians and Dominicans and had to learn not to become embroiled in these altercations (PP p. 94). The Japanese families that were distributed to other colonies of the country (six out of eight were located on the *línea fronteriza*) encountered similar problems. Dominican priorities shifted in 1961, after Trujillo's assassination and the ensuing political unrest, and the discontent of the colonists forced the Japanese government to begin a process of voluntary repatriation: of the 1319 Japanese who had arrived in the Dominican Republic between 1956 and 1959, only 276 remained in the country (PP pp. 92, 94–5).[30] Those who decided to stay came, for the most part, from former colonies of Japan and had few family ties left in the mother country, so they were ready to '*bear the unbearable*' and make do '*with whatever the country could offer them*' (PP p. 97; italics in the text).[31]

The hardship of these Japanese settlers is not forgotten in their country of origin: in *Sayonara, watashi no yon yo!* ('Farewell, my books!,' 2005), a novel by the Japanese Nobel Prize winner Kenzaburo Oe, the old and sick writer Kogito Choko (Oe's alter-ego) refers to the poor quality of the land that was allocated to those who migrated to the Dominican Republic while showing to his friend Shigeru Tsubaki a picture of one of the colonies' allotments, where the soil is clearly 'rough' and 'full of big rocks.'[32] Choko's plan is to include this picture in *Choko-Symptom*, a sort of 'diary' in which he aims to collect evidence – in the shape of 'signs' or 'symptoms' – of the ongoing decline of the world; in the book, the above-mentioned picture is to be accompanied by the commentary of a ruthless civil servant who told the disappointed settlers that those rocks will soon turn into 'fertilizer.'[33] According to Choko's catastrophic vision, people abandoned in the way in which the Japanese settlers were abandoned in the Dominican Republic end up being 'annihilated, with no hope of recovering'; at the same time,

---

[29] Horst and Asagiri, 'Japanese Colonists', p. 342.

[30] Horst and Asagiri, 'Japanese Colonists', pp. 342–7.

[31] Horst and Asagiri, 'Japanese Colonists', p. 347. In 2006 the Japanese who had remained in the Dominican Republic to work demanded compensation from the Japanese government for having abandoned them to their own devices after encouraging them, with false promises, to migrate. The Japanese government agreed to compensate them and those who decided to repatriate and issued a public apology for the way they had been treated (PP pp. 99–100).

[32] Kenzaburo Oe, *¡Adios, libros míos!*, trans. T. Ryukichi (Barcelona: Editorial Seix Barral, 2012), pp. 373–4. I have availed myself of the Spanish translation because *Sayonara, watashi no yon yo!* has not yet been translated into English.

[33] Oe, *¡Adios, libros míos!*, pp. 373–4, 366.

Figure 13. Monument built in 1981 which celebrates the 25th anniversary of the arrival of Japanese settlers in the colony of La Vigía (Dajabón) (photograph: Maria Cristina Fumagalli).

he continues, the 'idiotic' words of the civil servant also anticipate the catastrophe as they can be pronounced only by 'a broken human being' who has lost 'all hope' of stopping his own and the world's decline.[34]

Reyes, instead, presents us with a more positive scenario and reveals that the descendants of those who arrived in 1956 in La Vigía were well integrated into the life of 'their' village: intermarriages between them and Dominicans were not infrequent and, according to demographic statistics available at the time, the number of individuals with double nationality (Dominican and Japanese) was on the increase. The older members of the community are still very attached to their traditions but this does not prevent them from feeling proud of being *Dajabóneros*. In 1981, he explains, on the 25th anniversary of their relocation in the Dominican Republic, the colonists of La Vigía built a monument to celebrate their arrival right in the centre of the village (PP pp. 81–2, 99).[35]

---

[34] Oe, *¡Adios, libros míos!*, p. 374.
[35] Horst and Asagiri, 'Japanese Colonists', p. 351.

Some of the Japanese who decided to stay have in fact done well for themselves and the majority of these families have moved out of the precarious accommodation provided for them by Trujillo: these houses are now abandoned, or, ironically, occupied by impoverished Haitians – that is, by the very same people the dictator had tried to keep away from his country by inviting the Japanese migrants to establish themselves in the borderland.[36]

✶✶✶

In the aftermath of the massacre things were also rather difficult for those who had survived *el corte* and relocated in Haiti, a country that some of them had never seen before or had left many years earlier, and where many had no family left. In the second part of *The Farming of Bones*, Danticat describes the way in which these refugees felt betrayed and unsupported by the Haitian government: the financial settlement between President Sténio Vincent and Trujillo was inadequate to begin with but, to make things worse, the Dominican state did not pay the whole of the agreed sum. Danticat's protagonists (Amabelle and Yves) are among the many who never received any compensation and were left to fend for themselves. In *El Masacre se pasa a pie*, discussed in the previous chapters, Prestol Castillo also points out that the Haitian mulatto elites 'educated in Paris' were prepared to betray their compatriots if Trujillo bribed them with enough money and suggests that in Haiti the indemnity was mainly used to refurbish mansions in rich and residential areas while the 'thousands of amputees wandering around the eroded land of Haiti resorted to steal what they had previously sown in Dominican territory' (p. 152).

The Haitian government, however, did use some of the money paid by the Dominican state to establish agricultural colonies where the survivors of *el corte* were invited to settle and work. Unfortunately, none of these colonies was a success.[37] In *Les semences de la colère* ('The seeds of anger,' 1949) the Haitian writer, journalist, and politician Anthony Lespès, an agronomist who founded the Parti Socialiste Populaire in 1946 and who worked for the Ministry of Agriculture in the early 1940s, when new methods to protect the soil were being investigated, exposes the unsatisfactory conditions in the colony of Billiguy, a village situated in the Département du Centre and not too far from the border with the Dominican Republic.[38]

---

[36] Horst and Asagiri, 'Japanese Colonists', p. 354.

[37] Price-Mars, *La República de Haití y la República Dominicana*, vol. 2, p. 786.

[38] Anthony Lespès, *Les semences de la colère* (Port-au-Prince: Deschamps, 1949). Page references will be in parentheses in the text.

In 1938 Lespès was put in charge of the colony of Billiguy so, even if he does not appear as a character in *Les semences de la colère*, it is reasonable to assume that this third-person narrative, which covers the years from 1938 to 1943, is largely based the author's personal experience and that he shares the deep sympathy that the narrator feels for the peasants/ settlers.[39] The aim of Billiguy and the other colonies established in Haiti at the time was to make sure that the experienced farmers who had lost everything during *el corte* would remain in the country and contribute to its agricultural development. In Billiguy the state had planned to relocate 300 families and to provide them with tools, accommodation, seeds, and managers with different skills to assist them in the project (i.e. a director, agronomists, topographers, builders). There were also plans for a church, a school, a clinic, a police station, a metereological station, a hangar for the tools, buildings related to agricultural activities, a generator, a park and other amenities, and a big market where the peasants could sell their produce (p. 11). Sadly, things did not go as intended.

Billiguy, to begin with, had been selected not because it was a particularly fertile area but simply because it was one of the few places where there was a piece of land big enough for this enterprise: in post-independence Haiti, in fact, most of the large estates had been partitioned into individual smallholdings (p. 9). Lespès's book informs us that, in fact, most of the land surrounding Billiguy was not good for agriculture: the area suffered from prolonged droughts and the peasants could rely only on rain to irrigate the fields. *Les semences de la colère* describes three years in the life of the settlers during which a combination of drought, unexpected torrential rain, hail, the omnipresence of ineradicable weeds called 'Madame Michel,' and other external factors conspired to turn this particular colony into a disaster. Moreover, the number of families the land had to sustain was far more than the planned 300 – at some point the author reports the presence of 412 (p. 33) – so what the land did produce was never sufficient to support all those who depended on it: many lived at the point of starvation, feeding themselves only with boiled leaves (p. 154). Unlike the settlers described by Reyes, their counterparts in Haiti could not even organize a *coumbite* – a form of collective work where everyone helped everyone else by taking turns – because nobody had enough to buy *cléren* or even feed those who would have volunteered to help (p. 95). The question of ownership of the land was also a problematic issue: the settlers were given allotments to cultivate but they were told that before properly 'owning' their allocated

---

[39] Edith Wainwright, *Culture Haïtienne à travers des texts choisis: manuel d'enseignement* (Coconut Tree, FL: Educa Vision, 2001), p. 50.

plot they had to look after it and make it productive for at least two years. The land, however, was often of such bad quality that the peasants felt that no matter how much hard work they put into it, they would achieve very little or no results; moreover, when they were told that they would never be able to sell the land that was given to them but only to pass it on to their children, they felt even more sceptical about the scheme: 'This entire business is suspicious,' complained one of the men, 'we are asked to work for free' (pp. 40–42).

As noted above, *Les semences de la colère* is written in the third person, but it includes very harrowing first-person accounts of the 1937 killings, which had traumatized all the survivors who hoped to begin a new life in Billiguy, most of whom lost family and friends in horrific circumstances. Yet, in spite of their terrible experiences and despite being aware of the high degree of hostility they would have to face there, we are told that many of them eventually decided to go back to *Dominicanie* to search for a better life. Their desire to return can be better understood if one considers that many had lived for a very long time in the Dominican Republic (in some cases more than thirty years) and that their children were born there: when they first arrived in the colony, they spoke Spanish among themselves and some continued to do so a year or two after their arrival (pp. 30; 160). Many, we are told, never felt that they belonged in Haiti, a country which had previously 'spewed them onto the frontier' (p. 153) and where they continued to feel betrayed and unwelcome. The narrator, in fact, presents us with the lack of sympathy with which the survivors of the massacre were regarded by the Haitian elite and by the original inhabitants of the area, who feared that their livestock would no longer be able to graze on the land that was being allocated to the settlers. According to the narrator, the Haitian elite's prejudices against the peasants were not so different from those which had characterized Trujillo's murderous policy: he describes a short visit to Billiguy by some members of the Port-au-Prince's elite who came to see how the survivors lived as if they were 'animals in a zoo' (p. 25). Significantly, while the settlers arrived on foot, these visitors arrived by car and, while looking at the peasants from a distance, they describe them as lazy and dirty Vodou practicioners interested only in cockfighting and other wicked activities and whose behaviour brought shame to the country (p. 26). Their presence in the Dominican Republic is described as a 'slow invasion' (p. 27) which could understandably generate anxiety for their neighbours, whose attempt to preserve their racial superiority and their 'noble *hidalgo* blood' is considered entirely legitimate (p. 27).

As the narrator explains, the Haitian elite could sympathize with Trujillo because, affected by what Jean Price-Mars had called 'collective

Bovarism,'[40] they felt the need to state their superiority vis-à-vis the peasants; he offers us the example of a young journalist who not only considered Trujillo's policy as 'defensible' but goes as far as describing him as 'a patriot' who unfortunately failed to differentiate between the Haitian masses and the elite and whose real error was to kill 20,000 people all in one go: he should instead have eliminated them in small groups over a protracted period of time; in that way, he continues, nobody would have known or, indeed, complained (p. 28). In *El Masacre se pasa a pie*, Prestol Castillo had also argued that the 'mulatto landowners who studied in Paris' hated their poorer and blacker 'brothers' and were happy to exploit them for profit (p. 104). Despite the different political agendas which characterize the two authors, the Haitian and Dominican texts here concur in suggesting a disturbing across-the-border continuity between the anti-Haitian and anti-borderland discourses promoted by the Dominican oligarchy to justify the 1937 massacre and Haitian internal racism and classism.

The settlers, however, were ostracized also by the locals, who initially regarded them with suspicion and even blamed them for the drought which began to afflict the area as soon as the newcomers moved there. The hostility manifested itself in a series of conflictual exchanges, threats, sabotage against the colony, and even murder: for example, a starving settler who had killed and eaten a stray ox which belonged to one of the original inhabitants of the area was killed with a powerful poison by the cattle owner (pp. 84–91;127–33). In such a tense climate, it is no surprise that the settlers began to perceive the landscape itself as unwelcoming and even menacing: the lack of fertile land and the omnipresence of weeds were soon complemented by the ongoing danger posed not only by poisonous snakes but also by *galipotes* and *loup-garous* or were-wolves (pp. 46–7; 79–83).

At the end of the story we are shown how, in 1943, the settlers quickly prepared to defend themselves with everything they had against an attack which, they were told, had been launched by the Dominicans who had crossed the border at Elias Piña/Belladère. It soon transpired that the rumour was false: there was only a minor incident at the border where two people had been killed and ten wounded. Yet, the speed with which the news spread and the fact that an attack of this kind was considered entirely plausible testifies to the persistence of the trauma caused by the 1937 massacre and to the deep sense of alienation and insecurity that the Haitian settlers experienced in Billiguy.

---

[40] Price-Mars, *Ainsi parla l'Oncle*, p. 8.

***

The next two texts to be studied here are two recent memoirs, *Mis 43 años en La Descubierta* ('My 43 years in La Descubierta,' 2000) and *Memorias de Pedernales: Vencedor Bello y Alcoa Exploration Co* ('Memories of Pedernales: Vencedor Bello and Alcoa Exploration Co,' 2013). Both are important local documents which introduce us to the effects of 1937 on the central and southern sector of the Dominican borderland and describe the way of life in these communities.[41] In *Mis 43 años en La Descubierta* the story is narrated in the first person but it is Gisela Ramírez de Perdomo who has collected her father's memories of a life spent in La Descubierta, a small town near the border with Haiti. Jesús María Ramírez arrived in La Descubierta in 1921, when he was still a child, because his father was a *Montimpector* – that is, a member of a special corps of border guards created during the North American occupation who were supposed to prevent smuggling. Ramírez witnessed the negative effects of the Dominicanization of the central section of the borderland on its population and, operating as a government official, he remained in La Descubierta until 1964, contributing to the project of modernization of the area masterminded by Trujillo.[42]

At the core of Luis Vencedor Bello Mancebo's *Memorias de Pedernales*, instead, is the life of the author's father and the role he played in the exploitation of bauxite carried out in the southern portion of the borderland by the North American company Alcoa (Aluminium Company of America). The presence of Alcoa in the area, as we will see, was also the subject of a piece of travel writing by the New Zealand journalist and writer Bernard Diederich, who visited the Alcoa compound with the English writer and literary critic Graham Greene in 1965. Among other things, this visit inspired Greene to denounce the exploitation of the locals by the North American company in ways which chime with the grievances presented by Luis Vencedor Bello Mancebo in relation to his father's experience and the price that he and others had to pay for the post-1937 plan for modernization of the borderland.

In 1921, Jesús María Ramírez recalls, La Descubierta was a village with a few small farms, apiaries and goat pens.[43] The binational market was crucial to the local economy and social life: Haitian buyers and sellers

---

[41] For more information on La Descubierta see also Alberto Perdomo Cisneros, 'La Descubierta. Frontera y Mercado', *CLÍO – Órgano de la Academia Dominicana de la Historia*, 173 (2007), pp. 247–75.

[42] Perdomo Cisneros, 'La Descubierta. Frontera y mercado', p. 263.

[43] Jesús María Ramírez, *Mis 43 años en La Descubierta*, ed. Gisela Ramírez de

took an active part in it (we are told that across-the-border trade had been flourishing since the 1870s), the merchandise was generally paid in *gourdes*, and business transactions took place 'half in Spanish and half in *patois*' (italics in text; p. 17). Haiti exported all sorts of products to the Dominican Republic but Ramírez remembers, in particular, doors and windows made in Port-au-Prince which adorned the houses of some of the wealthiest inhabitants (p. 21). The young Ramírez went to Haiti often and thoroughly enjoyed visiting Port-au-Prince, which he describes as an impressive and bustling city with great shops, markets, and social interactions still unknown in Santo Domingo; he explains that, at that time, it was much easier (and more desirable) for those who lived in La Descubierta to cross the border and go to Port-au-Prince rather than to other Dominican towns in the same province, such as, for example, Comendador/Elias Piña (p. 23). Many families who lived in the vicinity of La Descubierta were mixed and had Haitian ancestors, and Ramírez reminds us that Haitian people often lived and worked in the Dominican Republic: he remembers the case of a well-known and respected Haitian teacher who operated in Neyba, a town where Ramírez lived before moving to La Descubierta and which is located further from the border (p. 52). Across-the-border cultural exchanges between the two countries are also brought to the fore (albeit indirectly) by Ramírez's repeated use of Haitianisms: notably, in the very first page of the book, he recounts his first visit to La Descubierta in 1921 and uses the Haitianism '*cu*' to describe a neighbourhood formed by people of the same family (p. 13).

Things, however, were bound to change. In 1937, news of the killings which took place in Dajabón and Montecristi reached the central portion of the borderland, whose inhabitants were also informed that, by the end of 1938, all the 'Haitians' living in the area would have to relocate in Haiti as part of a process which became known as *el desalojo* (or 'evacuation'): it was painful, he recalls, to see friends and former collaborators leave their homes and their families being dismembered. Ramírez also explains that the majority of those who refused to go were killed, mostly in June and July of that year (p. 65). Soon afterwards, however, some of these evacuees came back to steal cattle and other produce from the now empty farms that they had been forced to leave behind and in some cases they formed criminal bands which terrorized the locals with their activities (pp. 66–7; 70, 73). Ramírez, however, highlights that Haitian livestock was also stolen by Dominicans. When he became the respected local president of Trujillo's party, he made sure that the stolen cattle were returned to the Haitian

Perdomo (Santo Domingo: Editora Centenario, 2000), p. 15. Page references will be given in parentheses in the text.

authorities in what he remembers as a friendly meeting along the border where the two flags waved side by side (p. 74).[44] The two governments, he reveals, tried to organize a binational market in the same spot in which the exchange of cattle had taken place: this failed as a commercial enterprise but, while it lasted, it allowed friends and relatives who had been separated by what Rueda has called the *línea* to briefly get together again (p. 75).

In 1942, Ramírez was summoned by Trujillo, who gave him the task of funding and developing a Dominican colony in the southern province of Pedernales, in front of the Haitian market of Tetagló; Ramírez and his men were given passes to cross the border and acquire everything they needed for this enterprise (pp. 77; 81–2). In 1943, with the arrival of the settlers, the Dominicanization of the Pedernales began: the colony funded by Ramírez was christened 'Francisco del Rosario Sánchez' and the Haitian name of the nearby hill of Letó was changed to 'Flor de Oro' to celebrate Trujillo's daughter. Concomitantly, Ramírez continues, all the Haitian names of the southern borderland were changed: for example, 'Marrosó' became 'Ángel Féliz'; 'Sabambón' was substituted by 'Sabana Real,' 'Touissant' by 'Granada' (p. 83). Renaming is obviously a fundamental part of any form of colonization, as it has the function of erasing any trace of previous occupants and of a previous history. Significantly, Ramírez remembers that one of the names chosen for another colony in the area was '*Tierra Virgen.*' Far from being a never previously inhabited 'virgin land,' however, this was clearly a place which used to belong to 'Haitians': when he and his fellow explorers arrived *in loco* they found stoves left behind during *el desalojo* and enjoyed the ripe fruits from trees that had been planted there before the 'evacuation' and that nobody had picked for years (p. 86). In 1955, Ramírez was also put in charge of finding an appropriate space for a Japanese colony in the area between Pedernales and Bánica, but the Japanese officials who inspected the land found it inappropriate for the purpose because of the lack of proper roads (p. 117).

In *Mis 43 años en la Descubierta*, Ramírez is ambivalent towards the process of modernization which was underway in the borderland and in which he played an important role: he praises the plan of Dominicanization – which, however, he hastens to delink from the *desalojo* – because it helped develop agriculture and the overall economy in a region which had been traditionally neglected (p. 146), but, at the same time, he devotes an entire chapter to the moment in which, in 1956, the salt water of Lake Enriquillo,

---

[44] Interestingly, in *Les arbres musiciens*, Alexis also refers to Dominican cattle thieves who steal from Haitians. See especially pp. 111–13 and 191. I will go back to this novel in Chapter 10.

situated a handful of kilometres south of La Descubierta, began to rise uncontrollably: as a result, the road to Jimaní was submerged and the fertility of the surrounding land seriously compromised. Up to that point, Ramírez insists, the shores of Lake Enriquillo were extremely productive and he reveals that many, at the time, attributed this disaster to the fact that the structure of the Cristóbal Canal – built in 1955 in order to irrigate the fields of Neyba, Cabral, and Duvergé – had not been able to withstand the force of the swollen River Yaque del Sur and had emptied its waters into the lake for days (p. 127).

As noted above, *Memorias de Pedernales*, by Bello Mancebo, focuses instead on the agricultural colony of Pedernales, which was founded in 1909 but was utterly transformed by the arrival of Alcoa in 1944, two years after Ramírez contributed to the development of the area as a government official.[45] The book's protagonist is the author's father, Vencedor Bello, who was born in 1904 in Duvergé, a small town on the shores of Lake Enriquillo and not far from the Haitian border. Vencedor Bello, we are told, began his incursions into the Pedernales area in 1919 when, his son claims, he discovered the presence of bauxite but ignored its value (p. 63). Vencedor Bello spoke *patois* fluently – a fact that reaffirms the close relationship between Haitians and the inhabitants of the central and southern sections of borderland also highlighted by Ramírez. Bello Mancebo reports that 'Haitians' were also massacred by Dominican guards in the Southern provinces and adds that some Dominicans bravely protected them in this part of the borderland too (pp. 139–40). After 1937, however, Bello Mancebo recalls that the border was strictly guarded on both sides and explains that there were absolutely no Haitians in town: he saw his first Haitian person as late as 1961, when a woman from Anse à Pitre walked through the streets of Pedernales, where she was observed with curiosity and suspicion by local youngsters, who had been instructed by anti-Haitian propaganda to consider Haitians as enemies, evil-doers, and invaders (p. 141). Annoyed by the onlookers' behaviour, the woman from Anse à Pitre replied by throwing stones at the youths, who also reacted aggressively; this exchange turned the first encounter between Haitians and Dominicans that the author can recall into a violent episode (p. 141). Anti-Haitian propaganda, moreover, is repeatedly foregrounded: in the late

---

[45] Luis Vencedor Bello Mancebo, *Memorias de Pedernales: Don Vencedor Bello y Alcoa Exploration Co* (Santo Domingo: Editores Asociados, 2013), p. 188. Page references will be given in parentheses in the text. Incidentally, Japanese settlers are also mentioned by Bello Mancebo who recounts that, in 1962, they came to Pedernales to play baseball, the most popular sport in the Dominican Republic (p. 188).

1940s, when one of his relatives fell into what the author now defines as a 'schizophrenic state,' he recalls that her condition was attributed to the action of an 'evil Haitian spirit' (p. 59). Bello Mancebo also adds that, after Trujillo's death, the Haitians who came to Pedernales continued to be attacked by Dominicans who were made to feel that they had to defend their nation from a pernicious invasion (p. 141).

Bello Mancebo explains that the establishment of Alcoa in the Pedernales area had some positive effects, as it triggered the development of the local infrastructure (proper roads, an airport, a school, telephone lines); he also suggests that this business venture enabled the Dominican government to settle the country's foreign debt (pp. 79; 171; 87). However, he also insists that modernization came at a price: for example, Alcoa decided to establish its headquarters in the same site where the settlement of Boucán Polo was situated, causing the displacement of all its inhabitants (pp. 75-7). Moreover, the deforestation which currently afflicts the southern borderland, he asserts, can be partly attributed to the contract that Trujllo's government stipulated with the North American company in 1945, which gave Alcoa the right to deforest the area without the need to ask for further permission nor the duty to plant trees to replace those felled (p. 172).[46] Local workers, Bello Mancebo contends, had to fight for a decent salary: during the first phase of the exploration, he reports, in order to minimize strikes, Alcoa permanently dismissed all the workers who had participated in them (p. 67). The injustice suffered by his father Vencedor Bello who, according to his son, had assisted Alcoa from the start in the exploration of the territory and in the exploitation of bauxite only to be unlawfully dismissed and stripped of his properties after thirty years of work, is described in detail. The reversal of fortune experienced by Vencedor Bello is partly explained by a change in management which brought a new director to the helm of the local branch of Alcoa. The new manager, Mr Patrick Hughson, is described as an abusive, arrogant, cunning, and, ultimately, unfair man who allowed those who were racially prejudiced against Vencedor Bello to discriminate against him – it is worth remembering that Alcoa was committed, by contract, to contribute to the 'whitening' of the borderland by 'importing' into the Dominican Republic exclusively 'Caucasian' executive managers and directors.[47] According to Bello Mancebo, Hughson also plotted against his father and violated his employer's rights by taking advantage of his illiteracy (pp. 114, 108-10, 118, 231-50, 262-70).

---

[46] For the catastrophic effects of Trujillo's regime on Dominican woods in general see Moya Pons, *La otra historia dominicana*, pp. 233-234.

[47] Perdomo Cisneros, 'La Descubierta. Frontera y mercado', p. 271.

Alcoa and Mr Hughson also appear in Diederich's account of his 1965 stopover in the Alcoa compound. Diederich had arrived in Pedernales with Greene and another friend after an adventurous journey along the border which had begun in Dajabón (I will briefly refer again to this journey in Chapters 9 and 10). Since the 'decrepit lodging places' in Pedernales did not look 'inviting,' Diederich decided to ask Hughson, whom he had previously met in Santo Domingo, for hospitality on the Alcoa site. Hughson was extremely unwelcoming: initially he refused to let the three men through the gates of the chain-link-fenced complex. When he finally agreed to put them up for the night, he offered the tired travellers only 'dry ham-and-cheese sandwiches' and 'Coca-Cola'; when Greene asked for whisky, Hughson reluctantly offered a single glass to each of his guests. Greene, Diederich reports, found Hughson a 'bloody awful fellow' and a 'dreadful chap [with] no humanity,' but when the mortified Diederich apologised for the appalling behaviour of their host, Greene replied: 'on the contrary, this is interesting.'[48]

Mr Hughson's unfriendliness and the visit to the Alcoa compound did, in fact, inspire Greene: at the end of *The Comedians* (1966), a novel in which he famously excoriates the Duvalier regime, the protagonist crosses the border from a very troubled Haiti into the then still 'peaceful' Dominican Republic (the scene is set before the 1965 civil war and United States' intervention) and later goes for a job interview in a mining estate run by a North American company. The name 'Alcoa' is not mentioned but if one considers the location in which the mining company is situated and the road the character drives along in order to reach it, it is obvious that, when he wrote this chapter of the novel, Greene had in mind the visit he had paid to Alcoa a year earlier. The most striking feature of the modern mining compound, depicted by Greene as a 'luxurious trailer park,' is its seclusion from the surrounding area, another characteristic it seemed to have shared with the Alcoa complex described by Diederich as a 'forbidding enclosure.'[49] In the novel, the manager of the estate is called Schuyler Wilson and his unfriendliness exactly replicates Hughson's – including his 'inadequate' offer of Coca Cola.[50] Schuyler Wilson appears worried about the 'propaganda' that was entering his mining complex from 'under the wire' in the form of leaflets which aimed at making workers aware of their

---

[48] Bernard Diederich, *Seeds of Fiction: Graham Greene's Adventures in Haiti and Central America, 1954–1983* (London: Peter Owen, 2012), p. 82.

[49] Graham Greene, *The Comedians* [1966] (London: Vintage, 1999), p. 271; Diederich, *Seeds of Fiction*, p. 80

[50] Greene, *The Comedians*, p. 271.

labour rights – the very same rights which, according to Bello Mancebo, Alcoa failed to respect not only in his father's case but also in others.[51]

Greene's Schuyler Wilson appears utterly uninterested in what was happening outside the enclave of his compound, beyond its many gates, his private landing ground, and the private bauxite port which, when Greene visited the 'real' Alcoa, had reminded him of James Bond thriller *Dr No!*.[52] In conversation with the novel's protagonist, Schuyler Wilson declares that he has never heard of the *Tontons Macoutes* and hastily brands all Haitian insurgents as 'Communists.' At that point Greene's annoyed protagonist retorts: 'insurgents are not always Communists until you make them so,' an answer that chimed with Greene's own condemnation of the United States' support for murderous regimes such as Trujillo's or Duvalier's in the name of anti-Communism.[53]

It is safe to say that Shuyler Wilson is distrusted by Greene's protagonist (and his readers) as much as Hughson was distrusted by his hosts; the character's exploitative relations with employees is unsurprising but deplorable and readers cannot help but feeling that his lack of interest in the political situation of Haiti is at best disgraceful and at worst suspiciously and reprehensibly expedient. It is worth noting that, while the protagonist of *The Comedians* visits the mining estate on his own, Greene shared Hughson's (lack of) hospitality with Diederich and another travel companion, the exiled Haitian Catholic priest Jean-Claude Bajeux, an anti-Duvalierist who had relocated in the Dominican Republic to help, both spiritually and materially, the Haitians who had escaped from the regime. Bajeux had joined Greene and Diederich in an attempt to find some 'missing' Haitians, including members of his own family, that Duvalier had 'disappeared' in retaliation for the 'subversive' activities of their exiled relatives. Before visiting Hughson, in fact, the three men had gone to look for the Haitians, but to no avail, in another famous 'enclosure' not too far from the Alcoa complex: the prison of Pedernales.[54] At that time, Pedernales was the penitentiary capital of the Dominican Republic where, occasionally, Papa Doc sent Haitian prisoners (notably, they were among the very few Haitians who were allowed to cross the border at that time), who were almost invariably accused of being 'Communists.' Pedernales might have been chosen by Duvalier to destroy the spirit of his 'opponents' by making them feel alienated, isolated, far from home, and well beyond the reach of help from friends and relatives.

---

[51] Greene, *The Comedians*, p. 272.
[52] Diederich, *Seeds of Fiction*, p. 81.
[53] Greene, *The Comedians*, p. 272.
[54] Diederich, *Seeds of Fiction*, pp. 68, 80.

Annihilation of the spirit was soon to be followed by obliteration of the body since such trips, Bello Mancebo explains, invariably ended with a death sentence. Significantly, he reports having seen the following words, engraved by one of these inmates on the wall of one of the cells in Pedernales: 'O cursed Pedernales! Graveyard of living men, where men are broken and friends are forgotten!'(pp. 192–3). A civil nonentity, undone as a human being, depersonalized, and facing certain death, this prisoner in and of the borderland seems to be afraid, most of all, of being forgotten. It is impossible not to wonder if this particular fear was magnified by the location to which he was transported – that is, a place that many have often described and, as we will see, continue to describe, as remote, isolated, neglected, and, indeed, forgotten.

Chapter Eight

The forgotten heart-breaking epic of border struggle

Diego D'Alcalá, *La Frontera* (1994), Manuel Rueda, *La criatura terrestre* (1963) and *Las metamorfosis de Makandal* (1998), *Perico Ripiao* (2003) directed by Ángel Muñiz and written by Reynaldo Disla and Ángel Muñiz, Maurice Lemoine, *Sucre Amer: Esclaves aujourd'hui dans les Caraïbes* (1981), Gary Klang, *L'île aux deux visages* (1997)

The preceding chapter ended with a desperate inmate calling the prison of the southern border-crossing of Pedernales a 'graveyard of living men, where men are broken and friends are forgotten!,' a sentiment arguably amplified by its *locus* of enunciation. This chapter gives detailed attention to two novels, a long poem, a film, and a piece of investigative journalism which concentrate on different ramifications of what, in *La criatura terrestre*, Rueda has called 'the *forgotten* heart-breaking epic of [...] border struggle' (p. 26; emphasis mine). In addition, some of the works under scrutiny here remind us of particularly vulnerable border-crossers, namely the Haitian *braceros* working in Dominican *bateyes*. Their predicament was brought under the spotlight in 1979 by the London Anti-Slavery Society, which broke the silence and the strategic collective amnesia surrounding their condition. Backward looks will not be infrequent but, generally speaking, the texts and contexts at the core of this and the following chapters will deal with Hispaniola from the 1960s onwards.

In 1998, in his introduction to the *Antología Literaria Contemporánea de la Frontera*, Francisco Paulino Adames forcefully complained about the state of neglect suffered by the Dominican borderland.[1] Adames was not alone in holding such views: four years earlier, in his novel *La Frontera* ('The Frontier'), the Dajabónero Diego D'Alcalá also lamented the state of

---

[1] Adames, 'Presentación', p. 3.

abandonment in which the central powers had traditionally left his native province.² In his short preface, in fact, D'Alcalá explains that, as a work in progress, his novel had a different title, along the lines of 'the novel of forgotten and/or omitted things.' In *La Frontera* D'Alcalá describes the hardship of the inhabitants of the northern borderland, especially in Macaboncito, Dajabón, and Ouanaminthe, and offers his analysis of border relations between the Dominican Republic and Haiti. Anxious to record as many 'forgotten things' as possible, the author does not follow a particular order or chronology when making both his views and his characters' experiences available to readers: often one particular story begins or ends *in medias res*, only to be concluded (or indeed, started) a few pages later, after the narration has focused, for a while, on entirely different characters or topics. As if to counteract the divisive nature of what its title represents, D'Alcalá's *sui generis* text is not divided into chapters governed by thematic or spatio-temporal categories but presents itself as a continuous (at times, very chaotic) narration sustained for 379 pages and complicated by multiple plots interrupted by various digressions in which the narrator delves into local history, politics, and the toponomy of the area. The narrator's comments, political tirades, and descriptions of local habits, never signposted, can often catch readers unawares and continuously blur the line which separate fact from fiction.

Overall, the narrator – who seems to be giving voice to the author's own concerns – speaks from the perspective of the early 1990s, making references to events such as the ousting of Aristide and the embargo imposed on Haiti by the Organization of the American States and the United Nations or, albeit less often, to crucial moments in the history of the region and the island, such as the United States' occupation, the 1937 massacre, and Osorio's *devastaciones* (pp. 118, 254, 278–9, 67). As noted above, the novel also provides its readers with a window on the daily life of the people of the borderland and an insight into its human and physical geography: among other things, we are told how wild bulls were domesticated (pp. 1–2) and shown, repeatedly, that concubinage was extensively practised in the area; we are made aware, on almost every page, of the devastating effects of drought on agriculture and cattle raising, and introduced to the damages caused to local inhabitants by the unhealthy habit of chewing or smoking *güeva*, a kind of rustic tobacco (pp. 176–82). We are also provided with an outline of the cultural and economic profile of Dajabón (pp. 9–11) and the origin of local toponyms is revealed to us – for example, according to D'Alcalá's narrator,

² Diego D'Alcalá, *La Frontera* (Santo Domingo: Editora Taller, 1994). Page references will be given in parentheses in the text.

Canca la Reina was originally named Canca las Ñatas after a woman who had a nasal voice moved there after being bought by a Spanish colonist from a Dutch trafficker in the sixteenth century. As time went by, the women of Canca las Ñatas became 'as beautiful as queens,' so the name of the place was changed to reflect this (p. 69). D'Alcalá's novel also constantly exposes us to (and challenges us with) the speech patterns and the oral tradition of the *frontera*, with its peculiar expressions, the most recurrent of which is *según la lengua e lo palo* ('according to the language of trees, sticks, or, more likely, the long-drums of African origin called *palos*'), an *escamotage* introduced during the Trujillato to say something potentially controversial without fully committing to it. Above all, however, we are constantly reminded of the influence that, throughout the century, the proximity of the border had on different aspects of life and on the day-to-day lives of the people of the borderland.

The main fictional plot revolves around the relationship between the young Mártires Socías and the old Artemio Nabales, also known as '*el español*' or '*el Catalán*' ('the Spanish or Catalan man'). At the beginning of the twentieth century the young Nabales moved to the Dominican Republic from Catalonia and, after an initial stay in Montecristi, he bought lands in the Dajabón area (p. 372). At the time when the first part of the novel is set, while his wife lives permanently in the elegant city of Santiago de los Caballeros Nabales spends a considerable part of the year supervising his huge *hatos* close to the *frontera* with Haiti. Mártires Socías, who works for Nabales, was born and lives on the Spaniard's land and the novel begins by outlining the four different roles that, at different stages of his life, Mártires plays in their relationship. In his childhood he is a *compaicito* ('little mate'); he then becomes a *cachorro* ('puppy') as a teenager, a *compai* ('mate') as a young man, and later, an *amigo* or 'friend.'[3] As *amigo* he is invited to share with Nabales the secret of a treasure buried nearby by the Spanish General Buceta during the War of Restoration, a treasure which, however, will never be retrieved (pp. 3–4, 58–9). What the novel does not reveal until page 154, however, is that Mártires is in fact one of the many illegitimate children of Nabales's or, as the Spaniard puts it, his '*hijos de tropezones*,' born out of wedlock or 'by mistake' (p. 4). In a move that might suggest a possible overlapping between the pair D'Alcalá–Mártires, the novel is dedicated to 'all the illegitimate children of the borderland, of [his] country and of the

---

[3] '*Compaicito*' and '*compai*' are phonetic reproductions of the words '*compadrito*' and '*compadre*' as they are pronounced by D'Alcalá's characters – in the northern borderland, in fact, people tend to substitute the 'r' followed by another consonant with 'i' – see Murray, 'Lenguaje y raza', p. 256.

world.'[4] Other important characters include Tocha (Mártires's mother and Nabales's concubine), the old Román Zapata, Solimán Montero, the *Alcade* of Macabón León Durán – all local employees of Nabales – and the General Divino Mateo, with whom Durán embarks on a difficult journey south to seek the help of a *bocó* who lives in a different portion of the Haitian–Dominican borderland. Most of the dialogue between these characters seems to be a faithful transcription of the way in which the people of the borderland sound when they speak to one another, as the author records on the page many of the contractions, elisions, and peculiarities of local speech.

A substantial part of the plot is set in 1959: the novel contains references to the anti-Trujillo military expedition of Costanza, Maimón, and Estero Hondo and to Fidel Castro's Revolutionary Cuba (pp. 5, 43, 159, 213), as well as ample evidence of the constant harassment by military forces and civil authorities suffered by the local population during Trujillo's dictatorship. Nabales, for example, has to endure the requisition of one of his most fertile *fincas* ('land properties') in La Vigía,[5] while another part of his land, turned by the army into a vast shooting range, becomes impossible to use as grazing land (pp. 17, 160). Given the climate of sheer terror in which Dominicans live, when Mártires becomes *cachorro*, Nabales advises him that the safest course of action is '*ver, oír, callar*'('to watch, to listen, to keep quiet,' p. 41) or, even better '*ver, oír, callar [y] correr*' ('to watch, to listen, to keep quiet [and] to run,' p. 54). However, the novel makes it progressively clearer that Nabales is not only deeply angered by the usurpation of his property in La Vigía but also fiercely opposed to Trujillo. When some emissaries of the regime try to fine him for using out-of-date stamps on his official papers, Nabales declares that he refuses to buy new stamps until Trujillo pays him off for La Vigía. As a result of a protracted arm-wrestling match with the authorities, the old Spaniard ends up in prison, from where he is freed by his friends who, unbeknown to the proud Catalan, organize a collection to pay for his fine (p. 135).

Extreme violence against the so-called 'enemies of Trujillo,' the novel insists, was an everyday occurrence in the borderland. Yet, many members of the military and self-defined 'Trujillistas' protect Nabales in various ways and contribute to the collection to free him; he also has the support of most

---

[4] Mártires and D'Alcalá also seem to have a similar lives and academic careers: they were both born in Macaboncito and attended the Colegio Agrícola de Dajabón and the University in Santiago.

[5] The novel never explains the purpose of this requisition. In actual fact, as we have seen in Chapter 7, in 1956 at least part of a portion of land near Dajabón called La Vigía became one of the Japanese colonies established by Trujillo.

of his employees and of some of his upper-class friends in both Santiago and Dajabón (pp. 22–3, 28, 43–7, 135, 168). This brings to the fore an alternative and powerful local network of allegiances that, according to Reyes, also protected one of his uncles when he was in trouble with the regime and erodes the notion of Trujillo's absolute control of the territory, at least as far as the borderland is concerned (FR pp. 115–19). Nabales is not the only borderland-dweller who defies, more or less openly, the regime. A short anecdote recounts that when the *alcade* ('mayor') Durán is given the order to display ten portraits of Trujillo in the area, he entrusts Zapata to deal with the matter. To maximize visibility, Zapata sticks five of the portraits in plain view on a fence from where, unfortunately, they mysteriously disappear. Very anxious for his safety, the *alcade* concludes that they must have been eaten by the mule Guararé (pp. 40–41), and he is so afraid for his life and so annoyed with the mule that he has it killed. Luckily, Mártires finds five more portraits with which to substitute those that had been eaten to avoid problems with the military, but both he and Zapata are concerned about Durán, who might reveal to the military that the original portraits had been destroyed and, to further exonerate himself, lie and insinuate that Zapata had located them on purpose where he knew the mule could help himself to them. In a panic, Mártires and Zapata consider exhuming the mule to allow its carcass to be devoured by wild pigs: in so doing, should they be interrogated by the army, they would be able to 'prove' their allegiance to Trujillo by showing that not only had they punished the mule for what it did but, by denying it its burial, they treated it as all the enemies of Trujillo who, customarily, were not permitted to have a proper grave (pp. 40–49). At the end of the novel, however, we discover that it was actually Zapata who had destroyed Trujillo's portraits in revenge for the death of his son at the hands of the military, letting Guararé be blamed in order to save his own life (p. 310).

The narrator explains that, among the 'enemies of Trujillo,' the communists and the *contrabandistas* were punished with particular cruelty: yet, he also shows that the harsh persecution of the communists did not deter some peasants, who listened in secret to Radio Cuba, which continuously broadcast messages encouraging Dominicans to rebel (pp. 21, 43). When they were captured, smugglers were generally killed on the spot, left unburied next to a bottle of *Tusita* (Haitian rum which was often smuggled across the border; p. 252), and identified with a sign which read '*contrabandista*' (p. 83). Nevertheless, from Mártires's and other characters' accounts, the border seems to be very porous – 'traces' of 'trespassing' Haitians are highlighted as early as page 2 – and the smuggling of contraband appears to be widely practised in the area. The narrator is also careful to point out that not all the members of the military were keen to follow Trujillo's orders (p. 90) and that the violence of the army against the population could also have negative effects on some of its perpetrators. For example, we are informed that whenever General Mateo finds himself in the vicinity of one of the many sites where he had hung or otherwise eliminated one or more 'enemies of Trujillo' he is struck by a strong nausea and cannot prevent himself from vomiting (p. 88).

Such a debilitating condition, D'Alcalá writes, prompted Mateo to look for help from a *bocó* who '*liboriaba*' in Palma Sola and who is referred to as a *brujo* whose abilities derive from his exposure to Haitian influence (pp. 84, 111). In D'Alcalá's novel Liborio and Olivorism are never explicitly mentioned but are clearly evoked by the location in which the action takes place (Palma Sola), the verb used by D'Alcalá ('*liboriar*'), and the General's full name (Divino Mateo). D'Alcalá is rather ambivalent about this *bocó* and his charms, but overall *La Frontera* testifies to how important the area around San Juan de la Maguana was from a 'spiritual' perspective, despite the fact that, throughout Trujillo's rule, Olivorismo was forbidden and many Olivorista were accused of witchcraft and put in prison.[6] In D'Alcalá's novel Durán and Mateo are in fact initially very secretive and nervous about their visit, but when they are persuaded that the *bocó* is an effective healer they even consider the possibility of recommending him to Trujillo, who, behind the official façade, often resorted to the assistance of the supernatural (p. 148).[7]

The activities of the *bocó* of Palma Sola are described in detail: first of all, Mateo has to follow a complicated ritual that consists of a 'cleansing' bath with water in which various potions and different types of leaves had been left to brew (p. 94). This probably took place in the nearby Spring of St John, or *La Agüita*, whose waters are still considered to have healing powers and to be able to rid people of their sins. This spring has been the object of intense worship for centuries and, like La Surza, the 'spa' described by Deive and Saint-Méry in Chapter 4, is part of an important network of holy sites located in the borderland; as a matter of fact, the fact that *La Agüita*

---

[6] Lundius and Lundhal, *Peasants and Religion*, p. 155. In another part of the novel, which reveals the narrator's own ambivalent attitude also towards Haitian magic, he explains that, when their husbands betray them with other women, Dominican *damas* ('ladies') cross the frontier to resort to what he calls the 'false gods derived from the transculturation of the west of the island' (p. 243).

[7] In 'El caso de Trujillo y el bocó', Rafael Emigdio Caamaño Castillo recounts that Trujillo once visited a *bocó* in Port-au-Prince with the Haitian President Paul Magloire: on that occasion, the *bocó* predicted Trujillo's assassination in 1961 see *Antología Literaria Contemporánea de la Frontera*, pp. 120–21.

is near Liborio's birthplace is said to have assisted the spiritual leader in finding popular support. Pilgrimages to *La Agüita* reached their peak in 1962, three years after the events narrated in the novel are supposed to have taken place, when the *Mellizos* of Palma Sola used to direct people there to take purifying baths.[8]

After his bath Mateo has to visit three of the sites which bring about his vomiting sickness, kick the air three times, and throw a specially treated lemon given to him by the *bocó* in each of them (p. 147). Upon their first visit there is no time for Durán to take the purifying bath, so he has to go back to the *bocó* one more time. On that occasion we are told that Mateo, satisfied by the way in which the *bocó*'s spell has worked in the three places in which he performed the prescribed ritual, gives Durán a big sack full of lemons (one for each person he had killed for Trujillo) to be 'treated' by the *bocó* in order to protect him from the 'persecution' of his other victims. This sack was so big that, when he was carrying it, Durán was hardly visible behind it (p. 196). The lemons are then 'prepared' by the *bocó* and *La Caballo* ('The Horse'), his assistant, who cover each fruit with a piece of black cloth. Durán notices that the altar of the *bocó* is literally covered with lemons dressed in black, only twenty-four of which are reserved for Mateo: the others are to be distributed to the *bocó*'s best clients whom, we are told, are stationed at the different fortresses, prisons, checkpoints, and sites along the border where both Haitians and Dominicans are killed for crossing illegally (p. 197). 'From this, one must infer,' interjects the narrator, 'how similarly both regimes treated their citizens' when they broke the official laws that regulated border crossing (p. 197). In 1959, in fact, the agreement that François Duvalier and Trujillo had signed in 1952 to regulate the influx and repatriation of Haitians in the Dominican Republic had just been renewed: for each of the workers that he supplied every year to the neighbouring country, Duvalier received a substantial cut and he therefore had a vested interest in 'discouraging' clandestine, unregulated, and occasional emigration.[9] During a discussion with Mártires which takes place in the 1990s Nabales also seems to have this in mind when he asserts that the Haitians were no longer slaves of the French but of 'dictators' who have been plunging them into 'the most cruel servitude and poverty' for years (p. 189).

If General Mateo and other military men resort to the supernatural to deal with their sense of guilt, the *alcade* Durán, much less concerned about his own abusive behaviour, looks for assistance to change his luck and escape from his poverty in a manner similar to that of many other civilian

---

[8] Lundius and Lundhal, *Peasants and Religion*, pp. 327–8.
[9] Matibag, *Haitian-Dominican Counterpoint*, p. 155.

clients of the *bocó* of Palma Sola (p. 234). Here the narrator intervenes from the vantage point of the early 1990s and wonders: 'which government from Trujillo onwards has really improved the conditions of the humble and manipulated of our society?' (p. 234). In fact, if the narrator's overall rating of Trujillo is definitely negative, it is fair to say that he is not much more generous with the 'puppets' who followed him (p. 286). At the end of an anecdote which describes the ordeal of two prisoners who, during the Trujillato, were obliged by the *alcade* Durán to carry, for a very long distance and barefoot, a stretcher on which lay one of his friends who needed medical care, the narrator explains that, at that time, in the borderland, 'prisoners had no shoes, the poor had no ambulances and the *alcades* had no conscience' (p. 36). However, the novel also reveals that, years later, after Trujillo's death and in 'fully-fledged democracy,' one of the ex-prisoners in question became blind and found himself in an even worse predicament, as he had to turn to begging to survive. The narrator then concludes: 'how ugly democracy is when there is hunger and corruption!' (p. 37).

Corruption, hunger, and violence play centre stage in the part of D'Alcalá's novel that deals more specifically with the 1980s and 1990s: here the plot is frequently interrupted by what can be read almost as lists of events taken from the crime section of local newspapers. For example, we are told that Haitian and Dominican girls are being smuggled from Dajabón into Haiti to work in brothels (pp. 104–8), and the narrator condemns the fact that poor Haitians are being deprived of their *pepés* (second-hand clothes sent to Haiti from foreign charities), which are sold on Dominican territory for a profit (p. 78).[10] He continues by pointing out that, in 1985, in the mountains near Cayuco, one of the best-known illegal border-crossings points where, it was rumoured, Haitian immigrant girls were often attacked and violated, passers-by could sometimes come across stray dogs quarrelling over bones and other unidentifiable and unreclaimed human remains. We are told that in 1992 always in Cayuco, a young Haitian was hanged with his belt after his pockets had been emptied; on the night of 12 October 1992, the narrator continues with uncanny precision, some thieves visited the house of a Luis Aybar and took: 'a Honda 50 CC, a radio, a television, various

---

[10] '*Pepés*' were initially called 'Kennedy' because they began to arrive in Haiti during the Kennedy administration; the rise of the *pepés* market took place in the 1980s. See 'Haiti's Pepé Trade: How Secondhand American Clothes Became a First-Rate Business', http://www.youtube.com/watch?v=h2ZD1EQu7_U [accessed 18 February 2014]. In the early 1990s Haitian women began to work as cross-border traders of pepés or *pepeceras*, selling the clothes to Dominican buyers (Wooding and Moseley-Williams, *Needed but Unwanted*, p. 61).

pitchers and pans, a big mirror and [Aybar's] neighbour's dog'; in addition, the ruthless murder of a good friend of Mártires's, the evangelical priest Martín Tavárez, killed and beheaded by criminals who were after his car, is repeatedly referred to (pp. 227–30, 247, 187, 244–5, 255).[11]

In the northern borderland, criminal activities, the narrator laments, have become a 'form of subsistence which is both illegal and institutionalized' (p. 184). He is particularly disturbed by what he calls 'river business,' which consists of the smuggling of petrol across the River Massacre. As a result of the embargo imposed on Raoul Cédras's Haiti, both Dajabón and Juana Méndez/Ouanaminthe were literally 'drenched in' petrol, which was hidden everywhere ready to be sold to the highest bidder.[12] The embargo was decreed for the first time by the Organisation of American States the day after the *coup d'etat* of 30 September 1991 which removed President Aristide from office. It was confirmed in November 1991, after long hesitation, and was reconfirmed in October 1992. It was adopted by the Security Council on 16 June 1993, lifted after the Governor's Island agreement on 3 July, reimposed on 18 October, and reinforced by Resolution 917 of the United Nations Security Council on 22 May 1994. The fact that multiple versions of the embargo had to be decreed shows that previous orders were not respected and that the passage of contraband across the Haitian–Dominican border became a large-scale operation facilitated by the Dominican army and the Haitian army.[13]

The presence of so much badly stored petrol, D'Alcalá reports, was clearly hazardous, and was at the root of many fires, which often caused the deaths of many innocent people (pp. 183–8). In the novel, the main victims of this unlawful commerce are the Haitians who, owing to the unfair embargo, end up paying more than $100 for a gallon of gasoline; moreover, the plastic containers in which they carry the gasoline are routinely punctured to force them to buy more, they are sold gasoline diluted with other cheaper substances, and they are robbed and/or killed if they do not have enough money to pay the 'toll' to those 'border vigilantes' who take advantage of their desperation (pp. 185–7). Nabales condemns the embargo and tells Mártires that 'the impoverished masses are starved to

---

[11] It is never specified if this or other incidents reported are fact or fiction.

[12] Juana Méndez is the Spanish name of the Haitian town of Ouanaminthe.

[13] André Corten, 'The Dominican Republic Elections and the United States Embargo against Haiti', in *Haiti, the Dominican Republic and the United States*, University of London Institute of Latin American Studies Occasional Papers 6, pp. 1–18, pp. 5–7, http://sas-space.sas.ac.uk/3400/1/B62_-_Haiti_The_Dominican_Republic_and_the_United_States.pdf. [accessed 27 November 2014].

death in the name of the blockade' (p. 189). Nabales's words are followed by the howls of the famished stray dogs of Juana Méndez and Dajabón, who, Mártires explains, cry, respectively, 'for the thousands of children who have died in Haiti because of the embargo' and 'for those who have died in the [Dominican] province because of the embargo and for all the innocent people cowardly murdered in the borderland' (pp. 254–5). At this point Mártires also compiles a page-long list of all the borderland victims he can remember, an act of memorialization which effectively turns this part of the novel into an alternative cenotaph which enables readers to imagine a different (transnational) community from the one conjured up by the rhetoric of the Altar Votivo de la Republica Dominicana built by Trujillo after the 1937 massacre in the centre of Dajabón, a few steps away from the customs and the official border crossing into Haiti and from the site from where Mártires delivers his speech. Some of the victims on the list have been mentioned earlier in the novel and some are new to the reader but, according to Mártires, all of these deaths have in common the fact that they are 'ignored,' 'omitted,' and forgotten by the central powers of both sides of the border, like the rest of the borderland's inhabitants and the borderland itself (pp. 255, 227).

Later in the novel Mártires talks to a group of Haitians who were running away from Cédras's Haiti and witnesses other migrants begging the authorities to be killed on Dominican territory rather than being repatriated: he is both impressed and moved by their honesty, dignity, willingness to work, and complete desperation. These encounters are followed by new accounts of rapes of girls as young as eleven who were fleeing from Haiti where, after Aristide's 1991 deposition, democracy was but 'a wounded dove' (pp. 356–68, 312–13, 311, 363–4). The narrator is adamant that those who are ultimately responsible for this appalling situation are the '*blancos*' from a 'far away […] white house' (p. 187). His accusations against the United States are reinforced when he urges the borderland-dwellers to buy beehives to defend themselves because the '*blancos*' are afraid of bees (p. 187). The reference is to the battle of Barranquita where, in 1916, outnumbered Dominican troops managed to push United States invaders back (albeit temporarily) by strategically deploying barrels full of bees.[14] What is most interesting, however, is the fact that the narrator seems to be using the word '*blanco*' to identify the North Americans but not exclusively as a skin colour descriptor: in other words, a '*blanco*' is a 'foreigner,' and in this case a common enemy of Dominicans and Haitians, not just a 'white' person.

---

[14] See 'Battalla de la Barranquita' *Enciclopedia Virtual Dominicana*, http://www.quisqueyavirtual.edu.do/wiki/Batalla_de_la_Barranquita [accessed 18 February 2014].

The same ambiguity can be detected when '*blanco*' is the appellative with which some of his employees refer to the white-skinned Catalan Nabales who wants to die Spanish (that is, as a 'foreigner') and refuses to become Dominican (pp. 158, 139). The novel performs another intriguing revisitation of traditional pigmentocracy when, a few pages later, all inhabitants of Hispaniola are collectively identified by Mártires as '*hombres negros*' or 'black men' (p. 263). Significantly, when D'Alcalá was writing, in the Dominican Republic the adjective *negro* had long been replaced by the more acceptable *indio*; *negro* was generally used to refer exclusively to Haitians and, primarily, as an offensive term. Significantly, D'Alcalá's subversive reappropriation and rehabilitation of a disparaged term (*negro*) and his simultaneous distancing and stigmatization of a time-honoured descriptor (*blanco*) also seem to extend the Haitian way of identifying foreigners (*blan*) and Haitians (*neg*) to Hispaniola as a whole and is better appreciated if put in the context of the question of legitimacy (and usurpation) which preoccupies Mártires for most of the narration.[15]

When Mártires and Nabales discuss Hispaniola's past in *La Frontera*, they take two different positions. For Nabales the Spaniards brought 'culture' to the New World, Europeans are worthy of homage, and one day the entire world will have to kneel in front of them as '*hombres blancos*' or 'white men' (p. 203). Nabales not only displays a Eurocentric approach to history (to him America, compared with Europe, is a *compaicita* or 'little girl,' p. 140) but also promotes a white/Hispanophile supremacy of the kind that sustained Balaguer's decision to build the *faro a Colón* or Columbus Lighthouse to commemorate the quincentennial of the 'discovery' of the Americas only two years before *La Frontera* was published.[16] Mártires, instead, explodes white supremacist discourses by asserting that the *blancos* have always caused problems for the people of Hispaniola dating back to the arrival of the *conquistadores*, who annihilated the indigenous population; he wonders: 'were they burning the indigenous people alive because they had no soul? Because they had no merits?' (p. 263).

The question of 'merit' is directly relevant to Mártires's personal predicament as one of the many children that Nabales had with his borderland concubine(s). When Mártires asks Nabales if he and the other

[15] For *indio* vs *negro* see Sagás, *Race and Politics*, p. 35. For *blan* vs *neg* see Murray,' 'Lenguaje y raza', p. 263; for the Haitian use of *blan* and *nèg* to mean 'foreigner' and 'native' imposed by Dessalines in 1805 see Dayan, *Haiti, History and the Gods*, pp. 24–5.
[16] The estimated costs for the *faro* oscillate between US \$40 million and US \$250 million and its construction caused the eviction of almost 2000 families from the area in which the lighthouse was placed – see Ferguson, *Dominican Republic*, p. 39.

illegitimate children will ever be recognized by their father, Nabales explains that they had to '*hacer meritos*' – that is, to strive for recognition and prove themselves worthy of it. When the (illegitimate) son queries what this might entail, his biological father replies, rather puzzlingly, that it means to 'do things when they cannot be done!' (p. 140). Mártires then begins his personal quest into the significance of these words, consulting many of Nabales's friends, who provide him with different answers. In the meantime, he succeeds in the seemingly impossible task (or rather in 'doing things when they cannot be done') of forcing Nabales to review his Eurocentric stand and to appreciate that if the Spaniards brought their culture to Hispaniola they also found a culture there, the culture of the indigenous population that they destroyed (p. 199). The ugly face of European 'civilization' is further condemned when the narrator celebrates 'Enriquillo, Tupac Amarú, Hatuey, Caupolicán' for resisting 'oppression and inhumanity' and underlines a continuity between the oppression of the natives and slavery when he excoriates the Europeans for their inhumane habit of cutting their slaves' tongues as a form of punishment (pp. 218, 60). It should be emphasised, in fact, that D'Alcalá's insistence on the cultural validity of the indigenous heritage is not a move to disavow the African presence in the national makeup, as testified also by his mobilization of the controversial term '*negro*' to identify all the inhabitants of Hispaniola.[17]

Nabales's Eurocentrism is first eroded when Mártires finds a '*carita de barro*,' a little face made of clay by the indigenous population of Hispaniola which was buried in Nabales's land, significantly, in a place called 'the shrub of the seven negroes' because seven Haitians took refuge there during the Haitian–Dominican war (p. 199). This clay artefact, in a way, becomes the real 'treasure' for him, not the gold (allegedly) buried nearby by a *Spanish* soldier during the War of Restoration which he had planned many times to secretly unearth with Nabales: significantly, at the end of the novel, Mártires is no longer interested in digging it up. In the last pages of *La Frontera*, in fact, Mártires appears to have found an answer to his personal quest and confronts his father by reading him the story of Ishmael, son of Abraham and his Egyptian concubine Aghar, in which we are told that, despite his 'illegitimate' status, God made Ishmael 'into a great nation'

---

[17] In *Antología Literaria Contemporánea de la Frontera*, instead, the African heritage is never acknowledged in the introductory remarks to the different provinces of the Dominican borderland apart from in Rubén Darío Villalona's 'La cultura en Dajabón' (p. 53). The *Antología*, however contains poems which celebrate the indigenous heritage – see, for example, Rafael Emigdio Caamaño Castillo's 'Indoamericano' (p. 122) and Julio César Dotel Pérez's 'Indio de raza' (p. 141).

(*Genesis* 21:8–21; 21:18).[18] The 'great' nation represented by Ishmael did not require Abraham's legitimization to prosper; similarly, the 'illegitimate' and forgotten borderland community that Mártires stands for does not need Nabales's recognition and is characterized by the rejection of 'official' Dominican discourses of anti-Haitianism and Hispanophilism according to which 'black Haiti' was the antithesis and the nemesis of Santo Domingo. Even if *La Frontera* is not always pro-Haitian – it contains, for example, disparaging remarks about Haitian Vodou (pp. 274, 313–16) and recounts some episodes of Haitian violence perpetrated against Dominicans during the Dominican war of Independence against Haiti (pp. 92–3) – it seems animated, overall, by a sentiment of across-the-border solidarity among the poor and downtrodden. The peasant great-grandmother of one of the characters, in fact, encourages the people of the borderland to forgive the violence they perpetrated against one another in order to move on: in reference to 1844 and 1937, she asserts 'these things belong to the past. It is now clear that we have to forgive each other in order to live in peace' (p. 274). Most importantly, Mártires is persuaded that it is possible to talk about Haitians not only 'as friends': they are in fact 'brothers' (pp. 145–6).

✶✶✶

The Montecristeño Rueda was also deeply disturbed by the nationalistic and xenophobic discourses which created a gulf between the peoples of Hispaniola: in Chapter 5 we have seen how, in the poem 'Cantos de la frontera,' the *línea* superimposed on the geography of the island divides in two the Artibonite River (whose sources are in the Dominican Republic but which empties on the Haitian coast) and turns the border into a highly militarized barrier constantly scrutinized and traversed by armies. On this vertical interface, as Muir would call it, we are told that even the birds singing from the two different sides do not dare to respond to each other's lament.[19] However, if the the *línea* divides the island, the *raya*, the *horizontal* borderland, works in the opposite direction and has traditionally kept

---

[18] *Genesis* 21:8–21 and 21:18 in *The Holy Land Bible containing Old and New Testament, King James Version 1611* (Jerusalem: The Bible Society in Israel, 1962), pp. 16–17.

[19] Rueda, *La criatura terrestre*, p. 17 and Muir, *Modern Political Geography*, p. 119. Rueda's aversion to the *línea* is evident not only in the content but also in the form of his poetry: in fact he is the founder of a poetic movement called 'pluralismo' which frees both poem and reader from being subjected to a unique, fixed line. In his poems he explodes the line into a plurality of lines which aims to expand the field of vision and enrich the experience of the reader (See Rueda, quoted in Vicenta Caamaño de

Hispaniola's internal circuits open.[20] Despite the trauma of division, in fact, in 'La canción del rayano' the woods of the borderland can still 'recognize their inhabitants' and the one eye of the divided poet which, post-partition, remained on the 'other' side of the border can still cry for his estranged children 'washing away [with tears] their stigma of foreignness.'[21] Even in the dispiriting 'Cantos de la frontera,' looking across the border from his bank of the Artibonite the poet cannot see, let alone recognize, the 'enemy of a long time and blood.'[22] Rueda, it is important to clarify, does not advocate the political unification of the island: he is aware that the 'opprobrium of a line' has now somehow become necessary[23] but he also realizes that Hispaniola as a whole has to better understand itself, its components (*raya*, *línea*, and sea), and the nature of their interactions. In his last book, *Las metamorfosis de Makandal*, a long poem divided into five sections (1998), Rueda triangulates the vertical border (*línea*), the horizontal borderline (*raya*), and the sea which embraces the island in order to explore often neglected – or, rather, occluded – connections which criss-cross Hispaniola while investigating, among other things, the crucial role that the sea can play in the spiritual emancipation of the islander.

In *Las metamorfosis de Makandal*, Rueda refers to the sea which circumvents Hispaniola as 'the sea into which all waters flow.'[24] In so doing he seems to echo Édouard Glissant, who describes the sea of the Caribbean archipelago as 'the estuary of the Americas' – that is, the place where the three great rivers of the Americas – the Mississippi, the Orinoco, and the Amazon – flow into the Atlantic.[25] 'In this context,' Glissant argues, 'insularity takes another meaning […] each island embodies openness,'[26] and his assertion clearly aims to disengage insular space from a stifling and impermeable particularity while opening it up to the cross-cultural process of creolization. For Rueda, however, the waters which flow into the

---

Fernández, *El negro en la poesía dominicana* (Santo Domingo: Editora Corripio, 1989), p. 164.

[20] In Dominican common parlance 'línea' and 'raya' are interchangeably used – the distinction I propose here is based on some of the poems by Rueda analysed in this chapter.

[21] Rueda, *La criatura terrestre*, pp. 33, 32.

[22] Rueda, *La criatura terrestre*, p. 37.

[23] Rueda, *La criatura terrestre*, p. 26.

[24] Rueda, *Las metamorfosis de Makandal*, p. 39. Page references will be given in parentheses in the text.

[25] Édouard Glissant, *Caribbean Discourse: Selected Essays* (Charlottesville, VA: University Press of Virginia, 1989), p. 139.

[26] Glissant, *Caribbean Discourse*, p. 139.

sea which surround Hispaniola are also the waters of the rivers Massacre, Artibonite, and Pedernales, which run along the border between Haiti and the Dominican Republic. Rueda's project, therefore, is directed to bring about not only inter-island but also, crucially, *intra*-island openness, and to formulate answers to a particular configuration of local issues and to a specific problematic place (the island of Hispaniola) with its distinctive history, imaginary, and urgencies.

The poem's beginning takes us to an integral, pre-partition time focusing, as it does, on the birth of the island in its entirety – crucially, not on the birth of either of the two nations which now share it. First of all, Rueda rejects the Eurocentric notion that the sea was a homogenous empty space – *aqua nullius* – until mapped by Europeans: for example, for the seagulls who flew above it since the time of Creation and the 'man of the islands' who watched the stars in their thousands while navigating the Caribbean Sea and the Atlantic Ocean, the sea was clearly a place crowded with clues (pp. 15, 18). When the poet zooms in on the island from a planetarian perspective, he sees it as a 'bellowing rock at the edge of time,' 'a wing in the route of migrations,' 'the paw of the quadrupeds' (p. 14). In other words, if the sea is what, ultimately, defines the island while preventing its coasts from 'shipwrecking,' Rueda also insists on the mutuality of the process: the little island, shaped like the limbs of the animals that populate it, imparts definition to the sea, its presence prevents the waters from collapsing into a boundless and homogenous space where all locality dissolves (p. 17). As Rueda puts it, despite, or, rather, because of its smallness, the island 'saves us' (p. 13).

Rueda, therefore, does not advocate a nostalgic, impossible return to a *timeless* sea as a way to heal the wounds of the troubled history of the island and of the region; rather, he invites us to confront the colonial history which has traversed the sea while providing the tools to transcend it. In the very last lines of his collection, Rueda appears committed to inspiring change in the social dynamics of the island and explains that he has written 'this book of the beginning and the end to leave a testimony to all that should have been … but never was' (p. 214). Furthermore, with a move that negates 'progress,' boycotts periodization, and underlines continuities, Rueda shows the effects of European colonialism to be manifold, reaching well into the post-colonial period.

Las metamorfosis de Makandal evokes slavery and the Middle Passage, the 1937 massacre but also the life of contemporary Haitian migrants in Dominican *bateyes* who still work and live in appalling conditions; the poem refers to the *conquistadores* but also to the protagonists of what Rueda calls the 'new History': 'Business / and the trafficking of children and drugs / and bank transactions performed / by masked people at midnight' (pp. 121–4;

192; 65; 18; 100). Presiding over this new history are the national leaders and presidents of the Dominican Republic, who Rueda controversially equates to '*ratas*' or 'female rats': among them are easily identifiable the anti-Haitian Trujillo ('the rat with the bicorne,' p. 93) and Balaguer ('the blind rat,' p. 93).[27] Rueda also brings to the fore the relationship between neocolonialism and the sugar industry and the role played by the United States in the transformation of the borderland into a national frontier by underlining the collusion between the rats and 'Washington' (p. 93). The rats traverse the corridors of the '*Palacio*' – that is, the *Palacio Nacional* or National Palace of the Executive Power – and thrive in the underbelly of the city (pp. 93, 94). The National Palace was built under Trujillo's rule: its construction, significantly, commenced on 27 February 1944 to commemorate the centenary of the end of the Haitian occupation of the Dominican Republic. The corrupted city, Rueda insists, is infected by the presence of the rats, unlike the 'honest villages' of the borderland where he grew up (pp. 97, 200), setting up a contrast which highlights the diffidence, contempt and, resentment with which his rural borderland traditionally regarded the central power, located in the capital city, which masterminded the transformation of the horizontal, transnational, community-based *raya* into the vertical opprobrium of a *línea*.

The internal border of Hispaniola, however, is also presented as a legacy of European colonialism and as a product of the sea: when the 'the man of navigation' arrives with maps and compass he lacerates the oceans and divides up land, bringing death, pain, blood, misery, and lamentation (p. 18). Later, the man of navigation is also identified as the one who 'confused the paths,' 'gave new names to the wind,' and 'traced the line of the opprobrium': as a result, the island, originally 'one land,' 'bifurcates like the tongue in a snake's mouth' and becomes a 'island of two memories' (pp. 124–5). The island has two memories because each colony/country has its own official memory, shaped by nationalistic discourses and aimed at keeping the border as tightly sealed as possible. It also has two memories because, alongside this authorized memory predicated on exclusion, there is another unofficial recall which has kept disavowed circuits unbroken and still connects, deeply, the people of the island.

Makandal, the central figure in the poem, comes from the sea like the men of navigation, but in a 'slaveship' (p. 122). According to one version of his story, after his hand was amputated when it was caught in the

---

[27] In his official portrait in uniform Trujillo often wore a feathered bicorne. Balaguer suffered from glaucoma for many years and when he became president of the Republic for the third time in 1986 he was almost completely blind.

machinery of a sugar mill in French Saint Domingue, he escaped from his plantation and for eighteen years was a maroon leader whose master-plan was to poison the water of all the houses in Le Cap and overthrow the white regime. Makandal, who, as anticipated in Chapter 2, had created an impressive network of allies, was captured just before he could bring his plans to fruition and then burnt at the stake. However, many believed that he managed to escape by metamorphosing into a fly. He was expected to return one day to fulfil his prophecies:[28] for example, when Napoleon's army was decimated by malaria and yellow fever, many believed that the mosquitoes which carried the disease were in fact metamorphoses and reincarnations of Makandal himself.

It is crucial to remember that, unlike Anacaona (discussed in Chapter 3), Makandal is not a pre-partition notable: he lived and operated in *French Saint Domingue and is a prominent figure in Haitian history*: for instance, his image appeared on a twenty-gourde coin minted in 1967 to celebrate the 210-year anniversary of the revolt he led in the French colony in 1757. He is also a key figure in Haiti's 'unofficial' memory, where his name has become identified with many forms of supernatural powers: Vodou priests, for example, are often referred to as 'makandals.'[29] Rueda, however, firmly anchors 'the hero of his fantasies' to the *raya* when he recalls how he encountered Makandal as a child, when he was exposed to the 'miracles,' 'wonders,' and 'fears' of his people and when, in his native Montecristi, Makandal whispered in his ears when he was dreaming (pp. 127, 175, 181). In other words, Makandal, the 'wandering bird / of the two fatherlands' (p. 132), embodies the possibility of restarting the conversation between the birds from the two sides of the River Artibonite which, as Rueda lamented in 'Cantos de la frontera,' was tragically interrupted by the tracing of the *línea*.[30] By claiming Makandal the 'islander,' 'the borderland miracle man,' 'the demon of the frontier' (pp. 182, 178, 35) as an inspiring ancestor for all the inhabitants of Hispaniola, and not just the Haitians, Rueda powerfully erases the border which divides the island and transcends officially sanctioned memories; moreover, here the poet acts fully in accordance with the spiritual freedom of the *rayano*, who fluctuates between two countries without deciding to settle for one.[31]

A revisitation of the representation and demonization of Vodou plays an important part in Rueda's poem, which evokes powerful spirits or *luases* of

---

[28] Fick, *Making of Haiti*, pp. 60, 62–3.
[29] Fick, *Making of Haiti*, pp. 62–3.
[30] Rueda, *La criatura terrestre*, p. 36.
[31] Rueda, *La criatura terrestre*, p. 26.

Dominican Vodú such as Anaïsa, Makandal's lover, but also, significantly, one of Makandal's cross-gender incarnations or metamorphoses (pp. 27, 46). Anaïsa appears in the poem alongside, among others, Candelo Sedifé, in whose fire Makandal loses himself when he sings his love song to Anaïsa, and Damballah-wedó, whose intervention helps Makandal change shape and save himself during his execution (pp. 28, 118). These *luases* belong to a pantheon which is a fusion of African and creole Gods, the spirit of deified ancestors, and syncretized manifestations of Catholic saints (Anaïsa/St Anne; Candelo/St Charles Borromeo,[32] and Damballah/St Patrick) but which also, as highlighted in Chapter 4, is a powerful manifestation of internal open circuits, as two of the pantheon – Damballah and Candelo – also exist in Haitian Vodou, albeit with slightly dissimilar attributes. Anaïsa, instead, is so different from Anaïs, the daughter of the Haitian *lwa* Ezili Danto, that some anthropologists have identified her as exclusively Dominican.[33] Yet, on a few occasions, Rueda resorts to the compound Anaïsa-Ezili (pp. 30, 95, 120), coupling Anaïsa with Ezili who, in Haitian Vodou, manifests herself as Ezili Freda and Ezili Danto and, in Dominican Vodú, is Metres Ezili or Metré Silí.[34] Importantly, the hyphenation allows him to bring the *lwa* and the *lua* together while, at the same time, maintaining their individuality: a model for pacific cohabitation of two separate entities which, Rueda's work seems to suggest, would work well for Hispaniola itself.

In Rueda's poem the mutual desire of Makandal and Anaïsa is very strong: their flesh crawls 'between Dajabón and Juana Méndez' – that is, at the very heart of the northern borderland (p. 27). Their union and, even more so, the fact that Makandal at some point metamorphoses into Anaïsa and becomes one with her ('I, the strong Makandal, / am Anaïsa!,' p. 46) not only signpost their profound connection but also show how the transcorporeal conceptualization of the self which characterizes Vodou enables Rueda to erase the 'self vs other' binarism introduced by the *línea* and to enhance the reciprocity and mutuality of the *raya* by positing the temporary identification of a legendary male figure in Haitian culture with the female Dominican *luas* Anaïsa.[35] As a 'divided I and a multiple

[32] The Dominican border town of St Charles Boromé was one of the sites of the 1937 massacre, as Haitians visited it as a religious site: see Castor, *Migración y relaciones internacionales*, p. 26.

[33] Deive, *Vodú y magia*, pp. 175–6.

[34] Deive, *Vodú y magia*, p. 177; Davis, '*Vodú* of the Dominican Republic', pp. 75–90, p. 83.

[35] Unlike Descartes's unitary soul, the immaterial aspect of this Afro-Diasporic self is multiple, external, and removable: see, for example, Roberto Strongman, 'Transcorporeality in Vodou', *Journal of Haitian Studies*, 14.2 (2008), pp. 4–29.

l' Makandal the metamorphoser, moreover, transcends not just gender but also colour and race: we are told that he is neither black nor white but of all colours, like the sea (pp. 125, 57, 58–9). The shape-shifter Makandal, an 'enraptured form of infinite alchemy,' is in fact a creature who comes from the sea but belongs to and is at home in different elements (p. 62): he is a 'man halfway between land and sea' who addresses us while 'standing on the sea' and whose flights are also 'aquatic pirouettes' (pp. 24–5). On the day of his execution he is consumed but, at the same time, saved by fire, and flies in the sky with the truncated wing of his only arm (p. 119). His hybrid and amphibious status recalls the 'ambidextrousness' of the poet's self in 'La canción del rayano,'[36] which, in *Las metamorfosis de Makandal*, is reflected in the hybrid nature of Hispaniola, an island which Rueda describes as 'an amphibian who believed it was an island' (p. 60).

Poignantly, Makandal, is also an 'animal-man' (pp. 91, 131) who metamorphoses into a series of animals of different species (birds, fishes, mammals, amphibians) and into hybrid and mythological creatures such as the *galipote*. *Galipotes* – which in Haiti are often referred to as 'makandals' – are shape-shifters which, in the Dominican Republic, as we have seen in Chapter 4, are at times associated with blackness and described as being genetically Haitian. *Ciguapas*, mythological female creatures with a human form, backward facing feet, and very long hair which serves as a garment for their naked bodies, are instead considered 'Indian' and Dominican in 'essence.'[37] Such distinctions obviously reflect dominant negrophobic and xenophobic discourses which go hand in hand with Rueda's abhorred *línea* and which aim at negating the presence of African and Haitian culture in Dominican territory at the same time as identifying its inhabitants exclusively as the descendants of the Spanish and the indigenous Taíno population. In Rueda's poem, however, *ciguapas* are wild creatures who inhabit the hills of the *raya* and, crucially, announce the arrival of (the *galipotean*) Makandal (p. 179). Poignantly, Rueda's *galipotes* and *ciguapas* are not differentiated in terms of race, ethnicity, or origin but coexist side by side, testifying once again to his desire to go against the ideological divisive grain.

The fact that Makandal metamorphoses into various beasts also signposts the porosity of the boundary between humans and animals in a rural society where, as Reyes has also pointed out, interspecies interactions are both intimate and complex: at one point the rabbit is the uncle of the poet-persona and the widgeon his 'godmother' (p. 81), while human language

---

[36] Rueda, *La criatura terrestre*, p. 32.
[37] Rodríguez, *Haiti and Trans-Caribbean Literary Identity*, p. 191.

can be confused with the grunt of '*puercos cimarrones*' ('wild pigs,' p. 101). The Spanish adjective *cimarrón* further blurs the human–animal boundary: it is the word from which the English 'maroon' derives, and in Spanish it denotes both wild beasts and runaway slaves like Makandal himself. The pig is therefore an obvious choice for Makandal's transfigurations and in the poem it appears in both its wild (*cimarrón*) and domestic forms (pp. 71,72, 73, 106, 134). Pigs, like bulls, goats, and chickens – also mentioned in the poem in various ways (pp. 25, 133, 134, 72, 118, 25, 31, 61, 108) – often become offerings in Vodou and Vodú ceremonies which, in the Dominican Republic, are mainly devoted to divination and healing: in Rueda's poem, interestingly, the pig is invoked as an antidote to the power of the city and its 'rats' (pp. 71–3).[38] In open polemic with the favouring of the urban dimension which characterizes Dominican urban elites, this invocation of the rural dimension represents Makandal's and Rueda's positive engagement with a lifestyle and with an integrated, inclusive, and rebellious borderland which opposed the penetration of state apparati and the transformation of the *raya* into a *línea*: as an official put it at the beginning of the twentieth century, 'the revolutionary and the pig are the two principal enemies of the country.'[39]

Makandal's most frequent incarnation, however, is as a '*pájaro*' ('bird or sparrow,' pp. 33, 40, 43, 47, 58, 161, 180, 194, 196) or as another type of bird, such as kingfisher, colibri, dove, guaraguao, quail, gannet, sparrowhawk, or turkey buzzard (pp. 31, 47, 57, 56, 39, 56, 58, 194). Significantly, most of these creatures, like Makandal, can fly over the *línea* and, for some of them, in particular the guaraguao, rats are among their favourite food.[40] Arguably, Rueda's celebration of Makandal and his zoomorphic metamorphoses could also be seen as a way to subtly subvert the anti-Haitian dehumanizing rhetoric – evident, as we have seen, in Prestol Castillo's works – according to which, unlike the 'civilized' Dominicans, the primitive Haitians lived 'like animals.'[41] Rueda's Makandal also embodies and gives concrete form to the mesh of possibilities inherent in the *raya* by metamorphosing into weird hybrids such as the 'caterpillar-fish' (p. 131) and the 'snake-manatee' (p. 194), a creature which brings together Damballah, the patriarchal divinity of Haitian Vodou and Dominican Vodú, with one of the indigenous animals of Hispaniola decimated by the arrival of the Spanish *conquistadores*.

---

[38] Davis, '*Vodú* of the Dominican Republic', 78.

[39] 'Párrafos de las memorias presentadas por D. Emiliano Tejera en su calidad de Ministro de Relaciones Exteriores de la República Dominicana en los años 1906–1907 i 1908', quoted in Derby, "Haitians, Magic, and Money', p. 499.

[40] Reyes, *Cuentos y leyendas*, p. 255.

[41] Castor, *Migración y relaciones internacionales*, p. 89.

Overall, therefore, Rueda's *Las metamorfosis de Makandal* rethinks and reshapes official and unofficial memories while revisiting and bringing to the fore occluded syncretic systems of belief. Rueda's land and sea are in constant dialogue – the island is a 'bone of the sea' and 'palpitating flesh on which the sea has tattooed itself' (pp. 36, 26) – and are engaged in a broader conversation which includes both the divisive, shameful *línea* and the *raya*, a territory marked by the mutual desire of Makandal and Anaïsa. Makandal, 'spirit of the two lands and four seas,' is elected to be the *genius loci* of Hispaniola, the key figure in Rueda's 'geography of living flesh' and in his 'book of borders [...] and of a geography gone crazy' (pp. 9, 184, 10) and, more broadly in what, in *La criatura terrestre*, he had called 'the heart-breaking epic of our border struggle.'[42] His protean nature, in fact, both restores the 'hope for resurrection' which seemed lost in 'La canción del rayano'[43] and provides Rueda with the coordinates for a remapping of the island which celebrates and gains strength from marine and across-the-border continuities, connections, mutual influences, and shared – if disavowed – empowering memories and experiences.

✷✷✷

The borderland area around Rueda's Montecristi and Dajabón is also central to the 2003 film *Perico Ripiao* ('*Merengue* Trio'), directed by Ángel Muñiz, written by Reynaldo Disla and Ángel Muñiz, and starring Raymond Pozo (Francisco), Manolo Ozuna (Mauricio), Phillip Rodríguez (Manuel), Giovanny Cruz (General Contreras), and Miguel Céspedes (Quepis). *Perico Ripiao* recounts the adventures of three ex-inmates of the Dajabón prison who criss-cross the northern Dominican borderland in order to escape the military forces which are after them and (allegedly) police the border. Like Deive's *Viento Negro*, *Perico Ripiao* is a comedy which raises serious issues, investigating, as it does, nationalism, corruption, human rights abuse, traditional representations of the Haitian–Dominican *frontera*, the oppressive presence of state power on the territory and on the borderland, the movement of contraband, and border relations.

Perico Ripiao is mostly set at the very end of Joaquin Balaguer's second presidency (1966–78) – his portrait is visible in various offices of the military forces – a time characterized by authoritarianism, anti-Communism, and state repression, often violent and at the hands of the military. In 1966, Balaguer created the Consejo Estatal del Azúcar (CEA or 'State Sugar

---

42   Rueda, *La criatura terrestre*, p. 26.
43   Rueda, *La criatura terrestre*, p. 33.

Council') to manage the nationalized sugar- producing estates which
had previously belonged to Trujillo's family and signed an accord with
the Haitian government to regulate the migration of Haitian *braceros*
in Dominican territory. This agreement was different from those which
preceded it (as explained in Chapter 6, the first of such exploitative bilateral
agreement between the sugar companies and the Haitian and Dominican
governments was signed in 1952) because it sanctioned that the Dominican
government, rather than the private sugar companies, was responsible for
paying the Haitian state for organizing recruitment centres for *braceros* in
Haiti.[44] In 1972 Balaguer also signed various agreements with the Haitian
government that encouraged 'simplified trade transactions' between the two
neighbouring countries.[45] As we will see, the military portrayed in Muñiz's
film seem to take very seriously the task of 'simplifying transactions' while
maximising (their) profits.

The film begins with the narrator (José 'Pancho' Clisante), who, surrounded
by cacti and agaves, addresses the audience from a dusty, unpaved road
scorched by the sun in the desertic and semi-arid landscape of the northern
Dominican borderland. His Homeric white beard and the fact that he
speaks in verse (namely, in *decimas*) brings to the fore the Dominican oral
tradition while introducing us to the location in which the story takes place.
From the country as a whole, which is described as 'divine' despite being
a place where lies and the truth are easily confused, we are quickly invited
to zoom in on the *dichosa frontera*, literally the 'happy,' 'fortunate,' but also
'damned frontier.' This multivalence of meaning is intriguing and, as we
will see, *Perico Ripiao* capitalizes on it. After the *decimero*'s introduction, we
see a dilapidated *guagua* which connects Dajabón to Montecristi travelling
on the same unpaved road where he was previously standing.[46] Among
its passengers, mainly women, we find a group of soldiers from a nearby
barracks and three prisoners: Francisco (who is black), Mauricio (who is
white), and Manuel (a mulatto). Some of the passengers are singing and
dancing to the rhythm of Dominican traditional music and drinking
alcoholic drinks – Brugal is particularly highlighted – under the threatening
gaze of Commander Quepis who decides *when* and *if* to continue with, or
stop, the *fiesta*. Dance and laughter, therefore, cannot really be seen as a
brave attempt to celebrate life in a repressive and militarized society since

---

[44]   Martínez, *Peripheral Migrants*, p. 47.

[45]   Matibag, *Haitian-Dominican Counterpoint*, pp. 158–9.

[46]   This road was at the time known as the Carretera Sténio Vincent, and was named
by Trujillo in 1936 (a year before *el corte*) as a sign of 'friendship' towards the Haitian
president and the neighbouring nation.

everyone seems afraid of Quepis, who will later be described as a *diablo* (a devil): dancers and singers move their hips or open and close their mouths according to his wish. When the *guagua* breaks down, the driver, a hopeless, bespectacled buffoon who grins manically to exorcize his fear of the military, goes in search of spare parts while soldiers and prisoners wait for him in a nearby cockpit (*gallera*). The traditional rhythm of *merengue*, the *gallera*, and the Brugal are well-known markers of Dominican identity and what is underlined here is the pervasive presence of these national markers in the northern borderland which, contrarily to traditional depictions of it as a remote and alien place, does not appear to be 'out of step' with the rest of the nation. Arguably, the film questions traditional representations of the *dichosa frontera* as a 'damned' place, completely *sui generis* and eccentric: what happens there, *Perico Ripiao* insists, simply brings to the fore all that is reprehensible about the management of the country as a whole and, indeed, of the entire island. In this context, the positive meanings of the adjective '*dichosa*' are more difficult to explain but, I will argue, by the end of the film, their usage might be justified.

From a broader perspective, the constellation of Dominican 'national' symbols (*merengue*, *gallera*, *Brugal*, etc.) also points, perhaps counter-intuitively, to what we could call 'structural similarities' between the two sides of Hispaniola which can transcend the forms in which the two countries express their specificity and, to borrow Benedict Anderson's words, imagine themselves as nations.[47] In the case of cockfighting, for example, structure and form are almost identical, as cockfighting is a national sport in the Dominican Republic *and* in Haiti: as Michele Wucker has eloquently put it, in Hispaniola it is 'a powerful symbol of both division and community [...] Dominicans and Haitians practising the national sport of their countries also celebrate brotherhood by their unified devotion to the rituals and code of honor without which the sport and betting around it could not take place.'[48] *Brugal*, on the other hand, is the name and brand of a variety of Dominican rum: in their advertising campaigns the Brugal company has often identified their rum with Dominicanness.[49] Yet, as suggested also by the Dominican poet Pedro Mir, sugar-derived alcoholic drinks such as rum are common in the entire Caribbean archipelago.[50] Haiti is no exception, of course: the advertisement for Barbancourt, Haiti's

---

[47] Yunén (*La isla como es*) makes a similar point on p. 96.

[48] Wucker, *Why the Cocks Fight*, pp. 12–13.

[49] Austerlitz, *Merengue*, p. 102.

[50] 'There is a country in the world', he writes, referring to the Dominican Republic, 'situated [...] in an improbable archipelago / of sugar and alcohol.' Pedro Mir, 'Hay un

leading brand of rum, explains that rum is 'the spirit of Haitian life.' The majority of Haitians, however, cannot afford a bottle of Barbancourt and drink instead the much cheaper and very popular *clerén*, which is also used in Vodou ceremonies and, like Barbancourt, is extremely popular in the Dominican borderland.

Merengue, too, is a pan-Caribbean musical genre which, as acknowledged in Chapter 6, has become strictly linked to Dominican national and racial identity. In a Brugal advertisement, for example, *merengue* was played as a soundtrack to reinforce the link between the rum and national identity.[51] Different regions in the country had different types of *merengue* but, as Veloz Maggiolo's *El hombre del acordeón* reminds us, the version that gained national prominence and became an expression of nationhood is the one referred to in the film's title. As previously highlighted, the origins of *merengue* are uncertain and debated and different theories epitomize deep-rooted feelings about Dominican identity: Eurocentric theories stress *merengue*'s European elements and Afrocentric ones emphasize its African roots, while others point to its syncretic nature by highlighting a fusion of European-derived ballroom dance music with local African-derived elements. Some theorists, however, link *merengue* to the Haitian *mereng*, a national symbol in Haiti, which evolved from a fusion of different types of slave music such as *chica* and *calenda* with ballroom forms related to the French *contredanse*.[52]

All the national symbols mobilized at the beginning of the film (Brugal, *merengue*, cockpits) can represent ways in which the Dominicans have learnt to 'imagine' themselves as members of a specific nation but, if articulated in a different way, these very same symbols also highlight a network of connections that emphasize how this 'imagined' nation inextricably belongs to a cultural continuum which, going beyond its national boundaries, can also delineate a transnational, island-based 'imagined community.' Significantly, *Perico Ripiao*'s focus is firmly on the late 1970s Dominican Republic and its northern borderland: Haiti never appears in the film, the Haitians are mere extras as far as the development of the plot is concerned, and the film does not bring to the fore a from-below across-the-border solidarity between the disenfranchised. The pre-1937 fluidity celebrated by Veloz Maggiolo is not present but 'structural continuities' between Hispaniola's two countries are explicitly highlighted at the level of state

país en el mundo', in *Poesias (casi) completas* (México, D.F.: Siglo Veintiuno Editores, 1994), pp. 63–77, p. 63.
[51] Austerlitz, *Merengue*, p. 102.
[52] Austerlitz, *Merengue*, pp. 2–4.

apparati and by the film's insistence on the callousness and corrupted nature of official authorities and of their agents operating on both sides of the border. Nonetheless, despite its 'narrow' focus, or, rather, because of it, the film compellingly proves that one cannot fully understand the cultural, social, political, and economic dynamics of the Dominican Republic (and crucially, not just of one of its border region) without putting it in the broader context of the island.

In *Perico Ripiao* the Dominican soldiers who (allegedly) police the frontier are represented, for the most part, as corrupt, opportunistic, dishonest, abusive, and devious but also, in a crucial undermining and disempowering move, as rather stupid. For instance, when the three convicts are forced to push the broken-down *guagua* to make it start, they are simply left behind and forgotten by the guards who, for a while, happily continue their journey without them. No longer under custody, the prisoners try to secure their freedom by crossing a stream, probably a tributary of the River Massacre if not the Massacre itself. Attacked by leeches, they have to desist and will later be recaptured. The fact that the blood-sucker leeches are to be found in a river which divides *and* connects Haiti and the Dominican Republic and which is the theatre of much of the legal and illegal traffic between the two countries highlights the dishonesty and collusion of Dominican *and* Haitian border officials. As we will see, however, the film also shows us that those who unscrupulously mastermind business transactions and illicit trade and, ultimately, really 'call the shots' are in fact very 'close' to the Dominican (and, implicitly, the Haitian) capital and central government. In other words, *Perico Ripiao* reveals how the illegal activities and social dynamics of the frontier in fact characterize the national territory and the island as a whole and are simply 'conjugated' in a particular way because of the border's distinctive function.

In the next scene, which takes place seven years later and at the end of Balaguer's first twelve years of presidency, we see the three convicts playing at a party in the prison of Dajabón, where we are introduced to the sleazy General Contreras and an equally dishonest Haitian official. Performing in a typical nasal singing style and swinging their hips with studied licentiousness, the three men play the accordion-based *merengue* called *perico ripiao* (literally 'ripped parrot'). Paul Austerlitz argues that the name might derive from a brothel in Santiago (and therefore contain sexual innuendos) or from the fact that it was a simple kind of accordion-based music.[53] A *perico ripiao merengue*, in fact, normally requires the use of three main instruments: the *güira*, a metal musical instrument probably of Taíno

---

[53] Austerlitz, *Merengue*, p. 63.

origin and played here by Francisco; the *tambora*, an African two-headed drum here played by Mauricio; and the accordion, Manuel's instrument, which is said to come from trade with the Germans for tobacco.[54]

This reinscription of *merengue* in the film is characterized by crucial differences: seven years before, in the *guagua*, Quepis was the one who presided over and regulated the 'fun' and the three convicts were hostages to fortune and his whims; now, the three men are still imprisoned but, being accomplished performers, they are beginning to 'own' their music and to be empowered by it in important ways. While they play, Quepis records their music in order to enrich himself by producing and selling tapes of their performances; when the three detainees boldly approach him to ask for a cut of the profit, he refuses to comply and threatens to kill them. In retaliation, they warn him that they know about the disappearance of fellow inmates who are forced to do 'small jobs' for him and then are never seen again, and tell Quepis that they will inform Contreras that the Commander is secretly running a 'business' from which the General has not been allowed to profit. We know that the convict–musicians have managed to overturn, at least temporarily, the power relation between prisoners and chief guard when Quepis, frightened, yields to their blackmail. Such weakening of the state machinery is crucial because it takes place within one of its more constraining spaces (a prison) at the hands of particularly disempowered subjects (detainees) and is further enhanced by the presence, among the guests at the party, of undercover journalists who dance to the convict–musicians' rhythm while investigating smuggling, military abuses, and the 'disappearance' of inmates from the prison in Dajabón.

Merengue's crucial part in the prisoners' resistance, and, as we will see later, in their emancipation, is better appreciated in the context of the political function that it had in the history of the Dominican Republic. As already discussed, *merengue* was central to the country's resistance to North American domination: it was during the United States' occupation that the Cibao elite became interested in what they had previously considered to be an inappropriate rural and licentious genre. While armed insurgents (*gavilleros*) waged guerrilla warfare, upper-class Dominicans in the Cibao region engaged in a programme of diplomacy and propaganda against the foreign occupation which relied on a cultural movement which celebrated Dominicanness and embraced *merengue cibaeño* as a *national* symbol.[55] It is well known that Trujillo later appropriated *merengue cibaeño* for his own purposes but it is important to remember that, after Trujillo's death,

[54] Wucker, *Why the Cocks Fight*, pp. 45–6.
[55] Austerlitz, *Merengue*, p. 31.

merengue was not discarded because of its connection with the dictatorship. Many believed that, disassociated from reactionary influences and from the capitalist music industry which denatured it, *merengue* could still promote a progressive vision: in 1974, acclaimed *merengueros* were among the numerous artists who performed at a large music festival organized to challenge Balaguer's regime.[56] The genre gained further popularity during the 1970s and the 1980s – that is, when Muniz's film is set – and the success of Quepis's recording enterprise highlights this.

Evidently, like *El hombre del acordeón* (which was also published in 2003), *Perico Ripiao* aligns itself with a complex national symbol which has overcome regionalism, straddled class as well as the urban and rural divide, and can accommodate both Afrocentrism and Hispanophilism – as we have seen, three players in the film represent the mixed racial nature of the Dominican population. Having been both at the service of the state and a national symbol mobilized in fierce opposition to a repressive *status quo*, it is apparent that *merengue* can be appropriated and redeployed for different purposes. In the film, despite the limitations intrinsic in their condition as prisoners, the three *merengueros*, empowered by their music, reaffirm their ownership of it and, as we will see, will use their ability to perform as a means to free themselves from the despotic socio-political order that the military supports and embodies; most importantly, the 'happy ending' of the comedy *Perico Ripiao* will be strictly connected to the redemptive power of their music.

In the scene following the party in the prison of Dajabón, we see Contreras and the same Haitian official standing at a desolate section of the border between their two countries to oversee the arrival, in Dominican territory, of an illicit cargo (presumably drugs), of a group of Haitian migrants destined to become *braceros*, and of a Chinese man who is entering the Dominican Republic illegally, hoping that he will be able to obtain permanent residency.[57] The fact that the Haitians are handed over to the military suggests that their entrance to the Dominican Republic was not officially organized by agents of the sugar companies but rather a clandestine passage, and that the Haitian official is working as a *pase* or 'border guide' remunerated by the migrants themselves, who are also paying bribes which go to the Dominican authorities (here the military), to whom they are unofficially transferred. The military would then pass on the migrants (for a

---

[56] Austerlitz, *Merengue*, p. 109.

[57] According to Moya Pons, nobody really knows the history of the Chinese people who began to arrive in the Dominican Republic at the end of the nineteenth century, probably from Cuba. See *The Dominican Republic*, pp. 170–72.

fee) to sugar estates in need of harvest labourers.[58] Alternatively, they might
be directed to Contreras's own property: high-ranking officers in the army
often owned vast *fincas* for which they procured manpower illegally. Every
year, in fact, about 4000 of the 15,000 *braceros* officially recruited were made
to 'disappear' by immigration officers and relocated to private companies
which supplied themselves at the expense of the CEA. The CEA paid 86
pesos per worker but private companies – such as the one Contreras might
be running here – by supplying themselves directly and on location, paid
a reduced fee of 11 pesos per worker.[59]

Ironically, the Haitian man and Contreras should prevent the smuggling
of contraband and illegal commerce but they readily agree that, as the
General puts it, 'borders are for business.' The film, however, puts the
smuggling of illicit substances, the exploitation of migrants escaping from
the impoverished and repressive Haiti of Jean-Claude Duvalier, and the
smuggling of human beings for profit in the context of the many illegal
activities and human rights abuses perpetrated in the Dominican Republic
and, implicitly, in Haiti, where the migrants are coming from. The narrator,
in fact, intervenes again to inform us, with another *decima*, that, while
innocent people suffer, the guilty ones prosper and enjoy their lives at the
expense of others – a comment that perfectly suits both Duvalier's Haiti
and Balaguer's Dominican Republic, where social injustice and political
repression were rife. Moreover, the narrator's political stance signposts the
existence of borderland *cuenteros* who, unlike Veloz Maggiolo's Vetemit, are
in fact very critical of the status quo. As the *decimero* explains, Francisco,
Mauricio, and Manuel have been in jail for over seven years without being
able to see their families, they never had a proper trial, and their files are
now 'lost;' in fact, he laments, they were 'erased without remorse.' A series
of flashbacks inform us of their 'crimes.' Manuel was imprisoned for having
accidentally shot dead his wife's lover during a fight which occurred after
he walked in on them. Mauricio admits, on a number of occasions, to have
worked as a hit man for an international criminal organization which had
strong links with Miami but adds, however, that he was among the lowest
in rank and that he was actually framed when he was captured. Francisco
is a political prisoner: he is a self-proclaimed Communist but a very naive
and inexperienced revolutionary who, on his first political protest, ended up
lighting his Molotov cocktails at the wrong time. As a matter of fact, the
Molotovs were not actually thrown by him but by a last-minute 'accomplice'
he encounters *in situ* and who was in fact an informer of the government

---

[58]   Martínez, *Peripheral Migrants*, p. 8.
[59]   Lemoine, *Bitter Sugar*, p. 122.

who subsequently denounced him to get a reward. During their protest the two 'accomplices' shout names of both various revolutionary figures from Che Guevara to Mao Tse Tung and national icons such as the Mirabal sisters, Mama Tingo, and Liborio. The scene is hilarious – they are goofy, insecure, and scared, confuse Sandino with Somosa and end up cheering '*que vivan todos*' ('long live everyone!) when they run out of inspirational names – but the constellation of Dominican figureheads we are offered is an interesting one.

Mama Tingo, the most recent of Francisco's heroes, was an inspirational figure killed, only a few years earlier, in the struggle against the expropriation of the *campesinos* of Hato Viejo de Yamasá.[60] The Mirabal sisters were very vocal opponents of Trujillo assassinated by the regime in 1960. They are among the best-known emblems of Dominican resistance: Salcedo, the province where they were born, was renamed in 2007 as Hermanas Mirabal Province, and they appear on the 200 Dominican pesos note. Papa Liborio, as we have seen, was a healer, a spiritual authority, a charismatic leader, a representative of the borderland resistance to central power, and a nationalist icon who still inspires Dominicans 'to fight venomous politicians, corrupt patrons and a diabolical state.'[61] The reference to other icons such as Mama Tingo and the Mirabal sisters invites us to put the experience of Liborio and his followers in the context of Dominican resistance to abuse while Liborio's connections with the Haitian Cacos (Chapter 6) signpost the existence of across-the-border cooperative links forged by those fighting against repressive regimes on both sides of the island.

During another party where Contreras tries to arrange more illicit business across the border, the three prisoner–musicians are forced to dress up as soldiers to play *merengue* for his guests. Their disguise is involuntary but significant because it further blurs the very questionable distinction between criminals and law-and-order enforcers which the film presents us with. Disguise-wearing is frequent and instrumental in comedy, where it perverts or abolishes the expected relations on which society relies in order to function; on a deeper level, it can offer a carnivalesque alternative social space, an upside-down world characterized by equality, justice, and freedom. In *Perico Ripiao* it is initially mobilized to invite us to acknowledge the fact that the world in which the three fugitives operate is itself an 'upside-down' world where the military are the real criminals and the alleged criminals are

[60] See Guaroa Ubiñas Renville, *Historias y Leyendas Afro-Dominicanas* (Santo Domingo: Editora Manatí, 2003), pp. 139–44.

[61] Derby, *The Dictator's Seduction*, p. 238. Interestingly, Derby reports that Anacaona now serves the same function.

Figure 14. *Perico Ripiao* (2003) directed by Ángel Muñiz and written by Reynaldo Disla and Ángel Muñiz; producer Leticia Tonos. The convicts Manuel (Phillip Rodríguez), Mauricio (Manolo Ozuna), and Francisco (Raymondo Pozo) playing *merengue* in soldiers' uniforms.

actually 'good people,' as one of the characters points out. The emancipatory possibilities intrinsic in carnivalesque subversion, however, will soon begin to materialize.

During Contreras's party, in fact, the three convicts manage to run away with their instruments, which, they hope, will help them raise enough money to fund their escape. If they were obliged to wear military uniforms in order to fit into Contreras's plans, the fugitives quickly learn how to take advantage of the position of power in which their disguises put them. Dressed as soldiers, for example, the three have no difficulty in obtaining a lift from a truck driver who is hiding, in the back of his vehicle, the Chinese man and the Haitian migrants we have seen crossing the border. It goes without saying that his driver works for General Contreras: when the name of the General is mentioned at a military checkpoint they are allowed to pass with no questions asked. During a phone call to Contreras the truck driver realizes that he is in fact harbouring three fugitives and receives the order to kill them. The man does not hesitate to obey: in fact, he draws his gun straight away only to find that, at that point, the ex-convicts have already run away; when he asks the Haitians and the Chinese man where the prisoners have gone they respond to him in Creole and Chinese and he cannot understand a word, despite their intense gesticulation. The scene is played for comedy but while we are laughing we cannot fail to notice how the driver (an armed civilian) does not think twice about murdering three people in Contreras's name. In other words, the members of Contreras's organization do not seem to be any less dangerous or violent than the criminal gang Mauricio used to belong to.

Mauricio, Francisco, and Manuel, still dressed as soldiers, find momentary refuge in the house of a *campesino*, who feeds them and gives them his horses to facilitate their journey. The landscape here becomes green and lush as they move away from the desertic and dusty plains of Montecristi. The narrator reappears at this point in order to praise the generosity of the Dominican peasants, but the film also shows other members of Dominican society in a positive light, including a member of the military who helps the two journalists who are preparing an exposé on the disappearance of prisoners in Dajabón's jail, on across-the-border smuggling, and on the three fugitives. Their bravery is highlighted as the soldier and the journalists reveal that they are well aware that they could be killed for doing this. At some point the ex-convicts find a job as musicians in a brothel not too far from Puerto Plata, where they finally change into civilian clothes. The owner, however, is another accomplice of Contreras, who reveals to the General that the three are hiding in his 'club.' When the military catches up with them a distressed Manuel recognizes, among the soldiers, none other than Arcadio, his wife's lover, the man he thought he had murdered and for whose (presumed) death he had been put in prison. It goes without saying that Arcadio, who had engineered Manuel's condemnation with Contreras, becomes even more determined to capture and kill Manuel to make sure that this story does not enter the public domain.

The three fugitives manage to elude the military once again, only to re-encounter and overpower Arcadio and his men later in the film and, more precisely, in a sugar cane field close to one of the *bateyes* of the northern borderland. At this point Manuel takes a little revenge against Arcadio while Francisco convinces Mauricio to let their companion express his anger. In the meantime, in fact, the ex-hit-man Mauricio has found God, repented for his sins, and preaches forgiving, peace, and love. Kicking the tied-up Arcadio, Francisco explains, is a legitimate action because, as reported in the gospel according to Mark, Jesus reacted violently against the 'thieves' in the temple. His words are once again in line with comedy's reversal of roles, as the characters representing the 'thieves' here are clearly the guards and not the ex-prisoners; besides, in the context of *Perico Ripiao*, the gospel's 'cave of thieves' can be taken to define the Dominican Republic as a whole, a place the fugitives had previously described as 'a good country but very, very badly governed' and 'a rich country very poorly ran.' Yet, the fact that Francisco quotes from Mark's gospel in a sugar cane field next to one of the *bateyes* where Haitian migrants worked and lived (and in most cases still work and live) in hopelessly appalling conditions signposts once again the collusion of the Haitian and Dominican governments in the exploitation of Haitian labour, thus extending the definition of 'cave of thieves' to the entire island.

The fugitives' luck changes when the undercover journalists we had seen dancing in the Dajabón prison publish their article on the abuses perpetrated by the military. Contreras suddenly receives a phone call from someone speaking from a luxury villa who orders him to make sure that nothing happens to the ex-prisoners because the scandal has to be silenced. This person, who obviously has very close links with the political establishment, also arranges a way out for Contreras: he will be removed from Dajabón only to be promoted and sent to Panama as a consul or military attaché; his job on the frontier will be given to Arcadio, who will carry on illegal activities to maximize his profit and the profit of his superiors. All ends well, therefore, for Contreras, Arcadio, and their boss, none of whom are punished; they are, in fact, rewarded for their wrongdoings. It is important to remember here that the film is anchored, very firmly, to a precise historical moment in the history of the Dominican Republic: at one point we distinctly hear a radio announcing that Antonio Guzmán, the presidential candidate for the Partido Revolucionario Dominicano, has just been elected. His election was fiercely contested by Balaguer, who also resorted to the military to invalidate it, but to no avail. Guzmán's electoral campaign was founded on 'change' and initially he seemed to be a force for the good: he re-established formal liberties denied during the Balaguer's regime, freed many political prisoners, and raised the minimum salary to 125 pesos a month; he also tried to limit the power of the army and declared that he wanted to solve the situation of the *bateyes*.[62] Soon, however, many Dominicans became disillusioned with the Guzmán administration, which, as his critics highlighted, perpetuated corruption and social inequalities, forbade Haitian immigrants from participating in anti-Duvalier political activities, doubled the Armed Forces' budget, and simply ignored the problem of the *bateyes*: if anything, in 1980 there had been an increase in the unregulated traffic of undocumented workers and the *braceros*' condition deteriorated further owing to inflation.[63] Guzmán also appointed his children and other members of his family to key government positions and many of them governed to their own advantage. In other words, by showing us how Contreras and his accomplices continued to benefit from and actively sustained a corrupted

[62] Lemoine, *Bitter Sugar*, p. 260–61; Moya Pons, *Dominican Republic*, p. 405.
[63] Lemoine, *Bitter Sugar*, p. 261; Matibag, *Haitian-Dominican Counterpoint*, p. 159; Martínez, *Peripheral Migrants*, p. 48; Moya Pons, *Dominican Republic*, p. 406.

state of affairs, *Perico Ripiao* highlights the continuities rather than the discontinuities between Balaguer's and Guzmán's government.

At first sight, therefore, in *Perico Ripiao* comedy seems to have been mobilized to reveal a rather bleak or damning picture of the island; in what appears to be a rather reactionary and defeatist move, this bitter 'happy ending' seems to reconstitute and strengthen the social and political order that the three fugitives have been resisting and antagonizing throughout the film. The outraged and disgusted *decimero*, however, intervenes in the story to solicit, once again, the viewers's repulsion at the dominant social and political interests which, to maintain the status quo, engineer these kind of 'happy endings.' Most importantly, his interjection also confirms that the reconciliation of the forces at play, also a characteristic of comedy, is here both unattainable and utterly unpalatable. *Perico Ripiao*, however, seems to harbour some hope for the borderland, for the Dominican Republic, and for Hispaniola as a whole. We last see the three ex-prisoners coming out of a brothel wearing women's clothes – presumably because they do not yet know that they are no longer 'wanted criminals.' More poignantly, though, their cross-dressing can be interpreted as a further elaboration on the theme of disguise-wearing on which the film has often relied to convey perverted power relations on the island and their arbitrary but, ultimately, relative nature. The three musicians in drag embody the subversive potential of carnivalesque cross-dressing which creates at least the chance for a new perspective and a new order of things. Their sartorial excess matches their final outburst of laughter which disfigures the re-established order.

This is particularly true because, while laughing, they reappropriate a space similar to the one in which, at the opening the film, they were detainees under the control of the military and on their way to prison. Mauricio, Francisco, and Manuel are last seen boarding the Dajabón–Montecristi *guagua* driven by the same bespectacled and terrified driver who appeared at the beginning of the story: crucially, he immediately recognizes them – confirming that the drag has no disguising purpose – but, far from being afraid of retaliation from the military if he accepts them on board, he boldly invites them on his vehicle and joins with them in a final liberating and defying laugh. As Chicha Calma in Philoctète's *Le peuple des terres mêlées*, this borderland *guagua* boarded by the three cross-dressed ex-convicts represents a form of 'every day utopia,' a 'promising' place where daily life is both experienced and performed in imaginative, counterhegemonic ways, and which anticipates a conceivably tangible better future.[64] In the next scene the *decimero*, walking in the arid landscape where the film started,

---

[64] Cooper, *Everyday Utopias.*

informs us that the three musicians went their separate ways, never to meet again, but the audience can still hear, loud and clear, their music playing in the background while the image of the three laughing musicians boarding the *guagua* is still very vivid. The *decimero* also adds, with exultation, that their *merengue* still resonates in the *frontera* where nobody ever heard such a good *perico ripiao* again: when he stops talking we only hear the music and the desolate landscape is transformed in a soundscape which is no longer qualified by illicit business, prevarication, corruption, exploitation, and abuse but by a tangle of possibilities. In other words, the *frontera* is still *dichosa* but in a different way: it is 'happy,' 'fortunate,' no longer 'damned.' And a happy and fortunate frontier in this context implies, necessarily, a better country, epitomized by national symbols which, while enhancing national identity, can also promote a healthier, more invigorating, and unperverted way to inhabit and 'imagine' the nation as an inextricable part of the island as a whole.

***

In 1979, one year after the election of the social democrat Antonio Guzmán as president of the Dominican Republic – the historical moment in which *Perico Ripiao* is set – the London Anti-Slavery Society denounced to the United Nations the conditions of slavery in which Haitian *braceros* were working in the *bateyes* of the Dominican Republic. Two years later, the French investigative journalist and human rights activist Maurice Lemoine painted a damning picture of Guzmán and his politics on border relations in *Sucre Amer: Esclaves aujourd'hui dans les Caraïbes* (1981). We are shown how, to begin with, the election of Guzmán brought hope to the Haitian *braceros*: 'Under Balaguer it was different, but with Guzmán things are going to change. It's another story,' says one of them, 'Another thing altogether. Balaguer was a bad president, an old friend of the dictator Trujillo [...] Guzmán, the new president [...] is going to do big things for the Kongos.'[65] These optimistic *braceros*, however, soon realise that their hopes are misplaced and, through the harrowing account of the life of one of them, Estimé Mondestin (the name was changed but, Lemoine insists, his story is not fiction), we are told, step by step, how they were bought, sold, and ruthlessly exploited. Lemoine's criticism of the Guzmán administration is not restricted to the situation in the *bateyes*: he also informs us that Haitian dissidents were disappointed by its lack of condemnation for the Duvalier regime and by the fact that Haitian immigrants were forbidden

---

[65] Lemoine, *Bitter Sugar*, p. 29.

to participate in any anti-Duvalier political activities; he also provides us with a long list of anti-Duvalierists who were expelled or threatened with expulsion but saved, at the last minute, by the vigorous protests of Dominican democrats.[66] In *Sucre Amer*, however, Lemoine also declares that, under Guzmán's administration, the Dominican Republic became 'a nation where political crime and brutal repression ha[d] disappeared. For some,' he adds, 'that's a lot.'[67]

The Haitian writer Gary Klang, an anti-Duvalierist who had to leave Haiti in 1960 to avoid political persecution, is definitely among those who judge Guzmán's presidency in more positive terms (or, at least, did so in 1997), as witnessed by *L'île aux deux visages* ('The island with two faces,' 1997), a novel the second part of which is set during Guzmán's presidency (1978–82), while the first part is set in 1965, just before and during the United States' invasion of Santo Domingo.[68] In short, this historical thriller, reminiscent of Ira Levin's *The Boys from Brasil*, recounts the story of a group of Haitian insurgents who plan to overthrow the evil Haitian dictator Faustin (a pseudonym for the Duvaliers) but end up fighting alongside the Dominicans in 1965 and then support the Dominican president Pedro Guztal (a pseudonym for Guzmán) with the hope of exporting democracy to their own country. In the meantime, the three also discover and destroy a network of former members of the Gestapo who had been hiding under false identities in the Dominican Republic since 1935 and who are conspiring to turn the entire island into a gigantic *batey* where black people will be returned to slavery and worked to death for the benefit of the Reich. While denouncing foreign meddling in Hispaniola's affairs (not only the conspiracy of former Gestapo members but also the less fictional but equally sinister and pernicious political and economic influence of the United States), *L'île aux deux visages* explores the impact of the Dominican Republic on Haitian politics and vice versa and forcefully argues that, in order to bring stability to the island, it is important to understand how the border functioned in the past and how it can be negotiated in the future.

As one would expect from a historical thriller, *L'île aux deux visages* mixes fact with fiction and historical characters with fictional ones: the nazi conspirators are invented but many characters/names are authentic and some are only slightly different from the originals. For example, Trujillo, Balaguer, Aristide, Juan Bosch, and Jimmy Carter are all referenced by their

---

[66] Lemoine, *Bitter Sugar*, pp. 261–4.

[67] Lemoine, *Bitter Sugar*, p. 266.

[68] Gary Klang, *L'île aux deux visages* (Ville de Brossard, Québec, Canada: Humanitas, 1997). Page references will be given in parentheses in the text.

names and in more or less historically accurate terms. Peña Gómez, the Dominican politician of Haitian descent (see Chapter 6) who was (at least initially) an ally of Guzmán, three times candidate for presidency of the Dominican Republic but always defeated mostly thanks to the fraudulent manoeuvres of his opponents, appears with a slightly different name, Peña Gornez. The Duvaliers are collapsed into a single fictional dictator called Faustin who has a direct line to former members of the Gestapo in the Dominican Republic; as already mentioned, Antonio Guzmán is called Pedro Guztal and discrepancies between reality and fiction in his case are numerous and go beyond the fact that, while Guzmán committed suicide, his novelistic counterpart is assassinated by former SS agents.

Klang's biography might at least partly explain the writer's decision to offer a positive picture of Guzmán. In the Avant-Propos of *L'île aux deux visages*, the Haitian Klang reveals that the Dominican Guzmán was in fact his uncle and explains that he wanted this book to be a tribute to the man who 'introduced his country to democracy' (p. 7). In the same preface he also pays tribute to other people: first of all to those Haitians and Dominicans who fought side by side in Santo Domingo in 1965 against the United States' invasion, among whom he mentions, primarily, the Haitian Gérard Lafontant, a close friend who, he writes, 'fought very hard for the liberation of both countries' (p. 7). He is also keen to celebrate Peña Gómez and Aristide, who, at the time of writing, was Haiti's president and had, as Klang puts it, freed Haiti from the 'fascist yoke' of the Duvaliers. Klang's own family relations and circle of friends might have underpinned his commitment to a transnational approach to Hispaniola's history and the creation of what one of his characters describes as a much needed '*épopée commune*' or 'shared epic' for Haitians and Dominicans (p. 88; italics in the text). In Klang's mind, the contemporary figures he considered to be among the heroes of this shared epic (i.e. Guzmán, Peña Gómez, Aristide, Lafontant) belong in fact to a much larger pantheon which also includes common people such as those involved in the 1965 resistance and legendary Haitian and Dominican leaders. In a scene in the novel which could easily be interpreted as self-reflective, Klang shows us a Peña Gornez who, just before inciting the people of Santo Domingo to resist the United States' invasion (as Peña Gómez did, famously broadcasting from Radio Santo Domingo in 1965), reaches for history books for inspiration. Significantly, he chooses volumes on Toussaint, who unified Hispaniola in 1801, and Dessalines, the first ruler of Independent Haiti. Importantly, Toussaint united the island under 'French' domination (Chapter 4), prefiguring the Haitian Jean-Pierre Boyer's unification of the island between 1822 and 1844, which is also mentioned by Peña Gornez a few lines later in conjunction with the massacre of 1937.

At this point the character acknowledges that the Haitian unification and the *perejil* massacre are the events that are normally referred to in order to justify the reciprocal hostility of the two countries, but he insists that, *precisely because of* these facts, the two peoples should join forces and fight against the reoccurrence of abuse across the border and throughout the island. He then turns towards 'glorious moments' (p. 88) in Dominican history, namely to the deeds of the three *Padres de la Patria* Juan Pablo Duarte, Francisco del Rosario Sánchez, and Ramón Matías Mella, and reads an account of the events of 27 February 1844, when Sánchez declared the end of the Haitian domination and proclaimed the independence of the Dominican Republic.[69] It is significant that such an extract on Dominican independence is in Spanish and appears untranslated in the text, as the appearance of different languages on the page – *L'île aux deux visages* also includes some words and proverbs in Creole (all translated in notes)[70] – aptly celebrates the multilingual and multicultural nature of the island.

At this specific moment in the narration, however, the extract in Spanish also serves another purpose: it sanctions Peña Gornez's and, by extension, Peña Gómez's, 'Dominicanness.' As pointed out in Chapter 6, Peña Gómez's Haitian descent was used by his political enemies as a weapon against him, especially during the presidential elections of 1994, when the electoral campaign of his opponent, Balaguer, heavily relied on anti-Haitian rhetoric. It was insinuated, in fact, that Peña Gómez, who was nicknamed, disparagingly, *el haitiano*, would not only be disloyal to his country but, evoking the spectre of the Haitian invasion, would engineer the fusion of Haiti and the Dominican Republic. Balaguer won the 1994 election but only marginally and, as it soon emerged, fraudulently: he remained in office but agreed to hold new elections in 1996 and not to present himself as a potential candidate – notably, he was eighty years old at the time. In 1996, Peña Gómez received the greatest number of votes but did not obtain a sufficient majority. The runner-up Fernández won in the second round because he obtained the joint support of Balaguer and Juan Bosch, a former ally of Peña Gómez. It is possible that Bosch turned his back on Peña Gómez because of a personal grudge or political disagreement – they

---

[69] The text here has 28 February as a date: this is one of the many inaccuracies I found in the book. Considering the nature of the text, I am not entirely sure if/when such inaccuracies are deliberate (I fail to see the purpose of such an alteration here) or are due to poor proofreading. In this context, I am wondering also if Peña Gornez for Peña Gómez or Red Cobral for Reid Cabral might not also be recurrent typos. Should this be the case, however, my analysis of the text would not be affected.

[70] For example, *daiva* p. 68, *dodines* p. 76; *précaution pas capon* p. 70 and, crucially, *kamokin* throughout.

were both members of the PRD until Bosch formed a new party, the PLD, in 1973 – but it has also been suggested that his alliance with Balaguer was based on 'misguided anti-Haitianism.'[71]

In *L'île aux deux visages* Klang is keen to reveal the pitfalls of the defamatory campaign against Peña Gómez by insisting that his novelistic counterpart's commitment to the democratization of the island did not make him any less Dominican: apropos of Peña Gornez, one of Klang's Haitian characters confidently states that he is a Dominican citizen who 'has not a bit of Haitian in him' (p. 44), a rather problematic statement which somehow reinforces nationalistic impermeability. Overall, however, despite its many problematic traits, one could say that Klang's novel at times provides a refreshing antithesis to ultra-nationalist and xenophobic Dominican texts published in the 1990s, such as Manuel Núñez's *El ocaso de la nación dominicana* or Luis Julián Pérez's *Santo Domingo frente al destino*. In *Santo Domingo frente al destino*, for example, Luis Julián Pérez characterizes the 1937 massacre as a regrettable but necessary act of self-defence and the Dominicans who took part in it as exasperated victims of an intolerable, 'chronic,' and 'ancestral' situation caused by a disorderly invasion of immigrants who threatened their personal safety.[72] Pérez also endorsed the mechanization of the sugar industry to reduce the need for *braceros* and called for the erection of a wire fence to keep as separate as possible the two peoples who, according to him, had absolutely nothing in common.[73] *El ocaso de la nación dominicana* and *Santo Domingo frente al destino* echo, in many ways, nineteenth-century nationalistic discourses later institutionalized by Trujillo and disseminated by Balaguer with *La isla al revés*, which became an important vehicle to promote his anti-Haitian views during his electoral campaigns, including the one against Peña Gómez. Klang's *L'île aux deux visages*, in contrast, does not demonize one side of the island but is animated by an internationalist, island-based, and anti-fascist spirit which insists that Haitians and Dominicans can live together in harmony and peace only if democracy is established both in Haiti and in the Dominican Republic. In other words, the two faces of the island, while keeping their distinctive features, have to share the same commitment to democratic values and equalitarian principles.

The novel begins with a group of Haitian insurgents who are hiding near Ouanaminthe, on the border with the Dominican Republic, where they plan

---

[71] Howard, *Coloring the Nation*, p. 167.

[72] Luis Julián Pérez, *Santo Domingo frente al destino*, pp. 91–103. See brief discussions of Nunez and Balaguer's books in the Introduction and in Chapter 6.

[73] Luis Julián Pérez, *Santo Domingo frente al destino*, pp. 268, 48, 56, 59–72.

to attack the *Tontons Macoutes* in their barracks to begin an armed revolt aimed at overthrowing Faustin. One of the commandos, Philippe Rivière, is a relative of some of the victims of a massacre which had previously taken place in Jeremie.[74] Julien Leclerc, another insurgent, was born in the Dominican Republic – more precisely, in a *batey*. During the 1937 massacre he was saved, with his family, by a brave Dominican who confronted Trujillo's killers and escorted the Haitian fugitives to the border, which they crossed into safety: this virtuous Dominican was none other than Pedro Guztal (p. 81). When he was in Paris as a student, Leclerc became a close friend of Peña Gornez, who was also born in a Dominican *batey* and whose Haitian parents were killed during <u>the *perejil* massacre.</u> Like the historical Peña Gómez, whose family was also killed in 1937, Peña Gornez was then adopted by a Dominican family and became a Dominican citizen (p. 44). The third member of the group of rebels on which the novel focuses is Richard Parame, the intellectual and 'educator of the masses': he can read Spanish and is particularly intrigued by the horror stories of a fictional Dominican writer called Plinio Mendoza, whose negative representations of Haitians are reminiscent of those of a number of Dominican writers animated by anti-Haitian sentiments.[75]

When we are introduced to Leclerc, Parame, and Rivière, they and their group are ready to attack the *Tontons Macoutes* but do not know that their enemies, alerted by an informer, are actually waiting for them. The Haitian rebels' spies, however, warn them of the danger, and the *kamokins*[76] decide to postpone their attack and to hide in the Dominican Republic to wait for a better occasion. There they can count on the protection of Guztal and Peña Gornez, leaders of the Partido Revolucionario Dominicano, who are struggling against Balaguer to impose democracy in the country. Assistance will be reciprocal: in order to prevent *macoutisme* from spreading

---

[74] In August, September, and October 1964 a real massacre had taken place in Jérémie, where the Duvalier regime ordered the assassination of the family members and the participants of the group 'Jeune Haiti,' who aimed to overthrow the dictator: in total, twenty-seven people were killed.

[75] See, for example, Marcio Veloz Maggiolo, 'Tipologia del tema haitiano en la literatura dominicana', in *Sobre cultura dominicana y otras culturas (ensayos)* (Santo Domingo: Editora Alfa y Omega, 1977), pp. 93–121.

[76] In the novel a note on p. 25 explains that this is the name of Faustin's opponents but, in reality, they were Duvalier's opponents. According to Bernard Diederich, *kamokin* or *kamoken* derives from the word *Camoquin*, the name of an anti-malaria pill sold in Haiti which gave people a yellow complexion, and the term was used to describe the first anti-Duvalier invaders who were mulattoes and whites: see Diederich, *Seeds of Fiction*, p. 32.

throughout the island, the Haitian rebels decide to help their neighbours to establish democracy in the Dominican Republic (p. 43). The novel makes it very clear that what happens on one side of Hispaniola deeply influences what goes on in the other. Significantly, the first meeting between Peña Gornez, Guztal, Leclerc, Parame, and Rivière, where they all agree that they will fight together for their common cause – democratization of the island – takes place under a map of Hispaniola (p. 76).

In reality, border relations were rather complicated at the time in which the action is set: after Bosch's swearing-in as president in February 1963 the two nations were virtually on the verge of war, despite his intention to reconcile with Haiti. In April, Duvalier raided the Dominican embassy and the residence of the Dominican ambassador, who had given sanctuary to anti-Duvalierists. The Haitian dissidents were captured and executed despite the fact that Bosch demanded safe-conduct passes for the rebels; the Organization of American States had to intervene to prevent a war between the two countries. In May 1963, Bosch discovered that Haitian dissidents were trained in clandestine camps in Dominican territory that were run with the support of the Dominican military: he shut three of the camps down but also supported General Léon Cantave, whose exiled army of around a hundred people attacked the military post in Ouanaminthe on 5 August 1963. A few weeks later the OAS intervened and sent the rebels back to Dajabón. Three Dominican invasions then took off from Dajabón but, failing to win backing from the United States, they did not amount to anything. On 25 September Bosch was overthrown in a coup which replaced the president with a military *junta*. Subsequently, an armed 'constitutionalist' insurrection against the *junta* and in support of Bosch broke out on 24 April 1965 and violent revolts broke out in the streets of Santo Domingo, where the demonstrators were bombed. The constitutionalist insurrection, led by Colonel Francisco Alberto Caamaño and Manuel Ramón Montes Arache (both mentioned in *L'île aux deux visages*), brought about a civil war in which the United States marines intervened, landing in Santo Domingo on 29 April 1965. Their intervention was supported by OAS and Duvalier's Haiti had voted in favour of it.

In *L'île aux deux visages*, Klang describes the strenuous struggle which saw Haitians and Dominicans fighting side by side against the military *junta* on Duarte Bridge, the bridge which connected the part of the capital in the hands of the insurgents with the military which supported the *junta* and were stationed at the San Isidro Air Base (pp. 91–7). In Klang's novel, time is compressed and the Haitian plot to attack Ouanaminthe's barracks, the arrival of the rebels in the Dominican Republic, and their involvement in the struggle of the 'constitutionalists' against the military

and the United States all take place during a shorter period of time.[77]
Klang's transnational agenda, however, is not as well supported when he
focuses on Guzmán/Guztal and, as we will see, in other parts of the novel.
Guztal is a valiant adversary of Faustin, an inspirational figure for his
opponents, including Aristide (p. 143), and a protector (and 'accomplice')
of anti-Faustian dissidents, as well as a politician very concerned with
the predicament of the *braceros* – not only did he save Leclerc's family in
1937, but he mentions their suffering in his inaugural speech (p. 117); we
will later discover that Guztal has approved some measures to help them,
but the rich landowners, led by a certain Werner Brooks, blatantly refuse
to apply them (pp. 129–30). As I have already pointed out, not everyone
considers Guzmán to be as inspirational as Klang's Guztal: Guzmán's
government was seen by his critics as a political fraud in which he had
exploited his party in order to enrich himself and his family.[78] Furthermore,
during his presidency, Lemoine writes, anti-Duvalierists were not safe in
the Dominican Republic and were under constant threat of expulsion; he
also adds that, overall, the Dominican president had 'friendly' relations with
Duvalier.[79] Guzmán always denied the charge of enslaving Haitian *braceros*
moved against his government by the Anti-Slavery Society but Lemoine's
Sucre Amer confirmed and supported the Anti-Slavery Society's findings.[80]
On this point, Klang seems to rebuke Lemoine and other members of the
press who denounced the predicament of the *braceros* in the late 1970s
and early 1980s when he mentions that, unlike his predecessors, Guztal
actually opened the doors to journalists who, in their exposés, blamed his
government for the *bateyes*, forgetting that that problem had been created
by Trujillo (p. 130). Klang also argues that it was extremely difficult for
Guztal to go against the interest of the oligarchy who benefited from
the exploitation of Haitian *braceros* (p. 130), a fact that Lemoine was
also prepared to take on board in relation to Guzmán, but only up to a
point: 'it is true,' he writes, 'that any intervention in this crucial domain
would require radical measures involving a head-on conflict with existing
structures, the institutionalized corruption, the established privileges,' but,
Lemoine writes, 'Guzmán wasn't about to take the step.'[81]

---

[77] Philippe Rivière, who takes part in the fighting in the novel, might be a fictional
counterpart of François Andre Rivière, a Haitian who went into battle alongside
Dominicans in 1965 to fight for the freedom of the entire island: see Lemoine, *Bitter
Sugar*, p. 258.

[78] Moya Pons, *Dominican Republic*, p. 410.

[79] Lemoine, *Bitter Sugar*, pp. 262–5.

[80] Martínez, *Peripheral Migrants*, p. 48.

[81] Lemoine, *Bitter Sugar*, p. 261.

The situation of the *bateyes* in the Dominican Republic was in fact a very complex one: when Guzmán was president, sugar plantations belonged to three main owners. The CEA, which represented around 50 per cent of the Dominican production, was directly dependent from the Dominican state and plagued by inefficiency, corruption, and incompetence. The CEA also bought crop from a number of small private companies which, as mentioned, procured their manpower illegally and at the expense of the CEA. Every year, with the support of the armed forces, about 4000 of the 15,000 *braceros* officially recruited by the CEA were 'relocated' to these private companies.[82] The CEA is known to have also made use of forced recruits – that is, Haitian men rounded up by the Dominican army in border towns and farms or even across the country: these detainees (most of whom had no intention of working in *bateyes*) were generally transferred to agents of the CEA together with those who had entered the country illegally and were assigned, for a fee, to estates in need; this also happened, repeatedly, when Guzmán was president.[83] The remaining 50 per cent of Dominican sugar production was divided between the Vicinis – a family which has been involved in the Dominican sugar industry since the late nineteenth century – and the Gulf&Western multinational (40 per cent), whose agents organized the voyages of the *braceros* from Haiti. Needless to say, working and living conditions in the private sector were abysmal too, but Gulf&Western paid wages which were 25 per cent higher than those of the CEA.[84]

The complexity of the *batey* situation, the role of the CEA, and the corruption of those who – operating from *within* the state apparati – benefited from this 'business' do not transpire in any way in Klang's novel, where the *braceros* appear to be exploited exclusively by private companies such as the one owned by Brooks, who declares himself proud to own slaves (p. 39). It turns out that the evil Brooks is also a former Gestapo member who arrived in the Dominican Republic in 1945; he was preceded, ten years earlier, by his leader, a mysterious man called El Jefe who had been sent to Hispaniola by Hitler himself with a precise mission. The fact that Brooks owns huge and profitable plantations explains why *braceros* were spared during a killing spree targeting Haitians living in Dominican territory and organized by former SS members in 1965 (p. 71). According to a reformed member of the Nazi organization, the killing of Haitians in 1965 was aimed at decimating and discouraging those opponents of Faustin – with whom the Nazis were allied despite the fact that they disparaged him for being black –

---

[82] Lemoine, *Bitter Sugar*, p. 122.
[83] Martínez, *Peripheral Migrants*, p. 9; Lemoine, *Bitter Sugar*, pp. 273–5.
[84] Martínez, *Peripheral Migrants*, p. 8; Lemoine, pp. 122, 270.

who were hiding in the Dominican Republic (p. 170). The Gestapo, the same
informer reveals, was also involved in the 1937 massacre, during which – in
Klang's reconstruction but contrary to historical evidence – *braceros* were
specifically targeted. The Gestapo, we are told, had organized *el corte* with
Trujillo hoping that the Haitian president would react at such outrage. A
violent response would have given the Dominican dictator (who wanted
to take revenge for the 1822–44 occupation) an excuse to invade Haiti. At
that point, the Nazis would have eliminated Trujillo and taken hold of the
entire island, which they would have turned into a gigantic *batey*: this was
in fact the Führer's plan and El Jefe and Brook still hoped to make Hitler's
dream come true at the very end of the 1970s (p. 170).

Historians have investigated the existence of certain connections
between *el corte* and Nazist ideology[85] but to assert that the 1937 massacre
was masterminded by the Nazis, especially in a fictional account which
constantly engages with historical facts and people, is a highly problematic
move. Arguably, such an assertion does not reinforce – in fact, it considerably
weakens – Klang's attempt to create a 'shared epic' for the island which, to
fulfil its purpose, cannot be based on such radical and simplistic denials
of history and on the depiction of its inhabitants as mere puppets in
the hands of foreign powers. We have also seen how the novel seems to
engineer the canonization of Guzmán through the depiction of a righteous,
unblemished, and virtuous Guztal, a 'martyr' ruthlessly eliminated by the
Nazis because he wanted to bring democracy to the entire island. This is at
best a simplification and at worse a travesty of the very important historical
moment in which Guzmán operated and of the many contradictions which
characterized his time as a president, a distortion of the truth which does
a real disservice to what seems to be the author's genuine commitment to
a transnational agenda.

Klang's representation of the *braceros* as a homogeneous disenfranchised
group unable to fight for their rights – or to even understand that they had
rights – is neither helpful nor entirely accurate. As we have seen, Guzmán's
arrival initially brought hope to the country and those who wanted to bring
democracy to the island but it also worried people such as Duvalier, who
had invested nearly nine million dollars to support Balaguer.[86] Duvalier was
so concerned about Guzmán, and so keen to weaken his position, that he
tried to boycott him by sending to the Dominican cane fields a higher class
of *braceros* than those who normally accepted work in the *zafra*, or sugar
harvest. Lemoine's Estimé is one of these men who, in 1978, left behind

[85] Vega, *Trujillo y Haití*, vol. I, p. 403.
[86] Lemoine, *Bitter Sugar*, p. 261.

reasonably well-paid jobs such as shopkeepers, craftsmen and taxi drivers (as in Estimé's case) because they were told, by Duvalier's propaganda, that a huge amount of money was waiting for them in *Dominicanie*. When these men saw the appalling conditions in which they were supposed to work and live, and realized how little money they were really going to make, many refused to work and left the *bateyes* (even on foot, as Lemoine recounts), causing problems for the CEA, which had to repatriate them and then resort to desperate illegal migrants with lower standards.[87] In Klang's novel there is no trace of this: the *braceros* are all victims who 'unfortunately, do not harbour any real desire to rebel' (p. 84) and the Haitian protagonists/insurgents, regrettably, decide to focus on helping the virtuous Guztal rather than the people of the *bateyes* (pp. 113–14). At the end of *L'île aux deux visages* all we know is that the *kamokins* manage to eliminate the threat posed by the former Gestapo members; the novel provides no insight into what happens after that. This is perhaps not surprising, as it is very hard to understand how social equality and democracy could thrive on the island if the 'shared epic' that Klang's novel offers to the people of Hispaniola is one in which, ultimately, its most vulnerable inhabitants are not allowed to voice their views, let alone take centre stage, as it was the case, instead, for the 'forgotten heart-breaking epic[s] of [...] border struggle' presented in D'Alcalá's *La Frontera*, in Lemoine's *Sucre Amer*, in the film *Perico Ripiao*, and in Rueda's *Las metamorfosis de Makandal*.

---

[87] Lemoine, *Bitter Sugar*, pp. 75–97; Martínez, *Peripheral Migrants*, p. 48.

Chapter Nine

Some are born to endless night: structural violence across-the-border

Hulda Guzmán, *Some are born to sweet delight* (2011), Máximo Avilés Blonda, *Pirámide 179* (1968), Alanna Lockward, *Un Haití Dominicano: Tatuajes Fantasmas y Narrativas Bilaterales, 1994–1998* (2010), Louis-Philippe Dalembert's *L'Autre Face de la mer* (1998), Evelyne Trouillot, *Le bleu de l'île* (2005), Jean-Noël Pancrazi, *Montecristi* (2009), *Jean Gentil* (2010), written and directed by Israel Cárdenas and Laura Amelia Guzmán

I n Chapter 1 we saw how, in the eighteenth century, standing beside the Massacre River, Moreau Saint-Méry was struck by the fact that on the French side he could see 'settlements where everything bespoke an active industry,' 'a degree of wealth,' and even 'objects of luxury,' while the Spanish side was just a 'barren' wasteland.[1] A century later, as highlighted in Chapter 5, José Martí had a similar experience: he found the Haitian town of Ouanaminthe to be flourishing and 'cheerful,' while Dajabón, on the other side, was both poor and 'sad.'[2] Nowadays, standing roughly on the same spot, one can have a similar experience – if not as dramatic as that of Saint-Méry or Martí's – but with a crucial difference. The Dominican painter Hulda Guzmán has encapsulated this in a 2011 painting entitled *Some are born to sweet delight*,[3] a line from a fragment of William Blake's *Auguries of*

---

[1] Saint-Méry, ms, vol. I, pp. 10–11; PE, vol. I, pp. 206–7.

[2] Martí, 'War Diaries', pp. 361–2.

[3] In 2013 Hulda Guzmán took part in the art exhibition *On Common Ground: Dominican Republic + Haiti* (Museum of the Americas, Washington). When she was asked 'What comes to mind when you hear "Dominican Republic/Haiti?",' Guzmán replied 'Unification: One Love and One Future'. See Brian Schaaf, 'On Common Ground: Haiti and the Dominican Republic,' *Haiti Innovation – Choice, Partnership, Community*, 17 April 2013, http://haitiinnovation.org/en/2013/04/17/common-ground-haiti-and-dominican-republic [accessed 25 November 2014].

Figure 15. Hulda Guzmán, *Some are born to sweet delight* (2011) (photograph: Hulda Guzmán).

Innocence: 'Every night and every morn / Some to misery are born, / Every morn and every night / Some are born to sweet delight. / Some are born to sweet delight / Some are born to endless night.'[4]

In *Some are born to sweet delight* all is 'luxury, leisure and pleasure' (as Baudelaire would have it[5]) on the Dominican side, while Haiti is destitute and in ruin. This painting was produced after the 2010 earthquake – the shattered house is an obvious clue – and Guzmán's binarism draws our attention to the unsustainability of the current scenario. Yet, as the juxtaposition of Guzmán's piece with Saint-Méry's and Martí's words exemplifies, Haiti – crucially not just Saint Domingue – has not always been the poorer country on Hispaniola. Clearly, Guzmán's painting is deliberately deprived of nuances: in reality, as Guzmán knows very well, poverty is still widespread in the Dominican Republic (the borderland

---

[4] William Blake, 'Auguries of Innocence', in *The Complete Poems* (Harmondsworth: Penguin, 2004), pp. 506–10, p. 510.
[5] Charles Baudelaire, 'L'Invitation au voyage', in *Les Fleurs du Mal* (Paris: Flammarion, 1991), pp. 99–100, p. 100.

provinces, in particular, are among the poorest in the country), not all Haitians are destitute, and the Haitian earthquake did not destroy the entire nation. The limitations of binary oppositions, especially those which depict Haiti as the poorer, and often parasitical, neighbour of a wealthy Dominican Republic, are implicitly, but effectively, revealed, and the incorporation of Blake's words casts the situation of the island as a whole as a paradox. The unacceptable conclusion foregrounded by the poem indirectly discloses an important truth: uneven distribution of resources and riches is definitely an issue but poverty, deprivation, and injustice or, more broadly, what, in 1969, the Norwegian sociologist Johan Galtung poignantly called 'structural violence' often straddle the border of Hispaniola rather than being ring-fenced by it. 'Structural violence,' Galtung explains, is a kind of violence which 'shows up as unequal power and, consequently, as unequal life chances.'[6] This kind of violence is clearly different from the ferocious killings of the 1937 massacre, the often cruel Haitian ruling of the Spanish side in 1822–44, or any of the atrocities committed, by either side, in those moments in the history of the island which can be taken to encapsulate the so-called 'fatal conflict model' discussed in the Introduction. Galtung, however, warns us that it is 'indispensable' to extend our concept of violence to include 'the cause of the difference between the potential and the actual.'[7] Structural violence, he continues, 'is silent, it does not show [...] may be seen as about us as the air around us.'[8] Yet, it is as harmful as any other form of violence and, as such, it needs to be brought to the fore. Captured, visually, in one of those instants in which the borderline in Karmadavis's *Línea Fronteriza Intermitente* (the image on the cover of this book) is 'switched off,' the often disavowed across-the-border continuity of structural violence on Hispaniola is analysed in this chapter, which has at its core two plays, one film, various pieces of journalism, and two novels, by authors and directors born in Haiti, the Dominican Republic, Algeria, and Mexico. All these works focus on the lives of border-crossers and borderland dwellers who are often 'persuaded' by 'those who have the power to decide over the distribution of resources' not 'to perceive' themselves at the receiving end of a form of violence.[9] Their experiences, however, highlight multiple across-the-border materializations (i.e. migration, prostitution, environmental degradation, centralization of resources, destitution, privatization of survival) of Galtung's structural

6 Galtung, 'Violence, Peace, and Peace Research', p. 171.
7 Galtung, 'Violence, Peace, and Peace Research', p. 168.
8 Galtung, 'Violence, Peace, and Peace Research', p. 173.
9 Galtung, 'Violence, Peace, and Peace Research', pp. 173, 171, 173.

violence. By underlining the significance of structural violence, the texts under scrutiny here insist that in order to eliminate it and turn the 'potential' into the 'actual' – to use Galtung's parlance, which here chimes, in significant ways, with Bloch's utopianism mentioned in Chapter 6 – it is imperative to confront, urgently and effectively, the across-the-border imbalance in power relations.

✦✦✦

In 1968 – that is, sixteen years before Guzmán was born – the Dominican poet and playwright Máximo Avilés Blonda highlighted precisely the often disavowed continuities between Haiti and his own country from the point of view of '*los de abajos*' – the poor and disenfranchised of both nations – in a play entitled *Pirámide 179* ('Pyramid 179').[10] Born in Santo Domingo in 1931, Blonda was professor of Dominican literature and director of the Experimental Theatre of the University of Santo Domingo for many years; he received the Premio Nacional de Poesía twice and in 1987, a year before his death, he was awarded the prestigious Grado de Gran Cruz Placa de Plata in the Orden de Duarte, Sánchez y Mella. Significantly, *Pirámide 179* takes place on the very border between Haiti and the Dominican Republic, more precisely by one of the 313 pyramids that, following the treaty of 1929, were placed along the borderline to mark the division between the two nations.

The play, which, significantly, is not divided up into acts or scenes, begins with the author's description of pyramid 179, which is not, 'geometrically speaking,' a real pyramid but simply a landmark whose inscriptions (179 RD and 179 RH 1929) are meant to signpost a demarcation which would otherwise be indiscernible: it stands, we are told, in a landscape characterized by 'aridity and silence' surrounded only by 'thorny bushes' and 'lost goats' (p. 137). The only other presences which signal a geopolitical division are occasional fugitive border-crossers and military men who permanently guard the border on both sides of the pyramid (p. 137). The militarization of the border is crucial to Blonda's play: among the very few props on stage are the rifles which are carried by the two actors who play the soldiers. Besides, the only character who is identified by a profession other than 'actor,' 'actress' or 'director' is the '*militar negro*' or 'black soldier' (pp. 137–8). Haiti and the Dominican Republic are not referred to directly, but it is made obvious that the 'black soldier,' the 'black actress,' and the 'black actor' are Haitians,

---

[10] Blonda, *Pirámide 179*, pp. 135–205, p. 197. Page references will be given in parentheses in the text.

while the 'young actor,' the 'old actor,' and the 'third actor' represent
Dominicans; significantly, in a move that highlights Dominican white
supremacist 'othering' discourses which associate 'blackness' exclusively with
the opposite side of the island, their skin colour is not specified.

  Pirámide 179 is, in essence, a metatheatrical piece in which a group of
actors and a director rehearse a play which takes place around this particular
pyramid. The setting is very sparse and, crucially, it is organized in the
sight of the audience: four different towers are brought on stage by the
actors, who position the two shorter ones at a distance from one another
and closer to the audience. The taller ones are situated farther upstage. In
order to highlight the artificial nature of the geopolitical division, the island's
partition is marked by the actors themselves, who use a *trapo* or 'rag'[11] to
signify the borderline while the director tries to 'naturalize' the border by
introducing a fish tank which stands for one of the rivers of Hispaniola
which have been 'frontierized'[12] and now mark the division between the two
countries (pp. 152–3). The actors then position themselves in the following
way: the 'young actor' armed with a rifle occupies one of the tall towers at
the back, while the 'black actor,' who also carries a weapon, stands on the
other. The 'second actress,' the 'old actor,' and the 'third actor' are positioned
on one of the towers closer to the audience, while on the fourth tower we
see the 'black actor' and 'the black actress' (pp. 154–5). The actor who plays
the director sits in the middle, on a block of stone with the number 179
painted on it, which descends 'from above.' Since his role is 'to unite and
divide,' for the entire duration of the rehearsal the director will be sitting
on this makeshift pyramid, openly mimicking the God who, according to
the script the actors have received, 'divided the island' and stubbornly kept
it divided even when he realized that it was not 'a good thing' (pp. 155–6).
A long speech delivered by the actor/director to a soundtrack of military
music and noise made by cannons and shackles posits the creation of the
línea as an act of God, like the creation of land and water. The audience,
however, is once again invited to question the presence of the border as
'natural' and as 'God-given' when the director adds that God enlisted the
help of ruthless businessmen, politicians and armed forces (both local and

---

[11] In Spanish, '*sacar los trapos sucios a relucir*' means 'to wash one's dirty linen
in public' – which, in a way, is what the play is doing by bringing to the fore the
disavowed fact that poverty does not stop at the geopolitical border.
[12] Carlos Altagracia Espada and Ramón Corrada del Río have coined this neologism
to underline that, far from being a 'natural' frontier, the River Massacre has been
assigned its role by political forces which have 'frontierized' it – see 'Quisqueya,
Frontera Fragmentada', quoted in Alexandre, 'Visión Haitiana', p. 134.

foreign[13]) whose main task was to prevent the people from the two different sides from 'uniting and loving one another like brothers' (p. 156).

The 'old actor' and the 'third actor' are seen accompanying the 'second actress,' a graduate from a university of the United States, in her inspection of the borderland which has the aim of selecting an appropriate site for the convention of A.D.L.D.Q.N.H.P.A. This impressive acronym stands for *'Ayudadores de los demás que no han pedido ayuda'* or 'Helpers of those who have not asked for help' (p. 158), and clearly underlines the unwelcome interference on the island of the 'Princes of the North' (p. 156). Repeating ultra-nationalist anti-Haitian discourses, the 'old actor' depicts those who live on the other side of the pyramid as 'animals' who are occupying land that used to belong to their neighbours and was lost owing to the incapacity and neglect of inept politicians.[14] He then proceeds to praise those 'noble' leaders who fought instead to assert their country's rights. His words are promptly contested by the 'third actor,' who highlights class division within the country and, addressing the audience directly, points out that those who actually 'fought' the wars referred to by the 'old actor' were the poor, reduced to cannon fodder to serve the interests of the elite (pp. 161–2). Dismantling the sharp differentiation that the 'old actor' affirms exists between the two nations, the 'third actor' also reveals to the 'third actress' that those on the other side are not much poorer than those on his side: poverty and exploitation are the same everywhere: 'this pyramid,' he continues, 'divides the land but not the misery of the people' (p. 168).

The two black actors are then given the spotlight while they engage in a conversation in which the woman exhorts her (reluctant) husband to put down the drums with which he sings his longing and allegiances to 'Guinea' in order to get involved in politics to change the predicament in which they, and their fellow countrymen and women, live (pp. 170–77). We are also informed that they are forbidden to speak to those who live on the other side of the pyramid, with whom they believe they share the same struggle for survival (p. 173). The next two actors who are brought to the fore are

---

[13]   The historical role played by the United States in the demarcation and enforcement of the internal border of Hispaniola is repeatedly highlighted by Blonda. Blonda's condemnation of the United States' interference in Dominican affairs is unsurprising, especially considering that only three years before the play was written the Dominican Republic had been invaded for the second time by the United States, and that they had previously supported Trujillo's dictatorship and were supporting the Duvaliers' regime in Haiti.

[14]   For details on the territorial dispute see, for example, William Páez Piantini, *Relaciones domínico-haitianas: 300 años de historia* (Santo Domingo: Imp. Mediabyte, 2006), especially pp. 240–46.

the soldiers who guard the pyramid and the borderline: they agree that they are luckier[15] than their respective compatriots because their job allows them to take advantage of the illicit traffic that takes place across the border and because, as soldiers, they are allowed to do what is not permitted to civilians, namely talk to one another (pp. 178–81, 197). However, while the 'black actor' rehearses the glorious history of Haiti, the 'young actor' from the Dominican side insists that they should focus instead on the present and the future of the island and behave 'as brothers' because, after all, they are both peasants who have been taught to kill their own brothers for the benefit of others (pp. 177–9). He is also convinced that they should prevent the pyramid from becoming insurmountable and is profoundly disturbed by the fact that the peoples from the opposite sides of the pyramid are not allowed to communicate. His interest in countering the verticality of the borderline by allowing the horizontality of the borderland to sabotage it, however, is not shared by the 'black actor', who considers the prohibition of exchanges between civilians to be an order they are not in a position to discuss and is committed to safeguarding and enhancing impermeability (pp. 178–83).

At the time that the play was written border water-tightness was being forcefully preserved, especially from the Haitian side, while Balaguer was (as ever) actively promoting anti-Haitianism and the Dominicanization of the frontier. In 1963, fearing an attack of anti-Duvalierists from across the border, Duvalier had forbidden anyone from living in its proximity and went as far as creating a no-man's land zone three to four miles wide along its entire length.[16] Many emigrants who tried to re-enter the country were sentenced to death for trespassing into what Duvalier considered 'a war zone' and their bodies were displayed as a warning to those who wanted to cross. Those who were previously living in the area had been escorted out of it with their livestock by the *Tontons Macoutes*, who proceeded to cut trees, slash undergrowth, and burn homes and crops.[17] On 29 September 1963, in 'The Nightmare Republic,' a long article he published in the *Sunday Telegraph* that brought to international attention the atrocities committed by the Duvaliers' regime, Graham Greene reported that during a visit to Haiti

---

[15] They use the expression '*más dichosos*,' which resonates well with *Perico Ripiao* and the *dichosa frontera* from which the General Contreras and his sidekick profited so much.

[16] Martínez, *Peripheral Migrants*, p. 46 and Robert Debs Heinl and Nancy Gordon Heinl, *Written in Blood: The Story of the Haitian People, 1942–1971* (Boston, MA: Houghton Mifflin, 1978), p. 638.

[17] Martínez, *Peripheral Migrants*, p. 46 and Diederich, *Seeds of Fiction*, pp. 61–2.

it took him two days to get permission to visit the south of the country, while the north of Haiti, 'because of the raids [of anti-Duvalierists] from the Dominican Republic, was forbidden altogether.'[18]

In a subsequent visit to Hispaniola in 1965, as we have seen in Chapter 7, Greene travelled along the border from Dajabón to Pedernales together with the exiled Haitian Catholic priest Jean-Claude Bajeux and the journalist Bernard Diederich, who had just been expelled from Haiti, where he had been living with his family since 1949. Bajeux and Diederich were also directly involved in some of the across-the-border anti-Duvalier activities which took place at the beginning of the 1960s and that are fictionalized by Klang in the first part of *L'île aux deux visages*.[19] Diederich's vivid account of this journey through the Dominican borderland – which ended with the above-mentioned visit to the Alcoa compound in Pedernales – describes the '*cordon sanitaire*' (Greene used to call it the 'Voodoo Curtain') created by Duvalier on the Haitian side of the frontier. Diederich depicts the borderland as an abandoned and deserted place where the three men constantly felt as if they were in the gunsights of the *Tontons Macoutes* and faced the possibility of encountering Duvalier's three most notorious border henchmen, namely Ludovic Nassard, Zacharie Delva, and André Simon, who were controlling the northern, central, and southern sections of the border. Thankfully, however, Greene, Diederich, and Bajeux were approached only by a guinea hen, Haitian children who begged for money, and a mysterious hitchhiker who never spoke to them. Even the once-thriving trade in contraband in which the local people had traditionally engaged, Diederich reports, 'had come to a standstill: Dominicans no longer dared buy Haitian *clairin* (raw rum), while Haitians couldn't acquire basic necessities.'[20]

Poverty is also emphasized in Blonda's play: after the exchange between husband and wife, the 'third actor' launches a tirade against private property which he considers to be at the origin of the division of the island and of all the divisions and injustices which plague the earth; he then refuses to leave the borderland with the 'old actor' and the 'second actress' and remains there on his own, looking sadly at 'the terrible division between two hungers which is marked by the pyramid' (p. 189). On the other side, in the meantime, the 'black actress' announces to her husband that she will be leaving soon to carry out a mission for a political organization which aims to overthrow

---

[18] Graham Greene, 'The Nightmare Republic,' *Sunday Telegraph*, 29 September 1963, quoted in Diederich, *Seeds of Fiction*, p. 28.
[19] Diederich, *Seeds of Fiction*, pp. 32–46, 57–8, 68–70.
[20] Diederich, *Seeds of Fiction*, pp. 56–64, 77. In *The Comedians* Greene's characters also comments on the poverty of the Dominican population (p. 246).

the government and reminds him once more that his home is not Africa but the country in which they are living and where they have to build 'something good for everyone.' At this point, pointing towards the pyramid, she asks him: 'do you think they live better than us?' (p. 195). Affected by her words, while the Chorus indicts private property and exploitation once again, the 'black actor' addresses the 'third actor,' who is looking at him from across the border, and asks his 'brother' how his harvest went (p. 200). In flagrant breach of the prohibition on communication, the two discuss their predicaments and agree that the pyramid should not exist. When the 'forbidden word' 'brother' is pronounced again, sadly, the 'black actor' is shot dead by the zealous 'black soldier' (pp. 200–202).

The play in the play ends here, with the actors exiting their roles and the scene; the setting remains as it is, with the pyramid at its centre dividing the space in two. Before leaving, however, the 'young actor' and the 'third actor,' acting as 'real men' and no longer in their given roles, exhort the audience to 'rebel'; their words are repeated by the chorus, which makes it clear that, for the benefit of Hispaniola, class division and the separation between the poor of the island – signified by the pyramid – should be cast aside (pp. 204–5). The director closes this Brechtian 'anti-audience play' (p. 145) by wishing the audience 'good night,' and leaves them in charge of the situation: any improvement that might occur is, from that moment on, their responsibility, and depends on their ability and will to reject the received 'script' of anti-Haitianism (pp. 204–5). Overall, therefore, Blonda's militarized borderland is, to begin with, reduced to being a mere borderline and a 'non-place' characterized by 'division, vigilance and misery' (pp. 176, 184, 179). Yet, once the 'invisible thread' (p. 196) which links the people who live on either side is seized and capitalized upon, the pluralist *raya* depicted by, for example, Rueda, Philoctète, Veloz Maggiolo, Danticat, and (indirectly) Alexis is re-energized and becomes both a place where an alternative way of life can be imagined and, hopefully, the origin of change.

✶✶✶

Significantly, when the 'black actor' in *Pirámide 179* suggests to his wife that they should relocate to the other side of the border to give their child a better chance in life, she refuses to follow his advice and renews her commitment to stay in Haiti and fight in order to improve things for its inhabitants and, ultimately, for all the oppressed people of Hispaniola (pp. 186–7). In 1968, when Blonda's play was published, Haitian migration to the Dominican Republic was being discouraged: between 1967 and 1970, in fact, Duvalier had suspended the contract that he had signed with

Balaguer in 1966 which committed the Dominican government to pay the Haitian state for organizing recruitment centres for *braceros* in Haiti. The sugar cane harvests of 1967–70 were carried out mainly by forced recruits, *viejos* ('old men' – that is, workers who had lived in the *bateyes* for years), and illegal migrants. Moreover, while Balaguer was boasting of having finally 'Dominicanized' sugar cane harvesting, the persecution of Haitians living in the Dominican Republic was becoming harsher.[21] The official recruitment of *braceros* was renewed in 1970 but since 1986 the Haitian government has no longer been officially involved in their recruitment. The number of migrants who cross illegally or *anba fil* ('under the wire') into the neighbouring country continues to be very high – even though, as we will see, they do not work exclusively in *bateyes*. Nowadays, in fact, the majority of immigrants to the Dominican Republic are from Haiti, one of the Caribbean countries with the highest number of emigrants: poverty, political turmoil, social insecurity, and environmental degradation – what Galtung would call structural violence – have traditionally encouraged the population to leave.[22]

Interestingly, those scholars who have objected to the 'fatal conflict' scenario which shapes studies such as Wucker's *Why the Cocks Fight* have admitted that, in fact, 'there *is* a struggle taking place on the island of Hispaniola [which] focuses on the specific issue of immigration. What is being struggled for is not the island but control over the immigrant population on one side of it.'[23] It is not surprising, therefore, that a quarter of the articles and interviews in Alanna Lockward's 2010 collection *Un Haití Dominicano: Tatuajes Fantasmas y Narrativas Bilaterales, 1994–1998*, published over the second half of the 1990s, are devoted to the Haitian migration to the Dominican Republic, the plight of Haitian *braceros*, the debate around immigration laws, and the policy of deportation (chapters 11 to 18).[24] Alanna Lockward is a Dominican journalist, writer, art curator, and classical ballet dancer who now lives and works in Berlin. She believes in the cultural interdependence of the two countries sharing Hispaniola, as testified, for example, by 'Pares y nones' ('Even and Odds'), an innovative art exhibition which she curated and which, between 2002 and 2008, presented

---

[21] Martínez, *Peripheral Migrants*, p. 47.

[22] Riveros, *Estado del arte*, pp. 20, 30–33, 56–7; Rodríguez Grullón, *Estado del arte*, p. 94.

[23] Martínez, 'Not a Cockfight', p. 94 (italics in the original).

[24] Alanna Lockward, *Un Haití Dominicano: Tatuajes Fantasmas y Narrativas Bilaterales, 1994–1998* (Santo Domingo: Art Labour Archive, 2010). Kindle version retrieved from Amazon.es. Reference to chapters will be given in parentheses in the text.

contemporary photography from Haiti and the Dominican Republic in the Caribbean, Africa, the United States, and Europe.[25] More recently, she has published *Marassá y la Nada* ('Marassa and Nothingness'), a novel which highlights the connections and continuities between the two sides of Hispaniola while telling the story of a family scattered between Paris, Santo Domingo, Haiti, and New York.[26]

As the title suggests, in *Un Haití Dominicano* Lockward offers us a rare insight into the life of some Dominicans who, in the 1990s, were living and working in Haiti. The number of Dominicans who migrate to Haiti is modest: recent figures estimate that the number in 2010 was 9668 – that is 0.7 per cent of the total of those who left their country in search of opportunities. Yet, it is still important to remember that the migratory flux in Hispaniola resulting from pervasive structural violence is not entirely unidirectional.[27] Lockward's focus, in fact, is on female migrants who were (and still are[28]) forced to migrate mainly because of the economic, social, and cultural repercussions of gender and class discrimination; her collection of articles contains a series of interviews with Dominican women, all originally from a very humble background, who live and work in Haiti.[29] Among Lockward's interviewees we find a successful hair stylist and a thriving esoterist, formerly a businesswoman in the tyre trade (chapters 3 and 6), as well as various sex workers, some of whom did not want to be identified because they knew that their occupation is stigmatized and had children and relatives in the Dominican Republic or the United States who did not

---

[25] In 'Pares y nones: igualdad invisible,' *Un Haití Dominicano* (chapter 33), Lockward explains the rationale behind her curatorial decisions and comments on the works of the artists included in the exhibitions (Elia Alba, Carlos Acero, Vinicio Almonte, Ricardo Briones, Olivier Flambert, Miguel Gómez, Adler Guerrier, Carl Juste, Fonso Khouri, Abraham Khouri, Roxanes Ledan, Daniel Morel, Darío Oleaga, Marc Steed, and Roberto Stephenson).

[26] Alanna Lockward, *Marassá y la Nada* (Santo Domingo: Editorial Santuario, 2013).

[27] Riveros, *Estado del arte*, pp. 39–40. According to *Listin Diario* the number of Dominican migrants to Haiti increased quite substantially during 2011, in the aftermath of the earthquake, and the new arrivals were, predominantly, experts in information and industrial technology: see 'Dominicanos en Haití: migrantes desconocidos,' *Listin Diario*, 20 November 2012, http://www.listin.com.do/la-republica/2012/11/20/255812/Dominicanos-en-Haiti-migrantes-desconocidos [accessed 28 November 2014]. See also Rodríguez Grullón, *Estado del arte*, pp. 52–3.

[28] Riveros, *Estado del arte*, p. 50 and Rodríguez Grullón, *Estado del arte*, p. 49.

[29] In 1987, Pedro Mir too had pointed out how some Dominican women had to resort to prostitution abroad when 'hunger' – a key word also for Blonda – began to force poor Dominicans to emigrate. Pedro Mir, *Historia del hambre: sus orígines en la historia dominicana* (Santo Domingo: Editora Corripio, 1987).

know about their line of work (chapter 2). All these migrants explained that they had a very negative picture of Haiti and the Haitians when they were in the Dominican Republic. After living there for months or even years, however, they had changed their minds and became rather fond of their adoptive country and its people. Most of these women invested part of the money they gained in property located in Santo Domingo but they were determined to remain in Haiti because they claimed that Haiti offered them possibilities which were not available in the Dominican Republic: thanks to the work they were doing there, their children could afford a better life and, in some cases, even a university education.

Lockward informs us that Dominican prostitution in Haiti began to prosper in 1928 and that, together with the Dominican sugar cane industry, it is another legacy of the United States' occupation. Seventy years later, Lockward adds, the presence of Dominican sex workers in Haiti was so established that their status was being discussed by the Secretaries of Foreign Affairs of both countries in the Bilateral Mixed Commission (chapters 2 and 4). According to Lockward, in the 1990s the demand for Dominican sex workers was high both in their country and abroad (chapter 5) and Natalia Riveros and Altair Rodríguez Grullón have confirmed that, nowadays, this still remains the case.[30] It is not surprising, therefore, that the figure of the Dominican prostitute might have shaped the way in which Haitian cane cutters working in the Dominican sugar industry perceive both the neighbouring country and themselves as border-crossers. Haitian *braceros*, in fact, often refer to the Dominican Republic as *peyi bouzen* ('hookers' country'), and Martínez has suggested that this synecdoche might be triggered by the *braceros'* anxiety at having 'prostituted' themselves by migrating to the Dominican Republic. They are very well aware, Martínez explains, that working in sugar estates will not provide them with long-term security and know that, in most cases, they have swapped a life as an independent cultivator (as deprived as such life might be) for work for wages that can be more profitable but are also more precarious.[31]

The figure of the 'Dominican prostitute' makes repeated appearances in literary texts, and those included here are no exception: Alexis's *Compère Général Soleil*, for example, opens with Hilarion walking through the red-light district of Port-au-Prince – intriguingly called La Frontière – in the 1930s, where drunken Dominican sex workers swear and sing in Spanish

---

[30] Riveros, *Estado del arte*, pp. 49–50 and Rodríguez Grullón, *Estado del arte*, pp. 55–56. According to Rodríguez Grullón and Riveros, all too often these women also become victims of trafficking.

[31] Martínez, *Peripheral Migrants*, p. 88 and 'Not a Cockfight', p. 93.

(pp. 9–10). One of the main characters in Jean-Noël Pancrazi's *Montecristi* (2009), as we will see later in this chapter, is a Dominican prostitute whose physical deterioration mirrors the decline of the city in 2005 and 2006. In Louis-Philippe Dalembert's *L'Autre Face de la mer* (1998) the bars of 1980s Port-au-Prince are full of Dominican hookers, and Marie-Claire, the prostitute who bestows her favours on the young boys of one of its neighbourhoods, comes from the other side of the River Massacre.[32]

Migration is also a central theme of Dalembert's *L'Autre Face de la mer*, a novel which explores the urge to migrate that has affected four generations of the same Haitian family at different times in history; at the end of the novel, the youngest, Jonas, leaves Port-au-Prince to better his condition in the chaotic years which followed the flight of Jean-Claude Duvalier from Haiti in 1986. Jonas has no illusions about what a foreign land can offer to him, and had previously rejected the idea of abandoning his country but, at that point, he seems finally persuaded that whatever he is going to find will be better than what he has at home (pp. 216–20). When Jonas, an educated young man, finally leaves, he travels 'to the other side of the ocean' (p. 223), not choosing the Dominican Republic as his destination as his great-grandfather had done when he emigrated with his wife and children in the 1930s. The United States' occupation and environmental degradation are presented as contributing factors in Jonas's great-grandfather's decision to relocate but not as its ultimate causes (pp. 29; 31–2). The family was not doing badly in Haiti; they had their own house and both great-grandparents had a job, but at the time, the narrator explains, people erroneously believed that on the other side of the River Massacre all their dreams would come true (pp. 31–2; 35). Unfortunately, the family was caught in the 1937 massacre and had to endure an attack of dogs and an attempt by Dominican guards to burn them alive; most distressingly, one of the children had a leg amputated by a machete and another had to be left behind because, being a wanderer, he was nowhere to be found when his parents and siblings had to rush away from the compound in which they lived and worked (pp. 41, 58).

The experience of *el corte* was so traumatic that Jonas's grandmother – who was a little girl at the time – resolutely decided that she would never leave Haiti again and would never give her blessings to any members of her family who decided to migrate: Jonas, in fact, leaves only after his grandmother's death. Dalembert follows Alexis and Philoctète in both praising courageous Dominicans who risked their lives to protect Haitians and creating a connection between sugar fields and the massacre of 1937, but he also puts

---

[32] Louis-Philippe Dalembert, *L'Autre Face de la mer* (Paris: Stock, 1998), pp. 92, 147. Page references will be given in parentheses in the text.

el corte in the broader context of other types of 'forced migration' which preceded it and followed it. Descriptions of the Middle Passage are to be found in separate one-page chapters interspersed throughout the narration, and the predicament of the boat people who left the coasts of Haiti under the Duvaliers is also brought to the fore. Dalembert – himself a diasporic Haitian since 1986, when he moved to Paris and then to various other locations in Europe, Tunisia, and Israel – does not paint a rosy picture of migration, which is presented as a condition where death and exploitation are always around the corner and as something that people are almost invariably 'forced' to choose; as mentioned, he presents us with a character who, in the aftermath of 1986, believes that leaving Haiti is, regrettably, his only option.

***

Le bleu de l'île (2005), a play by Evelyne Trouillot, also investigates the causes and effects of forced migration from Haiti and forcefully highlights the fact that migration deprives the country of important human resources. Trouillot belongs to one of Haiti's most productive literary families: her uncle is the historian Henock Trouillot and her siblings are the novelist Lyonel Trouillot, the anthropologist, historian, and political scientist Michel-Rolph Trouillot, and the Creole scholar and children's book author Jocelyne Trouillot. Born in Port-au-Prince in 1952, Trouillot left Haiti at an early age to study in the United States, but returned to her country in 1987, where she now teaches and writes her fiction and poetry. *Le bleu de l'île* is Trouillot's first play and was initially conceived as a novel;[33] it was performed for the first time in 2008 in Port-au-Prince by the Haitian company Dram'Art, won a contest organized by ETC Caraïbe, has received the Prix Beaumarchais du Theatre Francophone, and was given read-throughs at the Theatre du Rond Point in Paris in 2005 and, later, in Guadeloupe and Martinique.[34] In 2012 the play was published in the French Theatre magazine *Coulisse* and, in an English translation by Robert McCormick, in the *Journal of Haitian Studies*.[35]

Le bleu de l'île takes place on a truck in which twelve Haitian men and women are crammed and squashed together under a blue tarpaulin in order

---

[33] Personal communication with Evelyne Trouillot, 12 April 2012.

[34] Stéphanie Bérard, 'Dramaturgie Haïtienne de l'exil: *Le bleu de l'île* d'Evelyne Trouillot', *Journal of Haitian Studies*, 16.1 (2010), pp. 60–69, p. 68 and personal communication with Evelyne Trouillot, 12 April 2012.

[35] Evelyne Trouillot, *Le bleu de l'île* ('The Blue of the Island'), trans. R. McCormick, *Journal of Haitian Studies*, 18.2 (2012), pp. 213–64. Page references to this translation will be given in parentheses in the text.

to pass the frontier into the Dominican Republic. All come from Piment, a small village in the north of Haiti not far from Le Cap, and their aim is to enter the Dominican Republic illegally, passing by Dajabón. While the predicament of each of the characters is powerfully elucidated, Trouillot also presents their individual perception of the border of Hispaniola and offers us her own views on Haitian migration. *Le bleu de l'île* is opened by Francine, who introduces us to the powerlessness of the migrants crushed by structural violence: 'I don't have any power,' she says, 'I will always be weaker than misery' (p. 213). Francine is not on the truck with her Roland, the father of the child she is expecting: her voice and presence on stage are to be understood as a projection of the desire, nostalgia, and desperation that he feels while travelling to the east of the island in such appalling conditions. In 2005, Haiti was going through a very troubled time: at the end of February 2004 President Aristide had left the country as a result of a second bloody coup against his government. The United States maintained publicly that Aristide resigned in the face of former Haitian army soldiers rebelling against him and that he demanded to be rescued by the United States. Aristide's supporters, instead, labelled his departure as an abduction and insisted (backed by diplomatic cables obtained by WikiLeaks) that the 2004 coup was in fact supported by the United States and fomented by the Haitian elite and right-wing paramilitary forces.[36] In May 2004 Haiti also experienced the flooding of Fonds-Verrettes and Mapou, while, in September, tropical storm Jeanne destroyed the town of Gonaïves, causing the death of thousands of people and making hundreds of thousands homeless. Trouillot does not make any direct references to these specific events, however, and, as a result, the play investigates Haitian emigration and structural violence in more general terms.

Most of the characters in Trouillot's play have a relative or a friend who has left the country to go to the United States or the Dominican Republic. Trouillot does not hide the fact that Haiti's economy largely depends on remittances; as Lorette, one of Roland's fellow travellers, explains: 'If one's relative in Miami doesn't promise to send off the money for the dress and new shoes, the first communion is postponed until next year' (p. 218). Romaine, another woman who is trying to reach the Dominican Republic illegally with Roland and Lorette, points out that even September 11 was seen by those supported by Haitian migrants who live in New York as a potential threat to their welfare: if something had happened to their relatives

---

[36] Hallward, *Damning the Flood*, pp. 232–49 and Kim Ives and Ansel Herz, 'WikiLeaks Haiti: The Aristide Files,' *The Nation*, 5 August 2011, http://www.thenation.com/article/162598/wikileaks-haiti-aristide-files [accessed 25 November 2014].

in the United States they would have been lost (p. 247). Migrating to the United States is not easy: it requires, in fact, a fair amount of preparation or courage: generally, one has to be able to pay for a plane ticket and obtain at least a tourist visa; otherwise one has to be ready to risk one's life on a clandestine boat headed for the coast of Florida. *Le bleu de l'île*, however, focuses on the predicament of Haitian migrants who cross the border to migrate to the neighbouring Dominican Republic and shows that crossing the internal frontier of Hispaniola is not necessarily easier or less insidious despite the closeness of the two countries and the fact that Haitian illegal migrants enter the Dominican Republic on a daily basis. Some newcomers find their way through the border by resorting to the help of friends who have crossed before, but the play highlights human smuggling and trafficking.[37] Trouillot shows us the role that Dominicans from the lower classes can play in the illegal smuggling of Haitians: the journey at the core of the play is organized, as it is often the case, by Dominican *buscones* (informal scouts) who are paid by the migrants to help them cross the frontier by, among other things, bribing the border guards and the military personnel at the many checkpoints which punctuate the Dominican borderland. Usually, once in the Dominican Republic, the migrants are taken directly to the places where their labour is needed. Trafficking/smuggling migrants can be remunerative but it is also a rather dangerous activity: at the end of *Le bleu de l'île* the Dominican truck driver, along with five of the twelve illegal migrants, is shot by Dominican guards, while the Dominican organizer of the trip is taken away with those who survive the shooting, who are arrested in order to be repatriated.

---

[37] Smuggling is a serious crime but it is done with the consent of the person being smuggled and ends with her arrival at the point of destination. Smuggling, however, can lead to the violation of various human rights of the migrant being smuggled and it can also lead to trafficking, which is 'the recruitment, transportation, transfer, harbouring or receipt of persons, by means of the threat or use of force or other forms of coercion, of abduction, of fraud, of deception, of the abuse of power or of a position of vulnerability or of the giving or receiving of payments or benefits to achieve the consent of a person having control over another person, for the purpose of exploitation': 'Protocol to Prevent, Suppress and Punish Trafficking in Persons, Especially Women and Children, Supplementing the United Nations Convention against Transnational Organized Crime,' *United Nations Crime and Justice Information Network* (UNCJIN), http://www.uncjin.org/Documents/Conventions/dcatoc/final_documents_2/convention_ per cent20traff_eng.pdf [accessed 25 November 2014]. As we will see, the migrants in Trouillot's play did give their consent to be smuggled into the Dominican Republic but it is arguable that their consent lost its validity during the transportation: some of them, in fact, at one point, want to get off the truck but they are unable to do so (pp. 223–4).

The years preceding the writing of the play were characterized by two major peaks in repatriations (November 1999 and March 2000) and a sustained activity in deportation in the following years.[38] For example, a report produced by GARR (*Group d'appui aux repatriés et réfugiés* or 'Support group for Haitian refugees and deportees') covering January–March 2003 states that during the first ten days of January 2003 more than 3000 people (including children) were driven back to Haiti from the Dominican Republic, while on 3 February fifty people (again including children) were expelled at the border post Miguel (Savanette, Central Plain). The majority of those deported – who were all unable to bring with them any of their belongings and lost all they possessed – had been in the Dominican Republic for more than five years, two had been resident there for over eighteen, and a 65-year-old person had lived there for forty years. On 5 March, the report continues, the Dominican military invaded the market in Neyba and arrested around 300 'dark-skinned' people, most of whom were second or even third generation migrants who had never visited, let alone lived in, Haiti. Most of them were released when their relatives produced identity cards but forty people were expelled on the pretext that they were Haitian nationals.[39]

In a valiant effort to contrast the homogeneity of statistics, the anonymity of numbers, and the stereotype of the Haitian migrant as a poor agricultural male labourer, Trouillot presents us with a very heterogeneous group whose members, despite all being disadvantaged, cross the border for different reasons and belong to different layers of the social structure. When Trouillot was writing her play, the profile of Haitian migrants entering the Dominican Republic was beginning to change: small-scale peasants and artisans no longer predominated, being substituted by young people with a higher level of schooling.[40] Some of the migrants in *Le bleu de l'île* are educated (including one woman[41]), some are skilled workers (a builder, a baker, a seamstress, a mechanic), and all are multidimensional and complex individuals with their own personal aspirations. Moreover, five out of twelve passengers on the truck are women: four of them are travelling alone (the strong and determined Marie-Jeanne and Romaine, the defiant Violetta, and the fragile Lorette, who is fighting an ongoing battle with depression); Fifi, who is pregnant, is with her husband Edgar. By 2005, in fact, women made up a quarter of the migrant population: some entered

[38] Wooding and Moseley-Williams, *Needed but Unwanted*, p. 80.
[39] Wooding and Moseley-Williams, *Needed but Unwanted*, pp. 83–4.
[40] Wooding and Moseley-Williams, *Needed but Unwanted*, p. 60.
[41] Lorette the baker, we are told, went to school in Port-au-Prince (p. 217).

the Dominican labour market by themselves, generally heading for cities where they could find work more easily, while others migrated with their partners.[42] In order to counteract the anti-Haitian rhetoric of Dominican nationalists who frequently refer to the threat of a Haitian 'invasion' which would radically change the country's (alleged) purely Hispanic identity, Trouillot makes it clear that most of the migrants aboard the truck do not plan to relocate permanently in the Dominican Republic but intend to return to Haiti as soon as possible. In order to cope with the trauma of dislocation, they (need to) imagine the border as permeable, in both directions, at different times. Roland, for example, boldly declares that he is planning to be away from his family for 'only' five years (p. 215). Others do not think in terms of time but are, similarly, intending to come back as soon as they can: their plan is to make enough money to be able to give their family a better life both while they are away (through remittances) and when they return; for example, Marie-Jeanne, who, before leaving Piment, used to sell charcoal, wants to come back and open a corner shop (p. 240).

Marie-Jeanne, we are told, began to sell charcoal because her husband, who used to be a shoemaker, was put out of work after secondhand shoes began to be sent to Haiti by international aid programmes and, as it is often the case, she is the only provider for her family (pp. 239–40). Similarly, Fifi is a seamstress who lost her customers because of secondhand clothes arriving mainly from the United States (p. 233). In *Le bleu de l'île*, Trouillot also highlights globalized criminal networks which have transformed the island into a place of transit for drugs, mainly directed to the United States, and which are shown to play an important role in the moral bankruptcy of those individuals who have succumbed to the lure of easy money generated by illegal activities. Like most of his fellow migrants, Jean-Marie is looking for money and a better life, but, unlike his older brother Edgar, who is a builder and would be happy to find a manual job in the construction industry in the Dominican Republic, Jean-Marie scorns the idea of a respectable job: he wants instead to organize 'his own' across-the-border drug traffic. What Edgar and Jean-Marie share, however, is the aim to get back to Haiti as soon as they can. Jean-Marie's plan is to relocate to Port-au-Prince once he can afford a big house with a swimming pool, a terrace, a garden, air conditioning in all the rooms and, crucially, a light-skinned partner: if he plays his cards properly, he reckons that he will be able to achieve all this by his thirtieth birthday (pp. 248–50).

Despite the migrants' hopes, plans, and wishful thinking, the fear of never being able to return to Haiti is widespread and runs very deep. In a

---

[42] Wooding and Moseley-Williams, *Needed but Unwanted*, pp. 60–62.

moment of sadness, Roland admits: 'I'm leaving without knowing if I can really return' (p. 245). We are also told that Madeleine's husband Charlot, who had gone to the Dominican Republic in search of work a few years earlier, disappeared shortly after arriving there. He is not the only one; as Madeleine says, 'so many disappearances in the *bateyes*, the hills and the countryside [...] Who has the courage to begin counting the dead that are still standing?' (p. 226). The purpose of Madeleine's journey is to find Charlot and bring him back to Piment; she seems to know that he might not be alive but she is determined to go and look for him anyway. This is not a decision Madeleine has taken lightly: she had always refused to turn herself and her child into 'mincemeat [for] the Dominican guards' (p. 226), but now that her son has died of meningitis the two sides of the island are both marked by death and are no longer distinguishable to her. Her mindscape has radically changed: from an island divided by a border she was determined never to cross, Hispaniola has turned into a territory she feels entitled to explore in its entirety because she hopes (against hope) to find again at least part of the family she has lost: 'love,' she says, 'scoffs at borders' (p. 225).

Madeleine is not the only person on the truck whose loved ones live (or, in her case, might be dead) on the other side of the border and who crosses the frontier for a reason which is not exclusively economic. Enzo Gabriel simply wants to go back home, to his wife and children. It is not specified if his wife Carmencita is Dominican but her Spanish name and their children's names (Pedro, Felipe, José González) seem to suggest that Enzo Gabriel's might be one of the many mixed families that one can encounter in Dominican territory and along the borderland. Enzo Gabriel, in his mixture of Spanish and French, explains that, after fifteen years in the Dominican Republic, he did not expect to be deported to Haiti and informs us that he had a reasonably good life on the east side, where he had his own home and some livestock and land (p. 246). His predicament is not isolated: migrants of Haitian origin (and not necessarily just illegal residents), Haitian–Dominicans who were born or have lived most of their lives in the Dominican Republic, and even individuals who (allegedly) just 'look Haitian' are often under threat of expulsion, sometimes despite the fact that they might have valid Dominican documents.[43] Fifi and Edgar,

---

[43] Redon, *Des îles en partage*, pp. 224–5; Riveros, *Informe*, pp. 48, 56–7; Wooding and Moseley-Williams, *Needed but Unwanted*, pp. 50–51; Geneviève Sevrin, 'République Dominicaine: Un mirage pour les migrants Haïtiens', in *Esclaves au Paradis*, Céline Anaya Gautier (La Roque-d'Anthéron, France: Vents d'ailleurs, 2007), pp. 5–7, p. 6; Rodríguez Grullón, *Estado del arte*, pp. 69–71 and 105–11.

instead, epitomize the many Haitian couples who have children in the Dominican Republic but might not be able to secure them a proper future if their economic conditions force them to remain in the country for a long time or even forever. All too often, in fact, Haitian migrants have not been allowed, for largely arbitrary reasons, to register their children's births: since in the Dominican Republic children without a birth certificate are not allowed in schools, have no access to the public health system, and are not entitled to receive a *cédula*, or identity card, they are condemned to have no official documents to prove who they are, thus becoming more vulnerable to deportation and other forms of abuse.[44] Fifi's baby, however, will enter Dominican territory but will not require a birth certificate: as we will see, s/he dies inside his/her mother when his/her parents are shot by the Dominican military.

Évariste, another passenger on the truck, is as adamant as Enzo Gabriel that he does not want to return to Piment but for less sentimental reasons: his dream is to work as a hairdresser in Santo Domingo. It is true that he cannot make ends meet with the hairdresser's shop he has inherited from his father, but this is only half the story: three years earlier, he explains, he went to Santo Domingo for two months for a 'seminar on *hair design*. *("Hair design" is pronounced with ostentation in English)*' (p. 242; italics in the text) and he has been longing to return there ever since. He is reproached for his idealization of life beyond the border by the other passengers, who remind him of 'the billy clubs, the raids and the *bateyes*' while he can only think of the '*ciudad*, the asphalt and the hotels, the public places and the avenues, the streetlights and the sidewalks' (Spanish in the original; p. 243). Évariste is not prepared to work as a *bracero* in the Dominican sugar fields or to find a job in the countryside as an agricultural labourer. His intentions are clear: he wants to go straight to the capital. Unlike the other travellers on the truck, Enzo Gabriel and Évariste (albeit for different reasons) think and, most importantly, feel that they are on the wrong side of the border when in Haiti. Enzo Gabriel fully belongs with his family in the east side of the island while Évariste is forcefully drawn to the Dominican capital and considers himself out of place in the small village of Piment. In other words, they want the border to be porous enough to allow them back into the Dominican Republic but, once they have crossed it, they want the frontier to become as tight as possible to keep them on their chosen side.

Despite the sympathy that Trouillot feels and wants us to feel for her characters, she does not present them as 'flawless': for example, Évariste's

---

[44] Wooding and Moseley-Williams, *Needed but Unwanted*, pp. 50–51, 65.

urban aspirations, albeit not entirely contemptible, can make him look either extremely naive or extremely shallow. Violetta has a criminal record (she has been in jail for theft) and defiantly declares that she does not regret sleeping with many men to avoid starvation (p. 254). It is evident, moreover, that, for some of them, the Dominican Republic also offers the possibility of redemption or expiation.[45] As we will see, this is particularly true of Roland, whose journey across the border triggers a profound psychological transformation which clearly debunks the simplistic and improbable Hell(Haiti)-to-Heaven(Dominican Republic) trajectory. At the end of the play Roland confesses to the audience that he has appropriated all the money that his mother had left to him and his sister in order to open his own garage in Piment. The money was subsequently stolen by his wife's brother, who used it to go to the United States to fulfil his own dream, but Roland's dishonesty has forced the pregnant Fifi and her husband Edgar out of Piment because they indebted themselves in order to pay for the expenses for her mother's funeral (pp. 260–62).[46] Fifi, however, has secrets too: we are told that she had an extra-marital affair which ended up with an unwanted pregnancy and an abortion (pp. 234–6).

On the truck there is also a murderer, namely the peasant Josaphat. Clearly, his reasons for leaving Haiti are only indirectly economic: he has to escape from Piment because he has killed the woman who, he claims, had poisoned his wife and zombified their only son (p. 231). Like Madeleine, who reluctantly leaves the grave of her child in Piment's cemetery to go and look for her lost husband, Josaphat is determined to return to be close to his dead (and undead) loved ones once things have calmed down and he no longer risks being arrested by the police; and he, too, has no illusions about the Dominican Republic: he knows that Haitians are not welcome there but, he says, he is not prepared to be treated like a dog (p. 230). The reasons behind the murder of Josaphat's wife and the zombification of his son are mentioned only *en passant*: 'a patch of land and some stolen plantains' (p. 231). His story, however, reminds us that every little piece of land matters greatly in Haiti. One of the most overpopulated countries in the New World, Haiti covers less than one-third of the land of Hispaniola but houses almost two-thirds of the population of the island: in 2005 the

---

[45] Edgar explains that when his mother asked him to take his brother Jean-Marie across the border with him she probably hoped that the Dominican Republic would either redeem him or be his place of expiation for his errors (p. 249).

[46] As Métraux has pointed out, in Haiti 'even the most destitute family does not hesitate to sacrifice its last pennies to ensure a proper funeral for one of its members' (*Voodoo in Haiti*, pp. 243–4).

average population density approached 1000 people per square mile.[47] Access to cultivable land is therefore dramatically limited, so Josaphat's wife and her neighbour were really fighting for survival. The situation on the truck, where the twelve migrants are constrained and do not have enough space at their disposal, is an obvious reference to the Middle Passage but it also reproduces the sense of claustrophobia that one might feel in a country which is running out of space for its people.

The 'blue of the island' in Trouillot's play is the sky that the migrants are not able to see while in transit: stuck in the truck, they can see only the artificial blue of the tarpaulin which covers them and, the play suggests, they have clearly lost sight of the bigger picture, both literally and metaphorically. We are reminded that they are travelling from Haiti to the Dominican Republic as they are pushed around by the movement of the truck, repeatedly silenced (in Spanish) by the *buscón*, and terrified by the speed at which the driver La Volanta goes. Their journey is punctuated by two road accidents: a flat tyre (Act I scene ii) and a collision with a goat (at the beginning of Act II) but there are never any references to the landscape outside and the migrants' physical mobility is counteracted by their mental 'immobility.' Most of them are constantly focused on (or obsessed by) their life in Haiti. Seven different settings, representing seven different locations, light up alternately when each character tells his or her story and provide the background to their imaginary interactions with the relatives and friends they have left behind. The presence of these relatives on stage and the visualization of their surroundings make Piment or Port-au-Prince (where some of the characters had previously moved in order to study or work) a tangible reality for the audience. On the other hand, Évariste's mesmerizing Dominican capital, Madeleine's murderous *bateyes*, or Enzo Gabriel's domestic blissful scenario are only (briefly) evoked, are always off scene, and do not feel entirely 'real.'

Trouillot's migrants eventually do cross the frontier and some of them die or are captured in some unspecified location in the Dominican borderland. In actual fact, the journey by road into the Dominican Republic is probably the most dangerous part of the migrants' travel; only a few years before the play was written, in June 2000, in Guayubín, the second largest city in the province of Montecristi, a few soldiers from the Dominican army were accused of shooting at a truck full of Haitian migrants which was travelling between Dajabón and Santiago. Apparently, the guards knew that the truck was transporting Haitian migrants when they opened fire, killing

---

[47] Jared Diamond, *Collapse: How Society Choose to Fail or Survive* (London: Penguin, 2005), p. 330.

one Dominican and six Haitians and wounding twelve more people (five seriously), all under thirty years of age. First of all the guards fired at the truck's tyres and, when the driver lost control of the vehicle, which crashed in a ditch, they shot to kill those who had been thrown on the ground; finally, they took away the survivors, all of whom were deported to Haiti.[48] Trouillot has admitted that she was haunted, for a few years, by what had happened at Guayubín, especially because 'almost all [the deceased] were young and came from the same little village called Piment [...] young people dying so tragically because they were trying to find a better place to live.'[49] The final sequence of events in *Le bleu de l'île*, in fact, occurs at a fast and furious pace and is not too dissimilar from the incident in Guayubín in 2000.

While Roland is trying to summon the courage to confess to his sister how he has behaved dishonestly towards her, we suddenly hear the noise of shootings and the voice of the alarmed organizer, who tells the driver to slow down (p. 257). Crucially, this is not preceded by a clear indication of when the crossing from Haiti into the Dominican Republic has taken place; no sense of transition is conveyed, there is no reference to a threshold, nothing that signposts the migrants' exit from their native land and their entrance into a new country. The two nations blur into one: having crossed the border makes no difference to the characters' predicament, as they are constantly surrounded by the artificial blue of the tarpaulin. When the military start shooting, things happen quickly: the driver presses his foot down on the accelerator and starts going even faster, while the truck is hit by bullets. The truck then begins to swerve dramatically, the passengers are thrown from one side to the other, and the tarpaulin begins to move convulsively, resembling a blue monster breathing spasmodically (p. 257). In what is described as a 'blue inferno' (p. 258), the migrants hear the noise of cars braking and stopping nearby and, when the tarpaulin finally collapses (p. 259), some Dominican guards get out of their cars, approach the migrants, and start shooting them at close range. In the mayhem, Josaphat and Romaine manage to run away, Évariste, Madeleine, Fifi, Edgar, and the driver are shot dead, and Marie-Jeanne, Jean-Marie, Enzo Gabriel, Lorette, and the Dominican organizer are captured by the soldiers (pp. 260–61).

At the end of the play Trouillot takes momentary leave of the realistic depiction of the tragic end to these migrants' dreams and aspirations as the audience witnesses Roland's poetic and metaphorical exit from 'hell.' Surrounded by progressively neater silhouettes of playing children and by the dead bodies of some of his companions and of Fifi, who talks to

[48]	Wooding and Moseley-Williams, *Needed but Unwanted*, pp. 84–5.
[49]	Personal communication with Evelyne Trouillot, 12 April 2012.

him posthumously, Roland confesses to her that he stole her part of their mother's inheritance. He also adds that he would be glad to return it in order to bring her back among the living. Fifi's answer focuses him and the audience on the crucial importance of location: 'On which side of the island?' she wonders (p. 262). Initially, Roland sounds confused: 'A part of me will stay here with you,' he repeats (p. 262). At this point the children begin to sing the unofficial national anthem *Haïti Chèrie*, prompting and sustaining his psychological transition from this fatal site in Dominican territory (the 'here' where his sister and the others have died) to his native Haiti. Fifi then makes Roland promise that he will never forget 'the blue of the island' and that he 'will come back from the other side of the island' to look after both their families (p. 263). Finally, now that the artificial, hellish blue of the tarpaulin no longer impairs his vision and he can see the blue of the island sky that Fifi exhorts him never to forget, Roland realizes the error of his ways: 'It seems to me that we wanted to find a solution and we forgot that the blue sky doesn't change crossing the border' (p. 263). Crossing the border here does not bring personal and, by extension, collective improvement: the structural violence which is at the origin of so many of these migrants' journeys has to be eradicated and, echoing Blonda's, Trouillot's play insists that, in order to do so and initiate change, Haitians have to stay in Haiti, a country where, Roland says, there are 'so many things to do' and, as Fifi reminds him, 'so many children to be born' (p. 263). In the final scene, beaten and pushed by the soldiers, a renewed Roland says goodbye to the dead and directs his step towards Haiti. The stage becomes 'more and more blue, an almost unbearable blue' (p. 263), the dead rise to accompany him on his journey, and the children's silhouettes progressively grow in size, invading the entire background and beginning to walk 'towards the West' with him (p. 263). Trouillot's message is very clear: migration is not the solution. Yet, it is hard to blame migrants when they live in a situation where everything conspires against making ends meet. While Trouillot is adamant that 'migration does accentuate the problems at a collective, national level' she is also aware that, 'at an individual level, it constitutes a temporary solution. No one has the right,' she continues, 'to tell an individual or a family who is facing extremely difficult situations that they should stay in their country [...] The problems that force people to leave in such undignified, risky and inhumane conditions should be resolved [...] the play evokes the fact that for many Haitians there is no choice, they are forced to leave whether by oppressive regimes or by economical disasters.'[50]

---

[50] Personal communication with Evelyne Trouillot, 12 April 2012.

Trouillot does not mention environmental disasters, but the *Le bleu de
l'île* also hints at the link between environmental degradation, structural
violence, and 'forced migration': among those captured by the soldier, in
fact, is Marie-Jeanne, who, as we have seen, used to sell charcoal. In Haiti,
charcoal is the main fuel used for cooking and Marie-Jeanne's occupation
reminds us that the frontier between the two countries has often been read
in the very landscape of the island, despite the fact that the movement of
illegal migrants across the border somehow mocks its political division. It
has been frequently highlighted, in fact, that it is not unusual to see, when
standing on the frontier, luxuriant forests on the east side while, facing west,
one is more likely to see deforested fields; it has been estimated that not
even 1.5 per cent of Haiti is forested against the 20 or, depending on the
source, 28 per cent of the Dominican Republic.[51] This dramatic difference is
the result partly of a dissimilar climate but also of human intervention and
the distinct forms of exploitation of the land which have been practised on
the two sides of the island since colonial times. The Dominican Republic,
in fact, receives more rain than Haiti and has better soil, as its valleys,
plains, and plateaus are irrigated by rivers. Haiti is much drier, a high
percentage of its territory is mountainous with relatively infertile soils,
and a much smaller area is suitable for agriculture.[52] As highlighted in
Chapter 1, in the eighteenth century Saint-Méry had noticed the potential
of the (then mainly unexploited) Spanish side and repeatedly lamented
the fact that the Spaniards had not put their fertile land to good use. Yet
the Saint Domingue plantation system rhapsodized by Saint-Méry was to
become one of the reasons for the dramatic deforestation and consequent
decrease in rainfall, loss of timber, soil erosion, loss of soil fertility, and
loss of watershed protection and of potential hydroelectric power that are
currently plaguing Haiti.[53] The degree of wealth, even luxury, discerned
by Saint-Méry on the French side was a direct result of the flourishing
plantation economy of Saint Domingue which was sustained by the constant
influx of imported enslaved labour. In colonial times, Saint Domingue
had a population seven times higher than its Spanish neighbour despite
the fact that it occupied a much smaller portion of the island. High
population density and low rainfall, together with the establishment of

---

[51]   For example, according to Redon not even 1.5 per cent of Haiti is forested against
the 20 per cent of the Dominican Republic (p. 127) while for Diamond 28 per cent of
the Dominican Republic is forested against 1 per cent of Haiti (*Des îles en partage*,
p. 329).

[52]   Diamond, *Collapse*, pp. 339.

[53]   Diamond, *Collapse*, pp. 329.

coffee plantations in the mountains and European demand for Haitian timber, were the main factors behind the rapid deforestation and loss of soil fertility on the French side.[54]

Currently, cutting trees for firewood and charcoal is still the main source of revenue in the Haitian countryside (as for Trouillot's Marie-Jeanne) because, sadly, electricity or kerosene are available only in major cities and towns; this dependence on wood is at the basis of the ongoing deforestation of Haiti.[55] Haiti's hunger for charcoal, however, is also affecting the landscape and ecosystem of the Dominican borderland, where trees are illegally felled and turned into charcoal to be sold on the black market in the neighbouring country: it is not unusual, in fact, to see charcoal being smuggled into Haiti at official and unofficial border crossings while substantial portions of the Dominican borderland become increasingly deforested. This illegal traffic thrives on the fact that many poor Haitians, Haitian–Dominicans, or Dominicans who live near the border often have few opportunities to make ends meet, and provides further proof of the fact that, as Blonda put it, the borderline 'divides the land but not the misery of the people.' Structural violence, moreover, plays an important part in the deforestation of both countries. For example, Vikram Ghandi has recently argued that the deforestation of the central portion of the Dominican borderland is mostly due to the inadequate response of the government to the effect of an environmental disaster, namely the rising of the waters of Lake Enriquillo, which have submerged a substantial amount of land, depriving local peasants and farmers of their homes and livelihood. In a short documentary for *VICE News*, Ghandi explains that the displaced residents have been provided with new houses but were given no land to work and therefore no means to survive: he shows how, as a result, illegal deforestation is reaching alarming levels as the production of charcoal destined for Haiti has often become the only way in which many of the locals, who feel neglected by the Dominican authorities, can support themselves and their families.[56] The situation, Ghandi warns, is quickly deteriorating, as this indiscriminate felling of trees is damaging the ecosystem: the rain falling on deforested land reaches the lake more easily, thus contributing to the acceleration of the increasing size

---

[54] Diamond, *Collapse*, pp. 339–40.

[55] William Wheeler, 'Haiti's Dirty Habit: Can Smarter Stoves Heal Haiti?' *Pulitzer Center on Crisis Reporting*, 11 January 2011, http://pulitzercenter.org/articles/haiti-earthquake-energy-efficient-stoves-reduce-wood-fuel-demand [accessed 25 November 2014].

[56] See Vikram Ghandi, 'The Lake that Burned Down a Forest', *Vice News*, 27 July 2014, https://www.youtube.com/watch?v=s6322_yP-20 [accessed 28 November 2014].

of the lake, and washes away the topsoil, compromising the possibility of growing forests or crops in the area in the future. In Haiti, the despoliation of woodlands and an excessive centralization of resources are also crucial to the migration of Haitians to the United States, Canada, Europe, or the other, more fertile, side of Hispaniola, and to the concentration of the population in congested and precariously built urban centres such as Port-au-Prince. This concentration has also set the stage for the transformation of a 'natural' disaster such as the January 2010 earthquake into, in Janet Abramovitz's words, an 'unnatural' disaster – that is, a disaster made much more severe owing to human action – and into an event which has caused even more migration.[57]

In the last ten years or so the island of Hispaniola as a whole has had more than its fair share of (un)natural disasters: the terrible earthquake of 12 January 2010 is only one tragic case in point. Originally scientists thought that it had been caused by the Enriquillo–Plantain Garden fault line, but more recent investigations have both revealed a new fault line in the Léogâne area and confirmed that the Enriquillo fault, which runs along the southern side of the island, remains a significant seismic hazard which geologists have to monitor very closely.[58] Hurricanes are also frequent and often devastating, as are floods, another huge threat to the population. Hispaniola, however, has also been affected by entirely 'man-made' disasters such as, among others, the ongoing cholera epidemic in Haiti, which many experts believe was accidentally introduced by United Nations peacekeepers and, according to the Centres for Disease Control and Prevention, the worst cholera outbreak in recent history;[59] the contamination from a battery recycling plant that has dumped battery acid and lead for more than a decade into the soil of a neighbourhood of Haina, a Dominican town which, in 2007, a New York environmental group placed third on the list of the ten most polluted spots

[57] Janet N. Abramowitz, *Unnatural Disasters* (Worldwatch Paper 158, Worldwatch Institute, Washington 2001). Riveros, *Estado del Arte*, pp. 30, 60–64 and Rodríguez Grullón, *Estado del arte*, pp. 65–66. Riveros has also pointed out that the Dominican Republic is often used by Haitian migrants as a bridge to other destinations (*Informe*, p. 29).

[58] Tim Padgett, 'Underneath Haiti, Another Big Quake Waiting to Occur,' *Time World*, 19 November 2010, http://www.time.com/time/world/article/0,8599,2031863,00.html#ixzz2Kypojp5V [accessed 25 November 2014].

[59] 'Cholera in Haiti: One Year Later,' *Centers for Disease Control and Prevention* (CDC), 25 October 2011, http://www.cdc.gov/haiticholera/haiti_cholera.htm [accessed 28 November 2014]; Ed Pilkington, 'Haitians launch new lawsuit against UN over thousands of cholera deaths,' *The Guardian*, 11 March 2014, http://www.theguardian.com/world/2014/mar/11/haiti-cholera-un-deaths-lawsuit [accessed 28 December 2014].

on the planet;[60] or the illegal dumping of rock ash in the Dominican port towns of Montecristi and Arroyo Barril in 2003 and 2004.

✶✶✶

Montecristi (2009), written by the Algerian-born writer Jean-Noël Pancrazi, deals with the rock ash disaster but, rather than treating it as a single event, puts it in the context of an island plagued, in its entirety, by human rights violations and ecological vulnerability.[61] Pancrazi's *Montecristi* is difficult to characterize: poised between novel and memoir, it reads (at least up to the final pages, when the narrator leaves his fellow sufferers behind) as a harrowing testimonial narrative which recounts an ecological disaster with 'lyrical rage'[62] and is probably best described as a 'lament.' What is being lamented is not just the illness and death of those who, according to Pancrazi, were adversely affected by rock ash pollution in the border city of Montecristi: in a compelling and lucid way, Pancrazi grieves over an island where the very poor and disadvantaged are ruthlessly left behind to struggle (and even die) and where many contemplate migration as the only solution. In some respects, *Montecristi* could be viewed as a sequel to Pancrazi's previous novel *Les dollars des sables* (2006), set in the Peninsula of Samaná, one of the top tourist areas of the Dominican Republic.[63] Here Pancrazi focused on those who live on the margins of international tourism, but some of the characters in the two novels appear to be the same, above all the foreign protagonist, who recounts his experience in the border region in a first-person narration (and who has been identified with Pancrazi himself) and Noeli, his ambivalent Dominican lover who is married to a Dominican woman and whose dream is to migrate to Puerto Rico to make a fortune. *Montecristi*, however, reveals an even bleaker picture than the one depicted in *Les dollars des sables*.

---

[60] Frances Robles, 'Pollution sickens children in Dominican Republic,' *Miami Herald*, 13 March 2007, http://www.miamiherald.com/2007/03/13/v-print/39816/pollution-sickens-children-in.html [accessed 18 February 2014]. In 2011, however, Haina had gone 'green' and was 'held up as an example of what can happen to a neighbourhood when environmentalists, the international community, academics, the business sector and the government work together': see 'Paradise Remade: Dominican Republic Lead Polluter Goes Green,' *Miami Herald*, 17 May 2011, http://www.miamiherald.com/2011/05/17/2221443_p2/dominican-republic-lead-polluter.html [accessed 19 May 2011].

[61] Jean-Noël Pancrazi, *Montecristi: Roman* (Paris: Gallimard, 2009). Page references will be given in parentheses in the text.

[62] Niklaus Manuel Güdel, '*Montecristi*: une colère lyrique', in *Les Lettres et les Arts – Revue d'information culturelle francophone de Bâle et Nord-Romandie*, 1 (2009), p. 14.

[63] Jean-Noël Pancrazi, *Les dollars des sables* (Paris: Folio, 2007).

On the Edge

Pancrazi was born in 1947 in Algeria, where he stayed until 1962, when his family left in the aftermath of the proclamation of Algeria's independence. In France, as a *pied-noir*,[64] he felt rejected: he remembers his arrival in France, where he and his family felt lost, poor, and 'afraid of the North' (p. 71); they never felt they belonged and never really wanted to belong, and Pancrazi talks about 'a sad will of never wanting to feel French' (p. 70). Pancrazi has not returned to Algeria since 1962, despite the fact that he considers it his 'home,'[65] but in Montecristi, he tells us, he felt that, in a way, he *had* returned to Algeria: 'my real voyage of return was here' (p. 73). Montecristi is described by Pancrazi as a city where life is punctuated by frequent cuts in the power and water supply and which is 'harsh,' 'dry,' characterized by an 'absence of colour' provoked by a 'total dazzle,' and by a pervasive smell of 'cement, sulphur, malaria, police, naked flesh, crushed mangoes and dead palms, iron and incomplete roofs': a city, significantly, with 'no horizon' (p. 14). Montecristi's landscape, initially, is what allows Pancrazi's Algerian past to break through to his present: the 'scorching roads [...], the little houses, the dry grass, the swamps, darkness at 6 o'clock in the afternoon' trigger in him what we can call 'the shock of recognition' (pp. 73–4). A comparable landscape, however, is not the only thing that makes Algeria and Montecristi rhyme. Pancrazi's childhood in Algeria was marked by colonialism and the violence which characterized the transition of Algeria from French colony to independent nation, while in Montecristi he finds himself witnessing the equally lethal effect of another type of violence, namely Galtung's structural violence.[66]

Pancrazi's stay in Montecristi between 2005 and 2006 coincided with a further impoverishment of an already destitute area. As pointed out in Chapter 5, nineteenth-century Montecristi was a booming cosmopolitan centre which attracted many wealthy migrants from Europe and the rest of the Americas. In 1937, however, its province was one of the main areas in which the massacre of Haitians and Haitian–Dominicans was perpetrated and since then, apart from a couple of decades (1940s to 1960s) in which the Grenada Fruit Company created the company town of Manzanillo and many jobs, which attracted workers from all over the country and abroad, Montecristi has undergone a gradual but unstoppable decline; it has now

---

[64] A citizen of French descent who returned to mainland France when Algeria became independent in 1962.

[65] Jean-Noël Pancrazi, *Le Point*, 20 October 2007, http://www.lepoint.fr/actualites-societe/2007–01–20/jean-noel-pancrazi/920/0/61476 [accessed 25 November 2014].

[66] Galtung, 'Violence, Peace, and Peace Research', p. 171.

become the capital of one of the poorest areas of the Dominican Republic.[67] Owing to its proximity to Haiti, however, Montecristi is still one of the first ports of call for many Haitian migrants, mostly illegal; some stay and work in the port but often they use Montecristi as a stepping stone to migrate elsewhere (Santiago, Santo Domingo or Puerto Rico, Florida, the Bahamas) and, as a result of the economic crisis, the number of emigrants tends to surpass the number of immigrants.[68] Pancrazi's *Montecristi* offers us a snapshot of the city at a particularly difficult time, when the North American AES (Applied Energy Services) corporation, one of the world's largest power companies, had obtained permission from Dominican officials to deposit a cargo of coal ash in the port of Montecristi.

In 2002, AES built a coal-fired power plant in Puerto Rico which which produced almost 400,000 tons of toxic coal ash a year. As there was nowhere to safely dispose of the waste from 2003 to 2004 the plant dumped thousands of tons of coal ash along the beaches of Montecristi and Arroyo Barril, in the Samaná peninsula, without observing the correct protocol for the depositing and disposal of toxic material.[69] In the immediate aftermath of the illegal dumping the media began to report the deaths of several people who had developed cancer in the Montecristi area and whose illness was attributed to the presence of rock ash. In addition to deaths, it was also disclosed that many people were bed-ridden or suffering from cancer, respiratory problems, skin lesions, and shedding hair. The environment official of Montecristi confirmed that the situation was alarming and that, after many deaths had occurred, those who could were opting to leave.[70] Pancrazi argues that Montecristi was chosen as a dumping place partly because it is 'the only port with deep waters on that side of the country' (p. 51) but, most importantly, because of its proximity to Haiti. The choice of this border area, he argues, was expedient in order 'to designate as dangerous and cursed only one part of

---

[67] Herrera, *Montecristi entre campeches y bananos*, pp. 141–64.

[68] Jhonatan J. Liriano, 'Monte Cristi: grisácea realidad,' *Listin Diario*, 21 February 2011, http://www.listin.com.do/economia-and-negocios/2011/2/21/178353/Monte-Cristi-esta-a-la-espera-de-su-salto-al-desarrollo-economico [accessed 25 November 2014]; *IX Censo Nacional de Población y Vivienda. Informe Básico* (Santo Domingo: Oficina Nacional de Estadística, 2012), p. 13, http://censo2010.one.gob.do/resultados/Resumen_resultados_generales_censo_2010.pdf [accessed 28 November 2014].

[69] Lisa Evans, 'Tr-Ash Talk: Dumping on the Americas', *Earth Justice*, 25 May 2011, http://earthjustice.org/blog/2011-may/tr-ash-talk-dumping-on-the-americas [accessed 28 November 2014].

[70] 'Fear grips Dominican town for deaths blamed on rockash', *Dominican Today*, 14 June 2006, http://dominicantoday.com/dr/local/2006/6/14/14555/Fear-grips-Dominican-town-for-deaths-blamed-on-rockash [accessed 28 November 2014].

the country' which, he continues, is regarded with the same 'pitiful hostility' and is seen as a place which shares the same 'misfortune' that seems to typify Haiti (pp. 51–3). According to Pancrazi, when the news of what was happening in Montecristi leaked into the public domain a delegation from the government inspected the polluted area. The inspectors pretended to be more or less surprised and outraged depending on how much money they had been offered to ignore the scandal; when they realized that they could blame the previous administration for the decision to allow AES Corporation to dump their coal ash there they decided, as a matter of political expediency, to openly denounce their predecessors. At the same time, however, they also tried to prevent the rock ash scandal from becoming known abroad, so that it would not interfere with the tourist industry (p. 52). In Sánchez, on the southern coast of the Samaná peninsula, we are told by Pancrazi's narrator that all the fish suddenly died; he argues that, since the area was significant for the tourist industry, the blame for their death was officially put on 'natural disasters' such as hurricanes or tropical storms (p. 53).

In 2007, AES agreed to pay $6 million to settle a lawsuit in which the Dominican Republic accused the company of having conspired with Silverspot Enterprises – the company which removed the ash from Puerto Rico – and with Dominican Republic officials through a series of crimes, including bribery, subversion of customs laws, and threats of murder, in order to dump the toxic waste illegally in Dominican waters. It was the first time in the judicial history of the United States that a foreign state brought to a federal tribunal a North American company using as the foundation of its lawsuit the environmental law of the foreign state, clearly a legal victory for the Dominican Republic.[71] In exchange for the money, which was destined for the clean-up operation, the Dominican Republic agreed to dismiss the lawsuit and represent that AES committed no wrongdoing.[72] In the Dominican Republic some criticized this settlement because it did not compensate the victims for the damage caused and because, in their view, it allowed AES 'to get away with it.'[73]

In 2009, the same year in which *Montecristi* was published, the media reported damage to the Manzanillo mangroves, the death of hundreds of

---

[71] This point was emphasized by Max Puig, who was Environment Minister at the time (personal communication with Max Puig, 16 June 2013).

[72] Ron Zapata, 'AES Settles Waste Suit With Dominican Republic', *Law 360*, 1 March 2007, http://www.law360.com/articles/19606/aes-settles-waste-suit-with-dominican-republic [accessed 25 November 2014].

[73] Yanet Féliz, 'Ambientalistas rechazan acuerdo por rockash', *Listin Diario*, 4 March 2007, http://www.listindiario.com.do/la-republica/2007/3/4/5033/Ambientalistas-rechazanacuerdo-porrockash [accessed 28 November 2014].

palm trees in Samana, and the pollution of tropical waters where humpback whales come every year to reproduce; furthermore, it was also suggested that several cases of horrific birth defects in Arroyo Barril were connected to the presence of rock ash.[74] Dominican authorities and established scientists, however, insist that there is insufficient evidence to link, beyond reasonable doubt, the deaths, birth defects, and diseases which occurred in Montecristi and Arroyo Barril to rock ash contamination.[75]

The fact that *Montecristi* is a 'novel' – it says so on its cover – might further problematize its implicit claim to truthfulness. Pancrazi, who, in interviews, has referred to his stay in Montecristi as 'hell,' and to his characters as victims who kept their dignity intact in adverse circumstances,[76] nevertheless insists on a correlation between rock ash contamination and the death of some inhabitants of Montecristi. In his novel we are shown how, according to him, the people of Montecristi felt about and coped with rock ash pollution: their anger and desperation are palpable, their sense of impotence is distressing, and the overwhelming fear which governs their every word and move is deeply haunting. The novel informs us that, to begin with, the locals could not find a proper explanation for the different medical conditions which affected them, so they decided to attribute them to an unspecified *parasito* ('parasite') (p. 49). The narrator explains that, generally, the skins of those who had been contaminated by the *parasito* whitened (p. 55); moreover, it made its female victims completely exhausted, while the fishermen affected by it looked like 'lost, drunk or sunstroked survivors who had wandered the earth for months and could no longer recognize their home' (p. 51).

---

[74] 'Acusan en tribunal EE.UU a empresa AES por causar problemas de salud en RD,' *Diario Libre*, 6 November 2009, http://www.diariolibre.com/noticias/2009/11/06/i222440_acusan-tribunal-empresa-aes-por-causar-problemas-salud.html [accessed 28 November 2014]; Frances Robles, 'Coal ash from U.S. blamed for Dominican town's birth defects', *Miami Herald*, 6 November 2009, http://www.mcclatchydc.com/2009/11/06/78461/coal-ash-from-us-blamed-for-dominican.html#.Ubsrnb5wZ1s [accessed 25 November 2014]. 'Coal ash dumping may have caused deformities', *Miami Herald*, 6 November 2009, http://www.youtube.com/watch?v=ikYX9JADOqs [accessed 286 January 2014].

[75] See, for example, Osiris De Léon, 'Rockash y contaminación ambiental', *El Día*, 10 November 2009, http://eldia.com.do/rockash-y-contaminacion-ambiental-2/ [accessed 28 November 2014]. Max Puig, who was Environment minister at the time of the scandal, and Miguel Silva, Vicepresident of the Fundacion Naturalez Ambiente y Desarrollo, share Osiris de Leon's views (personal communication with Max Puig, 16 June 2013; with Miguel Silva 11 October 2013).

[76] 'Jean-Noël Pancrazi: écrivain de l'exil,' interview with Jean-Noël Pancrazi conducted by Niklaus Manuel Güdel, in *Les Lettres et les Arts – Revue d'information culturelle francophone de Bâle et Nord-Romandie*, 1 (2009), pp. 10–13, pp. 11, 12.

Montecristi also describes at length the downward spiral of a local prostitute. She becomes increasingly thin and weak, loses her hair, begins trembling, and pretends to be drunk when she can no longer keep her balance: in her line of business, being drunk is less damaging than being ill (pp. 50, 124). The narrator explains that she lost so much weight that she had become 'as light as the smallest sack of salt which one would not even have bothered to weigh on a scale' (p. 124). The comparison of the prostitute's wasted body with an insignificantly small quantity of salt very evocatively links the woman's decline to the city's: as highlighted in Chapter 5, in its heyday, Montecristi's prosperity was closely linked to salt production.[77] Distressingly, however, according to Pancrazi, those most affected by the *parasito* were 'those who had run in the sea more often' – that is, the children: they became blind, 'their eyes bec[oming] enormous, feverish and engulfed in fear' (pp. 53, 51).[78]

In biology, a parasite is an organism that lives in a close relationship with another organism and benefits from it at the expense of its host. The parasite is dependent upon its host to survive, grow, and multiply, often causing it harm. Arguably, this word, used by the locals to describe something they initially could not understand, is not entirely a misnomer and the narrator, who blames corrupted members of the Dominican political class as well as the AES corporation for this disaster, seems to agree with them. On a metaphorical level, in fact, the exploitative and damaging relationship that characterizes parasitism is fit to illustrate the predicament in which he believes those who were contaminated in Montecristi and Samaná were put by those who, in the name of profit, illegally dumped the coal ash in Dominican territorial waters. In other words, it is clear that *parasito* also stands for structural violence: being the product of an unequal distribution of power and resources, Galtung explains, structural violence is to be measured against 'avoidability' and 'unavoidablity' of sufferance: when suffering is unavoidable, violence is not present; conversely, 'when suffering is avoidable [as it is the case here and in other examples provided in this chapter], violence is present.'[79]

In Montecristi the narrator also witnesses effects of structural violence which do not derive from the parasite. Pancrazi's relatively comfortable stay in Montecristi is contrasted with the lives of the desperate poor, who take their chances at sea and resort to the help of ruthless traffickers in

---

[77] Herrera, *Montecristi entre campeches y bananos*, pp. 57–60.

[78] In 2008 the AES Dominicana Foundation inaugurated the new 'energy room' of the children's museum *Trampolin* in Santo Domingo with the purpose of educating the new generations in energy saving.

[79] Galtung, 'Violence, Peace, and Peace Research', p. 169.

order to reach the coast of Puerto Rico or Providence (Bahamas) to better their condition. For example, the narrator reports the story of a group of Dominicans who, after hours of navigation in precarious conditions, were told by their smugglers that they had reached the coast of Puerto Rico. There were too many rocks in the sea for the boat to approach land safely, so they were invited to jump out of the boat and swim towards the coast. When they reached the shore, however, they soon realized that they were still in the Dominican Republic, had been robbed of the money they had paid for their passage, and had to face a shameful return, empty-handed, to their homes (p. 37). Similarly, the narrator adds, the Haitians who arrive in Montecristi illegally are often met by 'rabatteurs de la misère' – literally, 'poverty pimps' – who offer them alcohol until they can no longer stand and then trick them into accepting any sort of empty promise or job proposition (p. 82). Haitian children who cross the border alone, he writes, are even easier to entice, especially if a woman shows maternal feelings towards them, washes their frightened faces, or buys them a can of Coke (p. 98).

Pancrazi also reveals that these conned children and adults are frequently amassed on trucks and taken to the various *bateyes* or company towns of the Dominican Republic, where they are made to work and live in what, for the most part, are unacceptable conditions, and where their dream for a better life comes to a bitter end. In *Montecristi* we are reminded of the presence of Haitian migrants on every page: the first group appears only two pages into the narration, when Pancrazi describes a coach full of Haitians (mostly illegal) who have just crossed the border. They carry no luggage in order to pretend that they are not there to stay but just in the middle of some sort of improbable 'outing' (pp. 12–13) and we get the sense that, for the narrator, this is a daily sight. This particular coach, he speculates, is crossing Montecristi on Christmas Eve in the hope that the police check-ups will be less frequent and less meticulous (p. 13). Pancrazi refers to these Haitian migrants as 'refugees' (pp. 13, 129) – an interesting choice of words if one considers that, officially speaking, Haitians in the Dominican Republic are categorized as 'economic migrants' and not as 'refugees' who 'owing to a well-founded fear of being persecuted for reasons of race, religion, nationality, membership of a particular social group, or political opinion, [are outside] the country of [their] nationality, and [are] unable to or, owing to such fear, [are] unwilling to avail [themselves] of the protection of that country.'[80] It is true that most of the Haitians who work in the Dominican

---

[80] *Convention and Protocol Relating to the Status of Refugees – The Refugee Convention (1951), United Nations High Commissioner for Refugees* (UNHCR), http://www.unhcr.org/pages/49da0e466.html [accessed 28 November 2014].

Republic declare that they have *chosen* to cross the border in order to support economically both themselves and their families but *Montecristi*, like Trouillot's *Le bleu de l'île*, clearly foregrounds the fact that for the poor, operating at the receiving end of structural violence, life choices or, rather, survival choices, are hardly ever *choices*. For example, Jean, a Haitian who arrives in Montecristi, crossing the River Massacre on foot, recounts to the narrator the death of his sister, who had been assassinated a month earlier in Haiti, probably because she would not or could not afford the payoff for water or electricity to the clan that controlled her neighbourhood, or as a form of punishment for sexual jealousy or, simply, by mistake (p. 80). Jean also tells the narrator and readers that Milot, where he was born, used to be a place where one could find employment as an agricultural worker, as a builder, or as a guide for those tourists who once visited Sans-Souci palace and the nearby Cittadelle Laferrière (p. 78). All this, however, was in the past: when he tells his story to the narrator, Jean explains, owing to centralization of resources, there are no more peasants in Milot and, owing to political turmoil, there are no more tourists in the region. All there is, he continues, are 'the tanks of foreign powers which traverse his town as if it were an occupied country' (p. 78). The reference is to the MINUSTAH, the United Nations Stabilization Mission in Haiti established in 2004 by Security Council resolution 1542. The MINUSTAH has remained in the country since then, despite the fact that many fail to see the necessity of a military presence in a country which is not actually at war.

Furthermore, far from arriving in a safe place (a 'refuge'), the Haitian illegal migrants who cross the Haitian–Dominican border often find themselves in an impossible situation. Most cannot live without fear of being repatriated and having to return empty-handed to one's village; going back for a while to visit one's family is not within their reach because, generally, they do not have enough money to pay for a visa to secure their return. The narrator mentions the case of Janika, who works as a domestic worker for him and other wealthy foreign residents of Montecristi: she longs to see her family again, 'counting, [...] silently and one by one, all the steps that she would have to take to return to Cap-Haïtien' (p. 19). She knows full well, however, that if she crosses back into Haiti she might never be able to return, and cannot afford to take that risk. Pancrazi, therefore, insists on the importance of taking on board political, criminal, and, ultimately, structural violence, as well as environmental degradation and the over-centralization of resources, in order to revisit the problematic categories of 'economic migrant' and 'refugee' and to acknowledge that the distinction between the two is not always self-evident and absolute. The word 'refugee' comes back again at the end of the novel, where it is used to describe the Haitian relatives and friends of a little boy called Chiquito at the moment of his burial (p. 129). Chiquito is an illegal Haitian migrant, a young boy who works as a shoe-shiner and whom the narrator got to know because he worked near the hotel where he usually had dinner. His illness and death, which were, according to Pancrazi, caused by rock ash contamination, are very movingly described in the novel. Chiquito's burial takes place almost in secret and without ceremony on one of the islets of the bay of Montecristi at five o'clock in the morning (p. 126). His unmarked grave, we are told, will be confused with those of the other diseased children who will soon be buried there with him (p. 129). Structural violence, Pancrazi insists, does not necessarily cease to exist when the migrant or refugee reaches his/her destination: in Chiquito's case it has affected him throughout his short life, brought about his death, and even denied him a dignified burial.

The migrant Chiquito, we are told, is buried with his first ever pair of shoes (p. 129). Migration is generally associated with movement, trajectories, and connections, but Pancrazi's long, beautiful, and meandering sentences are full of metaphors and images of confinement, captivity, and forced immobility, such as the one of Chiquito in his coffin with his new shoes. The screams of a woman locked up in the Fortaleza (prison) of Montecristi constitute an important aural leitmotif in the novel and her visual counterpart can be found in the recurrent appearance of an amputee woman in a wheelchair whose movements are circuitous and restricted to the central square of the city (p. 13). Even some ex-convicts that had escaped from the Fortaleza are immortalized in a condition of further segregation: having become stuck in the mangrove swamp, 'their arms have taken the shape of the roots of the trees and their hardened skin can be easily confused with bark' (p. 61). The ex-convicts hide in the mangrove swamps for months hoping to be able, one day, to cross into Haiti, regain their freedom, and start a new life. In the meantime, however, they become part of the still landscape without horizon that the novel associates with the area (pp. 61–2). These fugitive Ariels will eventually be 'freed' from their arboreal prison by a very ruthless Prospero: the lethal '*parasito*' which destroyed the mangrove swamp and, according to the narrator, claimed its victims throughout the community and also among the ex-prisoners (pp. 107–8).

Overall, Montecristi appears to be a city which is unable to deal, practically, with the parasite. Most importantly, however, it is a city which cannot even imagine a solution to the problem. The local doctors are powerless in the face of the contamination and the only remedy that local people believe in comes from outside in the form of a 'recipe' by a woman in Samaná. At the end of the novel, however, people begin to believe that, in order to be healed, the sick have to leave Montecristi and visit, *in person*, the woman of Samaná

(p. 63). One could argue that, in Pancrazi's novel, the peninsula of Samaná functions as a counterpoint to Montecristi: Samaná's lush vegetation, for example, creates a great contrast with Montecristi's arid and semi desertic landscape, but this polarization works only up to a point. Ultimately, in fact, both places are contaminated, the healing recipe of the woman of Samaná does not really work, and the 'hellish' and 'diseased' border city of Montecristi is simply revealed as a place where the symptoms of an island sickened and undermined, in its entirety, by social injustice, environmental degradation, and structural violence are more easily identifiable because of its poverty and ongoing decline. Concomitantly, *Montecristi* and, most importantly, the borderland and the city of Montecristi itself also explode the crude distinction between an impoverished and cursed Haiti and a wealthy Dominican Republic with which Guzmán provocatively presents us in *Some are born to sweet delight*. Watching his sibling die in what should have been their 'refuge,' Chiquito's brother describes Montecristi as 'an intermediary region' where he had 'saved and lost Chiquito at the same time' (p. 67). The differences between Haiti and the Dominican Republic are also further blurred when we are reminded that, only thirty years earlier, Haiti was a well-known tourist destination (p. 65). Chiquito's brother, who remembers these times, also imagines that one day it might be the Dominicans' turn to cross the border illegally 'with no luggage and no visa, running away after a *coup* […] a country in decline […] abandoned by tourists, devastated by one political crisis after another, by opportunistic tyrants and farcical regimes controlled by the Americans' (pp. 65–6). Crucially, however, looking now at his dying brother in this 'intermediary region,' he no longer knows 'where the misfortune was and where help could be found' (pp. 67–6).

In the midst of this bleak picture, Pancrazi also reveals the existence of solidarity among the disenfranchised which transcends nationality or origin and is their only weapon (unfortunately a very blunt one in this case) against the *parasito*, state apparati that are depicted as being more parasitic than representative, and structural violence. One of Chiquito's favourite words, we are told, was 'community,' and his little Dominican or Haitian–Dominican friends of the northern borderland, the narrator explains, were fond of him despite the fact that he came from 'another place' (p. 57). Towards the end of Chiquito's life the Haitian maid Janika spends all her time trying to save him by reciting endless prayers while administering the (allegedly) healing concoction from Samaná, purchased at a very high price by Chiquito's brother and brought to the little boy by the combined efforts of various *motoconcho* drivers.[81] Pancrazi also reveals, however, that the Dominican

---

[81] A *motoconcho* is a form of public transport which works like a taxi but which,

prostitute affected by the parasite deeply loved the little Haitian Chiquito who, to her, represented all the children she has had and who were scattered on the island: she became very distressed when she heard that he was sick too (p. 105).

After the death of Chiquito, we see an upset, defeated, and outraged narrator who fears for his life departing in haste from Montecristi: before doing so, however, he took a last look at the victims of the *parasito* who surrounded him, at the Fortaleza, where the screaming woman was still locked up, and at the woman in the wheelchair, who, he says, was perfectly motionless in the mist (p. 131). Once again, unequal power and unequal life chances are made woefully evident: unlike him, these people are all stuck there, in what Pancrazi has called a landscape 'without horizon' (p. 14). Most importantly, Pancrazi makes it clear that this lack of horizon affects not only a particular country or a particular region of Hispaniola but the island in its entirety. Unlike the diseased prostitute who, displaying a deep sense of humanity, never stops empathizing with those who are weaker than her ('she was so upset – why did children have to be affected too?' p. 105), the island that the narrator leaves behind at the end of the novel is, in his words, a 'big moral whore,' a place undermined, in its entirety, by structural violence, where ruthless exploiters and corrupt politicians thrive and are prepared 'to let [...] children die' in the name of profit and without thinking twice (p. 131).

✶✶✶

Structural violence in Hispaniola, however, does not manifest itself only in the blatant fashion described by the likes of Blonda, Pancrazi, Trouillot, or Lemoine. The film *Jean Gentil* (2010),[82] written and directed by the Mexican Israel Cárdenas and the Dominican Laura Amelia Guzmán (sister of the painter Hulda Guzmán), reveals that there are less obvious and, for this reason, perhaps more insidious ways in which structural violence crushes its victims, constrains their agency, and attacks the human dignity of those who migrate across the border in search of better fortune. *Jean Gentil* has been presented at twenty-five international film festival and has received seven special awards and prizes.[83] Cárdenas and Guzmán were

---

instead of being a car, is a motorbike.

[82] *Jean Gentil* (dirs. Israel Cárdenas and Laura Amelia Guzmán, 2010), http://www.jeangentil.com/2010_08_01_archive.html [accessed 25 November 2014].

[83] *Jean Gentil* – Festival and Awards, http://www.jeangentil.com/p/festivals.html [accessed 25 November 2014].

both born in 1980, in Monterrey and Santo Domingo respectively, and *Jean Gentil* is the second film on which they have collaborated. In 2007 they shared the script, photography, production, and direction of *Cochochi*, which had its world première at the Venice Film Festival Official Selection 2007 (Orizzonti Section) and won various awards. For *Jean Gentil*, the two writers and directors worked very closely with Jean Remy Genty, who plays the protagonist in the film and who, like all the other actors who appear in the movie, is not a professional actor. Jean Remy Genty is a migrant from Haiti who, at the time of filming, had been living in the Dominican Republic for fourteen years; he speaks five languages fluently and has a degree in education and one in accountancy, but has never had a proper job, a family, or a proper home. When he was interviewed in 2010 he declared that all he really wanted was a permanent job because this would allow him to get a home (at the time he was living on the roof of a house under a piece of tarpaulin) and, hopefully, a wife and family.[84] The film, loosely based on Jean Remy's life experience, sheds light on a more collective reality, but Cárdenas and Guzmán's focus on a particular individual allows them to question the legitimacy of the privatization and individualization of survival: as we will see, Jean Gentil finds himself in a tough predicament because of circumstances beyond his control but, despite the fact that his agency is constrained in many ways, his own survival is entirely his own responsibility.

Like the actor Jean Remy Genty, in fact, the protagonist of the film is a migrant of Haitian origin who lives in the Dominican Republic. He is in his late forties or early fifties and we meet him at a particularly difficult moment of his life. We first see him walking alone on a beach by a forest at the break of dawn. The next scene, however, takes place in Santo Domingo, but how we got to the capital city from the beach is entirely unclear. What is clear, instead, is that, in the hustle and bustle of the city, Jean Gentil looks and feels out of place. Jean Gentil is unemployed but the circumstances behind his unemployment are never revealed: since he has accommodation he can no longer afford to pay for, one might assume that he used to have a job in the capital that he has now lost. All we can gather is that, with his tie and

[84] Alfonso Quiñones, 'Jean Genty: quiero un empleo', http://www.jeangentil.com/p/press.html [accessed 25 November 2014]. After *Jean Gentil* was released, Genty hoped to become an actor and work in other films but, sadly, so far, this has not happened; moreover, his relationship with the directors/producers turned sour when he accused them of exploitation, an accusation Cárdenas and Guzmán have rejected as completely false. See Dago Sánchez, 'Jean Remy Genty', 13 October 2012, http://www.dagosanchez.com/jean-remy-genty/ [accessed 25 November 2014]. These unsubstantiated accusations, however, draw attention to the precariousness of his situation.

clean shirt, he is now looking for another position. We follow this polite and timid man in the air-conditioned lifts of the luxury office buildings of the capital where, in fluent Spanish and with his reading glasses on, he explains to potential employers that he is looking for a job as an accountant and leaves behind curricula and copies of diplomas. He does not seem to have any luck despite the fact that, at the time of filming, growth in the Dominican Republic was running at over 5 per cent a year and inflation had been brought down from 50 per cent to less than 10 per cent.[85] Importantly, Jean Gentil is not the stereotypical Haitian agricultural migrant worker and, at least on paper, he has more rights than many of his compatriots who cross the border of Hispaniola illegally because he is in possession of a *cédula* and therefore is (at least in theory) free to move around the country and to apply formally for other jobs.[86] However, he is not immune to abuse and his condition, as illustrated by Cárdenas and Guzmán, urges us to move beyond what Paul Farmer, using Galtung's work as a springboard, calls '"liberal" notions of nominal political freedoms' because, he continues, 'most victims of structural violence have such freedoms on paper.'[87] It is worth pointing out, in fact, that the real Jean Remy Genty also has a *cédula*. Yet, like the character Jean Gentil, he is denied the right to 'work and to protection against unemployment,' the right to have 'a standard of living adequate for his/her health and well-being [...] including food, clothing, housing and medical care,' and the right to 'marry and found a family.'[88]

Cárdenas and Guzmán show how those who operate in the name of market forces are prepared to treat vulnerable migrants and the film contains moments in which discrimination against Haitians, and their exploitation in the Dominican Republic, is also brought to the fore. For example, we see a group of Haitians working in a construction site. At night their workplace becomes their dwelling: it is an unfinished structure, muddy, with hardly

[85] 'After Leonel', *The Economist*, 26 May 2012, p. 46. It should be pointed out that *The Economist* also highlights the fact that 'nearly a third of Dominican still live in poverty, a higher figure than before the banking collapse.'
[86] It is true that migrants with *cédulas* have often been deported back to Haiti and that *cédulas* can be, and often are, destroyed by the authorities but, without a *cédula*, migrants are clearly more vulnerable to deportation and other forms of abuse and discrimination: see Redon, *Des îles en partage*, pp. 224–5; Riveros, *Informe*, pp. 48, 56–8; Wooding and Moseley-Williams, *Needed but Unwanted*, pp. 50–51, 65; Sevrin, 'République Dominicaine', p. 6; Rodríguez Grullón, *Estado del arte*, pp. 111–24.
[87] Paul Farmer, *Pathologies of Power: Health, Human Rights, and the War on the Poor* (Berkeley, CA: University of California Press, 2005), p. 8.
[88] United Nations (UN), *Universal Declaration of Human Rights*, articles 23, 25 and 16, http://www.un.org/en/documents/udhr/ [accessed 25 November 2014].

any walls, no sanitation and running water, and no beds (some of the men spend at least part of the night sitting on plastic chairs), and it is swept by wind and rain. Ironically, this building is destined to be a condominium of luxury apartments that these Haitians (but also most Dominicans) will never be able to afford. The fact that the Haitian builders sleep where they work suggests that they are probably illegal and that those who have recruited them need to minimize the possibility of these labourers being noticed and picked up by the police. Taking advantage of his (relative) position of power, the night watchman – who also appears to be 'Haitian' – actually charges the workers to sleep in this building site: he is not a member of the Dominican elite but his behaviour shows that many, from different walks of life, can take advantage of unregulated migration.

Overall, however, Cárdenas and Guzmán do not foreground Dominican anti-Haitianism. There is no hard evidence in the film that Jean Gentil lost his job or cannot find a new one *because* he is of Haitian origin. The Dominicans he interacts with do not just try to exploit him – on some occasions, some actually try to help him – and, overall, the film contains different examples of transnational solidarity across the colour divide. For example, while in Santo Domingo, Jean Gentil 'borrows' some money (although nowhere near the sum he actually needs) from a light-skinned Dominican businessman while it is a black Dominican woman who gives him shelter when he first leaves the city. The boss of a construction site in the countryside who befriends him is a Dominican who speaks English very fluently: he might be a returnee from the United States or a descendant of the West Indian *cocolos*,[89] or, considering that this part of the movie was filmed in the Samaná peninsula, his ancestors could be those African American freed slaves who, in the nineteenth century, moved to Samaná from the United States following a scheme initiated by Boyer. They fiercely maintained their African American names, manners, music, religion, and language and, nowadays, about 8000 of their descendants still speak American English.[90] Two young friends who give shelter to Jean Gentil in the Dominican countryside consider themselves to be of different

---

[89] This part is played by Nadal Walcott, also a non-professional actor who is in fact a *cocolo* and a well-established painter.

[90] The emigrants had their passage paid, economic support for the first four months of their stay, and land grants: see John M. Weeks and Virginia Ramírez Zabala, 'The Samaná Americans: Some Forgotten Philadelphians', *Penn Museum Research Notes*, 47.1, pp. 38–41, p. 38, http://www.penn.museum/documents/publications/expedition/ PDFs/47–1/Weeks.pdf, p. 1 [accessed 28 November 2014]; Harry Hoetnick, 'Americans in Samaná', *Caribbean Studies*, 2.1 (1962), pp. 3–22; Don E. Waliceck, 'Farther South: Speaking American, the Language of Migration in Samana', in *Just Below South:*

nationality: one calls himself 'Haitian' but he seems to have resided in the Dominican Republic for a while and his Spanish is very good; the other thinks of himself as 'Dominican' but, the film intimates, he might be of Haitian descent. Overall, all these different characters deeply challenge traditional assumptions about a 'pure' and stable Dominican identity and bring to the fore the often disavowed linguistic and cultural heterogeneity which also used to typify the borderland areas.

Throughout his journey Jean Gentil has to contend with a terrible migraine, which causes him great pain and discomfort and for which he has no analgesic. In the Dominican Republic one can find a good range of across-the-counter medicines, including some normally available only on prescription in Europe and the United States: one could argue, therefore, that Jean Gentil is condemned to suffer because he cannot afford to pay for his medication. His malaise, however, is not just physical: it becomes progressively clearer that Jean Gentil suffers from very serious depression for which he receives no professional help and no medical treatment. His mental condition makes him distant and withdrawn from what happens around him and, at times, he also feels suicidal. During a night that he spends on a building site in the capital he climbs to a high floor of a skyscraper under construction and we see, from a distance, his silhouette and the incomplete building's skeleton against the lights of Santo Domingo by night: his inability to engage with the world is evident as he turns his back on the city. When the camera gets closer, we spot a noose hanging from a beam just beside him. It has been argued that structural violence generates violent acts generally perpetrated by the strong against the weak,[91] but Cárdenas and Guzmán remind us that it can also be at the origin of the violence that, in desperation, the weak perpetrate against themselves.

In the next scene Jean Gentil is in a bus heading, significantly, for the countryside – that is, travelling in the opposite direction of most Haitians and Dominicans, who head for their capital cities in search of a better life. Centralization of resources and the rush to modernization have progressively marginalized the Dominican rural areas,[92] a point eloquently made in Chapter 8 by Rueda, who invokes the countryside (which, in his case, significantly overlaps with the borderland) as an antidote to the homogenizing and oppressive power of the city. Similarly, Jean Gentil's against-the-grain directionality signposts his decision to look for

---

Intercultural Performance in the Caribbean and the U.S. South, eds J. Adams, M. Bibler, and C. Accilien (Charlottesville, VA: University of Virginia Press, 2007), pp. 95–120.
[91] Farmer, *Pathologies of Power*, p. 9.
[92] Yunén, *La isla como es*, p. 68.

opportunities in a place whose way of life and models of coexistence have been traditionally considered backwards or dangerously disorderly. At the beginning of the twentieth century the countryside and its inhabitants were regarded by the political and intellectual elite as negative forces responsible for preventing the Dominican Republic from becoming an integrated and stable bourgeois nation. The peasants became internal enemies, destabilizing 'others,' apathetic and bloodthirsty savages over which 'the State should immediately exercise its regenerating and civilizing will'; the *campesinos*, in fact, had to be 'subdued if the country aspired to play its part in the great symphony of nations.'[93] This urge for modernization and homogenization also played an important part in the ostracization and Dominicanization of the borderland which, like the countryside, was earmarked as uncivilized, primitive, the antithesis of the way in which the nation was being imagined by those in power. Prestol Castillo's pronouncements on the Dajabón area and its inhabitants (Chapter 5) are a case in point: the area was a remote and (at best) half-civilized outpost; the people who resided there were described either as lazy, barbaric, backward, ancestrally apathetic, and with no notion of what their fatherland was or as an a hybrid population of *rayanos*, completely alien to Dominican authentic reality.[94] By the 1930s, the peasants who were relocating to the city in increasing numbers also began to be labelled as semi-savage social outcasts. Once again, Prestol Castillo's depiction of the urban 'vagrants' initially sent by the government to Dominicanize the frontier reveals the deep distrust and the disparaging attitude with which they were regarded: they are idle, morally corrupt, and addicted to alcohol and delinquency.[95] During Trujillo's regime the introduction of the identity card or *cédula* to police the mobility of the population and 'the ten *tareas* law which required all "unemployed" to have a small cultivated plot' were measures that aimed to eliminate 'vagrancy,' a predicament that, significantly, the wandering and homeless Jean Gentil clearly ends up epitomizing despite himself.[96]

Moving further and further into the Dominican countryside, Jean Gentil reaches a stream, undresses and, walking naked, enters its waters. This ritual of purification allows him to establish an intimate connection with the Dominican landscape and for the first time, floating in the water, he seems to be at home and in harmony with his environment. Importantly,

[93] San Miguel, *The Imagined Island*, p. 104.
[94] See, for example, Prestol Castillo, *El Masacre*, pp. 17–18, 84, 90 and *Paisajes y meditaciones*, pp. 31, 37, 39, 21.
[95] Presto Castillo, *El Masacre*, pp. 163–5.
[96] Derby, *The Dictator's Seduction*, pp. 70, 93.

Figure 16. *Jean Gentil* (2010) written and directed by Israel Cárdenas and Laura Amelia Guzmán; producers Pablo Cruz, Bärbel Mauch, Israel Cárdenas and Laura Amelia Guzmán. Jean Gentil (Jean Remy Genty) sharing a yam with his pupil Yanmarco (Yanmarco King Encarnación)

the landscape in which he finds himself at home is the overpowering green and lush landscape of Samaná, which is not so common on the side of the border from which he comes: we often see him looking around, overwhelmed and dazzled by what he sees, struggling to take it all in. After his bath, he finds a dilapidated shack, which he immediately begins to furnish with small objects he had retrieved from his previous urban accommodation, and where he boils a yam using his CV, his diplomas, his *cédula*, and a few small twigs to make a fire. On a symbolic level, the burning of all his identification documents clearly signposts that his old, urban life is unmistakably over; this is a new home which presupposes a new beginning. This fresh start, however, does not entail the complete erasure of the past and of the existence of the other side of Hispaniola. In his prayer Jean Gentil thanks God for the meal which has now been provided for him and asks God to feed his family back in Haiti, intimating that, while he is eating, just across the border they might well be starving.

Jean Gentil's attempt at rerooting himself in the wild bit of land he has claimed as his new home, his symbolic 'ten *tareas*,' is impaired when he discovers that he has trespassed on private property. This land, in fact, is overseen by a young man who accuses Jean Gentil of stealing when he sees him digging up yams. Jean Gentil then introduces himself as Professor

Jean Remy Gentil and, as soon as the overseer realizes that they are both
Haitians, they switch from Spanish to Creole. When they are joined by
another youth, who asks the professor to teach him Creole, Jean Gentil
resolutely picks up a yam he has just dug out of the soil, gives it to the
young man, and makes him repeat, in Creole, the following words: 'this is
a yam. I give you this yam. When you eat it, you'll remember me. When
you eat it, you will think of me.'

Yams are among those rich and varied products which, in colonial
Hispaniola, replaced bread for black and white creoles alike but, far from
being native of the Caribbean, they are African in origin. The yam, therefore,
has a crucial symbolic function here: it stands for the possibility of finding a
new home after displacement and resonates poignantly with the predicament
of migrant like Jean Gentil who have undergone multiple dislocations
(Africa to Haiti; Haiti to the Dominican Republic; Santo Domingo to the
countryside). Almost in a Proustian way and in an echo of the Gospels, the
ingestion of the yam is supposed to trigger the remembrance of a dislocated
migrant in the mind of the consumer: this presupposes the necessity of
reimagining the community in which both 'eater' and 'donor' belong as an
open and welcoming one where trespassing is substituted by inclusion, and
the exclusivity of private property by sharing.

The yam, however, also works as a bridge between the two nations that
the characters can be taken to represent – Haiti (Jean Gentil) and the
Dominican Republic (young man) – and epitomizes the reconfiguration of
their relationship. The Dominican youth, in fact, wants to learn Creole in
order to talk to a Haitian girl he is in love with but does not know how
to woo because she cannot speak Spanish yet. The way in which power
relations on Hispaniola are conventionally understood is complicated and
transformed into a more level playing field. Jean Gentil (Haiti) is not the only
one in need. Signposting the fact that Haitian migrants in the Dominican
Republic can enrich the country's cultural capital, the two characters (much
like the Dominican Republic and Haiti) here clearly need one another, while
both have something to offer. In a subsequent scene, we see the Dominican
boy paying a visit to his Haitian beloved: he gives her a yam and tells her
the words that Jean Gentil had taught him: she looks very pleased and he
is visibly delighted to have been able to impress her. This is obviously the
beginning of a transnational and bilingual romance which has the potential
to become as strong as the one which linked Pedro and Adèle, Philoctete's
'lovers of the border.' In the following days Jean Gentil and the young man
continue their lessons by walking into the forest, where they name what
they see around them in Spanish and Creole: 'if a branch is dry you call it
bois sec; if it is still green is *bois vet*'; '*camino* ('path') is *chemin*' and so on.

Renaming here is a crucial gesture of condivision which goes the opposite direction from the appropriative toponomastics highlighted by Ramírez in *Mis 43 años en La Descubierta* and which had the function of erasing the long-standing presence of Haitians or Haitian–Dominicans on parts of Dominican territory. Jean Gentil and his pupil engage in a process of sharing which contains a deep and complex desire to belong to a place and to the bilingual and bicultural communities (real and imagined, present and future) that this particular place holds. Moreover, while renaming their world in two languages, they recreate the transnational and bilingual character of Martí, Veloz Maggiolo, Alexis, Philoctète, Danticat, Ramírez, Vencedor Bello, and Rueda's pre-1937 *raya*, and evoke Anacaona's Jaragua, or the borderland 'from below' analysed in the previous chapters.

Towards the end of the film the troubled Jean Gentil seems to have finally found his place in the world: we see him with books, pencils, and exercise books on his lap while he teaches French to a Dominican girl. There is also more potential for romance: the girl is definitely interested, stays with him until it begins to turn dark, endures with a smile his embarrassed silences, and, highlighting once more the mutual advantages of exchange, teaches him the Spanish name of a bird they both hear croaking in the bushes. Yet again, the positive features of the pre-massacre borderland infuse this outpost in the Dominican countryside with the promise of a 'happy' ending, or, at least, of an ending in which the ability to create a connection between the two sides of the island one has had to translate oneself across, negotiating languages, cultures, and experiences, might be seen to form a solid platform for a new way forward.

The fragility of a pluralism which depends exclusively on the will of individuals, however, is brought to the fore and Jean Gentil's dream is shattered when structural violence intervenes, once again, to complicate the picture and neuter the positive effects of across-the-border exchange and transnational and bilingual sensibility. Left to his own devices, and despite trying very hard to combat his illness, Jean Gentil cannot shake off his depression and fails to pursue his love interest. Next we see him crying with his head in his hands on the very beach where the film began: with the breaking of a new dawn, he stands up and begins to walk by the sea only to suddenly collapse on the sand. At this point the camera starts shaking and moving away from his body, which becomes smaller and smaller while we get an increasingly broad view of the coastline. The continuity of the natural coastline which defines and keeps the island of Hispaniola together clearly contrasts with the man-made borderline that divides it in two, and which Jean Gentil had to cross in order to look (in vain) for a better life and has, since his arrival in the Dominican Republic, been constantly trying to negotiate on a cultural and psychological level. Progressively, we get closer to another part of the coastline, where we see a few trucks moving around: all is white and covered in dust and there are shattered buildings everywhere. This ghostly landscape of destruction is Port-au-Prince devastated by the earthquake of 12 January 2010. The death toll of this catastrophic event is still disputed: a year later, the Haitian government declared that the earthquake had killed 316,000 people, a number contested by other sources, which estimated as a more likely figure 158,000 or less than 100,000.[97] Even if there is no consensus on numbers, everyone agrees that those who perished died partly as a consequence of the earthquake's large magnitude and energy release but also as a result of poor building construction practices and the concentration of both resources and population in the capital Port-au-Prince, where many had migrated from a countryside impoverished by ongoing deforestation. The correlation between Jean Gentil's collapse and the Haitian earthquake set up by Cárdenas and Guzmán highlights what Blonda, Trouillot, and Pancrazi have also forcefully pointed out: misery, suffering, and deprivation are not exclusive to one side of the border and the lives of the most vulnerable inhabitants of both countries are constantly undermined by 'natural' disasters, 'economic' migration, individual vulnerability, and the privatization of survival or, in other words, by multiple manifestations of Galtung's structural violence. Transnational collaboration and mutual respect are clearly crucial to the creation of a less dysfunctional Hispaniola but Cárdenas and Guzmán, echoing Blonda, Trouillot, and Pancrazi, remind us that what has to be engineered on the island is a much needed social change that can counteract across-the-border structural violence only by putting people's social and economic rights, human dignity, environmental integrity, and sustainability before profit and market forces.

---

[97] Maura O'Connor, 'Two Years Later, Haitian Earthquake Death Toll in Dispute', *Columbia Journalism Review*, 12 January 2012, http://www.cjr.org/behind_the_news/one_year_later_haitian_earthqu.php [accessed 25 November 2014].

Chapter Ten

Borderlands of the mind: present, past, and future

Frank Báez, 'Ahora es nunca' (2007), Jacques Stephen Alexis, *Les arbres musiciens* (1957), Carlos Mieses, *El día de todos* (2008), Junot Díaz, 'Monstro' (2012)

T he previous chapter closed with harrowing images from the film *Jean Gentil* depicting the devastating earthquake that hit Haiti on 12 January 2010. The earthquake was also felt in the Dominican Republic, where, although the seismic activity was much reduced and did not cause any serious damage, its occurrence was a compelling reminder of the inescapable, but often disavowed fact that Haiti and the Dominican Republic share the same island. After the catastrophe, many Dominicans performed gestures of solidarity towards Haitians in need; one of the most publicized stories was the case of Sonia Marmolejos, a young Dominican woman who, on 14 January, was in the Darío Contreras hospital of Santo Domingo with her new-born daughter. Marmolejos became famous because she decided to breastfeed wounded, hungry, and dehydrated Haitian children who had been admitted to the hospital after the disaster. The Dominican government capitalized on this story, defining Marmolejos as a heroine, and used her actions as a metaphor to illustrate the charitable response of the country towards neighbouring Haiti.[1] Formerly considered a country where Haitian immigrant workers were denied their human rights, after the earthquake the Dominican Republic was determined to change its international reputation and refashion itself as Haiti's 'Good Samaritan.'[2]

Marmolejos's gesture has also been praised by the Dominican–American

---

[1] Rodríguez, *Las Nuevas Relaciones Domínico-Haitianas*, pp. 84–7.

[2] Bridget Wooding, 'Human Rights Across an Island: New Twists Following the Haitian Earthquake', *Múltiples: An Informative Bulletin by the Just Governance Group*, 10 (2010), pp. 5–7.

writer Junot Díaz in a long article entitled 'Apocalypse: What Disasters Reveal,' in which he acknowledges the prompt mobilization of the Dominican government and the generous response of Dominicans towards Haitians in need.[3] In his article Díaz points out that the word 'apocalypse' derives from the Greek *apocalypsis*, meaning 'to uncover,' 'to unveil,' and, using James Berger as his springboard, he calls the earthquake 'an apocalypse of the third kind' – that is, 'a disruptive event that provokes a revelation' and unmasks pernicious discourses 'that we as a society seek to run away from [and] hide behind veils of denial.'[4] In the context of the Dominican Republic, some of these pernicious veils of denial are simultaneously the product and the origin of anti-Haitian propaganda. This propaganda was redeployed in the immediate aftermath of the earthquake when some right-wing ultra-nationalists warned that a stampede of desperate Haitian migrants would cross the border illegally into the Dominican Republic and demanded prophylactic measures to seal the border and check the migrants' 'invasion.'[5] While Marmolejos's gesture is very significant – Díaz insists that it gave him hope for the future – it is evident that to really improve border relations in Hispaniola what is needed is a more systematic approach to the matter which begins by laying bare the device which sustains anti-Haitian discourses, posits cultural impermeability as possible and desirable, and, concomitantly, casts the borderland as a dangerous, threatening, and alien place.

Two of the works discussed in this chapter are characterized by a determination to contribute to the removal of pernicious 'veils of denial': they denounce contemporary forms of vilification, mystification, and 'erasure' of the borderland which rely on the mobilization of Gothic paraphernalia, and even tentatively locate, in the imagined borderland of a dystopic future in a permanent 'state of emergency,' a fragile, but precious, possibility for renewal. These two short stories, written by authors born in the Dominican Republic, one of whom is Junot Díaz, are put in dialogue with a novel by a diasporic Dominican which instead (re)foments the obsession with the 'forever impending' Haitian 'invasion' and reiterates anti-Haitian dominant discourses which continue to depict the borderland as the site where the

---

[3] Junot Díaz, 'Apocalypse: What Disasters Reveal', *Boston Review*, 1 May 2010, http://www.bostonreview.net/junot-Díaz-apocalypse-haiti-earthquake [accessed 28 November 2014].

[4] Junot Díaz, 'Apocalypse'.

[5] See, for example, Tania Hidalgo, 'Pelegrín sugiere más control en frontera', *Hoy*, 8 February 2010, http://www.hoy.com.do/el-pais/2010/2/8/313093 [accessed 25 November 2013].

dissolution of an essentialized 'Dominicanness' begins. Transnational local intensity and across-the-border cultural exchanges, instead, play a crucial role in the Haitian novel also included here. Written fifty years before the Dominican texts, it has at its core a central portion of the island which straddles the border and overlaps with Lake Azuei, Lake Enriquillo, portions of Anacaona's chiefdom, and the Bahoruco mountains. The novel's protagonist identifies with a pre-partition (hence pre-nation) past, with a (border)land, and with landmarks which, as we have seen in the preceding chapters, have been traditionally characterised by different forms of creolised heterogeneity; in so doing, he powerfully undermines essentialism and rejects the notion (and attractiveness) of cultural impermeability.

✳✳✳

In 'Ahora es nunca' (2007), a short story by the Dominican poet and short-story writer Frank Báez, the Gothic mode is put at the service of a critique of anti-Haitianism and the concomitant demonization of the Dominican borderland.[6] Born in Santo Domingo in 1978, where he still resides, Báez is the editor of the online poetry review *Ping Pong* and in 2009 founded, with Homero Pumarol, a 'spoken word band' called *El Hombrecito* ('The Little Man'); his collection of poetry, *Postales* (2011), won the National Poetry Prize Salomé Ureña in 2009, when it was still a manuscript. In 2002, Báez spent a few months working as a social survey supervisor in the borderland, especially in the provinces of Jimaní and Neyba. 'Ahora es nunca,' included in the short story collection *Págales tú a los psicoanalistas* ('As to the psychoanalysts, you can pay them!,' 2007) which won the First Prize for Short Stories at the Santo Domingo Book Fair, is heavily influenced by this experience.

In 'Ahora es nunca,' when a group of young *capitaleños* (Charles, Julia, Leo, and the unnamed female narrator) decide to visit Jimaní and its surroundings, their journey quickly turns into a nightmare. The story is told in a series of diary entries which begin at 6.30 a.m. on 29 November and end at 11.55 p.m. on 3 December of an unspecified year in the twenty-first century. Up to a point, the protagonists' trajectory is detailed and, despite its zigzagging, easy to follow on a map: on the first day they go from Santo Domingo to Jimaní along the northern shore of Lake Enriquillo and then, along the southern shore, to Duvergé; on the second day, travelling

---

[6] Frank Báez, 'Ahora es nunca', in *Págales tú a los psicoanalistas* (Santo Domingo: Editorial Ferilibro, 2007), pp. 37–56. Page references will be given in parentheses in the text.

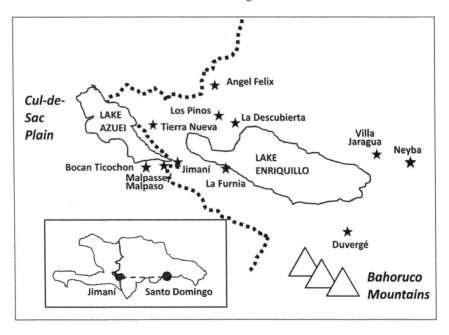

Figure 17. Map of the region of the lakes.

along the lake once again, they go from Duvergé to La Descubierta; from here they leave the lake behind and go up the mountain to Los Pinos and then down to Neyba; on the third day they visit the *bateyes* in the Neyba valley; on the fourth day, from Neyba, they head towards Ángel Félix, passing a number of villages on the north coast of Lake Enriquillo, such as Villa Jaragua and La Descubierta. From La Descubierta they go up the mountain, pass Los Pinos again, and then up to *la frontera* and a military outpost by Ángel Félix. At that point the account becomes confused and confusing and they (and we) lose all coordinates. The fact that the time of day and the geographical locations (at least up to a point) are meticulously noted, and that a map of the Dominican Republic is constantly referred to in the short story, might be seen as representing a (vain) attempt on the part of the narrator to bring order to a baffling, frightening, and, ultimately, self-destroying experience. Yet, the fact that the year in which the events take place is never mentioned allows the author to play fast and loose with temporality as he does with location. In fact, in this gothic fantasy, in which *The Blair Witch Project* meets *On the Road* passing by Alejandra Pizarnik's poetics of darkness, Báez offers us a geographical and cultural journey into the geographical borderland which is, simultaneously, an exploration of a

Figure 18. The road to Jimaní flooded by the waters of Lake Enriquillo, with submerged and dying vegetation visible (photograph: Maria Cristina Fumagalli).

borderland of the mind and an ironic commentary on the way in which the Dominican–Haitian border can be (mis)represented or, as we will see, even denied representation.

In 'Ahora es nunca' the negotiation between reality and fantasy is a complex affair. As we have seen, much of the journey takes place along the shores of Lake Enriquillo, which, when it is first mentioned, is 'rising and submerging the vegetation' (p. 39). This huge saltwater lake (375 km²), along which the characters travel, is an environmental mystery: at more than forty metres below sea level it is the lowest point in the Caribbean, and is famous for having submerged farmland, houses, roads, and one of the main highways linking Haiti and the Dominican Republic, which has been closed from time to time. At the time of writing, its waters are still rising, threatening the surrounding towns and villages.[7] The same problems are occuring on the other side of the border-crossing of Malpasse/

---

[7] In 'The Lake That Burned Down a Forest,' Vikram Ghandi forcefully argues that the rising level of the lake is a consequence of global warming (Chapter 9). In *Mis 43*

Jimaní, where the level of another lake, Lake Azuei, has risen ten metres in the last ten years, its area more than doubling in size. The most worrying aspect of this phenomenon is that nobody really knows why this is happening or how the two lakes may be prevented from submerging so much land.[8] Unavoidably, perhaps, the expansion of Lake Azuei has also been instrumental in various revisitations of the issue of a Haitian invasion of Dominican territory from a hydrographic perspective. José Gautier has pointed out how the rising of Lake Azuei is causing what he considers a grave political problem, namely the 'disappearance' of two of the pyramids (240 and 241) marking the borderline between Haiti and the Dominican Republic, which find themselves underwater, and the 'penetration' in between two further pyramids (250 and 251) of the waters of Lake Azuei at the border crossing of Malpasse/Jimaní. Blaming the 1929 treaty, which, he believes, penalized the Dominican Republic by giving Haiti absolute sovereignty over Lake Azuei, Gautier's contribution echoes numerous other interventions on the matter which have demanded that the Dominican state adopts adequate measures to deal with this problem (pp. 85–9).[9]

Fifty years before the publication of 'Ahora es nunca,' in 1957, the region of Lake Azuei also featured in Jacques Stephen Alexis's novel *Les arbres musiciens*, which focuses instead on a different territorial dispute and can be seen as playing an important part in the unravelling of Haitian nationalistic discourses.[10] The events described in the novel take place in 1941–42,

---

años en la Descubierta (Chapter 7), Ramírez talks about a flood which took place in 1956 and which he attributes to the inadequacy of a recently built canal (p. 127).

[8]   Alex McKechnie, 'Rising Waters in Haiti and Dominican Republic: Where will the Villagers Go?', *Drexel News Blog*, 25 April 2013, http://newsblog.drexel.edu/2013/04/25/rising-waters-in-haiti-and-dominican-republic-where-will-the-villagers-go/ [accessed 25 November 2014]. In 2013, Mimi Sheller, director of the Mobilities Center in Drexel's College of Arts and Sciences, along with a team of students and faculty members from City College of New York, installed environmental monitoring equipment in Lake Azuei, Lake Enriquillo, and three other locations in the mountain range south of the two lakes as part of a project entitled *RAPID: Understanding Sudden Hydro-Climatic Changes and Exploring Sustainable Solutions in the Enriquillo Water Basin* which seeks to understand the causes of rising water levels and the impact they have on the surrounding area and to identify potential mitigation strategies in response to this phenomenon.

[9]   José Gautier, 'Búsqueda y Localización de los Padrones Fronterizos Domínico-Haitianos Desaparecidos en las Aguas de la laguna de el Fondo', in *La Frontera: prioridad en la agenda nacional*, ed. Secretaría de Estado de las Fuerzas Armadas (Santo Domingo: Editora de las Fuerzas Armadas Dominicanas, 2004), pp. 85–9. See also Páez Piantini, *Relaciones domínico-haitianas*, pp. 240–46.

[10]   Alexis, *Les arbres musiciens*. References will be given in parentheses in the text.

during the campaign aimed at eradicating the practice of Vodou launched by President Lescot who, at the same time, was giving a North American company the right to confiscate lands belonging to Haitian peasants in order to plant rubber trees in the area surrounding Lake Azuei. Only a handful of years after *el corte*, the border here appears to be very porous: one of the protagonists routinely visits Dominican markets, another is a border official who lives with a Dominican girl and befriends his Dominican counterpart, and Haitian and Dominican Vodouisants work together and share the same political agenda (pp. 155, 189–91, 215, 221–3, 286–93, 175). The utopic plantation-based and ethnically diverse Macorís of *Compère Général Soleil* closely resembles this post-1937 rural borderland which becomes a bastion against materialism, the economic encroachment of the United States, and the complicity of foreign interests with the Haitian Church and State.

   Les arbres musiciens, in fact, reveals how, by destroying potential strongholds of peasant resistance, the anti-Vodou campaign had the aim of supporting the North American caoutchouc business; however, Alexis's reference to the presence of Dominicans at a meeting of Vodouisants in which a *local* response to Lescot's crusade was being formulated posits the existence of an across-the-border network. Further connections between the inhabitants of the Haitian–Dominican borderland are also brought to the fore and celebrated: despite the 'frontiers erected by violence and history,' the villages of the region of the lakes (Lake Azuei in Haiti, and Lake Enriquillo in the Dominican Republic) are 'brothers'; Haitian and Dominican peasants call each other 'cousin,' wish each other well for their respective harvests, and share 'the same heart [and] the same blood,' which Alexis describes as a mixture of black and Taíno (pp. 70–71).[11] The novel also evokes, with a deep sense of elation, the uninterrupted beauty and the common indigenous history which link the landscape around Lake Azuei, Lake Enriquillo, and the Bahoruco mountains (pp. 189–91). The irruption of the North Americans in this region – 'a cavalry of white men [...] on strange iron horses' – is compared to the disruptive arrival of the *conquistadores* in Anacaona's Jaragua, the *cacicazgo* which, as we have seen in Chapter 3, occupied roughly the same portion of Hispaniola in which *Les arbres musiciens* is set (p. 86). Significantly, Gonaïbo, a character who has lived all his life on the shores of Lake Azuei, suggests that he might be a direct descendant of Anacaona in the same breath in which

---

[11] The presence of *zambos*, 'a mixture of black and Taíno,' and of *onegas*, 'women of Indian descent of the borderland area,' is particularly highlighted – the terms are used on p. 70 and notes 1 and 2 on the same page provide readers with the above-quoted definitions.

he identifies himself with the land: 'He was the last son of the red earth of the kingdom of Golden Flower; he was *this land* itself [...]. He had the tastes, the colour, the face, the hair of the ancient men of Xaragua. Had their genes been passed on to him by some unexpected mixing of bloodlines?' (p. 89; italics mine). 'This land' (in French *'cette terre'*) has been generally taken to represent Haiti as a whole but, given the transnational geographical context outlined by the novel, and the fact that Gonaïbo is a border-crosser who routinely sells his artefacts at the Dominican and Haitian markets of Jimaní, Tierra Nueva, La Furnia, and Bocan Ticochon (pp. 43, 155, 215), Gonaïbo's primary identification might in fact be, at least in the first instance, with his *immediate* locality. 'This land,' understood as the region of the lakes which straddles the frontier – a borderland, as highlighted numerous times in the previous chapters, characterized by the presence of indigenous and African heritage and by various forms of across-the-border social interactions and cultural exchange – provides Alexis with the perfect platform from which to reiterate the importance of a transnational approach and to articulate the belief in creolization as a process which acknowledges all contributions to Caribbean culture. In other words, if, as Dash has astutely argued, Alexis firmly 'situated Caribbean man in the Caribbean -not exclusively in Europe or Africa,'[12] by setting his novel in the island's borderland Alexis also located Haitian men and women in Hispaniola *as a whole*, not exclusively within the boundaries of the Haitian nation. In so doing, he renewed his commitment to an understanding of culture as 'incessant happening' which transcends nationalism and which was crucial to the discussion of his work in Chapter 6.[13]

Overall, therefore, owing to its transnational, awe-inspiring, mysterious, and even menacing nature, the region of the lakes and the section of the Dominican borderland it presides over provides the perfect sublime background for Báez's 'Ahora es nunca,' a story also set in the interstices between known and unknown, terror and horror, materiality and hallucination, rationality and irrationality, borders and transgression, experience and projection, reality and delusion.[14] Significantly, while looking at Lake Enriquillo in all its magnitude, Leo, one of the characters of 'Ahora es nunca,' declares that what he has in front of his very eyes is in fact 'a panorama from the final scene of a movie' (p. 50), blurring all distinctions between the real and the reel. Furthermore, during their trip along the

---

[12]   Michael Dash, *Literature and Ideology in Haiti, 1915–1961* (London: Macmillan, 1981), p. 201.

[13]   Alexis, 'Of the Marvellous Realism of the Haitians', p. 255.

[14]   Diederich, *Seeds of Fiction*, pp. 76–7.

Figure 19. A panoramic view of Lake Enriquillo taken from the hillside where the pre-Taíno petroglyph of Las Caritas (La Descubierta) are located (photograph: Maria Cristina Fumagalli).

borderland, referred to in Chapters 7 and 9, Diederich, Greene, and Bajeux were also impressed by the eerie and 'spectacular view' of Lake Enriquillo surrounded by 'smoky, bluish haze.' They were also mystified by a strange encounter with a hitchhiker who suddenly appeared on the side of the road, got in the car, and never exchanged a word with them. When he reached his destination, he got out and 'simply walked away, disappearing into the dust.' Diederich refers to this episode as 'one of those ineffable Caribbean mysteries,' adding that in Haiti the 'mysterious stranger would have been considered a zombie.'[15]

Arguably, far from being a mere mysterious backdrop, the borderland surrounding Jimaní plays a very active part in Báez's plot as it constrains the protagonists, who repeatedly have to alter their plans and their trajectory owing to flooded roads and the unbearable presence of mosquitoes which, one should stress, in this particular locality, are not just a nuisance: the borderland, in fact, is still high-risk for dengue fever and malaria. The

---

[15] Diederich, *Seeds of Fiction*, pp. 76–7.

ultimate aim of the journey, however, is strictly linked to the flora of this particular area where (allegedly) grow special hallucinogenic mushrooms that nobody has used for more than 500 years and that Charles, the character who leads this 'expedition,' is very keen to find and try (p. 37). These mysterious fungi are not alone in signposting the pre-colonial and colonial past of the island also brought to the fore by the toponymy of the region (Jimaní, for example, is believed to have been a name of Taíno origin[16]) which, in its turn, signposts a long history of conflict and rebellion, what Casey would call the 'peculiar perduringness' of its antagonism to central power.[17] In *Mis 43 años en La Descubierta* Ramírez revealed that the current toponomastics of the area derives from the attempt to erase the Haitian presence, which was conspicuous before 1938; for instance, Ángel Félix, the last border outpost visited by the four youths in Báez's story, Ramírez explains, used to be called Marrosó (p. 85). Moreover, as Alexis's Gonaibo reminds us, we are in Anacaona's Jaragua and Lake Enriquillo is named after the (controversial) *cacique* who fought against the Spanish and established the rebel community in the nearby Sierra de Bahoruco. There are also pre-Columbian landmarks in the area: near La Descubierta one can still find caves with pre-Taíno petroglyphs. Owing to their strategic position – they overlook the lake – these caves are also called *Trono de Enriquillo* ('Enriquillo's throne') because Enriquillo himself is said to have camped there and, as underlined in Chapters 1 and 2, used them as hideouts. Incidentally, while crossing the Bahoruco, Diederich, Greene, and Bajeux reveal yet another layer in this area's history of resistance when they come across a thatched hut built by more recent rebels, namely the *kamokin* led by Fred Baptiste who, in 1963, found shelter in these mountains and turned them into the base from which to launch their incursions into Haiti.[18] This turbulent history of the region, however, does not interest in the least the four friends in 'Ahora es nunca,' who, in fact, take no notice of it in their search for the mushrooms.

The flora of the area, instead, takes centre stage again when plans for the expedition have to be altered following the ingestion, by some of the participants, of local hallucinogenic mushrooms (not the ones they were looking for) in Jimaní, and of a tea made with '*flores de campana*' ('angel's trumpets') near Los Pinos. The four travellers come across this plant while trying to negotiate their way up the mountain using what seems to be

---

[16] Rafael Leonidas Pérez y Pérez, *Apuntes para la historia de Jimaní: Contribución a su estudio* (Santo Domingo: Consejo Nacional de Fronteras, 2000).

[17] Casey, 'How to Get from Space to Place', pp. 25–6.

[18] Diederich, *Seeds of Fiction*, pp. 79–80.

a rather unstable temporary bridge to cross a flooded road. A bystander informs them that, during a wake for a dead child, some local people had made a tea with the leaves of these flowers and, after drinking it, they saw the child coming back from the dead, exiting her coffin and sitting among them. The consumption of *'flores de campana,'* like that of the 'lost' mysterious mushrooms Charles is looking for, dates back to pre-Columbian times, when they were used for divination: they contain powerful hallucinogenics which can induce a complete (and at times permanent) inability to differentiate reality from fantasy. When the friends prepare a tea with the leaves of the plant Julia is violently sick, Charles has a 'vision,' and Leo declares that he has remained unaffected – but we have to take his word for it. As for the narrator, we are not told if she has partaken of the tea or not, so it is up to the reader to decide if the narration that follows reflects reality or a hallucinatory dream.

Yet, if it is undeniable that the topography, landscape, and biota of the borderland prompt the protagonists' visit and deeply affect them when they are *in loco*, it is equally true that the search for the mushrooms can be seen as a pretext to explore a particular place which is also a space of the mind: the narrator, in fact, joins the expedition without even knowing what it is, exactly, that they are looking for. In the mind of the four friends, the borderland and what lies behind it (Haiti), are the ultimate 'uncanny' well before they arrive there: 'other,' yet so familiar; a fantasy, yet so real; occluded, yet so accessible; disquieting, yet so alluring. The youths' entrance into the 'other' world of the borderland is clearly signposted in the very first line of the short story when, at 6.30 a.m. on 29 November, they stop at the barrier to pay a toll for the highway which, from Santo Domingo, takes them, eventually, to the border town of Jimaní (p. 37). The fact that this is a threshold they will never cross back over flags up the anxiety that the frontier and Haiti can still engender in Dominican (metropolitan) society, an anxiety awakened (but not appeased) by the Gothic mode mobilized by Báez.

As soon as they arrive in Jimaní, Charles leaves the company to go and try local hallucinogenic mushrooms. While they wait for Charles, the scopophilic Leo asks Julia and the narrator to follow him to the nearby Malpasse to watch the Haitian vendors who come to sell their produce at the market. There, he adds, the Haitians drink *clerén* all day, and then, when they get drunk, 'butcher one another with their machetes' (p. 40). Julia reacts to this comment by branding him as a 'racist,' but, undeterred, Leo continues his speech, explaining that the Haitians who live in Jimaní put corn in rum bottles, leave it there for a few days and then feed it to pigeons. When the pigeons are drunk and unable to move, the Haitians capture them to either eat them or sell them (p. 40). It is not clear where Leo gets this information from, but it is evident that this is not something the characters directly witness during their expedition, although Leo definitely *expects* to see it. Leo's expectations are easily explained: the perception of Haiti as a savage and gory place and of Haitians as bloodthirsty primitive brutes dates back to the Haitian Revolution – incidentally, the foundational narrative of the Caribbean and American Gothic.[19] As we have seen, Dominican anti-Haitian discourse has traditionally appropriated and thrived on these tropes, mobilizing them to construct a Dominican identity and culture predicated on the negation of Haitian and Afro-derived influences and, simultaneously, transferring them to the discourse of the borderland to demonize the *cultura rayana* celebrated by, among others Rueda, Maggiolo, and Philoctète. In *La isla al revés*, for example, Balaguer (echoing, among others the works by Prestol Castillo analysed in Chapter 5) insists that the prevalently rural and poor population of the border region of the Dominican Republic is dirty, diseased, lazy, morally corrupted, and prone to delinquency owing to its proximity to Haiti and to the sustained influence of Haitians.[20] In other words, the borderland is not only identified as the place where the fabric of the 'Dominicanness' championed by Balaguer can come perilously loose, but is also made to encapsulate the terrors and horrors of various kinds of 'transgression' which are cunningly linked to a 'trespassing' of the geographical border and evoked in order to reassert dominant values and discourses.

When the four characters (possibly still affected by the '*flores de campanas*') cannot cross the bridge at Los Pinos, they decide to go in search of their mushrooms in the *bateyes* of the Neyba valley. The friends remain completely unaffected by the poverty and misery which surround them. They begin to pay attention to the locals only when a young boy explains to them that, one evening, he was sitting with his father in the very same spot where they are talking when, all of a sudden, they heard a loud noise of boots – namely, the noise that a military squad would make as they passed by (pp. 47–8). The sound of the steps came progressively closer but, the child continues, they could not see anyone. The father then told the child to escape into the house while he stayed outside, bravely confronting the noise (and what it represented) until it died out. At this point Charles intervenes to explain that

[19] See Dayan, *Haiti, History and the Gods*, especially 'Gothic Americas', pp. 187–267 and Fernando Valerio-Holguín, 'Primitive Borders: Cultural Identity and Ethnic Cleansing in the Dominican Republic', in *Primitivism and Identity in Latin America: Essays on Art. Literature and Culture*, eds Erik Caymand-Freixas and José Eduardo González (Tucson, AZ: The University of Arizona Press, 2000), pp. 75–88.
[20] Balaguer, *La isla al revés*, pp. 47–53.

the man was a *bisangó* (p. 48). In Saint-Domingue, a *bisangó* (or *bizango*) was the violent spirit of a warrior who protected the Bissagot slaves; more recently, it has become the name of a secret society with its roots in the maroon experience that protects a community from the exploitation of outsiders.[21] Charles's passing reference to Vodou and the fact that he has a French accent and pronounces Creole words perfectly (p. 48) can be taken to imply that he might be of Haitian origin; the short story, however, does not explicitly explore this possibility and its failure to do so tantalisingly suggests the disavowed proximity of what, traditionally, is so anxiously projected as 'other.' Vodou, as we have seen, has always played a central role in the demonization of Haitian culture as brutal, primitive, savage, and, ultimately, 'other,' a stigmatization that went hand in hand with the Dominicanization of the frontier.[22] In colonial (and neo-colonial) literature Gothic paraphernalia was mobilized to address, indirectly, the anxiety generated by the violence inherent in colonialism (and neo-colonialism) as Vodou and other African-derived belief systems were referred to in order to epitomize the savagism of the colonies and to reinforce their identification as threatening, brutal, and primitive places. Similarly, in his Hispaniola-based gothic fantasy, Báez refers to the *bisangó* to confront the troubling pasts and present encapsulated both in the *batey* – with its haunted cane field – and in the borderland as a whole: plantation economy, slavery, exploitation, human rights abuse, migration, border policing and corruption, violence, and anti-Haitianism are all conjured up while the *perejil* massacre loudly resonates in the steps of the ghost military squad. Once again, however, the youngsters are not willing to engage in any way with the history of the border, and Charles's explanation neither signals nor prompts (in him or the others) any interest in Haitian Vodou or Dominican Vodú nor in the complex socio-religious system of Gagá, a Vodou-derived cult which is well established in *bateyes* and along the Dominican side of the border.[23] All Charles and the others want to do, in fact, is to get high(er): when it is clear that the mushrooms they are looking for are not to be found in the *batey*, they speedily depart.

Clearly, this attitude and the cultural ideology which shapes their perception of the borderland pre-empt all possibilities to understand the place they find themselves in, let alone to engage with it in a productive manner. On the last day, when the increasingly confused narrator (allegedly)

---

[21] Laguerre, *Voodoo and Politics*, p. 81; Fernández Olmos and Paravisini-Gebert, *Creole Religions of the Caribbean*, p. 129.

[22] Moya Pons, *The Dominican Republic*, pp. 369–70.

[23] Rosenberg, *El Gagá*, pp. 43, 37.

sees a completely naked woman walking on the side of the road in the scorching hot mountains which overlook Enriquillo, she surrenders, simultaneously, to her vision and to the (ostensibly) disquieting borderland itself, and exclaims, in exasperation, 'what else could one do here?' (p. 50). We are only eighteen minutes away from the *frontera* and, for the first time during her journey, the narrator admits that she is scared and that what began as an absurdity is becoming more and more real (p. 50). After a stop at the border-crossing and the adjunct military outpost, the four continue to travel up a mountain. Suddenly, all geographical references dissolve as they get closer and closer to what the narrator describes as *la nada* ('nothingness,' p. 52). When they finally seem to have arrived to the place they were looking for, Charles, Julia, and Leo leave with shovels and torchlights while the narrator stays behind in the car. After more than two hours, she hears someone shouting from a distance and sees Leo running towards her. When she tries to go to him, she realizes that he is desperately signalling to her to get back into the car. She obeys and he disappears into the *nada* with the other two, mystifyingly erased by the landscape, like the land that Lake Enriquillo and Lake Azuei have been engulfing for years in their unstoppable and inexplicable rising. As night falls, the narrator finds a big knife in the glove compartment. At 11:53 p.m. the oxymoronic lines of the Argentinian poet Alexandra Pizarnik, 'even now is not now / now is never / even now is not now / now and always / is never' – which have been the leitmotif of the short story – begin to resonate in the head of a progressively incoherent narrator, who transcribes them in her diary at 11.53 p.m. The last entry, recorded at 11.55 p.m., reads: 'knife Charles pencil notebook' (p. 56) clearly indicating that any possibility of rendering this experience into a cogent narrative has now collapsed. As the *nada* engulfs her too, the narrator is no longer able to articulate: Báez's Gothic heroine/narrator, in fact, just lists words which insinuate the possibility of dangerous and alarming returns (Charles) or hint at terrifying and gruesome potential explosions of repressed violence (the knife suggests murder or suicide) which, evoked a few times – the Haitians who in Malpasse (allegedly) kill one another with their machetes; the steps of the ghost army-squad in the *batey*; the narrator inexplicably pricking her thumb with a pin to make it bleed (p. 45); Pizarnik's own suicide – has been latent in the text from the very beginning.

Arguably, it is the four friends' refusal to engage with the history and cultural complexity of the area and to face its reality – the fact that they are travelling in one of the poorest areas of their country, for example, is never acknowledged – which has obliterated the 'real' borderland, rendering it an ideological black-hole, a *nada* where temporality is suspended, where 'now is never / even not now / now and forever / is never,' as Pizarnik would have it. 'Ahora es nunca,' arguably, denounces from the very outset the violence of such obliteration while seemingly recording what one could define, in more than one way, as a trip to the *nada*. Crucially, in fact, the narrator begins her account with the following words: '*vamos con rumbo al sur*' ('we go towards the South,' p. 37). She should have known better: on a map like the one she and her friends frequently consult, Santo Domingo and Jimaní appear roughly on the same line. In other words, Jimaní is not south of Santo Domingo but, clearly, west. The narrator, however, is neither confused nor simply mistaken: her gaze is in fact unwittingly informed by (and, simultaneously, informs) what Yi-Fu Tuan would call 'mythical space,' a powerful 'intellectual construct' which here responds to the ultra-nationalist Dominican need to demonize or even deny representation to what lies on the other side of the border.[24] In the Dominican Republic the West is a 'lost' cardinal point; in colloquial terms, in fact, nobody ever refers to the West as a destination. A recent experiment performed by a group of visual artists led by the art historian, critic, and curator Sarah Hermann revealed that, in the Dominican Republic, the West is more often associated with John Wayne and the Hollywood industry than with the borderland – appropriately, Leo thought that they were watching a film (possibly one of John Ford's famous panoramic long shots) when they were looking at Enriquillo. The cardinal direction at the beginning of 'Ahora es nunca,' therefore, is much more than an innocent and convenient means to describe the territory: as Hermann herself has put it, 'the act of denying a cardinal point is one of the most violent acts that can exist.'[25]

---

[24] Yi-Fu Tuan, *Space and Place: The Perspective of Experience* (Minneapolis, MN: University of Minnesota Press, 1977), p. 99.

[25] I am grateful to Sarah Hermann for drawing my attention to this during a conversation in Santo Domingo in January 2013 and for showing me the draft of her unpublished paper 'Unconscious Curatorships,' from which is worth quoting at length: 'In the Dominican quotidian idiom, when you go to the north, you are going to Puerto Plata or Santiago; when you say you are going to the east you are going either to Higüey or La Romana; when going to the south it means that you are going either to the capital city, Santo Domingo, or to Barahona, 200 kilometers away; when going to the west ... wait, no we don't use that word ... we don't, in colloquial terms refer to the west. This is an anecdote, I know, but it illustrates very clearly how this definition by opposition, this binary polarity of the Dominican Republic and Haiti has permeated the language. The West does not occur in language, so as a consequence it does not really exist. I was adamant in trying to recognize this omission and embarked in a relatively simple research, a kind of survey on what *was the West* and *where people thought it was*. With a group of visual artists we asked many people, and recorded their answers. The results were clear: the West was more often associated with John

***

Some of the scaremongering Gothic trappings mobilized by Báez were also deployed in Juan Carlos Mieses's *El día de todos* ('The day of everybody,' 2008), a novel set in what is presented as the island's immediate future and which, arguably, reactivates the deep-seated Dominican fear of a Haitian invasion.[26] The Dominican poet, playwright, and literary critic Juan Carlos Mieses was born in Santa Cruz del Seybo, in the east of the Dominican Republic, in 1947, and lives in France, where he moved to study literature at the University of Toulouse: he began his literary career as a poet and his collections have won many awards (Premio Siboney – twice; Premio Pedro Henríquez Ureña; Premio Internaciónal Nicolás Guillén). *El día de todos* recounts a plan masterminded by the messianic Vodouist Papá Yoyó (previously a Catholic priest named Jean Pierre Bouchard) whose aim is to bring chaos to the Dominican Republic and initiate a mass exodus of Haitians to the eastern part of the island. After haranguing Haitian crowds, first in Port-au-Prince – where he refers to the island as 'one and indivisible' (p. 82)[27] – and then in the Cittadelle Laferrière, he eventually leads an 'invasion' of the neighbouring country where, he explains, his followers will find 'trees, woods, lagoons, marshes, mangrove swamps [and] rivers run[ning] happily towards the sea' (p. 134). Haiti, instead, he laments, is 'dying of thirst, of neglect [a place] where nobody thought anymore of a tree as a living entity but as a wood [and] charcoal' (p. 134). The novel ends with an image of Papá Yoyó, who, accompanied by the sound of the *congó*, *ibó*, *rada*, and *petró* drums and, most importantly, of the *Assotó* (a Vodou drum which bears the status of an Afro-Haitian God), guides a group of men dressed in blue and women dressed in red, followed by a huge crowd dressed in white, towards the Dominican Republic, 'the promised land reserved for them by their Gods' (p. 157). This exodus is witnessed by Ti'Karine, a little girl who lives by the semi-abandoned Carretera Internacional which links Restauración to Pedro Santana and runs along the border between Haiti and the Dominican Republic. Despite Papá Yoyó's rhetoric and rhapsodizing, Ti'Karine is not entirely convinced that '*Dominikaní*' is really a much better place than Haiti: on the other side of the border she can only see 'the same rocks, clay, dead trees, sun and sky that she could see from her village'

Wayne and the Hollywood industry than with geographical fact. For me the act of denying a cardinal point is one of the most violent acts that can exist.'

[26] Juan Carlos Mieses, *El día de todos* [2008] (Santo Domingo: Alfaguara, 2009). All page references will be in parentheses in the text.

[27] For more on the 'one and indivisible' question see Chapters 4 and 11.

(p. 57). Nevertheless, after being instructed by her grandmother about the seven most important days in one's life, Ti'karine recognizes the day of the 'invasion' as *'el día de todos'* ('the day of everybody'). In contrast with *'el día de nadie'* ('the day of nobody'), a day in which the bad spirits are all around and it is better to stay indoors, *'el día de todos'* appears to be a day in which the good spirits walk the earth (p. 89).

The Haitian Papá Yoyó, a charismatic and ruthless man on a (rather implausible) mission, is not the only character portrayed in a negative light in the novel. On the Dominican side of the border we are introduced to Captain Blas, a cruel, corrupt, xenophobic racist according to whom there are 'three classes of people: Dominicans, foreigners and, last, Haitians' (p. 29). He persecutes, abuses, and takes advantage of Haitians and Haitian–Dominicans despite the fact that they have birth certificates that prove they were born in the Dominican Republic. Mieses has explained that his decision to include bad and good people on both sides of the frontier is consistent with his resolve to show that, despite the fact that it is differences that are usually highlighted, Dominicans and Haitians have many things in common; he has also declared that he was determined to avoid 'stereotypes' and prejudices in order to make his fellow countrymen realize that the Haitians 'are people like us, with the same dreams and the same problems.'[28] Yet, good intentions notwithstanding, it is fair to say that Mieses presents us not only with an entirely preposterous plot but also with Haitians who, *for the most part*, are either entirely evil or mentally deranged (or both), and with Dominicans who are, *for the most part*, virtuous, noble, innocent: Blas is actually the only 'bad' Dominican that we encounter. Papá Yoyó's 'invasion' of the Dominican Republic, in fact, takes place after a command of fighters who follow his orders occupy the basilica de Nuestra Señora de la Altagracia in Higüey. This mission, which, as Papá Yoyó anticipated, ends with a bloodbath, is carried out by, among others, Bouteille, Marión, and Joëlle, all merciless assassins and sociopaths. We are told that Joëlle was an abandoned, deprived, and abused homeless child on the streets of Port-au-Prince when she met Bouteille and his men. They gave her food, clothes, a reason to live, and a sense of belonging, while Bouteille himself taught her how to survive and how to kill. The narrator explains that Joëlle kills people she does not know simply because Bouteille tells her to do so

---

[28] See Louis Martin Gómez, 'Diálogo con Juan Carlos Mieses', *Hoy*, 20 May 2011, http://hoy.com.do/dialogo-con-juan-carlos-mieses/ [accessed 28 November 2014] and Ruth Herrera, 'El conflicto domínico-Haitiano en una novela', *Hoy*, 20 June 2009, http://www.hoy.com.do/areito/2009/6/20/282299/El-conflicto-dominico–haitiano-en-una-novela [accessed 25 November 2014].

and that she finds the experience both rewarding, calming, and uplifting. Unlike Papá Yoyó, Bouteille does not seem to have a 'political' plan: he is just a violent criminal, a man full of 'rage' (like her) who is able 'to turn the worst nightmares into reality' (p. 115).

Marión, their accomplice, is a female assassin nicknamed La Perra ('The Bitch') who also does not seem to have a political agenda of any kind. During a killing mission, she hallucinates and shoots dead her partner Bouteille (who was plotting to kill her). Marión is a deeply disturbed character who has lost her sanity and lives in a world where reality and hallucination, past and present, continuously blur into one another. When she was a child named Mimi, she used to live in the Dominican Republic with her father, who was a Haitian legal migrant: she was happy then, and felt protected. Since her mother had previously died, after her father's death she went to live in Haiti with his relatives. It is not entirely clear why and when she became a killer and why and when she began hallucinating. The narrative, however, identifies both her father's funeral (where she witnesses, in deep shock, his separation from the Vodou *lwa* Agu) and her relocation to Haiti as negative events for Marión: in other words, her exposure to Haiti and Vodou practices seems to be posited as a damaging influence in itself.[29]

The hallucinating Marión kills Bouteille after the two of them slaughter the family of Colonel Cuevas, the military man in charge of negotiating with Joëlle and the Haitian command who have occupied the Basilica. Mieses creates a clear contrast between the occupiers' callous and frantic behaviour and the innocence of their victims. The two servants and Cueva's wife are slaughtered in their home before having a chance to even understand what is going on, while his terrified little girl dies reciting a prayer to her guardian angel after putting up a vain resistance. In the meantime, we are informed that her father, who firmly believes that 'nothing in the world could not be solved with a frank and open dialogue' (p. 116), has just managed, with the assistance of the Cardinal, to prevent, at least for the time being, a military attack on the basilica's occupiers. Cueva and the Cardinal are sympathetic to the plight of Haitian migrants in their country; they are conscientious and responsible men who try to limit as much as they can the possible social repercussions of the attack on the basilica. Things change, however, when Cueva is informed that his family has been murdered by the occupiers' accomplices. His reaction is cast in these terms: he feels that 'the demons had left their cave and were threatening to asphyxiate humanity'

---

[29] Puzzlingly, Mieses dedicates his novel to Alfred Métraux, author, in 1959, of *Voodoo in Haiti*, a book which aimed to counteract 'the morbid and hallucinatory character' which was often associated with Haitian Vodou (p. 15).

with a 'nauseating, thick, sticky and mortal vapor.' When he belligerently approaches the door of the basilica, we are left in no doubt regarding the righteousness of his plans: he is going to 'put an end to Evil' (pp. 116, 118).

This battle between 'good' and 'evil' takes place in one of the most important Catholic churches of the Dominican Republic and the first church in the Americas to be dedicated to the Virgin Mary. The novel clearly invites one to read the events as a confrontation between Vodou (evil) and Christianity (good). In the Dominican Republic the image of La Virgen de Altagracia (patron saint of the country) has been venerated for centuries: it was brought to Higüey by two Spanish noblemen who were among its original founders. As soon as the miraculous qualities of the painting became known – apparently, it disappeared and was then found in an orange tree which began to blossom out of season – the little sixteenth-century masonry church of Higüey became a pilgrimage destination for many believers who came to worship from all over the Caribbean, including Haiti. The monumental basilica which features in Mieses's novel was inaugurated in 1971 and the image of the Virgin was placed behind the High Altar in the midst of a group of orange trees carved in wood with gilded fruit and leaves.[30] The Virgin Mary, as highlighted in Chapter 2, was a crucial icon of Hispanic colonization, often referred to as 'Marian colonization.' The French, too, however, held Mary in high regard and, in 1718, they consecrated a cathedral in Cap-Haïtien to Notre Dame de l'Assomption.[31] The slaves were also drawn to the rituals associated with Marian worship and developed various forms of syncretism of the different manifestations of the Virgin Mary with female African spirits. In Haitian Vodou, for example, the Mater Dolorosa with her heart pierced by a knife is associated with Ezili Freda, while Ezili Danto is related to madonnas with children such as the Mater Salvatoris; in Dominican Vodú the Virgin of Altagracia has her counterpart in Metres Ezili Aila (Alaila) and shares with her 21 January as her feast day.[32]

In Chapter 2 we have seen how Romaine la Prophetesse, one of the leaders of the 1791 slave revolt in Saint-Domingue, appropriated Marian symbology in order to promote his own agenda; his strategy was copied, in the nineteenth century, by Henry Christophe and Faustin Soulouque.[33] In

[30] Manuel Rueda, *All Santo Domingo* (Santo Domingo: Fundación Dominicana de Desarrollo, 1984), pp. 117–21.

[31] Perry and Echevarría, *Under the Heel of Mary*, p. 31 and Rey, 'The Politics of Patron Sainthood in Haiti', p. 524.

[32] Fernández Olmos and Paravisini-Gebert, *Creole Religions of the Caribbean*, pp. 115–16 and Reyes, *Sincretismo*, p. 10.

[33] Rey, 'The Politics of Patron Sainthood in Haiti', pp. 526–9.

1842 the earthquake that, on 7 May, destroyed Cap-Haïtien, also created the waterfall of Saut-d'Eau, which became a centre of pilgrimage for the worship of the Virgin that rivalled the basilica of the Virgin of Altagracia in Higüey.[34] In 1882 it was believed that an epidemic of smallpox in Haiti was brought to an end by the intervention of the Virgin of Perpétuel Secours, whose icon had recently been introduced in the country: as a result, the Virgin became known as 'Queen of Haiti' and is still the most often addressed spirit in the Catholic pantheon in Haitian religion.[35] In 1942 the Virgin of Perpétuel Secours became patron saint of Haiti and the central figure in President Lescot's crusade to suppress Vodou, described by, among others, Alexis in *Les arbres musiciens*.[36] Marian devotion also played an important role in the anti-Duvalierist movement, and Maria was later mobilized by the *junta* led by General Raoul Cédras (1991–94), but, interestingly, also by those who opposed his rule: several murals prepared for the 1994 return of Aristide to Port-au-Prince portrayed him as the child Jesus embraced by Notre Dame du Perpétuel Secours.[37] Closer to Mieses's time of writing, in 2005, the Church of Notre Dame du Perpétuel Secours in Port-au-Prince was chosen to celebrate the mass in memory of the victims of the Bel-Air assault launched, on 30 September 2005, by the *de facto* government of Prime Minister Gérard Latortue and President Boniface Alexandre in order to crack down on those who had called for the return of Aristide, flown out of the country by United States troops on 29 February 2004.

Overall, therefore, it is evident that, for the Haitian popular masses, the patroness of Haiti has always been regarded as an empowering inspiration against socio-political subjugation, while oppressive regimes have appealed to her in order to legitimize their power and privilege.[38] This long-standing association between the Marian cult and Haiti is never brought to the fore in *El día de todos*, despite the fact that the basilica of Higüey has continued to play an important part in the life of Haitians: both Alexis and Philoctète, for example, reveal that the 'Miraculous Virgin of Higüey' is a crucial figure in the lives of their protagonists,[39] and her cult is compatible and not in contrast with other forms of belief they might profess. In *Le peuple des terres mêlées*, Pedro Brito, 'a man who respects the *loas* [...] never fails to make a pilgrimage, every year [...] to Higüey,' but he also goes to Saut-d'Eau,

34 Laguerre, *Voodoo and Politics*, p. 86.
35 Rey, 'The Politics of Patron Sainthood in Haiti', pp. 531–4.
36 Rey, 'The Politics of Patron Sainthood in Haiti', pp. 534–6.
37 Rey, 'The Politics of Patron Sainthood in Haiti', pp. 537–45.
38 Rey, 'The Politics of Patron Sainthood in Haiti', p. 541.
39 Alexis, *Compère Général Soleil*, p. 198.

always 'in devotion to the Miraculous Virgin' (pp. 197–8).[40] One of Mieses's rebels is visibly moved when he gets close to the painting of the Virgin of Altagracia in the basilica of Higüey, but the Virgin here is clearly mobilized as the counterpart of Legbá Pié Cassé, who 'had come from Africa to be with his blacks ('*negros*') at the time of their death' (p. 121). Being the God who opens the barrier which separates humans and spirits, Legbá, generally represented as an old man leaning on a crutch, occupies the most important place in Haitian Vodou and is always the first *lwa* to be evoked during ceremonies. Legbá 'reveals' himself to the occupiers of the basilica at the moment of the Dominican attack: up until then they all thought that he was simply a crippled old man who had joined their group. At that point it is also clear that some of the believers who had enrolled as armed commandos are dispossessed people who are easily manipulated and exploited by their leader: they seem to have become hostages rather than accomplices of Papá Yoyó's group. In other words, *El día de todos* depicts Haitians either as evil and deranged criminals or as wretched and suggestible people with no real agency and, as the Dominican critic Manuel Mora Serrano has put it, perennially hoping for a 'miracle.'[41]

The contraposition between Christianity and Vodou is further reinforced and connected more clearly to nationalistic discourses when, at the end of the novel, we are invited to contrast Papá Yoyó's Vodouist supporters and future invaders with a crowd of believers assembled by the Cardinal in the border town of Dajabón, where he is going to celebrate a mass. Arguably, the Cardinal's move echoes previous attempts to Christianize and Dominicanize the frontier which were traditionally disguised as self-defence. Consistently, Vodou is firmly associated with many evil practices in the novel. Papá Yoyó, in fact, also orchestrates a concomitant threat by giving one of his accomplices the task of infecting the people on the Dominican side of the border with a *wanga*, an evil charm in the shape of a magic powder that he was supposed to spread in public places in order to contaminate and kill. It is difficult here not be reminded of the way in which, in the 1980s, Balaguer insisted that the Haitians were infecting Dominicans with diseases such as malaria and syphilis[42] and of how, especially in the United States, Haiti and Vodou

---

[40] Incidentally, a statue of a crying Madonna also plays a central role in a short story by Danticat which features as its protagonist a Haitian survivor of *el corte*. Edwidge Danticat, 'Nineteen Thirty-Seven', in *Krik? Krak!* (New York: Random House, 1991), pp. 31–50.

[41] Manuel Mora Serrano, 'Lo que no se me ha perdido', 28 Agosto 2009, http://sanasanaculitoderana.blogspot.co.uk/2010/08/el-dia-de-todos-de-juan-carlos-mieses.html#.Ue6Xzr5wZ1t [accessed 25 November 2014].

[42] Balaguer, *La isla al revés*, pp. 43–4.

were blamed for the spread of HIV/AIDS and Haitians were indiscriminately identified as HIV carriers.[43] Confronted with the multiple threats orchestrated by Papá Yoyó, it is evident that the Dominican Republic – epitomized by the good-hearted Cardinal, the noble Cuevas, and his innocent family – urgently needs to defend itself and is clearly entitled to do so.

The Cardinal, in fact, is not the only one who goes to the border to counter the entrance of Papá Yoyó: political and military measures are also taken to fight against the Haitian menace. First of all we are told that bilateral summits between the Haitian and Dominican heads of state are suspended *sine die*.[44] Mieses also describes the way in which the Dominican army prepares to respond to Papá Yoyó's invasion: a gigantic digital map of the island is projected on a big screen illustrating the history of Hispaniola from 1492 to current times, marking the Spanish/Dominican side with blue dots and the French/Haitian side with red dots. The immediate future is dramatized by the entrance, en masse, of red dots into the blue area to create a new violet color (p. 139). As the dissolution of the blue area and the bastardization of what we can call the blue identity is broadcast on the screen, the Dominican national anthem, which plays in the background throughout the animation, is distorted to the point that it becomes an unrecognizable noise. This visual and aural demonstration of the imminent end of the Dominican Republic (which echoes Núñez's most catastrophic predictions) is concluded by the explicit warning that, should Papá Yoyó's invasion be successful, 'the Fatherland will never be the same again' (p. 139). This threat resonates, for the reader, with another scene in the novel where another map of the island takes centre stage: Papá Yoyó, in fact, plans his invasion on a leather map with a string of leather attached to it which represents the frontier. At one point he puts his finger on the River Artibonite, which marks part of the border between the two countries, and takes 'the string in his hands moving it with rage towards the east. His war had started,' we are told, 'but his enemy still ignored it' (p. 49). Most importantly, however,

---

[43] See Paul Farmer, *Aids and Accusation: Haiti and the Geography of Blame* (Berkeley, CA: University of California Press, 1993).

[44] Just a year before the publication of the novel, a study carried out by the European Community had highlighted the necessity to strengthen the Bilateral Mixed Commission which was considered as a crucial tool to improve border relations but which, up to 2008, had not been activated by the two governments: see Wilfredo Lozano and Franc Báez Evertsz, 'Políticas migratorias y relaciones domínico-haitianas: de la movilidad insular el trabajo a las presiones de la globalización', in *Los retos del desarrollo insular: desarollo sostenible, migraciones y derechos humanos en las relaciones domínico-haitianas en el siglo XXI*, eds Wilfredo Lozano and Bridget Wooding (Santo Domingo: FLACSO, 2008), pp. 237–76, pp. 263, 275.

Papá Yoyó's actions and the apocalyptic threat with which the Dominican Republic is presented are cast in no uncertain terms, as they are made to echo the long epigraph to the novel, a quotation from Paul Valéry's 'The Crisis of the Mind.' Here the French writer mourns the fragility and mortality of civilizations and explains that, sooner or later, everything 'falls into history's abyss' (p. 11).

At the beginning of his *Description de l'île Saint-Domingue*, Saint-Méry famously compared French Saint Domingue (whose social and political fabric, at the time of publication, had been dismantled by the rebels) to the past civilizations of Greece and Rome.[45] Similarly, echoing the apocalyptic prediction of Manuel Núñez, in *El día de todos*, Mieses equates his country to a civilization about to be annihilated. His depiction of Haiti, instead, follows a long tradition according to which the country is 'remarkable chiefly for its extreme isolation from the rest of the civilized world.'[46] As one of Mieses's characters (significantly, a Haitian, an attribution which is probably supposed to add extra credibility to the claim) declares: '*En Haiti todo podia suceder. Todo sucedia*' ('In Haiti anything could happen. Indeed, everything did happen,' p. 26). In *El día de todos* the annihilation of the Dominican Republic is clearly coming at the hands of those who inhabit the other side of the island – that is, the descendants of those who brought Saint-Méry's Saint Domingue to an end. The reader is alerted to this peril even before he opens the book: the terrifying ghost of the Haitian invasion is evoked on the back cover, where the words 'Why divide the island if it is one?' remind one of the 'one and indivisible' question, which, as we have seen, has for a long time been at the basis of Dominican anti-Haitianism.[47] Furthermore, Mieses seems to share Saint-Méry's ambition to intervene in current political debates and shape the future of the island. In an interview with the journalist Ruth Herrera, he explains how he conceived of the idea for the novel:

One night I dreamt about a gigantic wave which was crashing against El Seybo, my native city; then I saw that it was a living wave made of Haitian bodies. I knew that the arable land, water and forests of Haiti were disappearing at a frightening rate and that a movement called 'lavalas' – the word suggests a flood? – had seized power. The meaning of that dream was evident. This image gave me the idea of a massive immigration, a human wave, from which the novel originates.[48]

---

[45] PF, vol. I, p. viii. See also Chapter 1 for more on this.

[46] Farmer, *Aids and Accusation*, p. 4.

[47] See Chapters 4 and 11.

[48] Mieses quoted in Herrera, 'El conflicto dom
ínico-Haitiano en una novela'.

The reference to Lavalas enables us to identify Papá Yoyó with Jean Bertrand Aristide, who had been ousted only four years before the publication of *El día de todos* and was often accused by his critics of resorting to Vodou and to bands of criminal thugs (the so-called *chimères*) to eliminate his enemies. Aristide had never been popular among certain sectors of the Dominican Republic, especially since 1991, when he criticized the country to the United Nations for its mistreatment of Haitian braceros in Dominican *bateyes*.[49] Aristide's impassioned appeal followed an ABC 'Primetime Live' television exposé and the denunciation of human rights organizations such as Americas Watch which, in the later 1980s, had petitioned the trade representative of the United States to cease trade with the Dominican Republic because of its non-maintenance of labour rights.[50] In response to these accusations and in order to destabilize the Aristide administration Balaguer had issued decree 233–91, which ordered the immediate deportation of all illegal Haitians over sixty and under the age of sixteen (that is, those who were less useful as workers): in three months about 50,000 Haitians were deported and their possession confiscated by the military.[51] The Inter-American Human Rights Commission condemned these expulsions but the Dominican government did not intend to cooperate to ameliorate the situation. In September, Aristide gave voice to his frustration with his United Nations speech in which he reiterated the accusations previously made by ABC 'Primetime Live' and which he gave while the United States' trade representative was reviewing the eligibility of the Dominican Republic for the Generalized System of Preferences. Aristide's timing was crucial as 'an unfavourable decision [by the United States' trade representative] would have certainly meant economic disaster for the Dominican Republic.'[52] A few days later Aristide was overthrown by the military coup led by General Raoul Cédras: despite the fact that Dominican Republic officially supported the UN/OAS embargo against the military *junta*, it also allowed the entrance of all sorts of goods in Haiti across the border and it made little effort to consider political asylum applications from Haitians who escaped the repression of the Cédras

---

[49] Incidentally, in Mieses' novel, after the occupation of the basilica, a substantial number of Haitians try to escape from the island for fear of retaliation. The Dominican military considers this mass emigration as another aspect of Papa Boyo's plan to undermine the Dominican Republic, this time by bringing to international attention an issue which, up to that point, had been regarded more as a local one.

[50] April Shemak, *Asylum Speakers: Caribbean Refugees and Testimonial Discourse* (New York: Fordham University Press, 2011), pp.138–9.

[51] Sagás, *Race and Politics*, pp. 103–4.

[52] Sagás, *Race and Politics*, pp. 103.

regime.[53] Later, when Aristide returned to power, the Dominican Republic contributed military resources to destabilizing his administration and harboured and protected some of his exiled opponents, including Pinochet-admirer Guy Philippe who, in 2004, led the armed attack against Aristide which was launched from the Dominican Republic.[54]

In 2008, when Mieses published *El día de todos*, Aristide was still in exile in South Africa, but in the 2006 election the Haitian people had elected Aristide's former associate René Préval, who had been Aristide's prime minister during his first presidential mandate of 1991–95. It was clear that the majority of those who supported Préval in February of 2006 were in fact voting 'for the return of Aristide.'[55] Most of Aristide's supporters were disappointed by Préval's post-election behaviour but *Titid* (the name Haitians give Aristide) remained extremely popular among the masses: 'Viv Retou Titid' was a common graffiti mark seen across Haiti's urban poor districts.[56] The international community, moreover, was still putting pressure on the Dominican Republic regarding its handling of migration-related issues. For example, on 8 September 2005 the Inter-American Court of Human Rights handed down its decision in 'Yean and Bosico v. Dominican Republic,' a historical judgment in which it found that the Dominican government had violated the right to nationality of two young Dominican girls of Haitian descent by denying them birth certificates.[57] In 2006 Irene Kahn, the Secretary General of Amnesty International, wrote an open letter to the president of the Dominican Republic, Leonel Fernández, regarding arbitrary deportations and the deteriorating conditions of Haitian migrant workers and their descendants, while a delegation of the Senate of the United States which visited the *bateyes* found the working and living arrangements made for the labourers to be entirely deplorable.[58]

---

[53] Sagás, *Race and Politics*, p. 104 and D'Alcalá's *La Frontera* discussed in Chapter 8.

[54] Hallward, *Damning the Flood*, pp. 37, 122, 212–13.

[55] Ronald Saint-Jean, quoted in Hallward, *Damning the Flood*, p. 298.

[56] Wadner Pierre, 'Haiti: the Bel Air Assault', *Global Research*, 4 October 2007, http://www.globalresearch.ca/haiti-the-bel-air-assault/?print=1 [accessed 25 November 2014].

[57] 'Yean and Bosico v Dominican Republic', *Child Rights International Network*, 8 September 2005, http://www.crin.org/Law/Instrument.asp?InstID=1506 [accessed 25 November 2014].

[58] Irene Khan, *Letter to President Leonel Fernández*, 8 March 2006, http://www.amnesty-caribbean.org/en/do/sonstiges/AMR27_001_2006.html [accessed 25 November 2014]. Lozano and Báez Evertsz, 'Políticas migratorias y relaciones domínico-haitianas', p. 243.

In 2007, documentaries such as *The Price of Sugar* (dir. Bill Haney) and *The Sugar Babies* (dir. Amy Serrano) were released, together with the film *Haïti Chèrie* (dir. Claudio del Punta) and a book of photographic journalism by Céline Gautier entitled *Esclaves au Paradis*: all these texts denounced the inhumane treatment of Haitian *braceros* in the Dominican *bateyes*. Amnesty International also used *Esclaves au Paradis* as a springboard to launch a new campaign aimed at alerting international public opinion regarding the discrimination suffered on Dominican territory by Haitian migrants and Dominicans of Haitian origins.[59] The response of the Dominican establishment was mainly defensive: for example, it reacted very strongly against the accusation made by Father Hartley in *The Price of Sugar*, which was entirely devoted to the priest's attempts to improve the living conditions of Haitian cane-cutters working in the sugar plantations owned by the Vicini, one of the richest and most influential Dominican families.[60] The family, which wanted the film pulled from theatres, also filed a defamation suit in the federal district court in Massachusetts.[61] Father Hartley was then transferred from the Dominican Republic to rural Ethiopia, where he currently works: he insists he was forced out but the local bishop has denied that his removal had anything to do with his advocacy for Haitian *braceros*.[62]

---

[59] Céline Anaya Gautier, *Esclaves au Paradis* (La Roque-d'Anthéron, France: Vents d'ailleurs, 2007), pp. 5–7 and 'Haitian Migrants denied basic rights in the Dominican Republic', *Amnesty International*, 21 March 2007, http://www.amnesty.org/en/news-and-updates/report/haitian-migrants-denied-basic-rights-dominican-republic-20070321 [accessed 28 November 2007].

[60] Lozano and Báez Evertsz, 'Políticas migratorias y relaciones domínico-haitianas', p. 243.

[61] Barbara Bradley Hagerty, 'Family Accuses "Sugar" Filmmakers of Defamation', *National Public Radio*, 3 October 2007, http://www.npr.org/templates/story/story.php?storyId=14962748 [accessed 28 November 2014].

[62] 'Priest hails US report on conditions for Haitians in Dominican fields', *Catholic Sentinel*, http://www.catholicsentinel.org/main.asp?SectionID=2&SubSectionID=34&ArticleID=22479 [accessed 25 November 2014)]. The same article also asserts that Father Hartley felt vindicated in September 2013 by a report on the predicament of Haitian cane-cutters in the Dominican Republic prepared by the US Department of Labor, which highlighted how labour laws are routinely violated and how Haitian *braceros* are forced to live and work in unacceptable conditions. The report is available as 'Public Report of Review of U.S. Submission 2011–03 (Dominican Republic)', *Office of Trade and Labor Affairs*, 27 September 2013, http://www.dol.gov/ilab/programs/otla/20130926DR.pdf [accessed 1 March 2014] and a response of the Dominican Sugar Industry to this report can be found at 'Response of the Dominican Sugar Industry to the Department of Labor Public Report on Review of Submission 2011–03 (Dominican Republic)', December 2013, http://www.dominicansugar.org/uploads/DSI_Reponse_to_DOL_Report.pdf [accessed 25 November 2014].

It is perhaps possible to get a sense of the pressure felt by the Dominican government at the time if we consider that in July 2007 the secretary of foreign affairs Morales Troncoso went to London to discuss the situation with representatives of Amnesty International, Christian Aid, and Progressio. Troncoso was accompanied by the Dominican ambassador in the United Kingdom, Aníbal de Castro, and the political adviser, Alejandra Hernández, and delivered a speech that contained a rather embarrassed self-defence.[63] The reaction of Dominican ultra-nationalists to the international pressure and criticism was to give ideological prominence to the 'Haitian question' as a whole.[64] It is not surprising, therefore, that, in such a context, *El día de todos* has been read and championed by certain sectors of the Dominican intellectual and economic elite as a welcome indictment of Haitian migration and Haiti in general, and applauded as a text which usefully reiterates the existence of what Martínez has called 'the fatal-conflict model.' 'There is an eternal conflict between Haitians and Dominicans,' Mora Serrano argues in a review of Mieses's novel, in which the critic also delineates the political landscape against which (according to him) *El día de todos* should be read.

First of all, Mora Serrano asserts, we are dealing with the unusual scenario of two countries sharing one island: one of the two nations is 'very poor but has only itself to blame for this' while the richer country 'never invaded its neighbour's territory and was the first one to arrive on the island: nothing, therefore, justifies the hatred which is directed at it.' On the other hand, the poorer country has repeatedly invaded (pacifically and not) the territory of his neighbour, especially the border area; had it not been for Trujillo's decision to 'de-Haitianize the frontier' in 1937, Mora Serrano continues, invasions and prevarications would have carried on indefinitely. Mora Serrano condemns the cruelty and ferocity of Trujillo's massacre, which was 'comparable,' he says, 'only to the terrible genocides carried out by the Haitians on Dominican territory at the beginning of the nineteenth century,' but also adds that, despite his ferocity, Trujillo never crossed the border into his neighbour's land and always acted in self-defence. Predictably, Mora Serrano readily recognizes Aristide in Papá Boyo; he admits that the terrible crimes committed by the Haitians in the novel are not historical

---

[63] 'We accept that mistakes were made but we have acted upon them. Now is the time to look at the future and not at the past to establish an open dialogue, listen to your concerns, and improve those situations which affect the human rights not only of Haitians but also of Dominicans', in 'Aborda con ONGs el tema haitiano', *Hoy*, 19 July 2007, http://www.hoy.com.do/economia/2007/7/19/214913/Aborda-con-ONGs-el-tema-haitiano [accessed 25 November 2014].

[64] Lozano and Báez Evertsz, 'Políticas migratorias y relaciones domínico-haitianas', p. 246.

facts yet, he continues, they are events which 'could happen' because, in a rather unsophisticated reading of economic and power relations of the island of Hispaniola, he believes that Haitians are not likely to resign themselves to die of hunger when, on the other side of the island, they can find food.

El día de todos, Mora Serrano claims, is to be praised because it does not aim to delight but 'to make us "think"'; quoting the words of one of Mieses's characters as a warning, and, most importantly, almost as actual 'evidence' of the likelihood of a catastrophic scenario, he concludes: 'In Haiti anything could happen. Indeed, everything did happen' (p. 26). In other words, if the Haitian Revolution, as Michel-Rolph Trouillot has put it, 'entered history with the peculiar characteristic of being unthinkable even as it happened,'[65] within the parameters and strategies of anti-Haitianism the (forever) impending Haitian invasion of the Dominican Republic continues to gate-crash past and present political debates with the peculiar characteristic of being not only *thinkable* but a somewhat *tangible* event even as it does *not* happen. Despite Mieses's (puzzling) conciliatory declaration of intent, the readers of *El día de todos* are indeed encouraged, even urged, as Mora Serrano enthusiastically remarks, to think that this fantasized invasion is in fact an unavoidable, apocalyptic event which can be prevented only with the proclamation of a state of emergency and the adoption of extreme measures.

✳✳✳

At the end of *El día de todos* a member of the Dominican army stationed in Dajabón is depicted anxiously checking the bridge which separates the two countries 'as if he feared the arrival of a monster' (p. 140). 'Monstro' (a contraption of the Spanish word 'monstruo') is the title of a science-fictional short story by Junot Díaz[66] which addresses the strategically fomented fear of a Haitian invasion of the Dominican Republic but also posits the border as the place from which an oppressive order of things which has turned, as Walter Benjamin would have it, the 'state of emergency' into the rule, can finally be altered.[67] In both Mieses's fictional and Díaz's science-fictional accounts the (Haitian) monster throbbing at the border reminds one of the monstrous beasts which appear in the Book of Revelation and is a harbinger of the Dominican Apocalypse. One of the most acclaimed contemporary writers, Díaz was born in Santo Domingo in 1968 and remained in the

[65] Trouillot, *Silencing the Past*, p. 73. See also Chapter 2.
[66] Junot Díaz, 'Monstro', *The New Yorker*, 4 June 2012, pp. 106–18.
[67] Walter Benjamin, *Illuminations*, trans. H. Zorn [1955] (London: Pimlico, 1999), p. 248.

Dominican Republic until 1974, when, with his mother, he joined his father, who had previously migrated to New Jersey. Díaz is the recipient of, among other accolades, a MacArthur genius grant in 2012 and the Pulitzer Prize for the novel *The Brief and Wondrous Life of Oscar Wao* (2008), in which the protagonist shares Díaz's own interest in science fiction. Díaz has recently declared in an interview that 'Monstro' is in fact an excerpt from a science-fiction novel that he is currently writing; however, he is not entirely sure that this project as a whole will ever be completed.[68] 'Monstro,' therefore, might well be the enticing opening of a longer work but it can also be read as a short story complete in itself which contains a post-apocalyptic account of a mysterious viral outbreak in Haiti.

The first Haitians to be infected in Díaz's 'Monstro' are the poorest of the poor, who are housed in 'relocation camps' (p. 107). We are not told why these people had to be relocated and the short story takes place in a non-specified point in the future where most of the beaches of the Dominican Republic are submerged and the countryside is deserted because of the 'Long Drought' (p. 114). Yet, Díaz's camps clearly remind one of the relief camps created in Haiti after the 2010 earthquake. Díaz's futuristic setting seems to foresee that these camps will be there for a long time and, sadly, he does not seem to be excessively pessimistic if one considers that, five years after the earthquake and almost three years after the publication of 'Monstro,' hundreds of thousands of Haitians, namely the poorest of the poor, still live in appalling conditions in tent cities. These camps reveal a state of exception which has become the rule, as Benjamin and Giorgio Agamben would put it: in Agamben's theoretical analysis, in fact, camps are 'the materialization of the state of exception' which denotes the 'lasting crisis' of a nation-state.[69] As we will see, however, the imaginary camps described by Díaz inscribe themselves (metaphorically and not) on the transnational space where border relations on Hispaniola are negotiated. Moreover, in May 2011, when Díaz denounced the predicament of the earthquake's survivors in 'Apocalypse: What Disasters Reveal,' he also mentioned another calamity, namely the cholera epidemic which experts believe was introduced into Haiti by a Nepalese contingent of the United Nations and has so far killed

---

[68] John Joseph Adams and David Barr Kirtley, 'Junot Díaz Aims to Fulfill His Dream of Publishing Sci-fi Novel with *Monstro*', *The Geek's Guide to the Galaxy* – *Wired*, 3 October 2012, http://www.wired.com/2012/10/geeks-guide-junot-diaz/all/ [accessed 28 November 2014].

[69] Giorgio Agamben, 'The Camp as Nomos of the Modern', trans. D. Heller-Roazen in *Violence, Identity and Self-Determination*, eds Hent de Vries and Samuel Weber (Stanford, CA: Stanford University Press, 1997), pp. 106–18, pp. 113, 108.

thousands of people.[70] In its immediate aftermath the cholera epidemic also caused protracted closures of the border between Haiti and the Dominican Republic, turning, at least officially, Haiti *as a whole* into a camp in which to segregate, in the name of Dominican national security, the Haitian people who, in their turn, were transformed, en masse, into a lethal pollutant. It is no coincidence, therefore, that in 'Monstro,' when the situation gets out of hand, Dominican authorities decide to close the border to prevent the viral infection spreading to the Dominican Republic (p. 117).

Díaz, however, is keen to show that anti-Haitianism and the pathologization of Haitians does not characterize his native Dominican Republic exclusively but can also be seen to apply to his adoptive country: by featuring a lethal virus coming from Haiti, Díaz seems to be mocking the United States' early 1980s stigmatization of Haitians and Haitian–Americans as HIV-carriers, which was founded on the 1983 classification of Haitians as a 'risk category' by the United States' Centers for Disease Control (CDC). The subsequent erroneous identification of Haiti as the point of origin of AIDS, proposed by a number of medical journals and scholarly publications and then echoed in the popular press, was seen by some as one of the many manifestations of the Reagan administration's demonization of Haitians. After Reagan's election in 1981, in fact, the Coast Guard of the United States was authorized to interdict Haitian vessels bound for the United States and, in subsequent years, many Haitians arriving in the country have been imprisoned in special 'camps' such as the Krome Detention Center in Miami, where Edwidge Danticat's uncle died in 2004, or Guantánamo Bay in Cuba.[71] The narrator of 'Monstro,' moreover, also repeatedly insists on international neglect: since 'it was just poor Haitians types getting fucked up,' he explains, 'once the initial bulla died down, only a couple of underfunded teams stayed on' (p. 107). Later, when more clues about the mysterious diseased were revealing themselves, he adds, 'that should have alerted someone, but who paid attention to camp kids?' (p. 109); when the riots in the detention camps became 'a straight massacre' (p. 115) the United Nations Peacekeeping Mission 'waited a full two days for tensions to "cool down" before attempting to re-establish control' (p. 117).[72]

[70] Díaz, 'Apocalypse'.
[71] Farmer, *Pathologies of Power*, pp. 209, 211–14; Paul Farmer, *The Uses of Haiti* (Monroe, ME: Common Courage Press, 1994), p. 264; Shemak, *Asylum Speakers*, pp. 45–130; Nikòl Payen, 'Lavalas: the Flood after the Flood', *Callaloo*, 25.3 (2002), pp. 759–71; Nikòl Payen, 'Something in the Water ... Reflections of a People's Journey', in *The Butterfly's Way*, ed. E. Danticat (New York: Soho, 2001), pp. 66–82; Edwidge Danticat, *Brother, I'm Dying* (New York: Knopf, 2007).
[72] After the 2010 earthquake the UN had been accused by some of being sluggish and slow in its response: see Colum Lynch, 'Ban Ki-moon Katrina?', *Foreign Policy*,

The apocalypse the narrator of 'Monstro' presents us with, therefore, is a social and political disaster rather than simply a 'natural' one, a point Díaz also eloquently made about the 2010 earthquake.[73]

In Díaz's 'Monstro' the epidemic – the popular name of which is 'Negrura' or 'Darkness' – begins to manifest itself by making Haitians blacker: 'At first, Negroes thought it funny. A disease that could make a Haitian blacker? It was the joke of the year.' In Santo Domingo, Díaz's narrator continues, everybody was 'accusing everybody else of having it [...] Someone would point to a spot on your arm and say, Diablo, haitiano, que te pasó?' (p. 107). Here Díaz exposes and ridicules the pigmentocracy which goes hand in hand with anti-Haitianism: as soon as the skin of a Dominican becomes slightly darker, he is immediately addressed as '*haitiano*.' Paradoxically, however, the 'Negroes' the narrator mentions in the opening sentence of the short story are in fact Dominicans. Díaz's choice of words reveals the contradiction experienced by diasporic Dominicans: in the mother country they were socialized into thinking of the Haitians as the only 'blacks' of the island, while in the racially polarized United States they had to learn to see themselves as 'black' and use the word 'Negro' to display a confrontational 'political' awareness of their own 'blackness.' From its inception, therefore, the short story seems aimed at dismantling the conflation of Hispaniola's geopolitical border with pigmentocracy but, indirectly, it also reveals the paradoxes of identity politics in the United States when the narrator, a self-defined '*morenito*' ('black') applies the word 'Negro' to his multi-millionaire friend, also a diasporic Dominican who appears to be so light-skinned that he could easily pass for 'Spanish, Italian or [even] gringo' (pp. 115, 110).[74] We are also informed that Haitian–Dominicans and Haitians living in the Dominican Republic began to be 'deported over a freckle' (p. 113), an open criticism of the way in which the Dominican government has been using arbitrary deportations (often targeting dark-skinned individuals regardless of their status) as a means to control and regulate 'Haitian' immigration, and, more specifically, of the resumption of deportations after the cholera epidemic as a prophylactic measure.[75]

---

19 January 2010, http://turtlebay.foreignpolicy.com/posts/2010/01/19/ban_ki_moons_katrina [accessed 28 November 2014].

[73] Díaz, 'Apocalypse'.

[74] The narrator's friend was 'more than just a rico, turned out he was a fucking V–, son of the wealthiest, most priv'ed-up family on the Island' (p. 110). Díaz only gives us the initial 'V' which puts one in mind of the Vicini family, the sugar barons accused by Father Hartley of exploiting Haitian labourers in *The Price of Sugar* (dir. Bill Haney, 2007).

[75] 'Dominican Republic Resumes Deportations of Haitians', *BBC News Latin America*

As the narrative progresses we are told that, in Haiti, after turning the infected into a quarantined homogenous mass progressively able only to let out a series of shrieks at the unison, the epidemic suddenly transforms the diseased into unmanageable bloodthirsty murderers who quickly gain full control of the twenty-two camps in the vicinity of the quarantine zone (p. 115). The infected, one could argue, represent what Agamben would call 'bare life,' an army of *homini sacri* banned from the *polis* who, however, seem keen (and able) to reclaim subjectivity rather than remaining mere objects of political power.[76] When the belated interventions of the United Nations Peacekeeping Mission and the Unites States Rapid Expeditionary Force fail to bring the situation under control violence escalates and Haiti *as a whole* is placed under quarantine. Most importantly, the internal border of Hispaniola is militarily 'sealed' and, therefore, turned into a place where power negotiation between bare life and sovereignty are bound to take place (p. 117). Despite the border closure, however, some evacuees from Haiti manage to reach the Dominican Republic, and they describe the scenario they left behind in graphic terms. The first reaction of their interlocutors is disbelief:

> Initially no one believed the hysterical evacuees. Forty-foot-tall cannibal motherfuckers running loose on the Island? Negro, please.
>
> Until a set of soon-to-be-iconic Polaroids made it out on one clipper showing what later came to be called a Class 2 in the process of putting a slender broken girl in its mouth.
>
> Beneath the photo someone had scrawled: Numbers 11:18. *Who shall give us flesh to eat?* (p. 118)

In order to make fun of the paranoia instilled in the Dominican population by right-wing anti-Haitian extremists who predicted a post-earthquake mass invasion of the Dominican territory which, however, did not actually take place, Díaz refers to the Old Testament and then projects this paranoia onto a futuristic and dystopic scenario which identifies the border with Haiti as a dangerous threshold beyond which, as Mora Serrano insists in his review of Mieses' *El día de todos*, lies all that is evil, savage, vicious, and foreboding.[77]

& Caribbean, 7 January 2011, http://www.bbc.co.uk/news/world-latin-america-12132514 [accessed 28 November 2014].

[76] Giorgio Agamben, *Homo Sacer: Sovereign Power and Bare Life*, trans. D. Heller-Roazen (1995; Stanford: Stanford University Press, 1998).

[77] Various organizations have registered a substantial increase in the number of those who have entered the Dominican Republic from Haiti after the earthquake but it is

The apocalyptic nature of 'Monstro,' however, is instrumental to Díaz's determination to make the most of the radical and progressive potential of science-fiction – a genre whose artistic framework was established by the Gothic mode mobilized by Báez and, to a lesser extent, by Mieses, and which has traditionally been preoccupied with the creation and, simultaneously, the eradication of Otherness. In other words, Díaz's apocalypse of the third kind or 'revelation' here is aimed at excoriating anti-Haitianism rather than promoting it or hiding it 'behind veils of denial.'[78]

Eventually, in order to put an end to the threat posed by the infected and infectious *homini sacri*, the 'Great Powers' – namely, the United States – organize a 'Detonation Event' which destroys Haiti and changes the entire world after turning it 'white' (p. 117). As a result, thirteen million Haitians 'threaten[..] the border' with the Dominican Republic, determined to redefine the parameters which, up to that point, have excluded them as 'bare life' or 'life that does not deserve to live.'[79] The renegotiation of these parameters is a reconfiguration of power and sovereignty which has to explode the exclusionary discourses which have supported the creation of the camps and the sealing of the frontier. As in Mieses's novel, we are informed that 'Dominican military units had been authorized to meet the *invaders* – the term the gov was [...] using – with ultimate force' (p. 118; italics in the text). The short story ends with the narrator heading towards the border with a friend who is a keen photographer 'just in case [...] something happens': we are not told what exactly will happen there but it is clear that the border is the very place where, to prevent protracted warfare and bloodshed, a new order will have to be devised for Hispaniola.

---

impossible to establish the exact number of migrants because the figures presented by these organizations fail to include illegal border-crossers and to differentiate between those who enter the Dominican Republic on a daily or short-term basis and those who relocate there. Rodríguez Grullón, *Estado del arte*, pp. 65–6.

[78] Díaz, 'Apocalypse'.

[79] Agamben, *Homo Sacer*, especially pp. 136–43.

Chapter Eleven

The writing is on the wall: towards an open island and a complete structure

Francisco (Pancho) Rodríguez, *Que si fuere mil veces* (2012), Rita Indiana Hernández and Los Misterios, 'Da pa lo do' (2010) and 'Da pa lo do', video directed by Engel Leonardo, Jean Philippe Moiseau, *Palm Mask* (2009), *Metal Mask* (2011) and *Les rêves du cireur de bottes/Los sueños del limpia botas/Yon chanj kap reve* (2012), David Pérez Karmadavis, *Isla cerrada* (2010), *Isla abierta* (2006), *Lo que dice la piel* (2005), *Trata* (2005), *Simétrico* (2006), *Al tramo izquierdo* (2006), *Estructura completa* (2010)

In the immediate aftermath of the Haitian earthquake Junot Díaz was not the only one who hoped that the earthquake could turn into an opportunity to improve the relationship between the two nations which share Hispaniola.[1] Many writers and artists tried to play a central role to support and promote solidarity and the kind of cultural exchange which could make a difference: for example, in July 2011 the *Caravan Cultural de la Isla/Karavan Kulturèl Zile* saw more than a hundred artists from both Haiti and the Dominican Republic travelling from Santo Domingo to Jimaní and performing in Oeste, Baní, Cabral, and Jimaní. In Jimaní, the route to Port-au-Prince was declared the 'The Route of Solidarity' and, combining music, dance, theatre, painting, photography, and literature, the artists continued their journey across the border to Port-au-Prince through Fond Parisien, Gantier, Croix-des-Bouquets, and the camps for those displaced by the earthquake in Karadé.[2] In 2012 the Dominican poet Basilio Belliard

---

[1] Díaz, 'Apocalypse'. See also, for example, Rodríguez, *Las Nuevas Relaciones Domínico-Haitianas*.

[2] Rafael Feliz,'RD realizará el evento artistico más importante para la historia

and the Haitian poet Gahston Saint-Fleur compiled *Palabras de una isla / Paroles d'une île*, the first anthology of poems featuring, side by side, Haitian poems translated into Spanish and Dominican poems translated into French.[3] Incidentally, the volume is dedicated to the poet Jacques Viau, who was born in Port-au-Prince and moved to the Dominican Republic in 1948 with his father. He was killed in 1965, at the age of twenty-three, by American troops when Haitians and Dominicans fought together on the side of the *constitucionalistas*, an important moment of transnational solidarity also celebrated by Klang in *L'île aux deux visages*. In one of his poems, Viau famously declared his allegiance to both countries and to the island as a whole, paving the way for the kind of sensitivity that these post-earthquake interventions aimed to foster: 'I have tried to talk to you about my fatherland / About my two fatherlands / About my island / That was divided by men a long time ago.'[4]

In 2012 Sarah Hermann curated the exhibition *A los lados del límite* in Santo Domingo, which saw the participation of Haitian and Dominican photographers: the Dominican photographers were taken to visit Port-au-Prince while the Haitians went to Santo Domingo. The photographs that the artists took in the two capitals highlighted differences but, above all, continuities and similarities between the two cities and various facets of the human experience (informal trade, urban graffiti, popular markets, impoverished areas) which characterize them.[5] From February to May 2013, at the Museum of the Americas in Washington, an exhibition called *On Common Ground: Dominican Republic + Haiti*, featured contemporary artwork by emerging artists from Hispaniola who aimed to 'address misconceptions surrounding its two nations' complex relationship with one another, imagining a brighter future.'[6] The rest of this concluding chapter is

---

dominico-haitiana', *Pasandoeltiempo*, July 2011, http://pasandoeltiempo2.blogspot.co.uk/2011/06/rd-realizara-el-evento-artistico-mas.html [accessed 29 November 2014].
[3] Basilio Belliard and Gahston Saint-Fleur, eds, *Palabras de una isla / Paroles d'une île: Primera antología póetica de República Dominicana y Haití / Première anthologie poétique de la République Dominicaine et Haïti* (Santo Domingo: Ediciones de Cultura, 2012).
[4] Jacques Viau-Renaud, 'Estoy tratando de hablaros de mi patria', in *Poesía Completa* (Santo Domingo: Ediciones del Cielonaranja, 2006), pp. 68–71, p. 71.
[5] Carlos Acero Ruiz, '*A los lados del límite*: una experiencia inolvidable', *Cuadernos de Comunicación*, 5.4, March 2013, pp. 15–21.
[6] *Art Museum of the Americas*, http://www.museum.oas.org/exhibitions/2010s/2013-oncommonground.html [accessed 29 November 2014]. The Dominican artists were Natalia Ortega Gámez, Hulda Guzmán, Gustavo Peña, Engel Leonardo, and Julio Valdez; the Haitian artists Killy Patrick Ganthier, Marc Lee Steed, Emmanuel Jean,

concerned with various video performances, a musical video and the song lyrics it illustrates, a painting, two sculptures, and a poem by Dominican and Haitian artists who, in the wake of the earthquake, have contributed to the debate by asserting, or in some cases *re*asserting, that 'a brighter future' depends on a willingness to confront head on some of the misconceptions and disabling continuities which characterize pre- and post-earthquake Hispaniola and continue to hamper across-the-border dialogue.

✳✳✳

In 2012 the Dominican artist and photographer Francisco (Pancho) Rodríguez was selected to present *Que si fuere mil veces* ('For if it were a thousand times,' 2012), a performance documented with a video, at the XXIV Concurso de Arte Eduardo León Jimenes in Santiago de los Caballeros (October 2012–January 2013). Rodríguez, who has received a number of prizes for his photographic work, was born in 1979 in Santo Domingo, where he currently lives. In *Que si fuere mil veces*, the writing, or more precisely, the hand-writing 'is on the wall,' as it were, and, as in its biblical counterpart (Book of Daniel, chapter 4), it presupposes imminent doom or misfortune and a distressingly predetermined future. The biblical story, in fact, relates that, at a banquet hosted by the Babylonian King Belshazzar and attended by those who profaned the sacred vessels pillaged from the Jerusalem Temple, a disembodied hand appeared and wrote a mysterious message on the palace wall. The prophet Daniel was summoned and he interpreted this message as the imminent end for the Babylonian kingdom. That night King Belshazzar was killed and the Persians ransacked the capital city.

For his performance Rodríguez visited various Haitian communities in Santo Domingo and asked them to tell him one thing that they would really like to say to Dominicans; he then selected some of the over 100 texts he received from his Haitian interviewees and juxtaposed them against some lines inspired by Pedro Mir's poem 'Hay un país en el mundo' ('There is a country in the world'), one of the most famous Dominican poems dedicated to the country.[7] Rodríguez then asked an artist to intermittently write these texts as graffiti on a wall of one of the main arteries in Santo Domingo for thirty-two days. He initially wanted a Haitian person to perform this action

---

Manuel Mathieu, and Pascale Monnin; and the exhibition was curated by Gaël Monnin.

[7] 'There is a country in the world / situated right in the sun's path [...] in an improbable archipelago / of sugar and alcohol'; 'its two scars come from the sugar mill' in Mir, 'Hay un país en el mundo', pp. 63 and 71.

Figure 20. Detail of Francisco (Pancho) Rodríguez, *Que si fuere mil veces* (2012) (photograph: Pancho Rodríguez).

but those he approached were either too afraid or unable to commit for the entire duration of the performance.[8] The graffiti was left on the wall for one day and then, the following day, Rodríguez had it erased: both inscriptions and erasures were captured by a surveillance camera placed in front of the wall. The texts which were inscribed and deleted are all powerful reminders of the fact that Haiti and the Dominican Republic share the same island and history: 'We are siamese twins united by the same land' or 'by the same sun's path,' 'our common history is scarred twice by the sugar mill,' 'united by an improbable history of sugar and alcohol,' and, over and over again, 'the island is one and indivisible.' The question of the island as 'one and indivisible,' as we have seen in Chapter 4, is still a very sensitive one in the Dominican Republic but the uproar caused by Martelly's confused remarks on the unification of the island in 2011 should also be considered in the context of ultra-nationalist propaganda warning against the dangers of an imminent post-earthquake Haitian mass invasion, highlighted in Chapter 10.[9]

---

[8] Personal communication with Pancho Rodríguez, 9 April 2013.
[9] For Martelly's pronouncement and the ensuing debate see Chapter 4.

In Rodríguez's performance the biblical reference which recalls the end of the Babylonian kingdom might initially seem to suggest the imminent 'fall' of the Dominican Republic as a consequence of a Haitian offensive. Rodríguez, however, is instead suggesting that *the island as a whole* might be doomed if the 'writing on the wall' is not decodified correctly (as in the Bible) and change does not take place. The title of the installation *Que si fuere mil veces* suggests the act of doing something over and over again and is a quotation from the national anthem which insists that the Dominican Republic will always be able to free itself no matter how many times (*Que si fuere mil veces*) it will be rendered 'slave' to another power. The national anthem, as mentioned in Chapter 3, refers to the country as 'Quisqueya' and to the Dominicans as 'Quisqueyanos' in line with the discourse of indigenism deployed in the Dominican Republic to deny the African presence on the territory.[10] By resorting to what was then taken to be another indigenous name for the entire island (Quisqueya), the author of the lyrics of the anthem also seems to echo the decision taken by Dessalines in 1804 when he renamed French Saint Domingue using the indigenous word 'Haiti,' as if to erase the colonial presence from the island in a powerful and symbolic way. It is indicative that the two nations of Hispaniola have resorted to two different names (Haiti and Quisqueya) that in fact (or fiction) used to denote the *entire* island in order to define and imagine themselves: both nation-building processes seem to have been shaped by a desire to erase the existence of the other side of the island from the collective imaginary of the people. Paradoxically, however, if the word Quisqueya was the name for the entire island, the 'valiant' Quisqueyanos who are addressed in the national anthem of the Dominican Republic should also comprise the Haitians from whom the anthem actually celebrates independence, as the reference to the patriots Sánchez and Duarte clearly signposts. Furthermore, as much as Haitians *are* Quisqueyanos, Dominicans *are*, in fact, Haitians.

Interestingly, after twenty days the surveillance camera that Rodríguez was using to record his inscriptions and erasures on the wall was actually stolen. This was not programmed, but the remaining days of no recording are now incorporated in the work to signpost, very effectively, a 'stolen' history. As Rodríguez himself writes in the caption to *Que si fuera mil veces*:

> That the Quisqueyanos are Haitians, or that Haiti and not Quisqueya
> was the name of the island is a secret in our history that no secondary

---

[10] Anthem of the Dominican Republic, *National Anthems*, http://www.national-anthems.info/do.htm [accessed on 29 November 2014].

school ever taught me. Our history is a history of blacks and mulattos, of citizens who paint themselves white and with this act deny the truth.

[...]

Since it is desirable to sing Quisqueya a thousand times, as if a thousand times were sufficient to make it true, should we conclude that if the truth is erased a thousand times it becomes less true?[11]

This question is even more poignant if one considers that the coat of arms of the Dominican flag features a bible opened to the Gospel of John, chapter 8, verse 22, which reads 'The truth shall make us free.' In his post-earthquake interventions, therefore, Rodriguez reiterates that for the island to become a home for all its inhabitants it is necessary to lift what Díaz has called 'veils of denial' while reclaiming a 'stolen' history, or, as Klang has put it, 'a shared epic.'

The need for an empowering shared epic is also acknowledged and, arguably, met, in both 'Da pa lo do' ('There is enough for both'), a song by the Dominican singer, artist, and writer Rita Indiana Hernández, and by the video which accompanies the song and was directed by the Dominican artist Engel Leonardo, who also took part in the 2013 exhibition *On Common Ground: Dominican Republic + Haiti*.[12] 'Da pa lo do' is included in *El Juidero*, the first recording that Hernández issued with Los Misterios, a group whose name refers to the saints, beings, or *mysteries* of Dominican Vodú and which is famous for revisiting *merengue* with alternative rock and electronic music.[13] The lyrics contain references to slavery, the Middle Passage, and Dominican *bateyes* but focus on the story of two little brothers who share un *pedasito* (a little piece) of (presumably) bread but, metaphorically, of (is) land. Initially, they fight over it but then they realize that they are brothers

---

[11] Francisco (Pancho) Rodríguez, *Que si fuere mil veces*, in *Veinticuatro – Concurso de Arte Eduardo León Jimenes – Catálogo de Obras* (Santiago de los Caballeros, República Dominicana: Centro León, 2012–13), pp. 116–23, p. 117.

[12] The artists who participated in the exhibition were asked to respond to some questions related to border relations and when he was asked 'What comes to mind when you hear "Dominican Republic/Haiti?",' Leonardo replied, 'There's enough for both.' See Schaaf, 'On Common Ground'.

[13] Rita Indiana Hernández and Los Misterios, 'Da pa lo do', *El Juidero* (2011), compact disc.

and share the across-the-border embrace of the same ancestors, from Juana Méndez to Maimón. Dajabón, the Dominican counterpart of Juana Méndez, is mentioned in the following sentence but the reference to Maimón brings to mind the failed anti-trujillista expedition of Constanza, Maimón, and Estero Hondo, thus emphasizing the island's history of rebellion against oppression.

The positive vibrations which characterize the northern borderland at the end of *Perico Ripiao* inform this post-earthquake video, which is also set in the same semi-arid landscape surrounding Montecristi and Dajabón, underlining, in no uncertain terms, the decisive role that the borderland can play in positing Hispaniola as a place where one could develop a national identity in relation with and not in opposition to one's neighbours. The video relies on a cluster of complex symbols and icons and begins with a majestic tree which divides its surrounding territory in two: the partition of the frame provides a visual counterpart not only to the geopolitical division of the island but, most importantly, to those divisive discourses which posit and promote utter incompatibility between the two countries. The video, however, sabotages one of the most important assumptions on which such irreconcilability is predicated: that is, the suggestion that the African presence in Dominican culture is nonexistent or negligible. The very title of the song, thanks to the Dominican contraction 'Pa Lo' for 'Para los' (literally 'for the'), reminds one of the *palos*, the long drums of African origin used for syncretic rituals and also associated with Liborism.[14] The existence of a shared African heritage in Hispaniola is reinforced by the fact that, moving away from the tree, the camera focuses on two young Afro-Caribbean soldiers, one for each country, wearing ancient uniform jackets, one red and the other blue.[15] They also carry old-fashioned weapons and appear eager to engage in combat on the northern border, a reminder of the many military disputes which have characterized this area over the centuries. The two then arrive on the opposite shores of a river, probably the

---

[14] See *Papá Liborio: el santo vivo de Maguana* (*Papa Liborio: the living saint of Maguana*), (dir. Martha Ellen Davis, 2003), Contents in English – Study Guide, http://ufdcimages.uflib.ufl.edu/UF/00/08/74/00/00004/Liborio_contents_summary-Engl.pdf [accessed 25 November 2014]. For Liborio see also Chapter 6 and 8. Some scholars and musicologists have repeatedly suggested that *palo* music should be adopted as Dominican national music (Fradique Lizardo quoted in Austerlitz, *Merengue*, p. 109) and in 2008, just before Hernández's song was released, the *palo* music of the Afro-Caribbean Cofradía del Espíritu Santo de lo Congos ('Brotherhood of the Holy Spirit of the Congos') of Villa Mella was declared by the UNESCO a masterpiece of the intangible cultural heritage or 'living heritage' of humanity.
[15] Meaningfully, *both* colours feature in *both* national flags, so the two uniforms signify the two soldiers' differences but also their similarities.

River Massacre or one of its tributaries: the two men then strip themselves to the waist, effectively disrobing themselves of the mutual hostility signified by their uniforms. At the same time, through a series of cuts, we see Hernández travelling on a *motoconcho* wearing what, from a distance, looks like a Virgin Mary's costume.

As we have seen in Chapters 2 and 10, the Virgin Mary is an important figure both in the Dominican Republic and in Haiti. When the camera zooms in on her, the light-skinned Dominican Hernández appears to have a blackened face, reminding us of the dark-skinned Haitian *lwa* Ezili Danto, the incarnation of Ezili Freda as mother who has Metresilí as a counterpart in the pantheon of Dominican Vodú.[16] Hernández/Virgin Mary/Ezili Danto/ Metresilí also wears the *vévé* of the Sacred Twins or Marassá around her neck, which, while highlighting the filial nature of the relationship which links the island (mother) to the two countries which share it (her soldier sons), concomitantly signposts the existence of a strong kinship between the two sides of the island. The disavowal of this twinship/kinship – which, as Danticat has pointed out in *The Farming of Bones*, can have dire consequences – often occurs on the very race and colour grounds that Hernández's blackened face implicitly critiques and disables by identifying both race and colour with performance. This crucial move problematizes racial identifications and self-identifications, questions the viability of race and/or colour as markers of stable identities or nationality, and implicitly explodes the attribution of any particular status to either of them.

As we discern more and more clearly the image of Hernández/Virgin Mary/Ezili Danto/Metresilí reflected in the river, the two soldiers '(re)baptize' themselves in its waters, acquiring a different identity no longer predicated on hatred: with this ceremony of purification the River Massacre itself becomes a symbol of transnational solidarity and fraternity rather than a site disfigured by conflict and anti-Hatianism. At this point the two young men, who are both bare-chested and with identical white trousers, finally drop their weapons and embrace each other by the tree which appeared at the beginning of the video while the refrain *es que somos hermanos* 'we are brothers' is repeated five times. Hernández/Virgin Mary/Ezili Danto/ Metresilí materializes in front of the tree accompanied by six children dressed in white, three on each side: they all dance to the same music, prefiguring a more peaceful future where each nation 'imagines' itself as part of the island as a whole and moves following a shared, overarching rhythm. The fact that there are three children on each side brings about a Trinitarian logic which counteracts the potential negativity of doubling intrinsic in the

---

[16] Davis, '*Vodú* of the Dominican Republic', p. 83.

figure of twins. The *vévé* of the Marassa wore by Hernández, shaped roughly as a 'M,' introduces a third element in the middle of the two 'twins' which reminds us of the triad formed by the two soldiers and the tree in their midst. The song ends with Hernández/Virgin Mary/Ezili Danto/Metresilí dancing alone and superimposed on the tree so that they almost become one: her presence and the music which engulfs the semi-arid northern borderland transforms the region into a syncretic place of communion and unity which, as was the case at the end of Veloz Maggiolo's *El hombre del acordeón* or *Perico Ripiao*, can bring about an alternative to hostility, violence, divisiveness, exploitation, and prevarication.

The tree with which the video began also undergoes a process of resignification similar to the borderland's; it becomes a symbol of the island's Afro-Caribbean heritage and of Hispaniola's own 'shared epic' of resistance, two components of the national make-up which, Hernández insists, have to be fully acknowledged in order to move Hispaniola further. After his capture in 1802, and less than a year after becoming governor-general of the entire island, Toussaint Louverture had warned his enemies that the 'tree of the liberty of the blacks' they thought they were uprooting would instead grow back because its roots were 'deep and numerous.'[17] The tree in the video pays homage to Toussaint but also reminds us that, on Hispaniola, its 'roots' predate not only the 1791 revolt but also the 1777 partitioning of the island, and go back as far as the beginning of the sixteenth century, when the first slaves taken by the Spanish ran away from their masters.[18] In addition, Toussaint's tree 'branches' influenced the creation not only of the Haitian state in 1804 but also of the Dominican state in 1844, when the immediate and definitive abolition of slavery was promulgated with a series of decrees which also stated that, upon setting foot on Dominican soil, slaves coming from abroad would become automatically free. Hernández's and Toussaint's tree, therefore, evokes what Torres Saillant has called the 'good story' of Dominican blackness, which reveals to us a 'Santo Domingo setting the pattern of the struggle for freedom and racial equality in the Americas.'[19] Hernández and Engel Leonardo's video encapsulates this 'good' but seldom foregrounded 'story' and revisits it alongside the more widely circulated 'bad story' of anti-Haitianism and negrophobia. 'Da Pa Lo Do,' however, goes even further as Hernández makes it very clear that this 'good story' can be claimed and celebrated by *all* inhabitants of Hispaniola, regardless of their

---

[17]   Dubois, *Avengers of the New World*, p. 278.

[18]   Carlos Andujar, *The African Presence in Santo Domingo*, trans. Rosa Maria Andujar (East Lansing, MI: Michigan State University, 2012), p. 39–40.

[19]   Torres Saillant, 'Blackness and Meaning in Studying Hispaniola', p. 182.

Figure 21. Rita Indiana Hernández and Los Misterios, 'Da pa lo do' (2010), video directed by Engel Leonardo and set in the province of Montecristi.

somatic traits, colour, or nationality: importantly, Toussaint was neither Dominican nor Haitian.[20]

✳✳✳

The Haitian artist Jean Philippe Moiseau also firmly believes in claiming the entire island and not just one of its nations as his homeland. Born in Haiti in 1962, he moved to the Dominican Republic in 1994 and now lives in Santo Domingo. To promote his work Moiseau resorts to the visual rhetoric of national flags, not with the customary purpose of dividing and distinguishing but with the aim of emphasizing similarities and continuities between the two sides of the island. Moiseau's logo, in fact, reminds us that Haiti and the Dominican Republic utilize the same colours in their flags and, incidentally, also display similar symbols in their coats of arms – namely, a royal palm in the Haitian flag and a palm frond in the Dominican one.

The similarities between the two flags are not without an explanation. The Dominican flag was designed by Sánchez, Duarte, and Mella, the patriots who engineered Dominican independence from Haiti in 1844, but Moiseau's insistence on the continuities between the two flags foregrounds collaboration rather than fatal enmity between the two countries. His logo reminds us that the period of unification with Haiti, so often identified as one of the founding moments of the Haitian–Dominican conflict, derived

---

[20] Blas Jiménez also insists on this in *Africano por elección, negro por nacimiento*, p. 24.

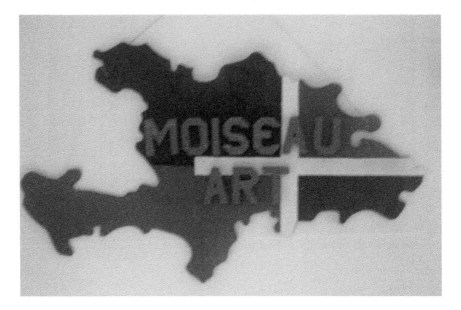

Figure 22. Jean Philippe Moiseau, *Logo* (photograph: Jean Philippe Moiseau).

in fact from a Dominican attempt to preserve freedom for colonial rule
and that the Dominican war of liberation can also be seen as a moment in
which Dominicans and Haitians collaborated, at least to an extent, in order
to overthrow unpopular dictators.

On 15 November 1821 the border cities of Montecristi and Dajabón
proclaimed their independence from Spanish rule and their leaders asked
the commander of Cap-Haïtien for the protection of Haitian laws and for
weapons and ammunition with which to defend themselves. This fact pushed
the Dominican Independentist leader Núñez de Cáceres to proclaim the
creation of the *Estado Independiente de Haití Español* on 1 December. The
Estado Independiente de Haití Español, however, did not have the support
of the pro-Spain elites and the majority of the population, which was
mulatto, was favourably disposed to the unification with Haiti (especially in
Dajabón, Montecristi, Santiago, Puerto Plata, Cotuí, La Vega, San Francisco
de Macorís, Azua, San Juan de la Maguana, and Neyba). Núñez de Cáceres,
therefore, invited Boyer, albeit reluctantly, to annex Santo Domingo to
defend it from an attack by colonial powers.[21] No blood was shed and no
opposition was met when Boyer, backed by his troops, was welcomed in

---

[21] Moya Pons, *La dominación haitiana, 1822–1844* (Santo Domingo: Librería La
Trinitaria, 2013), pp. 26–33.

Santo Domingo: actually, some accounts indicate that he was received with enthusiasm by Dominicans.[22]

As Toussaint had done in 1801 (see Chapter 4), Boyer immediately abolished slavery in Spanish Santo Domingo, gaining the support of the blacks and mulattoes. However, when Boyer took over all Dominican public properties and ecclesiastical holdings he inevitably gained enemies among the clergy and the oligarchy who, effectively, 'owned' some of those properties. His land reforms, moreover, became deeply unpopular on *both* sides of the island because they were aimed at compelling agricultural workers to work on plantations in condition not too dissimilar from slavery. To make things worse, Boyer also restricted free movement: land labourers, for example, were tied to the plantation and not allowed to freely circulate. Widespread discontent in unified Haiti increased when the high taxes imposed by Boyer, partly to finance the sizable indemnity that he had agreed to pay to France in 1825 to allow Haiti access to global trade, were made unbearable by an economic downturn. In 1843, Boyer was obliged to resign by the Haitian anti-Boyer movement, which worked together with those Dominicans who were also conspiring against the president.[23] Boyer's successor, Rivière Hérard, committed the same tyrannical acts against the people which had caused Boyer's deposition and, as a consequence, he too became extremely unpopular. On February 1844 the Dominican patriots Duarte, Sánchez, and Mella declared their independence from Rivière's Haiti. A few months later, in May, the Haitians got rid of Rivière, who was replaced with a new president.[24]

The two countries also worked together again in order to emancipate the entire island from colonial rule when the Dominican Republic was reannexed by Spain as a colony in 1861: Dominican patriots, in fact, turned for assistance to the Haitians and Haitian *rayanos* united with Dominican insurgents to fight the colonial power. Haiti, moreover, gave both sanctuary and weapons to the insurgents who, in 1865, permanently declared their independence from Spain.[25] In other words, Moiseau's vexillology counteracts those nationalistic and xenophobic discourses which are responsible for many erasures, occlusions, and mystifications in the history of the island and

---

[22] Moya Pons, *La otra historia*, pp. 276–8; Rayford Logan, *Haiti and the Dominican Republic* (New York: Oxford University Press, 1968), p. 32.
[23] Moya Pons, *La dominación haitiana*, pp. 35–107; Dantes Bellegarde, *Histoire du peuple Haïtien, 1492–1952* (Port-au-Prince, 1953), pp. 137–9.
[24] Moya Pons, *La dominación haitiana*, pp. 109–27; Bellegarde, *Histoire du peuple Haïtien*, pp. 144–5.
[25] Moya Pons, *The Dominican Republic*, pp. 210–18; Matibag, *Haitian-Dominican Counterpoint*, pp. 123–4.

which are instrumental in the erection of divisive barriers which prevent a more sustained dialogue between the two peoples. Moiseau's concern with a mystified and erased history is also consistent with his practice of creative recycling and his choice of materials which is informed by a determination to make permanent what would otherwise be lost. In particular, in the works in which he deals specifically with the island as a whole he often incorporates newspaper cuttings from the Dominican and Haitian press where the juxtaposition of languages creates a visual counterpart of the heterogeneous world of the borderland celebrated by Rueda, Philoctète, Veloz Maggiolo, Danticat, Alexis, and Ramírez. Many of these works are masks made with palm leaves (a symbol which, as we have seen, appears on both the Haitian and the Dominican coats of arms), which he treats in a special way in order to harden them and preserve them in time. The first palm mask ever prepared by Moiseau has the island of Hispaniola as its core.

In *Palm Mask* (2009) the colours blue, red, and white once again remind one of the two flags. The articles included by Moiseau deal with events which, at the time of production, had just affected the two countries. For instances, there are cuttings from articles on Hurricane Ike and on the Dominican narcotrafficker Ernesto Quirino. The reference to Hurricane Ike underlines Hispaniola's vulnerability to natural disasters.[26] Ike was the last of four hurricanes in 2008 which caused floods, widespread destruction, a large number of wounded and evacuees, and many deaths – 800 in Haiti and ten in the Dominican Republic. This disproportion in the numbers of deaths can be only partly explained by variations in the intensity and/or direction of hurricanes and tropical storms: as mentioned in Chapter 10, the ongoing deforestation of Haiti and its centralization of resources put the Haitian poor on the front line of exposure to what it is no longer possible to simply call 'natural' disasters.[27] Clearly, to counter environmental degradation and loss of biodiversity which turn natural disasters into unnatural ones, Haiti and the Dominican Republic should collaborate more and act in a coordinated way. Some promising steps have been taken, especially since the 2011 earthquake,[28] but when the mask was made there was still very little

---

[26] 'Le Group Villedrouin aide des Archelois sinistrés', *Le Nouvelliste*, 14 October 2008, http://lenouvelliste.com/lenouvelliste/article/63186/Le-Groupe-Villedrouin-aide-des-Archelois-sinistres [accessed 1 November 2013].

[27] Rory Carroll, 'We are going to disappear one day', *The Guardian*, 8 November 2008, http://www.theguardian.com/world/2008/nov/08/haiti-hurricanes [accessed 29 November 2014].

[28] See, for example, the *Estudios e iniciativas piloto para promover la sostenibilidad ambiental en República Dominicana y en Haití*, http://www.pilotinitiativesquisqueya.org/index.html [accessed 29 November 2014]. See also Bridget Wooding and Marcos

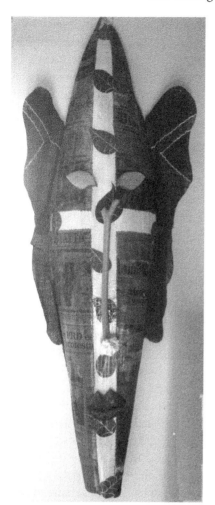

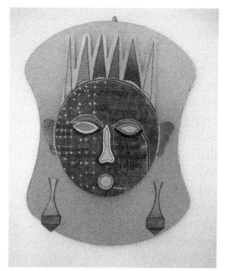

Figure 23. *left* Jean Philippe Moiseau, *Palm Mask* (2009) (photograph: Maria Cristina Fumagalli).

Figure 24. *above* Jean Philippe Moiseau, *Metal Mask* (2011) (photograph: Maria Cristina Fumagalli).

coordination between the two countries as far as environmental policies are concerned. Across-the-border 'coordination,' however, was not missing in Quirino's criminal network. Quirino, a.k.a. 'El Don,' is an ex-captain of the army of the Dominican Republic who became the boss of a drug-trafficking organization responsible for importing tons of cocaine into the United States between 1997 and 2003. The organization used a variety of routes to send

Morales, *Migración y medio ambiente: una reflexión pertinente – Migration Policy Brief* (Santo Domingo: Editora Búho, 2014) and *Migración y sostenibilidad ambiental en Hispaniola* (Santo Domingo: Editora Búho, 2014) and Rodríguez Grullón, *Estado del arte*, pp. 94–8.

the cocaine from the Dominican Republic and/or Haiti towards Puerto Rico and to the United States, and the borderland was crucial to these criminal activities. Quirino, who had strong connections with the highest levels of the Dominican military and political parties, financed the construction of an airport of the Dominican Airforce close to his residence in Elías Piña, which was routinely used for his criminal import–export activities owing to its strategic proximity to Haiti. Quirino's 'career' benefited from widespread corruption and from the fact that the border between Haiti and the Dominican Republic can easily become porous in the name of profit, legal or, as in this case, illegal.[29]

In *Metal Mask* (2011), which is also covered in Haitian and Dominican newspapers, Moiseau used as the centre piece an article focused on the reconstruction of Haiti published six months after the earthquake. Aptly, this mask is shaped as a post and lintel structure. The lintel or architrave is characterized by the word *reconstrucción* (reconstruction) right in the middle; one can also discern 'Préval' (then president of Haiti) on what we could call the 'Haitian side' of the mask, and *difícil* ('difficult') on the 'Dominican side.'[30] Significantly, the basis of the pillar on the Haitian side is a 2007 article published in *Le Nouvelliste* detailing a response to Dr Michael Worobey's (in)famous assertion that Haiti was the springboard for the spread of HIV in the United States and which reveals how the scientist's findings were distorted by a preconceived, negative image of Haiti.[31] On the other side, the Dominican side, *Hoy* reports the views of Pelegrin Castillo (*Fuerza Nacional Progresista*) on the role that the Dominican Republic should play (or not play) in Haiti's reconstruction. In particular, it highlights Castillo's fears that the Dominican Republic found itself in 'an extremely dangerous situation which could compromise, once and for all, its territorial integrity, economic development and the national identity of its people': a distressingly well-known refrain.[32]

As far as post-earthquake border-coordination is concerned, it is worth

---

[29] Vinicio A. Castillo Semán, 'Respuesta al presidente del PRD', *Listin Diario*, 12 January 2009, http://www.listindiario.com/puntos-de-vista/2009/1/12/87444/Respuesta-al-presidente-del-PRD [accessed 29 November 2014].

[30] 'Préval: reconstrucción difícil', *Hoy*, 13 July 2010, http://hoy.com.do/preval-reconstruccion-dificil/ [accessed 25 November 2014].

[31] Jean Marie Romain, 'Haïti à l'heure des grands débats', Le Nouvelliste, 27 November 2007, http://lenouvelliste.com/lenouvelliste/article/50913/Haiti-a-lheure-des-grands-debats.html [accessed 25 November 2014].

[32] 'Postura de Leonel Fernández hacia Haití es perjudicial para el país', *Hoy*, 22 August 2010, http://hoy.com.do/postura-de-lf-hacia-haiti-es-perjudicial-para-el-pais/ [accessed 25 November 2014].

remembering that when, during his election campaign in 2011, Martelly appeared to support the idea of political unification of the island and said that 'his dream' was to eliminate the frontier between the two countries (see Chapter 4), he mainly insisted on the necessity of intensifying 'commercial exchange.'[33] Arguably, he had something precise in mind. The Dominican journalist Nuria Piera has reported that, over the course of 2011, Martelly, as a candidate, president-elect, and president of Haiti, received close to $2.6 million from the Dominican Senator Félix Bautista. The alleged bribes were connected to securing three post-earthquake multi-million public works contracts dubiously won by Dominican construction companies controlled by Bautista.[34] Interestingly, therefore, while the Dominican Republic was sealing itself off from Haiti, stepping up military patrols on the border (allegedly) in a bid to stem the cholera epidemic, and increasing the number of collective repatriations of Haitians and Haitian–Dominicans (in 2011 they were five times higher than on 2009[35]), the frontier with Haiti was once again kept wide open for illegal and lucrative business. Overall, Moiseau's message is therefore very clear: an architrave can stand only if the two pillars on which it rests are solid. Similarly, 'reconstruction' can happen only if the negative ways in which Haiti is perceived in the Dominican Republic (and the world at large) are altered for good and if Haiti and the Dominican Republic make a concerted effort to develop healthier, mutually advantageous, and corruption-free border relations. A very difficult balance (the word *difícil* actually appears on the piece) but, the mask insists, not an unachievable one – its vibrant colours are there to remind us that Moiseau believes that Hispaniola, as a whole, has the power to bounce back.

Newspaper articles are also included in a post-earthquake painting by Moiseau entitled *Les rêves du cireur de bottes/Los sueños del limpia botas/ Yon chanj kap reve*. Here they contribute to shaping the different narratives which the painting displays and simultaneously foster further meditations on the permeability or impermeability of the border. A shoe-shiner appears, surrounded by his dreams (a car, a woman, a satellite dish). At bottom right we can see the *vévé* of Twins or Marassa which, as in the 'Da pa lo do' video and in Danticat's *The Farming of Bones*, invites us to see the two sides

---

[33] See 'Haitian President Michel Martelly wants to unify Haiti and Dominican Republic', Martelly interviewed by Nuria Piera.

[34] 'Nuria Revela que Félix Bautista y amigos regalaron millions de dólares a Martelly', *Acento*, April 2012, http://www.acento.com.do/index.php/news/14740/56/Nuria-revela-que-Felix-Bautista-y-amigos-regalaron-millones-de-dolares-a-Martelly.html [accessed 25 November 2014].

[35] Riveros, *Informe*, p. 30.

Figure 25.
Jean Philippe
Moiseau, *Les
rêves du cireur
de bottes/Los
sueños del limpia
botas/Yon chanj
kap reve* (2012)
(photograph:
Maria Cristina
Fumagalli).

of Hispaniola as if they were twins. This (and the fact that the title of the
painting is in the three languages spoken on Hispaniola) brings to the fore
the existence of common problems across the island, namely the extreme
poverty in which some of its people live – as we have seen in Chapter 9,
despite the fact that in the Dominican Republic life is generally 'easier' than
in Haiti nearly a third of Dominicans still live in poverty. In Haitian Vodou,
the *vévé* of the Marassa also represents children's sacredness and, arguably,
the painting addresses the serious issue of child labour. It is very easy to
spot very young *limpia botas* in the parks and main thoroughfares of the
Dominican Republic and, although shoe-shining is not the most common
form of child labour, shoe-shiners can also be found in Haiti, especially in
urban centres.

On another level, however, the 'little' shoe-shiner in Moiseau's painting
seems to stand for Haiti itself: the words '*sire soulye ou*' next to '*kiwi*' (a
brand of shoe polish) are in Creole and mean 'clean or shine your shoes.'
Provocatively, Haiti is represented here as the ultimate infantilized and

powerless subaltern. In point of fact, when it is not demonized as a cursed land of Vodou and savagism, or pathologized as a diseased and contaminating place, Haiti is often patronized as a country too 'immature' to govern and administer itself and in constant need of 'tutelage.' Paternalist discourse is one of the primary cultural mechanisms which have sustained and still sustain the meddling of foreign powers in Haiti – from the US occupation of Haiti (1915–34[36]) to the removal of the democratically elected President Aristide (twice) and the deployment on its territory of MINUSTHA, a presence that, as Pancrazi points out in *Montecristi*, many Haitians have long regarded as a military occupation. Interestingly, the newspaper articles that Moiseau has included towards the top of the painting refer to different types of 'tutelage': military, spiritual, political, and 'humanitarian'. More precisely, the first article refers to Martelly's problematic promise to reinstate the Haitian army dissolved in 1995 by Aristide because it had primarily been used against the Haitian people – a promise that, as the article dated May 2012 explains, ex-members of the army are determined to make him keep.[37]

The second newspaper cutting reports on Martelly's visit to Pope Benedict XVI in November 2012 – one of his many public 'affiliations' to different religions and fraternities, such as Protestantism, Catholicism, Vodou, and freemasonry to which the Haitian president has, directly or indirectly, entrusted the future of Haiti. Most importantly, the intermission of Jesus, the Virgin Mary, or other forms of supernatural interventions are invoked by Martelly while, under his presidency or 'tutelage,' nepotism, corruption, authoritarianism, kidnapping, and murders have increased, and it is becoming more and more evident that those responsible for law enforcement are the first ones who do not respect the law and can act with impunity.[38]

---

[36] Mary Renda, *Taking Haiti: Military Occupation and the Culture of US Imperialism, 1915–1940* (Chapel Hill, NC: The University of North Carolina Press, 2001), especially pp. 89–130.

[37] 'Exsoldados Haití insisten Martelly reinstale ejército', *Hoy*, 14 May 2012, http://hoy.com.do/exsoldados-haiti-insisten-martelly-reinstale-ejercito/ [accessed 29 November 2014].

[38] 'El Papa recibe a Martelly', *Hoy*, 23 November 2012, http://hoy.com.do/el-papa-recibe-a-martelly/ [accessed 29 November 2014]; Roberson Alphonse, 'Martelly mixe les religions', *Le Nouvelliste*, 23 novembre 2012, http://lenouvelliste.com/lenouvelliste/article/111070/Martelly-mixe-les-religions.html [accessed 29 November 2014] and 'A better class of dictator? Rebelling against the lies and illegalities', *Haiti Support Group – Haiti Briefing* 73, February 2013, http://www.haitisupportgroup.org/index.php?option=com_content&view=article&id=722:a-better-class-of-dictator-rebelling-against-the-lies-and-illegalities&catid=99:analysis&Itemid=256 [accessed 29 November 2014].

The third article focuses again on natural disasters and on the humanitarian aid promised to Haiti after Hurricane Sandy, in particular that offered by the Food and Agriculture Organization (FAO) of the United Nations. While the assistance of FAO and of other NGOs is welcome in principle, the article highlights how important questions have been asked (and continue to be asked) about the sustainability and the effectiveness of such help, especially after the 2010 earthquake, which has revealed how, in many cases, international humanitarian aid can make things worse rather than improving them.[39] Overall, in fact, the role and tutelage of the many NGOs, and of the United Nations itself, in Haiti is becoming increasingly controversial, in particular after the United Nations announced that Haitian claims for compensation for the cholera epidemic, which many believe was introduced by MINUSTAH troops, were not 'receivable' because of the United Nations' diplomatic immunity.[40]

The fourth article included by Moiseau suggests a different way to approach the shoe-shiner, namely as a Haitian or Haitian–Dominican working in the Dominican Republic. In the border region, for example, on market day, many Haitian shoe-shiners cross the border into the Dominican Republic to offer their services there. In the short film *I do not think we are equal* (2012), the Haitian director Dominique Telemaque has pointed out that the predicament of (especially undocumented) Haitian and Haitian–Dominican shoe-shiners in the Dominican Republic is often worse than that of their Dominican counterparts: while the money made by the Dominican shoe-shiner he features in his film will go towards paying for his education, the Haitian boy is seen giving all his money to an unidentified exploiter and it is made abundantly clear that he will never attend school.[41] The fouth article chosen by Moiseau, however, brings to the fore a different scenario, dealing,

[39] 'FAO ofrece a presidente de Haití ayuda "sostenible" para el desarrollo', *Hoy*, 22 November 2012, http://hoy.com.do/fao-ofrece-a-presidente-de-haiti-ayuda-sostenible-para-el-desarrollo/ [accessed 29 November 2014]. For an analysis of the (lack of) effectiveness of international humanitarian help in post-earthquake Haiti see, for example, Jonathan Katz, *The Big Truck That Went By: How the World Came to Save Haiti and Left Behind a Disaster* (London: Palgrave Macmillan, 2013) and the documentary *Haiti, Where Did the Money Go?* (dir. Michele Mitchell, 2012).
[40] 'UN rejects Haiti cholera compensation claims', BBC News, 21 February 2013, http://www.bbc.co.uk/news/world-latin-america-21542842 [accessed 25 November 2014].
[41] *I don't think that we are equal*, (dir. Dominique Telemaque, 2012), http://www.youtube.com/watch?v=QtIwtuvj-T4 [accessed 29 November 2014]. For the relationship between statelessness and education see also *Left Behind: How Statelessness in the Dominican Republic Limits Children's Access to Education* (Washington, DC: Georgetown Law Human Rights Institute, 2014).

Figure 26. Haitian shoe-shiner crossing the border from Ouanaminthe to Dajabón on a market day.

as it does, with the predicament of twenty-five Dominicans of Haitian origin who, in November 2012, were appealing against the decision of the civil authorities to deny them their identity cards and electoral certificates despite the fact that they are in possession of all the documents required by the law. This article emphasizes the reclaimed agency of these young people, who refused to be discriminated against, and supports a reading that counteracts both 'tutelage' and 'subalterneity.'[42] I will go back to the notion of denied citizenship and denationalization in my conclusion; here, however, it is important to highlight how the inclusion of this fourth article emphasizes the brave battles that some Haitians and Haitian–Dominicans fight in the Dominican Republic to defend their rights and suggests that across-the-border allegiances and coordination of a different kind from those forged by Quirino can be key to bringing social justice to Hispaniola as a whole.

---

[42] Iván Santana, 'Presentan recurso de amparo', *Hoy*, 14 May 2012, http://hoy.com.do/presentan-recurso-de-amparo/ 2012 [accessed 25 November 2014].

✶✶✶

David Pérez Karmadavis, born in 1976 in Santo Domingo and author of
Línea Fronteriza Intermitente, the work on the cover of this monograph,
is another artist who has always shown a deep interest in border relations:
many of his major works deal, directly or indirectly, with the predicament
of Haitian migrants in the Dominican Republic and, more broadly, with
border politics in Hispaniola. This concern did not diminish when the artist
moved to Guatemala in 2006: as we will see, among his latest works are
vigorous and sharp commentaries on the post-earthquake situation as he
sees it. Karmadavis is a talented painter and illustrator but the works under
scrutiny here are a poem and six *acciónes performaticas*, or performances
which are captured in photographs or videos in order to be shared with a
broader audience. In 2010, when the Dominican Republic was being praised
by, among others, the Governor General of Canada, Michaëlle Jean, who is
of Haitian descent, and the actress Angelina Jolie, Goodwill Ambassador
for the United Nations High Commission for Refugees (UNHCR), for the
way in which it generously helped his neighbour in need in the aftermath
of the earthquake of 12 January, Karmadavis wrote a sharp and insightful
poem entitled *Isla cerrada* ('Closed island'), where he argued that, despite
the massive post-earthquake media coverage, Haiti was still invisible to
certain sectors of Dominican society.[43]

Isla cerrada begins by focusing on Hispaniola as a geographic, organic
whole and as a political entity: he presents it as a *cuerpo* (a single body)
divided into two nations which are united by a common native soil and
separated by a frontier; he also adds that both governments of these nations
profiteer from them. The two countries share a long history – the selectively
remembered past of nationalistic narratives and the lived past of contradictory
contingencies. Haiti, Karmadavis continues, rehearsing much of what is
frequently said about it, is seen as a *periferia* (periphery), a country plagued
by racism and a tragic history of dictatorship, and a wounded and looted
region with a terrible need for help to overcome the poverty in which the
majority of its people live. However, he adds, Haiti shares these characteristics
and needs (Karmadavis uses the Spanish verb *compartir* here) with *el otro
extremo* (the other side) of the island, thus highlighting poverty, political
abuse, and instability in his native country. Karmadavis's views are in direct
opposition to those held and promoted by the Dominican oligarchy, which

[43] Karmadavis, *Isla cerrada* (2010), http://hemisphericinstitute.org/hemi/
en/e-misferica-71/karmadavis [accessed 25 November 2014].

wants the nation to perceive itself and to be perceived as the centre and *motor* (engine) of the island and not as a country with problems. Karmadavis also brings to the fore his country's vulnerability when he highlights how both its present and its future depend on foreign investments and the tourist industry. The Dominican Republic, Karmadavis adds, is also a country with a strong addiction to a deep-rooted nationalism that sees the other side of the island with doubt, fear, and resentment. He concludes his poem by saying, controversially, that 'From Haiti the Dominican Republic is seen as a *solución* (solution) while, from the Dominican Republic, Haiti is seen as '*un problema ... o simplemente, no se ve*' (as a problem ... or, simply, is not seen at all.)

Haiti is not 'visible' from the Dominican Republic because of distorting screens which have been in place for a long time; these have always depicted Haiti as a nation with which the Dominican Republic has nothing in common and vehemently dismissed the presence and contribution of Haitian culture in the Dominican national make-up. The people of Haiti, as we have seen in the previous chapters, are cast as half-civilized and hopeless victims of poverty, 'superstition,' corrupt local politicians, endemic violence, and, more recently, (un)natural disasters and tragic epidemics; their only dream (allegedly) is to flee to the Dominican Republic to escape their miserable condition. At the same time, the fact that the Dominican economy heavily depends on the work of Haitian migrants (legal and illegal) is a reality that many members of the elite, often those involved in the exploitation of Haitian migrants, are not prepared to acknowledge and give 'visibility' to. It is evident, therefore, that seeing Haiti for what it really is also implies seeing the Dominican Republic for what it really is: as Karmadavis insists, they share a long history and one cannot talk about one *sin mencionar* (without mentioning) the other. Border relations in post-earthquake Hispaniola, according to Karmadavis, are still hampered by vested interests and false conceptions, perceptions, and self-perceptions which have to be urgently challenged and profoundly altered, a point made, in different ways, by many texts examined here.

Significantly, on the site of *e-misférica*, the flagship online publication of the Hemispheric Institute of Performance and Politics, where *Isla cerrada* was published in *Seeing Haiti*, a dossier included in a special issue of the journal, the poem is accompanied by two photos of Karmadavis's arms receiving an intravenous cannulation for a 2006 *acción performatica* entitled *Isla abierta*. *Isla abierta* also aimed to raise awareness of the fact that, despite constant attempts to disavow reality, the Dominican Republic is part of the island of Hispaniola, an entity greater than the nation.[44] For *Isla abierta*

[44] Karmadavis, *Isla abierta* (2006), http://performancelogia.blogspot.co.uk/2007/08/david-prez-isla-abierta.html [accessed 25 November 2014].

Figure 27. David Pérez Karmadavis, *Isla abierta* (2006), Calle El Conde, Zona Colonial, Santo Domingo (photograph: Karmadavis).

Karmadavis performed an intravenous cannulation in both his arms, left the catheters open and walked along one of the main thoroughfares in Santo Domingo shedding his blood in order to (literally) embody the principle that Hispaniola's two separate 'arms' (Haiti and the Dominican Republic) belong in fact to the same body and are sustained by the same blood. Blood, it is worth remembering here, was crucial for colonial taxonomists of colour such as Saint-Méry who, in the eighteenth century, 'recorded' 128 parts of blood which, according to various combinations, produced different nuances of colour and other physical characteristics among the population.[45] Purity of blood, as we have seen in Chapter 1, was also what the French and Spanish creoles of Hispaniola accused one another of lacking.[46] Karmadavis here powerfully explodes Saint-Méry's elaborate system of gradation and erases all (fictitious) distinctions based on blood (and by extension, colour) which have traditionally been used to differentiate the people of Hispaniola: the same blood, he insists, sustains both countries and both peoples.

---

[45] PF, vol. I, pp. 70–99.
[46] PE, vol. I, p. 59. See also Sánchez Valverde, pp. 245–6.

The location Karmadavis chose for his performance is crucial. Situated at the heart of the colonial city, El Conde is a pedestrian road which connects Parque Colón (Columbus Park) and the Cathedral of Santa María la Menor, the oldest of the Americas, with the Puerta del Conde, one of the old city gates which is dedicated to Don Bernardino de Meneses y Brancamonte, count of Peñalba, who, in 1665, saved the city from an attempted English invasion. The Puerta del Conde was the scene of the proclamation of Dominican Independence from Haitian rule on 27 February 1844 and the place where the Dominican flag flew for the first time. The remains of Sánchez, Duarte, and Mella, the founders of the Republic and the so-called Fathers of the Nation, are sheltered in the *Altar de la patria* (Altar of the Fatherland), which is located a few steps away from the Puerta del Conde in what is now called Parque Independencia (Independence Park). At the other end of the Conde, next to Columbus Park, one also finds a bust of Bartholomew Columbus, founder of Santo Domingo, which was dedicated to him by the governor of the Indies, Nicolás de Ovando, in 1502. Significantly, for a short time after 1844 El Conde was rechristened Avenida de la Separación ('Separation Street') to celebrate the separation of the Dominican Republic from Haiti.[47] Walking from Columbus Park and the cathedral to Independence Park, therefore, amounts to a walk through the history of the Dominican Republic, where one's stepping stones are a set of icons that has been deployed to forge a Hispanophilic and anti-Haitian notion of Dominicanidad and to encourage the Dominican people's identification with the colonial masters. While the cathedral clearly stands for Catholicism, Columbus Park signposts the Hispanic heritage. It also gestures, to a lesser extent, towards the 'Indian' heritage: Anacaona is represented in the statue dedicated to Columbus which is found at the heart of the park. Anacaona, however, does not share the Admiral's pedestal but is positioned on the side of the column on which he stands; she is much smaller than him (roughly half his size) and cast in a submissive posture, climbing and longing to touch him but unable to reach even his feet. Karmadavis's decision to walk and bleed around both these monuments and their rhetorical function in order to foreground the notion of an 'open island' and to promote a multicultural, holistic, and island-based perspective which is neither tainted by anti-Haitianism nor predicated on the sealing of the frontier was, clearly, a particularly provocative act.

Karmadavis's walk along the Conde also highlights other contradictory

---

[47] Information displayed in January 2013 on a public information board situated on the Conde and prepared by the Santo Domingo City Council and the Santo Domingo Tourist Board.

dynamics which characterize the island as simultaneously closed and open. The Conde lies at the heart of the commercial and tourist district of Santo Domingo and, in Figure 27, one can see in the background a seller of souvenirs with the recurrent theme of the Dominican flag. Flags, souvenirs, and markets of typical products all concur to make the tourists feel that they have entered a specific nation whose difference from the rest of the world is encapsulated in this commodified iconography. Everywhere in the *Zona Colonial* one is surrounded by all sorts of maps of the Dominican Republic (which, unsurprisingly, fail to acknowledge the existence of another side to the island) and the Conde is full to the brim with Dominican artefacts on sale to tourists. In 2009 I purchased a painting with a very colourful depiction of a country village. Like many of the other paintings on offer among Dominican souvenirs, it actually looks 'Haitian' and an internet search of the artist's name does indeed confirm that the person who painted it is a *Haitian* whose works are categorized as *Haitian* naïf paintings. Of course I cannot establish if the one in my possession is an original or a counterfeit, nor if the artist is in fact a Dominican pretending to be a Haitian to take advantage of the popularity and marketability of Haitian art … but this is beside the point. What matters here is the deep irony behind all this. The sale of Haitian products next to Dominican flags signposts – rather unequivocally – that the two countries do share the same island. Yet, the fact that *Haitian* products are made to pass (at least tacitly) for *Dominican* souvenirs on the Conde as well as in other areas catering for tourists, such as the *Mercado Modelo*, which is only a few yards away – in an area known as *Petit Haití* or Little Haiti owing to the high number of Haitian migrants who live there – reminds one of ultra-nationalist discourses that disavow the many contributions of Haitian culture in the Dominican Republic and want to keep the border as sealed as possible.

In the photograph which documents the intravenous cannulation for *Isla abierta*, one can discern a tattoo on Karmadavis's arm. Karmadavis received this tattoo in 2005 as part of another performance entitled *Lo que dice la piel* ('What the skin says'), for which he explored the collusion between Haitian and Dominican oligarchies in the exploitation of the Haitian workforce.[48] The artist asked a person of Haitian origin to write his views on the socio-political conflict which has characterized and still characterizes the relations between Haiti and the Dominican Republic. This person's words were then tattooed onto Karmadavis's arm and, as a result, his body became the medium of communication between the two nations.

---

[48] Karmadavis, *Lo que dice la piel* (2005), video by Regina José Galindo, http://www.youtube.com/watch?v=GKahAn3TxKk [accessed 25 November 2014].

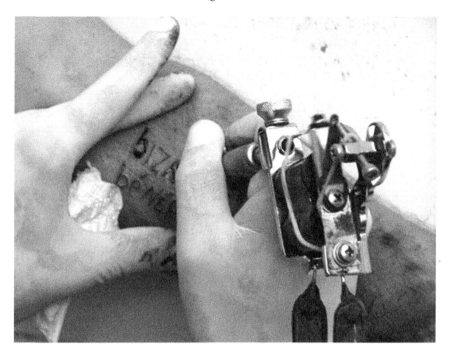

Figure 28. David Pérez Karmadavis, *Lo que dice la piel* (2005) (photograph: Karmadavis). The tattoo on Karmadavis's arm is in Haitian Creole and reads: '*Biznis gouvenman benefis gouvenman*' ('the business of the government benefits the government').

Significantly, the words Karmadavis had tattooed on his arm were: 'Biznis gouvenman *benefis gouvenman*' – that is, 'the business of the government benefits the government' – a clear indictment of the collusion between governments and dominant classes in the exploitation of poor Haitians. We are not told the gender, colour, or race of the Haitian person Karmadavis gives 'voice' to but we do know that the language in which s/he decides to express his/her ideas is Haitian Creole. By foregrounding Creole, Karmadavis is embracing rather than demonizing the diversity that characterizes the two parts of the island and which ultra-nationalistic discourses present instead as incommensurable and irreconcilable differences.

It is also poignant that the part of the body that Karmadavis puts at this Haitian's disposal is his skin because of the peculiar relationship that Dominicans can have with skin colour and national and racial identity. As we have seen, 'whiteness' in Dominican society signposts European culture and civilization and the Dominican white supremacist, negrophobic, and anti-Haitian conservative elite has always identified Dominicanness with whiteness and Hispanic origins. Most importantly, they have been powerful enough to perversely persuade of the validity and legitimacy of such a conflation both blacks and mulattoes, who constitute the great majority of the population. Coloured Dominicans, in fact, have often joined the white minority in their embrace of Eurocentricism and Hispanophilism and in their dismissal of the importance of the African heritage in the national culture, often attributing it solely to the presence of Haitian migrants. What has saved the majority of Dominicans of African descent from the deep alienation that the anti-Haitian and anti-African discourse might have instilled in them is what Torres Saillant has called a 'deracialized consciousness' which goes hand in hand with (self)decolourization.[49] Both deracialization and decolourization have hampered the development of a discourse of black affirmation in the Dominican Republic and have generally favoured negrophobic discourse. Concomitantly, because of deracialization and decolourization, it became impossible to create racial polarities such as those along which identities conjugate themselves in the United States, where diasporic Dominicans have realized for the first time that they were 'black' but also that anti-Haitianism is both wrong and 'impractical.'[50] In 2000 Torres Saillant wondered if upholding a sense of racial identity stemming from the imposition of one's environment (namely the United States) can really be liberating considering that polarized racial discourses disregard the complexity of Dominican national experience. His conclusion was that Dominicans could not afford the luxury of such subtleties. If the main purpose was 'to rid the country of the white supremacist thought and negrophobic discourse [...] and allow finally a celebration of our rich African heritage' then the 'long struggles for equality and social justice by people of colour in the United States have yielded invaluable lessons from which Dominican people in the diaspora and in the Dominican Republic have drawn and may continue to draw empowerment.'[51]

Karmadavis's *Lo que dice la piel* might offer an alternative to what Torres Saillant seems to regard as a 'foreign' template by capitalizing on those aspects of the Dominican experience that could serve his own agenda. For a long time Dominicans have been taught to repudiate their African ancestry and to deracialize and decolourize themselves. However, if race and colour can be so sidelined that Dominican blacks and mulattoes can be made to ally with white supremacists, then race and colour might not (and

---

[49] Silvio Torres Saillant, 'The Tribulations of Blackness: Stages in Dominican Racial Identity', *Callaloo*, 23.3 (2000), pp. 1086–111, pp. 1091, 1102.

[50] Torres Saillant, 'The Tribulations of Blackness', pp. 1108–9.

[51] Torres Saillant, 'The Tribulations of Blackness, pp. 1108–9.

in fact have not) always become an obstacle to different types of alliance and identification. In the presidential election of 1994, as Torres Saillant himself has pointed out, the Dominican people overwhelmingly voted for Peña Gómez despite a massive defamatory campaign which casted doubt on his Dominicanness on account of his Haitian ancestry and blackness.[52] As mentioned in Chapters 6 and 8, Peña Gómez in fact never became president because of the fraudulent interventions of Balaguer's government, but the fact that the majority of Dominicans did not deem it unpatriotic to elect *el haitiano*, as Peña Gómez was referred to at the time by his opponents, is a clear indication of how a deracialized consciousness might not always work in favour of negrophobia and anti-Haitianism. Similarly, when Sonia Marmolejos – the Dominican woman who, as pointed out in Chapter 10, become famous for breastfeeding Haitian children after the Haitian earthquake – was approached by a Dominican journalist who asked her: 'what do you think about the Haitians?' she replied: 'I think that the Haitians are people like us. We should not make a racial distinction based on prejudice because they are dark-skinned and we are light-skinned.'[53] Marmolejos here does not fully reject dominant discourses – she does refer to the colour of the skin as a reliable marker to differentiate between the two people – but she seems both ready and keen to transcend them.

Significantly, the frontier between the two countries has been defined as 'the epidermis of [Dominican] nationality'[54] and, in *Lo que dice la piel*, Karmadavis' skin, imbued by the Haitian's untranslated words, becomes the living embodiment of the porosity of this epidermis and of the bilingual and fluid borderland revisited and recreated by, among others, Rueda, Philoctète, Veloz Maggiolo, Danticat, and Ramírez. Simultaneously, the content of the tattoo reminds one of the long history of resistance towards central power and of collaboration between the inhabitants of the *raya*, a history which has been routinely occluded by ultra-nationalistic discourses or upheld as an unpatriotic national disgrace.[55] Bringing to the fore across-the-border dialogue, and the possibility of transnational alliances and identifications, Karmadavis's *Lo que dice la piel* echoes Franco's belief that, ultimately, the Haitian and Dominican elites have made sure that the people of both nations have interiorized conflicts which originated instead with the dominant classes.[56]

---

[52] Torres Saillant, 'The Tribulations of Blackness, pp. 1108–9.
[53] Rodríguez, *Las Nuevas Relaciones Domínico-Haitianas*, p. 87.
[54] Soto Jiménez, 'La Frontera en la Agenda de Seguridad, Defensa y Desarrollo Nacional del Estado Dominicano en el Siglo XXI', p. 4.
[55] Balaguer, *La isla al revés*, p. 48.
[56] Franco, *Sobre racismo y antihaitianismo*, p. 67.

Figure 29. David Pérez Karmadavis, *Trata* (2005), Plaza de España, Zona Colonial, Santo Domingo (photograph: Karmadavis).

Moreover, it also foregrounds a Dominicanness which goes against and beyond xenophobia, raciological categories, and pigmentocracy and is forged in relation with and not in opposition to Haiti.

Another crucial stepping stone in Karmadavis's journey to the heart of the border question is *Trata,* an *acción performatica* which took place in Santo Domingo in 2005 but reaches into the island's colonial past and into the way in which that past has been disavowed in order to posit the border between Haiti and the Dominican Republic as a frontier which separates two incompatible and profoundly different countries which never shared a common history.[57] Owing to its historical and symbolic resonance, the location in which this performance took place, as we will see, enables Karmadavis to work with different temporalities at the same time, forcing his audience to face occluded and unpalatable pasts and present. The title *Trata* translates as 'slave trade' or 'human trafficking.' *Trata* was realized in two different moments. First of all, a Haitian labourer peeled 500 sugar canes, which were then transported to Plaza de España in Santo Domingo, a square which is directly in front of the Alcázar de Colón, the palace built by Christopher Columbus's son

---

[57] Karmadavis, *Trata* (2005), http://www. karmadavis.com [accessed 26 November 2011 – website no longer available].

Figure 30. David Pérez Karmadavis, *Simétrico* (2006), Barceló Gran Hotel Lina (photograph: Karmadavis).

Diego at the heart of the *Zona Colonial*.[58] Here, the artist performed his part, which was to chew sugar cane after sugar cane until physical exhaustion had the better of him. In other words, *Trata* brought slavery to the middle of the Plaza de España, reiterating (as Deive does in *Viento Negro, bosque del caimán*) that slavery *did exist* in the Spanish colony and was not a practice restricted to the French side of the island. A reintegration of slavery into the country's history implies recognition of the African heritage dismissed by ultra-nationalistic, negrophobic, and anti-Haitian discourses which tend to minimize the importance of slavery in order to associate Africa exclusively with Haiti, and Dominicanness exclusively with Spain. Karmadavis's sugar cane, moreover, points towards more recent forms of abuse and oppression. Haitian *braceros*, as we have seen, are still exploited in Dominican sugar fields, even if the sugar business is no longer central to the country's economy, and, despite their hard work, they remain unprotected against illegal practices such as human trafficking or collective repatriation. It is worth mentioning that in August 2003, two years before Karmadavis performed *Trata* in the streets of Santo Domingo, the Dominican government had approved new legislation on people trafficking and exploitation or, in Spanish, *trata*. The

---

[58] Personal communication with Karmadavis, 18 November 2011.

Dominican government, however, was mainly concerned with the treatment of Dominicans in the rest of the world, not with the *trata* of Haitians in the Dominican Republic, but Karmadavis's work clearly insists that the legislation should also be applicable to crimes and irregularities perpetrated against Haitian nationals who cross the border into his native country.[59]

The predicament of Haitian migrants in the Dominican Republic is also central to *Simétrico* ('Symmetrical'), a performance which took place in a hotel in Santo Domingo in 2006. Evoking the concept of symmetry, the title presupposes both harmony and a patterned similarity between the parts engaged in a symmetrical relationship. The performance testifies once again to Karmadavis's belief that, as he has put it, 'the only way forward for the two nations sharing Hispaniola is finding a way to live together,' and, as we will see, it recreates the 'common ground' encapsulated by the pre-1937 borderland.[60] For five days Karmadavis shared a room in the hotel with a Haitian man he had never met before: throughout this time their interactions were filmed and available to the public. In a short video where their life together is condensed into a little less than eight minutes, we initially see them on opposite sides of the room, timidly folding clothes, each one near his own bed as though the room were split in two by an invisible border. The two strangers, however, slowly begin to transcend the mental boundary which divides them, get closer to each other and interact: they sit together at the table and discuss (in Spanish) the reasons behind Haitian migration and the effects that such a cheap workforce has on the Dominican economy. At the same table they also share their food and pray together before eating. Later, we see Karmadavis trying to teach the Haitian man how to play a musical instrument and are shown a notebook with a drawing of a map of the island with the two nations differently marked and the name of the Gaga 'group' *Tou Ba Doo*, which highlights the island's syncretism. The notebook also contains basic words scribbled in Creole and translated into Spanish and vice versa (*dlo – agua* 'water'; *du fè – fuego* 'fire'; *aire – vent* 'wind'; *tierra – tè* 'earth') illustrating how, like Jean Gentil and his pupils, the two have embraced bilingualism while trying to find a common language in which to communicate.[61]

---

[59] Blas Jiménez makes a similar point about slavery in Santo Domingo and a comparison between past and present in *Africano por elección, negro por nacimiento*, pp. 107–15 and 20–21.

[60] Karmadavis, *Simétrico* (2006), http://performancelogia.blogspot.co.uk/2007/08/david-prezsimtrico.html [accessed 25 November 2014].

[61] Karmadavis, *Simétrico* (2006), video by Regina José Galindo http://www.youtube.com/watch?v=HO7tB3UTZCc [accessed 25 November 2014].

Figure 31. David Pérez Karmadavis, *Al tramo izquierdo* (2006), public transport, Santo Domingo (photograph: Karmadavis).

If *Simétrico* recreates the fluidity of the borderland, *Al tramo izquierdo* ('On the Left-Hand Side,' 2006) reconstructs instead the enforcement of the borderline. In a public bus in the Dominican Republic, Karmadavis filled the left-hand side with people of Haitian origin so that the other side would be occupied by Dominicans.[62] It is worth pointing out that, while the picture disseminated on the web presents us with a very neat division, the video which documents the performance shows the confusion that this partition created in the passengers: some of them, not entirely sure on which side to sit, ended up standing between the two rows of seats, on what we could call the hybrid space of the *raya*. Also evident is the way in which the people on the bus readily cooperate to find seats for one another, trying to make sure that nobody is penalized by this experiment.

Across-the-border collaboration is also the focus of Karmadavis's *Estructura completa* ('Complete structure'), a 2010 *acción performatica* presented as a video to the 54th Venice Biennale in 2011 which forcefully demonstrates that, for Karmadavis, Hispaniola is a living organism in

---

[62] Karmadavis, *Al tramo izquierdo* (2006), ESCALA, http://www.escala.org.uk/publications-and-editions/publications/escala-research-paper-3-karmadavis-art-justice-transition [accessed 25 November 2014].

Figure 32. David Pérez
Karmadavis, *Estructura
Completa* (2010), Calle
del Sol, Santiago de los
Caballeros (photograph:
Karmadavis).

need of all its parts to function properly.[63] This performance features a
blind person of Dominican origin carrying in his arms a disabled person
of Haitian origin whose legs have been amputated. Their walk took
place through the streets of post-earthquake Santiago de los Caballeros
(the second largest city of the Dominican Republic), Bávaro (a luxury
tourist destination on the opposite side of the island from Haiti), and
Santo Domingo. Historically, Santiago is the theatre of the second major
battle of the Dominican War of Independence (30 March 1844), in which
Dominican troops defeated an outnumbering portion of the occupying
Haitian army, and is another sacred site for anti-Haitian rhetoricians.
Bávaro, on the other hand, incarnates the typical image of the Dominican
Republic as a string of sumptuous and expensive all-inclusives. *Estructura
completa* is especially provocative because the performance/walk took place

---

[63] Karmadavis, *Estructura completa* (2010), http://vimeo.com/28311549 [accessed 25
November 2014].

while Santiago and Santo Domingo were deeply troubled by anti-Haitian demonstrations which demanded the repatriation *en masse* of Haitians who were all accused of both having arrived illegally after the earthquake and spreading cholera.[64] The cholera emergency and its related witch-hunt was also a sensitive topic in Bávaro since the first confirmed case of cholera in the Dominican Republic (November 2010) was in fact a Haitian man who worked in the construction industry in Higüey, near the tourist area of Bávaro-Punta Cana, a fact that caused alarm in the tourist industry.[65] According to Karmadavis, the two people featured in *Estructura completa* 'symbolize the deficiencies and the similarities of the two nations in a single structure.'[66] The video, moreover, draws attention to the fact that collaboration can transcend impairment rather than lingering on the disabled bodies and their inadequacies. We see the structure from different angles: at times it comes towards us from a distance; at times it becomes progressively closer; and at other times it is far away again. The two people are confronted by different obstacles (passers-by, walls, steps, traffic) which they manage to overcome only when they cooperate and when he listens to her advice, which is imparted across languages (he speaks Spanish and she speaks Creole) and via gentle (or vigorous, depending on the situation) tapping on the shoulder.

Building on his lifetime commitment to the improvement of border relations, with *Estructura completa* Karmadavis offers an incisive comment on post-earthquake Hispaniola and its potential as a watershed moment in the redefinition of the relationship between Haiti and the Dominican Republic. The disabled woman with amputated legs may be seen as an embodiment of the earthquake as well as a powerful reminder of what had just happened across the border. The mutilated bodies of Haitians wounded during the earthquake were not an uncommon sight in the Dominican Republic in the immediate aftermath of January 2010, when many received medical treatment in their neighbouring country. However, Karmadavis insists, this woman is not a victim of the earthquake; her disability, in

---

[64] Ricardo Santana, 'Vecinos amenazan con botar a haitianos indeseables de barrios', *Listin Diario*, 28 December 2012, http://listin.com.do/la-republica/2010/12/28/171584/ Vecinos-amenazan-con-botar-a-haitianos-indeseables-de-barrios [accessed 25 November 2014].

[65] 'Dan a conocer primer caso del cólera en RD', *Diario Libre*, 16 November 2010, http://www.diariolibre.com/noticias/2010/11/16/i268561_dan-conocer-primer-caso-del-clera.html [accessed 29 November 2014] and 'El cólera preocupa al sector hotelero de RD', *Diario Libre*, 25 January 2011, http://www.diariolibre.com/noticias/2011/01/25/ i276969_clera-preocupa-sector-hotelero.html [accessed 29 November 2014].

[66] Personal communication with Karmadavis, 18 November 2011.

fact, predates it.[67] Thus, she does not represent post-catastrophe Haiti but forcefully signposts that Haiti had serious problems and something to offer well before the earthquake – and 'visibly' so, one may add. The Haitian earthquake, Karmadavis's 'casting' seems to suggest, can become a key moment in border relations only if it is seen in the context of the island's history and not as an isolated event, a 'natural' disaster with no solutions other than emergency (hence temporary) 'Good-Samaritanesque' ones.

Once again, Karmadavis insists on the need for a shift not just in perception and relations between the two countries but in self-perception, and stresses the concrete advantages of collaboration for *both* parties, not just Haiti. Significantly, Haiti is not pigeon-holed as just a 'burden,' 'the problem,' or the 'neighbour in need' of a more or less self-sufficient and generous Dominican Republic. *Estructura completa* does not urge Dominicans to look at the suffering of the Haitians and become 'Good Samaritans' – as a matter of fact, the man representing the Dominican Republic is not at all represented as a 'Good Samaritan.' Equally, Karmadavis's piece does not invite Haitians to look at the Dominican Republic as the solution to all their problems. The blind man carries the woman around but he is far from independent and autonomous; in fact, without her assistance, he could not move forward, at least not at the same pace. *Estructura completa* promotes a truly transnational, *isla-abierta* approach. Here both countries/figures are characterized by what Karmadavis calls '*carencias*' or 'deficiencies,'[68] and are perfectly aware of their deficiencies and of the deficiencies of their partner. They both know, however, that they have something to offer and that their partner has something to offer too, and they are committed to make their partnership work. Most importantly, they have clearly understood and accepted that neither can really go anywhere without the other.

---

[67] Personal communication with Karmadavis, 18 November 2011.
[68] Personal communication with Karmadavis, 18 November 2011.

Conclusion
The rejection of futures past: on the edge of an attainable acceptable future?

Polibio Díaz, *Manifiesto* (2013)

I n August 2013 the Dominican artist Polibio Díaz, whose 1993 photograph *Rayano* was discussed in Chapter 5, received an award from the Santo Domingo Museum of Modern Art for his video-performance *Manifiesto*, which was presented at the Dominican Republic's National Biennial of Art.[1] It features two illegal Haitian immigrants reading *The International Immigrants Movement Manifesto* in the back seat of a car while they are driven around the city of Santo Domingo on 18 December, International Migrants Day.[2] We see and hear the man reading the *Manifesto* in Spanish and occasionally helping the woman next to him to translate it into Creole.[3] The itinerary they cover is highly significant and it is crucial that all the places that the car drives by are seen by the audience from inside the car. In fact, the contours of the car windows are often visible in the frame and partly obstruct our view; as a result, while we listen to the immigrants reading and translating we are placed in the car *with* them and are forced

---

[1] Polibio Díaz, *Manifiesto*, 8 August 2013, http://www.youtube.com/watch?v= ViSY9v0k-uI [accessed 29 November 2014].

[2] *Immigrant Movement International*, 2011, http://immigrant-movement.us/ wordpress/migrant-manifesto/ [accessed 29 November 2014].

[3] Polibio Díaz has attracted my attention to the way in which the man generally pronounces the Spanish 'r' competently – a fact that demonstrates that he has been in the Dominican Republic for a long time – and has provocatively added that the man might have 'passed' the '*perejil* text' in 1937. Personal communication with Polibio Díaz, 11 February 2014.

to share their perspective. The first building they pass by, houses the offices of the *Junta Central Electoral* ('Central Electoral Committee'), the institution which, traditionally, has arbitrarily refused birth certificates to the children of Haitians born in the Dominican Republic. As Wooding and Moseley-Williams have pointed out, this systematic discrimination has been 'the institutional policy of the *Junta Central Electoral*' for a long time: during Balaguer's administration it was also the official line of the government while, taking advantage of the fact that *Junta Central Electoral* is an autonomous body, subsequent governments have tended to 'duck the issue,' leaving the matter in the hands of the Supreme Court.[4] A birth certificate, as we have seen, is the most important document in the Dominican Republic because, in its absence, one is denied name, nationality, citizenship, and access to health care and education, has serious difficulties in finding a 'formal' job, securing a pension fund, getting married, registering one's children's births, opening bank accounts, purchasing a house, and obtaining inheritance – in short, a life without a birth certificate is the life of 'an underclass non-citizen.'[5]

After the offices of the *Junta Central Electoral*, the car in Díaz's *Manifiesto* drives through a big flea market which takes place every Sunday in Santo Domingo: the camera focuses in particular on the numerous stands which sell clothes, many of which look like second-hand garments or re-exports, probably arriving from Haiti. It is significant that a large number of viewers thought that this part of the video-performance was filmed in Port-au-Prince or in one of the binational markets located alongside the frontier, where these products are also bought and sold.[6] Indirectly, therefore, the audience is either surprised by, or invited to ponder on, continuities and correspondences between the two countries and between the demonized borderland and the urban capital which in actual fact appear much less dissimilar than ultra-nationalistic discourses would care to acknowledge.

Leaving the flea market behind, the car passes the monument which was erected in the spot in which Trujillo was killed and which here reminds viewers of the massacre of 1937 and the violent anti-Haitian policy adopted

---

[4] Wooding and Moseley-Williams, *Needed but Unwanted*, p. 51. The Supreme Court was superseded as the highest court in the land since the 2010 Constitution allowed for the setting up of the Constitutional Court.

[5] Kåre Kristensen and Bridget Wooding, 'Haiti/Dominican Republic – Upholding the rights of immigrants and their descendants', *Norwegian Peacebuilding Resource Centre (NOREF)*, October 2013, p. 5, http://www.peacebuilding.no/var/ezflow_site/storage/original/application/273b4770daf48a18c60d724a641f0470.pdf [accessed 25 November 2014].

[6] Personal communication with Polibio Díaz, 29 December 2013.

by his regime. This monument is situated on the *malecón* of Santo Domingo and, while the car moves along, the camera remains focused on the sea – that is, on the seascape that is shared by Haiti and the Dominican Republic and celebrated in *Las metamorfosis de Makandal* and *Jean Gentil* as a unifying agent. The next portion of the journey takes place in Little Haiti, an area of Santo Domingo where many Haitians live and work. Once more, the very existence of Little Haiti brings to the fore not only across-the-border continuities but also the fact that the cultural syncretism which characterized Rueda's and Veloz Maggiolo's *raya* and Philoctete's *terres mêlées* is now to be found across the nation, and illustrates one of the ways in which, according to Torres Saillant, the Dominican experience itself has become 'fundamentally *rayana*'.[7]

In the last thirty seconds of the video-performance, which lasts about eleven minutes, the two immigrants read the final line of the *Manifesto*, which declares that 'dignity has no nationality,' get out of the car and begin to walk down the pedestrian street El Conde, surrounded by Dominican and Haitian souvenirs, which are sold side by side. *Haïti Chèrie*, the unofficial Haitian national anthem, is played as a soundtrack, creating an intriguing contrast between what the audience can hear – a celebration of Haitian identity – and what it can see – two figures disappearing among the crowd of Santo Domingo, entirely indistinguishable from the other pedestrians. Moreover, while the two are walking towards the Cathedral of Santa María la Menor and Parque Colón (Columbus Park), two icons of Hispanophilic and Christian Dominicanness, the lyrics of *Haïti Chérie* refer to the Cittadelle Laferrière, one of the icons of Haitian independence. The simultaneous evocation of these different emblems of national identification here does not presuppose antagonism but complementarity. The cathedral, Columbus Square and the Cittadelle signpost the shared history of a 'complete structure,' namely the island; they are powerful symbols of the complex identities which inhabit Hispaniola and their juxtaposition re-energizes what Rueda called the '*spiritual* freedom of the *rayano* who fluctuates between two countries without deciding to settle for one.'[8]

On 23 September 2013, only a month after Polibio Díaz received his award for *Manifiesto*, the Dominican Constitutional Court ruled that Juliana Deguis, who was born in the Dominican Republic in 1984 to

---

[7] Torres Saillant, 'La Condición Rayana', p. 227. For the use of the word 'rayano' as a metaphor to explain the identity of Dominicans in the twenty-first century see also Ramón A. Victoriano-Martínez, *Rayanos y Dominicanyorks: la dominicanidad del siglo XXI* (Pittsburgh, PA: Instituto Internacional de Literatura Iberoamericana, 2014).

[8] Rueda, *La criatura terrestre*, p. 26. Italics mine.

Haitian parents, had been wrongly registered as Dominican at her birth and ordered the *Junta Central Electoral* to search all birth registries from 1929 for people who had been (allegedly) wrongly registered as Dominican citizens. Deguis's birth certificate was seized by the *Junta Central Electoral* in 2008, when she applied for an identity card, because her name was 'Haitian.'[9] The attempt to denationalize Dominican citizens of Haitian ancestry, however, does not date from September 2013. Between 1929 and 2010 the Dominican state, where *ius soli* or birthright citizenship was in force until 2010, was supposed to grant nationality to all children born in the country except for those whose parents were diplomats or 'in transit' (that is, present in the territory for less than ten days) at the time of their birth. In reality, as mentioned, the *Junta Central Electoral* has often arbitrarily refused to issue birth certificates to the children of Haitians born in the Dominican Republic.[10]

In 2004 a new Migration Law redefined people with expired residency visas and undocumented migrant workers as 'foreigners in transit.' The law was also intended to affect, retroactively, Dominican-born children of Haitian parents who had already received Dominican nationality. Since 2007, Dominican authorities have used administrative procedures to remove Dominican nationality from an increasing number of Dominican citizens of Haitian ancestry who had previously been granted Dominican identity documents.[11] In 2010 the Dominican Republic changed its constitution and a new exclusionary clause was made to *ius soli* by which the right to Dominican citizenship is granted only if a child born in the country has a parent who is a 'legal resident.' Dominican state representatives hold that most Haitians' and Haitian descendants' ancestors entered without proper permission but many among the older generations were recruited by state agents, and most of the forms of immigration restrictions that they supposedly evaded did not exist until the turn of the century.[12] Nevertheless, since its ratification

---

[9] 'Dominican Republic must retract ruling that could leave thousands stateless', *Amnesty International*, 18 October 2013, http://www.amnesty.org/en/news/dominican-republic-must-retract-ruling-could-leave-thousands-stateless-2013-10-18 [accessed 29 November 2014].

[10] 'Without my identity card, it's like I'm dead', *Amnesty International*, 18 October 2013, http://www.amnesty.org/en/news/without-my-identity-card-it-s-i-m-dead-2013-10-18 [accessed 25 November 2014]; Wooding and Moseley-Williams, *Needed but Unwanted*, pp. 50–51.

[11] 'Without my identity card, it's like I'm dead'; Kristensen and Wooding, 'Haiti/Dominican Republic', p. 5.

[12] For a study of the implications of statelessness (especially from a gender perspective) for people of Haitian descent living in Dominican *bateyes* see Allison Petrozziello,

of human rights conventions, the Dominican Republic remains obliged to
grant citizenship to a child born on its territory who would otherwise be
stateless.[13]

Predictably, this Constitutional Court's sentence has been strongly opposed
by many within and without the Dominican Republic: as Torres Saillant
rushed to emphasize, the two women judges who cast dissenting votes in
the Court's decision impugned the ruling as one causing 'denationalization',
'statelessness' and 'disrespect for human dignity.'[14] Various journalists,
intellectuals, lawyers, human rights groups, faith-based organizations, and
NGOs have expressed concern and have been working hard to positively
influence official thinking even if, especially in the immediate aftermath of
the sentence, many of those who were opposing it have been branded as
'betrayers of the nation' and have been suffering serious intimidation.[15] In
the week between 2 and 6 December 2013 the Inter-American Commission
on Human Rights visited the Dominican Republic to monitor the effects of
the Constitutional Court's ruling and concluded that it arbitrarily deprived
thousands of people of their nationality, in violation of their right to a
juridical personality. The Inter-American Commission on Human Rights
also observed that the situation affected in 'a disproportionate manner
those of Haitian descent who are also people of African descent and
often identified on the basis of color, a fact that constitutes a violation
of the right to equality and non-discrimination.'[16] In the same week the
organizations and personalities who support the group *Dominican@s por
Derecho* ('Dominicans for Human Rights') and the *Comité de Solidaridad con
las personas desnacionalizadas* ('Solidarity committee with denationalized
people') organized *Abrazo Solidario* ('Solidarity Embrace'), a one-day event

Amelia Hintzen, and Juan Carlos González Díaz, *Género y el riesgo de apatridia para
la población de ascendencia haitiana en los bateyes de la República Dominicana* (Santo
Domingo: Editora Búho, 2014).
[13] Kristensen and Wooding, 'Haiti/Dominican Republic', p. 5.
[14] Silvio Torres Saillant, 'Denationalizing Dominicans of Haitian Ancestry? Santo
Domingo's Anti-Dominican Authorities', *The National Institute for Latino Policy*, 27
October 2013, http://campaign.r20.constantcontact.com/render?ca=e7ddcf9c-13bc-4699-
923e-55c999e3284d&c=65e0e960-32a8-11e3-8638-d4ae52753a3b&ch=66a91b60-32a8-
11e3-873b-d4ae52753a3b [accessed 29 November 2014].
[15] 'Comisión Interamericana de DDHH visitó RD para medir impacto de Sentencia
TC', *Observatorio Migrantes del Caribe* (OBMICA), 6 December 2013, http://obmica.
org/index.php/actualidad/23-derecho-a-nacionalidad/68-comision-interamericana-
de-ddhh-visito-rd-para-medir-impacto-de-sentencia-tc [accessed 29 November 2014].
[16] 'CIDH culmina visita a República Dominicana', *Organización de los Estados
Americano* (OAS), 6 December 2013, http://www.oas.org/es/cidh/prensa/comunicados/
2013/09 7.asp (accessed 29 November 2014).

attended by 2000 people which was aimed at publicly supporting all those who are affected by the ruling.[17]

As far as writers and artists are concerned, while it is too early for a properly articulated response, it is worth noting that some have been very vocal in their condemnation of the ruling. The writers Chiqui Vicioso, Avelino Stanley, Alanna Lockward, and Junot Díaz (among others) have publicly supported the initiative *Abrazo Solidario* and are members of the *Comité de Solidaridad con las personas desnacionalizadas*; the poet Rhina Espaillat reacted to the Constitutional Court's ruling by 'burst[ing] in anger': she felt 'nauseous' and labelled it a 'disgusting nonsense' and a 'stain on the conscience of the Dominican Republic.'[18] The writer and singer Rita Indiana Hernández intervened in the debate immediately after the ruling with an article published in *El País Internacional* in which she condemns the exploitation of Haitians, points out that they 'have done more for the country than the thousands of ghosts cashing cheques without going to their jobs in the big haunted house that is Dominican bureaucracy,' and insists that their rights should be respected and not denied.[19]

In an article entitled *Los parias del Caribe*, the Peruvian writer and Nobel prize winner Mario Vargas Llosa – author of *La Fiesta del Chivo* (2000), a novel which recounts the assassination of Trujillo and recreates the oppressive time of the dictatorship – calls the ruling a 'legal aberration' and goes as far as comparing it to the Nazi laws of the 1930s which deprived German Jews of their German nationality. Vargas Llosa, however, is cautious not to accuse all Dominicans of discrimination and not to end on a negative note: he acknowledges the many voices from Dominican civil society which oppose this ruling and celebrates the many acts of solidarity in which the Dominican people engaged after the Haitian earthquake of 2010.[20] The

---

[17] 'Comisión Interamericana de DDHH visitó RD para medir impacto de Sentencia TC', *Dominicanos x Derecho*, http://dominicanosxderecho.wordpress.com/ [accessed 29 November 2014]; 'La República Dominicana: *Comité de Solidaridad con las Personas Desnacionalizadas* – Síntesis Ejecutiva, Documento Constitutivo', *Episcopal News Service*, 5 November 2010, http://episcopaldigitalnetwork.com/ens/2013/11/05/la-republica-dominicana-comite-de-solidaridad-con-las-personas-desnacionalizadas/ [accessed 4 February 2014]. Notably *Comité de Solidaridad con las personas desnacionalizadas* is a bilingual label.

[18] Torres Saillant, 'Denationalizing Dominicans of Haitian Ancestry?'

[19] Rita Indiana Hernández, 'Magia negra', *El País Internacional*, 9 October 2013, http://internacional.elpais.com/internacional/2013/10/09/actualidad/1381345925_372245.html [accessed 29 November 2014].

[20] Mario Vargas Llosa, 'Los parias del Caribe', *El País*, 3 November 2013, http://elpais.com/elpais/2013/10/31/opinion/1383233998_965346.html [accessed 25 November 2014].

fact that, a few days after this article was published, Vargas Llosa's books were publicly burnt in retaliation in Santiago de los Caballeros testifies to the deep tensions which shape this debate.[21] On 10 November 2013, Mark Kurlansky, Julia Alvarez, Edwidge Danticat, and Junot Díaz published a letter in the *Los Angeles Times* to jointly condemn the sentence and accuse the Dominican government of institutionalized racism.[22] The letter drew fierce criticism: Díaz and Alvarez were subjected to personal attacks and invited not to interfere with Dominican affairs because, according to their detractors, their status as Dominican–Americans deprives them of the right to make pronouncements in Dominican affairs.[23]

Unsurprisingly, the ruling was also condemned by the Haitian government and by many of the country's intellectuals, among others the ex-minister and former consul general of Haiti in the Dominican Republic, Edwin Paraison (*persona non grata* to Dominican ultra-nationalists), the historian Weibert Arthus, the sociologist Roger A. Matiba, and Jean Thomas Philippe and Colette Lespinasse from GARR ('*Group d'appui aux repatriés et aux refugiés*' or 'Support group for refugees and repatriates'), who also highlighted that the Haitian government had to be careful that its protestations were not capitalized upon by Dominican ultra-nationalists and treated as an implicit admission that those denationalized in the Dominican Republic are in fact Haitian nationals.[24] At the beginning of 2014 the Dominican Republic and Haiti engaged in various meetings with the participation of CARICOM, the European Union, and the government of Venezuela in order to solve the

---

[21] Jean-Baptiste Marckenson, 'L'écrivain prix Nobel de littérature Mario Vargas Llosa, victime de la pyromanie dominicaine', *Parole En Archipel*, 17 November 2013, http://parolenarchipel.com/2013/11/17/lecrivain-prix-nobel-de-litterature-mario-vargas-llosa-victime-de-la-pyromanie-dominicaine/ [accessed 25 November 2014].

[22] Mark Kurlansky, Julia Alvarez, Edwidge Danticat and Junot Díaz, 'In the Dominican Republic, suddenly stateless', *Los Angeles Times*, 10 November 2013, http://articles.latimes.com/2013/nov/10/opinion/la-oe-kurlansky-haiti-dominican-republic-citizensh-20131110 [accessed 25 November 2014].

[23] 'Ocho escritores ponen en duda la dominicanidad de Junot Díaz y lo acusan de "ofensivo"', *7 Dias*, 29 November 2013, http://www.7dias.com.do/portada/2013/11/29/i152926_ocho-escritores-ponen-duda-dominicanidad-junot-diaz-acusan-ofensivo.html#.UydCcDpF3Pc [accessed 25 November 2014]; 'Why Is Giovanny Cruz Crapping on Fellow Dominicans Junot Díaz and Julia Álvarez?', *Latino Rebels*, 3 December 2013, http://www.latinorebels.com/2013/12/03/why-is-giovanny-cruz-crapping-on-fellow-dominicans-junot-diaz-and-julia-alvarez/ [accessed 25 November 2014].

[24] Amos Cincir and Dominique Domerçant, 'Que faire pour assurer la paix insulaire ?', *Le Nouvelliste*, 25 November 2013, http://lenouvelliste.com/lenouvelliste/article/124277/Que-faire-pour-assurer-la-paix-insulaire.html [accessed 29 November 2013].

issue.[25] The debate on the right to Dominican nationality, however, should not be a matter of dialogue between Haiti and the Dominican Republic and international efforts to frame it in this light can be seen as misplaced.[26]

The issue of Haitian immigration in the Dominican Republic is a complex one and proposals for the regularization of foreigners who have been long-term residents in the Dominican Republic are urgently needed in order to improve the situation and reduce statelessness for future generations. Partially as a result of international pressure, in November 2013 the Dominican Republic announced a National Plan for the Regularization of Migrants (Plan Nacional de Regularización de Extranjeros) aimed at regularizing the status of long-term migrants with irregular status in the country. In May 2014 the Dominican Congress passed a new law to address the situation of those persons who had been denationalized by the controversial ruling of the Constitutional Court in September 2013. Some cautiously regarded both measures as steps in the right direction but there have always been serious reservations regarding their fairness, arbitrariness, and efficaciousness. This long and complex process of regularization and restoration of fundamental rights is still under way and numerous experts continually draw attention to its many shortcomings, which, they insist, are condemning it to fail.[27]

[25] 'Dominican Republic must urgently face up to its human rights responsibility', *Amnesty International*, 9 May 2014, http://www.amnesty.org/en/library/info/AMR27/007/2014/en [accessed 29 November 2014].

[26] Personal communication with Bridget Wooding, 30 July 2014.

[27] See, amongst many, 'Naturalization law: a step in the right direction, but still a long way to justice in the Dominican Republic', *Amnesty International*, 3 June 2014, http://www.amnesty.org/en/library/info/AMR27/009/2014/en [accessed 25 November 2014]; 'Immigrantes y sus descendientes: tres procesos en marcha sin garantías de lograr ninguna solución', *Dominican@s por Derecho*, 26 June 2014, http://dominicanosxderecho.wordpress.com/2014/06/26/inmigrantes-y-sus-descendientes-tres-procesos-en-marcha-sin-garantias-de-lograr-ninguna-solucion/ [accessed 25 November 2014]; 'MIP repite patrón implementación plan de registro ley 169-14 que demostró ser inefectivo', Dominican@s por Derecho, 18 November 2014, https://dominicanosxderecho.wordpress.com/2014/11/18/mip-repite-patron-implementacion-plan-de-registro-ley-169-14-que-demostro-ser-inefectivo/ [accessed 28 December 2014]; 'Demandan juicio político al presidente de JCE e interpelación ministro de Interior por violación ley 169-14', Dominican@s por Derecho, 2 October 2014 https://dominicanosxderecho.wordpress.com/2014/10/02/demandan-juicio-politico-al-presidente-de-jce-e-interpelacion-ministro-de-interior-por-violacion-ley-169-14/ [accessed 30 December 2014]; '#Plataforma169 denuncia decreto 250-14 no se está cumpliendo', Dominican@s por Derecho, 27 August 2014 https://dominicanosxderecho.wordpress.com/2014/08/27/plataforma169-denuncia-decreto-250-14-no-se-esta-cumpliendo/ [accessed 30 August 2014].

Moreover, the recent Dominican Constitutional Court's ruling that the country's recognition of the competence of the Inter-American Court of Human Rights (IACHR) is unconstitutional – a decision taken after the IACHR ordered the Dominican state to revoke the September 2013 ruling and to adopt legislative measures to regulate a simple and accessible birth registration process in accordance with international human rights law – has once again drawn international attention to the matter and re-emphasized the global repercussions of the predicament of Haitian-Dominicans and, more broadly, the global dimension of Hispaniola's border relations.[28]

Notably, in their interventions, most of those opposing the 13 September ruling have mentioned as a sinister precedent the 1937 massacre and have referred to Trujillo's policy of Dominicanization of the frontier which was further supported by Balaguer. Haitian–Dominicans, however, no longer live predominantly along the borderland or segregated in *bateyes* but are spread throughout the national territory, and the *raya*, as we have seen, is no longer a geographical area but an intercultural reality that exists everywhere, in urban and rural contexts alike. It is no coincidence that Polibio Díaz's *Manifiesto* was filmed in Santo Domingo, that the 'writing on the wall' in Rodríguez's *Que si fuere mil veces* was partly contributed to by Haitians who live in the Dominican capital, and that Karmadavis's *Estructura completa* was performed in Santo Domingo, Santiago de los Caballeros, and the tourist resort of Bávaro. The ruling, therefore, could be seen as an attempt to Dominicanize the entire Dominican Republic according to a homogeneous and monolithic notion of Dominicanness which excludes the very possibility of interculturality that the borderland represented before 1937 and, for some, has continued to represent ever since, at least as a powerful symbolic 'cultural archive' and as a 'hinge' around which revolve the questions of citizenship and nationality.[29]

---

[28] 'Dominican Republic: Reaction to Court ruling shows shocking disregard for international law', *Amnesty International*, 23 October 2014, http://www.amnesty. org/en/news/dominican-republic-reaction-court-ruling-shows-shocking-disregard-international-law-2014-10-24 [accessed 28 December 2014]; 'Dominican Republic: Withdrawal from top regional human rights court would put rights at risk', *Amnesty International*, 6 November 2014, http://www.amnesty.org/en/news/dominican-republic-withdrawal-top-regional-human-rights-court-would-put-rights-risk-2014-11-06 [accessed 28 December 2014]; 'UN rights office voices concern over Dominican Republic's ruling on regional court', *UN News Centre*, 7 November 2014, http://www. un.org/apps/news/story.asp?NewsID=49285&Kw1=Dominican+Republic&Kw2=Human+Rights&Kw3=#.VKKv-8DpADA [accessed 28 December 2014].

[29] See Torres Saillant, 'La Condición Rayana', pp. 220–27 and Pérez, 'Leer la Frontera Hoy: Un Espacio para la Interculturalidad', pp. 157–71.

Figure 33. Polibio Díaz, *Manifiesto* (2013), Calle El Conde, Zona Colonial, Santo Domingo (photograph: Polibio Díaz).

The literary texts and artistic interventions contained in *On the Edge* form part of the *inter*cultural archive of the borderland and outline empowering models of coexistence which counteract the violation of 'spiritual freedom' that derives from violent enforcements of Rueda's *línea*, to be understood here both as a geopolitical and psychological barrier. The everyday interactions which shape Alexis's transnational Macorís in *Compère Général Soleil* and the patterns of identification with the land and its history which characterize Gonaïbo's celebration of the region of the lakes in Alexis's *Les arbres musiciens* and Yaquimex's flight to the Bahoruco mountains in Métellus's *Anacaona*, for example, find a powerful counterpart, at the end of Veloz Maggiolo's *El hombre del acordéon*, in the image of Honorio Lora rising from his grave to join all those who had died in 1937 in transnational, interethnic, and 'transcolour' solidarity. Philoctète's 'new world to build' for the people of the mixed and troubled (*mêlées*) lands of Hispaniola, Karmadavis's 'open island' and 'complete structure,' Hernández's celebration of communality and continuities in 'Da pa lo do,' and Báez's and Díaz's ironic deconstructions of dominant conceptualizations of the borderland are all powerful articulations of Rueda's 'geography of living flesh.'[30] Most

---

[30] Rueda, *Las metamorfosis de Makandal*, p. 214.

importantly, perhaps, intercultural archives such as *On the Edge* make past experiences available to those who want to engage fully with the present, refuse to comply with the idea that an acceptable future is unattainable, and do not accept inhabiting what Koselleck has called 'futures past'; as a matter of fact, all the texts under scrutiny here might be seen as solid stepping stones towards a better Hispaniola: after all, being 'on the edge' also means being at the point at which something is likely to begin.

Bibliography

IX Censo Nacional de Población y Vivienda. Informe Básico (Santo Domingo: Oficina Nacional de Estadística, 2012), http://censo2010.one.gob.do/resultados/Resumen_resultados_generales_censo_2010.pdf [accessed 28 November 2014].

'A better class of dictator? Rebelling against the lies and illegalities', *Haiti Support Group-Haiti Briefing 73*, February 2013, http://www.haitisupportgroup.org/index.php?option=com_content&view=article&id=722:a-better-class-of-dictator-rebelling-against-the-lies-and-illegalities&catid=99:analysis&Itemid=256 [accessed 29 November 2014].

'Aborda con ONGs el tema haitiano', *Hoy*, 19 July 2007, http://hoy.com.do/aborda-con-ongs-el-tema-haitiano/ [accessed 25 November 2014].

Abramowitz, Janet N., *Unnatural Disasters*, Worldwatch Paper 158 (Worldwatch Institute, Washington, 2001).

Abreu, Dió-genes, *Perejil: el ocaso de la 'hispanindad' dominicana, celebracion de la multiplicidad cultural desde New York* (República Dominicana: Imp. Mediabyte, 2004).

Acero Ruiz, Carlos, 'A los lados del límite: una experiencia inolvidable', *Cuadernos de Comunicación*, 5.4, March 2013, pp. 15–21.

'Acusan en tribunal EE.UU a empresa AES por causar problemas de salud en RD', *Diario Libre*, 6 November 2009, http://www.diariolibre.com/noticias/2009/11/06/i222440_acusan-tribunal-empresa-aes-por-causar-problemas-salud.html [accessed 28 November 2014].

Adames, Francisco Paulino, 'Presentación', in *Antología Literaria Contemporánea de la Frontera*, ed. Francisco Paulino Adames (Santo Domingo: FUDECESFRON, 1998), pp. 3–5.

Adams, John Joseph, and David Barr Kirtley, 'Junot Díaz Aims to Fulfill His Dream of Publishing Sci-fi Novel with *Monstro*', *The Geek's Guide to the Galaxy – Wired*, 3 October 2012, http://www.wired.com/2012/10/geeks-guide-junot-diaz/all/ [accessed 28 November 2014].

Adams, Paul, Steven Hoelscher and Karen Till, 'Place in Context: Rethinking Humanist Geographies', in *Textures of Place: Exploring Humanist Geographies*, eds Paul Adam, Steven Hoelscher and Karen Till (Minneapolis, MN: University of Minnesota Press, 2001), pp. xiii–xxxiii.

'After Leonel', *The Economist*, 26 May 2012, p. 46.

Agamben, Giorgio, *Homo Sacer: Sovereign Power and Bare Life*, trans. Daniel Heller-Roazen [1995] (Stanford, CA: Stanford University Press, 1998).

—, 'The Camp as Nomos of the Modern', trans. Daniel Heller-Roazen in *Violence, Identity and Self-Determination*, eds Hent de Vries and Samuel Weber (Stanford, CA: Stanford University Press, 1997), pp. 106–18.

Alexandre, Guy, 'Visión Haitiana sobre la Frontera de Cara al Siglo XX', in *La Frontera: prioridad en la agenda nacional*, ed. Secretaría de Estado de las Fuerzas Armadas (Santo Domingo: Editora de las Fuerzas Armadas Dominicanas, 2004), pp. 125–34.

Alexis, Jacques Stephen, *General Sun, My Brother*; original title: *Compère Général Soleil* [1955], trans. Carrol F. Coates (Charlottesville, VA: The University Press of Virginia, 1999).

—, *Les arbres musiciens* (Paris: Gallimard, 1957).

—, 'Of the Marvellous Realism of the Haitians', *Presence Africaine*, 8–10 (1956), pp. 249–75 (English translation).

Alix, Juan Antonio, 'Dialogo cantado entre un Guajiro dominicano y un Papá bocó haitiano in un fandango en Dajabón' (1874), in *Poesia popular dominicana*, ed. Emilio Rodríguez Demorizi, (Santiago, República Dominicana: Universidad Católica Madre y Maestra, 1979) pp. 267–86.

Alphonse, Roberson, 'Martelly mixe les religions', *Le Nouvelliste*, 23 November 2012, http://lenouvelliste.com/lenouvelliste/article/111070/Martelly-mixe-les-religions. html [accessed 29 November 2014].

Andujar, Carlos, *The African Presence in Santo Domingo*, trans. Rosa Maria Andujar (East Lansing, MI: Michigan State University, 2012).

Anthem of the Dominican Republic, *National Anthems*, http://www.national-anthems.info/do.htm [accessed on 29 November 2014].

Anzaldúa, Gloria, *Borderlands/La Frontera: The New Mestiza* (San Francisco, CA: Aunt Lute Books, 1999).

Aquino García, Miguel, *Holocausto en el Caribe: perfile de una tirania sin precedents, la matanza de haitianos por Trujillo* (Santo Domingo: Editora Corripio, 1995).

Art Museum of The Americas, http://www.museum.oas.org/exhibitions/2010s/2013-oncommonground.html [accessed 29 November 2014].

Austerlitz, Paul, *Merengue: Dominican Music and Dominican Identity* (Philadelphia, PA: Temple University Press, 1997).

Báez, Frank, 'Ahora es nunca', in *Págales tú a los psicoanalistas* (Santo Domingo: Editorial Ferilibro, 2007).

Balaguer, Joaquín, *La isla al revés: Haití y el destino dominicano* [1983] (Santo Domingo: Editora Corripio, 1994).

Balcácer, Juan Daniel, '¿Cuál es el nombre de nuestra isla?', *Diario Libre*, 29 September 2012, http://www.diariolibre.com/juan-daniel- balcacer/2012/09/29/i353742_cual-nombre-nuestra-islaa.html [accessed 25 November 2014].

'Battalla de la Barranquita', *Enciclopedia Virtual Dominicana*, http://www.quisqueya virtual.edu.do/wiki/Batalla_de_la_Barranquita [accessed 18 February 2014].

Baudelaire, Charles, 'L'Invitation au Voyage', in *Les Fleurs du Mal* (Paris: Flammarion, 1991), pp. 99–100.

Bellegarde, Dantes, *Histoire du people Haïtien, 1492–1952* (Port-au-Prince, 1953).

Belliard, Basilio, and Gahston Saint-Fleur, eds, *Palabras de una isla / Paroles d'une île: Primera antología póetica de República Dominicana Haití / Première anthologie poétique de la République Dominicaine et Haïti* (Santo Domingo: Ediciones de Cultura, 2012).

Bello Mancebo, Luis Vencedor, *Memorias de Pedernales: Don Vencedor Bello y Alcoa Exploration Co* (Santo Domingo: Editores Asociados, 2013).

Benjamin, Walter, *Illuminations*, trans. Harry Zorn [1955] (London: Pimlico, 1999).

Bérard, Stéphanie, 'Dramaturgie Haïtienne de l'exil: *Le bleu de l'île* d'Evelyne Trouillot', *Journal of Haitian Studies*, 16.1 (2010), pp. 60–69.

'Bernardo Vega y Edwidge Danticat discuten la matanza de 1937', *Hoy*, 5 June 2004, http://hoy.com.do/bernardo-vega-y-edwidge-danticat-discuten-la-matanza-de-1937 [accessed 27 November 2014].

Blake, William, 'Auguries of Innocence', in *The Complete Poems* (Harmondsworth: Penguin, 2004), pp. 506–10.

Blonda, Máximo Avilés, *Pirámide 179*, in *Teatro* (Santo Domingo: Ediciones de la Sociedad de Autores y Compositores Dramáticos de la República Dominicana, 1968).

Bongie, Chris, *Islands and Exiles: The Creole Identities of Post/Colonial Literature* (Stanford, CA: Stanford University Press, 1998).

Borders of Lights, http://www.borderoflights.org/ [accessed 25 November 2014].

Bradley Hagerty, Barbara, 'Family Accuses "Sugar" Filmmakers of Defamation', *National Public Radio*, 3 October 2007, http://www.npr.org/templates/story/story.php?storyId=14962748 [accessed 28 November 2014].

Buck-Morss, Susan, *Hegel, Haiti and Universal History* (Pittsburgh, PA: Pittsburgh University Press, 2009).

Caamaño Castillo, Rafael Emigdio, 'Himno a Comendador del Rey', 'Fucilado per equivocación', 'El caso de Trujillo y el Bocó' and 'Indoamericano', in *Antología Literaria Contemporánea de la Frontera*, ed. Francisco Paulino Adames (Santo Domingo: FUDECESFRON, 1998), p. 113, p. 119, pp. 120–21, p. 122.

Caamaño de Fernández, Vicenta, *El negro en la poesía dominicana* (Santo Domingo: Editora Corripio, 1989).

Carpentier, Alejo, 'Preface', *El reino de este mundo* (Lima: Editora Latinoamericana, 1958).

Carroll, Rory, 'We are going to disappear one day', *The Guardian*, 8 November 2008, http://www.theguardian.com/world/2008/nov/08/haiti-hurricanes [accessed 29 November 2014].

Casey, Edward, *The Fate of Place: A Philosophical History* (Berkeley, CA: University of California Press, 1998).

—, 'How to Get from Space to Place in a Fairly Short Stretch of Time: Phenomenological Prolegomena', in *Senses of Place*, eds Steven Field and Keith H. Basso (Santa Fe, NM: School of American Research Press, 1996), pp. 13–52.

Cassá, Roberto, *Movimiento obrero y lucha socialista en la República Dominicana: desde los origins hasta 1960* (Santo Domingo: Editora Taller, 1990).

Castillo Semán, Vinicio A., 'Respuesta al presidente del PRD', *Listin Diario*, 12 January 2009, http://www.listindiario.com/puntos-de-vista/2009/1/12/87444/Respuesta-al-presidente-del-PRD [accessed 29 November 2014].

Castor, Suzy, *Migración y relaciones internacionales: el caso haitiano-dominicano* (Santo Domingo: Editora Universitaria-UASD, 1987).

Cauna, Jacques, 'Les sources historiques de Bug-Jargal: Hugo et la Revolution Haitienne', *Conjonction: Revue Franco-Haitienne*, 166 (1985), pp. 21–36.

Certeau, Michel de, *The Practice of Everyday Life* [1984] (Berkeley, CA: University of California Press, 1988).

Chancy, Myriam, *From Sugar to Revolution: Women's Visions of Haiti, Cuba and the Dominican Republic* (Waterloo, Ontario: Wilfrid Laurier University Press, 2012).

Charlevoix, Pierre-François-Xavier de, *Histoire de l'Isle espagnole ou de Saint-Domingue* (Amsterdam: F. L'Honoré, 1733).

'Cholera in Haiti: One Year Later', *Centers for Disease Control and Prevention* (CDC), 25 October 2011, http://www.cdc.gov/haiticholera/haiti_cholera.htm [accessed 28 November 2014].

'CIDH culmina visita a República Dominicana', Organización de los Estados Americanos (OAS), 6 December 2013, http://www.oas.org/es/cidh/prensa/ comunicados/2013/097.asp [accessed 29 November 2014].

Cincir, Amos, and Dominique Domerçant, 'Que faire pour assurer la paix insulaire?', *Le Nouvelliste*, 25 November 2013, http://lenouvelliste.com/lenouvelliste/article/ 124277/Que-faire-pour-assurer-la-paix-insulaire.html [accessed 29 November 2013].

'Coal ash dumping may have caused deformities', *Miami Herald*, 6 November 2009, http://www.youtube.com/watch?v=ikYX9JADOqs [accessed 28 November 2014].

'Comisión Interamericana de DDHH visitó RD para medir inpacto de Sentencia TC', *Observatorio de Migrantes del Caribe* (OBMICA), 6 December 2013, http:// obmica.org/index.php/actualidad/23-derecho-a-nacionalidad/68-comision- interamericana-de-ddhh-visito-rd-para-medir-impacto-de-sentencia-tc [accessed 29 November 2014].

Convention and Protocol Relating to the Status of Refugees – The Refugee Convention (1951), UN High Commissioner for Refugees (UNHCR), http://www.unhcr.org/ pages/49da0e466.html [accessed 28 November 2014].

Cooper, Davina, *Everyday Utopias: The Conceptual Life of Promising Spaces* (Durham, NC: Duke University Press, 2013).

Corten, André, 'The Dominican Republic Elections and the United States Embargo against Haiti', in *Haiti, the Dominican Republic and the United States*, University of London Institute of Latin American Studies Occasional Papers 6, pp. 1–18, pp. 5–7, http://sas-space.sas.ac.uk/3400/1/B62_-_Haiti_The_Dominican_Republic_ and_the_United_States.pdf [accessed 27 November 2014].

Crassweller, Robert, *Trujillo: The Life and Times of a Caribbean Dictator* (New York: Macmillan, 1966).

D'Alcalá, Diego, *La Frontera* (Santo Domingo: Editora Taller, 1994).

Dalembert, Louis-Philippe, *L'Autre Face de la mer* (Paris: Stock, 1998).

Dalmas, Antoine, *Histoire de la revolution de Saint Dominque*, 2 vols [1793?] (Paris: Mame frères, 1814).

'Dan a conocer primer caso del cólera en RD', *Diario Libre*, 16 November 2010, http://www.diariolibre.com/noticias/2010/11/16/i268561_dan-conocer-primer- caso-del-clera.html [accessed 29 November 2014].

Danticat, Edwidge, *Brother, I'm Dying* (New York: Knopf, 2007).

—, *Anacaona: Golden Flower: Haiti, 1490* (New York: Scholastic, 2005).

—, *The Farming of Bones* [1998] (New York: Penguin 1999).

—, 'We Are Ugly but We Are Here', *The Caribbean Writer*, 10 (1996), http://www2. webster.edu/~corbetre/haiti/literature/danticat-ugly.htm [accessed 26 November 2013].

—, 'Nineteen Thirty-Seven', in *Krik? Krak!* (New York: Random House, 1991).

Dash, Michael, *Literature and Ideology in Haiti, 1915–1961* (London: Macmillan, 1981).

Davis, Martha Ellen, 'Vodú of the Dominican Republic: Devotion to "La Veintiuna División"', *Afro-Hispanic Review*, 26.1 (2007), pp. 75–90.

Dayan, Joan, *Haiti, History and the Gods* (Berkeley, CA: University of California Press, 1998).

De Léon, Osiris, 'Rockash y contaminación ambiental', *El Día*, 10 November 2009, http://eldia.com.do/rockash-y-contaminacion-ambiental-2/ [accessed 28 November 2014].

Deive, Carlos Esteban, 'The African Inheritance in Dominican Culture', in *Dominican Cultures: The Making of a Caribbean Society*, ed. B. Vega (Princeton, NJ: Markus Wiener Publishers, 2007), pp. 87–130.

—, *Diccionario de Dominicanismos* (Santo Domingo: Ediciones Librería Trinitaria/ Editora Manatí, 2002).

—, *Viento Negro, bosque del caimán* (Santo Domingo: Editora Centenario, 2002).

—, *La mala vida: delincuencia y picaresca en la colonia española de Santo Domingo* (Santo Domingo: Fundación Cultural Dominicana, 1997).

—, *Los guerrilleros negros: esclavos fugitivos y cimarrones en Santo Domingo* (Santo Domingo: Fundación Cultural Dominicana, 1989).

—, *Vodú y magia en Santo Domingo* (Santo Domingo: Fundación Cultural Dominicana, 1988).

—, *Heterodoxia e inquisición en Santo Domingo* (Santo Domingo: Editora Taller, 1983).

'Demandan juicio político al presidente de JCE e interpelación ministro de Interior por violación ley 169-14', Dominican@s por Derecho, 2 October 2014 https:// dominicanosxderecho.wordpress.com/2014/10/02/demandan-juicio-politico-al-presidente-de-jce-e-interpelacion-ministro-de-interior-por-violacion-ley-169-14/ [accessed 30 December 2014].

Derby, Lauren, *The Dictator's Seduction: Politics and the Popular Imagination in the Era of Trujillo* (Durham, NC: Duke University Press, 2009).

—, 'Haitians, Magic, and Money: Raza and Society in the Haitian-Dominican Borderlands, 1900 to 1937', *Comparative Studies in Society and History*, 36.3 (1994), pp. 488–526.

Derby, Lauren, and Richard Turits, 'Temwayaj Kout Kouto, 1937 / Eyewitness to the Genocide', in *Revolutionary Freedoms: A History of Survival, Strength and Imagination in Haiti*, eds Cecile Accilien, Jessica Adams and Elmide Méléance (Coconut Creek, FL: Caribbean Studies Press, 2006), pp. 137–43.

Diamond, Jared, *Collapse: How Society Choose to Fail or Survive* (London: Penguin, 2005).

Díaz, Junot, 'Monstro', *The New Yorker*, 4 June 2012, pp. 106–18.

—, 'Apocalypse: What Disasters Reveal', *Boston Review*, 1 May 2010, http://www.bostonreview.net/junot-Díaz-apocalypse-haiti-earthquake [accessed 28 November 2014].

Díaz, Polibio, *Manifiesto*, 8 August 2013, http://www.youtube.com/watch?v=ViSY 9v0k-uI [accessed 29 November 2014].

—, *Rayano* (1993).

Diederich, Bernard, *Seeds of Fiction: Graham Green's Adventures in Haiti and Central America 1954–1983* (London: Peter Owen, 2012).

Dilla Alfonso, Haroldo, 'Pensar la frontera', *Cuadernos de Comunicación*, 5.4 (2013), pp. 5–11.

—, ed., *La frontera dominico-haitiana* (Santo Dominigo: Editora Manatí, 2010).

—, 'La nueva economía fronteriza', in *La frontera dominico-haitiana*, ed. Haroldo Dilla Alfonso (Santo Dominigo: Editora Manatí, 2010), pp. 95–130.

—, 'Palabras preliminares', in *La frontera dominico-haitiana*, ed. Haroldo Dilla Alfonso (Santo Dominigo: Editora Manatí, 2010), pp. 9–13.

'Dominican Republic must retract ruling that could leave thousand stateless', *Amnesty International*, 18 October 2013, http://www.amnesty.org/en/news/dominican-republic-must-retract-ruling-could-leave-thousands-stateless-2013-10-18 [accessed 29 November 2014].

'Dominican Republic must urgently face up to its human rights responsibility', *Amnesty International*, 9 May 2014, http://www.amnesty.org/en/library/info/AMR27/007/2014/en [accessed 29 November 2014].

'Dominican Republic: Reaction to Court ruling shows shocking disregard for international law', *Amnesty International*, 23 October 2014, http://www.amnesty.org/en/news/dominican-republic-reaction-court-ruling-shows-shocking-disregard-international-law-2014-10-24 [accessed 28 December 2014].

'Dominican Republic Resumes Deportations of Haitians', *BBC News Latin America & Caribbean*, 7 January 2011, http://www.bbc.co.uk/news/world-latin-america-12132514 [accessed 28 November 2014].

'Dominican Republic: Withdrawal from top regional human rights court would put rights at risk', *Amnesty International*, 6 November 2014, http://www.amnesty.org/en/news/dominican-republic-withdrawal-top-regional-human-rights-court-would-put-rights-risk-2014-11-06 [accessed 28 December 2014].

'Dominicanos en Haití: migrantes desconocidos', *Listin Diario*, 20 November 2012, http://www.listin.com.do/la-republica/2012/11/20/255812/Dominicanos-en-Haiti-migrantes-desconocidos [accessed 28 November 2014].

Dominicanos x Derecho, http://dominicanosxderecho.wordpress.com/ [accessed 29 November 2014].

Dotel Pérez, Julio César, 'Indio de raza', in *Antología Literaria Contemporánea de la Frontera*, ed. Francisco Paulino Adames (Santo Domingo: FUDECESFRON, 1998), p. 141.

Dove, Rita, 'Parsley', *Poetry Foundation*, http://www.poetryfoundation.org/poem/172128 [accessed 27 November 2014].

Dubois, Laurent, *Avengers of the New World: The Story of the Haitian Revolution* (Cambridge, MA: Harvard University Press, 2004).

Eames Roebling, Elizabeth, 'Haiti–Dominican Republic: Cholera Chokes Off Border Trade', *Global Issues*, 17 January 2011, http://www.globalissues.org/news/2011/01/17/8204 [accessed 25 November 2014].

'El cólera preocupa al sector hotelero de RD', *Diario Libre*, 25 January 2011, http://www.diariolibre.com/noticias/2011/01/25/i276969_clera-preocupa-sector-hotelero.html [accessed 29 November 2014].

'El Papa recibe a Martelly', *Hoy*, 23 November 2012, http://hoy.com.do/el-papa-recibe-a-martelly/ [accessed 29 November 2014].

Estudios e iniciativas piloto para promover la sostenibilidad ambiental en República Dominicana y en Haití, http://www.pilotinitiativesquisqueya.org/index.html [accessed 29 November 2014].

Evans, Lisa, 'Tr-Ash Talk: Dumping on the Americas', *Earth Justice*, 25 May 2011, http://earthjustice.org/blog/2011-may/tr-ash-talk-dumping-on-the-americas [accessed 28 November 2014].

'Exsoldados Haití insisten Martelly reinstale ejército', *Hoy*, 14 May 2012, http://hoy.com.do/exsoldados-haiti-insisten-martelly-reinstale-ejercito/ [accessed 29 November 2014].

'FAO ofrece a presidente de Haití ayuda "sostenible" para el desarrollo', *Hoy*, 22 November 2012, http://hoy.com.do/fao-ofrece-a-presidente-de-haiti-ayuda-sostenible-para-el-desarrollo/ [accessed 29 November 2014].

Farmer, Paul, *Pathologies of Power: Health, Human Rights, and the War on the Poor* (Berkeley, CA: University of California Press, 2005).

—, *The Uses of Haiti* (Monroe, ME: Common Courage Press, 1994).

—, *Aids and Accusation: Haiti and the Geography of Blame* (Berkeley, CA: University of California Press, 1993).

'Fear grips Dominican town for deaths blamed on rockash', *Dominican Today*, 14 June 2006, http://dominicantoday.com/dr/local/2006/6/14/14555/Fear-grips-Dominican-town-for-deaths-blamed-on-rockash [accessed 28 November 2014].

Félix, Carlos Julio, 'Pedernales: Breve reseña historica', in *Antología Literaria Contemporánea de la Frontera*, ed. Francisco Paulino Adames (Santo Domingo: FUDECESFRON, 1998), pp. 165–7.

Feliz, Rafael, 'RD realizará el evento artistico más importante para la historia dominico-haitiana', *Pasandoeltiempo*, July 2011, http://pasandoeltiempo2.blogspot.co.uk/2011/06/rd-realizara-el-evento-artistico-mas.html [accessed 29 November 2014].

Féliz, Yanet, 'Ambientalistas rechazan acuerdo por rockash', *Listin Diario*, 4 March 2007, http://www.listindiario.com.do/la-republica/2007/3/4/5033/Ambientalistas-rechazanacuerdo-porrockash [accessed 28 November 2014].

Ferguson, James, *Dominican Republic: Beyond the Lighthouse* (London: Latin American Bureau, 1992).

Fernández Olmos, Margarite, and Lizabeth Paravisini-Gebert, *Creole Religions of the Caribbean: An Introduction from Vodou and Santería to Obeah and Espiritismo* (New York: New York University Press, 2003).

Fick, Carolyn E., *The Making of Haiti: The Saint-Domingue Revolution from Below* (Knoxville, TN: The University of Tennessee Press, 1990).

Fischer, Sybille, *Modernity Disavowed, Haiti and the Cultures of Slavery in the Age of Revolution* (Durham, NC: Duke University Press, 2004).

Floyd, Troy, *The Columbus Dynasty in the Caribbean, 1492–1526* (Albuquerque, NM: University of New Mexico Press, 1973).

'Foro de Discusíon', in *La Frontera: prioridad en la agenda national*, ed. Secretaría de Estado de las Fuerzas Armadas (Santo Domingo: Editora de las Fuerzas Armadas Dominicanas, 2004), pp. 229–31.

Fouchard, Jean, *The Haitian Maroons: Liberty or Death*, trans. A. Faulkner Watts [1972] (New York: Edward W. Blyden Press, 1981).

Franco, Franklin, *Sobre racismo y antihaitianismo* (Santo Domingo: Sociedad Editorial Dominicana, 2003).

Galtung, Johan, 'Violence, Peace, and Peace Research', *Journal of Peace Research*, 6.3 (1969), pp. 167–91.

Galván, Manuel de Jesús, *The Cross and the Sword*, trans. Robert Graves (Bloomington, IN: Indiana University Press, 1954); original title: *Enriquillo: novela historica* (1882).

Garraway, Doris, *The Libertine Colony: Creolization in the Early French Caribbean* (Durham, NC: Duke University Press, 2005).

Garrigus, John, 'Redrawing the Colour Line: Gender and the Social Construction of Race in Pre-Revolutionary Haiti', *Journal of Caribbean History*, 30.1–2 (1996), pp. 28–57.

Gautier, Céline Anaya, *Esclaves au Paradis* (La Roque-d'Anthéron, France: Vents d'ailleurs, 2007).

Gautier, José, 'Búsqueda y Localización de los Padrones Fronterizos Domínico-Haitianos Desaparecidos en las Aguas de la laguna de el Fondo', in *La Frontera: prioridad en la agenda nacional*, ed. Secretaría de Estado de las Fuerzas Armadas (Santo Domingo: Editora de las Fuerzas Armadas Dominicanas, 2004), pp. 85–9.

Geggus, David, 'Slave Resistance in the Spanish Caribbean in the Mid-1970s', in *A Turbulent Time: The French Revolution and the Greater Caribbean*, eds David Gaspar and David Geggus (Bloomington, IN: Indiana University Press, 2003), pp. 131–55.

—, *Haitian Revolutionary Studies* (Bloomington, IN: Indiana University Press, 2002).

—, 'Les esclaves de la plaine du Nord à la veille de la Révolution Française, part III', *Revue de la Société haïtienne d'histoire*, 144 (1984), pp. 15–44.

Ghandi, Vikram, 'The Lake that Burned Down a Forest,' *VICE News*, 27 July 2014, https://www.youtube.com/watch?v=s6322_yP-20 [accessed 28 November 2014].

Glissant, Édouard, *Poetics of Relation*, trans. Betsy Wing [1990] (Ann Arbor, MI: University Press of Michigan, 1997).

—, *Caribbean Discourse: Selected Essays* (Charlottesville, VA: University Press of Virginia, 1989).

Glover, Kaiama, *Haiti Unbound: A Spiralist Challenge to the Postcolonial Canon* (Liverpool: Liverpool University Press, 2010).

Gómez, Louis Martin, 'Diálogo con Juan Carlos Mieses', *Hoy*, 20 May 2011, http://hoy.com.do/dialogo-con-juan-carlos-mieses/ [accessed 28 November 2014].

González, Nancie L., 'Desiderio Arias: Caudillo, Bandit, and Culture Hero', *The Journal of American Folklore*, 85.335 (1972), pp. 42–50.

Graves, Robert, *The Cross and the Sword* (Bloomington, IN: Indiana University press, 1954).

Greene, Graham, *The Comedians* [1966] (London: Vintage, 1999).

Güdel, Niklaus Manuel, 'Montecristi: une colère lyrique', *Les Lettres et les Arts – Revue d'information culturelle francophone de Bâle et Nord-Romandie*, 1 (2009), p. 14.

Guzmán, Hulda, *Some are born to sweet delights* (2011).

Haïti Chèrie (dir. Claudio del Punta, 2007).

Haiti, Where Did the Money Go? (dir. Michele Mitchell, 2012).

'Haitian Migrants denied basic rights in the Dominican Republic', *Amnesty International*, 21 March 2007, http://www.amnesty.org/en/news-and-updates/report/haitian-migrants-denied-basic-rights-dominican-republic-20070321 [accessed 28 November 2007].

'Haitian President Michel Martelly wants to unify Haiti and Dominican Republic', Piera, Nuria, interview with Michel Martelly, 9 April 2011, http://www.youtube.com/watch?v=kvaU-4zZwis [accessed 27 November 2014].

'Haiti's Pepé Trade: How Secondhand American Clothes Became a First-Rate Business', *ReasonTV*, 23 May 2012, http://www.youtube.com/watch?v=h2ZD1EQu7_U [accessed 18 February 2014].

Hallward, Peter, *Damning the Flood: Haiti, Aristide, and the Politics of Containment* (London: Verso, 2007).

'Have you guys read what lunatic said?', Dominican Republic Forums (DR1), http://www.dr1.com/forums/general-stuff/112313-have-you-guys-read-what-lunatic-said.html [accessed 27 November 2012].

Heaney, Seamus, 'Song', in *Field Work* (New York: Farrar, Straus and Giroux, 1979), p. 56.

Heinl, Robert Debs, and Nancy Gordon Heinl, *Written in Blood: The Story of the Haitian People, 1942–1971* (Boston: Houghton Mifflin, 1978).

Helena Campos, Ramón Emilio, 'La botija', in *Antología Literaria Contemporánea de la Frontera*, ed. Francisco Paulino Adames (Santo Domingo: FUDECESFRON, 1998), pp. 41–7.

Henríquez Ureña, Max, *Panorama histórico de la literatura dominicana* (Santo Domingo: Librería Dominicana, 1966).

Henríquez Ureña, Pedro, *Diccionario dominicano* (Santo Domingo: Editorial del Nordeste, 1983).

Hermann, Sarah, 'Unconscious Curatorships', January 2013, unpublished paper.

Hernández, Rita Indiana, and Los Misterios, 'Magia negra', *El País Internacional*, 9 October 2013, http://internacional.elpais.com/internacional/2013/10/09/actualidad/1381345925_372245.html [accessed 29 November 2014].

—, 'Da pa lo do', *El Juidero* (2011), compact disc.

Herrera, Rafael Darío, *Montecristi entre campeches y bananos* (Santo Domingo: Editora Búho, 2006).

Herrera, Ruth, 'El conflicto domínico-Haitiano en una novela', *Hoy*, 20 June 2009, http://hoy.com.do/el-conflicto-dominico-haitiano-en-una-novela/ [accessed 25 November 2014].

Herrera y Tordesillas, Antonio de, *Historia general del los hechos de los castellanos en la islas y tierra firme del mar Océano* [1726] (Madrid: Academia de la Historia, 1935).

Hiciano, Eudaldo Antonio, *Cronología de un pueblo: antología de mitos* (Santo Domingo: Alfa y Omega, 1998).

Hidalgo, Tania, 'Pelegrín sugiere más control en frontera', *Hoy*, 8 February 2010, http://hoy.com.do/pelegrin-sugiere-mas-control-en-frontera/ [accessed 25 November 2013].

Hoetnick, Harry, 'Americans in Samaná', *Caribbean Studies*, 2.1 (1962), pp. 3–22.

Hoffman, Léon-François, 'Un Myth national: La cérémonie du Bois-Caïman,' in *La République haïtienne: Etat des lieux et perspectives*, eds Gérard Barthélemy and Christian Girault (Paris: Karthala, 1993), pp. 434–48.

—, 'Victor Hugo, les noirs et l'esclavage', *Francofonia: studi e ricerche sulle letterature di lingua francese*, 31 (1966), pp. 47–90.

Holguín-Veras, Norma, 'Antesala de la Patria' and 'Evocaciones', in *Antología Literaria Contemporánea de la Frontera*, ed. Francisco Paulino Adames (Santo Domingo: FUDECESFRON, 1998), pp. 93, 94.

Holguín-Veras Belliard, Norma, 'Sabana Larga', in *Letras del Sol*, ed. Carlos Reyes (San Francisco de Macorís: Angeles de Fierro/Editora Nacional, 2009), p. 77.

The Holy Land Bible containing Old and New Testament, King James Version 1611 (Jerusalem: The Bible Society in Israel, 1962).

Horst, Oscar H., and Katsuhiro Asagiri, 'The Odyssey of Japanese Colonists in the Dominican Republic', *Geographical Review*, 90.3 (2000), pp. 335–58.

Howard, David, *Coloring the Nation: Race and Ethnicity in the Dominican Republic* (Oxford: Signal Books, 2001).

Hugo, Victor, *Bug-Jargal*, trans. and ed. Chris Bongie (Peterborough, Ontario: Broadview, 2004).

Hulme, Peter, *Cuba's Wild West: A Literary Geography of Oriente* (Liverpool: Liverpool University Press, 2011).

Hurston, Zora Neale, *Tell My Horse: Voodoo and Life in Haiti and Jamaica* [1938] (New York: Harper and Row, 1990).

I don't think that we are equal (dir. Dominique Telemaque, 2012), http://www.youtube.com/watch?v=QtIwtuvj-T4 [accessed 29 November 2014].

Immigrant Movement International, *Migrant Manifesto*, 2011, http://immigrant-movement.us/wordpress/migrant-manifesto/ [accessed 25 November 2014].

'Immigrantes y sus descendientes: tres procesos en marcha sin garantías de lograr ninguna solución', *Dominican@s por Derecho*, 26 June 2014, http://dominicanosxderecho.wordpress.com/2014/06/26/inmigrantes-y-sus-descendientes-tres-procesos-en-marcha-sin-garantias-de-lograr-ninguna-solucion/ [accessed 25 November 2014].

Ives, Kim, and Ansel Herz, 'WikiLeaks Haiti: The Aristide Files', *The Nation*, 5 August 2011, http://www.thenation.com/article/162598/wikileaks-haiti-aristide-files [accessed 25 November 2014].

Jean Gentil (dirs. Israel Cárdenas and Laura Amelia Guzmán, 2010).

Jean Gentil, www.jeangentil.com/2010_08_01_archive.html [accessed 27 February 2014].

Jean Gentil, Festival and Awards, http://www.jeangentil.com/p/festivals.html [accessed 25 November 2014].

'Jean-Noël Pancrazi: écrivain de l'exil', Niklaus Manuel Güdel interviews Jean-Noël Pancrazi, in *Les Lettres et les Arts – Revue d'information culturelle francophone de Bâle et Nord-Romandie*, 1 (2009), pp. 10–13.

Jiménez, Blas, *Africano por elección, negro por nacimiento* (Santo Domingo: Editora Manatí, 2008).

Karmadavis, *Estructura completa* (2010), http://vimeo.com/28311549 [accessed 25 November 2014].

—, *Isla cerrada* (2010), http://hemisphericinstitute.org/hemi/en/e-misferica-71/ karmadavis [accessed 25 November 2014].

—, *Al tramo izquierdo* (2006), ESCALA, http://www.escala.org.uk/publications-and-editions/publications/escala-research-paper-3-karmadavis-art-justice-transition [accessed 25 November 2014].

—, *Isla abierta* (2006), http://performancelogia.blogspot.co.uk/2007/08/david-prez-isla-abierta.html [accessed 25 November 2014].

—, *Simétrico* (2006), http://performancelogia.blogspot.co.uk/2007/08/david-prezsim trico.html [accessed 25 November 2014].

—, *Simétrico* (2006), video by Regina José Galindo, http://www.youtube.com/ watch?v=HO7tB3UTZCc [accessed 25 November 2014].

—, *Lo que dice la piel* (2005), video by Regina José Galindo, http://www.youtube. com/watch?v=GKahAn3TxKk [accessed 25 November 2014].

—, *Trata* (2005), http://www.karmadavis.com [accessed 26 November 2011 – website no longer available].

Katz, Jonathan, *The Big Truck That Went By: How the World Came to Save Haiti and Left Behind a Disaster* (London: Palgrave Macmillan, 2013).

Keegan, William F., *Taíno Indian Myth and Practice: The Arrival of the Stranger King* (Gainesville, FL: University Press of Florida, 2007).

Khan, Irene, *Letter to President Leonel Fernández*, 8 March 2006, http://www. amnesty-caribbean.org/en/do/sonstiges/AMR27_001_2006.html [accessed 25 November 2014].

King, Stewart, 'The Maréchaussée of Saint-Domingue Balancing the Ancient Régime and Modernity', *Journal of Colonialism and Colonial History*, 5.2 (2004), http:// muse.jhu.edu/journals/journal_of_colonialism_and_colonial_history/toc/ cch5.2.html [accessed 25 November 2014].

Klang, Gary, *L'île aux deux visages* (Ville de Brossard, Québec: Humanitas, 1997).

Koselleck, Reinhardt, *Futures Past: On the Semantics of Historical Time* (New York: Columbia University Press, 1985).

Kristensen, Kåre, and Bridget Wooding, 'Haiti/Dominican Republic – Upholding the rights of immigrants and their descendants', *Norwegian Peacebuilding Resource Centre* (NOREF), October 2013, p. 5, http://www.peacebuilding.no/var/ ezflow_site/storage/original/application/273b4770daf48a18c60d724a641f0470. pdf [accessed 25 November 2014].

Kurlansky, Mark, Julia Alvarez, Edwidge Danticat and Junot Díaz, 'In the Dominican Republic, suddenly stateless', *Los Angeles Times*, 10 November 2013, http://

articles.latimes.com/2013/nov/10/opinion/la-oe-kurlansky-haiti-dominican-republic-citizensh-20131110 [accessed 25 November 2014].

'La República Dominicana: *Comité de Solidaridad con las Personas Desnacionalizadas – Síntesis Ejecutiva, Documento Constitutivo*', *Episcopal News Service*, 5 November 2010, http://episcopaldigitalnetwork.com/ens/2013/11/05/la-republica-dominicana-comite-de-solidaridad-con-lasersonas-desnacionalizadas/ [accessed 4 February 2014].

Lacroix, Pamphile de, *Mémoires pour servir a l'histoire de la Révolution de Saint Domingue*, vol. 1 (Paris: Pillet ainé, 1819).

Laforgue, Pierre, '*Bug-Jargal* ou de la dificulté d'écrire in *style blanc*', *Romantisme*, 69 (1990), pp. 29–42.

Laguerre, Michel, *Voodoo and Politics in Haiti* (London: Macmillan, 1989).

Lamb, Ursula, *Frey Nicolás de Ovando, Governador de Indias (1501–1509)* (Madrid: Consejo Superior de Investigaciónes Científicas, 1956).

Las 21 Divisiones – Dominican Vodou, http://las21divisiones.com/ [accessed 25 November 2014].

Las Casas, Bartolomé de, *A Short Account of the Destruction of the Indies* [1522] (London: Penguin, 1992).

'Le Group Villedrouin aide des Archelois sinistrés', *Le Nouvelliste*, 14 October 2008, http://lenouvelliste.com/lenouvelliste/article/63186/Le-Groupe-Villedrouin-aide-des-Archelois-sinistres [accessed 1 November 2013].

Lefebvre, Henri, *The Production of Space*, trans. D. Nicholson-Smith [1974] (Malden, MA: Blackwell, 1991).

Left Behind: How Statelessness in the Dominican Republic Limits Children's Access to Education (Washington, DC: Georgetown Law Human Rights Institute, 2014).

Lemoine, Maurice, *Bitter Sugar*, trans. Andrea Johnston (London: Zed Books, 1985); original title: *Sucre Amer: Esclaves aujourd'hui dans les Caraïbes* (1981).

León, Viviano de, 'DR será de negros, blancos y mulatos', *Listin Diario*, 11 November 2011, http://www.listin.com.do/larepublica/2011/11/11/210557/RD-sera-de-negros-blancos-y-mulatos [accessed 25 November 2014].

Lespès, Anthony, *Les semences de la colère* (Port-au-Prince: Deschamps, 1949).

Linebaugh, Peter, and Marcus Rediker, *The Many-Headed Hydra: Sailors, Slaves, Commoners, and the Hidden History of the Revolutionary Atlantic* (Boston, MA: Beacon Press, 2000).

Liriano, Jhonatan J., 'Monte Cristi: grisácea realidad,' *Listin Diario*, 21 February 2011, http://www.listin.com.do/economia-and-negocios/2011/2/21/178353/Monte-Cristi-esta-a-la-espera-de-su-salto-al-desarrollo-economico [accessed 25 November 2014].

Lizardo Lasocé, Luis Francesco, *Palma Sola: La tragedia de un pueblo* (Santo Domingo: Editora Manatí, 2003).

Lockward, Alanna, *Marassá y la Nada* (Santo Domingo: Editorial Santuario, 2013).

—, *Un Haití Dominicano: Tatuajes Fantasmas y Narrativas Bilaterales, 1994–1998* (Santo Domingo: Art Labour Archive, 2010), Kindle version retrieved from Amazon.es.

Logan, Rayford, *Haiti and the Dominican Republic* (New York: Oxford University Press, 1968).

Lozano, Wilfredo, and Bridget Wooding, eds, *Los retos del desarrollo insular: desarollo sostenible, migraciones y derechos humanos en las relaciones domínico-haitianas en el siglo XXI* (Santo Domingo: FLACSO, 2008).

Lozano, Wilfredo, and Franc Báez Evertsz, 'Políticas migratorias y relaciones domínico-haitianas: de la movilidad insular el trabajo a las presiones de la globalización', in *Los retos del desarrollo insular: desarollo sostenible, migraciones y derechos humanos en las relaciones domínico-haitianas en el siglo XXI*, eds Wilfredo Lozano and Bridget Wooding (Santo Domingo: FLACSO, 2008), pp. 237–76.

Lundhal, Mats, *The Haitian Economy: Man, Land and Markets* (New York: St Martin's Press, 1983).

Lundius, Jan, and Mats Lundhal, *Peasants and Religion: A Socioeconomis Study of Dios Olivorio and the Palma Sola Movement in the Dominican Republic* (London: Routledge, 2000).

Lynch, Colum, 'Ban Ki-moon Katrina?' *Foreign Policy*, 19 January 2010, http://turtlebay.foreignpolicy.com/posts/2010/01/19/ban_ki_moons_katrina [accessed 12 March 2014].

McD Beckles, Hilary, 'Caribbean Anti-Slavery: The Self Liberation Ethos of Enslaved Blacks', *Journal of Caribbean History*, 22.1–2 (1988), pp. 1–19 rprt in *Caribbean Slavery in the Atlantic World*, ed. Verene Shepherd and Hilary McD Beckles (Kingston: Ian Randle, 2000), pp. 869–78.

McKechnie, Alex, 'Rising Waters in Haiti and Dominican Republic: Where will the Villagers Go?', *Drexel News Blog*, 25 April 2013, http://newsblog.drexel.edu/2013/04/25/rising-waters-in-haiti-and-dominican-republic-where-will-the-villagers-go/ [accessed 25 November 2014].

Madiou, Thomas, *Histoire de Haiti* [1814–1884] (Port-au-Prince, 1947).

Maeseneer, Rita de, *Encuentro con la narrativa dominicana contemporánea* (Madrid: Iberoamericana, 2006).

Marckenson, Jean-Baptiste, 'L'écrivain prix Nobel de littérature Mario Vargas Llosa, victim de la pyromanie domanicaine', *Parole En Archipel*, 17 November 2013, http://parolenarchipel.com/2013/11/17/lecrivain-prix-nobel-de-litterature-mario-vargas-llosa-victime-de-la-pyromanie-dominicaine/ [accessed 25 November 2014].

Martí, José, 'War Diaries: Part I – From Montecristi to Cap-Haïtien', in *Selected Writings*, trans. and ed. E. Allen (New York: Penguin, 2002), pp. 350–414.

Martínez, Samuel, 'Not a Cockfight: Rethinking Haitian-Dominican Relations', *Latin American Perspectives*, 30.3 (2003), pp. 80–101.

—, *Peripheral Migrants: Haitians and Dominican Republic Sugar Plantations* (Knoxville, TN: The University of Tennessee Press, 1995).

Matibag, Eugenio, *Haitian-Dominican Counterpoint: Nation, Race and State on Hispaniola* (New York: Palgrave Macmillian, 2003).

Mejía Tirso, Ricart, 'Haití en la formacion de la nacionalidad Dominicana', *Eme Eme: Estudios Dominicanos*, XIV.79 (1985), pp. 61–75.

Métellus, Jean, *Anacaona* [1986] (Paris: Éditions Hatier International, 2002).

Métraux, Alfred, *Voodoo in Haiti* (New York: Oxford University Press, 1959).

Mieses, Juan Carlos, *El día de todos* [2008] (Santo Domingo: Alfaguara, 2009).

Mignolo, Walter, *Local Histories/Global Designs: Coloniality, Subaltern Knowledges, and Border Thinking* (Princeton, NJ: Princeton University Press, 2000).

'MIP repite patrón implementación plan de registro ley 169-14 que demostró ser inefectivo', Dominican@s por Derecho, 18 November 2014, https://dominicanos xderecho.wordpress.com/2014/11/18/mip-repite-patron-implementacion-plan-de-registro-ley-169-14-que-demostro-ser-inefectivo/ [accessed 28 December 2014].

Mir, Pedro, 'Hay un país en el mundo', in *Poesías (casi) completas* (México, D.F.: Siglo Ventiuno Editores, 1994), pp. 63–77.

—, *Historia del hambre: sus orígines en la historia dominicana* (Santo Domingo: Editora Corripio, 1987).

—, *Tres leyendas de colores: ensayo de interpretación de las tres primeras revoluciones del Nuevo Mundo* (Santo Domingo: Editora Taller, 1984).

—, *El gran incendio* (Santo Domingo: Editora Taller, 1974).

Moiseau, Jean Phiippe, *Les rêves du cireurs de bottes. Los sueños del limpia botas / Yon chanj kap reve* (2012).

—, *Metal Mask* (2011).

—, *Palm Mask* (2009).

Mora Serrano, Manuel, 'Lo que no se me ha perdido', 28 Agosto 2009, http://sanasanaculitoderana.blogspot.co.uk/2010/08/el-dia-de-todos-de-juan-carlos-mieses.html#.Ue6Xzr5wZlt [accessed 25 November 2014].

Moreau de Saint-Méry, Médéric Louis Élie, *Description Topographique, Physique, Civile, Politique and Historique de la partie française de l'Isle Saint-Domingue*, 3 vols, 3rd edition (Saint-Denis: La Société Française d'histoire d'outre-ner, 2004).

—, *Description Topographique, Physique, Civile, Politique and Historique de la partie française de l'Isle Saint-Domingue. Avec des Observations générales sur la Population, sur le Caractère & les Mœurs de ses divers Habitans; sur son Climat, sa Culture, ses Productions, son Administrations de cette Colonie et un Tableau raisonné des différents parties de son Administration &c, &c. Accompagnées des details les plus propes à faire connaître l'état de cette Colonie à l'epoque du 18 Octobre 1789; Et d'une nouvelle Carte de la totalité de l'Isle*, 2 vols (Philadelphia, PA: chez l'auteur, 1797–98).

—, *Description Topographique et Politique de la partie espagnole de l'Isle Saint-Domingue. Avec des Observations générales sur le Climat, la Population, les Productions, le Caractère & les Mœurs des Habitans de cette Colonie et un Tableau raisonné des différents parties de son Administration; Accompagnée d'une nouvelle Carte de la totalité de l'Isle*, 2 vols (Philadelphia, PA: chez l'auteur, 1796).

—, *Description Topographique et Politique de la partie espagnole de l'Isle Saint-Domingue. Avec des Observations générales sur le Climat, la Population, les Productions, le Caractère & les Mœurs des Habitans de cette Colonie et un Tableau raisonné des différents parties de son Administration; Accompagnée d'une nouvelle Carte de la totalité de l'Isle*, 2 vols, manuscript (ms F^{3}102–103), Archives Nationales d'Outre-Mer, Aix-en-Provence.

—, *Description Topographique et Politique de la partie espagnole de l'Isle Saint-Domingue. Avec des Observations générales sur le Climat, la Population,* les Productions, le Caractère & les Mœurs des Habitans de cette Colonie et un Tableau raisonné des différents parties de son Administration; Accompagnée d'une nouvelle Carte de la totalité de l'Isle*, 2 vols, English translation by William Cobbett, manuscript (ms F³104–105), Archives Nationales d'Outre-Mer, Aix-en-Provence. Erroneously catalogued as part of the manuscript in French which appears as ms F³102–105.

—, *Considérations presentées aux vrais amis du repos et du Bonheur de France, à l'occasion des nouveaux mouvements de quelque soi-disant amis-des-noirs* (Paris, 1791).

Moya Pons, Frank, *La dominación haitiana, 1822–1844* (Santo Domingo: La Trinitaria, 2013).

—, *The Dominican Republic: A National History* [1998] (Princeton, NJ: Markus Wiener, 2010).

—, *La otra historia dominicana* (Santo Domingo: Librería La Trinitaria, 2009).

—, 'Las Ochos Fronteras de Haití y la República Dominicana', in *La Frontera: prioridad en la agenda nacional*, ed. Secretaría de Estado de las Fuerzas Armadas (Santo Domingo: Editora de las Fuerzas Armadas Dominicanas, 2004), pp. 441–6.

Muir, Richard, *Modern Political Geography* (New York: Macmillan, 1975).

Murray, Gerald, 'Lenguaje y raza en la frontera dominico-haitiana: Apuntes antropológicos', in *La frontera dominico-haitiana*, ed. Haroldo Dilla Alfonso (Santo Dominigo: Editora Manatí, 2010), pp. 241–82.

—, *Sources of Conflict along and across the Haitian–Dominican Border* (Santo Domingo: Pan American Development Foundation, 2010), http://web.clas. ufl.edu/users/murray/Research/Dominican_Republic/Dominican_Haitian_ Conflicts.pdf [accessed 25 November 2014].

'Naturalization law: a step in the right direction, but still a long way to justice in the Dominican Republic', *Amnesty International*, 3 June 2014, http://www. amnesty.org/en/library/info/AMR27/009/2014/en [accessed 25 November 2014].

Núñez, Manuel, 'La Frontera y la Fractura del Territorio Nacional: Obstáculos en la Percepción del Problema', in *La Frontera: prioridad en la agenda nacional*, ed. Secretaría de Estado de las Fuerzas Armadas (Santo Domingo: Editora de las Fuerzas Armadas Dominicanas, 2004), pp. 47–61.

—, *El ocaso de la nación dominicana* (Santo Domingo: Letra Gráfica, 2001).

—, *El ocaso de la nación dominicana* (Santo Domingo: Alfa & Omega, 1990).

'Nuria Revela que Félix Bautista y amigos regalaron millions de dólares a Martelly', *Acento*, April 2012, http://www.acento.com.do/index.php/news/14740/56/ Nuria-revela-que-Felix-Bautista-y-amigos-regalaron-millones-de-dolares-a-Martelly.html [accessed 25 November 2014].

'Ocho escritores ponen en duda la dominicanidad de Junot Díaz y lo acusan de "ofensivo"', *7 Dias*, 29 November 2013, http://www.7dias.com.do/portada/2013/ 11/29/i152926_ocho-escritores-ponen-duda-dominicanidad-junot-diaz-acusan-ofensivo.html#.UydCcDpF3Pc [accessed 25 November 2014].

O'Connor, Maura, 'Two Years Later, Haitian Earthquake Death Toll in Dispute', *Columbia Journalism Review*, 12 January 2012, http://www.cjr.org/behind_the_ news/one_year_later_haitian_earthqu.php [accessed 25 November 2014].

Oe, Kenzaburo, *¡Adiós, libros míos!*, trans. T. Ryukichi (Barcelona: Editorial Seix Barral, 2012).

Oviedo, Fernández Gonzalo de, *Historia general y natural de las Indias*, ed. Juan Pérez de Tudela Bueso [1535] (Madrid: Ediciones Atlas, 1959).

Padgett, Tim, 'Underneath Haiti, Another Big Quake Waiting to Occur', *Time World*, 19 November 2010, http://www.time.com/time/world/article/0,8599,2031863,00. html#ixzz2Kypojp5V [accessed 25 November 2014].

Páez Piantini, William, *Relaciones domínico-haitianas: 300 años de historia* (Santo Domingo: Imp. Mediabyte, 2006).

Pancrazi, Jean-Noël, *Montecristi: Roman* (Paris: Gallimard, 2009).

—, *Les dollars des sables* (Paris: Folio, 2007).

—, *Le Point*, 20 October 2007, http://www.lepoint.fr/actualites-societe/2007–01–20/ jean-noel-pancrazi/920/0/61476 [accessed 25 November 2014].

Papá Liborio: el santo vivo de Maguana (Papa Liborio: the living saint of Maguana) (dir. Martha Ellen Davis, 2003), Contents – in English: Study Guide, http://ufdcimages.uflib.ufl.edu/UF/00/08/74/00/00004/Liborio_contents_ summary-Engl.pdf [accessed 25 November 2014].

'Paradise Remade: Dominican Republic Lead Polluter Goes Green', *Miami Herald*, 17 May 2011, http://www.miamiherald.com/2011/05/17/2221443_p2/dominican-republic-lead-polluter.html [accessed 19 May 2011].

Payen, Nikòl, 'Lavalas: the Flood after the Flood', *Callalloo*, 25.3 (2002), pp. 759–71.

—, 'Something in the water … Reflections of a People's Journey', in *The Butterfly's Way*, ed. Edwidge Danticat (New York: Soho, 2001), pp. 66–82.

Perdomo Cisneros, Alberto, 'La Descubierta. Frontera y Mercado', *CLÍO – Órgano de la Academia Dominicana de la Historia*, 173 (2007), pp. 247–75.

Pérez, Carlos Federico, *Historia diplomática de Santo Domingo 1492–1861* (Santo Domingo: Escuela de Servicios Internacionales Universidad Nacional Pedro Henríquez Ureña, 1973).

Pérez, Luis Julián, *Santo Domingo frente al destino* (Santo Domingo: Editora Taller, 1990).

Peréz, Odalis, 'Leer la Frontera Hoy: Un Espacio para la Interculturalidad', in *La Frontera: prioridad en la agenda nacional*, ed. Secretaría de Estado de las Fuerzas Armadas (Santo Domingo: Editora de las Fuerzas Armadas Dominicanas, 2004), pp. 157–71.

—, *La ideología rota: el derrumbe del pensamiento pseudonacionalista dominicano* (Santo Domingo: Editora Manatí, 2002).

Peréz de Tudela, Juan, 'Política de poblamiento y política de contratación de las Indias (1502–1505),' *Revista des Indias*, 15.61–62 (1955), pp. 371–420.

Pérez y Pérez, Rafael Leonidas, *Apuntes para la historia de Jimaní: Contribución a su estudio* (Santo Domingo: Consejo Nacional de Fronteras, 2000).

—, 'Cultura de la Provincia Independencia', in *Antología Literaria Contemporánea de la Frontera*, ed. Francisco Paulino Adames (Santo Domingo: FUDECESFRON, 1998), pp. 147–9.

Perico Ripiao (dir. Angel Muñiz, 2003).

Perry, Nicholas, and Loreto Echeverria, *Under the Heal of Mary* (New York: Routledge, 1988).

Petitjean Roget, Henry, 'Notes on Caribbean Art and Mythology', in *The Indigenous People of the Caribbean*, ed. Samuel M. Wilson (Gainesville, FL: University of Florida Press, 1997), pp. 100–108.

Petrozziello, Allison, Amelia Hintzen and Juan Carlos González Díaz, *Género y el riesgo de apatridia para la población de ascendencia haitiana en los bateyes de la República Dominicana* (Santo Domingo: Editora Búho, 2014).

Philoctète, René, *Massacre River*, trans L. Coverdale (New York: New Direction Books, 2005); original title: *Le peuple des terres mêlées* [1989].

Picquenard, Jean-Baptiste, *Adonis suivi de Zoflora et de documents inédits*, ed. Chris Bongie (Paris: L'Harmattan, 2006); original titles: *Adonis, ou le bon nègre* (1798) and *Zoflora, ou la bonne negrèsse* (1801).

Pierre, Wadner, 'Haiti: the Bel Air Assault', *Global Research*, 4 October 2007 http://www.globalresearch.ca/haiti-the-bel-air-assault/?print=1 [accessed 25 November 2014].

Pilkington, Ed, 'Haitians launch new lawsuit against UN over thousands of cholera deaths,' *The Guardian*, 11 March 2014, http://www.theguardian.com/world/2014/mar/11/haiti-cholera-un-deaths-lawsuit [accessed 28 December 2014].

'#Plataforma169 denuncia decreto 250-14 no se está cumpliendo', Dominican@s por Derecho, 27 August 2014 https://dominicanosxderecho.wordpress.com/2014/08/27/plataforma169-denuncia-decreto-250-14-no-se-esta-cumpliendo/ [accessed 30 August 2014].

Popkin, Jeremy D., 'Facing Racial Revolution: Captivity Narratives and Identity in the Saint-Domingue Insurrection', *Eighteenth-Century Studies*, 36.4 (2003), pp. 511–33.

'Postura de Leonel Fernández hacia Haití es perjudicial para el país', *Hoy*, 22 August 2010, http://hoy.com.do/postura-de-lf-hacia-haiti-es-perjudicial-para-el-pais/ [accessed 25 November 2014].

Pratt, Mary Louise, *Imperial Eyes: Travel Writing and Transculturation* (London: Routledge, 1992).

Prestol Castillo, Freddy, *El Masacre se pasa a pie* (Santo Domingo: Editora Taller, 1973).

—, *Paisajes y meditaciones de una frontera* (Ciudad Trujillo: Editorial Cosmopolita, 1943).

'Préval: reconstrucción difícil', *Hoy*, 13 July 2010, http://hoy.com.do/preval-reconstruccion-dificil/ [accessed 25 November 2014].

The Price of Sugar (dir. Bill Haney, 2007).

Price-Mars, Jean, *Ainsi parla l'Oncle suivi de Revisiter l'Oncle* (Montréal, Québec: Mémoire d'encrier, 2009).

—, *La República de Haití y la República Dominicana: diversos aspectos de un problema historico, geografico y etnologico*, trans. Martín Aldao and José Luis Muñoz Azpiri, 2 vols (Santo Domingo: Editora Taller, 2000).

'Priest hails US report on conditions for Haitians in Dominican fields', *Catholic Sentinel*, http://www.catholicsentinel.org/main.asp?SectionID=2&SubSectionID=34&ArticleID=22479 [accessed 25 November 2014].

'Protocol to Prevent, Suppress and Punish Trafficking in Persons, Especially Women and Children, Supplementing the United Nations Convention against

Transnational Organized Crime', *United Nations Crime and Justice Information Network* (UNCJIN), http://www.uncjin.org/Documents/Conventions/dcatoc/final_documents_2/convention_%20traff_eng.pdf [accessed 25 November 2014].

'Public Report of Review of U.S. Submission 2011–03 (Dominican Republic)', *Office of Trade and Labor Affairs*, 27 September 2013, http://www.dol.gov/ilab/programs/otla/20130926DR.pdf [accessed 1 March 2014].

Quiñones, Alfonso, 'Jean Genty: quiero un empleo', http://www.jeangentil.com/p/press.html [accessed 25 November 2014].

Ramírez, Jesús María, *Mis 43 años en La Descubierta*, ed. Gisela Ramírez de Perdomo (Santo Domingo: Editora Centenario, 2000).

Récit Historique sur les Évenemens qui se sont succédés dans les camps de la Grande-Rivière, du Dondon, de Ste.-Suzanne et autres, depuis le 26 Octobre 1791 jusqu'au 24 Decembre de la même année. Par M. Gros, Procureur-Syndic de Valière, fait prisonnier par Jeannot, chef des Brigands, augmenté du Récit historique du Citoyen Thibal, Médecin et Habitant de la Paroisse Sainte-Suzanne, détenu prisonnier, par les Brigands, depuis 16 mois et de la Déclaration du Citoyen Fauconnet, faite à la Municipalité le 16 Juin 1792 (Cap-François: Chez Parent, 1793).

Redon, Marie, *Des îles en partage: Haïti & République dominicaine, Saint-Martin, Timor* (Port-au-Prince/Toulouse: Editions de l'Université d'État d'Haïti et Presses Universitaires du Mirail, 2008).

Renda, Mary, *Taking Haiti: Military Occupation and the Culture of US Imperialism, 1915–1940* (Chapel Hill, NC: The University of North Carolina Press, 2001).

'Response of the Dominican Sugar Industry to the Department of Labor Public Report on Review of Submission 2011–03 (Dominican Republic)', December 2013, http://www.dominicansugar.org/uploads/DSI_Reponse_to_DOL_Report.pdf [accessed 25 November 2014].

Rey, Terry, 'The Politics of Patron Sainthood in Haiti: 500 Years of Iconic Struggle', *The Catholic Historical Review*, 88.3 (2002), pp. 519–45.

—, 'The Virgin Mary and the Revolution in Sainte Domingue: The Charisma of Romaine-la- Prophetèsse', *Journal of Historical Sociology*, 11 (1998), pp. 341–69.

Reyes, Carlos, ed., *Letras del Sol: Antología de escritores de la Línea Noroeste* (San Francisco de Macorís: Angeles de Fierro/Editora Nacional, 2009).

Reyes, Sergio, *La Fiesta de los Reyes y otros cuentos de la frontera* (Santo Domingo: Editora Universitaria-UASD, 2004).

—, *Sincretismo: Formas de Expresión en la Frontera* (Santo Domingo: Editora Universitaria-UASD, 1999).

—, *Cuentos y leyendas de la frontera* (Santo Domingo: Editora Universitaria, 1996).

Reyes Arriaga, Sergio Hipólito, 'La Vigía: destellos del "Sol Naciente" en la frontera' (Tercer Lugar), in *Premio Periodismo Rafael Herrera* (Santo Domingo: Colleción Premios Funglode/GFDD 2009 Periodismo), pp. 76–103.

Riveros, Natalia, *Estado del arte de las migraciones que atañen a la República Dominicana 2012* (Santo Domingo: Observatorio Migrantes del Caribe/Editora Búho, 2013).

—, *Informe sobre la cuestión de la migración internacional en la República Dominicana para el año 2011* (Santo Domingo: Observatorio Migrantes del Caribe/Editora Búho, 2012).

Robb, Graham, *Victor Hugo* (London: Picador, 1997).

Robles, Frances, 'Coal ash from U.S. blamed for Dominican town's birth defects', *Miami Herald*, 6 November 2009, http://www.mcclatchydc.com/2009/11/06/78461/coal-ash-from-us-blamed-for-dominican.html#.Ubsrnb5wZ1s [accessed 25 November 2014].

—, 'Pollution sickens children in Dominican Republic', *Miami Herald*, 13 March 2007, http://www.miamiherald.com/2007/03/13/v-print/39816/pollution-sickens-children-in.html [accessed 18 February 2014].

Rodman, Selden, *Quisqueya: A History of the Dominican Republic* (Seattle, WA: University of Washington Press, 1964).

Rodríguez, Emilio Jorge, *Haiti and Trans-Caribbean Literary Identity / Haiti y la transcaribeñidad literaria* (Philipsburg, San Martin: House of Nehesi Editores, 2011).

Rodríguez, Francisco (Pancho), 'Que si fuere mil veces', in *Veinticuatro – Concurso de Arte Eduardo León Jimenes – Catálogo de Obras* (Santiago de los Caballeros, República Dominicana: Centro León, 2012–13), pp. 116–23.

Rodríguez, Manuel, *Las Nuevas Relaciones Domínico-Haitianas* (Santo Domingo: Centro de Información Gubernamental, 2011).

Rodríguez, Néstor E., *Escrituras de desencuentro en la República Dominicana* (Santo Domingo: Editora Nacional, 2007).

Rodríguez Demorizi, Emilio, *Poesia popular dominicana* (Santiago, República Dominicana: Universidad Católica Madre y Maestra, 1979).

—, 'Laveaux to García, November 1795', in *Cesión de Santo Domingo a Francia: Correspondencia de Godoy, García, Roume, Hedouville, Louverture, Rigaud y otros, 1795–1802* (Ciudad Trujillo: Impresora Dominicana, 1958), pp. 17–20.

Rodríguez Grullón, Altair, *Estado del arte de las migraciones que atañen a la República Dominicana* (Santo Domingo: Editora Búho, 2014).

Romain, Jean Marie, 'Haïti à l'heure des grands débats', *Le Nouvelliste*, 27 November 2007, http://lenouvelliste.com/lenouvelliste/article/50913/Haiti-a-lheure-des-grands-debats.html [accessed 25 November 2014].

Roorda, Eric Paul, *The Dictator Next Door: The Good Neighbour Policy and the Trujillo Regime in the Dominican Republic, 1930–1945* (Durham, NC: Duke University Press, 1998).

Rosenberg, June, *El Gagá: Religión y Sociedad de un Culto Dominicano: Un Estudio Comparativo* (Santo Domingo: Universidad de Santo Domingo, 1979).

Rueda, Manuel, *Las metamorfosis de Makandal* (Santo Domingo: Banco Central de la República Dominicana, 1999).

—, *Bienvenida y la noche: Crónicas de Montecristi: A novela* (Santo Domingo: Fundación Cultural Dominicana 1994).

—, *All Santo Domingo* (Santo Domingo: Fundación Dominicana de Desarrollo, 1984).

—, *La criatura terrestre* (Santo Domingo: Editora del Caribe, 1963).

Sagás, Ernesto, *Race and Politics in the Dominican Republic* (Gainsville, FL: University Press of Florida, 2000).

San Miguel, Pedro Luis, *The Imagined Island: History, Identity and Utopia in Hispaniola*, trans. Jane Ramírez [1997] (Chapel Hill, NC: The University of North Carolina Press, 2005).

Sánchez, Dago, 'Jean Remy Genty', 13 October 2012, http://www.dagosanchez.com/jean-remy-genty/ [accessed 25 November 2014].

Sánchez-Carretero, Cristina, '*Santos y Misterios* as Channels of Communication in the Diaspora: Afro-Dominican Religious Practices Abroad', *Journal of American Folklore*, 118.469 (2005), pp. 308–26.

Sánchez Valverde Ocaña, Antonio, *Idea del Valor de la Isla Española, y utilitades, que de ella puede sacar su monarquía* [1785], in *Ensayos*, ed. Andrés Blanco Díaz (Santo Domingo: Ediciones de la Fundación Corripio, 1988), pp. 8–304.

Santana, Iván, 'Presentan recurso de amparo', *Hoy*, 14 May 2012, http://hoy.com.do/ponderan-importancia-de-la-ley-de-libre-acceso-a-la-informacion/ [accessed 25 November 2014].

Santana, Ricardo, 'Vecinos amenazan con botar a haitianos indeseables de barrios', *Listin Diario*, 28 December 2012, http://listin.com.do/la-republica/2010/12/28/171584/Vecinos-amenazan-con-botar-a-haitianos-indeseables-de-barrios [accessed 25 November 2014].

Schaaf, Brian, 'On Common Ground: Haiti and the Dominican Republic', *Haiti Innovation – Choice, Partnership, Community*, 17 April 2013, http://haitiinnovation.org/en/2013/04/17/common-ground-haiti-and-dominican-republic [accessed 25 November 2014].

Schaffer, Wendell, 'The Delayed Cession of Spanish Santo Domingo to France, 1795–1801', *The Hispanic American Review*, 29 (1949), pp. 46–68.

Schuller, Mark, 'Challenges to Solidarity across Multiple Borders: Haiti's Free Trade Zone', *Caribbean Quarterly*, 58.4 (2012), pp. 87–110.

Scott, David, *Conscripts of Modernity: The Tragedy of Colonial Enlightenment* (Durham, NC: Duke University Press, 2004).

Secretaría de Estado de las Fuerzas Armadas, ed., *La Frontera: prioridad en la agenda nacional* (Santo Domingo: Editora de las Fuerzas Armadas Dominicanas, 2004).

Sevrin, Geneviève, 'République Dominicaine: Un mirage pour les migrants Haïtiens', in *Esclaves au Paradis*, Céline Anaya Gautier (La Roque-d'Anthéron, France: Vents d'ailleurs, 2007), pp. 5–7.

Shemak, April, *Asylum Speakers: Caribbean Refugees and Testimonial Discourse* (New York: Fordham University Press, 2011).

Silié, Rubén, 'The *Hato* and the *Conuco*: The Emergence of Creole Culture', in *Dominican Cultures: The Making of a Caribbean Society*, ed. B. Vega (Princeton, NJ: Marcus Wiener Publishers, 2007), pp. 131–60.

Silié, Rubén, and Segura Carlos, eds, *Hacia una nueva visión de la frontera y de las relaciones fronterizas* (Santo Domingo: Editora Búho, 2002).

Smartt Bell, Madison, 'Engaging the Past', in *Novel History: Historian and Novelists confront America's past and each other*, ed. Mark Carnes (New York: Simon & Schuster, 2001), pp. 199–200.

—, *All Souls' Rising* [1995] (New York: Penguin, 1996).

Sommer, Doris, *One Master for Another: Populism as Patriarchal Rhetoric in Dominican Novels* (Lanham, MD: University Press of America, 1983).

Soto, José Luis, 'Caos en el mercado binacional dominico-haitiano', *Teve Espacinsular*, 14 November 2010, http://www.youtube.com/watch?v=LCB7X7bd2TA [accessed 25 November 2014].

Soto Jiménez, Miguel, 'La Frontera en la Agenda de Seguridad, Defensa y Desarrollo Nacional del Estado Dominicano en el Siglo XXI', in *La Frontera: prioridad en la agenda nacional*, ed. Secretaría de Estado de las Fuerzas Armadas (Santo Domingo: Editora de las Fuerzas Armadas Dominicanas, 2004), pp. 3–16.

Stevens-Arroyo, Antonio, *Cave of the Jagua: The Mythological World of the Taíno* (Albuquerque, NM: University of New Mexico Press, 1988).

Strongman, Roberto, 'Transcorporeality in Vodou', *Journal of Haitian Studies*, 14.2 (2008), pp. 4–29.

Suárez, Lucía, *The Tears of Hispaniola: Haitian and Dominican Diaspora Memory* (Gainesville, FL: University Press of Florida, 2006).

Sugar (dirs. Anna Boden and Rayan Fleck, 2008).

The Sugar Babies (dir. Amy Serrano, 2007).

Taleb-Khyar, Mohamed B., 'Jean Metellus', *Callaloo*, 15.2, *Haitian Literature and Culture*, Part 1 (1992), pp. 338–41.

Tejeda Ortíz, Dagoberto, *El Vudú en Dominincana y en Haití* (Republica Dominicana: Ediciones Indefolk, 2013).

—, *Cultura popular e identidad nacional* (Santo Domingo: Consejo Presidencial de Cultura-Instituto Dominicano de Folklore, 1998).

Théodat, Jean-Marie, *Haïti/République Dominicaine: Une île pour deux 1804–1916* (Paris: Karthala, 2003).

Thompson, Peter, 'Introduction', in *The Privatization of Hope: Ernst Bloch and the Future of Utopia*, eds Peter Thompson and Slavoj Žižek (Durham, NC: Duke University Press, 2013), pp. 1–20.

Thompson, Peter and Slavoj Žižek, eds, *The Privatization of Hope: Ernst Bloch and the Future of Utopia* (Durham, NC: Duke University Press, 2013).

Thornton, John, '"I Am the Subject of the King of Congo": African Political Ideology and the Haitian Revolution', *Journal of World History*, 4.2 (1993), pp. 181–214.

Torres Saillant, Silvio, 'Denationalizing Dominicans of Haitian Ancestry? Santo Domingo's Anti-Dominican Authorities', *The National Institute for Latino Policy*, 27 October 2013, http://campaign.r20.constantcontact.com/render?ca=e7ddcf9c-13bc-4699-923e-55c999e3284d&c=65e0e960–32a-11e3-8638d4ae52753a3b&ch=66a91b60-32a8-11e3-873b-d4ae52753a3b [accessed 29 November 2014].

—, 'Blackness and Meaning in Studying Hispaniola: A Review Essay', *Small Axe*, 19.10 (2006), pp. 180–88.

—, *An Intellectual History of the Caribbean* (New York: Palgrave Macmillan, 2006).

—, 'La Condición Rayana: La Promesa Ciudadana en el Lugar del "Quicio"', in *La Frontera: prioridad en la agenda nacional*, ed. Secretaría de Estado de las Fuerzas Armadas (Santo Domingo: Editora de las Fuerzas Armadas Dominicanas, 2004), pp. 220–28.

—, *El tigueraje intellectual* (Santo Domingo: Editora Manatí, 2002).

—, 'The Tribulations of Blackness: Stages in Dominican Racial Identity', *Callaloo*, 23.3 (2000), pp. 1086–111.

Trouillot, Evelyne, *Le bleu de l'île* ('The Blue of the Island'), trans. R. McCormick, *The Journal of Haitian Studies*, 18.2 (2012), pp. 213–64.

Trouillot, Michel-Rolph, 'Bodies and Souls: The Haitian Revolution and Madison Smartt Bell's All Soul's Rising', in *Novel History: Historian and Novelists confront America's past and each other*, ed. Mark Carnes (New York: Simon & Schuster, 2001), pp. 191–2.

—, *Silencing the Past: Power and the Production of History* (Boston, MA: Beacon Press, 1995).

—, *Haiti, State against Nation: The Origins and Legacy of Duvalierism* (New York: Monthly Review Press, 1990).

—, *Nation, State and Society in Haiti, 1804–1984* (Washington, DC: The Wilson Center, 1985).

Tuan, Yi-Fu, *Space and Place: The Perspective of Experience* (Minneapolis, MN: University of Minnesota Press, 1977).

Turits, Richard Lee, 'A World Destroyed, A Nation Imposed: The 1937 Haitian Massacre in the Dominican Republic', *Hispanic American Historical Review*, 82.3 (2002), pp. 589–635.

Turner, Frederick Jackson, *The Frontier in American History* (New York: Holt & Co, 1920).

Ubiñas Renville, Guaroa, *Historias y Leyendas Afro-Dominicanas* (Santo Domingo: Editora Manatí, 2003).

'UN rejects Haiti cholera compensation claims', *BBC News*, 21 February 2013, http://www.bbc.co.uk/news/world-latin-america-21542842 [accessed 25 November 2014].

'UN rights office voices concern over Dominican Republic's ruling on regional court', *UN News Centre*, 7 November 2014, http://www.un.org/apps/news/story.asp?NewsID=49285&Kw1=Dominican+Republic&Kw2=Human+Rights&Kw3=#.VKKv-8DpADA [accessed 28 December 2014].

United Nations (UN), *Universal Declaration of Human Rights*, http://www.un.org/en/documents/udhr/ [accessed 25 November 2014].

Ureña de Henríquez, Salomé, *Anacaona* (Santo Domingo: Publicaciones América, 1974).

Valerio-Holguín, Fernando, 'Primitive Borders: Cultural Identity and Ethnic Cleansing in the Dominican Republic', in *Primitivism and Identity in Latin America: Essays on Art, Literature and Culture*, eds Erik Caymand-Freixas and José Eduardo González (Tucson, AZ: The University of Arizona Press, 2000), pp. 75–88.

Vargas Llosa, Mario, 'Los parias del Caribe', *El País*, 3 November 2013, http://elpais.com/elpais/2013/10/31/opinion/1383233998_965346.html [accessed 25 November 2014].

Vastey, Pompée Valentin de, *An Essay on the Causes of the Revolution and Civil Wars in Hayti* [1819] (Exeter, 1823).

Vega, Bernardo, *Trujillo y Haití*, 3 vols (Santo Domingo: Fundación Cultural Dominicana, 1988–2009).

—, *Dominican Cultures: The Making of a Caribbean Society*, trans. Christine Ayorinde (Princeton, NJ: Markus Wiener Publishers, 2007).

—, *Los cacicazgos de la Hispaniola* (Santo Domingo: Museo del Hombre Dominicano, 1980).

Veloz Maggiolo, Marcio, 'La dictadura y su magia', in *Los retornos del Jefe*, Bismar

Galán and Marcio Veloz Maggiolo (Santo Domingo: Editorial Santuario, 2009), pp. 9–45.

—, *El hombre del acordeón* (Madrid: Siruela, 2003).

—, 'Eulogio, inventor de memoria', in *La memoria fermentada. Ensayos biblioli-terarios* (Austin, TX, University of Texas Press, 2000), pp. 87–92.

—, 'Tipologia del tema haitiano en la literatura dominicana', in *Sobre cultura dominicana y otras cultura (ensayos)* (Santo Domingo: Editora Alfa y Omega, 1977), pp. 93–121.

Viau-Renaud, Jacques, 'Estoy tratando de hablaros de mi patria', in *Poesía Completa* (Santo Domingo: Ediciones del Cielonaranja, 2006).

Victoriano-Martínez, Ramón A., *Rayanos y Dominicanyorks: la dominicanidad del siglo XXI* (Pittsburgh, PA: Instituto Internacional de Literatura Iberoamericana, 2014).

Vidal, Francesca, and Welf Schröter, 'Can We Hope to Walk Tall in a Computerized World of Work?', in *The Privatization of Hope: Ernst Bloch and the Future of Utopia*, eds Peter Thompson and Slavoj Žižek (Durham, NC: Duke University Press, 2013), pp. 288–99.

Villalona, Rubén Darío, 'La cultura en Dajabón', in *Antología Literaria Contemporánea de la Frontera*, ed. Francisco Paulino Adames (Santo Domingo: FUDECESFRON, 1998), pp. 52–6.

Wainwright, Edith, *Culture Haïtienne à travers des texts choisis: manuel d'enseignement* (Coconut Tree, FL: Educa Vision, 2001).

Waliceck, Don E., 'Farther South: Speaking American, the Language of Migration in Samana', in *Just Below South: Intercultural Performance in the Caribbean and the U.S. South*, eds Jessica Adams, Michael Bibler and Cecile Accilien (Charlottesville, VA: University of Virginia Press, 2007), pp. 95–120.

Weeks, John M., and Virginia Ramírez Zabala, 'The Samaná Americans: Some Forgotten Philadelphians', *Penn Museum Research Notes*, 47.1, pp. 38–41, http://www.penn.museum/documents/publications/expedition/PDFs/47-1/Weeks.pdf, p. 1 [accessed 28 November 2014].

Wheeler, William, 'Haiti's Dirty Habit: Can Smarter Stoves Heal Haiti?', *Pulitzer Center on Crisis Reporting*, 11 January 2011, http://pulitzercenter.org/articles/haiti-earthquake-energy-efficient-stoves-reduce-wood-fuel-demand [accessed 25 November 2014].

White, Hayden, *The Content of the Form: Narrative Discourse and Historical Representation* (Baltimore, MD: The Johns Hopkins University Press, 2009).

—, *Metahistory: The Historical Imagination in Nineteenth-Century Europe* (Baltimore, MD: The Johns Hopkins University Press, 1973).

'Why Is Giovanny Cruz Crapping on Fellow Dominicans Junot Díaz and Julia Álvarez?', *Latino Rebels*, 3 December 2013, http://www.latinorebels.com/2013/12/03/why-is-giovanny-cruz-crapping-on-fellow-dominicans-junot-diaz-and-julia-alvarez/ [accessed 25 November 2014].

Wilde, Oscar, 'The Soul of Man under Socialism', in *Collected Works of Oscar Wilde: The Plays, the Poems, the Stories and the Essays including De Profundis* (Ware: Wordsworth Editions, 1997), pp. 895–922.

Williams, Raymond, *Modern Tragedy* (London: Verso, 1979).

—, *The Country and the City* (New York: Oxford University Press, 1973).

Wilson, Samuel M., *Hispaniola: Caribbean Chiefdoms in the Age of Columbus* (Tuscaloosa, AL: The University of Alabama Press, 1990).

'Without my identity card, it's like I'm dead', *Amnesty International*, 18 October 2013, http://www.amnesty.org/en/news/without-my-identity-card-it-s-i-m-dead-2013-10-18 [accessed 25 November 2014].

Wooding, Bridget, 'Human Rights Across an Island: New Twists Following the Haitian Earthquake', *Múltiples: An Informative Bulletin by the Just Governance Group*, 10 (2010), pp. 5–7.

Wooding, Bridget, and Allison Petrozziello, 'New Challenges for the Realisation of Migrants' Rights Following the Haiti 2010 Earthquake: Haitian Women on the Borderlands', *Bulletin of Latin American Research*, 32.4 (2013), pp. 407–20.

Wooding, Bridget, and Marcos Morales, *Migración y medio ambiente: una reflexión pertinente – Migration Policy Brief* (Santo Domingo: Editora Búho, 2014).

—, *Migración y sostenibilidad ambiental en Hispaniola* (Santo Domingo: Editora Búho, 2014).

Wooding, Bridget, and Richard Moseley-Williams, *Needed but Unwanted: Haitian Immigrants and their Descendants in the Dominican Republic* (London: Catholic Institute for International relations, 2004).

Wucker, Michele, *Why the Cocks Fight: Dominicans, Haitians, and the Struggle for Hispaniola* (New York: Hill and Wang, 1999).

'Yean and Bosico v Dominican Republic', *Child Rights International Network*, 8 September 2005, http://www.crin.org/Law/Instrument.asp?InstID=1506 [accessed 25 November 2014].

Yunén, Rafael Emilio, *La isla como es: hipótesis para su comprobación* (Santiago de los Caballeros, Dominican Republic: Universidad Católica Madre y Maestra, 1985).

Zapata, Ron, 'AES Settles Waste Suit With Dominican Republic', *Law 360*, 1 March 2007, http://www.law360.com/articles/19606/aes-settles-waste-suit-with-dominican-republic [accessed 25 November 2014].

Zimmermann, Rainer, 'Transforming Utopian into Metopian Systems: Bloch's *Principle of Hope* Revisited', in *The Privatization of Hope: Ernst Bloch and the Future of Utopia*, eds Peter Thompson and Slavoj Žižek (Durham, NC: Duke University Press, 2013), pp. 246–68.

Index

Printed and bound by CPI Group (UK) Ltd, Croydon, CR0 4YY

07/12/2022

03169678-0005